D1288895

MORE THAN 1,000 SOLUTIONS
FOR THE FRUGAL CONSUMER!

Super Saver Secrets

Easy Ways to Save Energy and Save Money

Reader's digest

The Reader's Digest Association, Inc.
New York, NY/Montreal

A READER'S DIGEST BOOK
99¢ Solutions

Save Energy Save Money!

ISBN: 978-1-62145-178-5

We are committed to both the quality of our products and the service we provide to our customers. We value your comments, so please feel free to contact us.

The Reader's Digest Association, Inc.
Adult Trade Publishing
44 South Broadway
White Plains, NY 10601

For more Reader's Digest products and information, visit our website:
www.rd.com (in the United States)
www.thefamilyhandyman.com

Printed in China

1 3 5 7 9 10 8 6 4 2

NOTE TO READERS
The contributors, editors, and proofreaders who created *99 Cent Solutions* have taken all reasonable measures to confirm and verify the accuracy of the information contained in this volume. However, new learnings and research often reveal that historical information long held to be true isn't. We welcome your input on any content within this book for which you have sound evidence that it may be incorrect; mail any such comments and/or evidence to the address above. We will research all queries and make any necessary corrections in subsequent editions.

All do-it-yourself activities involve a degree of risk. Skills, materials, tools, and site conditions vary widely. Although the editors have made every effort to ensure accuracy, the reader remains responsible for the selection and use of tools, materials, and methods. Always obey local codes and laws, follow manufacturer's operating instructions, and observe safety precautions.

contents

99¢ Solutions

Easy Ways to Save Thousands of Dollars

Reader's digest

The Reader's Digest Association, Inc.
New York, NY / Montreal

Contents

Housewares 160

Ice cube trays? Bottle openers? Cheesecloth? You'd be amazed at the multipurpose uses these everyday items have, that will save you a bundle! Unclog a stubborn drain with a wire hanger. Detail a car with a coffee filter. Separate eggs with a funnel...and much more!

Notions 198

Baubles and beading bore you to tears? They shouldn't! Notions can do double duty almost anywhere in the house. Fix curling wallpaper with adhesive fabric spray. Quilt your windows with batting to save on heating bills. Keep a pot from boiling over with a handful of buttons.

School and Party Supplies 232

That white school glue? It's not just for your grandkids anymore! Use a dab to remove a splinter. Keep your plants toasty during the winter with bubble wrap. Remove scuff marks with an eraser. Pick up spilled beads with masking tape. You'll never spend unnecessarily again!

Tools 268

Tools can be used for a lot more than what they're meant for. Use a bungee cord as a yoga strap! Remove white furniture rings with car wax! Seal waterproof boots with duct tape! Wear a painting mask when you cut onions. Why buy something you don't need to?

Lunch Counter Legends 302

It's the icing on your cake...the cherry on your banana split...the chocolate in your egg cream: It's the lunch counter, where every one of us has treated ourselves to real cooking, at its very best. Lip smacking chili? The perfect, classic grilled cheese? Crispy delicious hash browns? They're all here, along with some surprising tales of how they came to be our favorite dishes.

Index 326

Saving Money, the FIVE-AND-DIME WAY!

WHY BUY PURPOSE-SPECIFIC ITEMS WHEN ONE SIMPLE TOOL CAN ACCOMPLISH SO MUCH?

We've all had this experience, from as far back as we can remember, regardless of where we lived, or what the store was called.

We walk into our local five-and-dime (or 99 cent store, Dollar Store, Woolworth's, or McCrory's or even our neighborhood general store that seems to sell far more than just nuts and bolts), and we begin to wander the aisles. We mosey up the notions aisle, transfixed by bolts of colorful fabric and buttons, and down the health and beauty aisle, with its jars of cold cream and boxes of analgesics. We stroll through the tool section and maybe visit the school supply or toy aisle, and uncover everything from glue to marbles to pencils. And then, maybe we stop for a grilled cheese sandwich or a cherry Coke to bolster a shopping trip that has turned into a walk through an institution that really hasn't changed since our grandparents' day.

In my own family, my grandmother would pick me up at the school bus and together—rain or shine, sleet or snow or hail—we would walk down a long boulevard until we arrived on a cross street that had not one, but *two* dime stores on it: McCrory's on the western side of the street, and Woolworth's on the eastern. On some days, we'd visit McCrory's for a sandwich or a slice of cherry pie, and we'd stroll the aisles, looking at odd nicknacks that ran the gamut from the sublime to the positively silly. On other days, we'd pop into Woolworth's, which was decidedly more *serious*; you could buy bicycle tires, little

red wagons, thread, Play-Doh, skeins of yarn, tooth powder, buttonhole-makers, yo-yos, jacks, cans of (white) tennis balls, knee socks, tube socks, anklet socks, support hose, peds, nail files, chewing gum in every flavor, plastic guitars, strings for plastic guitars, Flutophones, glassware, Pyrex dishes, Christmas ornaments, holiday greeting cards, baby lotion, Corelle ware, rain boots, Keds, potato chips, baked goods, tools, bicycles, and everything in between. What we didn't know (or took for granted, anyway) was that Woolworth's was, at one time, also the largest seller of restaurant food in the world.

Other dime store operators included Samuel Kress, whose Memphis store first opened in 1896, and who eventually built his chain up to 262 branches nationwide, with $168 million in sales. Sebastian Kresge, another mogul, had over 150 stores to his name by the middle of the First World War, and then branched out into self-service discount stores called (you'll never guess!) K-Mart! Even Sam Walton launched his first retail business with a Ben Franklin store in Newport, Arkansas, and when he was unable to convince management to open discount stores, he launched...Walmart!

Famous DIME AND DISCOUNT STORES in History

- **W.T. Grant**
- **H.L. Green**
- **McLellan Stores**
- **G.C. Murphy**
- **Neisner's**
- **J.J. Newberry**
- **Ben Franklin Stores**
- **Kresge's**
- **Kress**
- **Woolworth's**
- **McCrory's**
- **The Dollar Store**
- **Dollar Tree**
- **S.H. Knox & Co.**
- **Dayton's**
- **Woolco**

Today, many of these famous stores are gone... but not one of the things that continues to make the survivors famous: That almost everything you can find in a 99 cent store can save you money—*gobs* of money.

Think about it: Say you need a new screwdriver to replace that old rusted one sitting in your toolbox, so you pick one up at the five-and-dime. Maybe you paid a dollar for it, or maybe you paid a little bit more. Guess what? You have just bought yourself a tool that will help you accomplish *dozens* of other jobs—everything from opening a can of paint to planting seeds in packed soil to chipping ice for your annual barbecue. Why buy purpose-specific items when one simple tool can accomplish so much?

The possibilities are endless:

A simple cleaning bucket can be used to store your extension cords, create a mini-garden, and provide a convenient shower when you're camping.

A tub of car wax can make your wheels gleam, but also can fight bathroom mildew, keep fingerprints off appliances, and wax your snow shovel.

A roll of adhesive tape can help remove a splinter, emboss your library card, find the beginning of plastic wrap, and protect your wood floor.

Party balloons can help keep a bandage or cast dry when you shower, keep cats off the couch, and function as an instant icepack.

Aspirin can stop your grandson's acne, get rid of your athlete's foot, and give you a spa facial at home.

Baby powder can clean your carpet overnight, squash the squeak in your wooden floor, and help you undo a knot.

That's dozens and dozens of dollars saved, right there. And right here, in the pages of *99 Cent Solutions*, we provide you with over a thousand ways to save big, just by scouring the aisles of that old-fashioned store you've come to know and love. Read on, and watch your dollars grow!

Elissa Altman, *Executive Editor*

MOST DOLLAR STORES CARRY AN EXTENSIVE selection of nonperishable foods, but do pay attention to make sure you're not buying something for a dollar that would cost less than that in the grocery store—canned beans, for example. With that warning aside, dollar store food aisles can be a terrific place to trawl for bargains. The selections can change frequently, depending on what the wholesaler has on offer, so you may find imported chocolates and jams or your favorite brand of breakfast cereal for low, low prices. Once your pantry is fully stocked with all these goodies, their uses don't stop at the kitchen door. There's a whole lot more you can do with them, both on and off the kitchen table and all around the house and garden.

applesauce

Whether sold in handy individual serving packs or in a big glass jar, applesauce in the pantry opens a host of uses besides snacks. Go for the unsweetened varieties for better taste.

Replace the oil in baking

Fat makes baked goods moist and tender. It's also incredibly calorie-dense, and if you're cutting calories, it's an easy place to start. But say you don't like your cakes and muffins dry and tough? Then applesauce is the answer. Replace up to 2/3 of the oil called for in a cake or muffin recipe with applesauce, and you'll add moisture and flavor while ditching the fat.

Make holiday ornaments

Mix equal amounts cinnamon and applesauce to make fragrant ornaments. Start with 1 cup of each and mix, adding more cinnamon if needed to form a stiff dough. Mold holiday ornaments such as wreaths or hearts or roll it out 1/2-inch thick and cut shapes with cookie cutters. Be sure to make a hole with a chopstick or pencil for a loop of ribbon. Let dry completely for several days on a baking sheet or wire rack.

Add sweetness and fiber to oatmeal

You've gone to all that trouble to make a healthy breakfast of oatmeal so don't ruin it by slathering on butter, sugar and cream. Instead, stir in a few tablespoons of applesauce and a sprinkle of cinnamon. You'll add sweetness and flavor and even more fiber, making your breakfast both healthy and delicious.

baking soda

One of the most useful items in the pantry, baking soda is a super-item. It's inexpensive and incredibly potent, both inside and outside the kitchen.

Soften beans

Afraid those dry beans have been on the shelf too long? Help soften them by adding a pinch of baking soda to the soaking water. Add a fresh pinch to the cooking water, too, and you can significantly reduce the aftereffects of bean consumption.

Get rid of fishy odors

Been chopping something pungent? The smell of garlic or fish can linger on your fingers long after the food is gone. Avoid that by scrubbing your wet hands with baking soda, just as if it were soap, then rinse in warm water. Your hands will smell sweet—and feel softer, too.

Make a rainy day toy for kids

Kids stuck inside with nothing to do? Boil 2 cups baking soda with 1 cup cornstarch and 1 1/4 cups water until thickened. Remove from the heat and cool. It makes a fun, pliable modeling clay that's good for a day.

Deep-clean a dishwasher

Faintly funky smell in your dishwasher? You can sort that out fast with a baking soda wash. Put 1 cup of baking soda in the bottom of the dishwasher and run it on a rinse cycle. If the smell persists, sprinkle a few tablespoons on the bottom of the washer to sit there between loads. There's no need to rinse it out before running the next load.

Repel rain from a windshield

You know you need new wiper blades, but now there's rain in the forecast and you haven't replaced them yet. Dissolve a couple tablespoons baking soda in 2 cups of water, dip in a clean cloth, and rub it over the windshield. Rain will slip off more easily until you buy those new blades.

De-skunk a bottle or thermos

Can't get that smell out of a bottle or flask that has been stored with the lid on? Fill it with warm water and a few teaspoons of baking soda and soak it overnight. Rinse well and the smell will have evaporated.

Make a stove top sparkle

Cooked-on food stains are difficult to remove. But you don't need a commercial spray. Far faster, more effective, and more environmentally friendly is a sprinkle of baking soda. Wipe the stains with a wet sponge to dampen them, then sprinkle on baking soda. Scrub with the sponge, and the stains will lift right off. This is also perfect for the greasy black dirt that can build up around the edges of other kitchen appliances.

Salvage a burned pot

By the time you've thought, "What's that smell?" and then remembered you left the stove on, it's often too late. The bottom of the pot is a blackened mess. You can save it, though. Scrape out as much food as you can and then fill the pan a quarter full with water. Pour in 1/2 cup of baking soda and bring the pot to a boil. Turn it off and let it sit overnight. In the morning, you can clean off the black stuff with ease.

Keep garbage cans fresh

Before you put a new liner in the garbage can, sprinkle a dollop of baking soda. When you take out the full bag, turn the can upside down to dump any dry soda still left in there, and then add more before the new bag. You've got a natural deodorizer right where you need it most.

The Story Behind... Arm & Hammer Baking Soda

One of the longest-running and most recognized of all U.S. trademarks, Arm & Hammer Baking Soda dates back to 1867—just two years after the end of the Civil War—when the owner of The Vulcan Spice Mill of Brooklyn, New York, shut down the mill. James A. Church went into business with his father, a baking soda manufacturer, and reopened the plant as Arm & Hammer. It's said that the Arm & Hammer logo represents Vulcan, the Roman god of fire and metalworking.

Make tomatoes taste sweeter

If last year's garden tomatoes tasted dull, take action this year to ensure your garden harvest is as good as it can be. Sprinkle baking soda lightly on the soil around the base of your tomato plants. The resulting tomatoes will taste sweeter.

Save a mildewed book

Found mildew around the edge of a childhood classic you adored? If it's a mild case, you can arrest the growth and save the book with baking soda. Sprinkle it lightly between the pages, then put the book in a paper bag and dust the outside with more baking soda. Let it sit for several days, then remove, shake out and dust off the baking soda, and let the book get a shot of bright sunlight. It doesn't remove mildew marks, but if you store it in a dry place, no more mildew will grow.

Take the sting out of sunburn

You just want the itchy pain from a sunburn to stop. Soaking in a lukewarm bath helps, but help it a bit more with a cup of baking soda poured into the water. It will take the sting out and lessen the pain quickly.

Clean a glass-front fireplace

If the glass in front of your fireplace or woodstove is blackened with soot and smoke, it's time for baking soda. Crumple a sheet of newspaper, wet it in water, and dip it in baking soda. Scrub the glass—the black stuff will come right off. Wipe with a damp cloth. You can use the same technique to get soot off the glazed bricks lining the fireplace.

Stop a mosquito bite in its tracks

Slap! You killed the mosquito, but not before it got a good bite. Rush inside and pour a tablespoon of baking soda in your palm. Wet it with a few drops of water to make a paste, then smear it on the bite area. Let it dry and flake off. If you treat the mark this way as soon as you can, there will be no red welt from the bite, and the itching will subside almost instantly. The same treatment works for bee stings, assuming you have carefully removed any sign of the stinger.

Control cradle cap

The flaky scalp on infants known as cradle cap is harmless and will usually go away on its own, but most moms can't stand to look at it on the baby's head without trying to rub it away. Make a

Keep your garbage can fresh. Before you put a new liner in the garbage can, sprinkle a dollop of baking soda.

paste in your palm of a couple tablespoons baking soda and a teaspoon of water. Rub gently on the affected area, being careful not to get near the eyes, and then wipe off with a damp washcloth, using no soap or baby shampoo. Repeat for two to three days until the flakiness lessens. (If the baby's head is very red after this treatment, try rubbing in baby oil instead—the soda may be too abrasive.)

Soothe a canker sore

It's hard to believe how much pain a tiny sore on the inside of your mouth can cause. Soothe the pain away and help heal the sore faster by swishing every couple of hours with a solution of 1 teaspoon baking soda stirred until it dissolves into 1 cup warm water.

Soak your way to comfort

Hot, sweaty feet? Tired and achy toes? In the evening, plop your tootsies in a basin of cool water with baking soda stirred in. Soak for 15 to 20 minutes, then rinse and dry. Not only will this soothe your feet and help cut down on odor during the day, but it will also help dry up athlete's foot.

Soften hard-water washes

Add 1/4 cup baking soda to a hot white wash to boost the strength of your usual detergent and get your whites bright.

Ready your AC for the season

Before your window units go in, the filters should be washed. Brush off obvious dirt and dust, then lay the filters in a basin of water with several tablespoons baking soda mixed in. Swish them in the water to clean, then rinse and dry in hot sun before replacing in the unit.

Make fluffier omelets

Can't get your omelets as puffy as the restaurant kind? Add a scant 1/4 teaspoon of baking soda to every three eggs that you beat. The omelet will be light and fluffy. You can also use this trick to make big fluffy curds when scrambling eggs. Don't add too much or your eggs will taste bland, and be careful not to oversalt since the soda adds a slight salty taste.

Clean your brushes

Hairbrushes and combs should be washed periodically to remove the hair oils that build up. Remove any hair, then fill the sink with warm water and stir in a couple of spoonfuls of baking soda. Let the brushes and combs soak several hours, then rinse and air dry. You can also clean toothbrushes by letting them soak in a cup filled with warm water and a tablespoon of baking soda. Rinse well and air dry.

Discourage weeds in cracks

Hoping to keep grass and weeds out of the cracks between your paving stones? Sprinkle on baking soda and sweep it into the cracks. Grass will stick to the lawn instead.

Wash the dog's ears

Dirt or mites in your pet's ears can drive him nuts with scratching. Clean out the dirt and put an end to the mites with a cotton swab dipped in a mild solution of 1 cup warm water and 1 teaspoon baking soda.

10 More Nontraditional Ways to Use BAKING SODA

1 Eat Naked Fruit!

Give your produce a baking soda bath. Dampen fruits (or vegetables) with water, sprinkle a vegetable brush with baking soda, and then scrub before you eat them. Rinse well and dry. A baking soda wash removes wax from fruits like apples and reduces pesticides on fruits and veggies that a simple water rinse may not.

2 Be Tender to Tummies

If someone has a delicate stomach, careful use of baking soda can help you make food more palatable for them. A very tiny pinch in coffee, orange juice, or tomato soup, for example, can prevent an acidic stomach after eating. Be careful not to overdo it or food will taste bland.

3 Faux-Age Wood

Added an extension to your deck this summer? Does the new wood look funny and green next to the older boards? Faux-age that addition by stirring 1 cup of baking soda into a liter of water. Scrub the mixture into the wood with a stiff brush, then splash on cool water to rinse. When it dries, that fresh green look will have faded.

4 Miracle for the Microwave

Got a lot of gunk "baked" onto the walls of your microwave? Put 1 cup water and a few tablespoons of baking soda into a glass container. Microwave on high for 3 minutes. Use a damp sponge to wipe off all the loosened grime—it's that easy!

5 No Stick, No Rust, No Kidding!

They call it nonstick but stuff stuck. And your beloved cast-iron skillet has rust stains. Scrub the spots with a damp sponge sprinkled with baking soda. Make sure to wet the sponge well to dissolve the baking soda and avoid scratching your nonstick.

6 Revitalize Wallpaper

Did someone trail greasy little fingers down the wallpaper in the hallway? Rub the stain gently with a damp sponge sprinkled with baking soda, then rinse and pat dry. Your wallpaper will be good as new.

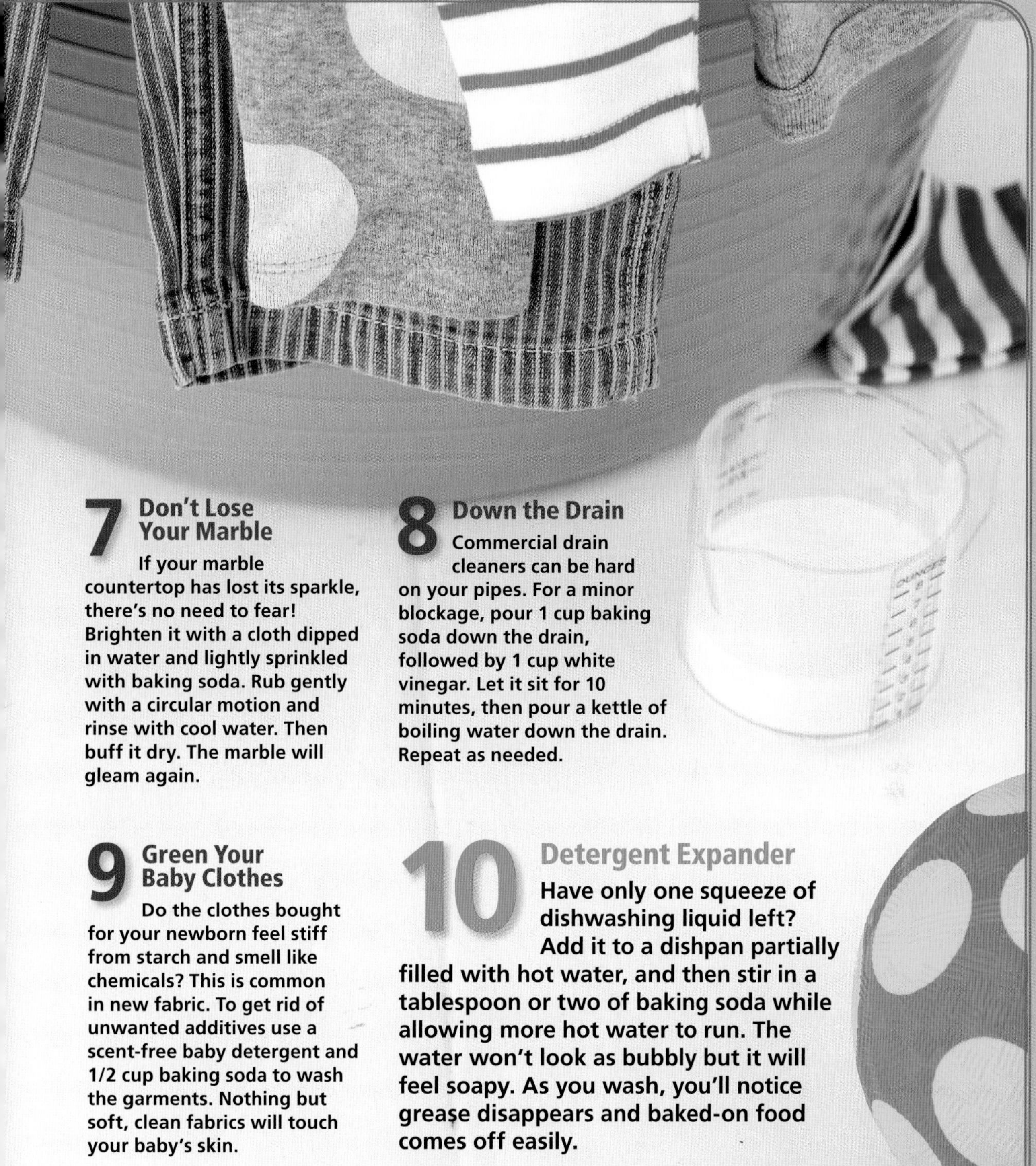

7 Don't Lose Your Marble

If your marble countertop has lost its sparkle, there's no need to fear! Brighten it with a cloth dipped in water and lightly sprinkled with baking soda. Rub gently with a circular motion and rinse with cool water. Then buff it dry. The marble will gleam again.

8 Down the Drain

Commercial drain cleaners can be hard on your pipes. For a minor blockage, pour 1 cup baking soda down the drain, followed by 1 cup white vinegar. Let it sit for 10 minutes, then pour a kettle of boiling water down the drain. Repeat as needed.

9 Green Your Baby Clothes

Do the clothes bought for your newborn feel stiff from starch and smell like chemicals? This is common in new fabric. To get rid of unwanted additives use a scent-free baby detergent and 1/2 cup baking soda to wash the garments. Nothing but soft, clean fabrics will touch your baby's skin.

10 Detergent Expander

Have only one squeeze of dishwashing liquid left? Add it to a dishpan partially filled with hot water, and then stir in a tablespoon or two of baking soda while allowing more hot water to run. The water won't look as bubbly but it will feel soapy. As you wash, you'll notice grease disappears and baked-on food comes off easily.

beans (dried)

Dried beans cost about the same at the dollar store as they do at the supermarket, but that doesn't mean you shouldn't stock up. In addition to being a delicious and cheap source of protein, they're great for a lot of other stuff, too.

Train a dog

Most dogs hate the sound of dried beans rattling in a can. Use that to your advantage when training a dog by putting a handful of beans in the bottom of an empty aluminum soda can. Seal the top with a strip of tape. When your dog misbehaves, shake the can a couple of times.

Make a close-fitting hot pad

Soothe aching muscles with a custom-made hot pad. Fill a long sock, such as a tube or athletic sock, with dried beans, and tie the top tightly closed with ribbon or string. Heat in a microwave on high for 30 seconds. Place it right on your painful spot. You can drape it around a stiff neck or wrap it around a sore wrist, and it will mold to you, providing faster relief.

Prevent a scorched pan

Got a lot of pans on the stove? Toss a small handful of beans in the bottom of a double boiler or a steamer, and as the water boils down, the beans will rattle. (This handy trick only works when you're boiling water for less than half an hour. Any longer and the beans will soften and cook!)

Make a beanbag

Put 1 cup of beans in the toe of a cotton sock, and tie a knot in the remaining material, pushing it down till the knot is close up against the beans. Make two more and you've got a terrific juggling set or the start of a bean toss for kids. Set up your youngsters with a few beanbags and a clean, empty wastebasket, and they're ready for hours of fun.

bread

Bread was long unavailable at the dollar store, but many chains have begun to expand their grocery sections to include a small selection of fresh foods. When you're looking for uses beyond a sandwich, packaged bread is often *more* useful than a crisp bakery loaf!

Sweeten the scent of cabbage

They're good for you and they taste good, but when they're cooking, cabbage and cauliflower and other cruciferous vegetables can release an odor that does not beckon people into the kitchen. Lay a slice or two of white bread on top of the cooking veggies and put on the lid—the scent will stay in the bread, not in the air.

Train your dog by putting a handful of beans in the bottom of an empty soda can. When your dog misbehaves, shake the can a couple of times.

Keep cookies fresh

Homemade chocolate chip cookies can go from tasting deliciously soft and cakey to feeling hard and crunchy in a matter of days. To keep your freshly baked cookies tasting...freshly baked, put a couple slices of bread into the tin or jar where you store the cookies, laying the bread right on top of the cookies. The bread will keep that just-out-of-the-oven flavor and texture intact for up to a week.

Prevent broiler flare-ups

Put a slice or two of stale bread in the bottom of the broiler pan, and it will absorb the grease as it runs off, stopping flare-ups and easing cleanup by preventing pan juices from getting stuck to the pan.

Butter corn on the cob

Corn on the cob, that summertime treat, wouldn't taste the same without a slather of butter on top, but it's hard to spread it evenly over the nubby cob, especially for kids. Instead, spread a slice of bread thickly with softened butter and cup the bread in your palm—butter side up! Turn the corn in the buttery slice for perfect coverage.

Clean smudges off suede

Suede jackets, shoes and handbags look great but they're prone to picking up dirty marks. Clean fresh smudges off quickly and easily before they set into stains by rubbing the suede gently with a piece of fresh white bread. Use a small, circular motion. You may need a second piece of bread to get the spot clean.

Take scuffs off wallpaper and flat paint

Scuffs, fingerprints, and other marks on painted wallpapers and non-glossy paint surfaces can be hard to clean: Water can leave marks if you scrub with a sponge. Try a fresh slice of plain white bread instead, with the crusts cut off so no color can transfer. Rub gently over the mark, using a fresh slice of bread if needed, until it gently rubs off, leaving the surface intact, unharmed—and clean.

WAY BACK WHEN...

It's a Wonder

The next time you use the expression, "It's the best thing since sliced bread," think of everyone's favorite white bread in the polka-dot package. The year was 1921 and the Taggart Baking Company of Indianapolis was planning to introduce its pound-and-a-half loaf of white bread to the public. Elmer Cline, the vice president of the company, looked low and high for a marketing hook—and the latter is where he found one! While attending the International Balloon Race at the Indianapolis Speedway, Cline was dumbstruck by a sky packed with colorful balloons. "It's wonderful," he thought....and then the lightbulb went off: Ever since that time, the red, blue, and yellow balloons are instantly recognizable as Wonder Bread's package.

butter

Like bread, butter is another fresh item that's only recently available in dollar stores. Once you're done slathering some on your toast, you'll be glad to have an inexpensive source of butter—both salted and sweet—for a lot of other uses.

Keep onions and cheese fresh

They're a world apart in flavor and texture, but both onions and cheese benefit from butter when it comes to storage. Rub the cut side of an onion with butter and wrap in plastic wrap—it will stay fresh for days longer, and you can dice the buttery parts right into your skillet. Hard and semisoft

Rub the cut side of an onion with butter and wrap in plastic wrap—it will stay fresh for days longer.

cheeses will stay mold-free for weeks if you rub the cut sides with softened butter, sealing them to keep the air out before rewrapping in plastic and storing in the fridge.

Get that medicine down

Doctor says you need to take that pill—but you're wondering if it's meant for you or a horse. Whether the pill is large or you just don't love swallowing pills, try a dab of butter to ease the job. Lightly rub butter all over the outside of the pill, and it will slip gently down with a sip of water, no sticking awkwardly in your throat. To your health!

Give dry hair a real salon treatment

Return your hair to the glossy tresses it had before all that blow-drying. Smooth and soften the cuticles of your hair with a super-rich butter treatment. Rub a handful of soft butter into dry hair, working it gently down to the ends. Wrap your hair in a towel or put on a shower cap and leave in for half an hour. Wash and rinse thoroughly, and run your fingers through your luxurious tresses.

Strip off sticky sap

Whether you've been stacking firewood or collecting pinecones, the tree sap on your hands is nearly impossible to get off. Unless you rub it well with butter. Use a generous amount and slather it on your hands like you're rubbing in lotion. Wipe it off with paper towel and wash with soap and water. All clear!

chamomile tea

Among the wealth of herbal teas on the shelf, chamomile is particularly useful. In addition to its mild and pleasant apple-like flavor and the calming effect it is said to have, there are a lot of useful things you can do with it besides drink a cup.

Repel mosquitoes

You may love the mild apple-like flavor of chamomile tea but mosquitoes absolutely hate it. Brew a very strong batch of chamomile tea and keep it in a spray bottle in the fridge. Before you relax in the back yard or run through the tall grass, spray exposed skin liberally. It's fragrant, potent, and totally safe for children.

Lighten your hair

Play up your blond highlights by using a weak solution of chamomile tea as the final rinse when you wash your hair. Combine a brewed cup of tea with two cups of cool water and pour this over your hair after rinsing out the shampoo and conditioner. Your golden highlights will gleam!

Tone your skin

If you have sensitive skin that feels dry and uncomfortable after washing with soap, try a facial toner with chamomile. It's far more soothing and effective than many expensive skin products. Boil 4 cups of water and soak 2 chamomile tea bags in it for 15 minutes. Discard the tea bags and cool the tea. Store in a glass jar in the fridge. To use, remove makeup with a soap-free remover, then soak several cotton balls in the cool tea and rub all over your face.

chewing gum

If your mother was always telling you to spit out that gum, that's probably because she didn't know how many other uses there are for gum—in addition to popping big bubbles!

Make a temporary repair

A piece of gum is more than a bubble waiting to happen. It's also the ideal material for a quick and temporary repair until you have the time and the tools to do it right. You can fill a crack in a dog's water bowl (on the outside, so the pooch doesn't accidentally suck it down!) or use a couple of wads as window putty if a pane of glass is loose. Ever have the lens pop out of your eyeglasses while you were out and about? Use a bit of chewed gum to hold them in place until you can get a proper repair.

Settle a sour stomach

Fresh out of antacids, and heartburn is making you miserable? Pop in a stick of minty gum and chew. Spearmint is ideal for settling stomach rumbles and burbles, and the increased flow of saliva from gum chewing can help neutralize stomach acids.

THE Story Behind... Chewing Gum

In 1869, Thomas Adams, a photographer from Staten Island, New York, invented modern chewing gum. His houseguest, General Antonio de Santa of Mexico, believed chicle, a natural gum from the sapodilla tree, could make rubber less expensive. Adams bounced this idea around, but when he noticed the general chewed the stuff, he was truly inspired. He created a chewing gum that wasn't paraffin-based, like all other gums on the market. A druggist agreed to carry it, the public responded well, and by February 1871 Adams New York Gum could be purchased in drugstores for a penny per piece. Today, Americans spend more than $2 billion per year on chewing gum.

Capture a crab

Crabbing is a favorite activity of kids who summer near docks and piers because all it takes is string, a net, and a lure. Crabs are notorious scavengers who tend to be keen to grab at a bit of raw bacon, but you'll catch aplenty with gum. The scent of a bit of freshly chewed and soft gum will call all the crabs in the area. Start that pot of water boiling; it's dinnertime soon!

club soda

Soda, seltzer, fizzy water...whatever you call it, it's cool and refreshing and immensely useful for many things besides drinking. Too bad the days are gone when you could get regular seltzer deliveries right to your doorstep.

Preserve a precious newspaper clipping

Newspapers aren't made to stay intact forever, but nobody wants a wedding or birth announcement to go brown and crumbly in just a few years. Make a preservative solution by mixing one tablespoon milk of magnesia with 2 cups club soda in a wide, flat dish. Soak the clipping for one hour, then pat dry with a paper towel and dry flat.

Make your diamond sparkle

Club soda gently and safely cleans precious jewels, whether it's your wedding diamond or your Great Aunt Ruby's emerald. Put the jewels in a glass and top with club soda. Let them soak overnight. The fizzing bubbles will lift away dirt and grime that dull the gleam. Dry and polish gently with a soft cloth.

Clean dentures overnight

Gone on a visit and forgotten your denture cleaner? Don't panic or go looking for a spare toothbrush. Instead, soak them overnight in a coffee mug topped up with club soda. The fizzy bubbles will lift away food particles and leave your teeth feeling clean in the morning.

Make a "submarine tank" for kids

Are the little ones bored at the restaurant table while the grownups chat? Kids need something to do! Make them a quick and easy game with a glass of club soda and a couple of raisins. Drop two or three raisin "submarines" in the water and let the kids watch the raisins go up and down. See if they can figure out that the bubbles in the club soda are lifting the raisins.

Fight tough stains on clothes and carpets

Just got a splash of red wine or a dribble of coffee on your cream-colored cashmere? Quick, splash it again, but this time with a dousing of club soda. There's no better way to stop the stain and prevent it from setting. You can do the same with spots on rugs and carpets—pour on the club soda and scrub gently with a towel or lint-free cloth.

Pancake and waffle batter, and especially
matzo balls, are much lighter when
you use club soda.

coffee

You can't do without a cup of coffee to start your morning or as a pick-me-up in the afternoon. But fresh coffee grounds provide more than caffeine, as you'll see in these fun tips.

Freshen a fridge

If something soured in your fridge or the freezer failed, clean it out, then fill a wide, shallow bowl with fresh coffee grounds and leave it in the fridge or freezer overnight. The strong scent of coffee will permeate the space, eradicating any hint of what went wrong.

Feed your plants

Used coffee grounds are full of nitrogen, so it's a shame to throw them away each day. Coffee is especially good for acid-loving plants, like camellias, evergreens, rhododendrons, azaleas, and rosebushes, so be sure they don't miss out on the occasional cup of coffee—grounds, that is.

Grow longer, stronger carrots

Carrot seeds are tiny to sow, and the beds require a great deal of cultivation so the soil is loose enough for the carrots to shoot downward as they grow. Increase the odds in your favor by working leftover coffee grounds into the soil as you prepare the plot, and then mix the seeds with damp grounds just before sowing them. The scent helps repel pests, and the added bulk of the grounds helps space out the tiny plants. What's more, that extra hit of nitrogen as the seeds sprout will give you a bumper crop.

Tamp down the ashes

A fireplace is a delight—until it's time to sweep out the ashes the next day, kicking up a cloud of dust and making you cough. Sprinkle the dead ashes liberally with moist coffee grounds and then sweep away. The dampness and weight of the grounds prevents clouds of dust dancing around your living room as you clean.

That takes the bait

Up bright and early for your fishing trip? Don't forget to bring the coffee. The grounds, that is. Stir the coffee grounds from your morning joe into the soil in your bait container. Whether it's the caffeine or the scent or perhaps the texture, worms love coffee grounds and they'll stay alive and lively all day.

cornstarch

Sure, you knew cornstarch was good for thickening sauces and puddings and also as a cooling, soothing alternative to talcum powder. But did you know it's good for all these other uses as well?

Untangle a shoelace

Junior got a knot in his sneaker and pulled and pulled until it became an impenetrable mass. Sprinkle the knot generously with cornstarch, and then work the knot again. The laces will start to slip and slide, and you'll be able to get the kinks out.

Clean up oily furniture

Got a little too enthusiastic when spritzing the side tables with lemon oil? Don't live with that sticky feeling. Sprinkle cornstarch over the surface and leave it for a few minutes to absorb the excess. Wipe up the cornstarch, then buff to a shine with a soft, lint-free cloth.

Remove a scorch mark

Left a brown scorch on a dress shirt with the iron? It can happen in the blink of an eye. The cleanup won't be quite that fast but it will be effective. Douse the scorch with water (presumably not on your ironing board!) then rub a generous amount of cornstarch into the stain. When the cornstarch dries, the stain will rinse out with the powder. This same technique works on bloodstains, though a second treatment may be needed before washing.

Make a gentle silver cleaner

Don't want to put harsh chemicals on Granny's old silver? Make a cleanser that's less harsh than commercial polishes—and one that won't remove all the tarnish from a complicated pattern, a look many silver lovers prefer because it throws a beautiful pattern into stunning relief. Mix cornstarch with water to make a thick paste. Rub it on the silver and let it dry. Buff off with a lint-free cloth to bring up the shine.

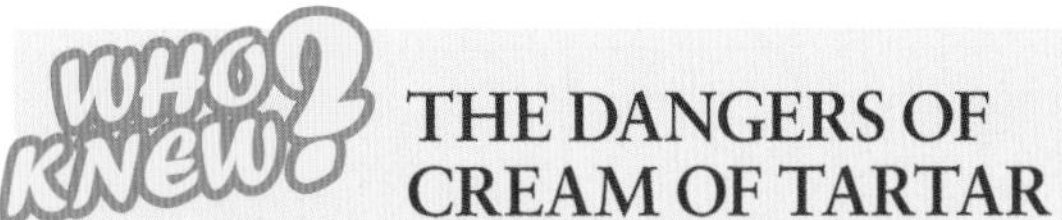

THE DANGERS OF CREAM OF TARTAR

Today you head out to the grocery store to buy cream of tartar; back in the 19th century you'd head to the druggist if you didn't want any trouble. In 1883, the *New York Times* covered the story of Manhattan grocer Henry V. Fuller, who, along with others, was charged by the City Board of Health "with selling cream of tartar." According to laws of the day, pharmacists sold cream of tartar (which could be used both medicinally and as a food) to ensure it was of the correct chemical makeup. Grocers could get in on the action—but they ran the risk of prosecution. Fuller claimed he bought "pure" cream of tartar at 164 Duane Street to sell as a food only. Interestingly, the street where he committed his "crime," along with its neighbor, Reade Street, became the birthplace of one of today's largest chain of drugstores: Duane Reade.

cream of tartar

Before the advent of reliable commercial baking powder, cooks made their own with varying mixtures of baking soda and cream of tartar, an acid salt that has many other uses besides making baked goods rise.

Create your own soft scrub

Got a surface that needs gentle cleaning, such as your elderly cast-iron tub or perhaps your brand-new designer sink? Make an effective cleanser that's devoid of harshness by mixing 2 teaspoons white vinegar with 2 teaspoons cream of tartar. Rub and scrub with a sponge, then rinse with warm water and buff dry.

Shine aluminum cookware

Aluminum pots conduct heat beautifully, but woe to the cook who lets acid touch the pan: Aluminum discolors like crazy. Remove discoloration and stains by putting 1 quart water and 2 tablespoons cream of tartar in the pan. Bring to a boil, and as it simmers for 10 minutes, you'll see the stains fade and disappear.

Take stains off tile and tubs

Got a bathtub ring that won't scrub off or stubborn stains on the tile? They're no match for hydrogen peroxide and cream of tartar. Put a few tablespoons of cream of tartar in a cup or jar, then add hydrogen peroxide by the drop to make a thick paste. (If you accidentally add way too much liquid, you may want to dump half the entire cup before stirring in more cream of tartar—otherwise you may find your container empty fast!) Spread on the stain and let it dry. Rinse off with warm water, and the stain should be history.

Repel ants

Sprinkle a thin line of cream of tartar across the path that ants are traveling to come in. Put it across the windowsill or in corners and cracks around the kitchen. As with boric acid, ants won't cross the line—but it's a much safer chemical to have out in your kitchen around foodstuffs and where children might be playing.

flour

You knew flour makes the bread that is our staff of life. But did you know that flour is also endlessly useful all around the house in a wealth of other ways?

Clean copper and brass

Mix 2 tablespoons flour with 2 tablespoons white vinegar and 2 tablespoons regular iodized table salt. Rub the resulting paste thickly on copper or brass (the uncoated kind; not anything with varnish on it) and let it dry. Use a soft, lint-free cloth to buff the dry remains off your metal object, and you'll find a smooth, mellow shine with an unharmed finish.

Buff up a stainless steel sink

Metal sinks look terrific when they go in, but the impact of daily use steadily dulls their luster until they look stained and worn. Bring the shine back to a steel sink by drying it with a dishtowel. Then sprinkle plain white flour over the surface—not too much, just a light coating—and rub it with a soft dry cloth. Rinse with warm water and polish with another dry cloth.

Restore a deck of cards

Your favorite, most winning deck of playing cards will gradually show the wear and tear of all those finger oils from you and your fellow players. You don't have to give them up, however. Put the cards in a ziplock bag and scoop in about a cup of flour. Seal and shake to coat every surface, then let the cards sit for 10 minutes so the flour can absorb the oils from the surface. Remove the cards and shake off the excess flour. You're ready to start clearing all the poker chips off the table again!

ketchup

It's on every table in every diner you've ever visited, and it's hard to find a fridge that doesn't hold a bottle. Ketchup is terrific for lots besides serving as a condiment for your burgers and fries.

Clean detailed silver patterns

Some people like a tiny bit of tarnish left in a complex silver pattern to throw the detail into relief, but if you want your silver to shine, shine, shine, without rubbing and wearing off the pattern, then ketchup is the way to go. The acids in ketchup will quickly remove every last speck of tarnish from an elaborate silver pattern, leaving it gleaming. Smear a few pieces at a time with ketchup and let them sit for several minutes. Rinse a piece to see how it's coming along. If needed, apply more ketchup, but keep checking so you don't do any damage with the acid. When the silver shines to your satisfaction, rinse with warm water and buff with a soft, lint-free cloth.

Banish chlorine green hair

Any blonde—whether natural or not—knows that too much time in the pool can leave a distinct green cast to light-colored locks, not to mention a decided smell of chlorine that builds up after days at the pool. To return your tresses to their rightful color and eradicate the chlorine, massage ketchup into your wet hair while in the shower and leave it for 10 minutes. Rinse well and shampoo as usual. The green will be gone, and you'll smell like nothing but freshly washed hair.

BAKING ROYALTY

THE HISTORY OF KING ARTHUR FLOUR

The year was 1790 and the place was Boston. The American Revolutionary War was over and wartime boycotts were lifted. Henry Wood, an importer and distributor, began to ship fine flour to Boston's Long Wharf, which extended into deep water, allowing large vessels to dock and unload directly to warehouses and stores. Over time, and with the addition of partners, the company became known as Sands, Taylor & Wood Co. **The company gave itself the mandate of selling only flour of the highest quality and purity.** To that end, they devised a process to bring to market flour that would rise but was unbleached and unbromated—in other words, additive-free. One of the partners, George E. Wood, impressed by a musical called *King Arthur and the Knights of the Round Table*, named the pure flour King Arthur Flour. It was introduced at the Boston Food Fair in October 1896 with canny marketing: **According to the *Boston Post,* attention was garnered by a knight clad "in glittering armor...as he rode a black horse through the streets of Boston."**

The image of a champion was prescient, because the company had trials to overcome. World War I caused quality wheat to be both expensive and in short supply; then mass production post-war led to housewives choosing "store-bought" bread instead of baking from scratch, and sales dwindled. Going from bad to worse, the Great Depression arrived. Turning again to savvy marketing, the company sponsored a radio show starring Marjorie Mills, known as New England's first lady of cookery and also the editor of the *Boston Herald-Traveler's* Women's Page. Broadcast in Massachusetts, Maine, Connecticut, and Rhode Island, the program promised five-pound bags of free flour to listeners who wrote to the show requesting purchase warrants. The company made it through the 1930s, but World War II again saw wheat being shipped to Europe, and flour production suffered—though not quality. The company maintained its standards, and by the 1960s, began a new advertising strategy. They started emphasizing the difference between natural and processed foods and called attention to the lack of bleaching and bromate exclusive to King Arthur Flour. King Arthur Flour's slogan, "Never Bleached—Never Bromated," seems all the more impressive given that it was created 100 years before we were concerned about carcinogens!

In 1984, the nation's oldest flour company relocated its headquarters to Norwich, Vermont. In 1996, it became employee owned, and by 1999 it changed its name to The King Arthur Flour Company. The King Arthur Flour Company is also an educator of home bakers, conducting tours that provide free instruction to thousands of bakers across the country.

To brighten up copper pots, smear a generous layer of ketchup all over the copper surface you want to clean.

Brighten the copper

While copper details on the exterior of a home look lovely as they take on an aged green patina, copper pots and decorative items inside the house look best when they're gleaming and bright. Rather than donning gloves to apply chemical cleaners, use your hands (or a sponge) to smear a generous layer of ketchup all over the copper surface you want to clean. The acidic coating quickly works to remove every speck of tarnish. Rinse with warm water and buff to a shine to make your brightwork bright again.

Kool-Aid

Powdered drink mixes, especially the Kool-Aid brand, are readily available, even though you might think these envelopes of potent drink mix might have outlived their usefulness in a world of soda pop. You would be wrong, as you'll find in these wide-ranging tips for using Kool-Aid.

Clean concrete

The same acids that make lemonade-flavored Kool-Aid taste good are a potent cleaning solution before you add water and sugar. Mix the contents of a package with 2 tablespoons hot water to make a paste, then rub that paste over rust stains in concrete. Scrub with a stiff cleaning brush and the stains will disappear. Rinse well.

Remove dishwasher rust stains

If you have hard water, the inside of your dishwasher will eventually get dingy, as iron and other minerals build up on the interior walls. Return your appliance to pristine condition by putting a package of lemonade Kool-Aid in the soap dispenser, then run a hot (or "heavy") cycle. The inside will gleam like new again.

Decorate a kid's room

Kids always want to have a say in decorating their own rooms, and here's a way to make their private space highly personal. Let your child choose the color and/or flavor of Kool-Aid he most prefers, and stir one or two packages into a quart of white, water-based paint. The strong dyes result in a distinctive paint that's perfect for brightening a wall of your child's room.

lemon juice

Bottled lemon juice is used for cooking, right? That's just the start. In particular, it's a great cleaner: Rub some on gold jewelry or copper-

bottomed pots and pans, and see how they glitter! Or mix equal parts lemon juice with water in a spray bottle for a handy all-purpose cleaner!

Cook fluffy rice

Add a tablespoon of lemon juice to the water when you're making rice. After it's finished cooking, fluff it with a fork. No more sticky rice!

Crisp up lettuce

Forgot to make a salad for supper the last few nights? Tonight you can redeem yourself, even if that head of lettuce seems soggy and sad. Put a couple tablespoons lemon juice in a bowl of cold water and let the lettuce leaves soak for 20 minutes. They'll be crispy and fresh again.

Remove stains from marble

Marble looks beautiful in the kitchen, whether you have a whole countertop of the stuff or a board for rolling pastry. If you've lived with marble, though, you'll realize its drawback: It stains. If you have a really stubborn stain, try scrubbing with a paste of lemon and salt. This ought to remove the stain, but don't scrub too hard, and rinse it very well so the acid doesn't damage the stone.

Clean a crusty microwave

Been awhile since you washed down the inside of the microwave? Don't spend ages scrubbing. Mix 2 cups of water with 1/4 cup lemon juice in a microwave-safe glass dish and cook on high for 8 minutes. The steam will loosen food particles on the walls and glass, making it easy to wipe clean with a few swipes.

Replace salt

If you have high blood pressure, omit salt from savory foods and sprinkle with lemon juice instead. This chef's trick really works!

marshmallows

What can you do with a marshmallow besides make a dessert treat from it? Here are some sweet ideas.

Top a cupcake

Anyone can make frosting. Be the coolest mom in school by bringing cupcakes topped with melted marshmallows! Once the timer goes off on your batch of cupcakes, open the oven door and put a single large marshmallow on the top of each cupcake. Return the pan to the hot oven for 1 minute, until the marshmallows soften and melt over the tops. Remove the pan and cool completely. Just before serving, melt 1 cup of chocolate chips in a glass bowl in the microwave for 1 minute on high. Whisk with a fork until smooth, then use the fork to drip a crazy pattern of chocolate stripes all over the surface of each cake.

WAY BACK WHEN...

Marshmallows Soothed Sore Throats

Today a marshmallow is a spongy treat cooked over campfires. Up until the mid-1800s, marshmallow candy was used medicinally. Doctors extracted juice from the roots of the marsh-mallow plant and cooked it with egg whites and sugar, then whipped it into a foamy meringue. This hardened and the resulting candy soothed children's sore throats. Eventually, advanced manufacturing processes replaced the root juice with gelatin, which eliminated any healing properties.

Drip-proof a sugar cone

Kids love ice cream in a cone but they rarely understand that the clock is ticking once you hand it over. Eat it or it's going to melt! Buy little ones some time to enjoy their cone by dropping a mini-marshmallow into a pointed sugar cone and pushing it down into the tip. Put a large marshmallow above it and push it down, too. You've just created two very effective barriers to the drips that always make their way out of the bottom and all over someone's shirt!

Preserve brown sugar

One day you have a lovely fresh bag of soft brown sugar, and the next time you go to make cookies, you've got a piece of brown granite. It's hard to keep brown sugar fresh, even in a sealed bag, but you can ensure easy scooping by putting two or three very fresh large marshmallows in the sugar bag before you seal it. If you add a few marshmallows *and* seal the whole thing up in a plastic container, you'll be ready to bake cookies at the drop of a hat for months to come.

mayonnaise

Lots of salads are nearly unimaginable without mayonnaise—from slaw to potato to egg—but once you've eaten lunch, you'll find plenty more to do around the house with that jar of mayonnaise.

Take crayon off polished wood

Did the kids color waaaay outside the lines on your varnished maple dining table? No problem—don't scrub it with water or anything scratchy and mar the surface. Just rub on a tablespoon or two of mayo with a paper towel and let it sit. Rub again and, presto, the marks are gone. Don't let your children know how easy it is to repair *that* mistake or they may try it again.

Take sap off auto paint

Parked your new car under a pine tree in spring? You may think you'll never get all those dots of pine sap off the hood. They're utterly impervious to soap and water, and you certainly don't want to scrub with anything abrasive. Mayonnaise is your car's new best friend. Rub a generous dab directly on each sap deposit and let it sit for 10 minutes. Use a soft, absorbent rag to remove the mayo and sap, then wash the car as usual. This same treatment will also remove road tar that can accumulate on the fenders. Now, don't park under that tree again!

Photo-worthy houseplants

Even a healthy houseplant looks sad and dingy when the leaves are coated with a fine layer of dust. Make the whole house look as verdant as a florist's shop by rubbing each leaf with a paper towel dipped in a little mayonnaise. Polish off with another paper towel and you'll have a gleaming, deep-green shine that will last for months.

Soften ragged cuticles

Housework making your nails look rough and ragged? Don't soak in dishwashing liquid! Put your digits in a dish of mayo for 5 minutes and then wipe off with a paper towel. Trim nails while they're slightly softer from the soak, and use an orange stick to push back raggedy cuticles. Wash with warm water, slather on some lotion, and you just saved yourself the price of a fancy manicure!

Two-for-one hair and skin treatment

Condition your hair and smooth your face at the same time with a mayonnaise treatment. Massage mayo into your dry hair and scalp, then wrap it in a towel or put on a shower cap. While your hair rests in this luxurious treatment, spread a thin layer of mayo over your freshly washed face, avoiding the eye area. Lie down with a couple of damp tea bags or cucumber slices over your eyes for 15 minutes and then step right into the shower to wash it all off. You'll feel like you're just back from the salon.

meat tenderizer

If that jar of meat tenderizer has been sitting on your shelf unused, take it down again. As you'll see here, you can do more with it than simply tenderize a steak.

Take the bite out of a mosquito attack

Got a bite on your face and a meeting in the morning? Make the itchy red bump of a bad mosquito bite disappear by slathering on a paste made by mixing a little meat tenderizer with a few drops of water. You can do this right in your palm and apply directly to your skin with your fingers. Let sit for 5 minutes before washing off. If you apply this paste within minutes of the bite, there will be no mark at all, but even if you do it hours later, you'll still reduce the redness and swelling significantly.

Ease a sting

The same trick works for a wasp or hornet bite, relieving the pain almost instantly and preventing or reducing swelling or hives. If the stinger is still in the skin, gently remove it with tweezers, being very careful not to squeeze it deeper into the wound. Apply the meat tenderizer and water paste and let it remain until it dries and flakes off, 15 minutes or so. The enzymes break down the toxins from the sting.

Soothe your lower back

Moving heavy boxes all day? Your back must be killing you. Mix 1/4 cup meat tenderizer with 2 tablespoons of water, adding a bit more as needed to make a runny paste. Have someone rub this right into the skin over your aching lower

THE Story Behind... Adolph's Meat Tenderizer

In 1949, two former GIs, Lloyd Rigler and Larry Deutsch, found a restaurant in Santa Barbara, California, that served tasty ***and*** inexpensive steak. The chef, Adolph Rempp, explained how he was able to release fine flavors in inexpensive cuts of meat: He sprinkled on a tenderizer of his own creation. One of the main ingredients was papain, an enzyme from papaya. The men saw huge commercial potential—the years after World War II were lean, and meat was expensive. They bought the recipe and Adolph's Meat Tenderizer was born. Rigler toured the country demonstrating the product to food critics. Rave reviews led to windfall sales. After the men retired, they became patrons of the arts. Adolph's Meat Tenderizer is still an artful way to stretch a budget.

back, and ideally cover the area with a washcloth dipped in hot water and squeezed out. After 10 to 15 minutes, you'll feel the muscles start to relax. Rinse off and take it easy.

Take on tough stains

Hot chocolate, coffee with milk, blood—these types of protein-based stains are usually nearly impossible to remove completely. If the stain is still wet, you've got the best chance. If not, wet the cloth and hope for the best. Sprinkle the area thickly with meat tenderizer, rub it in, and let it rest for an hour. Launder as usual.

milk

More and more dollar stores are carrying a limited selection of fresh items, usually basics such as bread and milk. Many stores already carried powdered milk in their grocery aisles, but whatever type of milk you find there, you'll find here some novel ways to use it.

Sweeten corn by adding 1 cup of milk to the pot of boiling water.

Shave your face

Use milk in place of shaving foam. Warm full-fat milk and pat it onto your skin. While you shave, continue to pat on more to keep your skin wet. For men, it's probably an emergency fix, but women shaving their legs may never go back!

Relieve a child's itching skin

Many parents hesitate to put hydrocortisone creams on children, but mild rashes can drive your kid crazy with the scratching. Mix powdered milk with just enough warm water to make it the thickness of heavy cream. Add a tiny pinch of salt and spread it over the affected parts. It will soothe the itch, and it's so mild that you can reapply as often as necessary to bring relief. Rinse off the previous application and slather on a new one.

You're soaking in it!

Cleopatra knew the benefits of a milk bath for the skin, and a couple thousand years later, it's still true. Milk moisturizes and softens the skin. Pour 2 to 3 cups of milk into the bath as the water runs (or use a cup of powdered milk) and add a little scented bath oil, if you like. Soak for at least 10 minutes for best results.

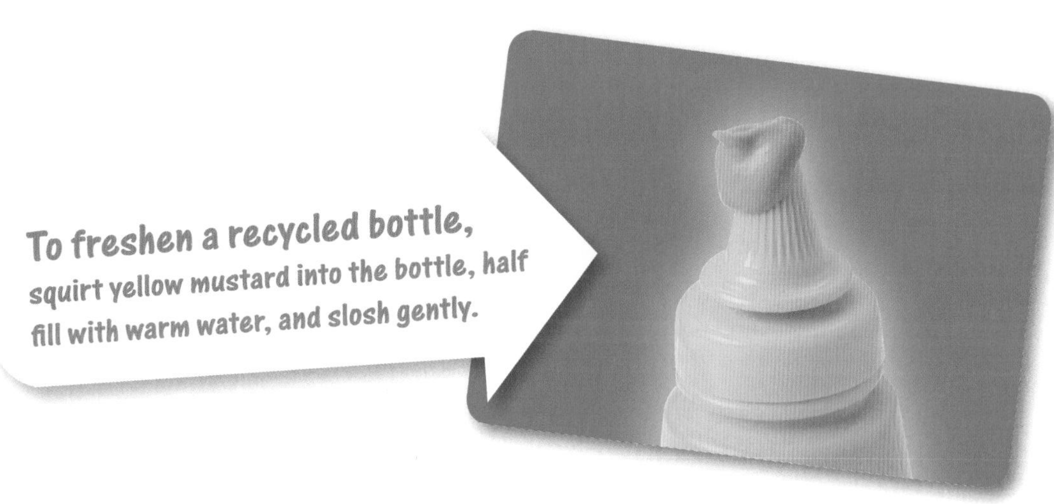
To freshen a recycled bottle,
squirt yellow mustard into the bottle, half
fill with warm water, and slosh gently.

Sweeten fish and corn

When you thaw a block of frozen fish, it can taste disappointingly watery. Avoid that by placing the unwrapped block in a shallow dish of milk and letting it thaw there—it will taste fresher when cooked. If you have corn on the cob that's been sitting in the fridge for a few days, add 1 cup of milk to the pot of boiling water, and you'll get sweeter corn.

Have a milk massage

If you like to use essential oils for your personal fragrance but don't like the greasy feeling of the carrier oil, use milk instead. Add a few drops to a little milk and spread it on your skin or use it in a bath. Make the solution up fresh when you need it.

mustard

You may find a tin of mustard powder in the food section, or you may be equally lucky and find a jar of prepared mustard. Either way, there are a lot of unexpected things you can do with it besides top a hotdog.

Soothe a chest cold

That awful feeling of congestion has settled right into your chest, and the cough is wearing you out. Sometimes Grandma really did know best, and what you need is an old-fashioned mustard plaster. Smear plain old yellow mustard (not Dijon or any other type) directly on your chest, then rinse a hand towel in hot water, wring it out, and lay it over the mustard. You'll feel that congestion start to break up.

Relax your muscles

Mustard can be very soothing for aching backs and weary muscles. While you run the hot water into the tub, add 3/4 cup yellow prepared mustard to the water and mix it in well. Soak for at least 15 minutes, and feel those tense muscles start to unwind.

Get the skunk out

Get sprayed by skunk? Wash with tomato juice. It's an old wives' tale that's also true. But what if your car runs over a skunk? Dead or alive, the scent can cling, and you can't splash tomato juice all over your car. But you can splash mustard. Mix 1 cup of dry mustard powder with a gallon of warm water, and slosh it all over the tires and underbody to get rid of the smell.

Freshen a recycled bottle

Want to use that nice wine bottle for cold water or that cold cream pot for a homemade cosmetic? That's a great idea, unless you can't get rid of the scent of whatever went before. Squirt yellow mustard into the bottle, half fill with warm water, and slosh gently. Let it sit for 15 minutes, then rinse and wash. The bottle will smell of...nothing.

oatmeal

Yes, you know it's one of the healthier breakfast options when you're starting your day. Now you can turn to oatmeal for help around the house at other times of day as well.

Tighten your pores

Oatmeal makes an extremely soothing face mask that tightens your pores and leaves your skin feeling soft and smooth. Grind 1/4 cup oatmeal to a fine powder in a blender. Add 1 egg white and 2 tablespoons honey. Pulse to combine, then smooth this mixture over your clean face, avoiding the eye area. Wear for 15 minutes, then rinse with warm water, pat dry, and apply a light moisturizer.

Scrub your hands

Been gardening and can't get that dirt scrubbed off your fingertips? Mix oatmeal—either quick-cooking or old-fashioned, but *not* the flavored instant kind—with enough milk to make a thin paste, and scrub your hands well with it. The dirt will come out, and your hands will feel softened and smooth.

Soothe itchy skin

Whether you've got chicken pox or poison ivy, oatmeal is what you need—not to eat, but to soak in. Grind a cup of oatmeal in your blender, food processor, or even a spice or coffee grinder until the oatmeal is a fine powder. Stir this powder into a warm bath and soak for as long as you like. For just a few pennies, this is the exact same thing you're getting when you buy special oatmeal baths at the drugstore. Oatmeal soothes and heals whatever ails you, and it's completely harmless and nonirritating, making it ideal for children with eczema.

Shampoo a shut-in

Oatmeal and baking soda make an excellent and effective dry shampoo that can be very comforting for someone who's bedridden or ill. It soaks up excess oils and neutralizes odors. Grind 1/4 cup oatmeal to a fine powder in a blender or spice grinder, then add 1/4 cup baking soda and pulse to combine. Put a towel around the shoulders of the person to be shampooed and another towel on the lap. Sprinkle a few tablespoons of this mixture over the scalp, working it to the roots with your fingers. Let it sit for 5 minutes, then gently brush it out over the towel.

olive oil

For years you've been hearing that olive oil is one of the most heart-healthy oils you can cook with. With these tips and ideas, you can also benefit from olive oil's goodness even if you're nowhere near the kitchen.

Mediterranean polish

Most modern furniture sprays and polishes are nothing but silicone, which leaves a quick shine but builds up to a sticky dullness over time. For a much more environmentally friendly polish for finished wood surfaces, simply wipe on a dab of pure olive oil with a soft cloth, then buff to a shine.

Rub three times for luck

Is your old baseball mitt in need of new life? Recondition it with olive oil and you'll bring softness and shine to that hard-worn old leather. Pour oil on a rag and then work it into the glove well, rubbing into cracks and crevices. Use a clean rag to buff off any excess, and then fly balls better watch out!

Repair damaged hair

Too much sun, chemicals, blow-drying, and curling can leave hair as dry and brittle as autumn leaves. Put hair in a time machine and undo severe damage with olive oil. Wash hair and rinse with warm water. Heat 1/2 cup of olive oil in a cup in the microwave for about 45 seconds, until it's warm but you can still hold your finger in it. Massage it all through your hair and then cover with an old shower cap or wrap your hair with a sheet of plastic wrap. Cover with a towel and wear it for 30 minutes. Shampoo and rinse well, and your hair will feel thick and silky.

peanut butter

Peanut butter is a cheap and healthy source of protein, and kids love it. But even if you have no intention of eating it on a sandwich, you shouldn't banish peanut butter from your kitchen cupboard, as you'll see from these useful hints.

Help the (pet) medicine go down

You've tried burying your dog's pill in his food but he finds it and spits it out every time. Who's the master here? Outmaneuver him with peanut butter! Take a teaspoon of peanut butter and push the pill into the center, then push the lump off with your finger and hold it out as a tempting treat. Down it goes, and Fido won't be any the wiser!

Catch a mouse

Mice don't want cheese; they want peanut butter. It's the best bait there is to lure the pesky critters into a mousetrap, and it won't dry up and harden like a piece of cheese. (Mice seem to prefer smooth to crunchy, but you can decide since you're serving up their last meal!)

Take off a price tag

Sure, WD-40 is terrific at removing price-tag adhesive, but you don't want to spray it on the outside of your kid's new plastic lunch box or beach ball. So use peanut butter instead. Rub on a dab, let it sit for a few minutes, and then wipe clean with a paper towel. The peanut butter wipes clean in seconds, and so do the remains of the glue.

Foil fried fish's odor

Frying fish can leave a strong odor lingering in the kitchen. Add a dollop of smooth peanut butter to the oil before you fry and it will absorb the smell, letting you enjoy fish for dinner—and not keep smelling it days later.

pepper

Black pepper is the seasoning most of us reach for right after the salt. You may be surprised to find that it has other uses besides perking up your stew. And when you're thinking pepper, don't confine yourself solely to the black stuff. Potent cayenne has lots of off-the-table uses as well.

Relieve arthritis in your hands

If your hands are stiff in the morning, make a warming massage oil to use like lotion: 1 tablespoon neutral oil (such almond oil or olive oil) mixed with 2 drops lavender essential oil and 1/4 teaspoon cayenne (or 2 drops pepper essential oil). Rub gently 'til your joints loosen.

Use peanut butter to remove a price tag. Rub on a dab, let it sit for a few minutes, and then wipe clean with a paper towel.

Fight off a migraine

Migraine sufferers usually know just before an attack is coming on, and some of them swear by this old-fashioned remedy that has averted many a painful headache. Briskly stir up to 1/2 teaspoon of cayenne pepper into half a glass of tepid water. Drink it down and lie down to rest. If you still feel the pain, repeat again in 30 minutes.

Break the grip of a cold

Id jer node stubbed ub? Cayenne pepper breaks up sinus congestion swiftly. Heat some chicken stock to boiling and lace it with a teaspoon of cayenne pepper (or less, depending on how much you can bear). Drink it from a mug, and be sure to sniff at the vapors as you sip. Soon that stuffed-up nose will be operating normally again.

Deter deer and groundhogs

Mix 1/4 cup cayenne with warm water in a spray bottle and mist it over the plants that the deer seem to be zeroing in on. If you can find the hole in your yard where that pesky groundhog hides in between eating your flowers, pour a liberal amount of cayenne down the hole (there's usually a second hole, too, that you should find and anoint), and he'll hastily make other habitation plans.

popcorn

You can buy unpopped kernels of popcorn to pop your own fresh at home, or you can sometimes buy ready-popped bags of popcorn in the food aisle, ready to be put to uses besides movie snacking.

Pad a package

If you're shipping a package overseas, popcorn isn't a recommended replacement for foam peanuts, but for domestic shipping, it's ideal. Cheap and environmentally friendly, it's also a terrific shock absorber. Wrap the object you're shipping in paper or plastic, and lay it down on a layer of air-popped popcorn on the bottom. Shake more popcorn all around to cover, then seal it. Ready to ship!

Decorate a tree

The old-fashioned look of a popcorn garland will remind you of childhood holidays at Grandma's house. Let your own kids and grandkids re-create those memories with a big bowl of popcorn and a couple of long strings or pieces of yarn attached to large plastic needlepoint needles.

Make a squirrel-unfriendly bird feeder

A couple loops of popcorn strung on thread and hung from a back porch make a tasty snack that birds can perch on and peck off, but squirrels will find too lightweight and unstable to climb.

potato chips

It's true that most uses of potato chips involve eating them, but there are a handful of useful kitchen tricks that expand the uses of a chip and may have you reaching for them more often.

Top a casserole

Crushed potato chips are a delicious casserole topping to use in place of bread crumbs. And they don't require any additional fat to crisp up. If your macaroni and cheese or green bean casserole looks naked going into the oven, grab a handful of chips out of the bag and crush them between your palms over the top. Bake as usual.

Give fried foods a crispy crunch

Out of bread crumbs to bread your pork chop, chicken fingers, or piece of fish? Roll the item in fine potato chip crumbs and fry as usual. The crust will be crisp, salty, and delicious.

Make a sandwich

In the British Isles, there's a phenomenon known as a "crisp butty" or "crisp sarnie," which is nothing more than two buttered pieces of bread enclosing a handful of salt and vinegar potato chips. Next time you think the larder is nearly bare, give it a try—it's strangely addictive.

Bake some cookies

Use your favorite butter cookie recipe, or the standard recipe for chocolate chip cookies, but instead of chocolate, add crushed, salted potato chips. If you love a mix of sweet and salty in your snack foods, you'll never look back!

salt

When someone is incredibly grounded and full of common sense and essential usefulness, we refer to them as "the salt of the earth." You may say the same about the huge variety of salty uses we've assembled here.

Salvage a pan

Is baked-on or burned food ruining one of your favorite pots or pans? Salt will bring it back into service. Sprinkle salt heavily on the stuck-on food and dampen it with a little water. Let the salt sit until the food lifts right off the pan, then wash.

Clean up a bubble-over

Fruit pies are especially guilty of bubbling all over the bottom of your oven. When you remove the pie, sprinkle salt thickly on the spill while it's still liquid. You can also do this with messy boil-overs on the stovetop. When the salted area cools, wipe it right up with a sponge.

Get dishwasher stains off glassware

Spots on glassware, such as Pyrex dishes or glass mixing bowls or heavy tumblers, can be very stubborn, but they're no match for salt. Mix

1 cup salt with 1 quart vinegar and soak the glassware in it overnight. Rub off the stain and wash as usual.

Clean fish more easily

Catching fish is half the battle. Cleaning is the rest! Sprinkle salt liberally on a fish before you start to descale it. You'll find that the scales flick off faster, making the whole job easier.

Polish your griddle

Pour a few tablespoons salt on the cold clean griddle and polish firmly with a paper towel, then discard and wipe before heating. The smoothly polished surface will prevent flapjacks from sticking.

Chase cabbage worms away

Every gardener knows the frustration of cabbage worms gnawing away just as the big heads of cabbage are ready to be harvested. Stop worms in their tracks with a mix of one part salt and two parts flour, dusted around the cabbages every few days as harvest approaches.

Whip cream higher

A tiny pinch of salt added to a bowl of whipping cream will make it whip up higher and fluffier. Same with egg whites and also with eggs you're whisking for scrambled eggs. They'll be fluffier.

CRUNCH!

A BRIEF HISTORY OF THE POTATO CHIP

In the 1850s, Saratoga Springs, New York, became the birthplace of the potato chip. A summer destination for those who love horse racing, Saratoga also boasted popular restaurants. One of these, Moon's Lake House, employed a chef named George Crum, a man who did not tolerate criticism of his cooking. Patrons who dared to send their food back were served repulsive substitutes; Crum himself would peek out of the kitchen to bear witness to the shocked reactions these awful "revenge" dishes elicited. One such evening, however, the tables turned—and history was made. A diner (possibly **Cornelius Vanderbilt, but this isn't certain) decided his French fries were too thick and not crispy enough.** He sent them back to the kitchen. Crum countered this affront by slicing the returned fries as thin as wafers and refrying them in hot grease. As an inspired final touch, he salted them excessively. Unaware that the dish was made out of spite, the patron tried the crunchy potatoes and loved them. The owner of Moon's Lake House saw an opportunity and Crum's "potato crunches" were officially added to the menu. Not long after, Crum opened his own restaurant, and sold the dish as "Moon Brand Saratoga Chips."

The tasty morsels caught on. Restaurants across the country renamed Crum's creation "potato chips," and they grew in popularity. **In 1895, William Tappenden began using a horse-drawn wagon to deliver them fresh to stores**

in Cleveland, Ohio. He made them on his kitchen stove. This was very common at the time; many entrepreneurs made chips in private kitchens and delivered them immediately to shops, because their shelf life was limited. Retailers dispensed the chips in bulk from cracker barrels or glass display cases, and consumers brought them home in brown paper sacks. This was a greasy affair, but the potato chip grew in popularity anyway.

In 1921, Earl Wise, the proprietor of Wise Delicatessen Company, located in Berwick, Pennsylvania, asked his mother to whip up a batch of potato chips as a way to get rid of excess potatoes. They quickly became a very popular sales item for him, and in 1923, Earl and his father designed and built a small factory to make Wise potato chips. As luck would have it, only a few years later there was a great leap in packaging technology. Laura Scudder, working in her own family-based chip business in California, instructed her employees to hand iron sheets of wax paper. After three sides were ironed to form a bag, chips were placed inside and then the fourth side could also be sealed. No more greasy brown paper! This same year, 1926, Wise enlarged their factory—they did so several more times as demand for Wise potato chips grew. **In 1946, Earl Wise created a logo for his product: an owl named Peppy.** Wise packaging still carries an image of Peppy's eye today.

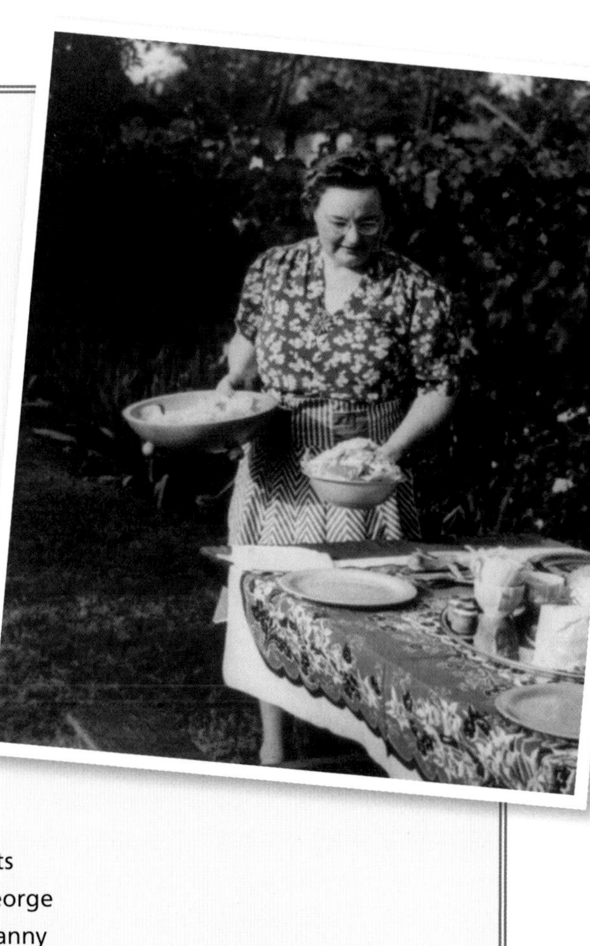

In 2009, in a turn of events that would make even George Crum happy, two men, Danny Jameson and Paul Tator, wondered why Moon Brand Saratoga Chips (which were sold commercially until the mid-1920s) were no longer available. The men researched the original recipe, decided to create a gourmet snack business in Saratoga Springs, and brought Saratoga Chips back to life!

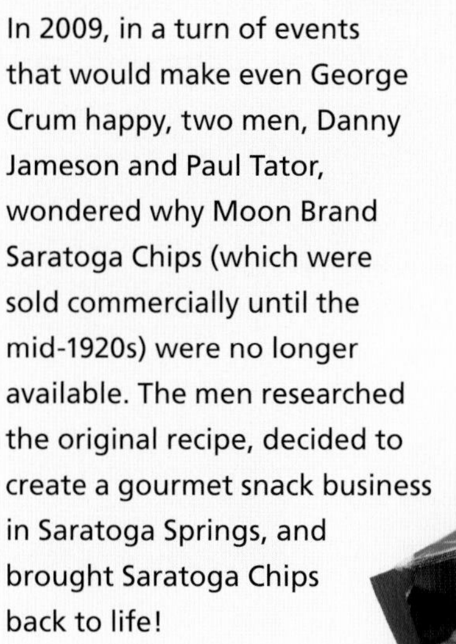

Stop a sudsy disaster

Ever put too much soap in a washing machine, or found that your trying-to-help kid used dishwashing liquid in the dishwasher? When the suds start to emerge from the door of the machine, you may think they'll never stop. Put a halt to the proceedings by sprinkling salt over the mountain of bubbles. They'll quickly subside so you can clean up fast.

Kill poison ivy

It's hard to fully destroy this dangerous vine once it takes hold, but salt will do the trick. Dissolve 3 pounds of sidewalk salt in a gallon of water and add a squirt of dish liquid. Saturate the plant and its roots. It will soon be gone.

shortening

Butter makes a tasty piecrust, but the real secret to a flaky one is shortening. Even if you're not making pastry, shortening is the secret to lots of useful household tips.

Make a magic snow shovel

Early snowfall catch you unaware? Before you start the backbreaking labor of digging out your car, smear a generous amount of solid vegetable shortening on your snow shovel. The snow will slide on and off much more quickly and easily, for a faster and more efficient job.

Restore a pair of galoshes

Grownups wear galoshes to keep our feet dry, but kids wear them as a license to walk through every mud puddle they see. And now your daughter's favorite pink princess galoshes are sadly scuffed and dull. Bring back the shine to your little princess's face and her boots by polishing the galoshes with a dab of shortening on a clean rag.

Soften your feet

The active ingredient in fancy foot creams is pretty much the same as the active ingredient in shortening: fat, or grease. That's what softens your skin. So save yourself more than a few bucks and soften with shortening. Before bed, slather it on your soles and put on socks. In the morning, you'll have satiny soft tootsies.

Remove tar from fabric

Is a drip of tar or pine resin ruining your favorite work jeans? Scrape off what you can with the edge of a credit card, then work shortening directly into the stain. Let it sit overnight, then dab up the excess with a paper towel and treat the whole area with a grease remover such as Wisk. Launder as usual.

Shine a pair of galoshes with
a dab of shortening on a clean rag.

Tell squirrels to take a hike

Is your standing bird feeder getting raided by hungry squirrels? Grease the pole of the feeder liberally with shortening. Squirrels will soon learn to forage elsewhere, and your favorite birds can return to the table.

soda and cola

When you're watching your sugar intake, you might find that it's best to cut back on your soda consumption. That's okay; there are still plenty of immensely useful things you can do with it besides drinking it.

Take rust off chrome

Got a car old enough to have real chrome on it? Then it's probably got a few rust spots, too. Crush a piece of tinfoil and dip it in cola, then scrub off those little dots of rust with ease.

Speed up a drain

Kitchen sink starting to drain slowly? You've probably got a clog waiting to happen. Make sure it never does by slowly pouring a whole 2-liter bottle of cola down the drain. The potent carbonic acid in cola will get things moving again.

Clean car battery corrosion

If your car battery has corrosion on the terminals, dip a rag in cola and wrap it around the terminals. Let it sit for several minutes and then scrub off the rust deposits and any cola residue with a damp sponge. The same trick works to loosen rusted-on nuts and bolts.

Restore stained porcelain

Got a toilet with a stain ring around the bowl? Pour in 1 1/2 cups of soda and let it sit for an hour. Scrub and flush—good as new.

BAKE A CAKE WITH SODA

Short on eggs and oil but yearning for a piece of cake? If you have soda in the house, you have no worries. Most packaged cake mixes direct you to add 3 eggs and 1/4 cup of oil to the mix. But the thing is, you don't *have* to. Here is a way to bake a cake without either eggs or oil that will result in a cake that is delicious—and lower in fat and cholesterol.

1. **Take out your packaged cake mix. Any flavor will work.**
2. **Grab a can of your favorite soda. Use diet soda for the fewest calories.**
3. **Ignore the directions on the box—don't add eggs, water, or oil. Just add one can of soda.**
4. **Bake for the amount of time suggested on the cake mix. You will have a delicious cake—and eat it, too!**

Get oil off concrete

Car leaked oil on the garage floor? That's a mess to clean, unless you have some cola. Sprinkle the spot liberally with sawdust or kitty litter, working it in with a broom. Leave for half an hour to soak up the grease, then sweep it up and discard. Pour on enough cola to cover the area, and work it in with a rag. Let sit for half an hour, then mop it up with 2 tablespoons each laundry detergent and bleach mixed with 2 quarts of warm water.

Keep flowers fresher longer

When putting flowers in a vase, add 1/2 cup of a clear soda, such as Sprite or 7-Up, to the water and the flowers will live for days longer than they will in plain water.

SPAM
Wipe a chunk of Spam across the mirror, then rub it off with a soft cloth; your mirror won't steam up again for weeks!

Spam

Spam has passed from being a survival food to a source of humor to simply a cultural icon. And in that time, its uses have expanded far beyond the limits of the kitchen.

Polish wood furniture

Cut off a chunk of Spam, wipe it across your wood tabletop, and polish it off with a soft cloth. You'll get a gleaming shine and no harmful chemicals. Best of all, there's no silicone buildup like most commercial polishes leave behind.

De-mist mirrors

Trying to shave but all the steam in the bathroom keeps thwarting you? Spam is the answer. Wipe a chunk of Spam across the mirror, then rub it off with a soft cloth. The light coating of oil it leaves behind is invisible, but your mirror won't steam up again for weeks!

Catch fish

Sure, worms are tasty, but any catfish or carp fisherman can tell you that what the fish really want is a chunk of Spam. Take along a can of Spam on your next fishing trip and you'll be pulling them into the boat! In fact, take two cans, and you can eat one for breakfast before you start the day.

spices

The selection of spices and dried herbs will vary widely, depending on your dollar store and its current stock. What won't change is all the many uses to which you can put these inexpensive items.

Discourage insects

The pungent fragrances that humans so enjoy in spices are the exact same scents that makes bugs scurry for cover. Keep ants and other insects out of flour and sugar by dropping a bay leaf into the container (the bay fragrance it imparts to your stores will be minimal). Put apple-pie spice into a small square of fabric and tie it tightly with a string. Hang this easy sachet in moist places such as under the bathroom sink or behind the washer to discourage silverfish.

Keep thermoses and storage jars fresh

Ever open a thermos to pour in coffee or soup and been horrified at the stale smell? Make sure it never happens again by dropping a whole clove into the bottom of a container that you usually store closed. Just be sure to discard the clove before using the container.

A sage solution to smelly sneakers

Crumble a bit of dried sage into each shoe before putting it on. Sage is not only gently fragrant, but it actually kills the bacteria that make your teenager's gym shoes smell so bad. Shake out the flecks at night, and add a new leaf the next day.

Keep dark hair glossy

To keep black, brown, and chestnut hair glossy, rinse weekly with an herbal tea of color-enhancing spices and herbs. In three cups of boiling water, steep 1 teaspoon each of dried rosemary, sage, cinnamon, and allspice, along with 1/2 teaspoon ground cloves. Strain through a paper towel–lined sieve or a coffee filter and let cool. Use as the final rinse after washing your hair.

sugar

Sugar makes baked goods tender and food more appealing and is an excellent preservative. It's also full of other completely nonfood uses that you'll be thrilled to try.

Scrub on a healthy glow

You can spend a fortune on a sugar scrub at a salon—or you can mix 1/4 cup olive oil with 1/4 cup granulated sugar and use it like soap in the shower, scrubbing your arms, legs, shoulders, and, gently, your face. Rinse well, pat dry, and moisturize. You'll glow like you just returned from a beach vacation! (This same mix will also safely scrub oil or paint off your hands after a job.)

Get rid of roaches

Toxic chemicals work to get rid of roaches, but particularly if you have children or pets, you don't necessarily want to use commercial roach products in your house. Instead, scatter corners and behind cabinets with a mix of half sugar and half baking soda for a nontoxic and highly effective "poison." The roaches come to eat the sugar, but also eat the baking soda and die. Replace often until the roaches disappear.

Cure a chile burn

Sprinkled on too much hot sauce? Found that salsa a bit hotter than you bargained for? Your next bite should be a spoonful of sugar. The chemical in chiles that burns is capsaicin, which bonds to the pain receptors in your tongue, and all the cold water in the world can't fix that. A taste of sugar, however, breaks those bonds right away.

Keep cheese fresher

Toss a few sugar cubes into the bag when you seal a lump of hard cheese. The sugar helps prevent mold from forming. Also add a few sugar cubes to the container before you seal up a cake or loaf of pumpkin bread, and it will also stay moist for days longer.

Prevent killer worms in the garden

If your garden is about 250 square feet, all you need is a 5-pound bag of sugar to keep nematode worms off all your plants. These microscopic parasites attack roots, destroying the plants and all your hard work. If your area is prone to nematodes, spread the sugar over the soil in the spring when you're preparing the ground, and the nematodes will never get started.

DINNER IN A CAN

THE STORY OF SPAM

In 1937, in Austin, Minnesota, the Hormel Company developed the first canned meat product that did not require refrigeration. Made of chopped pork shoulder and ham (a cut from the pig's buttock and thigh), it was marketed simply as "Hormel Spiced Ham." The public's response was anticlimactic. Other companies developed their own canned meats, and Hormel's product was soon at risk of getting lost in the shuffle. To save the day, a decision was made to offer a prize to the person who could think up a catchy new name. The winning entry was "Spam". Several versions of the name's meaning are in circulation—the two most credible are: **It's a blend of "spice" and "ham," and it stands for "Shoulder of Pork and Ham."** What is known for certain is that Kenneth Daigneau, a Broadway actor—and the brother of a Hormel vice president—submitted "Spam." As the contest winner, he was given a prize of $100.

What's in a name? In this case, a great deal. Spam stuck in consumers' minds. It was memorable, and the blue and yellow packaging (originally you had to open the can with a key) was pleasant to look at. Hormel actively marketed its jazzed-up product, and in 1940, Spam starred in what was likely the first singing commercial. The tune was set to the chorus of "My Bonny Lies Over the Ocean," and the lyrics were "Spam, Spam, Spam, Spam / Hormel's new miracle meat in a can / Tastes fine, saves time / If you want something grand / Ask for Spam!"

"Tastes fine" may not sound like a ringing endorsement, but during the 1940s, sales boomed. Spam was inexpensive and a convenient source of protein that was easy to store. Then, during World War II, Spam wasn't rationed, so its market expanded further as it became a staple in American meals. **It was also ideal for the military because it required no refrigeration and had a long shelf life.** Spam's span of influence grew and grew.

After World War II, Jay C. Hormel, the son of the company's founder and not a man to rest on his laurels, increased public excitement over Spam by creating the Hormel Girls, a musical traveling troupe 60 members strong. The women played instruments, sang, and praised Hormel products. They toured the country. The public was dazzled.

In the 1960s, Spam became available in different flavors, and eventually the can-key was replaced with an easier, modern pull-top. In the 1970s, a now-famous Monty Python sketch (Vikings sing a chorus of "Spam, Spam, Spam,") ensured that this luncheon meat was to be ingrained in the American psyche.

Today Spam is iconic. It is still an inexpensive source of protein that can stretch a budget; yet it is "famous" enough to have spawned fan clubs and cookbooks. It is known (sometimes by reputation and sometimes by taste) by Americans of all ages. As is fitting an icon, its packaging was accepted into the Smithsonian. **And if you travel to Austin, Minnesota, you can visit the Spam Museum, opened in 2001.** You will be welcomed by a variety of interactive and educational games, exhibits, and video presentations, all singing the praises of Spam, Spam, Spam, Spam....

Festive! Fun to make!
SPAM* UPSIDE DOWN PIE
SPAM* UPSIDE DOWN PIE
Line an 8-inch mold with Spam slices and fill with baking powder biscuit dough (prepared or home mixed) well laced with tiny cubes of Spam. Bake 40-45 min. at 425°F. Turn it out on a platter, fill center with a tart cheese sauce (or one made with tomato or horseradish).. and watch the family turn out and fill the table in a hurry!
SPAM
HORMEL
GOOD FOODS
COLD OR HOT... SPAM HITS THE SPOT!
*"Spam" is a registered trademark. It identifies a meat product—packed only in 12-ounce tins—made exclusively by Geo. A. Hormel & Co., Austin, Minn.

Rosebushes love the tannins in tea leaves. **Keep your tea leaves in a compost bowl by your kitchen sink,** and dump them around the rosebushes once a week.

tea

A nice cup of tea will perk you right up. But a nice handful of tea bags or tea leaves has even more uses that you'll be eager to try.

Keep the fridge fresh

An open box of baking soda in the refrigerator is the time-honored way to keep odors down, but did you know that tea bags do an even better job? Put three or four tea bags around the fridge, and odors will be readily absorbed. Change them every few weeks for best results.

Use tea in your smoker

Rip open a few tea bags and sprinkle the tea leaves over the soaked wood chips next time you're smoking fish or meat on the grill. The tea leaves impart a distinctive, unique flavor.

Help heal pinkeye

Children are more susceptible to pinkeye than adults, and they're also more apt to rub at their sore and tender eye while it's infected, making it likely they will spread the bacteria. Help heal pinkeye faster and give your child relief with a soothing tea bag compress. Wet a tea bag, squeeze out the excess, and have the child lie still for 10 minutes with the tea bag on the eyelid. The tannin helps the swelling go right down.

Brighten dark hair

Has summer sun and chlorine made your dark hair rough and dry? Soothe your sun-stressed tresses with a warm rinse of dark tea. Pour a quart through your hair after a mild shampoo. It will bring out highlights and make your hair feel soft again.

Freshen your feet

Sweaty, smelly feet ruining your shoes and your day? Every night, soak your feet in a basin of strong tea for 20 minutes. After a week or two, you should notice a real difference in both the sweat output and the odor.

Clean delicate Oriental rugs

Oriental and Persian rugs must be cleaned carefully to protect their valuable fibers and prevent damage to the patterned weave. Avoid major dirt and dust buildup by periodically cleaning the rug. Empty the contents of six tea bags into a bowl and sprinkle it with 1/2-teaspoon water. Sprinkle these barely damp leaves on the rug, and then brush them off vigorously with a clean broom. The tea leaves will draw out dust and dirt without leaving any stain or color on the rug.

Feed your roses

Rosebushes love the tannins in tea leaves, so if you're a regular tea drinker, keep your tea leaves in a compost bowl by your kitchen sink, and dump them around the rosebushes once a week.

Speed up compost

You're trying to compost your kitchen waste and not throw it all away, but it's not working as well as it should. If your compost pile seems sluggish, pour a few cups of strong brewed tea on it. The acidic tea will jump-start the compost, encouraging the acid-loving bacteria that make the whole thing work.

tomato juice

Canned tomato juice is handy to keep in the refrigerator for breakfast. It's even handier to keep around for any of these uses.

Freshen a fridge

If your power went on the blink while you were out of town, you can have a real mess in your fridge or freezer. Clean it out and get rid of any remaining odor by wiping down the fridge and freezer walls and shelves with undiluted tomato juice on a sponge. Rinse off with warm water and take a sniff. You may need to repeat once, but your major appliance will be saved.

Clean a cooler

You're not the only family that ever forgot a pack of hotdogs in a cooler after you came home from a trip. But you don't have to throw away an expensive item just because of one mistake. Clean it out and pour in a large can of tomato juice, undiluted. Rub it up the sides of the interior and under the lid with a sponge, then close the lid and let it sit in a cool place for a couple of days. Rinse and wash with dish soap and water and dry thoroughly. Sprinkle the inside with a little baking soda before you put it into storage.

Soothe a sore throat

The acids in tomato juice take the sting out of a sore throat. Make a solution of 1/2 cup tomato juice and 1/2 cup water, and add a couple drops of hot sauce. Gargle with this mixture several times, and the burning will subside in your painful throat.

Clean out the fridge and get rid of any remaining odor by wiping down the shelves and freezer walls with tomato juice.

vanilla

Pungent and fragrant, vanilla extract is the necessary flavor in so many baked goods. Without it, cookies and cakes can taste flat and dull. But it's also great to have on hand for a variety of uses even when you're not turning on the oven.

Sweeten a microwave

Wiped it down, washed the glass turntable, and yet still your microwave smells like all the dinners you've ever reheated? Vanilla is the answer. Pour a couple tablespoons of vanilla in a glass bowl and microwave on high for 1 minute. Let the vanilla in the bowl cool, then repeat. It will smell as sweet as freshly baked cookies.

Perfume the paint

Stir 1 tablespoon of pure vanilla into a gallon of paint before you start work. You won't completely eradicate the smell of fresh paint as it dries, but you'll make the whole experience a lot pleasanter!

Make a kid-friendly tick repellent

Children playing in long grass in summer are at risk of tick bites, which can lead to dangerous illnesses. Short of dressing them in haz-mat suits, it's hard to keep ticks off. But instead of toxic sprays, you can repel ticks with pure vanilla. Douse a cotton ball with real vanilla extract, and dab it liberally around ankles, wrists, and any uncovered skin on the limbs and trunk. The kids will smell great, too. Reapply as needed.

Sweeten the house

People who are allergic to air fresheners and sprays can still enjoy the benefits of a sweet-smelling house. Wet a cotton ball with vanilla and dab it very lightly on the outside of a regular light bulb (not a halogen bulb) in your lamps. When you turn on the lamp, the bulb heats up and a faint but alluring scent of vanilla drifts out.

Stir some vanilla into a gallon of paint before you start work. You won't completely eradicate the smell of fresh paint as it dries, but you'll make the whole experience a lot pleasanter!

vegetable oil

Plain vegetable oil makes a mild salad dressing and it's great for deep-frying and for making baked goods. It's also useful to have on hand for uses that have nothing to do with cooking.

Keep your birdbath operational

In summer, many people have to dump birdbaths after every rain to prevent mosquitoes from breeding in the standing water. But you can have your birdbath and keep water in it, too, if you float a few tablespoons of vegetable oil on the surface of the water. Birds don't care, but mosquitoes do. (Do change the water weekly, however, just in case.)

Give yourself a hot-oil treatment

You don't need a spa or special oils for silky hair! Heat half a cup of vegetable oil in the microwave for 20 seconds until it's just warm. Massage into your dry scalp and hair and wrap in a towel for 10 minutes. Wash as usual.

Remove water rings from wood furniture

Forgot to use a coaster yet again? Try this miracle cure: Spread a thin layer of vegetable oil over the affected area, and then sprinkle it lightly with cigarette ashes. Use a soft lint-free cloth to polish the oil and ash mixture gently into the ring and you'll see it steadily disappear.

Break apart tumblers without breakage

Who stacked the drinking glasses again? They can stick together as if they're stuck with cement. All you need is a thin drizzle of oil poured all around the top edge of the outside glass. Give it a few minutes to work in, and they'll separate with ease.

vinegar

Along with salt and baking soda, vinegar completes a powerhouse trio that no home should be without. With plain white vinegar and apple cider vinegar, you can perform near miraculous feats of laundry, housecleaning, health care, and more.

Perk up a rug or carpet

Foot traffic, dust, and dirt can wear down a carpet's fibers and dull the pattern and color. Bring back the life to a carpet with a solution of 1 gallon warm water with 1 cup white vinegar. Dip a clean broom in the mixture and brush it into the rug. Let it dry, and the fibers will stand up and the colors will revive.

Brighten wood paneling

How can wooden panels get dusty and grimy? But they do, and you'll be surprised at how bright they look when you wipe them with this mixture: 2 cups warm water, 1/4 cup white vinegar, and a glug of olive or vegetable oil. Wipe down the whole area, then rub with a dry cloth.

9 More Nontraditional Ways to Use VINEGAR

1 Bird Poo Voodoo

Have birds used your windshield as a target? Pour vinegar onto a rag and wipe those messes away with ease. Have winged friends left "gifts" on your patios and decks? Pour a little vinegar straight onto the spots and watch them dissolve like magic.

2 So Long Stickers!

Can't get the price tag off that glass vase? Get out some plain white vinegar. Soak the paper of the sticker in the vinegar, then scrape it off with a credit card or the edge of a plastic spoon. Use a dry cloth or paper towel to polish away the remaining glue.

3 Wave Good-bye to Odor

Get rid of smoke or cooking odors quickly and effectively by wetting a cloth in vinegar and waving it around the room you're trying to air. Soon you'll be able to take a big sniff of... nothing, Just like you wanted.

4 Spray It Proud!

Why use commercial cleaner when you can make an all-purpose wash that's cheap, simple, and green to boot? In a spray bottle, mix 2 parts water with 1 part white vinegar. You can spritz it on anything including grease spots, spills, and bathroom surfaces.

5 As Clear as Glass

Why buy a special spray to clean your glasses when you've got vinegar in the cabinet? Spritz your specs with white vinegar and polish with a soft cloth. It will work just as well as that tiny, overpriced bottle of cleaner.

6 Make Salt Surrender

Winter sidewalks leave unsightly white rings of salt on leather shoes and boots. There is a way to defeat sidewalk salt: Wipe your footwear as soon as you get inside with a cloth dipped in white vinegar. You will not only get rid of the rings, you'll also prevent damage to your shoes.

7 A Cut Above

Fresh-cut flowers are beautiful. Keep your blooms a-bloom for as long as possible by adding the following to the vase: 2 tablespoons apple cider vinegar and 2 tablespoons sugar. Then fill the vase from the tap and your flowers will be "drinking" something a cut above plain water.

8 Shiny Scissors

It's best not to clean good kitchen shears in water because it can rust the central fastener and dull the blades. Instead, dip a cloth in undiluted white vinegar and wipe the blades well. Dry with a towel.

9 Keep Water Bottles Fresh

If you're hiking in the heat all day, the water you carry can taste stale. Keep the flavor bright and bacteria down by adding a few drops of apple cider vinegar when you fill your bottle.

If you've forgotten to wash a paintbrush, you may be able to revive it by soaking it overnight in undiluted white vinegar.

Keep cats out of the sandbox

Don't let the neighborhood cats treat your child's sandbox like a public restroom. After your child is done playing for the day, drizzle a pint of white vinegar over the sand and stir it in with a spade. It will dry overnight, but cats will avoid the place for weeks.

Skip chips

Paint your clean bare nails with white vinegar and let it dry. When you apply the polish, it will stay on without chipping for days longer.

Clean dirt off blinds

Nobody wants to get into the job of cleaning window blinds, but now and then the grime and dust is too much and you have to give it a go. Make your life simpler by using socks and vinegar. Mix half and half water and vinegar, and draw a clean cotton tube sock loosely onto each hand. Dip the socks in the vinegar mixture and pull your hands along individual blinds, clutching top and bottom. The dirt will slip right off onto your socks. Dip them in clean water to rinse the dirt and back in the vinegar again for the next slat.

Avoid oven odors

When you use a potent chemical cleaner to scrub out your oven, it will emit a strong chemical smell the first time you use it again, no matter how well you rinsed. Avoid this odor, and don't let your baked food carry its taint, by soaking a clean sponge in white vinegar and using it for the final wipe-down after you've finished cleaning the oven. Let the vinegar dry completely before you turn the oven on again.

Fluff sweaters after washing

Wool and acrylic sweaters can look flat and dull after washing, and sometimes a hint of soap lingers in the fibers. Cut the soap and fluff up the fibers by adding 1/2 cup of white vinegar to the final rinse water, whether hand or machine-washing.

Clear the air of grease

It's an old southern trick to prevent a kitchen smelling of grease while chicken is frying: Put a small dish of white vinegar in the kitchen, and the grease will miraculously collect on the surface rather than hanging in the air. Try it and see.

Stop excessive barking

An exuberant dog can be a terrific companion on a walk, but excessive barking frays your nerves. Make an effective, low-tech deterrent by filling a spray bottle with water and adding a few tablespoons white vinegar. When your dog goes nuts because there's a squirrel about a mile away, spritz a little water in his direction, (being careful not to spray it in his face). He'll get the idea very quickly.

Eradicate a carsick odor

Young riders sometimes become carsick, even riding on the straightest of roads. Once you've cleaned up every trace, you may still find that the odor lingers, making everyone else feel a little carsick, too! Erase the smell overnight by leaving an uncovered bowl of half-full undiluted white vinegar on the floor of the car. In the morning, the odor should be gone.

Make your car gleam

You've got time to wash your car at home yourself, but not the whole afternoon to spend waxing it. Skip the wax step and use vinegar instead. A teaspoon of undiluted white vinegar in the bucket of soapy wash water will help remove road grit and tar from the paint. When you fill the bucket with clean water for rinsing, add another teaspoon of vinegar and pour this blend all over the car. For an added touch, wipe down the windows with vinegar to repel rain and frost.

Treat a cold sore

When you feel a cold sore coming on, get out the apple cider vinegar. Douse a cotton ball and dab your lip three times a day. If you already have the sore, do the same. The pain and swelling will subside, and the vinegar speeds healing.

Use as an aftershave

If you've got sensitive skin, commercial aftershaves with their strong scents can result in itching and irritation. Splash on a handful of plain white vinegar instead for a bracing tonic with no redness.

Save a paintbrush

Forgot to wash that brush? If the bristles are synthetic, you may be able to revive it by soaking overnight in undiluted white vinegar. Bend it as it starts to soften to work the vinegar in. When it's soft again, wash with hot soapy water.

Keep plaster pliable

Plaster dries quickly—so quickly, in fact, that if you're not experienced at plastering, you may find it has seized up before your job is done. Buy yourself some time by stirring a few tablespoons of white vinegar into the plaster as you mix. It will dry more slowly, giving you a few extra minutes to perfect your technique.

Protect plants from mildew

Powdery mildew or rust spots on your garden plants? The solution is simple: a quart of water and a tablespoon of apple cider vinegar, sprayed directly on the leaves, preferably in the early morning or evening so the leaves dry before they are hit by full sun.

AISLE 2 HEALTH AND BEAUTY

YOU MAY NOT MAKE A 99 CENT STORE THE first stop for your health and beauty products, but you should. You can find name-brand products for significantly less than at the grocery store or the drugstore and names you may not recognize (but are perfectly good) for a song. And so many of these items have purposes beyond their original intent—baby oil to polish your shoes, cotton balls to light a campfire, toothpaste to fight pimples—that you're bound to find an astonishing number of items that will make your life easier. Just consult the list that follows for endless possibilities.

NET WEIGHT
4 OZ
℮ 100g

adhesive bandages

Are adhesive bandages better than tape? In certain situations, you bet they are. How many different ways can *you* use them?

Test for allergies

Are you worried that you might be allergic to a product you just bought? Before you use it, test it on yourself. Put a little bit inside your wrist or elbow, and cover it with an adhesive bandage. Let it sit for 24 hours. Remove the bandage and check your skin; if your skin isn't red or irritated, the product is probably safe to use.

Stick it to your skin

Use adhesive bandages whenever you need to attach something to your skin. For example, you can get rid of a wart by taping a cotton ball soaked in vinegar to the wart for about two hours every day. Tape won't hold the cotton ball—but an adhesive bandage will.

Test your painting power

Have you cleaned your walls sufficiently before painting them? Is your primer a high enough quality for your project? To answer these questions before painting a large area, test your walls with an adhesive bandage. Paint a small, clean, inconspicuous spot with the paint you plan to use, and let it dry for two days. Put a bandage over the area, then strip it off. Did the paint come off? If so, you need to clean the walls more or use a better primer. If not, get to work!

Protect your fingertips

Thimbles save wear and tear on your finger, but they can be too rigid for many sewers. Ditch the thimble and put an adhesive bandage on your fingertip instead. You'll get the protection without the resistance.

antacid tablets

Antacid tablets work wonders for upset stomachs—and for healing and cleaning. Check out the surprising uses for these hard workers here.

Neutralize canker sores

Place an antacid tablet directly on the canker sore, giving it time to dissolve, or simply chew one. The medicine will stop the acids and enzymes in your mouth from attacking the tissue in the sore, and more importantly, it will stop the pain. (Be sure to check the product's label for correct dosage instructions.)

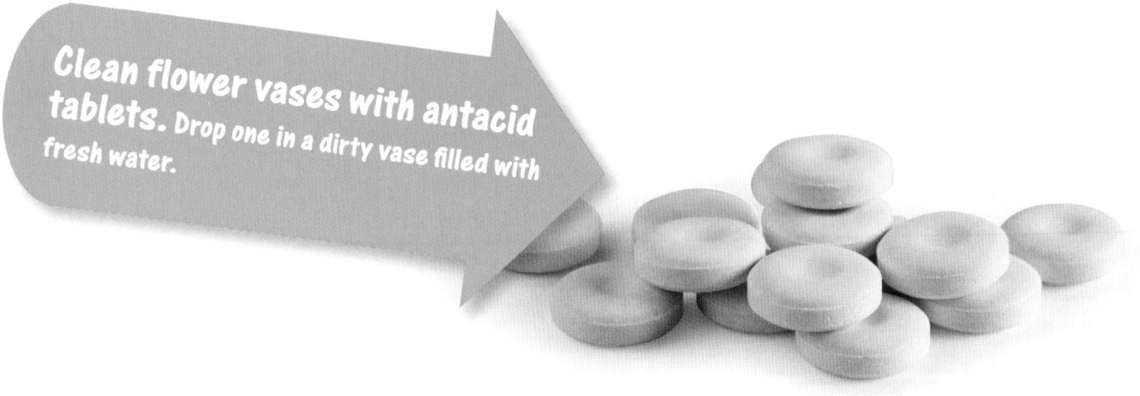

Clean flower vases with antacid tablets. Drop one in a dirty vase filled with fresh water.

Put the fizz to work

Clean your toilet with antacid tablets. As long as they contain sodium bicarbonate, two tablets will do the trick. Dissolve the tablets in the toilet bowl for 20 minutes, then scrub the bowl clean with a toilet brush. Flush and you're done.

Make a hot and cold cleaner

Cleaning out a thermos is always difficult, especially if its contents—generally coffee or tea—have been sitting in it for a while. Instead of trying to wedge your hand into the narrow opening to wipe it out, dump the contents, fill it with water, and dissolve four antacid tablets in it. Let the solution sit for an hour, then rinse and wash as usual. Your thermos will sparkle again!

Say so long to slime

Get rid of the brown and green slimy mess on your flower vase with a common antacid tablet. Drop one into the dirty vase filled with fresh water and give it five minutes to work. Wipe the inside with a sponge or cloth and rinse. Your vase will be ready for a new bouquet.

aspirin

It's hard to believe that one little white pill could have so many alternate uses beyond its original intent. From your face to your feet, aspirin can perform wonders.

Stop acne

Got an outbreak? Try taming it with one or two 325-milligram pills four times per day (after your doctor confirms you can take aspirin regularly). If you prefer a topical treatment, crush one aspirin, mix it with a little water to make a paste, and dab the paste on your pimple. Let it sit for a few minutes, then wash it off with soap and water. Repeat as needed.

Crush corns

How? Mix five crushed aspirin tablets with 1/2 teaspoon of water and 1/2 teaspoon of lemon juice. Swab the mixture onto the corn. Cover the corn with a patch of plastic wrap, and top that with a hot towel. Let it sit for 10 minutes. Remove the coverings and the mixture, and gently file down the softened corn with a pumice stone.

Make a homemade styptic pencil

Nicked yourself shaving? Ouch! Don't rummage for an old-fashioned styptic pencil to dry up the cut. Just crush a single aspirin, mix with just a few drops of water to make a paste, and dab it on the cut. As the paste dries, the cut will too.

Give your face a day at the spa

An aspirin facial will smooth and exfoliate far better than an expensive preparation. Grind six uncoated aspirin tablets into a coarse powder and combine it with a tablespoon or two of lemon juice if your skin is oily—or olive oil if your skin is dry. Smooth it on and let sit for five minutes, then rinse.

Get rid of athlete's foot

The salicylic acid in aspirin can serve as an antifungal. Crush two or three aspirin to a fine powder and mix with some cornstarch or talc. Sprinkle it on every morning when you put your socks on and your toes will be clear in no time.

baby oil

Baby oil isn't just for babies—and it isn't just for making skin soft or for tanning (which isn't recommended anyway). Instead, use it on your shoes and your ears and many other places you may never have considered.

Stop an earache

Baby your ear when it hurts. How? Hold a bottle of baby oil under hot running water for about a minute to warm its contents. Then place a few drops of the heated baby oil into the affected ear canal to soothe away the pain.

Improve your shoes

Give your shoes new life without spending anything on shoe polish. Dab a few drops of baby oil on your leather shoes, and rub the oil in with a soft clean cloth. You'll soften the leather as well as polish it. You can also use baby oil to freshen other leather and patent leather accessories: purses, belts, briefcases—even jackets! Just be sure to wipe off any excess oil when you're done.

Rip it off the right way

Pulling an adhesive bandage off your child's skin can be tough on both of you. Make it easier by rubbing the bandage with a cotton ball soaked in baby oil. Rub until you can easily pull the bandage off. This trick works well for adults with sensitive skin, too.

Give it a rub

Get rid of stubborn latex paint splatters on your face and hands (and anywhere else you may find them on your skin) by rubbing the area with baby oil. Once you've removed the paint, wash your skin with soap and water.

baby powder

Whether you call it baby powder or talcum powder—baby powder doesn't necessarily contain talc, which talcum powder does—the soft white stuff can work wonders around your house, in your garden, and with your jewelry. See how it can help you!

Dusting the bulbs with baby powder before planting helps keep rot and pests away.
Johnson's
baby
powder
CLINICALLY
MILDNESS
PROVEN
WORLDWIDE PARTNER

Squash the squeak

If your hardwood floor squeaks and you can see gaps between the boards, you can fix the problem with a dusting of powder. Sprinkle the powder in the cracks—or use a plastic ketchup bottle filled with talcum to aim the powder directly into the gap. Place a towel over the boards and work the powder into the cracks with your foot. Clean up the excess powder with the towel. Your room will seem very quiet!

Baby your bulbs

Put 3 tablespoons of medicated baby powder and five or six flower bulbs in a plastic bag, seal it, and shake. Dusting the bulbs before planting helps keep rot and pests away.

Clean your carpet overnight

Whether your carpet smells dank and musty because of a pet, a smoker, or a season of rain, take the odor out with baby powder. Using a flour sifter, spread the powder generously over the carpet. Let it sit overnight—a few hours will suffice, but overnight is better—and vacuum up the powder and the smells in the morning.

Undo a knot

It may seem as soft as a newborn, but never underestimate the strength of baby powder! It can undo the toughest knot in a jewelry chain. Just cover the knot with a light dusting of powder, then pry the knot apart with a straight pin. Wash the chain with a mild soap, rinse it, dry it, and wear it!

baby shampoo

Baby shampoo was designed to be gentle on babies' eyes, and its gentleness is a godsend for adult eyes, too. Here are several alternate ways to use this kind solution.

THE HISTORY OF JOHNSON'S BABY POWDER

The original Johnson's Baby Powder owes its existence to medicated plasters (bandages) that caused skin irritation. Johnson's sold these plasters with a container of talcum powder meant to eliminate friction and keep covered skin comfortable. The question arose: Could talc use be expanded? The answer came in 1893, when Johnson's Baby Powder, made with talc, became available in a metal tin that declared: "For Toilet and Nursery." The tins were a mainstay in baby's room until 1963, when plastic bottles arrived. Today, many pediatricians don't recommend talc; Johnson's also offers a cornstarch formula.

Baby your eyes

Don't let conjunctivitis get you down! Soak a cotton ball in a mixture of 1 part baby shampoo and 10 parts warm water, then simply use it to wash the crud out of your eyelashes.

Wet your dry hair

Dump those expensive shampoos and conditioners promising a quick fix for dry hair right down the drain, and wash your hair with ordinary baby shampoo instead. Baby shampoo is cheaper and may be even less drying than its more expensive cousins.

Wash your eyelids, along with your hair

If you get sties more than occasionally, you may want to take preventive steps to stop them in their tracks. The secret? Wash your closed eyelids once a day with a solution of warm water and no-tears baby shampoo.

TAKE TWO AND CALL ME IN THE MORNING

THE HISTORY OF BAYER ASPIRIN

For over a century, aspirin has worked wonders in relieving our aches and pains. What would we do without it?

As it turns out, a precursor to aspirin was already familiar to Hippocrates, the ancient Greek physician; he wrote about a fever reducer made from willow tree bark. In 1828, salicin was finally identified as the active extract that made willow bark effective. Salicin was manipulated into salicylic acid and sold as a painkiller. It worked, but caused such severe stomach irritation that for many it was intolerable—the cure was worse than the illness.

One such person, a man suffering with rheumatism who simply couldn't stomach salicylic acid, had a son who was a chemist at a German company called Bayer. The son's name was Felix Hoffman, and in 1897 he joined the search for a way to modify salicylic acid so the body could better absorb it. The result of Hoffman's labor was acetylsalicylic acid. It could reduce fevers, stop aches and pains—and it was easy on the stomach. One imagines his father was thrilled on several levels! **The discovery was named Aspirin: "a" for "acetyl" and "spirin" for Spirea, the genus name of the plant from which salicylic acid was obtained.**

When it entered the market in 1899, Bayer sent out small packets of powdered Aspirin to doctors, pharmacists, and hospitals to press into pill form. They encouraged

Gentle as a
Mother's Kiss...

...yet SO FAST you need a
stopwatch to time its speed!
Glass of water test proves amazing disintegrating speed of a Bayer Aspirin tablet. Test of time proves its gentleness.
Gentle relief and *fast* relief. Both are important when you're suffering with pain. And of all pain relievers, *only* Bayer Aspirin can offer you this *proof* that it gives you *both:*
Bayer Aspirin's gentleness is proved by time. It is so gentle that its record of safety—of safe use by millions of people—can be matched by no other pain reliever. So gentle, in fact, that doctors prescribe it even for small children.
Bayer Aspirin's speed is proved merely by dropping a Bayer Aspirin tablet in a glass of water. It starts to disintegrate almost instantly—so fast you need a stopwatch to time its speed. It does the same thing in your stomach. That's one reason why it makes you feel better—fast.
So when you have an ordinary headache, take Bayer Aspirin. And remember—if Bayer Aspirin does not relieve your pain—don't experiment—*it's time to see your doctor.*
THE BEST
IN PAIN RELIEVERS
BEARS THE NAME...

BAYER
BAYER ASPIRIN

feedback and asked clients to publish their findings about the drug's effectiveness. The high amount of positive responses convinced Bayer to secure patent and trademark rights. **Aspirin was patented in the United States in 1900**. The company soon switched from distributing Aspirin powder to producing its own water-soluble, standardized tablets—each bearing the Bayer name in a distinctive cross logo. In 1903, the company set up an American subsidiary in a converted factory in Rensselaer, New York. By 1915, the drug became available without a prescription, just as Aspirin's patent was about to expire. Anticipating a deluge of competition, Bayer began an all-out campaign to brand its product in the consumer's mind. An advertisement in 1917, the last year that Aspirin would need a capital "A," featured the tag line: "One Real Aspirin" and warned that "counterfeits and substitutes" could be harmful so "protect yourself by demanding Bayer tablets of Aspirin."

The advertising strategy worked. **Even though aspirin is now a generic term, Bayer Aspirin comes readily to mind when people have a headache.** For its 100th anniversary, professional mountaineers wrapped the high-rise building that houses the company's headquarters in Germany to look like a giant bottle of aspirin. There was no huge glass of water by its side—perhaps that's something to look forward to on the next centennial celebration.

Remove eye makeup

Stop spending money on expensive, less-than-sensitive eye makeup remover. If you have baby shampoo in your house, you already have the perfect solution for taking off your face at night. Dab a bit of baby shampoo on a damp cotton ball, wipe off your makeup, and rinse your face. It's gentle on your face *and* on your wallet.

baby wipes

Considering all the unusual uses for baby wipes, it's hard to believe that they were originally intended for the younger set. You can use them for cleaning carpets and cars and so much more. Even the container is handy!

Wipe it off with a wipe

Did a little one use your skirt as a napkin? If so, you can get the food off by blotting the area with a paper towel, then rubbing it gently with a baby wipe.

Stop it before it sets

Did baby (or someone who should have known better) spill on your carpet? If so, use a damp baby wipe to blot up the fresh mess.

Wipes for windows

Grime and dead bugs can quickly build up on your car's windshield, particularly when you don't have time to find a bottle of glass cleaner and a clean cloth. A more practical solution: Keep a container of baby wipes in your glove compartment, and use one every now and then to clean your car windows.

Dash away the dregs

Use baby wipes to clean sticky stuff off your dashboard—greasy handprints, spots of misdirected hand lotion, drips from juice boxes, and anything else that has found its way to the front of your car. If you really want your dashboard to shine, buff it with a little baby oil.

Take a swipe at your shoes

Don't let unpolished leather shoes turn your bright day dull. Use a baby wipe to quickly shine your shoes and brighten your day.

bath oil

Bath oil is an essential ingredient in a calming, luxurious bath—and, apparently, an essential ingredient for cleaning messes and repelling bugs. Who knew? You will, when you see the tips below.

Leave shower doors sparkling

Soap scum on glass shower doors can build up fast when you shower every day. If you never have time for a long, hot soak in the bathtub, you may

Keep your patent leather shoes sharp. Moisten a clean, soft cloth with a few drops of bath oil, and gently rub the oil on to the shoe.

as well put your bath oil to good use cleaning off the scum. Pour a little bath oil straight on a sponge and swipe it over the glass. The scum will wipe right off. Rinse the sponge and wipe the doors lightly.

Tell insects to buzz off

You don't need a particular brand of bath oil to act as a repellent for flies, mosquitoes, and other biting insects. A strongly scented oil, especially one with citrus, can do the same job. Rub it on exposed skin (if you have sensitive skin, test it on a small area first) and flying pests will look elsewhere.

Use oil to clean off oil

Maybe you got grease or oil on your hands from trying to fix the chain on your bicycle, or maybe you were solving a problem under the hood of your car. Maybe you don't know how the grease got there! But you can get the goo off easily by rubbing a little bath oil into your hands, then washing your hands in warm water with soap.

Protect your patent leather

Keep your patent leather shoes and purse looking sharp by getting rid of scuff marks. Just moisten a clean, soft cloth with a few drops of bath oil, and gently rub the oil into the patent leather. (A towel works well, too.) Polish the area with another dry cloth or towel, and you'll see new life in your old accessories!

bubble bath

What liquid can you use to clean your car, your plants, and your hands? Bubble bath! (And you can take a really fun bath with it, too.)

Give your car a bath

Stop buying all those fancy and expensive products for washing your car. You can give your car a luxurious bath—and a beautiful shine—by washing it with bubble bath instead. Add one or two capfuls to a bucket of water and wash away.

Shine on!

Bubble baths aren't just for kids—or adults. They can be for plants, too! Dilute a little bubble bath in water. Wash your plant's leaves with a clean cloth dipped in the bubble bath solution. The leaves will shine, and the plant will look healthier.

Replace your hand soap

Don't relegate bubble bath to the tub—use it at the sink as well. Pour it into liquid hand soap containers that need to be refilled. Bubble bath is an effective, inexpensive replacement for your regular soap.

calamine lotion

Calamine lotion is a lifesaver for skin problems well beyond poison ivy—though it's a lifesaver for poison ivy, too. You can even use it to disguise your skin at Halloween! Here's how.

A new use for an old remedy

You may think of the pink stuff to soothe poison ivy, but it also provides great relief for heat rash. Slather it on and feel the itching and irritation ease.

THE Story Behind...

Pond's Cold Cream

In the 1840s Theron T. Pond, a pharmacist from Utica, New York, observed Native Americans treat small cuts and other ailments with tea made from witch hazel. He founded the T. T. Pond Company and used an extract from this plant to produce a general heal-all cream called Golden Treasure, later renamed Pond's Extract. It was the first commercial use of witch hazel. In 1905, Pond's Cold Cream—specifically made for the face and still containing witch hazel—was introduced. Cold cream had been around since ancient times, but Pond's created ad campaigns featuring celebrities and royalty, and soon Pond's became *the* brand to buy for face care.

Get relief from hives

It's a good idea to take an antihistamine to get relief from hives, but don't forget that you can get even more relief from itching by slathering the hives with calamine lotion.

Beat back blisters

Dab a healthy dose of calamine lotion onto blisters to dry them out. The lotion draws the moisture out of the blisters as it dries.

Think pink for Halloween

Going as a ghost to this year's Halloween party? Dab a few layers of calamine lotion on your face with a cotton ball to achieve a ghostly white pallor. Be sure to apply it evenly; you don't want to end up as a ghost with splotchy pink skin!

chest rub

It prevents and treats bug bites, relieves sore feet, and makes you feel so much better when you're sick. Is it a bird? Is it a plane? Is it chest rub? You bet it is!

Kick the cough!

Buy a chest rub containing camphor or menthol, and spread it over your chest and throat. Along with relieving the pain in your chest caused by coughing, it will help stop the cough itself. (Don't take it internally.)

Steam away your stuffiness

Add a teaspoon of vaporizing chest rub to a pot of water, and bring it to a boil. Remove the pot from the stove. Lean over the pot—keeping your face about 18 inches from the water—and place a towel over your head and shoulders so that it forms a dome over the water. Breathe in the air trapped by the towel. Your sinuses should feel better shortly.

Chest rub for your feet

Maybe you danced a little too much last night. Maybe you walked a little too far. Whatever the reason, pamper your sore feet with chest rub at night. Cover them with the goo, put on a pair of socks to protect your sheets, and go to bed as usual. You'll have happy dogs in the morning!

Tick off ticks (and other pesky bugs)

Don't give ticks, gnats, and mosquitoes a chance to bother you next time you venture into the great outdoors. Slather a healthy dose of chest rub on your legs and pants to repel the bugs. Like many humans, they want to stay far away from that smell!

cold cream

Cold cream, sour cream, heavy cream—which is the most versatile? Try these ideas for using cold cream, and then you'll know.

Remove bumper stickers, not just makeup

Is that bumper sticker from the last election starting to look silly on your car? Cover it with a thick layer of cold cream. Let it sit for 3 or 4 minutes, then scrape it off with a dull table knife or a credit card.

Take off temporary tattoos

Street fairs, carnivals, and parties are fun for your kids, especially when they get temporary tattoos—but removing them isn't fun for you. Make it easier on yourself by slathering cold cream on the tattoo and then gently rubbing it with a clean cloth until it comes off.

Kiss that stain good-bye

If you got a lipstick stain on your blouse as well as on your glass, remove it the way you remove makeup. Rub cold cream into the fabric (try it in an inconspicuous corner of the fabric first), then wash with washing soda, an alkaline compound used to remove stubborn stains from laundry. The stain should disappear.

comb

A comb seems so ordinary that it could have only one use—to comb your hair. Right? Wrong! Here are some fun ideas for using a surprisingly useful tool.

The hair of the dog

Consider buying a new comb, even if you already have one—just put it to a different use. Your dog or cat will thank you for the new belly-scratching tool (even though it's really designed for your locks)!

Comb more than your hair

Don't despair if you have an itchy back and no back scratcher (and no way to reach the itch). Rubbing your comb across the affected area will help relieve the problem quickly and easily. It's effective on other itchy parts of your body, too!

Thwart thieves

Use an ordinary comb to foil pickpockets. How? Fold your wallet in half, and put your comb in the middle of the wallet, with the teeth sticking out. Secure the comb to the wallet with a rubber band, running it around the wallet and through the teeth of the comb. Now put the wallet in your pocket. If anybody tries to steal the wallet, the comb will catch on your pocket so it will be harder to remove—and you'll know exactly what's happening.

Hold a nail

Stop hitting your fingers every time you hammer a nail in place. Use the teeth of an ordinary comb to hold the nail while you hammer.

Protect your shirt

Cutting a button off a shirt without cutting the shirt can be tricky. Make it easy by sliding a comb under the button, then cutting through the button's thread with a razor.

cotton balls

Liberate cotton balls from the linen closet—even from the house—and let them work at a campsite, on a plane, in a car, and many other places. Let them show you what they can do!

Light my fire

You may have heard of using lint from the dryer to start a campfire, but what about cotton balls? Rub petroleum jelly over a bunch of cotton balls—making sure they're completely covered—and store them in a ziplock bag. Take the bag with you on your camping trip, along with a lighter or waterproof matches. When it's time to light the fire, pull a few strands of fiber out of the cotton ball, place the ball into your pile of tinder and wood, and light the cotton ball. Instant fire starter!

Calming cotton balls

Take a little of the misery out of air travel by packing in your carry-on luggage some cotton balls designed to bring the stress down a notch. Before you leave for your trip, dribble lavender oil or clary sage onto a few cotton balls, then place them in a small ziplock bag. Take them out during the flight for instant tension release.

The fresh express

Take the stale stink out of your car with cotton balls. Soak a few in eucalyptus oil, tea tree oil, or vanilla extract, and transport them to your car in a plastic bag. Take a few out in the car—you can hide them in the cup holder or any other storage container—to refresh your ride.

Squash bugs with cotton balls

You may not need insect repellent when you travel, so you don't want to bring a bottle of it—but then again, you might need it. Leave the cans and bottles at home and instead bring a ziplock plastic bag containing a few cotton balls soaked in the repellent. Dab the cotton ball on your skin when you sense trouble. The small bag is easier to carry, and you'll avoid any potential spills in your luggage.

Have a ball with bleach

Forget about using elbow grease! Tackle mildew in crevices in your bathroom with cotton balls soaked in bleach. Put them in areas you can't normally reach—behind faucets, for example—and let them sit for a few hours. When their job is done, remove them and rinse the area with warm water.

cotton swab

Think of a cotton swab as a tool you can use around the house as well as in your beauty regime. These little swabs have big ambitions, as you'll see.

Simplify your makeup routine

Use one less makeup brush—substitute a cotton swab for an eye shadow applicator. It's even better than the real thing, capable of smoothing on the shadow, softening eyeliner, and smudging colors into each other. It's disposable, too!

Splint a bent stem

Push a cotton swab into the garden's dirt to make a splint for a bent flower stem. Wrap transparent tape loosely around the swab and the plant to hold the stem in place.

Use as a tiny duster

Crevices, cracks, and small spaces are a challenge for anyone trying to keep a home dust-free. Use your regular dust cloth for big and medium surfaces and cotton swabs for the tight spots: between the number keys on a phone, on the inside of photo frames, and all around a computer keyboard. Don't forget that swabs work equally well with household cleaners to clean difficult spots, such as on and around oven knobs and the base of the hot and cold faucets.

Swab your way to a professional look

Use cotton swabs the next time you give yourself a manicure or pedicure, and bump your technique up to a professional level. Use swabs with nail polish remover to get rid of the old nail polish wedged into your cuticles, and use them to wipe the new polish off the skin that borders your nails.

dental floss

Even if you don't floss daily as your dentist recommends, you should still buy dental floss to use in the kitchen, in your purse, and on a picnic. You may even want to buy it in bulk!

It cuts like a knife

Dental floss, that is. Hold it taut to cut butter, brownies, cakes, soft cheeses, and many other soft foods. Move it side to side to make a clean cut. Now you don't have to worry if you forget to bring a knife to your next picnic!

Use one less makeup brush—
substitute a cotton swab for
an eye shadow applicator.

Make a lifeline for your keys

Stop fishing around your purse for your house keys every time you need them. Make them readily accessible by tying them into your handbag with dental floss. Measure the distance from the bottom of your purse to the bottom of your purse handle. Add 6 inches, and cut that length of dental floss. Tie your keys to one end with a tight knot, and tie the other end to the bottom of the purse handle, again with a tight knot. Now you can easily retrieve your keys by pulling on the line!

Get crafty

Don't spring for specialty beading wire or string the next time you feel the urge to create a beaded masterpiece. Just use dental floss (two strands for extra strength) for your bracelet or necklace—you'll save money and a trip to the craft store.

Button, button, who's got the button?

Sometimes it feels like buttons disappear as often as socks disappear from a dryer! Stop buttons from fleeing by sewing them on with ultra-durable dental floss, rather than ordinary thread. Use dental floss on coat and jacket buttons for a particularly strong bond.

WAY BACK WHEN...

The Ballpoint Pen Inspired Ban Roll-On

An anonymous inventor from Philadelphia trademarked the first commercial deodorant in 1888. Called Mum, (an acronym for "Morning Until Midnight") it was a cream that you applied with your fingers. Deodorant application didn't evolve until Helen Barnett Diserens joined Mum's production team. She developed an applicator based on the ballpoint pen. It was tested in 1952 and marketed under the name Ban Roll-On. This was a fantastic innovation, and today Ban is still a bestselling roll-on deodorant. Incredibly, the world would have to wait until 1965 for antiperspirants to enter the picture.

deodorant

Get rid of bug bites and moist feet along with body odor the next time you buy deodorant. It's more useful than you could have imagined!

Protect your feet

Roll or spray a little deodorant—specifically, an antiperspirant—on your feet for a change. Why? You'll keep them dry and keep blisters at bay.

Banish bug bites

Apply a dab of deodorant onto a bug bite to reduce itching and irritation. Many deodorants contain ingredients designed to reduce skin irritation. Yours may do the trick!

Say good-bye to sweaty palms

Whether you have an important business meeting or a big date, you don't want to have sweaty palms. Rub some antiperspirant into your palms, and don't sweat it.

emery board

Whether you buy an emery board by itself or a nail file as part of a manicure or pedicure set, you'll find plenty of new uses here for what you normally use on your nails.

Erase the eraser

Rub away smudges and scuffs on your pencil eraser with an emery board. Lightly rub it over the eraser until the mark is gone.

File seeds before planting

Rub off the hard coating on seeds using an emery board before you put them in the ground. They'll absorb moisture better and get a head start sprouting.

Steam away stains on suede

Whether you discover a stain on your suede shoes or your suede jacket, you won't be happy. Bring a smile back to your face quickly by rubbing the stain gently with the fine side of an emery board, then holding the suede item over steam from a pan. The stain will disappear! You can use the emery board again to freshen the nap.

Get to the point

Knives get dull. Scissors get dull. Even needles get dull. Make your needle sharp again by rubbing it against an emery board.

epsom salt

Sweat, splinters, raccoons, and roses—what do they have in common? Epsom salt! This product will amaze you with its many uses.

Salt your bathwater

Why? To get rid of rough patches of skin. Add 2 cups of Epsom salt to a tub filled with warm water, soak for a few minutes, then finish the job by rubbing additional salt on the rough spots. You'll be a smoother person when you emerge from your bath!

Season your toes

You know Epsom salt can relieve sore feet, but did you know it can also help prevent foot odor? Just add 2 cups of Epson salt to 2 gallons of warm water in a suitable container (a bucket or tub), then soak your feet in the solution twice a day, 15 minutes each time. You'll find your feet sweating less and smelling less.

Ditch the itch

Got a case of poison ivy? Soak in a tub of warm water and Epsom salt to dry out the rash. Check the label for soaking instructions.

Stop splinters

Make a paste of Epsom salt and water and apply it to the area harboring a splinter. The paste will pull the splinter to the surface of the skin in about 10 minutes. It will pull insect stingers out of your skin, too. A luxurious bath in Epsom salt will also help draw out the splinter or stinger.

Rub off the hard coating on seeds using an emery board before you put them in the ground.

Relish your roses

Sprinkle half a cup of Epsom salt around the base of your rose bush in early spring and in the fall for healthier roses. After the leaves appear and again when the roses appear, spray them with a mixture of 1 tablespoon Epsom salt per gallon of water. Gardeners in the know swear by it!

Rid yourself of raccoons

If those cute but annoying nighttime pests are getting at your garbage, sprinkle a few tablespoons of Epsom salt around your trash cans to drive them away. Remember to do it again after it rains.

foot powder

You may not be looking for foot powder when you visit a 99 cent store, but you should grab a container of it to keep around the house. Why? See below.

Power to foot powder!

You find a dark puddle on your garage floor and realize that oil is leaking from your engine, but you don't know the exact source of the leak.

Clean the engine with WD-40, then cover the sides and bottom of the engine with spray-on foot powder. You'll see the leak when it turns white.

Give fleas the boot

Sprinkle a light dusting of foot powder around the edges of each room and outside the doors leading into your house to get rid of fleas. If you have fleas in your yard, sprinkle some there, too. (But make sure no one in your house is allergic to the powder before using it, and don't use it if you have small children in the house. They may try to eat it.)

hairbrush

Whether it's a round styling brush, a flat brush, or a pocket brush, hair brushes are one of those things that we take for granted. But there are so many more uses for them than just doing the obvious!

Brush the cat

The kinds of women's hairbrushes you find at 99 cent stores are ideal for your hair—and for your cat. In fact, brushes with round-tipped plastic bristles work better on cats than the soft (and expensive) kind sold in pet stores.

Scratch your back

Can't reach that itch square in the middle of your back? Rubbing your back against a door frame may help, but using your brush as a back scratcher is more efficient. You'll be able to zero in on the offending spot faster.

Scrub a stainless steel sink

Stainless steel may be the material of choice when it comes to kitchen sinks, but it's also easily scratched. A 99 cent store hairbrush is perfect for gently lifting grime off the surface without scratching it.

Find a hair conditioner that contains lanolin, and use it to wash your car.

hair conditioner

Stretch your thinking about hair conditioner, and you'll find that it has many uses (other than conditioning hair) in the bathroom—and far outside of it. Can you use it on cars and tools? Why not?

Keep conditioning all day

Super-dry hair requires more than a casual rinse with conditioner in the shower. Spray wet hair—or dry hair slightly dampened—with a mixture of half hair conditioner and half water. Leave the conditioner in for the rest of the day.

Skip the shaving cream

Use hair conditioner for a smooth, clean shave—on your legs, under your arms, and (for men) even on your face. The conditioner will pamper your skin as well as your hair! You can also use hair conditioner as a soothing agent for legs irritated by shaving.

Condition with care

Keep your tools in tip-top shape by stopping rust before it starts. How? Rub hair conditioner onto screwdrivers, saws, and other tools before a problem erupts.

Wash and wax

Find a hair conditioner that contains lanolin, and use it to wash your car. You'll get a nicely waxed car—and one that will repel the rain.

hair spray

Hair spray has so many uses beyond its original purpose that you may think it was designed to help you all over the house, not just on your hair. Use it in the laundry room and in the kitchen, as well as in the bathroom. You may even forget why you originally bought it!

Preserve your bouquet

Spray the undersides of your cut flowers—leaves and petals—with hair spray to prolong their life. Be sure to stand about a foot away when you spray them for best results.

Stop static cling

If your pants or skirts or dresses are getting a little too friendly, spritz the underside of the garment with hair spray to stop it from clinging. You can also spray some hair spray on a paper towel, and then rub the paper towel on the inside of your clothes.

10 More Uses for HAIR SPRAY

1 Banish Bites

If a mosquito bite doesn't itch, it's almost like it isn't there. You have the power to make bug bites less irritating with a squirt of hair spray. One shot and the stinging feeling will subside.

2 No Running!

Having even a tiny run in your panty hose can spoil your outfit—especially if you don't have a spare pair. You can't make it vanish, but you can stop a run in its tracks by spraying it with hair spray.

3 Carpet Saver

If you spill nail polish on the carpet, take quick action to clean the mess by spraying it with water and then squirting on some hair spray. After a few squirts, the polish will get tacky, and you can blot it off your rug with a paper towel.

4 Zap Bugs

Don't panic if you discover you've run out of bug spray just as a winged insect is buzzing its way through your home. Grab a can of hair spray and take aim. You'll find it kills most bugs.

5 Preserve Polish

Here's a neat trick: After you polish your leather shoes, spray them lightly with hair spray. The shine will last longer.

6 Glue Glitter

If your child is making a project and doesn't have glue to add a touch of glitter, you can save the day with hair spray. Spray the surface that will be sprinkled, and the glitter will stick like magic.

7 Faux Dye

Want to add a shocking color to your hair for a holiday? A temporary and inexpensive way is to pick a powdered drink mix (like Kool-Aid) in a shade that suits your mood, sprinkle it over your hair, then moisten and hold it in place with hair spray.

8 Fur Fix

No time to vacuum? A quick way to remove pet hair from furniture is to spray a tissue with hair spray and then wipe. The hair will cling to the tissue, and you can toss the furry mess into the trash.

9 Chalk It Up

If you've carefully marked chalk lines for a home improvement, don't let them get smudged accidentally—spray them with hair spray. You can easily wash everything away when you want to, but until you do, that chalk won't disappear.

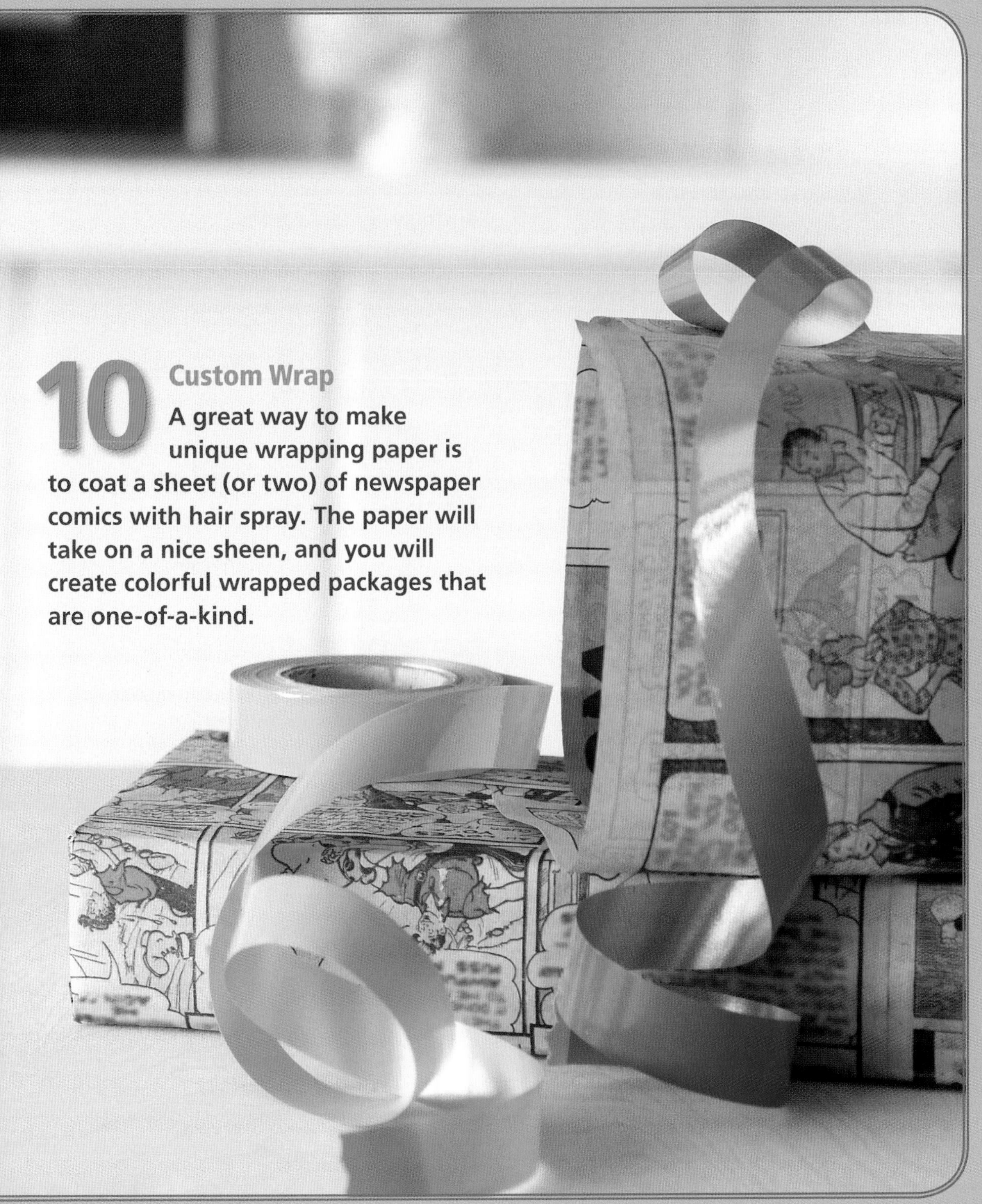

10 Custom Wrap

A great way to make unique wrapping paper is to coat a sheet (or two) of newspaper comics with hair spray. The paper will take on a nice sheen, and you will create colorful wrapped packages that are one-of-a-kind.

Zip it shut

Does your zipper refuse to stay shut? Show it who's boss! Put the item on, zip the zipper shut, then coat the teeth with hair spray, applying it with a cotton swab. The hair spray will act like invisible glue.

Remove the stink and the ink

If a pen leaked on your shirt or your child autographed you as well as her artwork, just spray the offending mark with hair spray and launder as usual (making sure the ink has disappeared before you dry the item).

Thread a needle

If you have trouble threading a needle, try spritzing the end of the thread with hair spray. It will stiffen the end and make it easier to push through the needle.

hemorrhoid cream

You may not think of your face when you buy hemorrhoid cream, but that may be the most logical place to use it. Rethink the purpose of your purchase, and make your face the beneficiary.

The eyes have it

Puffy, wrinkly eyes need help, and they can get it from expensive eye cream—or common hemorrhoid cream. Oddly enough, the hemorrhoid cream tightens the puffiness and the wrinkles and makes eyes look brighter and more alert. Mix scented lotion into it before applying it to your face if you're bothered by the smell. Rub it under your eyes, let it sit for 20 minutes, then wash the cream off gently and pat the area dry. And be sure to keep it out of your eyes.

Reduce swelling from pimples

Rub a dab of hemorrhoid cream into pimples to relieve the swelling that accompanies a breakout. You won't get rid of the redness, but you will get rid of the inflammation. The blemishes will look less obvious.

Laugh away facial lines

Apply a little hemorrhoid cream to laugh lines, frown lines, and worry lines on your face. The cream will help tighten those areas and soften the lines and wrinkles.

Remove a stuck ring

Warm outside? Retaining water and your wedding band is stuck? Simply massage your ring-bearing finger with hemorrhoid cream and wait 3 minutes. The ring should slip right off.

hydrogen peroxide

Heal and clean yourself with the hydrogen peroxide that you buy at a 99 cent store. It's one of the store's most useful bargains!

Stop bad breath

Kill the bacteria that cause bad breath by storing your toothbrush in hydrogen peroxide. Stick it head down in a plastic container filled with the liquid, rinsing it thoroughly before every use. Your friends and family will thank you!

Banish body odor

Don't despair if you suddenly run out of deodorant. Simply swipe a little hydrogen peroxide under your arms instead. You'll kill the bacteria that cause odors. Rubbing alcohol and vinegar work, too!

Kill the bacteria that cause bad breath
by storing your toothbrush in
hydrogen peroxide.

End ear pain

Use hydrogen peroxide to stop an earache in its tracks. Check the label to make sure you have 3 percent commercial-grade hydrogen peroxide, then place 3, 4, or 5 drops into the ear canal every 3 to 4 hours. The pain and inflammation will subside. Be careful not to let it drip on your clothes because it will remove color from fabric.

Tame a toothache

If you have a toothache, a fever, and a bad taste in your mouth, you'll benefit from a hydrogen peroxide rinse. Simply use 3 percent hydrogen peroxide as mouthwash to kill bacteria and temporarily provide relief from the toothache. Spit out the solution and rinse repeatedly with water. Be sure to see your dentist as soon as possible—you likely have an infection.

ice pack

Ice packs help keep cold food cold and frozen items frozen. They are also surprisingly helpful when it comes to noses and mouths, as you'll discover below.

Solve an inside problem from the outside

If your gums are swollen and painful, try treating the problem with an ice pack. Wrap it in a cloth and apply it to your cheek where the gums hurt. It's a twofer: The cold will both numb the pain and reduce the swelling.

Stop the flow

Don't let a nosebleed get you down. Stop the bleeding by placing an ice pack on the problem nostril. The blood vessels in your nose will react by narrowing, and the flow of blood will slow and eventually stop.

Numb your eyebrows

Make plucking your eyebrows much less painful by putting an ice pack on them until they're uncomfortably cold. At that point your skin will be numb enough to begin plucking. You won't even feel the tug!

BUBBLE, BUBBLE...

THE HISTORY OF HYDROGEN PEROXIDE

You can bleach a hat with it, change the color of your hair—or use it to fuel a rocket. What is this wonder substance? Hydrogen peroxide, of course. Discovered in 1818 by a French scientist named Louis Auguste Thenard, hydrogen peroxide is a compound that is very pale blue liquid at room temperature and consists of two oxygen and two hydrogen atoms: H_2O_2. **Essentially, it is water with an extra oxygen atom.** It can be found in nature in very low concentrations but was first produced by man by burning barium salt to produce barium peroxide and then dissolving that in water. Today, self-oxidation processes are used to produce hydrogen peroxide.

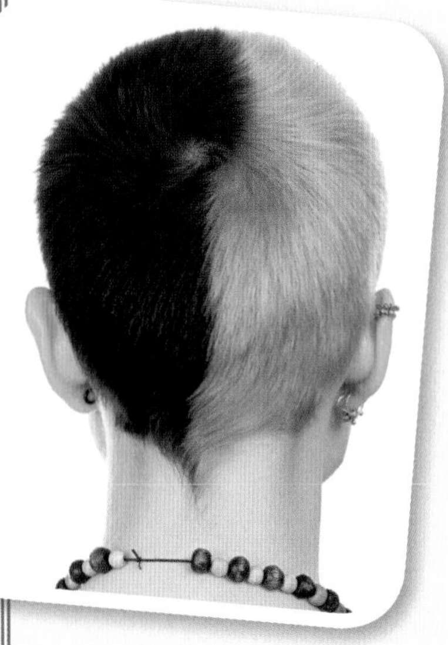

At the beginning of the 20th century, wearing hats was in fashion. A style that was particularly popular with both men and women was made of straw and called a "boater." These hats are familiar to us today—they are commonly seen on members of barbershop quartets. **One of the first commercial applications of hydrogen peroxide was bleaching these hats. Bleaching meant the color in the straw would be lost:** part of the hydrogen peroxide molecule would bond with the color-causing molecule in the straw and the resulting new molecule would not reflect light in the same way as the original. **Then those boaters**

wouldn't look like hay—they'd be bright and white!

Fashions inevitably change, and some women didn't want hats covering their hair. If they were brunette and wanted to be blonde, that could be arranged in the same way that a boater could be bleached. A dark hair pigment will be seen as much lighter if it is washed with hydrogen peroxide. **Many women followed the lead set by stars such as Jean Harlow and later Marilyn Monroe and bleached their hair to a platinum color using hydrogen peroxide.** Today's hair coloring products are made with a variety of ingredients, but a fair-haired woman who doesn't seem born that way may still be called a "peroxide blonde."

The hydrogen peroxide used on hats and hair is always diluted, for safety reasons. Even though it seems only slightly removed from water, undiluted hydrogen peroxide can ignite spontaneously if it come comes in contact with flammable substances. And if it is mixed, undiluted, with alcohol, it could explode. Spontaneous ignition is something to be avoided in almost all instances, and for this reason hydrogen peroxide is generally shipped only in diluted form. It is shipped often, as it is used today for a wide-ranging variety of uses, both household and commercial, from paper bleaching to laundry whitening to cleaning wounds.

What happens when it is used in an undiluted form? **In the early 1960s, Bell Aerosystems built a rocket pack for the U.S. Army. It was fueled by hydrogen peroxide!** The unit is on display at the Smithsonian Institution's National Air and Space Museum's annex.

lip balm

Your lips may be the last thing you touch with your lip balm after reading the tips below. Who knew lip balm could be so versatile? (And lipstick is as well—here's a tip for that, too!)

Tame the wild beast

If your wayward eyebrows or mustache make you look like you belong in a zoo, apply a little lip balm to calm them down. It's clear, waxy, and able to groom wild hair.

Lip balm for your hands

Hand lotion is a necessity in the winter, but it isn't always a miracle worker. If your hands still get chapped—particularly between your fingers—rub some lip balm on them at night before bed. You'll treat the rough spots and contribute to overall moisturizing.

WAY BACK WHEN…

Lipstick

Would you like to kiss crushed beetles, ants' eggs, and fish scales? Would it sway your answer to know that Cleopatra did? We know her lipstick contained these unsavory sounding ingredients. It was red (due to cochineal beetles) and had a high degree of shine (thanks to the scales). Modern lipsticks are made of less exotic ingredients, including castor, olive, and mineral oils—but cochineal is still used as a dye to this day, and a shiny, red kiss is timeless.

A bright idea

Prevent lightbulbs in outdoor fixtures—floodlights, porch lights, and motion detector lights—from rusting and resisting removal by coating the threads with lip balm. Apply the lip balm before you screw in the lightbulb and you'll have less trouble removing it when you need to replace it.

A faux finish

Don't let a chipped nail ruin your dinner date. Temporarily solve the problem by applying lipstick or lip pencil to the chipped area. Reapply as necessary until you can properly fix it.

Take the ouch out of shaving

Nick yourself while shaving? Lip balm is a pain-free alternative to styptic pencil. Just dab a bit on your cut and you'll be good to go.

lotion

Hand and body lotion was designed to moisturize your hands and your body (surprise, surprise). Here are alternate uses for the lotion. Some still involve your hands and your body, but with a twist.

Hand lotion for your hair

If you're having a particularly bad hair day because of dry hair, try rubbing your hands with lotion, then running your hands through your hair.

Shine your shoes

Give your shoes a quick polish with hand cream. Rub a little into your shoes and then briefly buff them. They'll look like they have a new life!

It's not so shocking

Slather yourself with body lotion in the morning and continue putting hand lotion on during the day, and you'll be less likely to receive those

Give your shoes a quick polish with hand cream. Rub a little into your shoes and then briefly buff them.

annoying static electricity shocks that often happen over the course of the winter.

Stop hanging out with hangnails

Get rid of annoying hangnails by rubbing hand or body lotion into your cuticles daily. The lotion will keep those troublesome areas soft and help prevent future hangnails.

maxi pads

Put those maxi pads that you bought at the 99 cent store to good use around your house. Here are some unusual ways to make them work.

A maximum idea

If you run out of window washing fluid in your car, you can wash your windshield without it—as long as you use a feminine hygiene maxi pad. Keep the sticky side next to your hand, and rub the windshield with the padded side. You might want to keep a box in the trunk if you're prone to running out of the fluid.

Feminine first aid

Suppose you cut your arm and an adhesive bandage isn't substantial enough to stop the bleeding. What's a good alternative? Try putting a maxi pad on your arm and wrapping it with an ace bandage. It will staunch the bleeding, and no one will be the wiser!

Quick-thinking solution

Your toilet starts to overflow and the only towels you have on hand are your good bath towels. What can you use to stop the overflow from flowing all over your bathroom? Maxi pads! Grab a bunch from under the sink (or wherever you store them in or near the bathroom) and stop the water in its tracks.

mirror

Remember "Mirror, mirror, on the wall?" One big mirror hanging on the wall is so old school. Try these ideas with mirrors to enlarge and brighten your world.

See yourself in a newly decorated room

You know a large mirror can enlarge and enhance a small room, but have you ever thought about using a collection of small mirrors to accomplish the same effect? Buy several small inexpensive mirrors, preferably in different shapes and sizes, and mount them on a single wall. (Experiment with various arrangements by using masking tape to mark the position of the mirrors before you mount them.) You'll suddenly have more space!

Add sparkle to your garden

Give your plants what they want—light—*and* add interest—dancing sunshine—to your shady garden by hanging a mirror on a fence or wall.

Think like a dentist

You know how your dentist uses a tool with a tiny mirror on the end to help see into the recesses of your mouth? Like your dentist, you can use a mirror to help see under the siding on your house when you're caulking cracks and gaps between your siding and your foundation.

Look into your reflection

Create a warm centerpiece by grouping different size and color candles on top of a mirror. (Use candleholders as usual.) The mirror will reflect the light from the candles, warming the atmosphere in your room.

mouthwash

Healing, cleaning, soothing feet—who knew mouthwash could do so much more than clean your breath? You will, after you read the tips below!

Give your toothbrush a bath

Kill viruses that lurk on toothbrushes by giving your toothbrush a daily bath in mouthwash. Your immune system will thank you. (Your mouth will too!)

Bite your tongue!

In fact, if you do bite your tongue, rinse your mouth with mouthwash. It won't help your tongue heal faster, but it will help keep infection at bay.

Refresh tired feet

Take this tip from marathon runners, who know that a ten-minute soak in a sugarless mouthwash will take your tootsies from tired to terrific. Alcohol invigorates and mint will make them smell sweet again.

Help heal a bruise

When you bump your arm or leg and you feel a bruise coming on, alleviate the pain and cut

Refresh your feet with a ten-minute soak in sugarless mouthwash.

down on the discoloration by rubbing the surface of the skin with a splash of an alcohol-based mouthwash.

Rinse away skin problems

Help your dog or cat recover from minor skin troubles with mouthwash. Dab a mouthwash-moistened cotton ball onto cuts and scrapes—even boils. The mouthwash will clean out the wounds and cool down the boils.

nail polish

You probably know to use nail polish to stop a run in your stockings, but did you know you can use it to fix a scratch on your car? This little bottle of varnish is worth its weight in gold, as you'll see below.

Mark keys

Don't fumble for your keys on a dark doorstep. Mark your front-door key or other important keys with a colorful dot of bright nail polish so you can pick it out of the bunch in a hurry.

Banish the green meanies

Have you ever had a beautiful piece of costume jewelry turn your skin an ugly shade of green? Try painting the inside of the next piece you buy with clear nail polish. Once you've covered the part that touches your skin, you'll eliminate the chance of green fingers, neck, and wrist.

Ditch the ding

If you find a scratch on your car, rub your fingers over it to determine its depth. If you can feel the indentation, you'll need to camouflage the scratch—with nail polish. Find a color that matches the color of your car, and carefully apply the nail polish to the scratch. Let it dry, and drive off in your shiny looks-as-good-as-new car. (If you make a mistake, remove the polish with a cotton swab dipped in nail polish remover. Let the area dry and start again.)

Tag a toothbrush

Will your kids use a toothbrush of any color, so long as it's purple? You can keep the peace by dabbing different colored nail polish on the end of each brush for easy identification.

nail polish remover

Superglue, gum, sap, and more—remove more than just nail polish with this super substance. Check out how much you can really do with nail polish remover.

Remove pain with polish remover

Don't let pain from shingles get you down. Mix two crushed aspirin with 3 tablespoons of nail polish remover, and stir until the aspirin disappears. Apply the concoction directly to shingles blisters with a cotton ball. Let air-dry.

Stop being sappy

Did your tree- and bush-trimming shears get covered with sap last time you worked in the yard? Get rid of the stubborn sap with nail polish remover. Put some on a clean cloth, and rub the sap off the tool.

Carefully clean chrome

First the caveat: Keep it away from the paint on your car. Now the solution: Clean chrome with a clean cloth moistened with nail polish remover. It works wonders!

Take the "super" out of superglue

Superglue is a great invention—until you can't get it off your hands. Don't rub it until you hurt your skin. Instead, thoroughly wet a cotton ball

ODORS AWAY

THE HISTORY OF MOUTH-WASH

"Can I be happy with him in spite of *that*?"

This was a tagline in a 1920s advertisement for Listerine, featuring a young woman pondering her potential husband's horrible breath. As you may imagine, it caught people's attention.

Romans and Egyptians were worried about halitosis, too. Records show they'd chew on plants like eucalyptus or spices like cinnamon and vanilla to freshen their sour breath. Many of our mouthwashes and oral rinses today have the same or similar flavors. Of course **the ancients also swished and gargled with donkey milk, animal blood, or, in the case of the Romans, human urine.** Happily those solutions have fallen out of favor, though the reason human urine may have worked was due to its ammonia content. At the most basic level, mouthwash is meant to kill odor by killing bacteria in the mouth—so some of today's mouthwashes do contain ammonia as an active ingredient. Rest assured it is of the synthetic variety, manufactured in laboratories so it is healthier and less, um, pungent than what the Romans used.

Health was what led to the development of Listerine. Dr. Joseph Lawrence and Jordan Wheat Lambert created it as a surgical antiseptic in 1879. They named it after Dr. Joseph Lister, a surgeon who applied Louis Pasteur's theory that germs caused infection and pioneered antiseptic surgery. Lambert, a St. Louis pharmacist, licensed the formula and formed the Lambert Pharmacal Company to manufacture and market Listerine. **Initially, it was sold as a multipurpose antiseptic, used for everything from cleaning cuts to curing athlete's foot.** By 1895, Lambert started selling the product to dentists as an oral antiseptic, but it wasn't until it was pitched as a solution to bad breath in 1921 that it really took off.

The first antiseptic mouthwash to be marketed commercially was in fact invented by a German man named Carl August Lingner. Called Odol, it is still available today, though it is not nearly as well known as Listerine. That is likely due to the social stigma Lambert ingeniously created through advertising. A Listerine advertisement that ran in 1928 sums it up: **"No matter how charming you may be or how fond of you your friends are, you cannot expect them to put up with halitosis** (unpleasant breath) forever. They may be nice to you—but it is an effort." Who wouldn't rush out to get the product that promised to cure such a crushing situation?

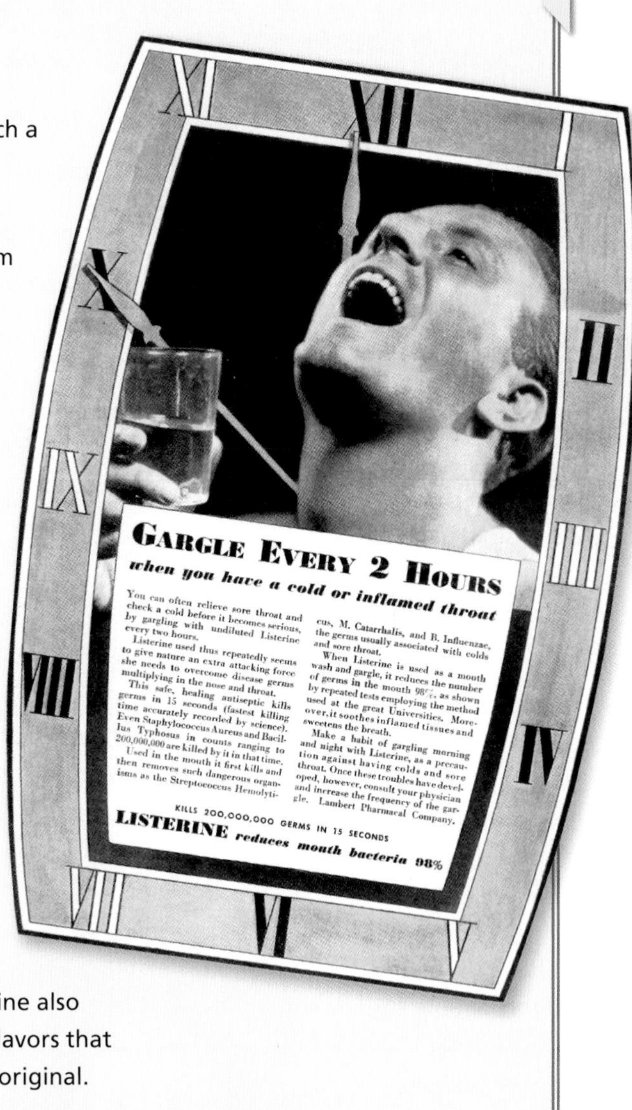

Though we have moved far away from the days of donkey milk, the taste of some mouthwash, including Listerine, has been a source of complaint. A relative newcomer to the market (compared to Listerine) is Scope. Hitting the shelves in 1966, it is now available in Original Mint, Cool Peppermint, Long Lasting Mint, and Mint Splash. For those with unbreakable brand loyalty, Listerine also comes in different flavors that are milder than the original.

To swish away bad breath has been a goal of people since ancient times. May the easy availability and variety of modern mouthwash ensure that none of us becomes an effort for our friends to speak to.

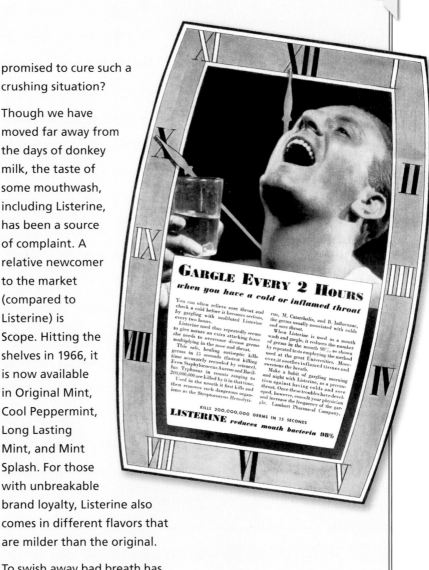

with nail polish remover (make sure it contains acetone), and hold the cotton ball against the superglue until it dissolves.

The Story Behind...

Vaseline

During an on-site visit to an oil well, Robert A. Chesebrough, a chemist born in London and raised in New York, noticed workers smearing the cuts on their skin with a residue wiped from their drills. Chesebrough experimented with the substance, and from it he extracted petroleum jelly. He patented it in 1872 and marketed it under the name Vaseline. Then he traveled his home state, injuring his skin in front of audiences and covering his wounds with petroleum jelly. People may have been horrified—he'd burn himself over an open fire—but they were also impressed. By the late 1880s, Vaseline was sold nationwide. Chesebrough lived to be 96 years old and credited his longevity to one simple fact: He ate a spoonful of Vaseline every day.

petroleum jelly

Petroleum jelly, how do I love thee? Let me count the ways—and let me count the different ways to use it! Here are a few to get you going.

Petroleum jelly spells relief!

You already know that petroleum jelly relieves chapped lips; now try putting some under your nose to relieve allergies. The goo will trap the pollen before it enters your nostrils, stopping an allergy attack before it can even start.

Paint perfectly

Coat door hinges and handles with petroleum jelly next time you paint a door. You won't have to remove the fixtures, and the paint won't stick—so your paint job will look great! Just wipe off the jelly when you're done painting.

Sometimes glue works *too* well

If you've ever had the cap of glue—wood glue, school glue, or any other type of glue—get stuck on the container of glue, just apply a thin veneer of petroleum jelly to the cap's threads, and you won't have trouble opening it again.

Protect cuts and scrapes

Apply a layer of petroleum jelly to your cut. It will soften the scab so you won't even *think* about picking at it. It protects the scraped skin, too.

Seal the deal

If you think your plunger isn't working up to its normal standard, try covering the rim with a thick coating of petroleum jelly. You'll get a tighter seal and better suction.

shampoo

You can always use shampoo to wash that man right out of your hair—or you can use it for really practical purposes that have nothing to do with hair. Here are some different ways to use shampoo.

Get rid of ring around the collar

Rub a little shampoo into shirt collars with an old toothbrush. (Shampoos containing ammonium lauryl sulfate work best.) Let the shirts sit for half an hour, then launder as you normally would. The rings will disappear.

Wash away hair spray

Your hairdo may look better with hair spray, but your vinyl floor doesn't. Mop your floor with a cleaner consisting of one gallon of warm water and a squirt of shampoo. Rinse with a damp mop.

Shampoo your silk

You can feel comfortable hand washing silk in cool water and a protein-based shampoo. Not only will the shampoo not destroy the silk, but it will actually give the silk more body and a longer life.

Forget about the fog

Driving with a foggy windshield is annoying and potentially dangerous. If the inside of your windshield tends to fog up in the winter, wipe it with a clean cloth moistened with shampoo. You'll clear out the fog and clean the glass at the same time!

Say good-bye to sap

Whether you're working in your yard or bringing in the annual Christmas tree, chances are good that you'll end up with sap on your hands. Zap the sap by washing your hands with shampoo.

shaving cream

Shaving cream has long been used by mischief-makers on Halloween, but you know there are much better alternative uses for it. Try the tips that follow instead—you're more likely to stay out of trouble!

Shave away the stain

Find a fresh stain on your carpeting? Blot up as much as you can, pat it with a damp cloth or sponge, then shoot shaving cream (the non-gel variety) onto it. Wipe the shaving cream and the stain away with a clean damp cloth or sponge.

Color it gone

If you find crayon markings on your wall, don't get mad—get shaving cream. Spray the shaving cream directly onto the offending artwork, and scrub it off with a toothbrush or scrub brush.

Stop soap scum

Spray shaving cream directly onto glass shower doors, then wipe it off with a clean dry cloth to prevent a buildup of soap scum. A bonus: The shaving cream creates a thin film that prevents the shower door from fogging.

Cut through the fog

Foggy glasses—which can happen when you come in from the cold or lean over a pot of boiling water—are both irritating and potentially dangerous. You need to be able to see! Prevent this problem by occasionally cleaning your glasses with white foamy shaving cream. It covers the lenses with a thin, invisible coating that repels water (also known as fog).

See clearly once again

Don't panic if you've accidentally sprayed your glasses as well as your hair with hair spray. Add some shaving cream to the mess, rub the lenses and frames gently with a clean cloth, and then wipe it all off.

7 More Uses for WHITE, NON-GEL TOOTHPASTE

1 Whiten Shoes
Squeeze toothpaste on a brush to clean and whiten the rubber on your sneakers. After scrubbing, wipe with a damp cloth and your shoes will look new.

2 Hide Holes
This is an old dorm room trick: A little white toothpaste can fill nail holes. Once it dries, paint right over it.

3 End Itches
Putting toothpaste over bug bites—including those from mosquitoes, fleas, and ants—will quickly lessen the itch.

4 Clean Sinks
If you've run out of bathroom cleaner and company is on the way, you may have a sinking feeling. Never fear! Use toothpaste instead and your basin will be sparkling clean in no time.

5 Magic Mirrors
Write a message to a loved one on the bathroom mirror using toothpaste. Then wipe it off. After your sweetie steps out of the shower, the message will appear outlined by the fog that covers the rest of the mirror—it will seem like magic.

6 Water Views
If you want to prevent "fog" in your swimming goggles, smear them with toothpaste and then wipe them clean with a dry cloth. When you dive into the pool you'll see clearly underwater.

7 Shine Silver
Don't buy an expensive polish: Toothpaste can bring out the shine in your silver.

shoe polish

Use shoe polish on your skin, your furniture, your picture frames, and your blinds—not just your shoes. In fact, forget about your shoes and try these tips instead!

Dash your rash

If you have poison ivy but no calamine lotion handy, dab a little liquid white shoe polish on your rash. The pipe clay (found in the old-fashioned bottle of liquid shoe polish) is cousin to one of calamine's main ingredients. You'll stop the itch.

Shine away the scratches

Hide light scratches in your wood flooring with shoe polish. Find a shoe polish color that closely matches the color of your floor, and use a soft clean cloth to apply it. Let the polish dry. Use a clean, damp cloth to buff it, and your secret is safe!

THE TRUTH ABOUT SHINOLA

For many years, the American Mining & Manufacturing Co. in Rochester, New York, supplied the world with Shinola shoe polish. Trademarked in 1929, the brand went out of business in the middle of the 20th century, but the name is immortalized in the saying: You don't know...poop...from Shinola. The original alliteration implied a person fooled by appearances. Shinola might have looked like a sidewalk gift from a canine—but between the two substances, only one would be advantageous on shoes, and the wise person would know which. Many people today have heard the phrase yet have no idea it was once the name of a shoe polish.

Picture this

Polish a new wooden picture frame for an antique look. How? Sand the frame, then apply a thin coat of brown or reddish-brown shoe polish. Lightly buff the frame. New will look old!

Polish your blinds

Venetian blinds are notoriously difficult to clean and, to make matters worse, easily soiled. Spruce up dirty spots on your white blinds with liquid white shoe polish.

shower cap

Though you should feel free to use a shower cap in the shower, you'll find even better uses for it outside the bathroom. Try it on your bike, in your suitcase, and on your kitchen counter.

Cover your camera

If you're planning to take pictures in the rain—even a slight drizzle—wrap your camera in a shower cap. Let the lens peek out through the opening in the cap. If the shower cap isn't clear, cut a small hole in it so you can look through the viewfinder or see the LCD monitor.

Don't leave home without it

Shoes can be a problem to pack, particularly if the soles aren't brand spanking new. Protect your clothes from your shoes next time you travel by encasing your shoes in shower caps.

Be ready for an unexpected shower

If you've parked your bike for a few minutes in threatening weather while you run into a store, cover your bicycle seat with a shower cap. You'll have a dry place to sit on your ride home if it rains!

Keep out dust—not just water

Cover the kitchen appliances you keep on your counter—your stand mixer, your food processor, and your bread machine—with shower caps to keep them free of dust.

Create a makeshift saucer

Does your hanging plant have a saucer beneath it to catch drips and protect your floor? If not, slip a shower cap across the bottom of the plant when you water it.

soap

Bars of soap are inexpensive—especially so at a 99 cent store—and can be used well beyond the kitchen or bathroom sink. So think beyond the sink!

Wash away your door troubles

If wooden doors in your house tend to swell and stick in humid weather, try rubbing their edges with a common bar of soap. The thin coating of hand soap will help the door open and close with ease.

These teeth have no bite!

If your zipper looks fine but doesn't zip up or down smoothly, try rubbing the teeth with a dry bar of hand soap. You'll be zipping up and down in no time.

Save your stockings

Stop a run in your stockings with soap if you don't have a bottle of nail polish handy. Rub a wet bar of soap—or dab some liquid soap—on the end of the run. The run will stop running when the soap dries.

Stop sewing snafus

Sewing on a button? Make tangles and knots easier to unravel by running the thread over a bar of soap before you even thread the needle.

toothbrush

Teeth and toothbrushes don't really have to go together, since toothbrushes have so many other uses. Here are a few of the best.

Put a toothbrush to grate use!

Use an old, hard-bristled toothbrush to clean cheese (or lemon zest or anything else) from the cheese grater. Scrub the grater with the wet toothbrush, then rinse the grater and the toothbrush and you're done. No muss, no fuss, and you haven't destroyed a sponge or cloth in the process.

Spruce up dirty spots on your white blinds with liquid white shoe polish.
KIWI
LEATHER
SHOE
WHITENER

Tame those brows

If your eyebrows go every which way, bring them under control with the tool for your teeth. Spray a new soft toothbrush with a light coating of hair spray, and brush your brows into shape.

Get dirt out of the grout

Use commercial grout cleaner to clean your grout—but with a twist. Apply the cleaner, let it sit for a few minutes, then use an old toothbrush to remove the cleaner and the dirt.

Brush *before* you eat

Clean craggy vegetables with a soft toothbrush before you cook them. Brush mushrooms, asparagus, and peppers before throwing them in a pot. You'll get rid of dirt that won't normally just wash off the vegetables.

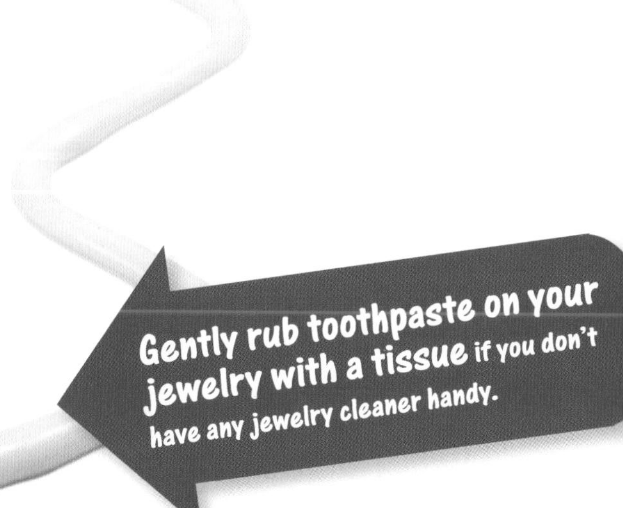
Gently rub toothpaste on your jewelry with a tissue if you don't have any jewelry cleaner handy.

toothpaste

Toothpaste does everything from clean jewelry to fix glass coffee tables. It's so versatile that it's undoubtedly one of the most valuable products in your 99 cent store. Buy a tube and try the tips below for yourself!

Clean your jewelry

If it can make your teeth sparkle...it can make your jewelry sparkle, too! Gently rub toothpaste on your jewelry with a tissue if you don't have any jewelry cleaner handy. Rinse under water and wear.

Brush away water rings on wood surfaces

Put a bit of white non-gel toothpaste on a clean rag, and rub away the water ring—gently, and in the direction of the wood grain. Though it may take some time, the ring will disappear. Let it dry, then apply furniture polish.

Make your glass gleam

If you discover small scratches in your glass coffee table, rub plain, white toothpaste into the glass top with your fingertip or a soft cotton cloth. (The "extra-whitening" kind is recommended.) Be sure to rub in a circle for best results. Let dry, then rub the area gently with a clean lint-free cloth to clean completely.

Soothe minor burns in the kitchen

Grabbed a hot pot handle or touched the edge of a baking sheet fresh from the oven? Keep a tube of white, minty toothpaste nearby to soothe a minor burn. First, run cold water over the burn, then gently pat dry and spread on a layer of toothpaste. The pain will quickly fade.

How to Stock Your MEDICINE CABINET

...THE 99 CENT WAY

Every medicine cabinet we know is filled with similar items: cotton balls, aspirin, Q-tips. But here is a quick roundup of (some surprising) must-haves that will make your bathroom storage work better for you and your family.

1
Baby Oil
It does everything from staving off an earache to making bandage removal painless.

2
Bubble Bath
Hand soap too drying? Decant bubble bath into a container, and keep it on the sink.

3
Chest Rub
Massage into your tired feet for a quick pick-me-up.

4
Cotton Balls
Soak them in bleach and clean out the gunky crevices in your bathroom and kitchen.

5
Cotton Swab
Substitute a swab for an eye shadow applicator.

6
Deodorant
Sweaty palms? Rub some antiperspirant into your hands and never be nervous again.

7
Hair Spray
Mosquito bites giving you an itch? One quick blast of hair spray will kill the sting.

8
Lip Balm
Dry nose? Rub a dab of lip balm on it the way mountain climbers do, and you'll feel better.

9
Mouthwash
Wash your toothbrushes instead, by soaking them for a few minutes every day.

10
Toothbrush
Bushy eyebrows? Spritz a spare toothbrush with hair spray and use it to tame them.

AISLE 3
GARDENING AND OUTDOORS

THE GREAT OUTDOORS HOLDS SO MANY possibilities—gardening, camping, barbecuing, and sports—and a number of responsibilities, too, including taking care of pets and cars. Your local dollar store has supplies for both the possibilities and the responsibilities. You'll find flowerpots for gardening, matches for camping, charcoal briquettes for barbecuing, golf tees for sports, cat litter for pets, and ice scrapers for cars. And best of all, each of the outdoor items listed here can be used for a wide variety of other practical purposes, too. So start digging into this chapter right away for innovative ways to stretch your gardening and outdoor dollars!

bandannas

Bandannas are part of every camper's arsenal. They're used for keeping your hair out of your face (particularly if you haven't had a shower in a few days), as a washcloth, a towel—even an emergency bandage. But bandannas aren't just for camping anymore. See where else they're handy!

Cure a headache

Stop a headache in its tracks with a bandanna. Tie one around your forehead, tightening it until you feel pressure at several points around your head. The bandanna will reduce the flow of blood to your scalp, which in turn will reduce the pain you feel from swollen blood vessels. For extra benefit, soak the bandanna in vinegar. You may not like the smell, but you'll like the added relief.

Wipe your mouth

Stop wasting money on expensive fabric napkins and use dollar store bandannas at casual meals instead. They're affordable and less likely to show stains than their fancy counterparts.

Wrap presents

Turn your wrapping paper into an additional present by using a brightly colored bandanna as the giftwrap. The recipient will love getting two gifts in one!

Turn it into a carryall

Keep a bandanna with you whenever you travel. You never know when you'll need a container—made by tying together the corners of the bandanna—to collect shells on the beach or pinecones in the forest.

Get a good night's sleep

If light at night stops you from sleeping, tie a bandanna around your eyes. You'll block out the bothersome rays until you're ready to see the morning light.

Make a bib

No need to run out to the store to buy a bib when young children visit. Just turn a bandanna into a bib with a clothespin.

buckets

Buckets have a reputation for being outdoor carryalls. They're perfect for collecting weeds, filling with water for cleaning the car, and toting around gardening tools. Give them a chance to do more, however, and they shine. Check out what they can do below.

Clean your room

Before you start the hard work of cleaning a room—dusting, vacuuming, and so on—you need to get rid of the clutter. Clear out the mess by walking around with a bucket, filling it with items you need to move to other rooms or sort through when you're done cleaning.

Soak dirty laundry

Rather than commandeering the sink for soaking dirty clothes, put the clothes, water, and detergent in a small bucket. You can simply remove the bucket when someone else needs to wash their hands, brush their teeth, or otherwise use the sink.

Make a container pot

Container gardening is all the rage, and container pots come in all shapes, sizes, and colors—and often with serious price tags. Skip the garden store and buy a few 5-gallon plastic buckets at the dollar store instead. Poke drainage holes in the bottom of each bucket with a hammer and a large nail. You can even decorate the buckets with enamel paint to give them a little pizzazz.

Keep car clutter to a minimum

Store a bucket in the back seat of your car to act as a catch-all for maps, directions, magazines, loose change, and anything else that finds its way into your car but never seems to leave. Cleaning out the car will be a cinch—just take the bucket out and empty it—and your passengers will always have room for a ride.

Tote your tools

Climbing a ladder? Carrying your hammer and screwdriver up the steps with you is dangerous. Put all the tools in a bucket, then attach a long rope to the bucket. Take the free end of the rope up the ladder with you—and simply haul the bucket and tools to your level when you're ready.

Organize an extension cord

Does the extension cord that you use outside get tangled every time you store it? If so, a plastic bucket can save the day. Drill a hole a little larger than the size of the cord's plug at the bottom of a 5-gallon bucket. Run the plug through the hole—from the inside to the outside—and pull a foot of the cord outside the bucket. Now coil the remainder of the extension cord inside the bucket and store it in its usual spot. All you have to do to use it is pull as much of the extension cord as you need out of the bucket—no tangles! When you're done, coil it back in the bucket.

Stop magazine clutter

Nothing makes a house look messier than hordes of magazines scattered across a prominent coffee table. Get rid of the clutter by storing rolled-up magazines in a bucket. You'll still have access to your favorites, and your house will immediately look cleaner.

Help your Christmas tree stand tall

Store-bought Christmas tree stands can be surprisingly annoying to use—screws that don't turn, water that sloshes out of the base—but the solution can be found in a bucket. Make your own Christmas tree stand by partially filling a bucket with sand or gravel and lowering the tree trunk into it. Now fill the bucket with more sand or gravel, then pour water on it to prevent the needles from dropping. Keep the bucket contents moist as long as the tree stands.

bungee cords

No longer only for thrill-seekers, bungee cords entered the mainstream a while ago. But they never really proved their worth to people who weren't interested in jumping off bridges. Here, though, they show exactly what they can do.

Protect food storage containers

Keeping containers of food that you bought on sale or at a warehouse store on open shelves in your pantry is smart; you saved money and probably extra trips to the grocery store. But all that food will go to waste if the containers topple

Hold appliances, chairs, and tables together with bungee cords while you make necessary repairs.

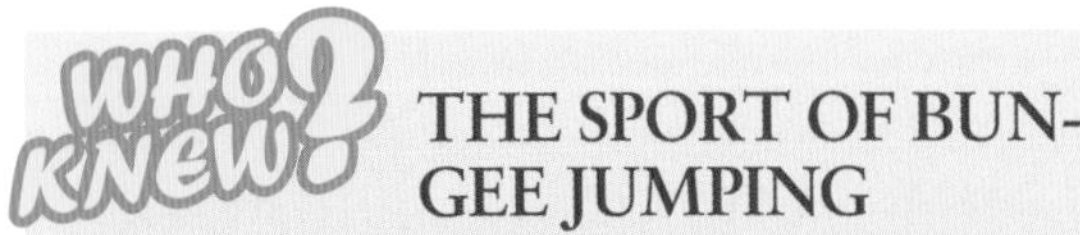

THE SPORT OF BUNGEE JUMPING

Modern bungee jumping as we know it started on April Fool's Day in 1979 when members of the Oxford Dangerous Sports Club jumped from the Clifton Suspension Bridge in Bristol, England. The enthusiasts were arrested—but this did not stop them from making a second jump off the Golden Gate Bridge in San Francisco.

off your pantry shelves and break open. Save yourself a headache by stretching a bungee cord across each shelf to corral the containers.

Use cords as clamps

Hold appliances, chairs, and tables together with bungee cords while you make necessary repairs. Attach several cords to each other to make one large clamp, and wrap a long cord several times around the item you're repairing to make a smaller one.

Keep trash cans covered

Stop raccoons and other hungry animals from opening your trash can and spreading garbage all over your lawn with the help of a bungee cord. Just attach the cord to the can's two handles and stretch it across the top of the can. Your lawn will stay clean.

burlap

A staple of gardeners everywhere, burlap protects new lawns and baby flowers and vegetables. But it's a lot tougher than you might think—it's even strong enough to move heavy objects!

Keep soil in pots

Prevent dirt from escaping from repotted houseplants by covering the drainage hole of each pot with burlap before you fill the pot with soil.

Create necklaces and bracelets

Tease out several threads from the burlap and weave them or braid them into unique pieces of jewelry. Add beads for an even greater special effect.

Store root vegetables

Turn a sheet of burlap into a burlap bag and use the bag to store potatoes and onions. The burlap lets the vegetables breathe.

Move heavy objects

Use a sheet of burlap to transfer heavy items like container plants from place to place in your yard or on your patio. The heavy weave makes it a solid workhorse.

candles

Whether you're repelling mosquitoes with a candle designed to keep your barbecue free of insects or illuminating the dark with a candle on a camping trip, you'll probably want to buy a few of these lights at the dollar store. Here's how to light up your life in even more ways with those dollar store candles.

Wax your windows

Do your double-hung windows have a bumpy ride every time you open or close them? If your windows don't slide up and down with ease, let a candle help them. Clean the insides of the window frame where the sashes travel, then rub the same area with a candle. The windows will have a much smoother journey.

Unstick dresser drawers

If your dresser drawers won't cooperate when you want to open or close them, take them out of the dresser and see if they move on wooden runners. If they do, turn the drawer upside down, and remove any dirt or other obstructions in the wooden tracks that hold the runners. Rub a white candle on the runners and, if possible, on the tracks. Return the drawer to its upright position, and put it back in the dresser. It will move with ease.

Silence sliced onions

Try burning a candle the next time you chop onions. It will burn off some of the fumes emitted from sliced onions and make for a more tear-free chore.

Mask a dusty room

Don't panic if you don't have time to dust before your last-minute guests arrive. Just turn down the lights in the dining room and living room and set out candles on side tables, windowsills, the mantel, a coffee table, and so on. The dim—but atmospheric—lighting will hide any housekeeping faux pas.

Save a stuck zipper

Have dirt and lint gummed up the teeth of your zipper? If so, you need to take two steps to get your zipper working again. First, get rid of the dirt and lint by brushing the teeth with a dry toothbrush. Second, lightly rub the clean teeth with the end of a beeswax candle. Your zipper will return to its usual ups and downs.

Test for drafts

Close the front door, back door, side door, and any other doors to the outside, then place a lit candle near them to see if a draft makes the flame move. If it does, consider installing a door sweep or weather stripping to stop the air from coming inside.

Protect mailing labels from rain

And sleet and snow, for that matter. Rub a white candle over the label you've addressed with a marker. The label will remain legible on its journey through the mail.

Make a home for pins

Don't let lost pins and needles put you on pins and needles! Make a pincushion out of a wide candle. Not only will the wax trap these pointy objects, it will also help them move more easily through fabric.

Squelch squeaks

Does opening and shutting a door hurt your ears? Take the door off its hinges and rub a candle over the hinge and other metal surfaces that touch it. Replace the door and enjoy the quiet.

Decorate Easter eggs

Before you dip your Easter egg in dye, use a candle to draw designs on it. The wax from the candle will repel the dye. You'll end up with a design in white. For a multicolored design, draw on the egg with the candle after each color dye. The candle will save the most recent color from disappearing.

car wax and polish

Who knew there were so many alternate uses for car wax and car polish? Maybe the dollar store did, because they stock a lot of them. You might want to stock up and use them for all these different purposes.

Clean window frames

Get rid of oxidation deposits on the frames of your aluminum windows by cleaning them with one of three things you can usually find in your house: a mild detergent, a light abrasive cleaner, or fine steel wool. Once the window frames are

THE Story Behind...

Armor All

Car wax defends the outside of your car; the inside of your auto found its champion in 1962 when Joe Palcher (a polymer chemist) created a formula to protect rubber, plastic, and vinyl. He sold it as "Tri-don" ("no dirt" spelled backward). Marketing expert Alan Rypinski redubbed the product Armor All Protectant, a name that is now internationally recognized.

clean, polish them with car paste wax. Keep them looking spiffy by reapplying the wax every year.

Spruce up patio furniture

If you have aluminum furniture on your patio (or if some of your patio furniture sports aluminum parts), make it look better by scrubbing it with detergent and water, then drying it with a soft absorbent cloth. Weatherproof it by coating it with car wax.

Keep dust off blinds

Venetian blinds are never a pleasure to clean, so a trick to keep them clean is a trick worth knowing. Here's what to do: Clean the blinds as you normally would, then apply a thin coating of car wax to the blinds. The wax will repel dirt and dust, so your next cleaning will be easier.

Stop a CD from skipping

How? Use car wax. Put some wax on a clean, 100 percent cotton cloth and wipe the CD. When the wax has dried, buff the disc with another clean cotton cloth. Be sure to buff it in straight lines from the center of the disc to the outside edges, not in a circular motion. Rinse the disc in water, let it air-dry, then enjoy your tunes again.

Hide countertop scratches

If you find superficial scratches on your laminate countertop, you can camouflage them with car polish. Follow the directions on the car polish container to apply it, then buff it with a soft cotton cloth.

Polish your refrigerator

Forget about fingerprints and other smudges on your white refrigerator and freezer. Wash and wipe the appliance dry, then apply a coating of car paste wax. Finally, buff it with a clean soft cloth. Your fridge will have a glossier finish and a smudge-free shine.

Wax your snow shovel

Shoveling snow is a big enough headache without snow sticking to your shovel. Stop the sticking by applying two thick coats of car wax to the shovel (but not the handle, obviously) before you start working. And don't forget to lift with your knees, not your back!

Keep tools rust-free

Prevent rust from attacking the tools you store in your garage—particularly if your garage is damp—by coating them with a light application of car wax. Petroleum jelly works, too.

Work away wood scratches

Does your dining room table have a high-gloss lacquer finish? Does it seem to scratch easily? Get rid of those small scratches with car wax. Once you've tested the wax on an inconspicuous section of the table (confirming that it won't hurt the finish), polish the table with a soft cloth dipped in it. Work in a circular motion for best results.

Rub away rust rings

Metal cans—containing vegetables, tomato sauce, shaving cream, or hairspray—are essential items in the kitchen and bathroom, but can leave nasty rings on countertops. Get rid of these rings by rubbing them away with car wax.

See clearly in the morning

Prevent fog from forming on your bathroom mirror when you take a hot shower. Before you step into the shower, rub a little bit of car wax on the mirror. Let it dry, then buff it with a soft cloth. You'll no longer be in a fog in the morning.

Buff out scorch marks

If you've accidentally scorched your laminate countertop—and who would harm it on purpose?—let car wax help you fix it. Assuming the burn is superficial, put some car wax on a clean cloth and buff the counter until the mark is gone. Don't use abrasive cleanser because it may remove the finish as well as the mark.

cat litter

Cat litter can be used for so much more than cats. And in so many different ways! Make your home smell better, your garage cleaner, and your car ride safer, all with a little kitty litter.

Save a cell phone

If you've ever dropped a cell phone in water, you know your heart sinks, too. But don't stand there. Whip the phone out, remove the battery and pat both dry. Wrap in a dish towel and push this lumpy package down into a clean new bag of litter. In three days, take it out and plug it in. You should be good to go.

Make your garage floor sparkle

Let kitty litter help you clean your garage. If you find a puddle of oil on your concrete garage floor, pour paint thinner over it, and then cover the area with kitty litter. (Make sure that the garage is

TIDY CAT KITTY LITTER

Prior to 1947, cat boxes were filled with ashes or sand. Then Edward Lowe of St. Paul, Minnesota, was asked by his neighbor: What would work better? He suggested Fuller's Earth, an absorbent clay he sold to machine shops. The neighbor loved the clay—no more ashy paw prints. Lowe packaged his "kitty litter," and by 1964, he had created the Tidy Cat brand.

well ventilated by keeping the garage door open, and don't let anyone smoke or strike matches anywhere near the affected area—and keep the cats away.) The kitty litter will absorb the oil. Just sweep up the mess and you're done.

Refresh your books

If, when cleaning your bookshelves, you find a book that has a musty smell, put it in a paper bag with some clean kitty litter and leave it in the bag for about a week. When you take it out, brush off any litter—and the musty smell.

Dry long-stemmed flowers

Most dried flower arrangements look better when they include long-stemmed flowers, as well as shorter versions. Here's a handy way to dry statice, snapdragons, and more: Fill a long airtight container about halfway with cat litter. Place the flowers on top of the litter, leaving some space between them. Put the lid on the container and put it away for a week to 10 days. Open the container and find the flowers dried and ready to arrange.

Scare off unwelcome rodents

This is a great use for *used* cat litter, something that rarely gets recycled! Pour it down the holes of burrowing rodents such as groundhogs or moles. The scent of predatory urine frightens them away!

Take the stink out of the garbage can

Pour about a cup of cat litter into the bottom of your garbage can before you toss in bags of garbage. Replace it every week or when it is damp. Your cans will stop smelling like trash.

Use as an air freshener

Does your closet smell musty? Or your entire basement? Get rid of that unpleasant odor by filling shallow boxes or aluminum pans with kitty litter and placing them in the closet or around the room. The air will smell fresher!

Dispose of paint

Chances are your garbage collectors no longer pick up cans of paint. If you need to get rid of latex or water-based paint, do it with kitty litter. Simply fill a paper bag with cat litter and pour the paint into the bag. Let the kitty litter absorb the paint, then toss the bag out with the trash. (Don't use this method to dispose of oil-based paint.)

WAY BACK WHEN...

Kingsford Charcoal

Henry Ford had an impact on grills other than those found on cars. Production of his Model T created a steady stream of wood scrap. In the 1920s, Ford built a factory to compress this by-product with a binder to form charcoal briquettes. Ford contacted real estate agent Edward G. Kingsford, the husband of Ford's cousin and a Ford dealer, to choose the site for the plant. The charcoal company was eventually named in Kingsford's honor, and Kingsford Charcoal still makes briquettes today.

charcoal briquettes

What can you do with charcoal briquettes other than start up your grill? Even Santa preferred coal over them! But Santa apparently never saw the multitude of alternate uses for this barbecue staple. Here's what he missed.

Get rid of refrigerator odors

You already know that baking soda will prevent bad smells in your fridge, and even absorb some odors already there. But what to do if you have strong, sour smells? Simple. Place a few charcoal briquettes on a dish—don't cover it up—and put the dish in the fridge for a few days. The odor will disappear.

Keep silver tarnish at bay

Since polishing silver is probably not your favorite way to pass the time, consider a novel way to delay the inevitable tarnish. Put a few charcoal briquettes—which absorb moisture—into your silver drawer or cabinet. You can go the extra distance by putting a briquette inside a silver teapot to prevent a build-up of moisture.

Lock rust out of your toolbox

Place a few charcoal briquettes in your toolbox to keep rust away from your tools. Chalk and silica gel packs (those small white packages that inevitably accompany a new pair of shoes) work well, too.

Stop bathroom smells

Place a few charcoal briquettes in clever spots in your bathroom—in a decorative vase, behind the toilet, or hidden in a corner—to stop moisture and odors. Don't forget where you put them, and replace them every few months. Your bathroom will smell fresher.

Protect your books

If you keep your books in a bookcase with glass doors, they may be more susceptible to mold and must because the doors keep moisture in. Get rid of the moisture—and the musty smell and the mold—by placing a piece of charcoal inside the bookcase. The books will stay dry and your problem is solved.

dustpan

Take the brush away from the dustpan and you're left with...just a dustpan, right? Wrong! You're left with a snow shovel and a craft tool and a toy picker-upper.

Shovel a little snow

Let young children shovel snow alongside you—they'll learn how to do it and may really help you when they're older—with a mini shovel. Give them a dustpan and show them just how much fun shoveling can be.

Clean up crafts

Pom-poms, sequins, and beads are all-important ingredients in many craft projects, but they can also be a headache to put away when the project is done. Use a clean dustpan to scoop up these little pieces and pour them into their containers. You'll save time and a trip to the medicine cabinet for aspirin.

Clean up small toys in one
fell swoop using a dustpan.

Pick up tiny toys

Little army men, doll accessories, and games like jacks can be annoying and potentially dangerous underfoot. Clean them up in one fell swoop using a dustpan. Drop the toys in the toy chest and admire the clean room.

flowerpot

You may think a flowerpot is a pot in which to plant flowers. That's true. But it's also true that flowerpots can be incredibly versatile tools in the garden *and* in the house—and in ways you might not have considered. Consider these!

Trap slugs

At night, put a piece of orange or grapefruit rind inside a flowerpot, then place the pot on its side in your garden. The slugs will enter the pot overnight, and you can get rid of them in the morning.

Plant a pot in a pot

Save yourself the expense of filling a large container pot with potting soil if you're planting shallow-rooted plants. Instead, turn a smaller flowerpot upside down at the bottom of the container pot—it will take up the space usually reserved for the soil.

Protect basil from the sun

Whether you're planting basil seeds or transplanting seedlings into your garden, you need to protect these babies from the strong sun. Water the seedlings well, then cover them with an upside-down flowerpot. Remove the pot after a few days—when the plants can handle the sun—and watch the basil grow.

Attract toads to your garden

Insects eat garden plants, and toads eat insects—so you'll want to make your garden into a happy home for toads. Give them water by placing a pan filled with rocks and water in the soil, and place a flowerpot—with a broken edge, so the toads can and come and go—upside down in the shade for shelter.

Kill off ants

If you find an entire colony of ants in or near your garden, you'll want to get rid of it. How? Cover the anthill with an upside down flowerpot. Pour boiling water through the hole in the bottom of the pot. You'll get rid of all the ants at once.

flowerpot saucers

Count on plastic flowerpot saucers to catch more than water from an over-watered plant. They can catch ketchup and cocktails and even hamburger meat. Give the saucers a chance to astonish you.

Stop sticky shelves

Keep refrigerator shelves clean by placing plastic flowerpot saucers under salad dressings, condiments, and other containers that can become sticky. Even if the container is a mess, your shelves will stay pristine.

Create coasters

Who ever has enough coasters for a party? Protect your wooden tabletops the next time you have many guests by using plastic flowerpot saucers as coasters. You'll keep your tables safe and have a conversation piece at the same time.

Freeze individual portions

Plan ahead for your next barbecue by creating your burgers now. Place each one in a small, shallow plastic flowerpot saucer, then stack the saucers on top of each other. Put the stack in a freezer bag and stick it in the freezer. You'll be able to separate the burgers easily when you're ready to grill.

Frisbee

The Frisbee is the ultimate toy—and an ultimate sport (called Ultimate Frisbee)—even if it started its life as a pie plate. So what can you do with it other than toss it or use it for pies? The ultimate answers are here.

Feed Fido on the road

Whether you're traveling with your pet or simply on an outing to the park, use a Frisbee as a dog food dish or a water dish for your pet. It's easy to carry and easy to clean.

Keep paper plates steady

Take several Frisbees on your next camping trip and use them as paper plate holders. Better yet, take an assortment of colors and assign each camper a color for the trip. No more soggy, floppy plates.

Create a paint palette

A Frisbee is the perfect paint palette. Flipped upside down, it has room for individual dabs of paint and room for mixing different colors together. The lip around the edge even keeps the paints in the palette, rather than dripping on your canvas.

Make a soap dish

Don't let your soap slide around your campsite. Give it a proper home by keeping it in an

The Frisbee

The Frisbie Pie Company of Bridgeport, Connecticut, sold pies. Local college students used the empty tins (embossed with the words "Frisbie's Pies") to play catch. In 1948, Walter Morrison and Warren Franscioni found a way to capitalize on this free toy by creating a plastic version called the Flyin' Saucer and later renamed the Pluto Platter Flying Saucer. (This was after the alleged UFO sightings in Roswell, New Mexico.) When the founders of Wham-O bought rights to the toy and renamed it Frisbee, sales truly went out of this world.

8 More Ways to Use FLOWERPOTS

1 Candy Garden

A plastic or terra-cotta pot can be made into a unique gift. Place a square of florist's foam into the bottom of the pot and stick lollipops (or any favorite candy on a stick) into the foam. Cover this base with green shredded paper. Your gift will look like a garden, and after the treat is gone the pot can be put to use!

2 Wind Chimes

Gather several terra-cotta pots in descending sizes. Thread a piece of nylon rope through the drain holes, starting with the largest pot on top; the progressively smaller pots should hang below. All the flowerpots must hang upside down. At the end of the rope, tie some beads to serve as the chime. This is a lovely way to add some "music" to your garden.

3 Fowl Fun

Two clay pots and a saucer can make a bath that will please backyard birds. Use pots that are around 18 or 20 inches in size, and a similar sized saucer. Glue the bottoms of the pots together, then glue the saucer to the top (smaller) pot to hold the water. It is best to coat the saucer in polyurethane before attaching it to the pots.

4 Hit the Beach

Plastic pots come in many sizes and work great as molds to build castles in the sand—either at the beach or in a sandbox.

5 Basket-less Gift

Make a flowerpot an integral part of a gift's presentation. Fill a terra-cotta pot with gloves, bulbs, seed packets—everything you know your favorite gardener will love.

6 Outside Ashtray

A way to ensure that cigarette butts end up in the proper place is to make ashtrays for your garden parties. You can do this on the cheap by taking terra-cotta pots, covering their drainage holes with duct tape, and filling the pots with sand.

7 Interior Decoration

Who says inexpensive terra-cotta pots can only be used outdoors? Paint them in shades to match your home décor using acrylic paints. Try special finishes like silver or copper. When your paint is dry, use a clear polyurethane sealer, inside and out. You can use your one-of-a-kind pot for plants or dried flowers.

8 Organize Kitchen Tools

Tired of fishing for your whisk in a drawer crowded with tongs, serving spoons, turkey basters, and slotted spoons? Get organized by keeping your kitchen tools in flowerpots.

upside-down Frisbee. You can use the Frisbee to hold your other personal cleaning supplies, too—shampoo, washcloth, and so on—if you need to transport them from your tent to the shower.

gardening gloves

What do babies, knickknacks, and chandeliers have in common? Gardening gloves! See what other kooky uses they have here.

Stop the swelling

Do you have stiff, swollen hands when you wake up in the morning because of arthritis? If so, try wearing form-fitting garden gloves to bed at night. They'll help reduce the swelling.

Dust your tiny treasures

Find a pair of soft fabric gloves and put them on the next time you dust your knickknacks. Clean your treasures with your fingers. You'll have more control over the cleaning—meaning you'll be less likely to knock over a knickknack and damage it.

Wear two pairs of gloves

If you suffer from eczema, you may have noticed that your condition gets worse—or at least doesn't get any better—when you wash dishes. Protect your hands by wearing rubber gloves over a pair of thin gardening gloves (but don't choose latex gloves because the latex may make your eczema worse).

Protect your nails

Do you have dry, brittle fingernails? If so, you can strengthen them by rubbing petroleum jelly or a thick hand cream into your nails at bedtime, then covering your hands with a pair of thin cotton garden gloves before you turn in for the night. The petroleum jelly or hand cream moisturizes the areas around and under your nails, and the gloves retain the moisture. Repeat as needed.

Wash slatted blinds

Overcome your dislike of cleaning blinds with a combination of a garden glove and fabric softener. Fill a small bowl with fabric softener, and put the glove on your power hand. Dip your gloved fingers into the fabric softener, then rub your first two fingers over the top, then bottom, of each slat. The fabric softener will not only clean the blinds but will also help keep dust at bay.

Get a grip on a baby

Babies and baths make a notoriously slippery combination. Keep your infant safe—and your grip firm—by wearing cotton gardening gloves when you give your baby a bath.

Clean houseplants

Put on old cloth garden gloves and run your fingers over the tops and bottoms of each leaf simultaneously. You'll have dusted the entire plant in no time!

Fool your fingers

Whether you scratch at night because of eczema or out of habit, you can trick yourself by covering your hands with garden gloves. You'll stop scratching in your sleep.

Give a chandelier new life

Soak a pair of cloth gardening gloves in window cleaner, put them on and wipe away any mess you find. Your chandelier will sparkle again.

golf balls

Fore! Well, actually here are three alternate uses for golf balls. If you've given up the game and have golf balls lying around the house or just bought some at the dollar store on a whim, you can put them to good use with these suggestions.

Place golf balls at the bottom of a pot or container before adding the soil and the plants to help the water drain.

Enjoy a warm bath

Don't let a missing tub plug stop you from luxuriating in a warm bath. Use a golf ball in place of the plug. It will keep the water in the tub—and you in heaven.

Drain potted plants properly

Place golf balls at the bottom of a pot or container before adding the soil and the plants. The golf balls will help the water drain—and the flowers grow.

Give yourself a hand massage

Place a golf ball in one palm, then place your other palm over it and interlock your fingers loosely. Now roll the golf ball around your hands, pressing your palms together at the same time. The tension in your hands will ease. Roll your bare feet over a golf ball for a few minutes for a soothing foot massage, too.

golf tees

Both golfers and non-golfers will want to buy golf tees to use in these creative ways—off the course, of course.

T marks the spot

A golf tee, that is. If flowers that normally bloom in the spring don't show up, mark the bald spots with golf tees. In the fall, plant new bulbs beneath the tees. You'll have a full complement of flowers next spring.

Fill an empty hole

If you're replacing a screw in a hole that's gotten too big for it, let a golf tee help you. Simply dip the tip of the tee into yellow carpenter's glue, then insert the tee into the too-big hole. If some of the tee juts out of the hole, trim it with a utility knife. Let the glue dry. Now drill a new hole for the screw and screw it in.

WAY BACK WHEN...

Golf Balls

Small, round, white, dimpled—these are images that may come to mind when one thinks of golf balls. However, the first golf balls, dating to the 1500s, were made of wood. By the 1600s, golf balls were made of goose feathers tightly packed into a small pocket of animal hide that would dry into a ball shape. If you wanted one, you asked for a "feathery." Imagine the misery if modern golfers were faced with such a thing today!

Organize your ties

Here's a handy idea for someone who can't find a tie in the morning or for someone who loves golf (and ties): make a tie rack out of golf tees! Grab a piece of pine board. Sand it, paint it, and drill 1/8-inch holes every 2 inches. Find a corresponding number of golf tees, and dip their tips into yellow carpenter's glue. Insert each tee in a hole, securing it with a hammer. Let the glue dry. Hang the tie rack on the inside of a closet door or on the closet wall, and watch your favorite golfer smile.

holiday lights

From protecting a plant to making your stairs safer, holiday lights have many uses far beyond the Christmas season. So turn your ho, ho, hos into oh, oh, ohs with these merry ideas for holiday lights.

Protect your plant from frost

Don't let an early frost damage a large plant you may have in a container outdoors. Save it with Christmas lights! Weave the lights around the plant, then cover it with a sheet. Turn on the lights. Your plant will not only look festive, it will also stay warm.

Light stairs for safety

String white holiday lights on the banister going up the stairs. Along with looking pretty, the lights serve as a night-light for the steps.

Outline walkways

Use bright white holiday lights to illuminate the border of a walkway at night. Guests will appreciate being able to find their way to their cars easily when they leave your party.

Make your own Christmas tree

Don't have room for a Christmas tree in your house or apartment? Make a two-dimensional one out of holiday lights! Outline the shape of a Christmas tree on a wall with a pencil, then place nails at each angle in the tree. String the lights around the nails, and a festive Christmas tree is born.

ice scraper

Bring your windshield scraper in out of the ice and snow and cold. Reward it for a job well done outside, and let it show you all the good it can do inside!

Level your floors

If you're filling small indentations in your wood floors with wood filler but worry that your floors will end up uneven, rest assured that no worry is necessary—if you have an ice scraper. Just pack wood filler into each gouge, then use an ice scraper to smooth out the work. Your floor will look as good as new!

Clean a gas stovetop

Food baked onto the top of a gas range can be a challenge to remove. Make your job easier by using a car's ice scraper. First and most importantly, turn off the pilot lights and burners. Next, spray the baked-on mess with WD-40, and give it a few minutes to work its magic. Then scrape the food off easily with a plastic ice scraper. To finish the job, wash the stovetop with hot soapy water and wipe it dry.

Replace a spatula

Have you ever had a spatula break in the middle of preparing a dish in a nonstick pan? Replace it pronto with a plastic ice scraper and calmly finish cooking.

Scrape off paint splatters

Don't fret if you've splattered paint on your acrylic bathtub while you painted your bathroom. Remove it easily and quickly—and without scratching the surface of the tub—with an ice scraper.

Wipe away baking messes

Whether you're making cookies or baking bread, you'll probably end up with some dough stuck to your work surface—no matter how much flour you've used to keep it from sticking. Use an ice scraper to clean off any gummy residue.

Remove ice inside

An ice scraper can work as well on a freezer as it can on a car window. If you don't feel like defrosting your freezer but want to get rid of some of the ice and frost, gently chip away at it with an ice scraper until you're happy with the space you've created.

kneeling pad

Kneeling pads were designed to make gardening a little more comfortable for people who spend a lot of time planting and weeding. But maybe kneeling pad designers had more ideas like this in mind.

Bring your plants to their knees

Protect your floor and tables from scratches caused by flowerpots by putting the pots on top of garden kneeling pads. The pads will keep your floors and furniture looking spiffy.

Kneel comfortably at bath time

Bathing a child in a tub can mean bubbles and giggles, but it can also mean sore knees. Give your knees a break by using a garden kneeling pad the next time you enter your child's soapy world.

Protect your wood floors

Cut a garden kneeling pad into small pieces and superglue each piece to the bottom leg of a chair or table. These tiny pads will keep your wood and other hard-surface floors free from scratches caused by tables and chairs.

Use a garden kneeling pad the next time you give your child a bath.

A SAFER SEASON

THE HISTORY OF HOLIDAY LIGHTS

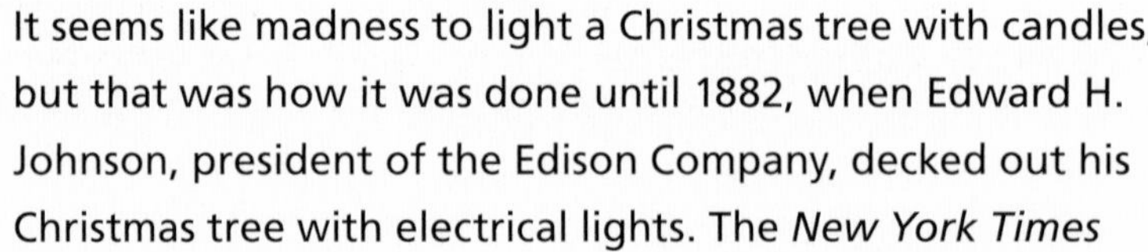

It seems like madness to light a Christmas tree with candles, but that was how it was done until 1882, when Edward H. Johnson, president of the Edison Company, decked out his Christmas tree with electrical lights. The *New York Times* wrote a story about the tree that described the marvel: "[It] dazzled persons entering the room. **There were 120 lights on the tree, with globes of different colors...."** Yet despite the improvement in safety, the "wow" factor, and, surely, bragging rights, electric holiday lights still cost too much for most Americans. The dangerous use of candles continued, and households that used them were wise to keep a bucket of sand or water near their trees.

General Electric began mass-producing electric tree lights in 1903. This reduced expense, and though they were still out of reach for most private homes, department stores in cities that had electricity could buy or rent them. The lights were sold with eight colored glass bulbs connected in series on wired porcelain sockets. **Strings were available with 8, 16, 24, and 32 lights. A strand of bulbs was called a "festoon."** Flyers for the product depicted happy children decorating a tree next to the words "simple, clean, safe." GE did not obtain a patent on this product, and this opened the door to competitors.

One of them was a teenager named Albert Sadacca, whose family was in the novelty business. Around 1917, he suggested manufacturing affordable holiday lights. Electricity was charging into more and more households, and sales grew steadily. **By the 1930s, electric Christmas lights had become a standard part of holiday decorating.** Sadacca and his brothers made their fortunes off of strings of light, and they organized the National Outfit Manufacturers Association (NOMA), a trade association that became NOMA Electric Company. Its members cornered the Christmas light market until the 1960s.

Today, holiday lights come in all shapes and sizes, and some blink and make noise. They are so affordable that **some homes are decorated to the extent that they may be visible from outer space** on dark December nights.

leaf bags

Paper leaf bags are more than grocery bags on steroids. They're gentle with your sweaters and protective of your car's windshield. They're versatile and useful, and you should always have some on hand. Here's why.

Make a temporary cover

Don't stop ironing just because the ironing board cover is useless. Make a new one by opening up a leaf bag or two, dampening the bags, and laying them over your ironing board. The bags will work as a temporary cover until you have time to buy a new one.

Protect your steering wheel

Actually, protect your hands from the steering wheel on a hot summer day. Cut a leaf bag in half, and place the bottom half—the half that still looks like a bag—over your steering wheel when you park the car. It will keep the steering wheel from overheating and hurting your hands.

Wrap a large present

Don't waste money on rolls and rolls of wrapping paper just because you need to wrap a large gift. Cut a leaf bag along one of the seams so that it opens out into a flat sheet of paper, and make sure that any printing faces you. Put your present on top of the bag and wrap it as you would wrap any gift. Decorate the brown paper with markers or tie it with a particularly colorful ribbon.

Stop snow on your windshield

Keep snow and ice off your windshield with leaf bags. If snow is forecast, get in your car and turn on the wipers. Turn the car off when the wipers are practically vertical. Place leaf bags that you've split open under the wipers and wait for the snow. Once the snow has stopped, simply remove the leaf bags—and the snow. (Be sure to remove the bags and the snow before you turn the car back on to avoid damaging the wipers.)

Reshape sweaters

Before you wash your favorite wool sweater, trace its shape onto a leaf bag—cut the bag along one seam and open it up if you need more room. After washing the sweater, place it on the outline to stretch it back into its original shape.

Keep spray paint in the bag

If you need to spray paint a small to medium-sized item but don't want to make a mess, reach for a leaf bag. Place the item in the bag, spray it as needed, let it dry, take it, out and toss the bag. You mess will be contained!

lighter fluid

Dollar stores sell lighter fluid with their barbecue supplies, but it can be used all around the house. Keep a bottle on hand, even if you never grill. (However, be sure to use it in a well-ventilated area. Don't use it near an open flame, and don't smoke around it because it is highly flammable. And of course, do not inhale or ingest it.)

Wipe away heel marks

Black heels marks on light-colored floors—or any colored floor, really—are a jarring sight. Get rid of them easily by rubbing them with a paper towel dipped in lighter fluid. The marks will quickly disappear.

Get rid of rust

Have rust spots sprouted on your stainless steel sink? If so, use lighter fluid to make them disappear. Rub the rust spots with a drop of lighter fluid, then wash it off with a combination of nonabrasive scouring powder and water.

Correct cooking-oil stains

Cooking oil belongs in the pan, not on your clothes—but accidents happen. If you discover a cooking-oil stain that didn't come out of a garment the first time you washed it, pour a capful of lighter fluid directly onto the stain before tossing it in the wash again. Kiss that stain good-bye!

Let labels go

Sometimes labels don't want to part from their friends—books, drinking glasses, or anything else that's individually marked in a store. And the thrill of buying a nice new item is significantly lessened if you can't get rid of the gummy adhesive that remains after you take off the price tag. Get the thrill back by removing the adhesive with a little bit of lighter fluid.

matches

Matches and matchbooks or boxes are an essential ingredient in barbecuing and camping. But your plants and your car and your knives can use them, too. Here's how.

Fix your lipstick

Throwing away a broken lipstick is like throwing away money. Fix it instead by using a match to warm the bottom of the broken piece (don't melt it completely) and the top of the piece that stayed in the tube. Put the two pieces together and slightly melt the edges of the break together with a new match. Put the lipstick in the refrigerator until it has completely cooled, then return it to your purse.

Unfreeze a lock

Does your car door or your front door freeze closed in the winter? Thaw out the lock by holding your key over a lit match, then putting the key in the lock. The lock should open.

Repair a hole

If you have a nail that won't fit back into its hole because the hole has gotten too big, get some matches to help. Break the tips off several matches and properly dispose of them. Stuff the remaining matchsticks one by one into the hole, until you can't fit in any more. Now hammer the nail back into its hole. It should stay snugly in place.

Smooth rough nails

Whether you break a nail barbecuing or realize while grilling that your nail is snagged, use a box or book of matches to smooth out the problem. Instead of striking a match against the emery-board-like strip, rub your nail on it.

Make your azaleas happy by adding sulfur from matches to the soil (to lower the pH).

LET THERE BE LIGHT

A MATCH AND A COLEMAN LANTERN

Do you remember your first camping trip? Maybe you also remember the Coleman lantern your family used when the moon or the stars weren't providing enough light. **Coleman has been lighting the night for people since the early 1900s.** The lamp that made them famous was introduced in 1914.

It was called the Arc Lantern, and it was specifically designed to be used outdoors. This lantern changed life in rural America. **Farmers were able to stay outdoors later into the evening.** Of course, they were working, not camping. This would have pleased the company founder.

William Coffin Coleman was a diligent worker. **In 1900, he needed a job to pay for his last year of law school.** He saw a gasoline-fueled lamp in a drugstore window in Alabama that gave off a fantastic amount of clean, white light. Sensing a profitable product, he bought up an inventory of the lamps, certain he could sell them to merchants in Oklahoma, where he was attending school. Shop owners declined, but the young man did not despair. **He ingeniously sold a lighting service instead of the lamps themselves.** It was a success; no one likes to be in the dark.

Coleman began manufacturing his own lamps in 1903. In 1916, he introduced the Quick-Lite Lantern. It was the first lantern you were able to light with a match.

As the country changed and we all gained more leisure time, outdoor activities became more adventure than chore. If you do remember your first camping trip, do you remember what you ate? **Coleman celebrated its 100th anniversary in 2001 by creating the world's largest s'more.** It weighed 1,200 pounds. It might not be exactly what you recall munching on, but doesn't thinking about it bring back the smell of a fire, the sound of crickets, and the memory of a Coleman lantern bathing you with a welcoming light?

Use a small rubber spatula to fill an indentation or hole in a plaster wall.

Feed acid-loving plants

Make your hydrangeas, azaleas, impatiens, and gardenias happy by adding sulfur to the soil (to lower the pH). Place matches torn from matchbooks into the holes before you plant these acid-lovers. They'll pay you back with vivid colors and bright whites later.

Sharpen knives

Bring a dull utility or craft knife back to life by rubbing its blade repeatedly on the strip of a matchbook that normally serves to light matches. Don't forget to sharpen both sides of the blade.

seeds

Vegetable and flower seeds may not have much of a life beyond the garden—unless you plan to use them in crafts—but the colorful seed packets can live on in unusual and exciting ways. Here are some to consider.

Make labels for your garden

Don't discard the seed packets you've bought for your vegetable garden once you've planted the seeds. In fact, plan to keep them for labels before you even put the seeds in the ground. Open the packet from the bottom—this way the packet will stand right side up in the garden—then plant the seeds as you usually would. Cover the packets with small, clear plastic bags, and attach them to Popsicle sticks or twigs that you stick in the soil. You'll always know what you've planted where!

File garden information

Use seed packets as mini files that contain everything you need to know about what you planted when and where. Keep a file—a seed packet—for each kind of plant, and you'll never be at a loss for detailed garden information again.

Create homemade greeting cards

The photos of flowers and vegetables on seed packets can be stunning. Cut off the front of a seed packet and glue it onto good-quality card stock (or even construction paper) to make a unique, old-fashioned-looking card.

spatula

Take the spatula away from the grill and it takes on a whole new life as a tool that protects and removes and repairs. Who knew such a simple tool had such a complex alter ego?

Remove old finish

Look no further than a spatula the next time you need help stripping finish off a piece of furniture. Hold the spatula by the blade—but upside down—and push it firmly and repeatedly in a straight motion. You'll be finished with the finish before you know it.

Pull nails out gently

If you're planning to pull a nail out of wood but worry that the hammerhead will hurt the grain, protect the wood before using the hammer. How? Slip a plastic spatula under the head of the hammer before you start the job.

Repair plaster

Use a small rubber spatula to fill an indentation or hole in a plaster wall. You'll find it more flexible than a putty knife—and, as a result, easier to use.

Scoop up unmentionables

Sometimes, it happens—especially if you have a young puppy or kitten running around your house. Buy one spatula and put it aside as your go-to tool if your pooch or kitty has an accident. Much easier than paper towels, and you only have to buy it once.

squeeze bottles

Plastic squeeze bottles are sold as containers for ketchup and mustard—perfect for an outdoor barbecue. But they're perfect in other jobs, too. Give them a chance to strut their stuff, and maybe they'll give you a friendly squeeze in return.

Pretreat your laundry

Pour your liquid laundry detergent into a plastic ketchup or mustard squeeze bottle. It will make pretreating spots easier—you'll control the amount of detergent you use, plus you'll be able to hit the stain on the spot.

Ration real maple syrup

Does it make your frugal heart constrict when your kids take that pricey bottle of Vermont maple syrup and upend half over a plate of French toast? Transfer that free-running syrup to a squeeze bottle to slow down their consumption. The portion you save may be your own!

Fill your iron

The hole you're supposed to use in your steam iron can seem impossibly small when you're using a measuring cup or drinking glass to pour in the water. Make your life easier by loading up a clean mustard or ketchup squeeze bottle with water and using it to fill your steam iron.

Decorate a cake

Fill a clean plastic mustard or ketchup squeeze bottle with icing, and use it to decorate your cake. You'll find that creating flowers, flags, balloons, and piping is much easier, and your words made of icing will be much clearer.

Fill a clean plastic mustard or ketchup squeeze bottle with icing, and use it to decorate your cake.

Keep vinegar in the shower

Vinegar enthusiasts swear by apple cider vinegar instead of soap and shampoo for washing sensitive skin and rinsing chemical buildup from hair. Put a bottle of undiluted apple cider vinegar in the shower and see if it works for you, too.

Adorn soups and desserts

Use a squeeze bottle the next time you cook to make your dishes extra fancy. Fill one with pesto or sour cream, and create squiggles on top of soups. Fill another with chocolate, and decorate the dessert you've just made or the plate you plan to present it on for a special effect.

Make a masterpiece in the snow

If you're not a big fan of snowball fights, try redirecting your children toward a different kind of snow play. Arm them with several squeeze bottles filled with water and a few drops of food coloring. They'll get a kick out of squirting colorful designs into the snow.

Think outside the squeeze bottle

Squeeze bottles can be used for so much more than ketchup and mustard. Fill some with honey, mayonnaise, and salad dressing. You'll save space—and sticky messes—in your refrigerator, and your dishwasher won't have to work so hard (no knives!).

Water your kids in the summer

Give your children a few squeeze bottles filled with water on a hot summer day and send them outside to play. They'll have a blast squirting each other, and they'll keep cool, too.

Make perfect pancakes

A squeeze bottle filled with pancake batter is the perfect tool for squeezing out silver dollar-size pancakes onto a griddle. If the nozzle is too small to let the batter flow, use scissors to snip off a bit. For camping, add a bottle half filled with dry pancake mix to the food pack. At breakfast time, add water, shake, and squeeze into the pan.

string

String is so versatile that it can be hard to remember why you bought it in the first place. Maybe you bought it to tie something together—or maybe you were so smart that you knew it had a bunch of different uses. Here are a few of the best.

Bundle kindling

Got string and pieces of twig and dried grasses? Then you've got the makings of little kindling bundles that will help get a cheerful fire started in no time. Toss one in the fireplace, prop a few small logs over it, and set it alight. You can make a basket of these to keep next to the fireplace, or give a basket to a friend as a welcome winter gift.

Trim a long hedge

Create a guide for trimming a hedge to the desired height by using two stakes and a piece of string. Drive one stake into the ground at each end of the hedge, then run the string between the two at the height you want for your hedge. Tie the string onto each stake at the corresponding height. Now trim your hedge down to the string. The top of the hedge will be level from end to end.

Truss a chicken

You don't need butcher's twine or fancy linen string to truss a turkey or chicken before roasting. A length of clean cotton string off a fresh roll will do the job perfectly. For the most straightforward truss, wrap the string around the drumsticks, which will hold any stuffing in place and help the bird keep its shape during roasting.

tennis balls

Tennis balls help you park and sand and even get a good night's sleep. Forget about bouncing them around on a tennis court—they're much too valuable elsewhere!

Relieve sore feet

Take a load off your aching feet and give them a treat. Put a tennis ball on the floor. Remove your shoes, and place your foot on top of the tennis ball. Now roll the ball around with your foot. You'll end up with a feel-good—and good for you—massage.

Massage your back, too

Drop a few tennis balls into a long tube sock and tie the end shut. Now pretend the tube sock is a towel, and move it across your back the way you would if you were drying off after a shower. Forget about getting dry—you'll get a relaxing back massage instead!

Make a mini toolbox

Cut a slit in a tennis ball, and squeeze it to widen the slit. Toss in some nails, then stop squeezing the ball to close your toolbox. Carry it with you around the house or in the yard and squeeze it open any time you need a nail.

Fluff up feathers

Throw one or two tennis balls into the dryer the next time you dry down-filled items like pillows, comforters, and jackets. They'll ditch the flat look they get from the washing machine and puff up again with pride.

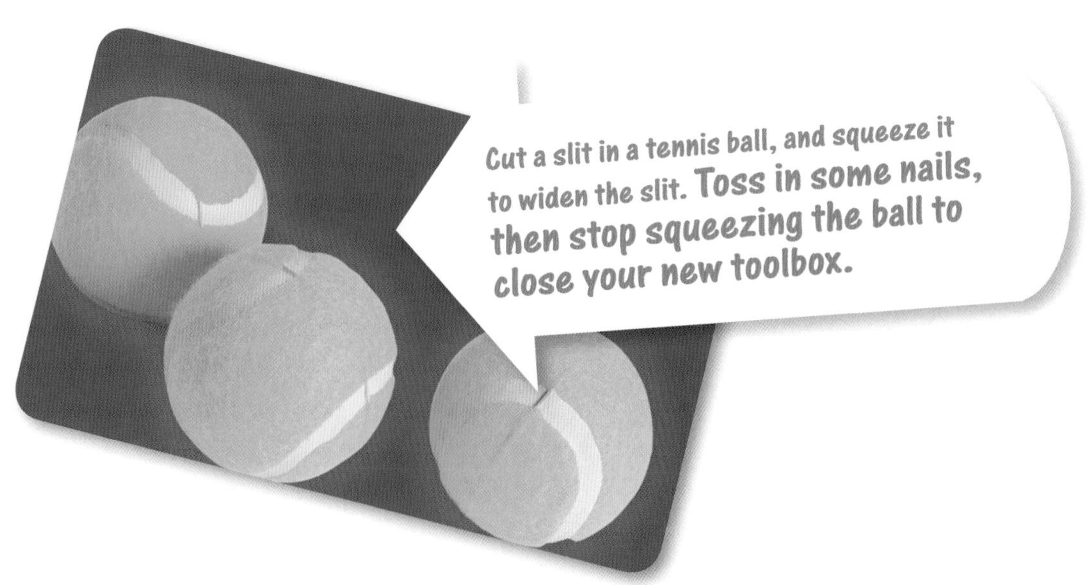
Cut a slit in a tennis ball, and squeeze it
to widen the slit. Toss in some nails,
then stop squeezing the ball to
close your new toolbox.

Save your socks

Don't toss your sock just because it has a small hole in the toe or the heel. Place a tennis ball in the toe or heel—wherever it needs to be mended. The tennis ball will stretch out the surface of the sock so that sewing it will be easier.

Keep your bike level

Help your bicycle's kickstand do its job—keeping your bike standing—and prevent it from sinking into the grass or mud by using a tennis ball. How? Cut a slit in the ball and slip it over the end of the kickstand. If you ever find yourself at the beach with your bike, this trick will stop the kickstand from sinking into the sand, too.

Open bottles with ease

Twist-off bottle caps never seem to twist off the way they should. Let a tennis ball help them do their job. Cut a ball in half, then cover the bottle cap with one half and twist it off without a problem.

Soften the hammer's blow

Whether you need to gently nudge some woodwork back into place or tap a nail into soft wood, place a tennis ball with a slit in the middle over your hammer. The tennis ball will treat your job gently.

Park perfectly

Parking your car in the garage is an art: You have to pull only so far forward—but far enough!—and only so close to each wall—but not too close! Take the guesswork out of the equation by hanging a tennis ball on a string from the ceiling or rafters of the garage so that it hits the center of your windshield when you park correctly. You'll never have to guess again exactly where the car goes.

Sand curvy furniture

Voluptuous furniture is pretty, but refinishing it can be an ugly job. Make it easier by covering a tennis ball in sandpaper and using the ball to sand the curves.

Stop snoring

People who snore tend to do so more often when they sleep on their backs. But how can you prevent someone from sleeping that way? Easily. Attach a tennis ball to the back of the person's pajama top by safety-pinning a sock onto the pj's and inserting a tennis ball. (Sewing a pocket in the back of the pajama top works, too.) When the snorer turns onto his back, the tennis ball will prevent him from getting comfortable, and he'll return to his side—where he'll snore less.

Stop doors from slamming by tying a piece of twine to the inside doorknob, running it across the edge of the door, and tying it to the outside doorknob.

twine

Twine is one of those handy-dandy items that you can use all around the house. Use it to tie up newspapers for recycling or tie up packages for shipping. Better yet, use it in these unusual ways.

Go fishing in your drain

Dropping a metal object—a fork or a ring, for example—down a drain is annoying because you can't retrieve it, and it's potentially dangerous if you have a garbage disposer. Get rid of your annoyance and danger by attaching a magnet to a long piece of stiff twine, and use the twine as a fishing line. You should be able to retrieve your belongings.

Close doors quietly

Don't let slamming doors give you a headache. Stop the slamming by tying a piece of twine to the inside doorknob, running it across the edge of the door, and tying it to the outside doorknob. The twine will slow the door down as it shuts, and prevent it from slamming.

Make a hanging planter

Cut two same-size pieces of twine. Cross the two pieces in the middle, then place a container where they cross and glue the container onto the twine. Fill the container with colorful plants, and use the four ends of the twine to hang it on a tree branch or a stake outside.

Create earthy jewelry

Braided twine can make unique natural-looking bracelets and necklaces. Add some beads for a stunning accessory to go with casual clothes.

Fix accessories

Did your shoelace break? Did your belt take a vacation without telling you? Show your accessories who's boss. Replace them with hardworking twine. The twine will keep your pants up and your shoes on.

twist ties

Garden twist ties look so little and defenseless—but they act like they're big and powerful. And they are, judging by all the different, practical ways you can use them around your house.

Keep your zipper up

Some pants have zippers that won't stay up, and you might not realize it until you take them off that night. If you have pants with a zipper that's a repeat offender, bring a twist tie to the rescue. Loop it through the zipper pull and twist it. When you zip up your pants, twist the tie around the button or snap and *then* fasten the button. An invisible repair!

Organize your keys

Quick: Which key on your key chain fits your back door? If you have several keys that look alike, differentiate them with different colored twist ties. Simply loop a colored twist tie through the hole in each key and you'll never go searching for the right key again.

5 More Ways to Use TWINE

1 Ribbon Replacement

If you've run out of ribbon, don't dash to the store—use twine! It looks rustic, like raffia, and will contrast nicely with wrapping paper.

2 Stack 'Em

Balls of twine have a very textural, organic appearance. You can make modern-looking holiday ornaments by stacking twine balls three in a row to create snowmen. Add arms with pipe cleaners, facial elements with beads, and you'll have a truly unique display.

3 Knit and Purl

You can knit twine! You wouldn't want to make a sweater, surely, but what about a utilitarian object—like place mats to be used when you are camping? They would definitely be conversation starters!

4 Modern Lighting

You've seen those ultramodern-looking string lamps. They're round and cool looking—and generally pricey. Why buy one expensively when you can make one cheaply? All you need is twine, craft glue, and a balloon or beach ball of the appropriate size. Blow up your round base. Dip twine in your craft glue and paste it crisscross all over the base. Allow the glue to dry, then pop and remove the interior. You'll be left with a hip lamp. A quick trip to the hardware store for a lighting kit will complete your creation.

5 On the Ball

Do you like those decorative balls in home-décor stores? You know the kind—made of twigs or colored sea grass? There is a simple way to make them yourself using twine, Styrofoam balls, and a glue gun. Take a ball and put a dab of glue on the top. Fasten the twine to the ball and then begin tightly coiling it around the ball, adding glue as you go. You will be amazed how expensive looking the finished product is! If you want something more colorful than natural twine, apply spray paint after the ball has dried.

Hold your place while knitting

If nobody will touch your knitting until you return to it, stop reading. But if you have kids, cats, dogs, or even a meddling spouse, push a twist tie through your last stitch and twist. You won't find your work undone when you return.

Reset a screw

If an unanchored screw in the wall has loosened significantly, the hole it's in has probably grown and you need to make it smaller. How? Bunch up several twist ties, then shove the ties into the hole. Once the hole is filled, reset the screw. It will stay in place.

Tie on a button

Help! A button popped off your shirt and you don't have the time or the supplies to sew it back on. What to do? Grab a twist tie, peel off the paper or plastic covering, then use the wire to attach the button. Push it from the inside of your shirt up through the hole made by the original thread, through one hole in the button, back down through another hole in the button, and then finally down through the second hole in your shirt. Twist the tie ends together so that the button stays in place, and bend them so they lie flat on the inside of your shirt. Done!

Make a fake shoelace

Shoelaces have a tendency to break at the most inopportune times—usually when you don't have another one on hand. Make a temporary replacement with a series of twist ties. Use one tie for each pair of eyelets, and twist it shut. Your shoes will stay on as you run to the store for new shoelaces.

Fix your glasses

The tiny screw that holds your eyeglass frames together has a very big job—but it seems to fall down on the job a lot. If the screw has fallen out and your glasses have fallen off, replace the screw with a twist tie. Tear or cut off the edges of the tie so that only the wire is left. Thread the wire through the screw's hole, twist it shut, then trim off the excess wire. You're good to go!

Grab a twist tie, peel off the paper or plastic covering, then use the wire to attach a button.

THE 99 CENT SOLUTIONS

TOP 10 GARDENING TOOLS

One of the things that constantly boggles the minds of our editors is the uselessness of so much expensive specialty stuff that's out there on the market. Instead, we scoured the aisles of our local 99 cent store.

1 Trowel

This ancient tool is our go-to favorite for planting perennials, potting plants, and burying bulbs.

2 Watering Can

Pick up an inexpensive plastic watering can for spot-watering delicate seedlings.

3 Pruners

You'll use them for everything from pruning shrubs and roses to the odd tree.

4 Scissors

Pick up a package of children's school scissors for cutting stems or removing dead flower heads.

5 Meat Fork

A meat fork will help you lift out the roots of established perennials or divide overgrown plants.

6 Transplanting Spade

Long, narrow, and super-useful, this tool doubles as a great bulb planter.

7 Trug

This big, plastic barrel drags dug-up weeds into the woods, or newspapers out to the recycling bin.

8 Wheelbarrow

Spend a few extra bills for one that is solid and doesn't teeter on its wheel. You'll use it forever.

9 Soaker Hose

A few good soaker hoses will save your roses. Hook them up, and watch your garden smile.

10 Gloves

Rubber gloves are great for weed pulling, but we prefer soft leather for everything else.

AISLE 4 CLEANING AND HOME SUPPLIES

IF YOU TALLIED THE COST OF ALL THE cleaning supplies and home supplies—like tissues, toilet paper, plastic bags, and toothpicks—that you had bought over the years, you would probably be horrified by the amount you had spent. But think about this: If you used those same products for uses you (and the manufacturers) never considered, you wouldn't be so horrified. And if you bought those products at a 99 cent store, you might even come out ahead! Check out the many different ways you can use what you once thought were expensive, one-shot deals.

aluminum foil

You'll run into foil again in an upcoming chapter. But in this case, forget about using it for leftovers. Instead, think about foil in terms of trees, seeds, couches, grills, and more.

Create a Halloween costume

Homemade costumes are always more fun than store-bought ones. Help your child wrap a large box in foil. Attach shoulder straps to the top and decorate with construction paper to make a robot costume. Or dress your kid with a little padding and cover him in foil. Poof! He's a baked potato.

Bug-proof a container

Wooden tea chests used to be lined with metal to keep insects out. Plastic has taken over in the kitchen, but you can still line boxes with foil before storing clothes or books.

Reflect heat on your grill

Grilling food such as a whole chicken or a roast requires a low and slow heat. Bounce all the heat upward by lining your clean, empty charcoal grill with foil, shiny side up, before you build your fire.

Make individual grill packs

On a square of foil, mound a handful of thin-sliced veggies. Top with herbs and butter, salt and pepper, and a little chicken broth or wine. Fold the packets over tightly and cook on the back of the grill rack until tender.

Scouring power

Backyard grilling and campsite grilling can be thrilling—until it comes time to clean the grill. If you forgot a scouring pad (or don't have one at home), just ball up some foil and use it to scrape grime off the grill.

Fill a stripped screwhole

If the screw keeps turning and turning in a piece of wood, push a bit of foil loosely in the hole and try again. It will grab tight.

Protect decorative buttons

Never risk losing a pricey button again! Before you send an item of dressy clothing to the cleaners, cover any decorative or engraved buttons with foil. They'll be protected during the cleaning process and won't get damaged.

Premier Aluminum FOIL
Line storage boxes with aluminum foil before storing clothes or books to keep insects out.

ammonia

Ammonia is one of those incredibly versatile cleaning products. It cleans more in your house than you could ever imagine—but it has a number of uses outdoors, too. Here are several ways you can use this miracle solution, inside and out.

Take it outside

Ammonia is a miracle worker in the house: It cleans almost everything, almost every time. But it can work wonders on your car, too. Mix 1/4 cup ammonia with 1 quart of cold water and use the solution to clean your windshield wiper blades. Lift each blade, wiping it with a soft cloth or paper towel that you've dipped into the mixture. Dry the blades with a clean dry cloth, and put them back in their place.

Whiten your sneakers

Mix a 50-50 solution of ammonia and water, dip a clean cloth into the solution, then rub your tennis shoes with the cloth. You can use this approach to cleaning any white shoes. (Be sure to test the ammonia mixture on an inconspicuous part of the shoe first.)

Water your lilacs

Lilacs, clematis, and hydrangeas are alkaline-loving flowering plants, and as such would love to be watered with ammonia. Mix 1/4 cup of ammonia into 1 gallon of water, and water them as usual. Cucumbers like this treatment, too!

Stop the itch

Don't let mosquito bites drive you crazy—even if you have more bites than anyone else at the picnic. Stop the itch with one or two drops of ammonia applied directly to the bite (unless you've already scratched the bite, in which case this is a painful remedy!).

Clean out your vegetable garden

Soak several sponges in ammonia and place them strategically in your vegetable garden to keep animals away. The animals may love the taste of your ripening vegetables, but they'll hate the smell of the ammonia more.

antistatic fabric spray

You probably use antistatic fabric spray to—not surprisingly—get rid of static that attaches your clothing to you. But when it comes to antistatic spray, stop thinking of clothing and start thinking of everything from your computer to your Christmas tree.

Prevent dusty blinds

Clean your blinds as you normally would, then spritz an antistatic spray on the blinds to keep dust at bay. You won't have to clean your blinds nearly as often.

Comb away scary hair

Save frightful looking hair caused by static electricity for Halloween. Get rid of it every other day by spritzing your comb with antistatic spray and combing your hair. You'll look less ghoulish immediately.

THE Story Behind...

Clorox Bleach

The Electro-Alkaline Company was founded in Oakland, California, to make bleach using electrolysis and brine from the salt ponds of San Francisco Bay. The resulting product—Clorox—was sold locally to businesses, but when a less concentrated household version debuted, the company really took off. Butch, an animated glass bottle, became famous nationwide as a "spokesperson" for the renamed Clorox Chemical Company, but he met his demise in the 1960s when plastic containers arrived.

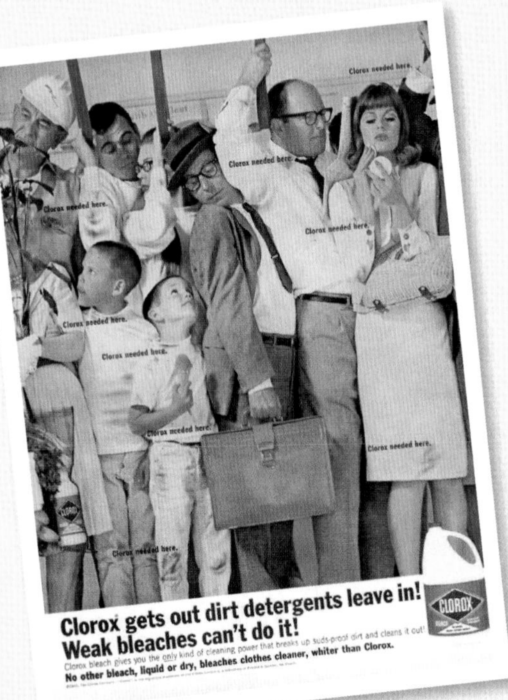

Clorox needed here.
Clorox gets out dirt detergents leave in!
Weak bleaches can't do it!
Clorox bleach gives you the only kind of cleaning power that breaks up suds-proof dirt and cleans it out!
No other bleach, liquid or dry, bleaches clothes cleaner, whiter than Clorox.
CLOROX
actually dissolves suds-proof dirt that makes clothes gray!

Tame tinsel

Does the tinsel on your Christmas tree have a tendency to attack you? If so, spray it with antistatic spray, and it will stay in its place.

Protect your electronic equipment

Spritz antistatic spray on the carpeting around your TV, computer, and other electronic equipment to protect them from static electricity. Be careful, though, not to spray any of your electronics directly.

Get rid of pet hair

If your cat has left a trail of hair on your pants, spray your slacks with antistatic spray. Let the spray work for a few minutes, then simply brush off the loose hair.

bleach

Like ammonia, bleach is a miracle worker around the house. And like ammonia, it has uses far beyond the interior of your house. Think outside the box—and outside your house—when you think about using bleach.

Clean and green

Odd as it sounds, you can make cut flowers last longer with bleach. Add 3 drops of bleach and 1 teaspoon of sugar to 1 quart of water. Pour the mixture into a vase to extend the good look and smell of your bouquet. If you don't have sugar handy, just add 1/4 teaspoon of bleach to a quart of water for the same effect.

The kindest cut

You're doing your trees and shrubs a favor by cutting off dead and dying branches, but you won't be helping them if you spread disease from one plant to another. Stop viral and fungal diseases in their tracks by dipping the blades of your pruning shears in a bucket of undiluted bleach each time you cut an obviously diseased branch. Better yet, use the bleach if you even suspect the plant has health problems.

Give plastics a bleach bath

Tomato sauce can stain your plastic containers quickly and—it seems—permanently. Fill the offending container with water and one capful of chlorine bleach. Let the bleach bath sit for at least an hour. Rinse with water, and reclaim your clean container! This trick works for white plastic spatulas, too.

Make glass sparkle

Whether you're washing drinking glasses or glass plates, give them an extra shine with bleach. Add a teaspoon of bleach to your soapy dishwater, and wash as usual. Rinse the glasses and plates well—you don't want bleach to be part of your next meal!—and dry with a soft towel.

Kill that moss

Moss and algae can make patios and walkways slippery and can create dangerous conditions for you and your guests. Make your home safe again by getting rid of the moss and algae on brick, stone, and concrete with bleach. Mix 3/4 cup bleach with 1 gallon of water and scrub hard (keeping the solution away from grass and flowers). Rinse well.

cedar chips

Cedar shavings and chips have come out of the cedar closet, and they're showing us how multitalented they are. Consider these new bug-related ways to use them.

Caterpillars, snails, and slugs, oh my!

If your garden is a haven for insects, caterpillars, snails, and slugs, spread a mulch made from cedar shavings and chips over it to repel these pests.

Repel fleas with cedar

Keep fleas out of your house by adding cedar chips to the stuffing in your pet's bedding. Keep them out of your dog's house, too, by hanging or nailing a cedar ring inside the doghouse.

Make a sachet

Wrap cedar chips in a piece of tulle, and keep it shut with a twist tie. You can use it in drawers or—using the twist tie—attach it to a hanger and use it in your closet. Your clothes will smell nice, and you'll repel moths, too!

Keep fleas out of your house by adding cedar chips to the stuffing in your pet's bedding.

clothespins

Clothespins are so popular that they can appear in more than one aisle...and they do. In this case, clothespins are doing just the opposite of ammonia and bleach—they're coming indoors! You can still use them outside in both their original and new ways, but you'll find several helpful hints here on how to use them indoors in ways you may not have considered.

Relief for a bloody nose

Give your fingers a break the next time you use the tried and true remedy for a bloody nose (pinching it shut). Sit up straight and tilt your head forward. Pinch the tip of your nose with a clothespin, and use it to hold your nose shut for at least 10 minutes. The flow should stop shortly.

Make garlic chips

Plain potato chips just don't satisfy sometimes. If you crave chips with a kick, put a peeled garlic clove in a bag of unflavored chips. Shut the bag with a clothespin, and stay away from it for 6 to 8 hours (though you can return occasionally to shake the bag to distribute the garlicky flavor). Open and enjoy.

Put a clothesline in your closet

Clothespins aren't handy just for an outdoor clothesline; they can do double duty in your indoor closet. Use them to secure tops and dresses with spaghetti straps to their wire hangers.

Keep your side mirrors clear

No more worrying about icy side mirrors on your car on cold winter nights. Cover the mirrors with plastic bags and hold them shut with clothespins. Take the bags off in the morning. No ice!

Clip shut drapes

Privacy can take a back seat at hotels when draperies won't shut tightly. Make sure you have lightweight plastic clothespins with you when you travel—you can use them to hold drapes shut (which will help keep out light when you're trying to sleep, too).

Make a mitten clothesline

Run a piece of string along the lower inside of your coat closet door and attach clothespins. Let your kids hang their mittens from the string—no more missing mittens!

A new kind of pin

Hemming a skirt made of loosely woven fabric can be a challenge: The stitches are more likely to show and the pins used to keep the hem in place while you're working are more likely to slip out. A better solution? Use clothespins rather than straight pins to hold the hem as you sew.

contractor bags

Contractor bags are multi-aisle players, too; they can often show up anywhere from housewares to tools. Nevertheless, they earn their keep around the house. They do the dirty jobs and lots of other jobs, too. See here what they can do.

Toss a gigantic salad

Throw the ingredients into a small new garbage bag as you cut them, close the bag with a twist tie, and shake to mix your salad. Best of all, you can toss the bag into the refrigerator until you're ready to serve your salad.

Wash your oven rack in a bag

Cleaning a greasy tub after you've soaked your oven rack in it is a nasty job, and one you don't have to do. You can still use the tub for the job, but instead of putting the rack directly in the tub, put it in a heavy-duty trash bag with 1/3 cup dishwashing liquid, 1 cup white vinegar, and lots of hot water. Put the sealed bag in the tub (that you've filled with warm water) and let it sit for an hour. Take the rack out of the bag, give it a good scrubbing, rinse it, and let it air-dry. You'll have a clean rack *and* a clean tub!

Create compost

Fill a large black plastic trash bag with autumn leaves, a small bucketful of soil, a handful of 10-10-10 fertilizer, and wet the leaves thoroughly. Close the bag with a twist tie, and scramble the contents a few times. Store the bag over the winter in a sunny spot. Open the bag in the spring and you'll find rich compost.

Protect your car

Stash trash bags in the trunk of your car and pull them out to protect your upholstery and floor mats when necessary. Muddy kids and dogs need a ride? Cover the seats and carpet with trash bags, and you're ready to roll.

Keep clothes dust-free

You know you won't wear your linen dress for several months, and you don't want it to attract dust and dirt while it sits undisturbed in your closet. Protect it from harm with a new trash bag. Cut a slit in the top for the hanger, and push the hanger—holding your dress—through. Hang it in your closet with complete confidence that it will stay clean.

dishwashing liquid

Dishwashing liquid isn't just for washing dishes anymore. It's for killing weeds and ants and washing air conditioner filters and your hair. It's enough to make you feel sorry for the dishes!

Dishwashing liquid is cool

Clean your foam or metal mesh air conditioner filters once a month during the summer—or whenever you routinely use your AC—with dishwashing liquid. Soak the filter in a bath of warm water and dish soap, then scrub it gently with a toothbrush. Once you've removed any debris, rinse it and dry it completely. Put it back in the air conditioner, and enjoy a sweat-free day.

Get rid of ants with a simple 50/50 solution of water and white vinegar with a dash of dishwashing liquid.

Kill weeds kindly

Be kind to the environment—not so much to weeds—by using a natural weed killer rather than harmful herbicides. Mix 1 teaspoon of dishwashing liquid with 1 cup of salt and 1 gallon of white vinegar. Pour the solution on weeds sprouting in the cracks and crevices of sidewalks, front walks, and patio pavers.

Wash away ants

Outdoor ants can be just as annoying as indoor ants, particularly if they've invaded the crevices in your patio where you eat. Get rid of them with a simple 50/50 solution of water and white vinegar with a dash of dishwashing liquid. (You can substitute glass cleaner for the vinegar if you want.) Spray the affected area with the mix, wait a few minutes, then happily return to your picnic.

Water your lawn with household liquids

Fill the reservoir of a 10- or 20-gallon hose-end sprayer with water and a 12-ounce can of beer or non-diet cola, 1 cup of corn syrup or molasses or household ammonia, or 1/2 cup mouthwash—*and* 1 cup of dishwashing liquid. The dishwashing liquid helps spread the concoction more evenly across your lawn, and as an added bonus, helps it stick to individual blades of grass. Water your lawn approximately every three weeks, and watch your neighbors turn green with envy—like your lawn.

Degrease your hair

If your locks aren't looking so lovely, try mixing a dollop of dishwashing liquid into your shampoo. It fights grease in hair, as well as on dishes!

Clean your blender

Forget about taking your blender apart to wash it thoroughly. Instead, fill it partway with warm water and dishwashing detergent, cover it, and run it for a few seconds. Empty it, rinse it, air-dry it, and call it a day.

dishwasher detergent

Dishwasher detergent is trying to get in on the "I can do lots of other things, too" act—and has succeeded! Add dishwasher detergent to your list of cleaning supplies to buy and use in new and different ways.

Wash your dishes—and your shower

Make the tiles in your shower sparkle with dishwasher detergent (either liquid or powder). Dissolve 1/4 cup of dishwasher detergent in warm water in a spray bottle. Cover the shower walls and floor with the mixture. Let it stand for several hours, then scrub with a sponge and rinse.

Clean screens and dishes

Window screens need to be thoroughly washed once or twice a year, and it's not a fun job. Make it easier on yourself by removing the screens from the window and washing them outside on a nice day. Scrub each side of the screen with a broad, soft brush and a mixture of hot water and lemon-scented dishwashing detergent. Rinse the screen with a hose and let the screen dry completely before putting it back in the window.

Stinky shoes? Place a dryer sheet in each shoe when you're not wearing them.

Banish burn marks

You try to make your pants look better by ironing them, but instead you end up scorching them with the iron. Don't get frustrated—get some powdered dishwasher detergent. Mix it with water to make a paste, and apply the paste to the scorched area. (Test it in an inconspicuous place on the fabric first.) Put your pants out in the sun to bleach away the mark. Launder as usual.

Get out grease stains

Soak garments stained with grease overnight in a solution of water and 1 cup of powdered dishwasher detergent. Wash the next day as usual, and watch the stains disappear. The dishwasher detergent boosts the cleaning power of your regular laundry detergent.

dryer sheets

A fabric softener dryer sheet does a great job reducing static cling as your clothes tumble around in the dryer. But it does a great job in other situations, too.

Save your soil

Houseplants generally aren't messy, but if soil escapes from the bottom of the pot through the drain hole when you water your plant, you have a dirty problem. Solve it by placing a used dryer sheet in the bottom of the pot the next time you repot a plant.

Solve stinky problems

Smelly hamper? Put a dryer sheet at the bottom of it, and change it every week. Stinky shoes? Place a dryer sheet in each shoe when you're not wearing them. Need to hold your nose near your wastebasket? Same solution: Keep a dryer sheet at the bottom, beneath the bag holding the trash. Your whole house will smell better, one dryer sheet at a time!

Stuff handbags for storage

If you save all your used dryer sheets, over the course of a few weeks of laundry you may well find you have plenty to fill a purse for storage. Bunched-up dryer sheets will not only keep a bag in shape but will also leave it smelling fresh, not musty, when you use it again.

Take dryer sheets on your travels

A hotel room with a musty air conditioner is not the most comfortable place for sleeping. Carry a dryer sheet in your suitcase. While you're traveling, it helps make clothes smell fresh. Once in the hotel, put it in front of the AC's vent to blow a better scent into the air.

7 Ways to Use DAWN DISHWASHING LIQUID

1 Launder Delicates

You don't need special detergent to hand wash clothes. Mix 1 teaspoon of dishwashing liquid into a gallon of water and let your delicate items soak. Then rinse with cold water. (Do not try this on items marked Dry Clean Only!)

2 Sparkling Shower

Getting soap film off of your glass shower door just got easier. Use dishwashing liquid, and you will be amazed at how quickly and easily the gunk comes off.

3 Vanishing Spots

Out of stain stick and ready to do a load of laundry? Don't worry—grab your dishwashing liquid and get to work. Gently rub the liquid on the stained fabric, let it sit, and then machine wash the item as usual. You'll find stains will disappear.

4 Foil a Rash

A poison ivy rash is diabolical in that scratching can make it worse. To find relief, rub exposed skin with cotton balls soaked in dishwashing liquid. It will strip the plant oils that cause the itchy rash—and cut down your suffering nicely.

5 Farewell Fleas

If you are combing fleas off of your dog or cat, keep a pan of water filled with dishwashing liquid at your side. Drop any fleas you find into the mixture, and they will quickly meet their demise.

6 Shiny Stove

Is there grease buildup on your stovetop or range hood? Squirt a little dishwashing liquid on a sponge and wipe it away with ease.

7 Patrol Pests

To rid your garden of pests without using harsh chemicals, make your own insecticidal soap by mixing 1 1/2 teaspoons of dishwashing detergent in one quart of water. Spray this on your plants and you will get rid of mites, whiteflies, and aphids.

Unpack packing peanuts

Opening a box filled with packing peanuts can be a trial at best. They leap out and attach themselves to you, your carpet, and your furniture. And they cling to your hands like magnets, preventing you from finding the contents of the package. Stop the madness by rubbing your hands with a dryer sheet before you open the box. The packing peanuts will stay away!

Stop knots in their tracks

Rub a fabric softener dryer sheet along your thread the next time you sew. It will help prevent knots and snarls. Soap works well, too.

fabric softener

Take fabric softener out of the laundry room, and see what it can accomplish in other rooms. You'll be amazed by its wide range of abilities, once you set it free.

A sterling solution to tarnish

Sterling silver jewelry is spectacular when it sparkles and dull when it is tarnished. Return dull jewelry to its former luster with fabric softener. Heat 4 cups of water in a pot on the stove, then turn off the heat. Dissolve 4 teaspoons of salt in the water. Mix in fabric softener until the solution becomes cloudy. Add the jewelry (unless it has stones set in it), and let it sit for an hour. Remove the silver, rinse it with warm water, and gently rub it with a clean dry cloth. Your silver should sparkle again.

Run away from runs

Add a drop or two of fabric softener to the water the next time you rinse out your panty hose to avoid future runs. The fabric softener helps the nylons stretch more easily, so you're less likely to run them the next time you pull them taut. Roll them in a towel to dry.

Banish burned-on food

Liquid fabric softener is your best friend when it comes time to scrub pots and pans soiled by your worst enemy, baked-on grime. Soak the offending vessel in water and a squirt of fabric softener. Let it sit for an hour. Wash and rinse it all away.

Free your walls from wallpaper

Whether you're painting or re-papering your walls, you need to get rid of the wallpaper already there—no matter how awful the job. Make your life easier by adding a capful of liquid fabric softener to a quart of water, and cover the wallpaper with it using a sponge. (Be sure to gently score the wallpaper with a wire-bristle brush or razor blade if it has a water-resistant covering.) Let it work its magic for 20 minutes, then simply scrape the old stuff off the wall.

Ready your brushes for their next job

Keep your paintbrushes soft and pliable and ready for the next can of paint coming their way. Clean them as you normally would, but rinse them in a quart of water that contains a drop of fabric softener. Swish the brush around, then wipe the bristles dry. Your brushes are ready to go!

furniture polish

Polish off a few additional household chores with furniture polish. Once you use it for things other than tables, chairs, and sofas, you'll want to add it to your stable of very versatile cleaning supplies.

Polish your shower door

Prevent soap scum buildup on your shower door with furniture polish. Clean your shower door, then apply lemon oil furniture polish to it with a soft cloth. Let it sit for two minutes. Using a clean dry cloth, gently rub off the excess polish. The oil from the furniture polish will keep soap scum away, shower after shower.

Make your bicycle sparkle

Unless you like to spend your free time polishing the nooks and crannies of your clean bike with liquid or paste wax, consider taking the easy way out. Simply spray your bicycle with a coat of furniture polish that contains wax. It will shine like new!

Oil squeaky hinges

Spray a little oil-based furniture polish on a squeaky door hinge, then open and shut the door several times to work the lubricant into the hinge. The furniture polish is a lot cleaner than the oil you'd usually use for a noisy hinge, and it works just as well to silence the squeak.

Shine your hubcaps

Furniture polish works well outdoors, too. Spray some on your car's hubcaps and other chrome features, and rub them well with a soft clean cloth. You'll make your car's details shine.

gallon bags

Big plastic bags are particularly helpful in the kitchen, but they can take on big jobs all over the house, too. Use gallon-size plastic bags (or gallon-size freezer bags) to do a wide range of duties.

Save a little paint

You finished painting a room, and have a small amount of paint left over that you want to save for future touch-ups. What's the best way to store less than half a can? Pour the paint into a ziplock plastic food bag, seal the bag (getting rid of the air inside as you go), then place the paint bag back into the paint can. Seal the can, and mark it with the color of the paint, where you used the paint, and when you bought it. If paint has obscured the paint's color and number on the outside of the can, add that too. Your paint will be fresh the next time you need it.

Protect your feet

It's only November and you haven't had time to buy snow boots—and you're faced with a winter wonderland. How can you keep your feet dry? Cover your feet with socks first and plastic bags second, then put your shoes on. If you have time, use duct tape to fasten the tops of the bags to the tops of your socks so that the bags don't slip down into your shoes. Now you're ready for snow!

Have bags, will travel

Pack your belongings in plastic bags the next time you take a trip. If you're traveling by plane, the bags let airport inspectors see your possessions without trawling through them. And no matter your method of transportation, they help you keep your clothing organized and easy to find in your suitcase.

glass cleaner

Glass cleaner can do so much more than just clean windows (though, thankfully, it does its primary job really well). In fact, it's a pro when it comes to jewelry, hardwood floors, bug bites—even your face.

WAY BACK WHEN...

Windex's Blue Color

You may picture a plastic bottle filled with blue liquid when you're thinking of Windex, but when it first hit shelves in 1933, the cleaner was combustible and had to be sold in steel cans for safety. Thankfully, after World War II the formula was improved, the packaging changed, and the recognizable blue dye was developed. Though transparency is good for clean windows, it's less useful for proprietary formulas. The patent application for Windex revealed the ingredients used to make the brilliant blue dye, and competitors immediately began to copy it.

Help for your hardwood floor

Has hairspray hit on your hardwood floor? Has furniture polish left it cloudy or peeling? Help has arrived—in the form of window cleaner! Wipe the floor with a clean damp cloth, then apply ammonia-free window cleaner to remove any remaining blemishes.

Make stones sparkle

If the gems in your jewelry have turned dull, revive their sparkle with window cleaner. Dampen a clean, lint-free cloth with glass cleaner, and gently wipe your jewelry. A bonus: The solution will also clean the metal surrounding the gems. (Don't use glass cleaner on opaque stones like opal or turquoise or on pearl or coral because it might discolor them.)

Relieve a bee sting

After taking out the stinger, spray the area with ammonia window cleaner. It will help reduce the swelling and soothe the pain. (Just never use a concentrated product.)

Dry out pimples

Assuming you will keep the window cleaner out of your eyes and have no allergies to the ingredients (which include ammonia, detergents, solvents, and alcohol), spritzing window cleaner on your pimples is a good way to dry them out and make them disappear.

Free your finger

If you thought your ring fit a little too snugly and it turns out that you were right—you can't get it

Marinate without a mess

Forget about using a bowl or pan to marinate your next barbecue meal. Instead, marinate the meat in a ziplock plastic bag. Put the seasonings and liquids in first—close the bag and shake it to blend the ingredients—then add the meat. Close the bag, and shake it again. Stash it in the refrigerator, turning upside down occasionally to mix the liquids, for as long as the recipe requires. Then grill and enjoy!

Keep your cookbook clean

Though spills on cookbook pages may bring back fond memories of special meals, they may also make reading the recipe a little too difficult. Keep cookbook pages spotless by covering the open book with a plastic bag or two. You'll protect the book and be able to easily wipe off any splatters.

off your finger—spray some glass cleaner on your finger, twist the ring several times, and slide it off.

Spruce up your shoes

If you need to shine your patent leather shoes before you step out for the evening, try spraying them with glass cleaner. They'll look spiffy in a hurry! Use glass cleaner on patent leather purses, too. Wipe dry with a paper towel.

lint roller

It's the perfect stocking stuffer and the perfect lint-picker-upper—and it achieves perfection in lots of other ways, too. Check out the range of a lint roller's abilities below.

Pick up pet hair

Brush your lint roller over couches, chairs, beds, and anywhere else pet hair tends to accumulate in your home. Toss the sheets once they're full, and admire your clean house!

Clean up crafts

Whether you've accidentally spilled glitter all over the craft table or need a way to easily pick up loose beads that didn't quite make it onto your necklace, a lint roller can be your best friend. Just roll it over whatever needs to be picked up and call it a day.

Get rid of bugs

Bring a lint roller on your next hiking trip and use it at the end of your hike to get bugs—specifically ticks—off your pants and shirt. Use it all over your clothing, including your socks, for best results.

Clean your bathroom floor

Roll your lint roller over your bathroom floor to pick up stray hair that the hair dryer has blown onto the tiles. Do this between your regular cleanings and your bathroom will look cleaner longer.

mothballs

Mothballs and moth crystals can repel so much more than moths, but we've all been trained to believe that mothballs are for...moths. Here are some ideas that prove otherwise.

Dash their dreams of dinner

There's no such thing as a free lunch for squirrels, chipmunks, and mice anymore if you protect your flower bulbs from them. Plant your bulbs as you normally would, but add a few moth crystals over them to spoil their predators' meal.

Kill potted plant pests

Get rid of bugs on houseplants using a dry cleaning bag and mothballs. Encase the plant—including the saucer—in the clear plastic bag, water the plant, add 5 or 6 mothballs, and close the bag tightly. Move it to a bright spot (though keep it out of direct sunlight). Remove the plant after a week. You and your plant will be rid of the bugs (and moths for a while, too!).

MOTHBALLS MORPH AS THEY WORK

Mothballs are pesticides that come in a solid form but change into a gas. In the United States they contain one of two active ingredients: naphthalene or paradichlorobenzene, both of which are toxic. If you have children or pets in the home, there are chemical-free ways to thwart moths: cloves, eucalyptus, lavender, cinnamon sticks, and bay leaves can keep your clothing safe. Simply wrap whichever one appeals most to you in a cheesecloth sachet, and store them along with your clothing.

Protect your vegetable garden

Rodents and (obviously) insects can't stand mothballs, so use them to your advantage when growing vegetables. Hang a mesh bag filled with mothballs from a trellis or a fence to keep the critters and pests away. (Don't put them directly on the soil or in shallow containers that could be knocked over; the chemicals in the mothballs can contaminate the soil.)

Give woolens a final rinse

Mothballs will protect your woolens from moths—it's a given. But did you know that by dissolving a few mothballs in the rinse cycle as you're washing the items you plan to store, you'll provide even more protection for your winter sweaters? Just make sure you do this the last time you wash your woolens before you put them away.

Drive bats batty

Chances are you think bats won't get into your house—until they do. Keep them away by leaving mothballs around the floor of the attic.

oven cleaner

Cleaning an oven is never a fun job, but if you bought oven cleaner, you really should use it—and now you can use it on a whole lot more than your oven! Here are several really useful ways to put off cleaning your oven.

Clean bricks like an oven

If the bricks on your fireplace, your front walk, or anywhere else sport dingy spots, you need to think outside the box—and into your oven. Spray a coating of oven cleaner on the bricks, and let it sit for 15 minutes. Attack the spots with a scrub brush. Repeat the process, then clean the area with water.

Help your hubcaps

Clean your hubcaps the easy way—with oven cleaner! Spray it directly onto each hubcap to remove any and all accumulated dirt and debris. Let the cleaner stand for a minute, then spray it off with a hose. Just be sure not to use it on painted hubcaps; it may remove the paint as well as the grime.

Hang a mesh bag filled with mothballs from a trellis or a fence to keep the critters and pests away from your vegetable garden.

Wash whitewalls

If your whitewall tires are looking tired, spray them with oven cleaner. Rinse them with a hose, and see your tires shimmer!

Remove burnt stains from non-aluminum cookware

Drips of food or oil can get cooked to a black, resinous finish on the base or sides of a pan, and it won't scrub off no matter how much elbow grease you apply. Instead, turn the pot upside down on a newspaper, and spray the outside with oven cleaner. Let sit for an hour, then scrub and rinse.

Clean caked-on window grime

Windows that haven't been washed for a long time can be very difficult to clean. When you've scrubbed off most of the dirt but can't get through the worst stains, bring on some oven cleaner. Spray the window lightly and let sit for a few minutes, then wipe away. The sun will shine through at last!

paper bags

Paper bags are hard workers that get little credit. But they should get lots of extra credit for all the extra jobs they do, like these here.

Iron your wood floor

If you accidentally dripped candle wax on your wood floor—or if your child colored on it on purpose—you need to remove the stain pronto. How? Place an ordinary brown paper bag over the offending mark, and run a warm iron over the bag until it soaks up the stain. The same strategy will work to remove wax stains on carpet, as long as you scrape off as much wax as possible before you start.

Sow paper bags

Protect your seedlings from the wind by planting them in paper bags partially filled with soil. Dig

a hole in your garden for each paper bag. Place the bag in the hole, but leave about 2 inches of the bag sticking out of the ground. The paper will protect your plant and will disintegrate as the plant grows, letting the roots unfurl into your garden's soil.

Hide the snap trap

If you have a mouse problem but the sight of a dead mouse gives you the heebie-jeebies, set the trap inside an open paper bag. Once you've caught the mouse, simply close up the bag and throw it—and what's inside it—in the trash.

Breathe better with a paper bag

Hiccups? Stop them before you start to hurt. Breathe in and out of a paper bag for a few minutes. You'll create a build-up of carbon dioxide in your lungs, which helps relax your diaphragm—whose involuntary tightening causes the hiccups in the first place. This trick works if you're hyperventilating, too.

Tame a toothache

Cut a piece from a brown paper bag and soak it in vinegar. Sprinkle black pepper on one side, and hold that side to your cheek. Your cheek will feel nicely warm—which may pull your attention

A DIFFERENT Solution

10 Ways to Use PAPER TOWEL TUBES

Once you run out of paper towels, don't toss away the roll! Look at all the things that you can do with it:

1 Baby Your Tomatoes

Keep cutworms away from your tomato plants by slitting a paper towel tube so that you can use it as a "collar." Depending on the height of your plants, you could get several collars from each tube. The cardboard is biodegradable, so you won't need to remove it.

2 Cord Storage

For neater, easier storage, fold your extension cords to the length of a paper towel tube and slide them in. You can label the tube with magic marker, indicating where the cord is generally used.

3 Bag It

If your kitchen is overflowing with plastic grocery bags, here's a way to get a handle on the situation. Stuff those bags into a paper towel tube and toss the whole thing in a drawer. It is a handy (and free!) way to get organized.

4 Boot Shaper

Before storing your boots for the season, slide a few paper towel tubes inside each boot. This will keep the tops from flopping over and causing creases in the ankle area.

5 Protect Paperwork

To store important paperwork, be it a marriage certificate or a treasured child's drawing, use a paper towel tube. Roll the document carefully and slide it inside to keep it from getting creased or torn. Before storing, you can write the name of the document on the paper tube for easy identification.

6 Have a Ball

Yarn is useless if it's in a tangle. Cut a paper towel tube in thirds and notch each end of the pieces. Secure one end of your loose yarn in a notch and wrap it tightly around the tube. Secure the other end in the second notch. You will have one neat ball; make two more with the rest of the tube.

7 A Knit Kit

Do you have more knitting needles than you know what to do with? Are they unpaired with all of the sizes mixed up? Take some paper towel tubes, label them according to needle size, and then get those needles of yours organized! You can stopper the ends with paper towels.

8 Hair Bands

Don't search all over for your hair bands; wrap them around a cardboard paper towel tube. Toss the tube in a drawer, and you'll always know where to find them.

9 Happy Hamsters

You can thrill hamsters by placing paper towel tubes in their cage. They enjoy running through them and shredding the cardboard. When the tube is demolished, you can replace it with a fresh one.

10 Banish Creases

Don't buy padded hangers. Instead, make a cut down the length of a paper towel tube, then slip it over a plain wire hanger, and it will protect your pants from getting sharp creases.

from the pain in your tooth. Of course, call your dentist as soon as you can to get rid of the pain permanently.

paper towels

Paper towels sound so fragile—how can towels of paper be strong? But strong they are. In fact, they're so strong that they can plug leaks and stop hiccups. Here's how.

Brighten the white

If your white porcelain enamel sink is looking a little down on its luck, bring back its shine with paper towels. Line the sink with them, then douse them with bleach. Leave the bleach-soaked paper towels in place for half an hour, then throw them away. Rinse away any residue with running water. Stand back and admire your sparkling sink. (Don't try this on colored porcelain, though; it may fade the color.)

Halt the hiccups

Put a stop to annoying—and occasionally painful—hiccups with a paper towel. Place it over the top of a glass of water, and take a few swigs through it. Your diaphragm—the villain causing the hiccups—will have to work harder to pull the water out of the glass, and the extra work may stop the diaphragm's involuntary muscle movements.

Line your crisper drawer

If you want the vegetables in your refrigerator's crisper drawer to truly be crispy, line it with paper towels. They will absorb the moisture in the fridge that can turn carrots, broccoli, and beans soggy. Replace the towels when they're damp.

Plug a leak around a window

If you detect a drafty window in the middle of winter, try to find the source of the leak—it's a good bet you'll find it along the top of the lower sash. If that's the case, put two paper towels together, and fold them up from the bottom, one inch at a time. Once you've made a thick inch-wide strip, place it over the leak and tape it down on all sides. You'll stop the leak—and high heating bills.

Clean out your ears (of corn)

Picking individual strands of silk from husked ears of corn is as time-consuming as it is annoying. Get your time and your pleasing temperament back by easily wiping away the silk. Dampen a paper towel

Line your refrigerator's crisper drawer with paper towels. They will absorb the moisture in the fridge that can turn carrots, broccoli, and beans soggy.

and rub it gently across the corn. The paper towel will quickly and calmly pick up the silk.

rubber gloves

Rubber gloves are a staple in your cleaning supply cabinet, but they actually can do a whole lot more than protect your hands while you do the dishes or the floors. Here are some of the other jobs rubber gloves can do.

Give the jar a hand

No more banging a jar on the floor to loosen a tight lid. No more running it under hot water. And no more fancy tools designed to do the trick—that somehow don't work. Just put on a pair of rubber gloves, and open the jar with ease.

Lend your broom a hand

Actually, lend your broom and your mop a finger from your rubber gloves. Cut off two fingers and put one over the end of the broom handle and one over the mop handle. They won't slip across the floor the next time you need to stand them up against a wall.

Handle hot potatoes

Don your rubber gloves if you need to take a hot potato out of the oven, move a roasted chicken from the pan to the serving dish, or handle prickly foods like pineapple. You'll protect your hands, and you won't drop your food!

Avoid creepy crawlies

Next time you have to clean up a cobweb or pick up a dead ant, put your rubber gloves on first. You won't be as creeped out by the bugs if your skin doesn't get anywhere near them.

Pick off pet hair

Dog and cat hair on a couch or chair can make your house look messy—or dirty—even when it isn't. Whip your house back into shape by getting rid of the omnipresent pet hair. Put a rubber glove on one hand, and rub your gloved fingers across your sofa, back and forth until a ball of pet hair forms. Just pick up the ball and continue on to your chairs.

WAY BACK WHEN...

Playtex Gloves

Ladies' undergarments may seem to have little to do with Playtex gloves. Yet Playtex began life as the International Latex Corporation. Founded by Abram Nathaniel Spanel, the company once produced girdles that were made completely of latex! Uncomfortable as that sounds, the company thrived, and in 1954 the product line expanded to include household utility gloves. Playtex gloves have been dominant in the market ever since. Incidentally, the gloves can be purchased lined with cotton—the rubber girdles were eventually lined for comfort, too.

Some like it hot

Make your own hot-water bottle out of a heavy-duty rubber glove. Fill the glove with hot water, seal it with a strong rubber band, and wrap it in a towel. You'll stay toasty warm!

rubbing alcohol

Like bleach and ammonia, rubbing alcohol is one of those amazing liquids that has a wide range of alternate uses around the house. Here are some that may help you.

Make mincemeat of mealybugs

If you find mealybugs on your houseplants, simply rub them away with rubbing alcohol. Dip a cotton

THE Story Behind...

Brillo Pads

Light, shiny aluminum pans were replacing heavy cast iron cookware in the early 1900s. Sales were brisk but the pots blackened with use. An enterprising cookware salesman consulted his brother-in-law (a jeweler), and the two men mixed jeweler's rouge (polish for jewelry) with beef tallow soap. They applied the mix to used pots with steel wool and the cookware shined like new. They secured a patent for the product under the name Brillo (Latin for "bright") and by 1917, the Brillo Manufacturing Company was packaging steel wool pads with a cake of the soap. Surprisingly, putting the soap into the pads did not happen until the 1930s.

swab in rubbing alcohol, and dab the swab on the bugs. You'll get rid of these common pests pronto.

Stretch your shoes

Help your feet adjust to your new leather shoes by stretching out tight spots with rubbing alcohol. Put your shoes on. Moisten a clean cloth with rubbing alcohol, and dab it on the areas that grip your feet too hard. You'll need to wear your shoes for a full day for the rubbing alcohol to soften the leather (which works best with the heat from your feet). If you can't wear them all day, stuff your shoes with socks to mold them as your feet would.

Care for your car

You've carried the most beautiful Christmas tree you've ever found home on top of your car—and you've carried the sap home, too. If you find sap on your car and can't get it off, apply a few drops of rubbing alcohol directly on the sap. Rub it into the finish with your fingers. The marks will magically disappear!

Rub out a rash

Work fast to prevent a poison ivy rash from developing if you know you've been exposed to the plant. Soak a washcloth in a bowl of rubbing alcohol. Wring out the washcloth, then use it to scrub the area you think may erupt into a rash. Don't be gentle: scrub hard. Take these steps immediately after being exposed. If you wait until the rash develops, this solution won't work.

Keep ice off your wiper blades

Getting in a cold car isn't the worst part of keeping your car outside in cold weather—frozen windshield wiper blades may take that award. Prevent ice by washing blades with a soft clean cloth doused in rubbing alcohol.

sponge

The lowly sponge can actually play several important roles around the house. Here is a range of ways you can use a sponge for more than just doing dishes.

Go natural with houseplants

Skip leaf shine products and wax when cleaning houseplants—instead, just use water and a wet sponge. The waxy store products can clog leaf pores and tend to make the plants look fake.

Wash away a fever

Take a break from washing dishes when you have a fever, and use the sponge on yourself to bring your fever down. Apply a sponge rinsed in cool water to the high-heat spots on your body: your armpits, wrists, neck, groin, and so on. Your body will cool—and your temperature will fall—as the water evaporates.

Soap-dish sponge

Forget about using a traditional soap dish to store your bar of soap—it turns your soap into a gloppy mess that you really don't want to use to clean your hands (or anything else!). Instead, rest your soap on a sponge. It wicks away moisture and leaves your soap clean and ready to use.

Keep your veggies crunchy

The point of a crisper drawer in the refrigerator is to keep your vegetables crisp. Help your fridge out by placing a few new kitchen sponges with the vegetables in the drawer. Squeeze them out when they absorb the excess moisture.

Wipe off pet hair

Clothing and upholstered furniture can be magnets for pet hair. Remove the hair easily by rubbing sofas, chairs, pants, and dresses with a slightly damp sponge.

Stand umbrellas on a sponge

Place a sponge at the bottom of an umbrella stand (or bucket or other type of makeshift umbrella stand) and let your umbrellas rest on it. The sponge will keep water from pooling in the stand. Best of all, you can take the sponge out and squeeze it dry when needed.

Perfect your pedicure

Keep your toes away from each other as you paint your toenails—you don't want the nail polish to smudge. Cut a sponge into small triangles and use the pieces to separate your toes.

Rest your soap on a sponge.
It wicks away moisture and leaves your soap clean and ready to use.

Make mini ice packs

Regular-sized ice packs can be too big for bumps and bruises on children. Cut a sponge into a few pieces, soak the pieces in water, and freeze them to make child-sized ice packs for kids.

spray bottles

At first glance, a spray bottle seems to have limited uses. But on second or third glance, a whole new world of possibilities opens up. What can you spray with it? Where can you use it? Here are some intriguing answers.

Spray bugs with vodka

Pour some inexpensive vodka in a clean spray bottle and take it with you on your next picnic. When mosquitoes start biting, spray them—and yourself—with the vodka. You'll kill the bugs and protect yourself from the bites.

Save money greasing your pans

Stay away from expensive nonstick cooking sprays and use olive oil in a clean spray bottle instead. You'll probably save calories as well as dollars!

Keep your counters cat-free

If you want to keep kitty off your kitchen counter, just spray her gently with water in a spray bottle. She won't like it: In fact, you'll eventually be able to just show her the bottle, and she'll jump off quickly!

Spritz your car windows clean

Keep a spray bottle filled with glass cleaner in the trunk of your car so you'll be ready to clean your car's windows, mirrors, and headlights at a moment's notice. (Be sure to throw a roll of paper towels in the trunk as well.) Add 1/2 teaspoon antifreeze to the cleaner in the winter—it will melt the ice on your windows and mirrors.

Water your pants

A spray bottle is always welcome in a laundry room. Use it to mist your clothes as you iron them, or use it as a container for stain removers. Once you start spraying rather than pouring on your stain remover, you can stop blotting the excess liquid from your clothes.

Spray your way to better baking

Use a spray bottle to lightly spritz your homemade bread with heavily salted water as it bakes. You'll end up with a deliciously crisp, salted crust. You can also use it to squirt a liqueur on a cake.

spray starch

Spray starch is the perfect example of a cleaning item that seems limited in its possibilities—to make pressed garments stiff and crisp—and a cost that you might consider giving up. But wait—you might need it for its other jobs!

Keep your walls clean

Whether you just painted your walls or simply want to keep the paint job you have looking fresh, try lightly coating your walls in busy areas with spray starch. You'll have an easier time getting rid of fingerprints, smudges, and other grime.

Protect your sneakers

Help your canvas or nylon sneakers stay dirt- and stain-free by coating them lightly with spray starch. They'll look cleaner longer.

Frame needlepoint more easily

Give your work of art a light coating of spray starch before framing, and it will hold up better than if you just frame it.

steel wool

It's strong enough to polish metal, yet gentle enough to clean dishes. This multi-aisle favorite can show up in more than one place in a 99 cent store because it's so versatile. Here are several other ways to use it.

Shine your car's chrome

Take a damp pad of ultrafine steel wool (grade 0000) and squeeze it into a bowl containing a little baking soda, mixing with the steel wool until a paste forms. Scrub the chrome trim, rims, and bumpers on your car with the steel wool, making small circles. Rinse the metal and wipe it dry with a clean soft cloth.

Keep mice out

Block small passages—in basement cracks or holes in kitchen cabinets, for example—with steel wool to keep mice out of your house. They won't even try to get around it.

Silence the squeak

Don't come unhinged if you've oiled a door hinge but it continues to make noise. It may just need a thorough cleaning. Prop the door closed with a book or a brick and remove the hinge pin. Scrub it with fine-grade steel wool—be sure to remove any rust and dirt that you can see—and blow off the debris and wayward steel threads. Rub it with oil, and replace it. Swing your door open in silence!

A ring you don't want

Get rid of water rings on a wood table with steel wool. Dip extra-fine steel wool (grade 0000) in lemon oil, and gently rub the ring. Once it disappears, polish the wood with more lemon oil and buff with a soft clean cloth.

Prevent a pet hair clog

Stuff some steel wool in your bathtub drain the next time you wash Fido. It will prevent your

dog's hair from clogging the drain. Just make sure that you don't press the steel wool too far down; you'll want to remove it when you're done.

sandwich bags

Sandwich bags aren't just for sandwiches (though it's always a good idea to keep a few on hand for lunches). These little bags have big ambitions, and they fulfill them every day.

Clean a showerhead

When you're looking forward to a nice, warm shower, nothing is more frustrating than facing a weak trickle of water. If a buildup of lime and mineral scale have reduced your shower to a fading stream and you to tears, fix the problem with vinegar, a plastic sandwich bag, and duct tape. Fill the bag with white vinegar and cover the showerhead with it, making sure that the head is covered by the vinegar. Tape the bag to the showerhead arm with the duct tape, and let it soak overnight. When you take it off in the morning, you'll finally get the shower you've wanted. (Test the vinegar on your fixture first; it can discolor some brass and other finishes.) The same strategy applies to clogged faucets, too.

Keep moisture out of outdoor padlocks in winter. Simply cover the locks with plastic sandwich bags.

Bag your photos

Photos of the family are de rigueur at reunions, get-togethers with long-lost friends, and other meetings of family and friends. Keep your pictures pristine by placing two back to back in a clear plastic sandwich bag. You can then show them with pride without worrying about fingerprints—or worse!

Protect padlocks

Keep moisture out of outdoor locks in winter. It freezes and thaws over and over until it damages the lock. Simply cover the locks with plastic sandwich bags. The bags help keep rust off, too.

Decorate a cake

Writing good wishes on a cake has never been easier! Just fill a plastic sandwich bag with the frosting, squeeze out the extra air, and seal the top. Cut a corner of the bag on a diagonal—make a small cut at first, since you can always enlarge it later—and squeeze out the words you want to write.

Cushion your treasures

Whether you're storing a fragile doll in the attic for your daughter's future children or shipping your favorite vase to your new home, you can protect your belongings with small plastic bags. Wrap your items as you normally would in newspaper, bubble wrap, or tissue paper, then surround them in the box with several plastic bags that you've inflated (by breathing into them with a straw) and sealed. The bags will protect your valuables from shifting in the box.

Polish sandals without a mess

Polishing shoes can be a messy undertaking, particularly when you're polishing sandals. Take the mess out of the equation by covering the hand holding the sandal with a small plastic bag.

string

String does so much more than tie things together. It polishes, measures—even waters plants. How? See below.

Polish silver forks

Silver knives and spoons aren't difficult to polish, but forks can be a challenge. How on earth can you get the edges between the tines to shine? Easy. Cut a piece of string about 6 inches long, and run it through silver polish. Now thread it between the fork tines. Mission accomplished!

Create the sound of silence

The constant sound of a leaky faucet—drip-drip-drip—might make you want to scream, but you can stay calm with a piece of string. Tie a piece of string to the spout so that it hangs from the end of the faucet down to the bottom of the basin.

The water will ride down the string quietly. Now call the plumber!

Water your plants

Let your plants drink up while you take a short trip. All you need is a large container of water and a few pieces of string. Place the water next to your indoor potted plants, and run a piece of wet string from the bottom of the water to each pot, burying the string in a few inches of soil. The string will deliver moisture to the soil as it dries.

Measure your waist

Or anything else that a ruler can't measure, for that matter. Then place the piece of string against a ruler (or yardstick) to determine the dimensions of your object.

toothpicks

Toothpicks are generally known for testing if a cake is done or playing a major role in a child's craft project. But these small sticks can do so much more. Let these little helpers help you in big ways.

A little lemon drop

Slicing a lemon in half to get a few drops of lemon juice for a dish just doesn't make sense. Get only the little bit you need by piercing the lemon rind with a toothpick and squeezing out a few drops. When you're done, tape over the hole and put the lemon back in the refrigerator to use again another day.

Nail bread to cake with toothpicks

Why, you ask? Because the part of the cake exposed to air—where it's been cut—can get stale quickly. If you attach a slice of bread to the exposed part with toothpicks, you'll protect the moist cake. The bread will get stale instead.

Tighten your glasses

The teeny tiny screwdrivers designed for glasses may be cute, but they're a waste of money. Tighten the screw that holds your frames together with a toothpick instead.

First aid for flowers

If your flower has a bent stem, tend to it using a toothpick as a splint. Stick the toothpick in the soil, then attach it to the stem with a loose circle of transparent tape.

Attach a slice of bread to the exposed part of a cut cake with toothpicks, and you'll protect the cake's moisture. The bread will get stale instead.

TAKING CARE OF THOSE CHOPPERS

THE HISTORY OF THE TOOTHPICK

Why would you buy something if you could make it yourself? This was a question that posed a challenge to Charles Forster, who began importing the picks from Brazil with the long-term goal of mass-producing them. Since people in New England were practical and could whittle, he had to rack his brain to find a way to create a large enough market for his venture to be profitable. Legend has it that **he found his answer in Harvard College students.**

The Union Oyster House, the oldest restaurant in Boston, had been open for business since 1826. Having been born in Charlestown, Massachusetts, Forster must have known the place well. **He paid for undergraduates to eat at this establishment**—but it wasn't truly a free lunch. After the students finished dining, they had to ask for a toothpick. And when they were told there were none available, they had to make a scene and express their outrage at being so deprived. The following day, per his master plan, **Forster would turn up offering to sell boxes of toothpicks.** The Union Oyster House may not have been born yesterday, but they bought toothpicks all the same. Today it recounts the whole experience fondly on its Web site.

Forster had shills repeat similar scenes in other restaurants. His wooden toothpicks soon became readily available as diners exited eating establishments, and **chewing them in public became fashionable.** After all, if you couldn't afford to eat at a restaurant, you could imply you were better off than you were by chewing a toothpick *outside* of the place.

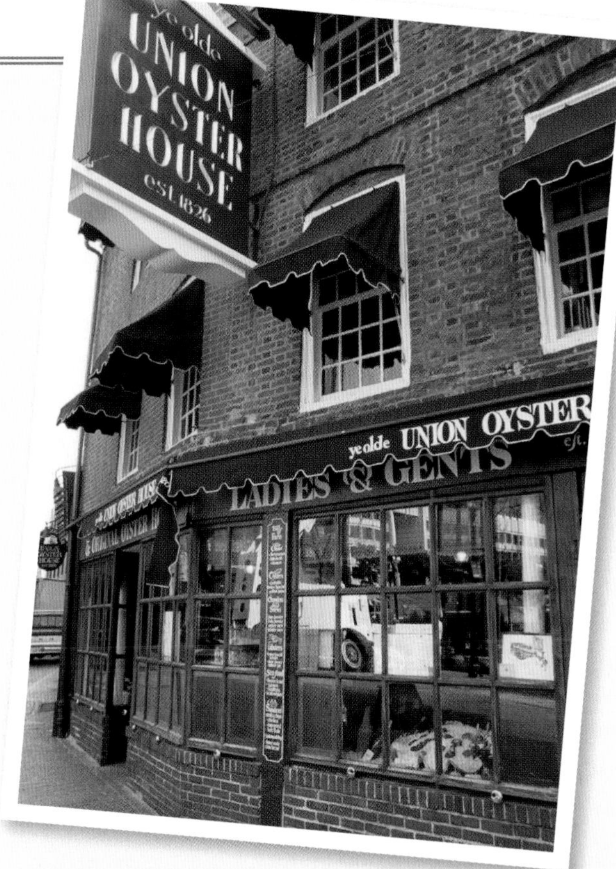

By 1870 Forster had a toothpick-making machine that was **capable of making millions of the little tooth cleaners a day.** As incredible as it seems, the toothpick he made then and the toothpicks we have now in the 21st century were quite alike: Both were made out of virgin white birch.

Until recently, the state of Maine manufactured 90 percent of this country's toothpicks, thanks largely to the enterprising Forster (who set up a factory there). Unfortunately, **"The Toothpick Capital of the World" made its last pick in 2003,** and now most are imported from China. Still, it is a happy event that they are still available in this world of floss. For we all get food stuck between our teeth in public, now and again. And many of us find ourselves politely stabbing tiny food on circulating platters at parties, especially around the holidays—where we may be asked, **"How many toothpicks can be made from a tree?"** An easy answer is, "It depends on the tree." If you want to prolong your conversation you can reveal that one cord of white birch wood can make 7.5 million toothpicks.

The toothpick test

Pretend your garden bed is a cake. How do you know if your cake has finished cooking? Insert a toothpick—if it comes out clean, it's done baking and ready to come out of the oven. Stick a toothpick in the soil of your garden, too, to see if it needs to be watered. If it comes out clean, it's ready to be watered. If it comes out with soil attached, you can wait and test it again the next day.

towels

Gone are the days when you only used a towel to dry yourself—or your dishes. You can use towels for your plants, your pants, a wine bottle, and more. Check them all out!

Use a towel to iron your pants

Metaphorically, anyway. If you have a wrinkled shirt but don't have access to an iron—but you do have access to a dryer—toss your shirt and a damp towel in the dryer. Run the dryer on air-dry for 10 or 15 minutes. Your shirt will be wrinkle-free and ready to wear.

WAX PAPER

Although wax paper may look like parchment paper, the two are quite different and not interchangeable—especially if you want to line cookie sheets. Wax paper is paper coated in wax. If you use it in a hot oven, the wax will melt. This will not add a desirable taste to your cookies. Parchment paper, on the other hand, is coated with silicone, is very heat resistant, and won't melt, stick, or add unwanted flavor. So don't get in a situation where you'll have to toss your cookies—keep wax paper out of the oven.

Keep your plants wet

Don't use towels to dry your plants—use them to water your plants the next time you go on vacation. Place already-watered, saucer-less plants on a damp towel in your sink or bathtub. Let cold tap water drip—and only drip—onto the towel. As long as you leave the water slowly dripping and as long as the pot's drain holes touch the towel, you'll return home to healthy, well-watered plants.

Don't whine about the wine bottle

Don't get discouraged if you can't get a cork out of your wine bottle. Instead, get a towel, soak it in hot water, and wrap it around the neck of the bottle. The neck of the glass bottle will expand slightly, and you'll be able to pull out the cork.

Ship packages with towels

Skip packing peanuts, bubble wrap, tissue paper, and newspaper the next time you ship a package. Instead, send an additional gift—towels! Use them to protect your cargo and fill the box so that the contents don't shift. The recipient will be happy to receive a package in one piece, and delighted to have packing material that she can use!

Support your back

Driving doesn't have to hurt your back, and it won't if you use a lower back support. Make your own with a towel and old panty hose. Fold a medium-size bath towel in half lengthwise, then roll it from one long end to the other. Cut the leg off a pair of stockings, and slide the towel in. Trim the stocking so it fits neatly around the towel. Place the support between the car seat and your lower back and drive away in comfort!

Speed dry your clothes

Say you're in a rush to get to a party but you need to wash your party outfit first. Run it through the washer, then put it in the dryer—with a few clean towels of a similar color. The towels will help speed up the drying process by absorbing the moisture.

wax paper

What's up with wax paper? It seems like it's not terribly handy around the house—can you name three ways to use it?—but it can surprise you with its worth. Here are a few alternate ways it can earn its keep.

Clean your radio antenna

Keep your car's radio antenna working like a dream by rubbing its length with wax paper. It will help repel dirt and grime, and the antenna will glide up and down with ease.

Keep your fridge clean

Cut a piece of wax paper to fit the bottom of the fruit and vegetable drawers in your refrigerator. When the drawers get messy—and they will!—just pull out the sheet of wax paper and replace it with another. It's much easier than pulling out the bins to wash them.

Give your chrome a shine

Make your chrome bathroom fixtures sparkle by rubbing them with wax paper after you've cleaned them. The wax paper will keep them spot- and smudge-free for longer than usual.

Protect your cookie sheets

You may be careful to use plastic spatulas on your no-stick cookie sheets, but do you protect them as well when you store them? Place a sheet of wax paper between each cookie sheet when you put them away, and you'll keep them from getting scratched.

Stop struggling with corks

Wrap your wine bottle's cork with wax paper the next time you have a drink, then put it back in the bottle. The wax paper will prevent chips of cork from getting in your wine, and will make opening the bottle for your next drink easier.

Repair your iron

If your iron is coated with a nonstick substance but still sticks to your clothes and even stains them, call in wax paper reinforcements. Crumple some wax paper into a ball and rub it over the warm soleplate. Your iron will stop sticking and staining.

Help ice cube trays slide

Liberate your ice cube trays from the freezer—they get stuck easily—by lining the freezer shelf with wax paper.

Place a sheet of wax paper between each cookie sheet when you put them away so they don't get scratched.

AISLE 5

HOUSEWARES

DOLLAR STORES ARE A PARADISE FOR shoppers seeking housewares. From basters and buckets to candles and coat hangers, this is the place to look for those everyday, utilitarian items we all need to run our homes. And part of the pleasure of shopping at a dollar store, once you've stocked up on certain staples, is that you never know what you'll find. A selection of variously shaped bottle openers, perhaps? Ice cube trays in cheery colors? Bathtub appliqués that look like circus animals? Whatever you find there, you'll be able to find a wealth of uses for it with these tips and suggestions.

aluminum foil

It has been many years since aluminum foil was tinfoil and actually made from tin. It has also been many years since we could do without this indispensable workhorse of the kitchen.

Keep your oven clean

Why do fruit pies always bubble over? By the time your dessert is done, there's a blackened mess on the bottom of the oven, and you'd better remember to clean it off before you turn on the oven again. Or, you could just line the oven with foil and discard the whole mess.

Make temporary hair curlers

You daughter wants her hair in curls for her school play tomorrow but it's been ages since you last saw your curlers. No problem! Tear off strips of foil, fold them over, roll a damp lock of hair around each, and fold them over. By the time her hair dries, she'll have perfect ringlets. Curl the whole head, or make pincurls to frame her face.

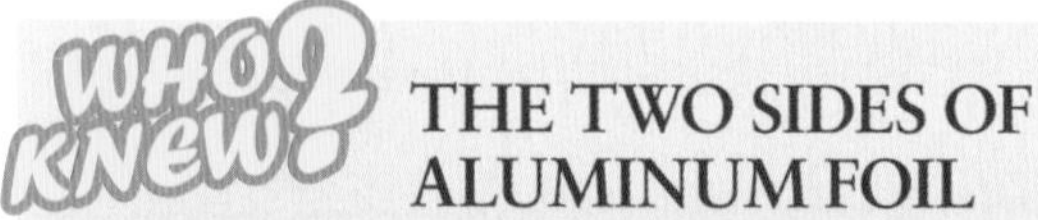

THE TWO SIDES OF ALUMINUM FOIL

The reason the two sides of your aluminum foil look different is a direct result of how the foil is made. During manufacturing, sheets of foil pass through giant polished rollers in layers; the side that contacts the rollers comes out shiny and the other side remains matte. The foil itself is made of aluminum—so why do so many people refer to it as "tinfoil"? It is a matter of habit: Household foil was made of tin until 1947. Some old habits are hard to break!!

Help soap last longer

Most of us let bars of soap melt away in water in the soap holder. Wrap a piece of foil around the bottom of the bar so when people swipe their wet hands against the top, the base won't end up in a puddle of water.

Cover stovetop drip pans

If you have removable drip pans beneath the heating elements on your stovetop, cover them in foil, shiny side up, to protect from drips. When they look dirty, discard and re-cover in clean foil. The shiny foil will also reflect heat when the elements are on.

Prepare a taco salad shell

Ball up a piece of foil on a baking sheet; the ball should be about 4 inches in diameter. Brush a large corn or flour tortilla lightly with olive oil and drape it over the ball. Bake at 350°F for about 10 minutes, until it's crisp. Cool and fill with your salad!

Make ironing more efficient

Lay a sheet of foil under your ironing board cover, shiny side up. It will reflect the heat back up, so you need fewer swipes to get your shirt smooth and wrinkle-free.

Wrap a gift

Use a sheet of foil, shiny side out, to wrap a present (ideally something in a box). Top with a sparkling metallic bow for a novel and arresting giftwrap.

Cut down on static cling

It's frustrating to find all your synthetic socks clinging for dear life to your pants and shirts when you remove them from the dryer. Reduce static in the dryer and avoiding peeling clothes apart by tossing a crumpled ball of foil in with the clothes.

Make a spare dustpan by simply cutting an aluminum pie pan in half.

Wrap a doorknob

Foil makes a tight seal to keep paint off doorknobs while you're painting. Press down the foil right up to the edge of the doorknob and its fitting, then run a utility knife around to make a neat edge you can paint right up to.

aluminum pie pan

You meant to make a homemade crust for that apple pie, but somehow you just ran out of time. No worry. With a readymade freezer crust, you get pie *and* a hugely useful item to have around the house.

Catch paint drips

No matter how carefully you think you wiped the edge after pouring, it's almost impossible to keep paint from dripping down the sides of a paint can. But keep an aluminum pie pan handy and set the can back down in it. It will still drip—but only into the pan!

Scoop up garbage

Why is there never a dust pan around when you need it? Make a spare by simply cutting an aluminum pie pan in half. The thin plate makes for a much sharper edge that will sit flat on the floor, letting you sweep even the finest crumbs right into the pan instead of underneath it.

Stack pies for storage

At the holidays, counter space can quickly get scarce with all the desserts arriving with visitors. Create some more room by turning one clean and empty pie pan upside-down atop a full pie pan. Now you can stack a second pie on that, then turn another pie pan upside-down to cover the stack.

Stop grease from spitting

Some brands of bacon "spit" hot grease when cooking more than others, no matter how carefully you fry. Protect yourself and the top of your stove by poking a few holes in the bottom of a pie pan, then turn it upside down over the spitting food. Use tongs to lift it when you're ready to flip the bacon, and discard (or recycle) the pan when you're done.

Tote dinner to a neighbor

If you share food with neighbors or friends who might be elderly or unwell, keep empty pie pans to serve as portable, disposable plates. Dish up the food as if it was a dinner plate, then cover with foil. It can go straight in the oven to reheat.

baster

Suction in the roast's juices to squeeze over the top or suction off the fat and discard—basters seem to be highly specific in their uses. If you think so, you might just be surprised at what else you can do with one.

Water hanging plants

Are you tired of pouring water down your arm when you're trying to reach a decorative plant hung high? Suck up water in a baster that you save for just this purpose and push the tip right into the soil. Squeeze gently—no more drips.

Clean an air conditioner

You can use your fish-tank cleaning baster for this job: If your AC is blowing musty air into the room, chances are the drain hole is clogged. Take off the front of the unit and use the baster to suck out any standing water you may see, then blow through the drain hole with the baster to clear the blockage.

Lower the level of coffee water

Half asleep while making the morning coffee and you overfilled the reservoir? Use a baster to suck out the excess, and soon you'll be happily brewing.

Make perfectly even cupcakes

Spooning batter into cupcake papers can be a messy job. Drips dot the pan, and woe to you if you spill a bit between the paper liner and the cup. And it's hard to get them all evenly filled, meaning some are short while others burst out like mushrooms. Use a baster to suck up the exact amount of batter and squeeze it into the paper liner with accuracy.

A no-spill way to handle paint

Pouring paint from a large can into a small one for touch-ups can be a messy job. Keep a dedicated baster as part of your paint supplies, and suction up the amount of paint you need. This also works for transferring paint to a roller tray. When you're done, rinse with water and let dry. You'll be able to use the same baster time and again for this job.

bathtub appliqués

While they might seem like an item from the past, people still have bathtubs, and dollar stores still sell the appliqués that make the floor of the tub less slippery. What you may not know is that you can do a whole lot more with them as well.

Make your slippers nonslip

Nearly broke your neck in a new pair of slippers or sandals? There's no need to throw them away. Cut pads out of the bottom of nonstick bathtub appliqués and apply them to the soles of your shoes. This is great for the slippery bottoms of a pair of kiddie "footie" pajamas.

Keep a sippy cup in place

A sippy cup banged down on a food tray wet with food has a good chance of hitting the floor. Cut a circle of bathtub appliqué to fit the bottom and stick it on. You've got a much better chance of Junior's juice staying on top of the tray.

Keep a baby comfortably in his high chair

Little ones wriggle and slip around in high chairs, especially when they first start sitting in them, and you can find your tot sliding down even if she's not trying to get out! Put a couple of appliqués on the seat of a high chair to keep baby from slipping around.

Make wading pools safer

Before you put water in that plastic baby pool, stick down a handful of bathtub appliqués so that little feet can get a better grip while they toddle around in the water.

Anchor your computer

Replace your computer's missing feet or add ones that you wish were there, by cutting out little circles of bathtub appliqués and applying them to the base of your laptop or keyboard. They don't need to be large to get the job done.

bottles and jugs

Whether you save old bottles and jugs and wash them out or buy specific sizes new at the dollar store, you can bet there are heaps of uses for them all.

Save on every flush

Even if you don't have a newer toilet that's designed to use less water, you can still live a little greener. Fill a clean, label-free 1-liter bottle with water and put it in the tank. You'll save water, and money, on each flush.

Design a string dispenser

Cut the bottom half off a 2-liter soda bottle and mount it upside down on the wall near your desk or kitchen—wherever you wrap packages or roasts or anything else that requires twine. Put a ball of string in the top so the end hangs down through the top of the bottle (which is now the bottom of your dispenser). You can easily pull out what you need, tangle-free.

Stay prepared for winter ice

Keep two gallon-size milk bottles full of grit, sand, or kitty litter in your car during the snowy season. If your wheels are ever caught spinning on ice or slush, you can pour the sand or grit in front of the tires to free your vehicle.

Make your freezer more efficient

A half-empty freezer is a freezer that's costing you more. Keeping it full of frozen items actually uses less electricity. If your freezer is on the empty side, fill in the empty spaces with plastic gallon jugs full of water (leave a few inches empty for the water to expand as it freezes). The freezer will run more efficiently, and you can also put one of these frozen jugs in a cooler as you pack a picnic.

Create a paint storage system

With a disposable funnel made from a soda bottle, pour leftover water-based paints into clean plastic milk jugs. Add a few marbles to the jug before screwing on the cap. When you need the paint again, you can shake the jug and the marbles will help mix the paint. Write the manufacturer, color name, and date directly on the jug with a permanent marker.

bottle openers

A simple bottle opener might seem like an unimportant item, unless you can't find yours! It's the only tool for that particular job. Fortunately, it does several other jobs as well.

Make a dedicated grill scraper

Grill brushes can easily wear down by the end of the season, but you can make a super-efficient one that will last and last with a church-key bottle opener and a metal file. File a notch in the flat end, and use it to scrape along each bar of the grill rack.

Make creative party favors

Make original and memorable party favors by customizing bottle openers for every guest. Use a hot glue gun to attach rhinestones or sequins, or paint designs (or names of the recipients) on each opener with brightly colored nail polish. String beads on a wire and loop it through the hole in the handle for added color.

Hull strawberries

The pointed end of a church-key opener is exactly the right size to hull strawberries. When you've been out picking berries and find that you need to clean a couple quarts of them fast to make jam, use the church key to nip out the leafy top without trimming off extra berry.

WAY BACK WHEN...

The Church Key Bottle Opener

Bottle openers became a necessity after William Painter invented a cap with a cork lining to seal beer bottles in the early 1900s. With one flat end and one pointed one, the brewing industry nicknamed bottle openers "church keys." It wasn't because the brewers believed opening their product was a gateway to a higher power, but because the gadget resembled ornate keys used to unlock heavy church doors. The cap also had a nickname—it was called a "crown" since it resembled the Queen of England's headgear.

buckets

A house can never have too many buckets. Big and small, dull metal or brightly colored plastic, they have endless uses—including some slightly more unusual ones.

Make a garden on your fire escape

No outdoor space in your apartment? Fill some brightly colored plastic buckets with some big stones, then pebbles, then potting soil and seeds or plants. You'll have enough of a drainage system from the rocks that you don't need to drill holes in the bottom.

Shower in the great outdoors

A large plastic bucket with holes punched in the bottom can serve as a shower when you're camping. Hang it from a sturdy branch, and fill with another bucket—ideally one you've left in the sun all day to warm up. Punching fewer holes means a slower drip but a longer shower!

Lock up your food

Bears are getting smarter and smarter at opening "bear-safe" food lockers at campsites. But there's still not a bear with the digital dexterity to open a sturdy 5-gallon plastic bucket with a tight-fitting lid, so it's a great way to store food on camping trips. The bucket also helps seal in the odors that summon bears to your campsite.

Store extension cords

However you wrap them, long extension cords are inclined to tangle. Coil them down into a bucket with a hole drilled in the side near the bottom to pull out the pronged end of the cord. The other end lifts out of the top, so you can pull out as much or as little as you need.

cans

You open a can of food, rinse out the can, and toss it into the recycling, right? Not so fast! Cans have so many special uses that you won't want to hurry to throw one away.

Stack it like a restaurant chef

If you remove the top and bottom of a clean tuna can, you're left with the same tool that high-end restaurant chefs use to "stack" food for beautiful presentations on the plate. Put the ring on a plate and make a mashed potato base topped by beef stew, for example, or put down washed mesclun mix and top with chicken or shrimp salad. Pull off the ring, and it's like you're dining in a fancy restaurant.

Poach eggs to perfection

That same tuna can ring can make perfectly round poached eggs. Bring a skillet of salted water to a boil and drop in three or four clean tuna "rings." Break an egg into each ring and your poached eggs will be beautifully even.

Plug a mouse hole

Old houses often have major holes in the floorboards or skirting that mice have gnawed over the decades. To really seal these up, you need metal, and a can lid is ideal. Carefully nail it over the hole (ideally from behind or underneath a carpet or rug) and your little visitors will be thoroughly foiled.

Lock table legs together

Remember back when you sat at the kiddie table at a family meal? More often than not, it was a couple of card tables stuck together. Make a kiddie table that's kiddie-proof by setting the adjacent legs of each table in empty cans. If those tables do move, they'll be in lockstep.

candles

It's always good to have a handful of candles on hand. Not only do they light the occasional pleasant meal, but they're good for emergencies when the lights go out. And with these tips, you can use them for other things, too.

Stop a saw from sticking

Here's a trick from professional carpenters' shops: When you're cutting wood, rub a candle over the saw blade. It will help it glide more easily through the wood. Reapply as often as needed.

Make sleds (and skis) slide faster

Rub the metal runners of the sled with a candle, and soon you'll be schussing down the hill at the head of the pack.

Fill a scratch

Got a hairline scratch in the surface of your dining room table or coffee table that resists all efforts to polish it out? Rub it with a white candle to fill the scratch, then buff to a shine with a soft, lint-free cloth.

Help a drawer slide smoothly

Kitchen drawer keeps sticking or squeaking? Remove the drawer and rub a candle all along the runners. The drawer will slide smoothly back into place.

Waterproof a postage stamp

When you use a marker to address a package, better hope it doesn't rain on your way to the post office. Marker can run at the slightest hint of moisture, and some ballpoints aren't much better. Waterproof your label by rubbing the writing with a white candle after you're done. The address will remain clear, and a stray shower won't disturb it.

cheesecloth

If you think a sheet of cheesecloth is little more than a flimsy dishtowel, you need to read these tips. You may soon find cheesecloth indispensable in your kitchen.

Create a fine-mesh strainer

Trying to clear a stock or drain yogurt to thicken it? Your regular colander won't do the job. Put a layer of cheesecloth in the bottom and you'll have a chef-worthy sieve.

Wrap bay leaves and herb sprigs

When a recipe calls for stewing a dish with several bay leaves or a sprig of fresh herbs such as rosemary or thyme or even whole cloves or allspice berries, you want to be able to fish out the stems or inedible bits with ease. Just wrap the herbs or spices in a small square of cheesecloth and tie with kitchen string. When you're done, remove and discard.

Avoid tiny items when vacuuming

A vacuum nozzle is a great way to clean up dust from the tops of bureaus or the edges of shelves, unless you sweep up earrings, marbles, or other tiny items. Fix a square of cheesecloth over the end of the nozzle with a strong rubber band and clean away! The cheesecloth filters out the items you don't want sucked up but lets the dust through.

Dry herbs for use all year

Drying herbs you grew yourself is such a romantic idea, until they're crumbling all over your kitchen. Wrap individual bouquets of the herbs you want to dry in cheesecloth and tie with kitchen string. Hang these upside down in a dry area such as the pantry. When you want to use some rosemary or thyme, untie the bag and take what you need.

coat hangers

Whether you get them free at the dry cleaner or buy them in bulk at the dollar store, coat hangers are endlessly useful for tasks other than just hanging coats.

Cultivate a window-box greenhouse

If you have a window box, you're halfway there. Bend several lengths of wire coat hanger into wide U shapes and insert each end on either side of the window box. Cover the wires with tough plastic, such as a storage bag you've cut for the purpose, and your seedlings will stay warm.

Make a bright mobile for a baby

Fit two white wire hangers together at 90-degree angles, twisting the hooks so they both point the same way, and secure them by wrapping ribbon around the hooks, overlapping it to cover the metal. Now you have the frame for a baby's mobile. Dangle pieces of brightly colored ribbon off the bottom and hang toys, such as tiny stuffed animals or shiny race cars, from the ribbon. Hang it well out of reach of the crib, where it can swing in a light breeze and enchant a little one.

Stopper a caulk tube

With a wire cutter, trim off a short piece of a metal hanger and twist it into a U-shape. When you're finished caulking a job, insert one end into the tip of the caulk tube. It will seal it completely, preventing leaks and preserving the rest of the tube unclogged for another job.

Unclog that drain

You know you dropped something down the sink or Junior tried to flush a toy or a washcloth got abruptly sucked down the bathtub drain. Don't panic. Untwist a wire hanger, keeping a small hook on one end, and probe the drain for the offending object. You might just loop it back up—and save yourself a fortune on a plumber!

coffee filters

The fine-textured, food-grade paper of the typical coffee filter makes it perfect for lots of things other than filtering coffee.

Make a disposable funnel

Need to pour something potentially messy, such as cooking oil, solvents, or motor oil? Avoid the cleanup by making a quick and effective funnel from a coffee filter. Snip off the bottom and fold it to fit the neck of the container you're pouring in. A filter has just enough stiffness to complete a speedy pouring job, and when you're done, no cleanup—just throw it away.

Keep the soil in the pot

Layers of rocks and pebbles let the water drip down in a potted plant, but over time, all that watering washes the soil down into the rocks, compacting it and washing it away out the drainage holes. Put that day off for a long time by putting down a layer of a couple of coffee filters before you pour in the potting soil. Water will filter through; dirt won't.

Apply shoe polish

Shoe polish can be a mess waiting to happen. Instead of risking stains when polish rags touch other items, simply apply the polish with a soft,

THE Story Behind... Melitta Coffee Filters

Amalie Auguste Melitta Bentz was living in Dresden, Germany, in the early 1900s. Thirty-five years old and busy raising children, she was displeased with the bitter grounds she tasted in her coffee each day. She was sure the metal and porcelain filters on the market could be improved—so she took a metal pot, punched holes in it, and lined it with paper taken from her son's notebook. Grounds-free coffee dripped out of the bottom. Benz took her invention to the Imperial Patent Office in Berlin. In June 1908, she was granted legal protection for her "filter top device with filtration paper." More than 100 years later, the German-based company manufactures its popular Melitta Coffee Filters in Clearwater, Florida, and at other factories around the world.

SAY CHEESE...

THE HISTORY OF CHEESE-CLOTH

Nobody really knows when the first cheese was made, but evidence of its existence has been found in Egyptian tombs dating back over 4,000 years. **What is known with certainty is that one tool necessary for making cheese is a piece of loose-woven cotton.** Cheesecloth, available in different weights and weaves, from light to heavy, loose to extra fine, has been used for straining excess liquid from cheeses-to-be for ages. Light but strong, it is an ideal fabric for this purpose because it does not fall apart when wet and does not transfer flavor to food with which it comes in contact. It has been used for generations in the kitchen for tasks such as straining stock and bundling herbs used to add flavor to dishes. As humble as it seems, this cloth has an interesting history outside the kitchen.

If you were visiting your dentist in the early 1900s, and serious mouth work was in your immediate future, your dentist would approach you with a metal device fitted with a piece of cheesecloth that had been dipped in chloroform. If that didn't cause you to flee the premises, the whole apparatus would be clamped over your nose and mouth, the soaked cloth would emit vapors, and you would drift off into another world. The dentist's office wasn't the only place where cheesecloth could transport one into another realm. **In Scotland in 1926, Helen Duncan began offering séances during which the dearly departed appeared as "ectoplasm."** Believers and skeptics alike described this manifestation as "a white substance" that emerged as if by magic from Duncan's mouth. Eventually, the London Spiritual Alliance investigated her, accused her of swallowing and regurgitating cheesecloth, and denounced her as a fraud. The authorities may have found her "cheesy" but Duncan had her supporters and continued to offer her services. In 1944, after several post-séance arrests, she became one of the last people to be tried under the Witchcraft Act of 1735.

A more uplifting use of cheesecloth is a modern one: **Underwriters Laboratories (UL) tests many electrical devices by wrapping them with cheesecloth.** Hazardous conditions (such as electrical surges) are simulated, and when the test is over, the cheesecloth is removed and inspected for burned or charred strands, which would indicate that sparks were emitted. To pass the test, the device can be destroyed—but it must not ignite the cheesecloth in any way.

From the spirit world to the kitchen, cheesecloth is an inexpensive kitchen staple that easily and inexpensively wraps its way into our lives.

basket-style filter (not a cone filter) and polish with a second, clean filter. Discard both after use.

Detail a car

The absorbent, lint-free paper of a soft pleated filter will get every last speck of dust and dirt off the dashboard and electronics in the interior.

Filter cooking oil

Those fritters were terrific at dinner, but now you've got a saucepan full of oil and floating bits of food. How to salvage it? Cool the oil and filter it through a coffee filter and you'll get every last bit of grit out. Use a second filter as a funnel, and put the oil back in the bottle. Live to fry another day!

Diffuse light for a photo

Avoid the harsh look of a flashbulb when taking closeup interior shots, especially of people's faces. Hold or tape a single thickness of a coffee filter over the flash. When you take the shot, you'll find that the faces will look more like a professional, softly glowing studio portrait, and not a police mug shot.

colanders

A bowl that won't hold water sounds totally useless. But call it a colander and you can do all sorts of things with it besides drain pasta!

Make a slow-drip watering system

If you've just planted delicate seedlings and need to water them, do this: Line a colander with one layer of coffee filters, place the colander right next to the seedlings, and pour in water to the top. It will drip through slowly, and your seedlings will be happy.

Keep bath toys fresh

When you gather up damp bath toys after a child's bathtime, storing them in a bucket or other container can quickly lead to mold. Gather them in a bright plastic colander, and they'll drip dry, remaining fresh bath after bath. During baths the colander itself is a great toy. It's equally at home in the sandbox.

Store grapes perfectly

Tucked away in a plastic bag, grapes will sag and mold quickly. But rinsed in a colander and stored uncovered in the colander in the refrigerator, they'll stay fresh longer, and they're right at hand, ready to eat.

Prep the pasta platter

Whether you're serving your pasta on a bowl or plate, you can serve it up piping hot with this simple trick. Put the serving dish in the sink and set the colander on top of it. When you drain the cooked pasta, the hot water pours right over the serving dish and heats it up. Pour off the water and wipe dry with a dishtowel before pouring on the pasta and sauce.

curtain rings

Metal curtain rings are especially useful when it comes to tasks other than hanging your shower curtain. Buy a pack and see for yourself.

Keep your keys nearby

Always fumbling in your bag for your keys? Loop a metal shower curtain ring through a fastener just inside your purse, such as the zipper on an inside pocket. When you put your keys away, open the shower curtain ring and slip on the keys. They'll be hanging just inside so you don't have to search around when you need them.

Improvise a baby lock

Special baby locks for cabinets can be expensive. Why spend all that money when your grandchild is only visiting for a few days? Keep busy little hands at bay temporarily with a metal shower curtain ring locked between the two handles of a lower cabinet. It might not keep a clever 2-year-old out forever, but it will give you time to get there first.

Organize your backpack

When camping or hiking, you can make extra space *outside* your backpack. Most metal shower curtain rings can hold just enough weight to make them useful for clipping a small flashlight or canteen to the outside of your pack. Hang items such as a pair of sneakers or leisure-time sandals on the outside and save valuable room inside.

dustpans

You've probably never given your dustpan a second thought. But if it wasn't there, you'd have problems! Keep it on hand for its basic job—and for all these other ones, too.

Make a scoop

A mini-dustpan, intended for quick cleanup jobs, can seem useless compared to the amount of kitchen floor you have to clean. But you're looking in the wrong place. A mini-dustpan is ideal for scooping cat litter or scattering salt on an icy sidewalk or spreading sawdust on a greasy garage floor.

Use to shovel sand

Headed out for a day by the waves? Pack a plastic dustpan for your little beachgoer. It's much more effective than those flimsy plastic shovels that usually come with beach sets.

Pick up toys by the shovelful

Ouch! No matter how good your little one is at cleaning up, there always seems to be a few sharp pieces of toy under your feet at the end of the day, whether it's plastic building blocks or doll furniture. Use a plastic dustpan to help gather it all up and put it in the toy bin.

flowerpots

A basic terra cotta flowerpot can do so much besides hold a plant. For many of these jobs, a decorative one will do the job very prettily.

Create a yarn dispenser

Some balls of yarn won't unspool smoothly when you're knitting, forcing you to stop every few rows and pull another length free. When you're faced with a stubborn ball of yarn, take out a clean flowerpot. Put the ball of yarn under the upturned pot and thread the end through the hole in the bottom. The weight of the pot holding it down lets the yarn pull free with ease.

Make an attractive container for kindling by putting a piece of duct tape over the hole in the bottom of a large clay flowerpot.

Line one pot with another

Turn a medium-size pot upside-down inside one of those large decorative pots and you can decrease the amount of soil you need to fill it, and thus decrease the weight—very helpful if you need to move it around or if it sits on a balcony.

Store kindling

Baskets for kindling are nice-looking, but they let dirt and dust from the kindling sift down onto your hearth. Make an equally attractive container by putting a piece of duct tape over the hole in the bottom of a large clay flowerpot, and store your kindling there. Nothing will sift out onto the hearth, and kindling and sticks will be readily at hand. Put a second large one on the other side of the fireplace and store logs there.

Give it a lift

Want to elevate a potted plant to give a space some height? Invert a taller pot and place the plant on top of it. Instant pedestal!

Make a drainage system

Even broken, a clay flowerpot has its uses. Use the shards to line the bottom of other flowerpots instead of stones and pebbles. They're lighter weight than rocks and naturally drain well.

funnels

Big, small, metal, or plastic—there's a huge variety of funnel types and a huge amount of things you can do with them.

Separate eggs with ease

It can be tricky to separate the whites from the yolks, and that foolproof trick—breaking it into your hands—is a big mess. Try this: Break the egg into a funnel. The whites will trickle out the bottom and you can pour the yolk into a bowl or cup.

Make a funnel phone

Despite the wonders of modern technology, kids still love a string telephone. Run a length of string up the bottom of each of two funnels, and tie each end firmly to a large button to hold the string in place. Instant funnel phone! Remind kids that the trick to a string phone is to pull the string tight between the rooms before talking into the funnel.

Dispense string

A plastic funnel makes a terrific dispenser for kitchen string. Nail or screw it to the wall and drop the ball of string in it with the end hanging down through the funnel. String is at hand whenever you need it, for tying up roasts or packages—or making funnel phones.

ice cream scoops

While ice cream scoops might seem designed to do one job and one alone, in fact they're great for a wealth of tasks.

Scoop potting soil

Once you move a plant to its new pot home, it's hard to top it off with dirt without spilling all over. A plastic ice cream scoop that you keep dedicated to gardening is ideal for putting dollops of soil all around the roots before patting it smooth.

Make a seed planter

A mini-scoop is perfect for making holes when you're planting seeds in spring. You can make holes of an even depth, sprinkle in the seeds, and cover back up with the scoop of dirt in your hand.

Shape butter

Patting softened butter into molds seems like such a throwback to the days when ladies had nothing to do but lunch. Nonetheless, shaped butter really *is* cute on a holiday dinner table. Use mini-scoops or melon ballers to make small rounds of butter to put on individual bread plates, or use a larger scoop to make an even round for a central butter dish.

Keep cookies round

Love those large, perfectly round chocolate chip cookies you get in bakeries? If you've always wondered how they get them so perfect, the answer is a full-size ice cream scoop. And you can do it too! Scoop up a level portion of dough and plop it down on your baking sheet, leaving several inches between each scoop so the cookies can spread.

Shape meatballs

Homemade meatballs are a treat but the task of rolling and browning can make you hesitate to start. Put meatballs back in your repertoire with the super-easy scoop method. Use a small scoop to put balls of the meat mixture right onto a baking sheet, and then brown them in a 350 degree oven for 15 minutes before adding them to your sauce. You skip rolling and the mess of pan-browning in several batches, which you may find is well worth the tradeoff of having a meatball that's flat on one side.

Make melon balls

There's no reason why melon balls (traditionally made with a melon baller, which is really just a miniature ice cream scoop) have to be tiny. A delightful way to enjoy watermelon is in balls, so use a standard ice cream scoop instead.

THE Story Behind...

The Ice Cream Scoop

Although the history of ice cream in America dates back to at least 1744, the first one-handed ice cream scoop wasn't invented until 1894, when Edson Clemant Baugham of Topeka, Kansas, patented a one-handed ice cream scoop. A spring rotated a scraper inside the bowl when the handle was squeezed. It was manufactured by the Kingery Company of Cincinnati and marketed as Kingery's Rapid Ice Cream Disher. A mere three years later, another man, Alfred L. Cralle, got a patent for his lever-operated, half-globed-shaped, ice cream scooper. Once one-handed scooping was discovered, there was no stopping people from finding ways to get at ice cream faster: Approximately 241 patents were taken out on scoops between 1878 and 1940. Some of them are quite collectible today, particularly those made in the 1940s. These have Bakelite handles and Art Deco carvings and are generally brightly colored. Ice cream itself will never be considered vintage, but a scooper like this is a fantastic way to decorate your kitchen, remember the past, ***and*** serve up something delicious with a hand to spare.

ice cube trays

All those neat and tidy little compartments in an ice cube tray must be good for something besides freezing water, right? Right. Read on for much, much more.

Freeze baby food

Any mom who has ever struggled to make homemade foods for her fussy little darling will know the value of this tip: Once you have gently steamed and carefully pureed that butternut squash, portion it out into ice cube trays and freeze. After it's frozen, pop the cubes into a ziplock plastic bag for storage. Not only does it make all your hard work go further, but the trays make the ideal portion size for baby's dinner.

Make flavored ice cubes

Tired of your cold drink getting diluted by melting ice? Make a tray of ice cubes out of whatever you're drinking, be it coffee, tea, lemonade, or anything else that's not fizzy.

Freeze leftover wine for cooking

Leftover glass of wine in the bottom of the bottle? Freeze it to add to a stew or sauce in weeks to come. When the cubes of red or white wine are solid, pop them out and store them in a plastic bag.

Have fresh herbs all winter

End of summer is approaching and you're going to miss plucking fresh parsley, sage, rosemary, and thyme in the garden. Chop the herbs coarsely and drop by tablespoon into the individual cubes of an ice cube tray. Top with a little water and freeze. When solid, pop them out into bags labeled with the herb's name. When you want to add "fresh" herbs to a dish, you have them at arm's reach. Plus, the freezer keeps them bright green.

jars

You can buy a huge range of different types of jars at the dollar store, from basic canning supplies to jars big and small for everything from storing flour to cutting cookies. You can do a lot more with them, too.

Bake big cookies

Want great big cookies like grandma used to make? Then you need her special cookie cutter. So use the wide mouth of a clean empty jar to cut out those cookies from your childhood.

Make a homemade piggy bank

Charity starts at home, they say. Let it start with a piggy bank that you and your child or grandchild can make together. Put the jar lid on a work surface and hammer a flathead screwdriver tip against it to make a slit for coins. You can file the inside edges to make it safe and smooth. Then let your child decorate the jar with poster paints or permanent markers. Make it a regular thing to put coins and money inside—some for the child, some for your favorite charity. You can see through the glass when enough has been saved to take it back out!

Store flours and grains

The best way to keep flours and grains fresh as the day you bought them is to decant them from their store packaging into jars. Place them in the refrigerator to keep them for up to six months.

Make a mini-terrarium

In a large mason jar, place about half a cup of potting soil. Using a skewer, make holes in the soil and carefully drop in seeds. Water, place in a sunny spot, and voila!

Organize a workbench

Large glass jars, such as pickle jars, are ideal for organizing the bits and pieces that clutter a workbench. Screw the metal lids directly to the underside of a wooden shelf, then fill the jars with nails, screws, bolts, washers—whatever is making your mess—and then turn the jar right into its lid. It's out of your way and your items are plainly visible.

Catch drips

Many condiments, such as honey and soy sauce, drip down the outside of the bottle after use, leaving sticky rings on your kitchen table and in your cupboards. Prevent the mess by storing the bottle in an upturned plastic or metal jar lid, both on the table and in the cabinet. The lid will catch and hold the stains, leaving the underside clean and un-sticky for storage.

jar lids

Jars are so incredibly useful that even the lids are indispensable. With the spares that you're not using to top a jar, try some of these tricks around the house.

Keep counters clean

A large metal jar lid is an ideal spoon rest. As you occasionally stir that simmering spaghetti sauce all afternoon, set the red-coated spoon down into the upturned jar lid. You won't get hard-to-scrub dried stains all over the countertop, and you can toss the lid into the dishwasher with everything else.

Organize earrings and pins

If you tend to take off your jewelry and toss it on the dresser top, you need a handful of metal jar lids. Put earrings in one, rings in another, pins and brooches in a third. No more fumbling for your favorites in the morning.

Protect tabletops

Even the best-intentioned family member can't help putting that sweating glass of ice tea down on your wood surfaces now and then. Remind them that you prefer no white rings on the tabletops by leaving out a few coasters, ready to use. Glue rounds of felt to the inside and outside of an attractive large metal jar lid, and keep one or two of these in potential trouble spots.

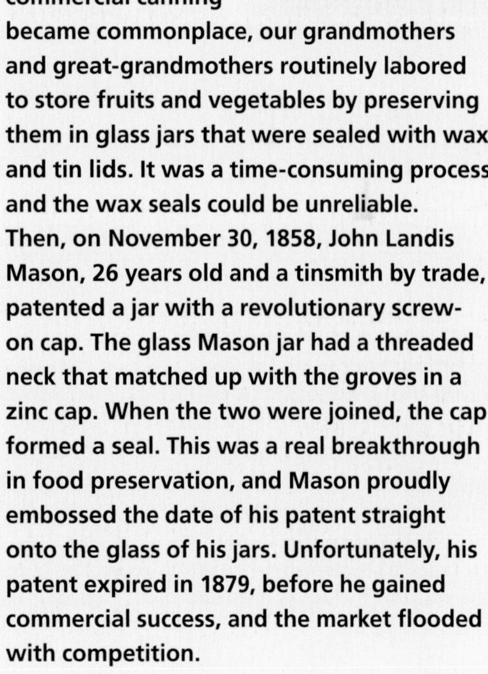

WAY BACK WHEN...

The Invention of the Mason Jar

Before refrigeration and commercial canning became commonplace, our grandmothers and great-grandmothers routinely labored to store fruits and vegetables by preserving them in glass jars that were sealed with wax and tin lids. It was a time-consuming process, and the wax seals could be unreliable. Then, on November 30, 1858, John Landis Mason, 26 years old and a tinsmith by trade, patented a jar with a revolutionary screw-on cap. The glass Mason jar had a threaded neck that matched up with the groves in a zinc cap. When the two were joined, the cap formed a seal. This was a real breakthrough in food preservation, and Mason proudly embossed the date of his patent straight onto the glass of his jars. Unfortunately, his patent expired in 1879, before he gained commercial success, and the market flooded with competition.

10 Nontraditional Ways to Use ICE CUBE TRAYS

1 Start Your Garden

Put some soil in each compartment of the tray, plant seeds, and get your season started early with indoor sprouting!

2 Treats for Tots

Ice cube trays make an excellent mold for Jell-O cubes. Make several trays, each a different flavor, and mix them together for a fun presentation of "finger foods" that kids will love.

3 Pair Up!

Searching for an earring is not the way to start your morning. Keep an ice cube tray (or two) in your top drawer and you have the perfect place to store earrings together. The trays can hold a dozen pairs and they stack nicely.

4 Egg Whites in a Hurry

Want to save time on your morning routine and still maintain your diet? On the weekend, crack some eggs and pour the whites into an ice cube tray. When frozen, pop them into a freezer-proof container. You can grab egg whites out of the freezer without having to crack a single egg—a great time-saver for your weekday morning rush!

5 Improve Canine Table Manners

If you have a toy breed of dog that eats so fast that indigestion is a problem, an ice cube tray can be a dog's best friend. Simply distribute your pet's normal portion of food between the empty cube holders. Your pooch will have to slow down to get at the food. It will take longer to finish the meal and this will aid in digestion.

6 Real Fruit Snacks

Try this for a delicious, healthy snack: Fill an ice cube tray with springwater and drop one seedless grape into each cube. Frozen grapes are low-fat and taste great. You can also freeze summer berries this way, and if you don't want to eat them individually, fill several trays and then store the berries in freezer bags. You can make a smoothie whenever you have the urge to snack.

7 Sweeten Tea

Simple syrup is a delightful way to sweeten cooled, freshly brewed tea. Make some ahead of time so that you'll have it quickly at hand. Simple syrup is made of 2 parts sugar to 1 part water. To prepare, bring the water to a boil. Dissolve the sugar into the boiling water; once it has dissolved completely, remove the pan from heat and allow the mixture to cool. Then pour it into your ice cube tray and pop it in the freezer—thaw when needed or simply put the sweet cubes directly in your drink.

8 Astonish Unsuspecting Friends

To liven up a party, fill an ice cube tray with water, and allow it to come close to freezing. Then place a Mentos candy into the middle of each cube and allow for a complete freeze. Serve these ice cubes to a (good-natured) friend in a glass of cola. As the ice melts and the candy becomes exposed, the drink will suddenly foam over for no apparent reason!

9 More Delicious Edges

Do you have an old metal ice cube tray? Then you're in luck! Remove the metal divider from the tray and insert it into brownie dough before baking. You can bake with the divider in place, and when the brownies are done and cooled, pull it right out. You will have precut brownies, and each piece will have a delicious, crispy edge.

10 Now That's a Tomato

Why is it that recipes call for 1 or 2 tablespoons of tomato paste when you've just bought a whole can? Don't throw the extra away. Freeze it in an ice cube tray, then transfer to plastic bags and store it in your freezer for future use.

Cover a glass or bottle

Kids left half a glass of milk on the table after lunch? Can't find the cap for the salad dressing bottle? A jar lid is just the thing. Cover the glass and put it in the fridge, so that milk can be drunk for dinner, or seal off that bottle—the cap will turn up one of these days!

paper bags

In addition to being an overall test of general ability ("He couldn't write/act/find his way out of a paper bag"), the paper bag has other, more practical uses.

Blackout your windows

Unless you want to spend big money for blackout curtains, the lower priced versions rarely do the job completely. But as any parent of a very young child will tell you, well-darkened windows can be the difference between a baby who wakes up at the first rays of dawn, and one who slumbers till 8 in the morning! Whether you're the tired parent of a toddler or a nightshift worker who needs some daytime shut-eye, darken your windows by taping up brown paper bags slit open.

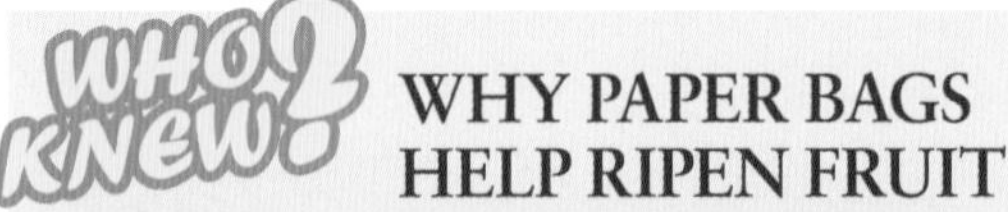

WHY PAPER BAGS HELP RIPEN FRUIT

Why does fruit ripen more quickly when stored in a loosely closed paper bag placed out of direct sunlight? The reason is simple: The bag helps contain ethylene, a gas fruit releases as it ripens. Ethylene triggers the creation of enzymes, which cause starches and acids in fruit to turn into sugar; they also break down cell walls, softening fruit. Paper trumps plastic, because plastic bags trap and condense too much moisture, causing spoilage. If you have unripe stone fruits and want to speed up the paper bag process just put an apple—which produces a lot of ethylene—in the bag along with your plums and peaches.

Wrap a gift

Homemade wrapping paper can be as precious to a grandparent's eye as what's inside. Cut open a large paper bag to lie flat, and let your child decorate it with markers, stickers, ribbon, paint, whatever you like. Then wrap the gift as usual and watch the recipient's eyes shine.

Microwave popcorn

Why spend money on pricey popcorn packs? Put 1/4 cup of kernels in a lunch-sized paper bag and fold the top down. Pop on high for a few minutes (it may take a couple of trial efforts to get it right) until you have fresh bag of fat-free, low-price popcorn.

Separate linens

Can't find the pillowcases that go with that sheet set? Avoid tearing apart the linen cupboard by storing the whole sheet set together in a paper bag after washing. The paper lets your linens "breathe" so they won't have the musty smell they can get from plastic storage, and you can even slip in a sachet or a dryer sheet so they smell sweet when you need them.

Clean up a wax spill

Tall tapers are lovely on the dinner table, but wax dripped on the tablecloth isn't quite so charming. Scrape off any excess, and then lay the wax-stained area over a heavy brown paper bag on the ironing board. Press the waxy area with a hot iron, melting the wax and transferring it to paper bag. Launder as usual to remove any remaining traces.

Contain a messy project

Cleaning a catch of crabs, peeling shrimp, or perhaps coring heaps of apples? Cut open a large paper bag and cover your work surface. When you're done, you can gather together the whole messy pile, paper and all, to discard (or toss on the compost pile).

Line drawers

Heavy-duty brown paper grocery bags make ideal drawer liners, both in the kitchen and the bedroom. Brown paper bags are sturdy, hard-wearing, inexpensive, and absorbent, keeping damp and odors from foodstuffs or fabric. Cut the bags to fit and lay flat in drawers. The heavyweight paper will lie flat, no adhesive needed.

Keep mushrooms fresh

As soon as you bring home mushrooms from the store, whip them out of their plastic or foam packaging and put them in a paper bag in the fridge. This way, you can keep them up to a week without the mushrooms browning or growing those large unappetizing "gills" on the underside.

Dry herbs

Trim the plants by the base and store them upside down in paper bags. Seal the tops and let them sit undisturbed in a cool place to dry. The bags let the herbs gently breathe, avoiding mold and mildew as they dry. Once they're completely dry, pick off the leaves and store in glass or plastic to keep them pungent.

Keep ice off windshields

Snow is easy enough to sweep away but ice on windshields is a hassle. Avoid the problem with a paper bag. Open a large paper bag and lay it over the windshield, holding it in place with the wipers. In the morning, just lift it off. You'll have clear windows and be ready to go.

paper plates

Every cupboard seems to have a pack of paper plates, way up in the back, kept for those pizza nights or when you just can't face the dishes. Now you can move that package closer to the front of the shelf and start using it for other jobs.

Microwave mess-free bacon

Microwaved bacon leaves a greasy mess on the plate, even when cooked between sheets of paper towels. Put a paper towel on a paper plate, then lay on bacon slices in one layer and top with a final paper towel. When you're done, eat the bacon and throw the mess away.

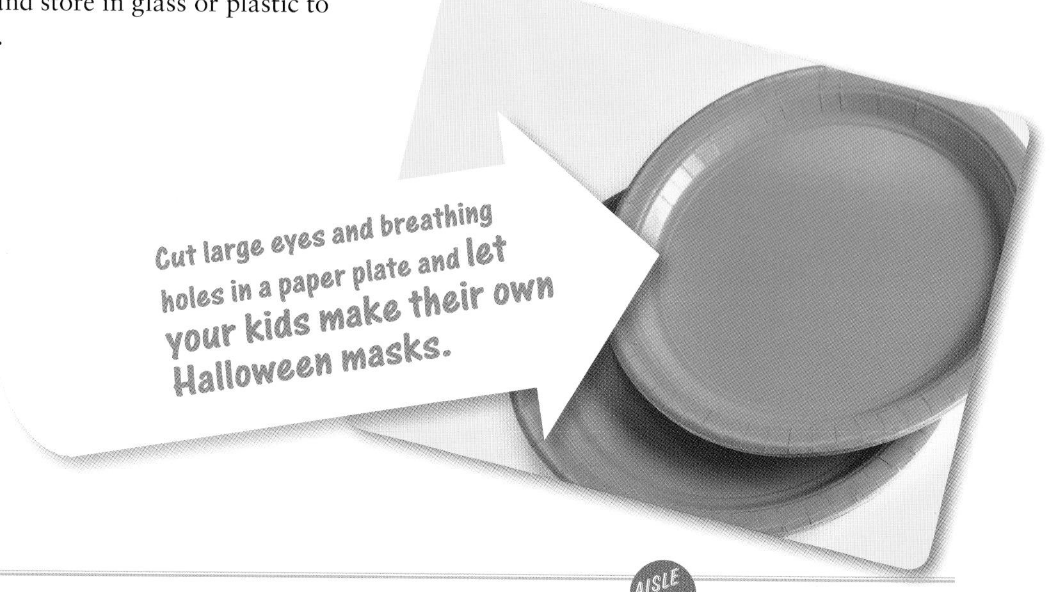
Cut large eyes and breathing holes in a paper plate and let your kids make their own Halloween masks.

Catch paint drips

A paper plate under an open can of paint will save a world of tears in spills and drips. As the paint drips down the side, the can will end up sticking to the plate. When you pick up the can to move it or to pour more paint into a roller tray, the plate will stay intact to prevent more drips when you set it back down.

Make kids' crafts

Kids stuck at home on a snow day? Give them a stack of paper plates, scissors, glue, and markers, and let their creative sides go nuts! Staple three together and trim around the middle and top plates to make snowmen. Put a handful of beans on one plate and staple another one on top, sealing the sides, for a tambourine.

Create a safe Halloween mask

Many parents worry about close-fitting plastic masks. Kids can't see well from odd-shaped eyeholes and they can't draw a deep breath through tiny mouth holes. Cut large eyes and breathing holes in a paper plate and let your kids make their own masks, scary or funny. They can glue on ribbons and feathers or make additions from construction paper.

Make crystal-clear stock

Even when you've poured off the solids from your homemade stock, you may find that it still has tiny bits of solids, not to mention a layer of fat. Clear your stock by pouring it into a fresh pot through a strainer lined with a paper towel. It will strain out any bits and a lot of the fat, too, for stock that's crystal clear.

De-grease a soup or stew

You're ready to eat but there's too much grease floating on top of your food. And it's too late to cool it down and wait for the fat to solidify. Remove excess grease by slowly dragging a paper towel over the surface. You want to soak up the grease, not the sauce. Discard the greasy towel and use another until the food is de-greased and ready to eat.

Remove the silks from corn

Once you peel the husks off fresh corn, the silks that remain can seem almost impossible to remove. Don't make yourself crazy picking them off one by one. Dampen a paper towel and wipe it along the length of the corncob. You'll find that the silk will pull off easily all down the length of the cob. Dampen a fresh paper towel if needed.

paper towels

You already knew that paper towels have a thousand uses in the kitchen every day, but here's a roll call of beyond-the-ordinary things to do with them.

Help thaw frozen bread

Before you freeze a loaf of bread, slide a paper towel between the loaf and the bag. When you thaw it, the ice crystals that have formed in the bag will melt and be absorbed by the paper towel, not the bread, leaving it dry and fresher-tasting, not soggy and freezer-burned.

pillowcases

Yep, just a plain cotton pillowcase. It keeps your pillow clean and makes a smooth, soft surface for sleeping. And it does dozens of other things, too.

Dry lettuce

Making a big salad for a large picnic? Nobody has time to wash and dry six heads of lettuce in a salad spinner—unless you have a really big spinner. Fill the sink with cold water, break up the lettuce heads, and wash all the leaves. Lift them into a clean cotton pillowcase, then take it out into the

Toss a clean pillowcase into your luggage the next time you travel, and you can shift dirty clothes into it each day.

backyard and spin your arm like a propeller. The water will fly in a big circle, and the pillowcase will get wet, but the lettuce leaves will be dry as a bone. Seriously, don't do this indoors.

Line a wicker basket

Why pay for fancy fabric-lined baskets when you can make your own. A pillowcase is the perfect size to line a small wicker wastebasket, ideal for holding items such as skeins of yarn, socks, or anything you like.

Make a dress for a little girl

If you have a pillowcase with an embroidered edge, you can make a darling dress for a child. Cut off the seam on the short end, and slit the side seams just enough to make armholes. Fold over the tops and make a deep hem. Thread with two lengths of ribbon to tie over the shoulders. You'll have perfect summer dress!

Cover a changing pad

The covers on baby's changing pads need washing frequently, which isn't surprising considering the use they get. Instead of investing in lots of pricey covers, slip a pillowcase over the pad, or even lay it flat on top. You can change it quickly as needed, and wash and dry with ease.

Travel with a laundry bag

Toss a clean pillowcase into your luggage the next time you travel, and you can shift dirty clothes into it each day, rather than having to pack them next to your clean clothes. Take another one to hold shoes, if you like, so you don't have to stack shoes directly on top of your shirts.

plastic bags

If you're just using plastic bags to line your garbage cans, you're missing out on a huge range of other things you could be doing with these versatile, inexpensive items.

Make a temporary mattress cover

Grandkids sleeping over or perhaps a family member is recovering from surgery? You can make a protective mattress cover for a few days by sliding a large plastic garbage bag over the mattress.

8 Nontraditional Ways to Use PLASTIC BAGS

1 The Cat's...Meow

Plastic bags make changing cat litter easier—dump the box into the bag and the bag into the trash.

2 Diaper Duty

Carry some bags when you're away from home with baby—they can contain soiled diapers.

3 Foot Protection

Considering shoes at a tag sale? They're not yours yet. Use plastic bags as a hygienic covering as you try on the footwear.

4 A Traveler's Tip

Use old plastic bags to stash your dirty clothes when you are traveling. This will keep your suitcase neater and smelling fresh. It also makes unpacking a breeze—carry your bags of dirty laundry straight to the washing machine.

5 You're Soaking in It!

Want a quickie mini-manicure? Coat your hands with a moisturizer and cover them with plastic bags for a quarter of an hour. The plastic will keep in your body's warmth, and your hands will emerge soft and smooth.

6 Bury Them!

If you have a large planter to fill, crumple plastic bags to fill the bottom of the container first (keep the drainage hole clear!). Then fill the rest of the planter with potting soil. The planter will be lighter and therefore easier to move.

7 It's a Wrap

Keep an eye out for colorful plastic bags. An unexpected way to wrap a gift is to triple or quadruple-bag a present—and then tie all the sets of plastic handles into a knot. Once everything is secured, cut the tops of the handle loops and fan the pieces out into a multicolored plume.

8 Ship 'Em Out!

Use the bags as packing material to ship fragile items. Stuff the box full to support the item enclosed, and your recipient will be grateful that you didn't use messy foam peanuts when she unwraps it with ease.

Make a garment bag

Need to protect a suit or dress for the season? Make a small slit in the middle of the bottom seam of a large plastic garbage bag and slide it down over the item on a hanger, letting the hanger's hook poke out through the slit. Leave the bottom of the bag open so the item can breathe.

Protect an antique vase

Love that vase from the antique store but you're not sure it's watertight? Don't risk it. Line the interior with a heavy-duty plastic bag, such as a ziplock bag, and fill it with water. After you add the flowers, push the top of the bag down below the rim of the vase so it's invisible.

Make steel wool last

One use and your piece of steel wool is already rusting by the sink. Keep it to scrub pots again and again by instantly sealing it in a ziplock sandwich bag after use. Shake out the water, then pop it in a bag and press out the air as you seal. No air, no rust.

Dispose of a holiday tree

There's nothing sadder after Christmas than dragging the dead holiday tree out the door, leaving a trail of sticky needles. Avoid the whole rigmarole by pulling a large plastic garbage bag over the tree from the top down. You'll have far fewer needles to vacuum.

Prepare crumbs easily

A ziplock bag is the ideal way to make crumbs neatly. Put cookies or graham crackers, cornflakes or dry bread, whatever you need, in a bag, seal it, and crush with your hands or a rolling pin. Store the extras in the same bag.

Tote an umbrella cover

Who wants to climb back in the car with a sopping umbrella dripping all over? Keep an appropriately sized plastic bag in the car and toss the umbrella in the bag as you climb in. You'll keep your seats and your floor mats dry and clean.

Keep a paintbrush wet

Time for lunch? Time to quit? Just because you're stopping a paint job for awhile doesn't mean you need to wash your brushes before the work is done. Wrap wet brushes tightly in a plastic bag and you can leave them overnight. If you want to stop for longer—say, several days or a week—stick the bag in the fridge.

plastic containers

There's an endless variety of plastic containers available at the dollar store, from tiny containers that could hold salad dressing in a lunch box to huge containers ready to transport a fleet of cupcakes. And somewhere within that variety is just the size you need for a home task that lets you think outside the (plastic) box.

Feed your dog on the road

A wide plastic container is an ideal dog dish for both food and water when you're traveling. They're lightweight and disposable. Take along a stack so you can toss one away or into the recycling bin when it gets dirty or worn.

Prevent ants on picnic tables

When you're having a picnic, ants are not invited to the party. Keep them from gate-crashing their way up the table legs by setting the picnic table legs into plastic containers. If you want to make doubly sure that no ants arrive, pour some water in the containers.

Give wasps the heave-ho

You can use a plastic container to make an extremely effective wasp trap that will keep your outdoor dining sting-free. Fill a small or medium plastic container with sugary water (3 parts water to 1 part sugar works well). Cut a hole in the lid and cover the container tightly. Wasps crawl in but can't crawl out.

Serve beer to slugs

Slugs love beer but it doesn't love them! Keep slugs off your plants by digging a hole in the garden and setting in a plastic container so that the rim is level with the ground. Fill with stale beer. If you like, you can put slices of potato around the rim to attract them. In the morning, you'll see slugs who have attended their last party.

plastic tablecloths

If you're decorating the room for a kid's birthday party, a plastic tablecloth is quick and makes for easy cleanup. But these inexpensive items can do much more than cover a table.

Collect leaves

You can get special leaf cloths, but why pay for such a specialty item when you can use a plastic tablecloth? Lay it next to the pile, rake the leaves onto it, and gather the edges to transport the leaves.

Dress up the bathroom

Can't find a shower curtain pattern you like? Look at the selection of plastic tablecloths, where you can find a wide variety of colors and patterns. Use a hole puncher to make 12 holes evenly spaced along the hem, 1/2 inch down from the edge. Loop shower curtain rings through the holes or use ribbon to tie it to the rod.

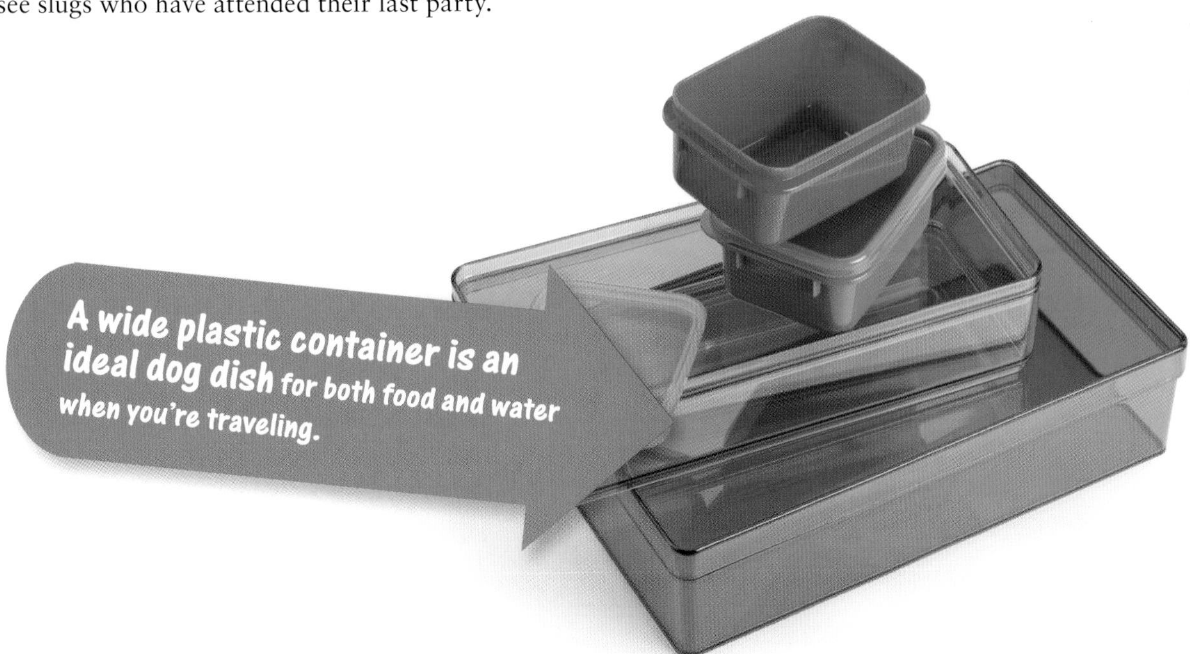

A wide plastic container is an ideal dog dish for both food and water when you're traveling.

THE Story Behind...

Saran Wrap

In 1933, Ralph Wiley, a lab worker employed by Dow Chemical, came across a vial used in experiments for developing a dry-cleaning product. The vial was covered in a film and had an offensive odor. Try as he might, he couldn't scrub the container clean. He dubbed the stuff "eonite," after an indestructible material in the comic strip *Little Orphan Annie*. The invincible substance was soon made into a greasy, dark green film, and renamed "Saran." The first practical use was military: Saran was sprayed on fighter planes to guard against salty seawater. Eventually Dow improved Saran's appearance (and odor), and by 1953 Saran Wrap was being marketed nationwide as the first cling wrap designed for household use.

Make a drop cloth

When you're done with using a plastic tablecloth for a meal, don't throw it away. Save it to serve as a painting drop cloth, or spread it under a toddler's high chair while she eats.

Upholster a vintage dining chair

Picked up a tag sale chair with a torn seat? Upholster it with a heavy-weight plastic tablecloth in a cool design. Remove the old seat, place it top down on the tablecloth, cut out the replacement plus 5 inches all around, and fasten with furniture staples. Fun, nifty, and easy to clean!

Have a picnic!

The very best picnic blankets aren't the plaid wool ones that we remember from our childhoods. Plastic tablecloths are absolutely perfect. They're easy to wash, inexpensive, and there's no reason to get upset when you accidentally dump your relish all over it.

plastic wrap

Besides covering food, plastic wrap is useful for some very surprising jobs *outside* the kitchen.

Protect your keyboard

Computer keyboards are like dirt magnets. Every bit of fluff that drifts by seems to get trapped between the keys. Make a simple and effective protector out of a sheet of plastic wrap. Cut it larger than the keyboard and tape it down loosely at the sides. Don't stretch it taut or you won't be able to push the keys. Replace as needed. It might feel funny till you get used to it, but if you spill a cup of coffee over your laptop, you'll be glad you had a protector on there.

Heat up a sports cream

When you spread a heating sports cream over aching muscles, you get relief for a short time, but the

Make a simple and effective protector for your keyboard out of a sheet of plastic wrap.
SARAN
Cling Plus
GREAT VALUE!
200 SQ FT

effectiveness often seems to cease before the pain is gone. Enhance the effect of a liniment by wrapping a sheet of plastic wrap around the affected area after you apply the cream. It will increase the heating effect and treat the pain better. (This treatment is so effective that you may want to test it on a small patch of skin to make sure it doesn't burn you.)

Keep a cast or a bandage dry

Don't fumble with plastic bags when you need to keep a cast or large bandage dry. Wrap the limb or area with plastic wrap, circling high above and below the area to protect. You can pull the wrap tight to keep water out during a brief shower, then dry the skin on either side and remove the plastic wrap quickly.

Roll up a (plastic) rope

Need a length of sturdy twine for a household job? Trying to tie up a package or box? Don't look further than the kitchen. You can pull out a long piece of plastic wrap and twist it into an extremely strong and flexible rope.

Seal a drafty window

Are winter winds blowing in a small window in your basement? Lots of heat can be lost that way. Food wrap is thinner than industrial plastic window sealers, but in a pinch, you can use three or four layers of food-grade plastic wrap to seal a drafty window. Tape it firmly to the sides with duct tape.

Popsicle sticks

Tongue depressors, Popsicle sticks, craft sticks, little wooden thingies—whatever you want to call them, craft sticks are great for more than just doctors' offices and frozen treats.

Use for finger paints

Most kids adore the mess they get to make with finger paints, but more than a few actually don't like sticking their fingers in the cold wet stuff. There's no need for them to miss out on the fun. Give your picky young one a handful of Popsicle sticks and let him paint with them to his heart's content.

Label the garden

Seed packages on a stick look charming, but by the time the seedlings are coming up, the packages have faded and blown away. Avoid the confusion by writing the name of each plant in permanent marker on a craft stick and stick it in the ground at the end of the row.

Keep a record of your house paints

By the time you need to make a spot repair on the living room wall color, that paint color's name will have escaped you. When you finish a paint job, dip a craft stick into the color and when it dries, use a permanent marker to write the color name and the room where you used it. Keep these memory sticks in a safe place on your workbench.

Make a temporary splint

Got a broken finger? You'll need to go to the emergency room to be sure. But until you get there, hold the injured digit stable by laying it against a craft stick and wrapping it with gauze.

Steady a bookshelf

Is that bookshelf rocking a little unsteadily? No need to go to the hardware store for shims. Just use one of these!

Make skewers for kids

Got a picky toddler? Make food fun by skewering healthy bites on an easily grabbed craft stick. Pieces of chicken breast, chunks of fruit—with food on a stick, every meal becomes a game.

Pack an impromptu "spoon"

Sending along a container of yogurt or pudding in your kid's school lunch but you're out of plastic spoons? Grab a craft stick and toss it in the lunch box to serve as a handy utensil for eating creamy foods.

Give a kid his own "knife"

Little ones always want to do what the grownups are doing, but you're still not comfortable handing down a dinner knife. Instead, let kids spread their own jelly or peanut butter with a craft stick. It does the same job as a metal knife, and you can throw it away when they're done.

pots and pans

Dollar-store pans aren't always made to last forever. The metal can be thin or the nonstick finish may chip. But those lightweight metal pans can be ideal for some things.

Catch the drips from your grill

When you're grill-roasting a large piece of meat, you need to put a pan underneath to catch the dripping fat so it doesn't flame up. Instead of using and throwing away a disposable aluminum pan each time, keep a metal baking dish as your grill pan, and use it over and over.

Improvise a grill

Grills don't have to be huge, high-octane affairs with enough surface space to cook for a football team. Take a page from the Japanese, whose tiny hibachi grills are just big enough to cook supper for a small family. Build a charcoal fire in a large old pot and cook on a rack set over the top. When you're done, use the lid to smother the fire.

Make a big scoop

A small saucepan with a narrow rim and a single handle is an ideal scoop for scattering grass seed out of a big sack or sprinkling lime or fertilizer over your yard. If you've got a big dog, use one as a dog-food scoop.

Change your oil

A large pot is just the thing for draining your car's oil. Stick it under the drain plug, empty out the old, and put in the new. Use a funnel to pour the old oil into the empty containers for disposal.

Make a birdbath

Set a wide pan on top of an overturned flowerpot and partially fill it with water. Your feathered friends will hone in on it instantly for a quick bath on their way to visit your bird feeder.

saltshakers

Usually found next to the pepper, a saltshaker is such an ordinary household item that you may not have realized that you can do more with it than season food.

Apply colored sugar

Want to get an even layer of colored sugar on top of your cookies or cupcakes? Pour the sugar into a clean saltshaker. If you're making holiday cookies, fill as many shakers as you have colors.

Keep a dedicated cinnamon-sugar shaker

Some people actually buy shakers of premixed cinnamon and sugar at the store. Don't even consider it. Make your own blend, with as much or as little cinnamon as you like, and store it in a shaker near the toaster. Refill as needed.

Dust with flour

When you just need a little flour, such as a dusting on top of a pork chop you're about to sauté, a saltshaker makes a convenient and speedy distributor. Mark it clearly with a label so you don't accidentally dump flour in your clear soup, but keep it by the stove so you can add a few teaspoons to a sauce or dust a chicken breast.

Cut down on your sugar use

A little sugar in your coffee, a sprinkle on your cereal, a dab on top of sliced fruit—pretty soon all those little bits add up. If you're trying to cut down on sugar consumption, put the sugar in a saltshaker, not in a sugar bowl, and you'll automatically use less.

sandwich and freezer bags

Small plastic bags, whether ziplock-style or fold top, have a lot of uses besides keeping your sandwich fresh for lunchtime.

Pack cosmetics for travel

Even when you're not flying, it's useful to keep cosmetics in a small sealable bag. Toothpaste can squeeze out, shampoo bottles can leak. Put individual items in sandwich bags in your cosmetic kit or bag to prevent messy drips and leaks.

WAY BACK WHEN...

If the Baggie Fits, Wear It!

Once upon a time, homemade sandwiches were wrapped in waxed paper, but this changed in 1957 when the Mobil Corporation introduced Baggies. Made of plastic, they were marketed as keeping sandwiches fresher. They helped the household in other ways, too. Savvy mothers discovered Baggies indeed kept sandwiches from getting stale—but they were slippery as well. Putting one on a child's sock-covered foot made it easier to get little feet into rubber boots and ready to go out in the rain or snow! This added benefit decreased when the "flaps" were replaced by plastic "zippers" in the 1960s. One can still find the original style Baggies today—but the "zipper bags" seem to be more plentiful.

WORTH YOUR SALT

THE INVENTION OF TABLE SALT

Do you recall seeing a tiny bowl in your grandmother's breakfront? Something that looked like it was made to serve fairies? Chances are you are remembering a salt cellar or "open salt." Today, salt shakers are ubiquitous and can be found in every shape and size, inspiring dedicated collectors to gather all types from the tacky to the sublime—but this wasn't always so. When household salt came in the form of cakes or large granules, salt cellars graced our tables. They looked like small bowls, were generally made of glass or silver, and came with a tiny spoon.

Then, in 1911, a veritable salt revolution happened. **The Morton Salt Company, incorporated in 1910 and located in Chicago, added magnesium carbonate (an anti-caking agent) to its product, creating a table salt that flowed freely, even in humid weather.** Soon after, the company created its now-famous Morton Umbrella Girl and the slogan, "When it rains it pours." Today we recognize Morton's slogan, but perhaps not the degree of innovation it involved. Back in the day, people never expected to pour their salt because the crystals were impacted by the weather—on a rainy day, they clumped. When this happened, you could mash up the salt with your fingers—or that little spoon. But the idea of getting salt from a covered shaker out of little holes? Unthinkable!

On the subject of holes—there is often debate as to whether your salt or your pepper shaker should have the larger number. This isn't an issue if there is an "S" or a "P" on the shaker (or forming the holes) but if there isn't, some believe salt should get more holes because it is used more than pepper; others advocate fewer holes to reduce usage. As there is no rule, "to each their own" applies.

The additive that prevents Morton salt from clumping has since been changed to calcium silicate. But some things about salt haven't changed at all. Quick: What do you do when you knock over a salt shaker and cause a spill? Throw the salt over your left shoulder with your right hand, correct? Why do so many people do this? Why is spilling salt considered bad luck? **An overturned salt cellar is included in Leonardo Da Vinci's famous painting, The Last Supper.** It is in front of Judas Iscariot, which may have contributed to the widespread superstition against salt spillage. Also, there is a belief that the devil lurks over the left side of the body (while guardian angels hover on the right). **So tossing salt over your shoulder is akin to tossing it in the eyes of the devil, which could balance out your bad luck (spilling) with some good (blinding the devil).** It is interesting to consider which toppled distribution method would ultimately be more effective: the old-fashioned cellar, which would spill crystals, or the modern shaker and its pourable contents. Perhaps it is aim that matters most.

In any event, it seems that everything old can become new. These days it is popular to expand one's taste from table salt to more exotic varieties that come in rocks or flakes. With red and pink salt crystals commonplace on dinner tables and in restaurants, could the salt cellar be challenging the shaker and making a comeback? Perhaps. Will this impact salt and pepper collectors? Not likely. Those who collect the shakers rarely store condiments in them. In this instance, it is the package and not the contents that matter most!

Waterproof a youngster's shoe

Does your little one want to walk in every mud puddle? Keep the wet out with a plastic sandwich bag. Pull one on over each sock, then put the bagged feet in the shoes. Her shoes may not be dry when she gets home but her feet will be.

Pipe frosting

Want to write "Happy Birthday" on top of a cake? You don't have to have a special piping bag and different sized tips. Spoon the frosting into a ziplock bag and push the frosting into one corner. Seal the top, pressing out as much air as possible, then cut a tiny piece off that bottom corner where the icing is bunched. Gently squeeze, and you've got a perfect "round tip" piping bag. Cut a tiny hole first and try it. You can always cut it larger if need be.

Grease cake pans

Getting a pan thoroughly greased to stop a cake from sticking can be a messy job. Make it tidier by putting your hand in a sandwich bag and scooping up some shortening or butter. Grease away; your hand will stay clean.

Carry a damp washcloth

Carry a sealed ziplock bag with a clean wet washcloth in it. You can wipe a dirty face and hands before mealtime with no funny aftertaste.

Stash clean and dirty clothes

Heading out the door with a small child without a change of clothes is a mistake. Pack the fresh clothes in a ziplock bag, and, after whatever spill or accident, pack the damp or messy clothes in there for the trip home.

Use as a rubber glove

A sandwich bag or two makes an perfect hand covering in a pinch. Whether you're working on a messy project (peeling beets, anyone?) or you need to answer the phone while kneading bread dough, slip your hands into a pair of plastic bags and you can do the job with ease, then discard the bags.

shower curtains

A large sheet of lightweight but sturdy plastic might be just the thing to keep the water in the tub while you shower. Then again, it might be good for a whole lot more, too.

Make a picnic tablecloth

Going on a picnic? Don't forget to take a shower curtain. A clean shower curtain can either cover the tabletop or a bench at a public park, or it can serve as a waterproof blanket to keep you dry and comfortable when you eat on the grass.

Protect a tabletop

Worried about people putting hot or wet stuff down on your walnut dining tabletop? Sure that the grandkids will turn over their milk glasses? Sometimes a tablecloth just isn't enough. Lay a clean shower curtain on top of the table and then place your tablecloth over it. Nobody will ever know it's there, and you can dine in peace, no matter what gets knocked over.

Line kitchen cabinets

A new shower curtain makes a sturdy liner for kitchen shelves. It's waterproof and durable. Cut to fit, and glue or tack in place, folding the front edges under for a smooth finish.

Keep weeds out of a flowerbed

Put a piece of an old shower curtain, cut to fit, on your newly cultivated flower bed. Cut large X-shaped slits through it to set in your bedding plants. Top with more dirt, and cover up with mulch to hide any hint of that shower curtain.

straws

Kids already know that ordinary drinking straws contain a world of fun. Besides blowing bubbles into chocolate milk, kids will always find more uses when they're playing with straws. Now you can put straws to other uses as well!

Arrange flowers

You weren't paying attention when you trimmed that bunch of flowers and now you don't have any taller ones for contrast. Push a few stems down into straws, and hide those plastic stems in the middle of the bunch.

Create a protective mat

Lay eight drinking straws side by side, and hold them at the top with a heavy book. Use yarn to weave in and out, over one straw and under the next, circling at the end and weaving back the other side. Use the resulting mat under planters, preventing water stains on furniture. The mat will eventually flatten out under the plant, but it's easily replaced by a new mat!

Make a dropper for liquids

If you need to add a little liquid to something, such as a drop of milk in icing to get the texture right, use a straw in the liquid and then put your thumb over the end to lift out a tiny bit.

toothpicks

Some people treat a toothpick almost like a chewable mint when they leave a restaurant, keeping it in the corner of their mouth for hours. They know that it has a value beyond the one contained in its name. Update your supply of toothpicks at the dollar store, and you'll find more to do with them, too.

Clean in the cracks

Like auto detailers who clean around the radio dial with a cotton swap, a toothpick will let you "detail" areas in your house that are hard to clean. Dip the tip in a little rubbing alcohol and run it around the dials on your stove, the cracks in the phone, the lettering on your fridge—anywhere those fine lines accumulate dirt.

To use a straw as a dropper, put the straw in the liquid, then put your thumb over the end to lift out a tiny bit.

Light candles

A paper match always burns down before you can light more than one or two candles. Use a round wooden toothpick when you're lighting up a room with candles. It will burn long enough to light a lot of them.

Mark steaks or burgers

Why can't everyone just eat medium? Or rare? Or well-done? But people are different, and we all want our food the way we want it. So the next time you're on the grill doubling as a short-order cook, use toothpicks to mark which steak or burger is which. One toothpick means rare, two mean medium, three mean well-done. Everyone can pick up whatever they want.

Clean the gaskets on a gas stove

If your flame is running yellow, it means that your gaskets are probably stopped up. Turn off the gas, remove the grate, and clean each gasket by sticking a toothpick in it.

twist ties

When you don't want a twist tie, they're lying all over the countertops—off the bread, from the potato bag, off those apples. When you want a fresh one, don't go scrounging. Just lay in a fresh supply from the dollar store, and you'll have them for uses beyond the kitchen.

Rein in your electrical cords

The back of your desk looks like a spaghetti junction with all those cords and cables hanging down. Use twist ties to gather them together, tying off coils or bundling together long falls of cord. It will be tidier and far less dusty than a jungle-like tangle.

Find your house key

Does your ring full of similar keys get confusing when you need to open a door in a hurry? Use different colored twist ties through the holes to mark the keys you reach for most often: a green twist on the front door, a red one for the security lock. You can stop fumbling for the right key and go on inside.

Secure Christmas ornaments

If you don't want Fluffy the kitten to bat your precious ornaments all over the house, secure them to the branch with a twist tie.

vegetable peelers

Whether they're swivel peelers, or fixed, you can use your trusty kitchen companion for far more than just carrots.

Sharpen an eye or lip pencil

Can't find your makeup pencil sharpener? Don't put your eye and lip pencils into the kids' pencil sharpener lest you get a graphite pencil shaving on the tip of your cosmetics. Instead, use a clean vegetable peeler to shave off enough to turn on the color.

Make chocolate curls

Ever wonder how pastry chefs make those elegant, delicate curls of chocolate? The answer is in your drawer. Chill a chunk of chocolate in the refrigerator for 20 minutes, then run along the surface lightly with a vegetable peeler to make curls. Make them thin or thick; you'll get the hang of it quickly. Shave right over a cake or onto a plate, and arrange them on the cake as you like. Don't handle them too much or they'll melt.

Butter toast with cold butter

Your toast is hot but your butter is cold and hard. Never mind! Get out a vegetable peeler and shave off a few thin scrapes of butter right onto the hot toast. It will soften right up, and you can spread it with ease.

wax paper

Sandwich bags are handy, sure, but there's nothing like unwrapping a sandwich from a crisp and crinkly square of wax paper. While you eat, digest these other uses for this versatile wrapping.

Clean garden tools

Crumple up a sheet of waxed paper and rub it briskly over the work surfaces of your garden tools before storing them. You'll remove the dirt and add just enough lubrication to protect from rust.

Grease your shower rod

Not many of us pay attention to our shower curtain rod until it starts to get a bit rusty. If you have metal shower-curtain rings, they might start to squeal like failing brakes when you shoot back the curtain. And the plastic rings will stick and bunch, perhaps causing you to nearly tear down the curtain as you pull. Keep your shower rod running smoothly by bunching up a handful of wax paper and rubbing it along the length of the rod. The rings will run smoothly along the slightly waxed surface.

Clean a can opener

Whether manual or electric, a can opener's gears will eventually get gunked up with all the bits of food that can leach out as you open cans. Keep your can opener operating smoothly by running a sheet of wax paper through it as if you were opening a can. The wax will clean away any grime and coat the wheels to keep the opener running smoothly.

Cover a cutting board

Experts recommend that you keep two cutting boards, one for meats, one for fruits and vegetables. But if you don't have a second, you can still keep meat juices and their potential bacteria out of the pores of your board by covering it with several sheets of wax paper every time you cut meat. When you're done, bundle up all the paper and scraps and throw it away. You should still wash your board before you use it for veggies again, but the risk of cross-contamination drops significantly.

Make a pastry bag

Don't have a special bag and tips for piping frosting onto cakes? You don't need one. Pull out a big sheet of waxed paper and fold it in half for strength. Roll it into a cone and spoon frosting into the open end. Twist shut, pushing the frosting down to the tip. Snip off the end, always starting with a small cut that you can enlarge as needed, and start piping.

AISLE 6

NOTIONS

IF THE WORD "NOTIONS" CONJURES UP something your mother shopped for while you loitered, bored, in the aisles as a child, you obviously haven't visited the notions section in some time. In case you haven't hit a craft or sewing store in awhile, notions are those sorts of small, lightweight items that facilitate domestic comfort and harmony—needles, thread, ribbons, buttons. These days, however, notions can mean so much more, from a huge range of craft and scrapbooking materials to beads and rhinestones, fasteners, felt and fleece. The extent of how many notions a 99 cent store carries may vary, but you can always find something that will inspire you either to create something new—or use the item for something completely different from the manufacturer's intent!

adhesive fabric spray

Originally sold in the notions aisle as a fast way to secure a fallen hem until you could fix it with needle and thread, adhesive spray has terrific uses in virtually every room of the house.

Fix it quick!

Spray adhesive might be great for putting down appliqués on fabric, but it works just as well for making minor home repairs. Wallpaper curling in a corner of the dining room? Piece of linoleum peeling up in the kitchen? Border in the bathroom beginning to come unstuck? Spray the back of the paper or tile lightly with adhesive, then spray the wall or floor behind it. Let dry for a minute or two, then press down firmly, smoothing from the inside edge outward to remove any bubbles, and you've got a fix that may well be permanent.

Make storage boxes

For a fraction of what you'd pay for them in a specialty store, you can make stylish fabric-covered boxes good for storing anything from family photos to baby booties. Cut a square of fabric that's 1.5 inches larger than the box all the way around. Spray adhesive all over the base, and center the box on the fabric. Press to smooth and continue around the sides, spraying and smoothing on the fabric for a tight fit. Fold the ends as if gift-wrapping a present, then fold and spray-glue the top edges inside. Do the same with the lid, spray-gluing a piece of batting on top first, if you like, for a padded effect.

Design your own labels

If you've got spray adhesive and paper, there's no need to buy labels ever again. Whether you're identifying a storage box of summer clothes or putting your own logo on a jar of homemade jam, make up your labels on any kind of paper, whether you're printing straight off the computer or hand-tinting a piece of rag paper for a special gift of peach preserves, then cut the paper to size, spray lightly with adhesive, and apply.

baskets

Old-fashioned, lidded sewing baskets are perfect for holding more than just needle and thread. The trick is finding them! Once you do (and you may have to look in unusual places, like a tag sale or even your own attic), you're in for a multipurpose organizer that works everywhere.

Create a towel holder

Make it clear to guests that yes, indeed, those fresh towels really are meant for their use by placing a basketful of small folded towels right next to the sink when you're having a party or gathering. To underline the point, if you have enough guest towels, you can toss a used towel into a second basket farther away from the sink, which will invite others to do the same.

Make a small-stuff tool kit

A few small tools are needed over and over around the house—tape measures, screwdrivers, hammers, picture hangers and nails, duct tape. Rather than taking up kitchen space with a large and ungainly tool chest, make a tool basket of the little things you need repeatedly. Tuck drills and larger items away elsewhere while keeping a basket of the little stuff right on your pantry shelf.

Never lose your mittens

In wintertime, the whole family comes in the door and shucks off mittens, gloves, hats, earmuffs, and scarves. While boots and overcoats can go in their appropriate closet, the smaller items of cold-weather gear tend to pile up higgledy-piggledy.

Designate a particular basket to hold all those much-needed items, making it easier for everyone to find their own gear each morning and giving you a storage container ready to be put away when spring comes again.

Make a makeup kit

It's too hard to rummage through a messy makeup drawer in the bathroom or to unpack your whole makeup bag when you're looking for that tube of pink lipstick that must have fallen to the bottom. Keep makeup in a basket on the bathroom counter where you can readily find the items you need. Sort other toiletries into different baskets, as necessary, so your cotton balls and hair bands aren't jumbled cheek-by-jowl with your nail clippers and eyelash curlers.

Create a remote holder

A basket is a far, far better place than deep inside the sofa cushions to keep the endless jumble of remote controls that build up around the living room. Put them all in one place—a basket kept right on the coffee or side table, for example—and perhaps you can add that week's TV schedule.

Prep an after-school snack basket

Kids come home ravenous each day, and whether there's a cook in the kitchen or not, they love to rummage through the cabinets, sometimes leaving a trail of destruction in their wake. Head them off at the pass with a designated snack basket that puts everything in plain sight. Fill it with fruit and packages of granola bars or cookies, along with drink boxes, and perhaps a note reminding them that carrot sticks or kid-friendly yogurt and juices are just inside the door of the fridge.

Build a thank-you note station

Even in an Internet age, many of us still try to write thank-you notes by hand and send them via snail mail. Make it easy on yourself by keeping everything you need in one place. With note cards, envelopes, pens, and stamps, along with perhaps a few dried flowers or sequins to drop into the envelope just before sealing, you can dash off a thank-you (or a casual missive to brighten someone's day) the moment you think of it, rather than wishing, too many days later, that you had gotten that note in the mail.

Tote a table-setting caddy

It's hard enough to get food on the table every weeknight, much less remembering to set the table before dinner is ready. It's the same old task night after night, and whether you're doing it or asking the kids to do it, it's easier if you keep it all in one place. Put placemats, napkins, knives,

Wrap your hot water heater in batting, then surround it with heavy-duty foil, taping it down with duct tape.

forks, spoons, coasters, candles, or anything else that's a regular at your table in a basket that you keep in the kitchen or pantry just for the purpose of getting dinner on the table with ease.

batting and fiberfill

There are many more uses for this notions aisle standby then just providing cushioning on chairs and the like. All it takes is a little ingenuity!

Make a dog bed for a small pooch

Cut two equal circles of toweling or sturdy scrap fabric a little larger than the dog when it's curled up. Stitch a thick layer of batting between the circles. Sew a couple of layers of batting to the back of a soft towel or a contrasting piece of fabric. Roll this piece up into a soft border for the bed and hand stitch it around the round base to make a cozy, cuddly sleep spot for your favorite dog.

Quilt your windows to keep costs down

Tired of that winter draft blowing in through your windows? They need blankets! Use lengths of lightweight batting to line curtains. Making "window quilts" that keep in heat and keep out the cold will help cut fuel bills and make your house cozy in cold weather.

Wrap your water heater

A plushy roll of thick polyester batting can provide as much insulation as natural down, especially when combined with a reflector such as aluminum foil. Wrap your hot water heater in batting, then surround it with heavy-duty foil, taping it down with duct tape. It's a cheaper and safer alternative to fiberglass insulation.

Baby-proof your living room

Anxious parents and grandparents can spend hundreds of dollars buying specialized products to prevent little ones from falling against the sharp edges of coffee tables or railings around the home. But the need for this kind of protection only lasts a few short months. Instead, use heavyweight fiberfill to wrap the edges of sharp furniture while baby is learning to toddle.

Make a homemade oven mitt

Use batting and pieces of felt and toweling to make a custom set of oven mitts. Whether you need to replace your own worn-out mitts or create a great homemade gift, trim felt into squares and stitch on a thick layer of cotton batting. Cover with a smaller square of cotton terrycloth, and fold the felt over the edges of the terry, using a decorative zigzag stitch to finish.

WAY BACK WHEN...

What Was in Grandma's Quilt?

Long before quilters and sewers could just stroll out to their local five and dime or notions department to pick up a roll of batting, they stuffed their quilts with whatever was available: old rags, children's clothes that had been outgrown, even used oilcloth. Always looking for a way to use absolutely everything, country folk often cut apart flour sacks for use as quilting pieces. (The next time you find an antique quilt, look at it closely for the telltale signs: flour company logos!)

beading

Doesn't matter if they're big or small: Dime-store beads are good for far more than embellishing fabric. Start right here to learn more!

Make a key saver

Tired of losing your keys all the time? Make a keychain that will help them really stand out. Tie two 8-inch lengths of twine or leather strips to your existing key ring, so that the four ends dangle loose. Then string on the chunkiest, funkiest beads you can find and tie knots at the ends. Your keys will never again disappear into the clutter on the hall table!

Count your calories

Make a bracelet that will remind you not to casually eat three cookies just before dinner and help you keep on track with your favorite diet plan. If you're trying to keep your daily calorie limit to 1,500 calories, for example, string 15 beads on a length of string or a leather strip. In the middle of the strip, tie a single knot that's just big enough for you to push a bead across it. Tie the two ends together to make the bracelet just tight enough to slide on and off your wrist. First thing each morning, put your bracelet on. As you eat approximately 100 calories (a slice of bread, an apple, etc.), push a bead across the knot. When all your beads have migrated to the other side, you're done eating for the day.

Build a bookmark

Tie a knot at one end of a narrow ribbon and wrap cellophane tape tightly around the opposite end. String on a handful of colorful beads, pushing them all the way to the opposite end, and tie a knot just above the beads to hold them in place. Then tie a knot 3 or 4 inches above the taped end, string on a matching or complementary pattern of beads. Remove the tape and tie off that end, and you have a bookmark with ribbon to lie between the pages and beads to show the place.

THE MEANING OF BEADING

The history of beads dates back a whopping 40,000 years! The word "bead" comes from the Anglo words *bidden* (to pray) and *bede* (prayer). Traditionally, beads have been used through the ages for prayers, protection, worries, money, and adornment.

Decorate a box

Bring fresh life to an old jewelry box or knickknack by gluing beads in a meandering pattern all over the surface. You'll have a unique item that's as lovely and decorative as the jewelry inside.

Score your golf game

Can't keep track of how many strokes you hit on one hole? String together 10 small beads on as thick a cord as will pass through them, and knot the cord on both ends. Tie it onto your golf bag or attach it to your belt loop, and with every stroke, move one bead down. Tally your score at the end of each hole.

bias tape and binding

Designed to be used on the raw edge of any material, bias tape and binding is very strong, hence its use on the most stressed part of a garment. Here are some other uses for this lifesaver!

Preserve a quilt top

Is the filling all bunched and lumpy in the quilt your grandmother made? Picking apart, relining and re-quilting is a huge job. Instead, save and preserve a favorite old quilt by using seam rippers to carefully detach the backing and batting. Then stitch a suitably colored binding or bias tape all the way around the outer edges and use the resulting lightweight blanket as a bedspread or coverlet. Your bed covering will be good as new, and only you will know the trick!

Replace a drawstring

Bias tape is cut at a 45-degree angle to the cross-grain of a fabric, providing the maximum possible strength and support. Thus double-fold bias tape, which is less likely to fray since the edges are folded inside, can take the place of string or straps in lots of places. Use brightly colored cotton bias tape to bring new life to a frayed drawstring bag or backpack.

Play baby blanket bingo

Looking for something special and practical to give to a new mother or a mom-to-be? Buy a bright colored blanket (pink or blue!) and cut it into four or six squares. Bind the edges with a wide satin binding in a matching or contrasting color, as you prefer, and the new mom will have a blooming garden of baby blankets to keep in the car, under the stroller, in the diaper bag, near the rocker—anywhere she likes.

Get hung up

Bias tape's strength and range of finishes can make it better than ribbon for some decorative uses. Strong and narrow, it's ideal for hanging Christmas ornaments or serving as a hanging loop on a potholder or dishtowel. Sturdy (and inexpensive to replace), it's also great for looping through the handles of kitchen tools so you can hang that stirring spoon or spatula right by the stove.

buttons

Whatever shape or size—big, little, round, square—buttons are a basic notions department find and can run the gamut from plain to gorgeous. But don't keep them hidden—use them all over your house!

Keep a pot from scorching

If you've ever let a steamer or double-boiler dry and burn, you'll never want to let it happen again. A few metal buttons in the bottom of a pot of boiling water will start to rattle and clank loudly as the water gets low, serving as an alarm to remind you it's time to refill the water.

Stitch on sock puppet eyes

When you're trying to get some work done, give your favorite preschooler a couple of old wool or tube socks, a very large plastic needlepoint needle threaded with a length of yarn, and a selection of coat buttons. Little fingers can be surprisingly adept at stitching on the big buttons to make sock puppets—and the challenge of sewing like a grown-up keeps small hands occupied for a long time!

Replace a game piece

Lost a few checkers or backgammon pieces? The fun doesn't have to end. Replace with large plastic buttons and the game goes on. With the huge range of colors available, you can likely find a button the same color as your missing piece.

Metal buttons in the bottom of a double boiler can serve as an alarm to remind you it's time to refill the water.

Decorate a frame

Eye-catching buttons such as those with glittering or pearly finishes make a striking decoration when glued around an inexpensive picture frame. The only limitation is your imagination, so have fun.

Perk up a planter

Glue plastic buttons in a swirling pattern all over the exterior of a clay plant pot to make a hard-wearing surface that will brighten a patio or porch. Blooming flowers in the pot will be icing on the cake!

Make a curtain

If you come across a large cache of mixed buttons, you're in luck. String them on heavyweight thread or dental floss—or single-fold bias tape, if the buttons' openings are large enough—to make a gleaming garland that will fascinate children and adults alike. Drape it around a Christmas tree or over a doorway. If you have enough buttons, make several ropes and tack or tie them to a wooden dowel. Affix it the top of a doorway or in the kitchen window for a shimmering curtain of buttons that both catches the light and discourages flies and other insects from entering a room!

Dress up a vintage jacket

Have an old jacket that you just love but find, well, a little bit drab? Replace the buttons with some pretty ones, and everyone will stop you and say, "Nice buttons!"

clips, d-rings, and fasteners

Used to secure fabric in clothing, bedding, and more, these handy dandy items have a host of other uses throughout the home.

Tie back curtains

Attach two D-rings to one end of a fabric tube or a ribbon, then tack it to the edge of a window frame to make a distinctive curtain tieback that you can open and close with ease each day.

Close a backpack or messenger bag

If Junior has broken the buckle on his backpack, you can repair it by attaching a strip of webbing or ribbon to the backpack—one side to the flap, another to the bag. Then put a pair of D-rings on the piece attached to the bag and thread the other

A BUTTONED-UP HISTORY

EVERYONE'S FAVORITE CLOSURE

Clothing today often comes with a card attached along with the price tag. This card contains thread that matches the garment and an extra button. Admit it, you toss it away, don't you? What would you do with it? There was a time in the thrifty 19th century when this question had an obvious answer:

Every home had a button box. If a new garment needed buttons or a repair could be facilitated with just the right adornment, women would rummage through their button boxes to find the item that would do the trick. The button box has all but fallen out of favor these days, living only in our memories of visits to the homes of grandmothers or great aunts who were generous and allowed us to explore and play with their stashes.

The word "button" stems from the French *bouton* (bud) or *bouter* (to push). **It was the French who first established a Button Makers Guild, in 1250, and by the middle of the 1300s, France was the button capital of Europe.** The guild members created elaborate and expensive buttons and serviced only kings, queens, and the aristocracy. Buttons were status symbols for the rich, and this continued for centuries, with commoners being strictly limited, by law, as to the number and quality of buttons allowed to keep their clothing on their person. By the 1700s, tailors wanted in on the guild's lucrative action. They began making buttons out of little balls of thread. It was...well, revolutionary. It was also the first salvo in *la Guerre des Boutons*—the Button War. Button makers, wild with rage, convinced the government to impose strict fines on tailors audacious enough to produce thread buttons. The government obliged, but the guild was not satisfied—they also wanted the right to search people's homes to locate and destroy the subversive cloth buttons.

Near the end of the 1700s, Napoleon introduced sleeve buttons to discourage soldiers from wiping their noses on garments. This sartorial choice can still be seen on men's jackets today. Unlike the button box, it hasn't gone out of style.

The 18th century produced buttons that were works of art—exquisite painted buttons and buttons crafted from silver or carved from wood. Louis XVI, married to Marie Antoinette, sported buttons so extravagant they drew condemnation from philosophers.

Perhaps the most popular button in history was the black glass button made in response to Queen Victoria's use of black jet buttons—mourning buttons—following the death of her husband. These are lovely "gems" to discover in a forgotten button box. **Another place to find them would be on "charm strings"—unmarried women collected buttons on a string.** When one thousand were amassed, it was believed a man would claim the string's owner as his bride.

After the introduction of plastic at the turn of the 20th century, novelty buttons were the rage. During the Depression, plastic buttons were made with realistic, unexpected shapes. They were amusing and inexpensive—easily purchased in a five and dime. Children sorting through button boxes particularly loved this type of button. Who expects to find a tiger or a hamburger in a box of buttons?

Today we take the fasteners on our clothing for granted. But perhaps the button box—or the charm string—can be brought back into vogue. What is a button box, after all, but a box of memories? Of all the things a family has, memories are the least expensive to enjoy—and the most dear.

Grip a nail with a clothespin. This way you can hammer the nail and not your finger.

end through—no homework will get lost on the way to school this way!

Fashion a belt from scarves or ties

Any distinctive piece of fabric can become a stylish belt with the addition of a pair of D-rings. Vintage men's ties that you pick up at a consignment shop make a belt that the hippest college student would be proud to wear. Attach two D-rings at the narrow end of the tie and thread the whole tie through your pants loops. If the wide end of the tie is too big to thread through the D-rings to fasten it shut, you may need to trim the sides and stitch that end down a bit narrower.

Seal a special book

Glue one end of a wide ribbon to the inside back cover, then stitch on two D-rings just where the ribbon leaves the book. Then loop the ribbon around the back and over the front cover and catch the opposite end in the D-rings on the back.

Close a gaping tote bag

Tired of losing things out of that open-top beach tote? Use four pieces of ribbon—two on either side—and D-rings or any dollar-store clips to seal the top in a decidedly stylish manner.

Put a new strap on a purse

Stitch one D-ring on either side of a purse with frayed handles, and attach a length of chain, a fabric tube, or a strip of leather to either end to breathe fresh life into your old handbag.

clothespins

Invented to hang up damp laundry on a clothesline, these babies were designed by the Shakers and date back to the early part of the 18th century. Their uses are widespread around the home, even in the playroom!

Get your shoe closet in shape

If your method of storing shoes is to open closet, throw in shoe, you need clothespins. You can still use your favorite technique, but before you toss that shoe, clip it to its mate with a clothespin. It will speed up the search each morning.

Build a better bib

So many baby bibs are tiny little half circles, when what kids learning to eat need is a drop sheet. Make a broader bib for your little food thrower by wrapping a dish towel around your child and clipping it at the back of the neck with a clothespin.

Fill in the (bulb) blanks

When a bulb in your carefully planted bed doesn't bloom in spring, press a wood clothespin into the dirt above the spot. When it's time to plant new bulbs in fall, you'll know exactly where to replace one.

Save your thumb

Trying to fit a nail into a hard-to-reach place or at a funny angle? Grip the nail with a clothespin, and that way you can hammer the nail and not your finger.

Seal a snack bag

You don't need specialty clips or sealers to close your chip bag. Pop on a clothespin or two when you fold down the top to keep snacks fresh.

Pin up Christmas lights

Deck that holly bush with lights, but don't wind them around the stems to keep them in place. Clothespins are tough enough to survive the winds of winter. You can clip them to gutters, trees, anywhere you like, and they'll keep your lights in place all holiday season.

dyes

They started out life as a way to turn old clothes into "new" ones, especially during the Depression. But today, dyes can be used in a myriad of ways. Here are just a few!

Paint unfinished furniture

Get a highly distinctive look on a piece of unfinished wooden furniture by carefully painting on fabric dye with a foam brush. (It's best to wear gloves to protect your fingers from the dye.) Paint the whole item, a section at a time, always moving the brush in the direction of the wood grain, then use a soft rag to rub off any wet patches before

THE Story Behind... Rit Dye

We've all seen these little boxes of dye, yet if it weren't for Don Price, a smart marketer for Best Foods, this product may have "dyed" in the '60s.

During the Depression, a thrifty way to make old clothing (or drapes or sheets) seem new was to dye them with Rit. As the country got more prosperous, Rit Dye was falling off of shopping lists. Price (who already had a star brand called Hellman's Mayonnaise that was selling itself) decided to use his free time to save Rit Dye. He approached artists in New York's Greenwich Village, dazzled them with the array of colors available from Rit, and invited them to use the dye as they saw fit. What came of it? Tie-dye. The psychedelic clothing worn by revelers at Woodstock can be traced back to the staid little boxes of Rit Dye. Today thrift is back, and a Rit ad from 1967 says it all: "Something you own right now is waiting to come alive with Rit."

13 Nontraditional Ways to Use CLOTHESPINS

1 Make a Coupon Holder

Glue a magnet to a clothespin and hang it on the fridge door. As you clip coupons, stick them in the clothespin, and you'll always have them in one place.

2 Fasten a Dryer Sheet

Before turning the machine on, fasten a dryer sheet to a piece of clothing. When you remove the clothes, the dryer sheet is easily found and reused for another load.

3 Clip Your Keys to Your Purse

Run a clothespin through the O-ring and clip to the inside of your purse to keep from misplacing your keys.

4 Clip Your Book Where You Left Off

Use a clothespin instead of a bookmark.

5 Keep Your Skirt on Its Hanger

Clip the corners and that skirt will never slip off again.

6 Clip Outgoing Mail to Your Purse

Never forget to mail a letter when you head out the door.

7 Clip a Tarp

Help keep tarps in place on outdoor furniture by anchoring them with clothespins.

8 Clip Those Mittens

Attach mittens to your kids' coats so they don't go missing.

9 Close a Bag of Dog Food

Got a big bag of pet food in the pantry? Keep it fresh by clothes pinning it shut.

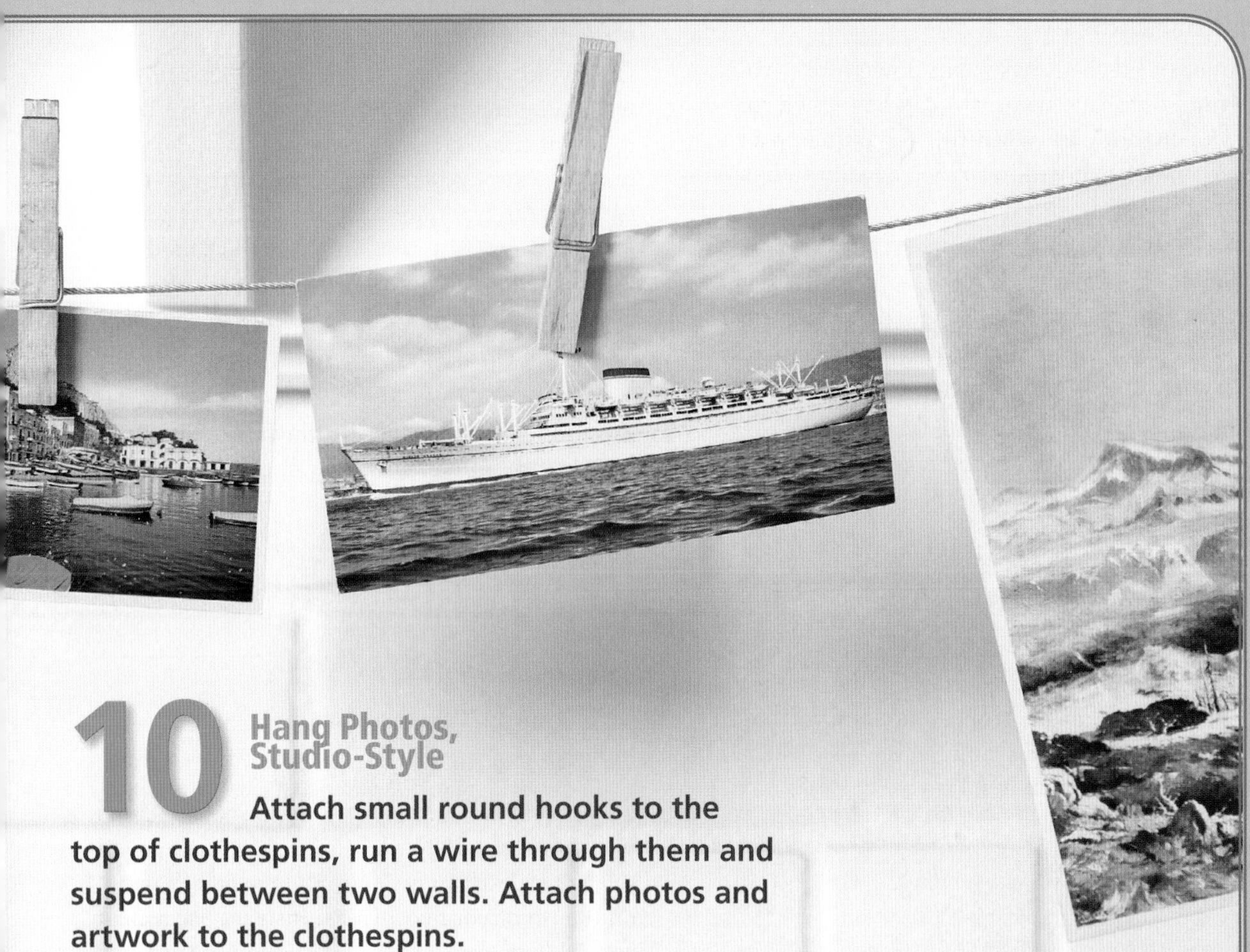

10 Hang Photos, Studio-Style

Attach small round hooks to the top of clothespins, run a wire through them and suspend between two walls. Attach photos and artwork to the clothespins.

11 Keep a Cookbook Open

Clip open the page, and the book won't shut while you're cooking.

12 Stand-in Barrette

If your hair is long and you're out of barrettes, just clip with a clothespin and keep hair out of your face.

13 Make a Car Seat Protector

Before you put Fido in the backseat, clip an old sheet in place, attaching it to side-hung seat belts.

beginning a new section. After the item dries, cover it with a few coats of a clear water-based finish.

Freshen up a slipcover

A small slipcover, such as for a chair or a loveseat, can be dyed in your washer if the slipcover is 100 percent cotton. Put the item in the washer, fill with hot water, and push the cover down until it's fully submerged. Follow package instructions to dissolve the appropriate amount of dye in the water, and then add it directly to the washer. Close the lid and allow it to agitate for a few moments before opening the lid and allowing it to sit for one hour. Allow the cycle to finish, and dry the item in the dryer.

Make custom tablecloths

Use a resist medium to paint figures or a design on a tablecloth border, then dye the fabric any shade you like to cast your masterpiece into beautiful relief. You can also mix a concentrated portion of dye and use a paintbrush to paint designs on placemats or a table runner. (Wear gloves and work on a well-protected surface with a thick covering of newsprint.)

elastic cord and tape

Elastic can be used to do everything from letting out trousers that have gotten a bit snug to attaching to the bottom of pants to keep them in place on a bike ride. What are some more uses?

Dress up a T-shirt

Cut off the hemmed neckline and sleeve edges of a dull, store-bought T and make it look like high couture by stitching fold-over elastic tape around the hems. Use a zigzag or straight stitch, whatever you prefer. Stitch the neckline flat, but you can gather the sleeves for an instant puffed sleeve.

Shape a bouquet

If your flowers—real or silk—keep falling over in the vase, use a length of elastic cord to shape and support them. Tie the bunch just under the rim of the vase where it will remain invisible to the eye as it keeps the flowers standing beautifully at attention.

Make a yoga band

A 24-inch strip of wide elastic tape serves perfectly as a yoga band for keeping your upper arms toned and stretched—and it costs a tiny fraction of what a yoga band will set you back at a sports store.

Bead a stretchy bracelet

Narrow elastic cord is perfect for letting kids make jewelry. Give them a handful of beads and several lengths of elastic, and they can make bracelets that easily slide on and off their wrists. It's also a fun project for a birthday party to let kids string round candy or mints with a hole in the center to make colorful edible bracelets.

embroidery hoops

Not so long ago, ladies would spend bucolic afternoons embroidering fabric that was held in place by a round, adjustable frame, which would stretch the fabric taut like a canvas. Well, you can still get those hoops, only now there's a lot more you can do with them!

Use them as frames

Use colorful plastic embroidery hoops just like you would a picture frame. You can showcase the piece of needlework you've just completed by trimming off the excess fabric and tying on a ribbon at the top for hanging, or you can fit the hoop over a picture your child has created on a piece of fabric with markers or fabric paint. Embroidery hoops can also frame paper, including wedding invitations and birth announcements. Fold and curve the paper's edges over the bottom loop of the hoop, then stretch it smooth with the enclosing top hoop and hang.

Create a Christmas ornament

Use the smallest size embroidery hoops to make personalized holiday ornaments. Hang them on your Christmas tree or make a garland of five small hoops over a doorway. Use your imagination to create a holiday series unique to your home. Use the hoops to showcase a series of patterned holiday-themed fabrics, such as a hoop with fabric showing bells, one with Christmas trees, and one with candy canes, for example, or you can create a holiday series of individual cross-stitch vignettes—perhaps a wreath, a candle, a reindeer, a gingerbread man, and a snowman.

Personalize a wall hanging

Put swatches of bright, eye-catching graphic fabric into a series of different sizes of embroidery hoops, from large to small, and hang them on the wall in a varied group. This is an excellent way to brighten a dark wall or decorate a nursery and also to highlight an exciting remnant of fabric that you couldn't resist buying. Craft hounds have a name for these beautiful groupings of embroidery hoop frames enclosing fabric with bold patterns: swatch portraits.

Make a door hanging

Stretch a piece of plain, light-colored fabric across a hoop and trim it close so no overhang shows in the front. Use fabric pens or glue to write and illustrate a message on it such as, "Welcome Home!" or "Let It Snow!" Decorate as you like by gluing on beads or buttons. Glue a length of lace trimming all around the front rim of the embroidery hoop and glue on a bow at the top, covering up the metal clasp. Use a pushpin to hang it on an interior door.

Hang up a kitchen towel

Paint an embroidery hoop a bright color. Tie a small piece of wire to the top of it and twist the ends, creating a loop. Hang the loop from a nail and a kitchen towel from the hoop.

fabric

They might be inexpensive remnants from a tag sale or on-sale bolts from the notions aisle. Either way, bits of fabric are perfect for many other uses, including these.

Make cloth napkins

Found a fabric remnant that you love, but it's too bright or the pattern is too busy for a dress or shirt? Cut it into 18-inch squares and hem them on all four sides, either with a machine or iron-on hemming tape, to make a stack of cloth napkins. They're good-looking, absorbent, and much greener to use than continually throwing away paper napkins. In some European countries, each family member ties his or her cloth dinner napkin in a distinctive knot and uses it for several days running.

Replace paper towels with clean rags

One way to go green in the kitchen with ease is to quit buying, using, and discarding paper towels. Cut up absorbent cotton, such as a T-shirt knit, into small squares and use them, unhemmed, for quick kitchen cleanups like spilled juice. Then throw these used kitchen rags into the wash. Save the paper towels only for the greasiest cleanups, such as draining cooked bacon.

Use cotton squares for mopping cloths

Those household mops and sweepers with disposable wipes fitted to the mop head seem like a great idea until you realize you have to buy replacement cloths over and over and over—they get expensive very quickly. Instead, cut absorbent cotton scraps into a suitable size replacement and use real fabric instead of those pricey store-bought replacements. To make a dry duster, spray the cloth with a bit of furniture polish. For wet mops, use a rectangular strip of terrycloth or toweling.

Clean your spectacles

Over time, tissues and paper towels can scratch the surface of your lenses when used to clean eyeglasses. Instead, cut 4-inch squares of soft, 100 percent cotton cloth. Store one in your eyeglasses case, one on your desk or by the bed—anywhere you might need to give your specs a rub. Gently polishing with these unhemmed squares, which can be easily replaced when soiled, will give your glasses longer life and give you a clearer field of vision!

FELT IS EVERYWHERE

Felt dates back to 6500 BC and is used everywhere from the automotive industry to children's storytelling (a felt board is a great way to tell a visual tale). It's also used on musical instruments. It wraps the bass drum and timpani mallets, and on drum cymbals, it protects the cymbals from cracking and ensures a clean sound. And those hammers on your piano? They're covered with felt!

Make a self-baster

Drape a square of cheesecloth over a turkey or chicken and drizzle it with melted butter before you put it in the oven. You may need to baste once more, but the absorbent cloth will keep the butter on top of the bird, not in the bottom of the pan. Before serving, peel off the cheesecloth and discard; the skin will stay in place.

Carry a coin purse

Tired of collecting change in big jars on the dresser? Start spending coins as you go instead of lugging them to the bank or rolling them. Make a small coin purse and seal it shut across the top with Velcro or snaps, then pull it out every time you make a purchase. No cashier minds waiting an extra second while you count out the change—and you'll likely find that the paper money goes a bit further when you eke it out with the coins.

felt

The oldest known fabric in the world, felt is created by matting, condensing, and pressing fibers together for a thick, dense result. It's used everywhere, from making children's toys to billiard tables. Here are a handful more uses!

Turn felt into a toy

Like paper dolls, but with felt! Turn felt scraps and a shoebox into a toy that kids will play with for hours. Use a pale color of felt such as light blue or beige to cover the lid of a heavy-duty plastic shoebox (a square-ish shoebox, such as those from a pair of boots, is ideal), tucking the ends under the inside of the box lid. Use different colored felt scraps to cut out shapes and figures that kids can stick to the felt board. Try a theme, such as "The Little Old Woman Who Lived in a Shoe," and cut out the old woman, a big brown shoe, and as many kids as you like, along with their pets and even mix-and-match clothes for each figure. Use markers for detail, or let kids decorate their felt figures themselves.

Stop wood floor scuffs forever

Use heavy-duty felt to cut out circles to fit under the feet of every piece of furniture you own that sits directly on a wooden floor. These protective pads, will prevent those inadvertent scratches and scrapes on wood that result from over-enthusiastic rising from an armchair.

Make an insole

Those new loafers were a terrific bargain, but they're a little loose around the heel. Pull out the insole and use it as a pattern to cut a layer of mid-weight felt the exact same size. Slide it into your shoe and return the insole over it. You may need one or two more layers to get comfortable. Real cotton felt won't make your feet sweat like synthetic liners, and your shoes will fit like a glove!

Top a table

Do you worry when guests set their hot cups on top of your grandmother's dining room table? A regular tablecloth can't protect the surface from the bangs of flatware and heat from dishes. Buy lightweight felt by the yard and use it to cover your tabletop completely. Then lay your tablecloth directly over the felt layer, for a smoothly padded, plushy surface that mimics the dining experience at the world's most expensive restaurants—and keeps your tabletop safe for generations to come!

Weather-strip windows and doors

Casement windows rattling in the wind? Wind whistling around an old wooden door? Cut strips of lightweight felt and use adhesive spray, double-sided tape, or glue to attach the felt to the jamb of the door or window. Use a neutral color such as beige, white, or gray—whatever matches your window or door frames most closely—or an appropriate contrast, such as dark-green strip against a mahogany door. When you pull the rattling parts shut, you'll get a snug, secure fit that keeps the heat in and the winter weather out.

Cut a bouquet that won't fade

Trim felt into a vibrant bouquet of flowers that will brighten your home year-round. Cut a simple flower shape, then trim two or three smaller ones and stitch them together, with the largest flower on the back. Finish them off with a bright button center, and attach them to a bamboo skewer for a stem.

Use heavy-duty felt to cut out circles to fit under the feet of every piece of furniture you own that sits directly on a wooden floor.

THE Story Behind...

Polarfleece

Polarfleece, the synthetic fabric that changed the way we dress for cold weather, was invented at Malden Mills in Lawrence, Massachusetts, in the late 1970s. The market was ripe for cold-weather clothing that was warmer, easier to care for, and less allergy-inducing than wool. Synthetic Polarfleece wicked moisture away from the body, it was warm, and it dried quickly—though it did pill after a few uses. Still, it was almost perfect. At about the same time, a company in Ventura, California, called Patagonia, was developing clothing for people who were serious about their outdoor sports. Malden Mills worked with Patagonia and improved its fabric to reduce pilling. Patagonia used the fabric in its clothing, and sales were fantastic. Today there are many makers of fleece, but the original fabric is now marketed in various forms under the name Polartec, the company which acquired Malden Mills.

fleece

Pound for pound, there is no other fabric as resilient or warm as manmade fleece (which is patterned after sheep's wool, which dates back thousands of years). The uses for fleece are endless and include the following.

Add absorbency

If you use cloth diapers for the baby in your life, putting one or two layers of fleece inside will add a lot of extra absorbency for nighttime or when you're going out. Cut the fleece into narrow rectangles to fit without adding a lot of extra bulk. Wash along with the diapers for repeated uses.

Make a comfy throw

With nothing but fleece, a few pins, and a pair of scissors, you can make a double-layer fleece blanket at lightning speed for a lovely handmade gift or to warm your own tootsies on a winter night. Cut two pieces of fleece to the same size—it's nice to use a solid color on one side and a complementary pattern on the other—and pin them together in several places to keep them from slipping while you work. Clip a fringe about 4 inches deep at 1-inch intervals all the way around the blanket. Tie the fringe together all the way around, remove the pins, and you're ready to snuggle.

Wrap up in a no-sew scarf

Cut a strip of fleece 12 inches wide and 3 to 4 feet long. Use scissors to trim each end into a fringe 3 inches long at 1/2-inch intervals. That's it—wrap it around your neck and hit the slopes!

Tempt Fifi with a fleecy toy

Your kitten or puppy will go nuts for a fleecy ball. Fleece is frequently sold in 60-inch widths. Cut four strips 1 inch wide and 60 inches long (if your fleece is 36 inches wide, cut seven or eight strips).

Hold one hand flat and wrap the fleece strips very loosely around your palm. Slide the ball of strips off your hand and tie it tightly around the center with a piece of string. Use scissors to cut through all the fleece loops on either side of the string and fluff them up into a big, soft round ball. Here, kitty!

Throw on a no-sew poncho

Perfect to keep a little girl toasty in cool weather, you can make a fleece poncho in less than an hour. Cut a 30-inch square of fleece, then fold it in half and cut a 5-inch slit from the very center for a neck hole. Open it and trim the edges all around into a fringe, as long or as short as you like. If you have time, you can string a bead on each strip of a narrow fringe and tie a knot in the bottom to hold the bead on. Voila! A stylish poncho in minutes.

liquid fray preventer

We've all had it happen: The edge of a favorite garment begins to fray and that shirt is history. But a little dab of fray preventer will help keep things where they're supposed to be. Even better? There are lots of uses for this miracle liquid. Here are just a few.

Stiffen a bow

Did you ever spend time tying a beautiful bow for a gift-wrapped package or holiday wreath only to watch the ribbon sag like an old balloon? A little fray preventer along the outer edge, once you've tied your bow to perfection, dries stiff and colorless and keeps it looking perfect throughout the holiday or until your gift is opened!

Repair a stuffed animal

If Junior's most beloved teddy starts to show wear at the seams, extend its life by stitching up any visible holes with a needle and thread, then anoint the joint with a few drops of fray preventer to toughen up the area. You might make the bear last long enough to get your little one to stop sucking that thumb!

Prevent button loss

Buttons always seem more likely to pop off a brand new shirt than an old one—the old ones have stood the test of time, while new ones are more likely to have been loosely stitched at the factory. Whether you've just finished a button repair or you're about to don a brand new shirt or cardigan, put one or two drops of fray preventer at the threads on the underside of each button to keep them locked firmly in place.

Appliqué any print

You can make your own appliqués by cutting out the picture from any type of printed fabric and stitching it directly onto the front of a pillow or the side of a backpack or bag without hemming the cut edges. Apply a thin band of liquid fray preventer all around the outside edge of the cut-out picture and you're done.

glue sticks

These familiar items started out life as a sewer's helper; place a little bit on a hem to use as a guide or to keep a hem taut, and then start sewing. Over time, they've found their way into school desks, but their uses go much further than that!

Wrap a gift

You've just squared the paper perfectly on the corner of a box you're gift-wrapping—but then you need two hands free to rip off a piece of tape. Instead, use a glue stick to secure the paper, and you have one hand to hold the paper down and one to apply the glue.

WAY BACK WHEN...

Elsie the Cow Meant More Than Milk

Before glue came in easy-to-use sticks, it came in a bottle. In 1947, Borden, primarily a food company with a charming bovine logo, Elsie the Cow, introduced the first consumer white glue under the name Cascorez Glue. It was packaged in glass bottles, and the company included wooden application sticks that attached to the bottle via rubber band. Hardly a "no-mess" experience, the glue caught on nevertheless and was repositioned under the name Elmer's Glue-All. The new logo was a bull—the "spouse" of Elsie. According to the corporate Web site, it is estimated that over 47 million elementary school students now use Elmer's Glue on a weekly basis.

Fold up an envelope

The handmade invitations for your spouse's birthday party are ready to go out, but it seems a shame to stick them in a white business envelope. Use colored paper and a glue stick to make your own envelopes—the glue stick holds immediately and doesn't need to dry like liquid glue, and it won't seep through and stick to the front of your invite.

"Pin" a seam

Use a swipe of a washable, water-soluble glue stick to hold together a simple seam instead of pinning it. Whether you're making a pillowcase or repairing the ripped edge of a shirt, it's far faster and easier to glue the edges together and stitch them up than to laboriously pin them first.

Make a wreath

Glue twists of brightly colored craft paper to a wreath shape to make seasonal decorations, whether you're using yellows, reds, and golds for autumn or pastels for spring. Push a pencil eraser down in the center of a square of paper and wrap the paper up tightly around the pencil, then use the pencil to press each twist of paper down as you glue it to a foam wreath or a flat wreath shape that you have cut out of a cardboard box. The base of each twist should be glued together closely, letting the ends of the twist bloom and curl around the wreath.

Secure a vase

Where there are animals and breakables, there is breakage. Rub the glue stick on the bottom of a vase and place it where you want it on display. If the table gets bumped, the vase will stay in place.

no-sew/iron-on hem tape

Ever step on your own pants leg and tear out a hem? This great product is designed to let you iron on a bit of special tape, with no muss or fuss. More uses? Absolutely.

Replace paper napkins

You bought that beautiful linen remnant with the idea of making some classy hem-stitched napkins, but the fabric sits and sits because you can never find the time to commit to that project. Don't drive yourself crazy—use iron-on hem tape instead to make napkins in a hurry. When making a set of napkins isn't such a laborious process, you can pick up other appealing fabric remnants and make a grab-bag of pretty napkins so your table is always set with something nice. (And it's greener than throwing away paper after every meal.)

Hem curtains

While iron-on hem tape is perfect for quick jobs like shortening a pair of pants you want to wear the next day, it's also acceptable for long-term jobs such as a hemming a set of curtains. Cut the curtains to length and iron in the self-stick hemming tape, using the hottest setting acceptable for the fabric. While hem tape isn't meant to last forever, well, neither are curtains—and your hem will likely last for years, no matter what the tape's label says.

Relax with a heating pad

Make a flexible and renewable heating pad by using hem tape to stitch up two sides of a rectangle of cotton fabric to make a pouch. Fill the pouch about half full with rice or dried beans, then fold over the flap and use hem tape to seal it (the filling can fall to the bottom while you iron the top). When your neck or shoulder aches, heat the bag in the microwave for 1 to 2 minutes, until the filling is warm to the touch, and drape it over your aching part, reheating as needed. A few cloves added to the mix will provide a soothing scent for many moons.

Make café curtains

A simple, durable pair of café curtains for a kitchen window can be yours in moments with hem tape. Find a cute pair of tea towels and use hem tape to iron on a 1-inch hem at the top of each. Thread a curtain rod through the hem and string 'em up! Since café curtains are intended to hang on the bottom half of a window, you won't need to hem the other side.

interfacing

This is the stuff that is sewn between a garment's lining and surface material. It helps protect both surfaces and provides warmth. But it also has more uses....

Prevent a pocket from wearing through

Men tend to keep their wallets, loose change, and keys in the same pocket of their pants, whatever pants they're wearing. And a heavy wallet, jingling coins, or a set of metal keys can wear through a lightweight pants pocket in no time flat. Turn the pants inside out and cut lightweight fusible interfacing to fit exactly around the pocket. Sew it up on three sides to make an interfacing pocket, then stitch it directly to the interior seam where the pocket attaches to the pants. Lightly iron to fuse the interfacing to the pocket.

Add life to upholstery jobs

If you're going to make the effort to recover a piece of furniture yourself, you want the job to last as long as possible. Before recovering a stool or chair seat with padding and fabric, wrap a layer of thick, heavy-grade interfacing around the surface of the wood or metal frame to be covered.

That additional layer of strong, hard-wearing interfacing prevents hard edges from rubbing through the surface.

Trace a pattern

Bought a multisize paper pattern you love but your family wears different sizes? Use interfacing to fit all concerned. Trace the pieces from each size on the pattern onto lightweight non-fusible interfacing and cut them out. Use the interfacing "pattern" you've now made to cut out the pieces in each size. You can also use this trick to extend the life of a pattern. The interfacing will last much longer than the delicate paper, letting you make that perfect pair of pants or dress several times without needing to buy the pattern again.

knitting needles

They are exactly what they say they are: needles for knitting. Here are a few additional uses that will save you time and money!

Put up your hair

Wooden or colorful plastic needles make a stylish coiffure when you use them to hold a bun or chignon in place. Twist your hair up behind your head and push in two matching or contrasting needles like hairpins to hold the bun in place.

Stuff a doll or pillow

Use the blunt end of a knitting needle to push fiberfill or batting into the far corners of an item you're stuffing. A knitting needle will let you reach and plump out those difficult edges, as well as the main body.

Test a cake

Keep a narrow-gauge wooden or metal knitting needle among your kitchen utensils and never be at a loss when the oven timer goes off. Press a knitting needle into the center of baked goods, and you'll know they're ready if the needle comes out with a few crumbs clinging to it in place of raw batter.

Turn a tube

Use a large-gauge needle to turn projects that have been stitched together inside out. A large needle helps you turn corners and narrow strips, such as the arm on a stuffed doll or the stitched tube of a purse handle.

Make kebabs

String chunks of cut fruit on colored metal knitting needles and serve them with a dip of melted chocolate or plain thick yogurt flavored with vanilla and a little powdered sugar. Children love the novelty, and it makes a lovely presentation for a party.

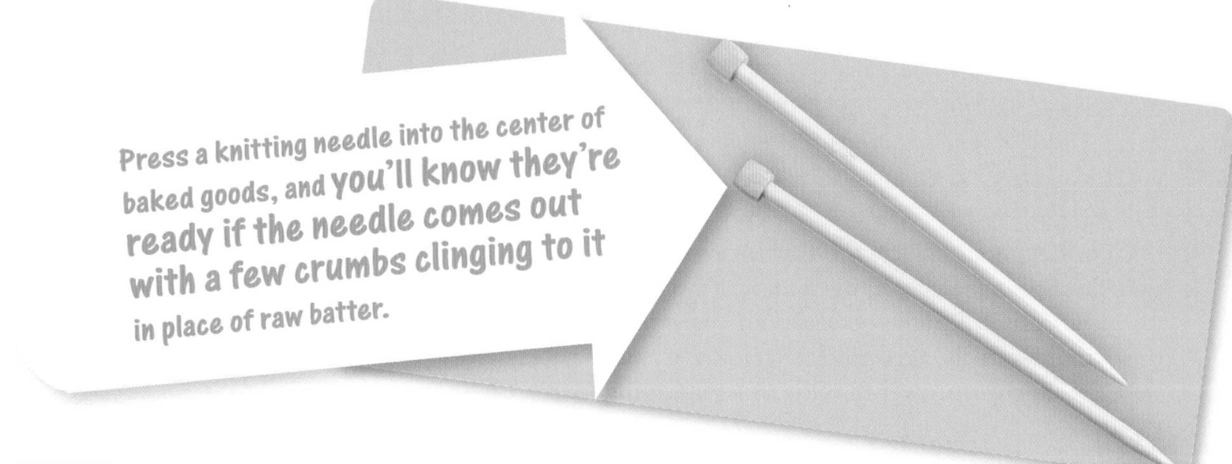
Press a knitting needle into the center of baked goods, and you'll know they're ready if the needle comes out with a few crumbs clinging to it in place of raw batter.

marking pens

Marking pens are a necessity in every sewing kit. But their uses outside of sewing are multitudinous.

Sign your work

Use a fabric marking pen to sign your name to the back or bottom of any handmade item such as a quilt or purse. Other artists sign their work—why shouldn't you record your authorship for posterity?

Decorate a T-shirt

A clutch of permanent fabric-marking pens in different colors can be used to make much more intricate designs than fabric paint. For a terrific birthday party activity, let children run riot with a white cotton T-shirt and a handful of colorful permanent fabric pens. Or you can do something a little more sophisticated, such as sketch a curling vine and a few blooming flowers around the sleeve or neckline of your favorite white V-neck.

Hide a repair

Does your pale thread show up on a seam you've repaired on a dark garment? Use a permanent marking pen that's a similar color to the fabric and "color" any visible threads to hide your stitches.

Create a needlework template

Use fabric marking pens to make your own designs for cross-stitching or embroidery. There's no need to buy preprinted kits when you can design your own, for a much more personal and distinctive piece of needlework.

Blow up (or shrink down) a design

Want to transfer an existing photo or design to your piece of fabric for needlework and make

your finished work either bigger or smaller than the original? Mark or overlay the picture with a 1-inch grid, then mark a 2- or 3-inch grid on your fabric (to enlarge) or a 1/4- or 1/2-inch grid on your fabric (to shrink). Then you can easily sketch what's in each box in the original into the corresponding box on your ready-marked fabric.

Cover a bleach spot

Accidentally splashed a dot of bleach on your favorite T-shirt? Color it in with a matching fabric pen. It may not totally disappear, but it will become far less noticeable. After you wash the shirt, color it in again.

oilcloth

Oilcloth was originally invented as a way to keep roofing and walls dry during construction. Today, it shows up everywhere from home porches to picnics. Where would you use this great material?

Weatherize porch furniture

That cushion on your wicker chair was supposed to be "weather resistant" but after a month of rain, it's got dark spots that won't wipe clean. Make your outdoor sofa and chair cushions

Use KNITTING NEEDLES in the Garden

Knitting needles are great if you knit. But what if you've inherited a big stash and prefer to crochet? Use them in the garden.

1 Make a Depth Marker

Make marks on the needle for required planting depths; poke the needle into the soil and you can be confident that all the holes will be uniform. The same needle can be marked for several different depths—you can differentiate them by using different colored markers.

2 Protect Plants from Critters

"Plant" needles, pointy sides down, into each corner of the area you wish to protect. Using scrap yarn make a "web" a few inches above the soil. Birds will be prevented from landing and snacking, and other creatures won't find the space convenient for toileting needs.

3 Mark Your Spot!

Make a hole in the bottom of a seed packet and use packing tape to attach it to a knitting needle. Use the needle to mark the row where the seeds are planted.

weatherproof, not merely resistant, by re-covering them with covers made of PVC-coated oilcloth. The same bright lengths that make such ideal washable tablecloths can be sewn easily into envelope-style, wipe-able cushion covers that will keep the rain out, extending the life of your outdoor furniture.

Make a place mat

Why waste money on place mats for the kitchen table, especially if you have young kids who spill food all over them anyway? Cut rectangles of a brightly patterned vinyl cloth and use them for place mats instead. To keep the edges from rolling, use scissors or pinking shears to cut a 1-inch fringe all around the edges. When the place mats get worn or dirty, cut fresh mats!

Line a drawer

Decorative kitchen paper for lining drawers and shelves can be pricey, but you can save yourself money and prevent wear and tear on your cabinetry by lining your kitchen storage with vinyl instead. Cut lengths to fit, and either tack down with thumbtacks or use a light spritz of spray adhesive under the corners.

Protect a baby's bottom

Many parents hesitate before setting their child into a shopping cart at the grocery store or before using a grubby high chair or booster seat at a restaurant, especially in winter, when colds and flu are rife. Plonk that little bottom down with impunity when you carry along a square of fabric-backed oilcloth. Just unfold and place it over the seat before putting down your precious cargo. You can also use your vinyl square as an impromptu changing pad when using public changing tables. When it starts to look at all worn or dirty, throw it away and cut a fresh square!

Cover a book

Just bought that new hardcover everyone is talking about? If you're getting ready to take a plane trip or a long car journey, chances are you're going to rip or scuff the paper dust jacket. Instead, cut a rectangle of vinyl that's 3 inches taller than the height of the book and 6 inches wider than the open book lying flat. Fold the long sides of the rectangle (the top and bottom) by 1 inch, gluing these folds flat with glue or spray adhesive, then fold in the edges to make a 2-inch wide flap on either side, gluing these just at the very top and bottom edges. Remove the dust jacket and insert the hardcover flaps in the edge flaps of your brand new, waterproof, wipe-able, reusable "travel jacket."

pipe cleaners

Traditionally, they're used for exactly what they sound like they're used for: as a way to clean a pipe. But there are so many more ways to use these familiar items.

Scrub in a tight space

True to their original use, pipe cleaners fit well into narrow spaces. But you don't need to limit their cleaning abilities to pipes. Use one to dust

Use a pipe cleaner to dust off your sewing machine's tight corners, clear a pressure cooker safety valve, or clean other tight spaces.

off your sewing machine's tight corners, clear a pressure cooker safety valve, or clean the dust from around the trackball of the computer mouse. You can also use one to clean the little vents on your gas stove top to keep the ring burning clear.

Keep your shoe on

Just busted a shoelace but you're on your way out the door? Grab a pipe cleaner and thread it through the top of your shoe just like a lace. It will keep your shoe on until you get to the store for a replacement. It's tougher than a twist tie—but a pipe cleaner can replace one of those, too!

Twist up a set of holiday napkin rings

Give the kids or grandkids a task while you finish preparing the meal. Have them twist together pipe cleaners of seasonal colors—use yellow, orange, red, and brown for Thanksgiving, for example—and tie up the napkins for dinner.

Keep kids busy on the road

Parents panic about what to take along to keep little ones entertained on long road trips or flights. Don't overlook pipe cleaners. Take along a colorful heap of them for kids to twist together into animal shapes or make necklaces and bracelets.

ribbons

Ribbons are among the very first materials used to adorn garments and date back beyond the Middle Ages. Even Geoffrey Chaucer mentioned "ribbands" in *The Canterbury Tales*. Overlooked and often forgotten, they are divine used in many other circumstances.

Hang a picture

For an old-fashioned look in your picture hanging, use a length of heavy, wide ribbon and tie the ends through the two metal D hooks on the back of a picture frame. Loop the top over a decorative hook (or even a nail) on the wall several inches above the frame, or use a longer length of ribbon for a more dramatic presentation and drape it high above off a picture rail.

Update a necklace

This season's fashion-forward style in jewelry includes necklaces that tie with ribbon rather than clipping with metal fasteners. Hang a favorite pendant off a narrow length of dark grosgrain ribbon and tie it to any length you like. For a more exciting and contemporary look, press grommets into one end each of two lengths of a wider ribbon, and suspend a length of an old

necklace between them. Use a twist of chain, a collection of funky beads, or a length of river pearls—any old necklace that needs a new look.

Personalize a photo, card, or note

Use a hole puncher to make holes in a photo mat, birthday card, or piece of notepaper. Use long and short lengths of ribbon either to tie bows between two holes or to weave back and forth through a series of holes for a fun, funky personalized look to any heavy piece of paper.

trimming

Trimming is used to add a bit of pizzazz to fabric on a garment, upholstery, curtains—everywhere. Buy it in bits and pieces to give a little zip to anything and everything around you.

Decorate a gift

Pre-tied bows and curling paper ribbons on a gift-wrapped present are so dull. Make your wrapped gifts highly distinctive by tying a length of decorative trimming around the box. From a run of tatted lace to a dangling golden fringe to colorful cotton bobbles, your package will shine on a table of ordinary gifts. With a colorful and cheerful length of trimming, you can even skip the paper. And the lucky recipient can put the trimming to his or her own use after opening!

Perk up a lamp shade

With very little effort, you can bring a whole new look to a living room or lounge by adding some striking trimming to the base of the lamp shades. Go for an elegant gold braid all the way around the top and bottom, or put a long fringe around the base of the shade on a tall standing lamp, or get a hip mod look by hanging bobbly fringe all over a little shade. Brightening up the lamp shades in a room is like dressing the room in new clothes. Your room will be ready to party!

Have a Victorian Christmas

Get an old-fashioned look by draping your holiday tree with yards and yards of wide lace trimming instead of tinsel or sparkling ropes. Make small paper fans out of folded craft paper and clip them to the branches. Finish the look with white lights and a few gauzy bows tied here and there. You'll hear a chorus of approval singing as you work!

Update a photo frame

Glue braid, bobbles, a strip of lace, or a short fringe all around an ordinary photo frame and make the picture inside spring to life!

Give a dress a swing

Make up your own flapper dress that's reminiscent of the 1920s by stitching row after row of long fringe all the way around a simple sheath dress. Whether you're wearing it for a Halloween party with a feather in your hair or simply to kick up your heels for a night on the town, you'll be the belle of the ball.

Velcro

Where would we be without Velcro? But who knew that it had so very many uses!

Replace duvet cover fasteners

It's hard enough to slip a full-size quilt or duvet cover back on after washing it, but worse is when you get to the bottom and realize you've buttoned the quilt cover on crooked and have to start all over. Replace your buttons or snaps with Velcro, and not only will quilt covers go back on with ease, but the ends won't poke out if you lose a button.

Keep a pen where you need it

Does your refrigerator pen always disappear the moment that you need to write something on your grocery list? Put a strip of Velcro directly on the door of the fridge and glue the other side along your favorite pen or pencil. Now you'll never forget to add peanut butter to the list while you rummage in a drawer for a pen.

Hang a smoke detector

To make it easier to take smoke detectors down twice a year to change the batteries, as recommended for fire safety, stick them to the ceiling with a wide strip of Velcro. You won't have to perch on a stepstool trying to jigger the detector down from its screws when you can just tear it away.

Secure a first-aid kit in your car

It seems like a good idea to keep a small first-aid kit in the car. It's there when you need it at soccer practice or when you have a flat and need a bandage after wrestling with the jack! But the plastic boxes slip and slide and end up all over the floor and eventually back in the house. Keep it firmly in place by putting a Velcro strip down in the back window ledge and putting the other side on the bottom of the kit. That bandage will be there when you need it.

Hold the car mat under the driver's feet

The floor mat that came with your car is usually carefully fitted so that it will lie flat under the driver's seat. But what if you get a replacement? Don't risk the dangers of a mat that slides under your feet or potentially bunches up under the brake pedal. When you put down a replacement mat from the auto store, be sure it's well secured on the left and right with Velcro. That way it will stay in place without question when you drive—and rip right up when it's time to clean.

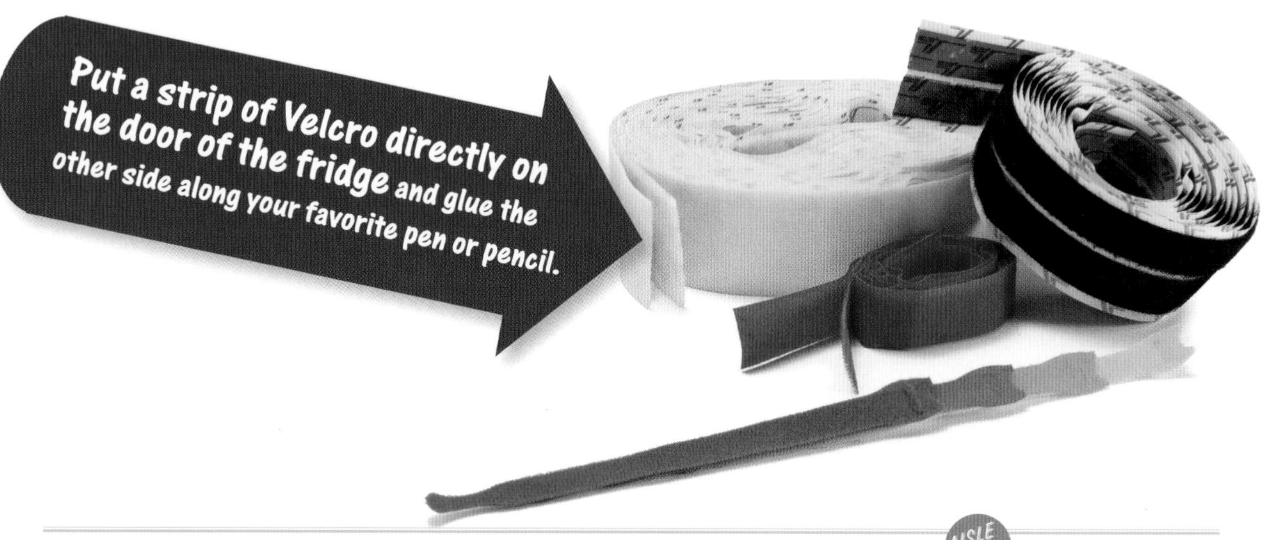
Put a strip of Velcro directly on the door of the fridge and glue the other side along your favorite pen or pencil.

RRRRRIP...

THE STICKY HISTORY OF VELCRO

Velcro looks space age, very modern. In fact, in the movie *Men in Black*, it is asserted by Agent K that aliens invented Velcro. This is not true. **Velcro was invented on Earth, by a dog.** George de Mestral, an engineer, and said dog (the canine's name has been lost to history) were walking together in the Alps in 1941. They returned home covered in cockleburs. At this juncture, the bulk of the inventing was carried forth by de Mestral, for it was he, possessing hands, who closely observed the spiky seeds on his clothing and on his dog's fur. **He unstuck one of the burs and put it under a microscope—he wanted to discover what made the annoying little things stick so well.** What he saw under magnification were small "hooks" perfectly designed to cling to anything that had tiny loops, such as the wool of his trousers and the coat of his Irish Pointer. It can be imagined that the vast majority of people would leave the microscope at this point, nod their head at the efficiency of nature (Ah, cockleburs! Spreading their seed in such an ingenious way!), and commence de-burring themselves and their pet. Not so George de Mestral. He had a brainstorm that would cause him to quit his job, get mocked by professional weavers, and ultimately create something new. He envisioned a man-made, two-sided fastener: one side with hooks like burs, the other with loops like fabric. It would rival the zipper as a clothing fastener. Although

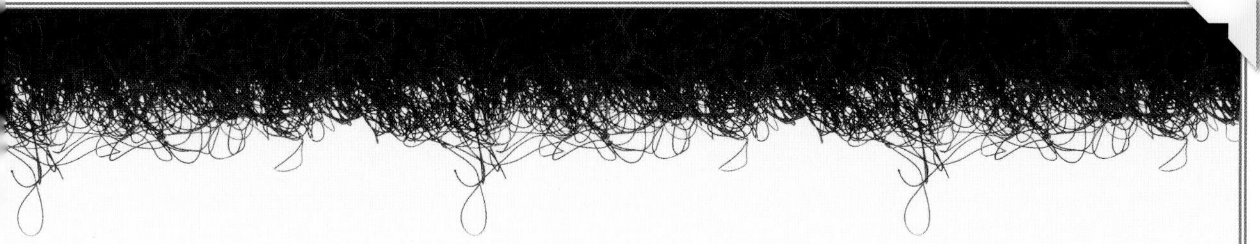

we don't know how long it took him to leave his microscope and begin the arduous task of grooming his dog, we do know that this idea germinated in him for several years. In 1952 de Mestral quit his engineering job, raised an impressive amount of capital (a sum equivalent to $150,000), and began his quest to re-create cocklebur hooks with fabric. He approached weavers in Lyon asking for their help. They scoffed at him. At last he convinced one weaver of the project's merit. The two men explored many materials to replicate the burs, including cotton. A prototype worked, but the cotton wore out too quickly to be viable. The search then turned to synthetic fibers. Luckily, nylon had recently been invented, and when sewn under hot infrared light, it formed hooks perfect for the "bur side" of the fastener—the trickiest part of the endeavor.

A patent was granted in 1955, and de Mestral named his product "Velcro"—a combination of "velvet" and "crochet," the French word for "hook."

When Velcro made it to market, it was a failure. Though de Mestral had envisioned his invention replacing the zipper, the finished product was undeniably ugly. It made an inelegant noise when pulled apart, and clothing designers did not want to incorporate it into their designs. Velcro could have died an ignoble death but for a bit of good timing: the growth of the aerospace industry. A spacesuit does not need to be stylish or silent—it needs to fasten and unfasten quickly and easily. Food and tools can float away in zero gravity; Velcro holds things in place. A lucrative market for Velcro existed after all.

Make a sink skirt

Put the zing back in a lifeless bathroom with a colorful sink skirt. Wrap the base of a plain porcelain wall sink with a wide strip of cheerful fabric that's long enough to reach the floor. Stick a strip of Velcro all the way around the base of the sink and stick on the skirt with the opposite side of Velcro. This way, you can whip it off in a hurry if you need to launder the skirt or dry it after a vigorous washing! Best of all, you can swap in a different skirt with ease if this one gets soiled or boring.

Replace buttons

Buttons on clothing can be very difficult as fingers get older and stiffer. Make dressing simpler for your older loved one by replacing tiny buttons or tricky snaps with small pieces of Velcro. For clothing, use the type that can be stitched on, not stuck on with double-sided tape, and be sure to use a small patch of Velcro to replace each closure, not a long wide strip. Too much Velcro can cling hard and make it just as hard to get clothes off as a stiff button.

webbing

Designed for use as belts, suspenders, sandals, and even back braces, polyester webbing has a plethora of other uses. Here are just a few!

Substitute for a bungee cord

Can't lay hands on your bungee cord when you need to strap luggage to your car's roof? Prefer to ensure that those bikes won't come off their travel rack on the back of your camper? Polyester webbing is strong and tough and can hold a knot well. Keep a roll of webbing in the back of your car and you'll have a strong, lightweight cord for any packing eventuality.

Weave a mat

Use natural jute webbing to weave a distinctive and hard-wearing floor mat or area rug. Weave over and under just like making the lattice top on a pastry, tacking down one end of each strip to your work surface so you can pull against it for a tighter weave. Use scissors to even off the edges

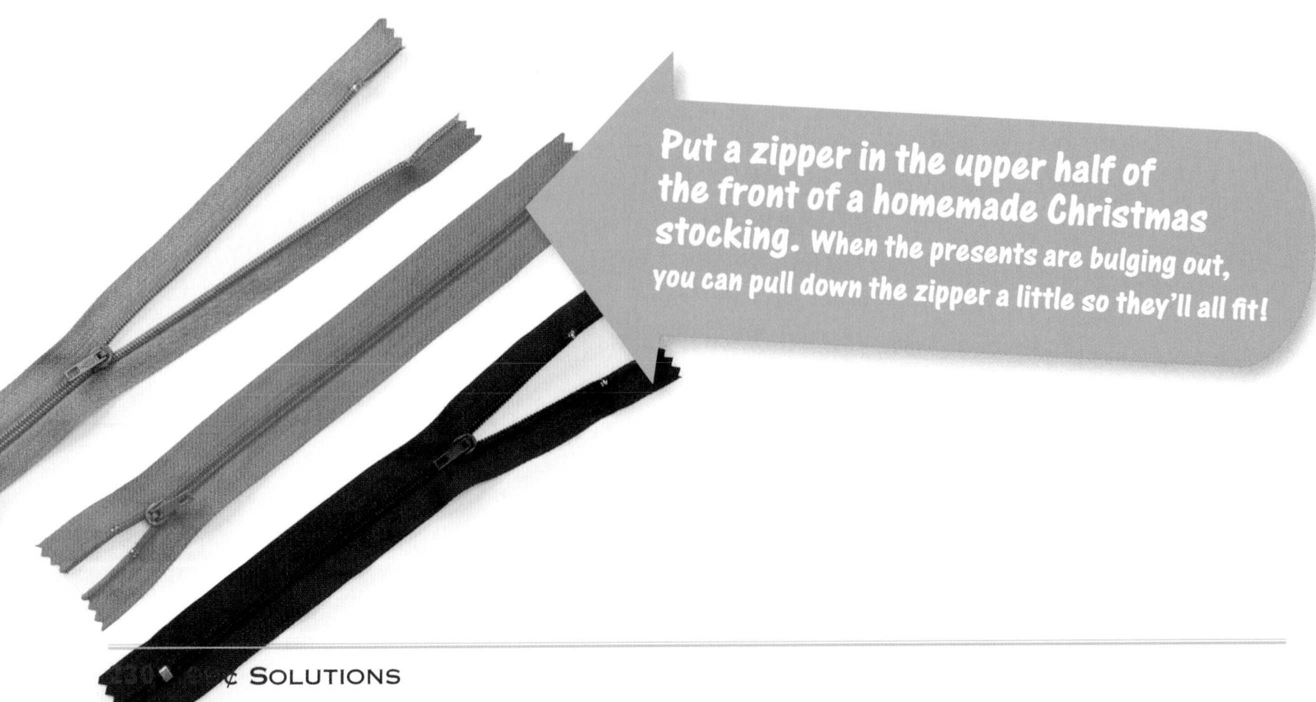
Put a zipper in the upper half of the front of a homemade Christmas stocking. When the presents are bulging out, you can pull down the zipper a little so they'll all fit!

of the finished mat and seal it all the way around with binding tape.

Make a tool belt

If you're a workman who needs a heavy-duty tool belt—well, chances are you've already got one. But if you're a weekend DIY warrior who just needs a hammer and screwdriver at hand while doing a few light home repairs, you can make a stripped down, lightweight belt that frees your hands while keeping indispensable tools nearby. Cut a long length of jute or polyester webbing that fits around your waist with an extra 2 feet to spare. Use a sewing machine to sew two loops into the webbing, about 5 inches each, just big enough to slip a hammer through and let it hang. When you need to do a few repairs, tie on your tool belt and get cracking.

zippers

Invented a good 12 years before the Civil War, the zipper was invented to, well, hold things together. They're everywhere now, but we've found even more uses for them than the obvious.

Pad a pajama pillow

Set a zipper up the front of a satiny pillowcase that's several inches larger than the pillow form that you have to stuff it. Then fit the oversize case over the pillow, leaving room inside for a folded pair of pajamas to recline on your bed all day.

Make a friendship bracelet

Perfect for the preteen set and an ideal activity for a girl's birthday party, make snazzy friendship bracelets by putting snaps or Velcro on the ends of 7-inch zippers. Kids can decorate the bracelets themselves with beads, sequins, buttons, and fabric markers.

Decorate a doll

Bring new life to an old rag doll by adding zippers. Put a zipper in an old dress to make it easier for little fingers to manage. And put a short zipper in place of the mouth on a rag doll's face and give new meaning to the phrase "zip your lips"!

Turn teddy into a secret safe

Use a seam ripper to open a discreet side or bottom seam on a stuffed animal such as a teddy bear. Remove a handful of stuffing—enough to make some space inside but not so much as to make the bear collapse. Stitch a zipper into the seam, and your secret home safe is ready for use. Put your jewelry into a soft bag and stuff it inside, or protect any cash you may have lying around. It's an easy way to hide anything you want in plain sight.

Zip up your (Christmas) stockings

For a charming and highly personal approach to holiday stockings, put a zipper in the upper half of the front of a homemade Christmas stocking. When Santa brings so many presents that they're bulging out, he can pull down the zipper a little so they'll all fit!

AISLE 7
SCHOOL AND PARTY SUPPLIES

THANK GOODNESS FOR DOLLAR STORES! They stock essential supplies for you and your house—soap, shampoo, rubber gloves, laundry detergent, paper towels, and so on—that you're likely to use on a regular basis. But don't forget that dollar stores can be fun to visit, too! Two aisles in particular provide items that are a blast to browse: school supplies and party supplies. Whether you're looking for snazzy notebooks for your child's first day of school or brilliant bows and ribbons to adorn your best friend's birthday present, you'll likely find a stunning array of products that you need and want. And don't forget that many of these items have uses well beyond what their manufacturers intended. Use your imagination—and the tips that follow—to get the most use out of your new school and party supplies.

adhesive tape

One of the most versatile school supplies available, adhesive tape can be used on everything from your face to your shoes and from your car to your cake. Forget about using it to stick two pieces of paper together. It's way too busy doing other more important jobs around the house!

Help flowers stand straight

If your cut flowers are a few days old and have started to droop, use transparent tape to bring them back to attention. Remove the flowers and fill the vase with fresh water. Place several pieces of tape across the top of the vase, leaving small gaps for the stems. Put the flowers back in the vase and enjoy several more days of your bouquet.

Remove a splinter

As long as the splinter is sticking out of your skin, you may be able to remove it without tweezers or a needle. Lay a piece of adhesive tape over the affected area, and rub your finger gently over the tape until it makes contact with the splinter. Pull the tape up, and the splinter may come with it. This method works particularly well if you find many small splinters near the surface of your skin. It also works if you need to remove small cactus prickles from your fingers.

Get rid of a furrow

If you're a deep thinker or a big worrier, you may have a deep furrow in your brow. And if you don't want it, you can get rid of it with tape. Just rub your regular moisturizer into the furrow at night before you go to bed, then pull the skin taut, and put a piece of tape across the smoothed-out wrinkle. Make sure the tape sticks onto dry skin, rather than on the moisturized skin, or it may not last through the night. Do this every night for a month, and you'll see results you like.

Protect your library card

And your bus pass, your lunch ticket, your car registration, and any other small piece of paper that you use repeatedly or need to protect in your wallet. Cover them with transparent tape. (Clear shipping tape works well, too.) Tape both sides of the card, then cut the excess tape at the sides of the card. You'll keep the card in good shape, and scanners will be able to read it well.

Think like a shoelace

Wrap the ends of string or ribbon tightly with transparent tape to make it look like a shoelace. Stringing beads, macaroni, or anything else you want will be much easier.

Nix the adhesive

Ignore the adhesive on the permit sticker that you need to attach to the inside of your car's windshield—it makes removing the permit messy and difficult. Instead, simply tape the permit where it belongs. You'll have no trouble removing the sticker when its time has come.

Keep your sweets safe

Protect your cakes, cookies, and other sweet treats from ants by surrounding the goodies with a circle of adhesive tape. Place the tape sticky side up and you—rather than the ants—will have a yummy dessert.

Clean your comb

Even if your hair is always as clean as a whistle, your comb will still need to be cleaned occasionally. Pick up loose hair and accumulated dirt between the teeth by pressing adhesive tape on one side of the comb and then removing it. To fully clean your comb, soak it in a bowl of warm water and shampoo or a bowl of white vinegar. Scrub it with a toothbrush, rinse it, and let it dry.

Find the beginning of plastic wrap

Anyone who has ever used plastic wrap has undoubtedly had trouble finding the beginning of it on the roll. Here's an easy way to avoid that trap: Wrap tape around your finger with the sticky side out. Tap your finger on the plastic wrap until you discover the edge, then use another piece of tape to lift the edge off the roll.

Help chains travel well

Cover your necklace chains with tape before you take them on the road. The tape will prevent them from tangling.

X marks the spot

Make an *X* out of tape on your wall the next time you hang a picture or drive a nail into the wall for any reason. The tape will keep the wallboard from cracking or the plaster from chipping. It will also keep the paint from peeling off if you need to remove the nail.

Protect your wood floor

Don't let your grandmother's rocking chair ruin the finish on your wood floor. Just place a piece of adhesive tape along the bottom of each rocker, and your floor will be safe.

balloons

Balloons may be colorful, whimsical, delightful decorations, but they're otherwise useless, right? Pop that thought right now, and consider all these jobs balloons can do.

Put your bouquet in a balloon

You won't have to wait until the last minute to buy a bouquet for your hostess if you know how to keep the flowers fresh as you travel. Here's the trick: Fill a balloon with 1/2 cup of water, and pull the mouth of the balloon over the ends of your flowers. Prevent the balloon from falling off by wrapping a rubber band around the top.

Run off rabbits

Cut deflated, used metallic birthday balloons into vertical strips and use them to scare rabbits, squirrels, and birds away from your garden. Hang them from poles near your plants to keep them safe.

Travel with a balloon

Toss an uninflated balloon in your suitcase on your next trip in case you need a cold or hot pack for a twisted ankle or sore muscles. If you need an

Toss an uninflated balloon in your suitcase on your next trip in case you need a cold or hot pack for a twisted ankle or sore muscles.

ice pack or a heat pack at your destination, just fill the balloon with very cold water or very hot water and place it on the problem area.

Keep your bandage dry

Helping a cut heal means keeping it clean and protected and dry. Getting through the day without getting a cut on a finger wet is almost impossible—unless you get help from a balloon. Slip a balloon over your affected finger when you need to get your hands wet (in the shower or doing dishes, for example) and you'll keep your cut dry.

Chase cats off the couch

Tie some small inflated balloons to your couch or chair if you want to keep your cat off the furniture. The loud noise of popping will scare off your cat and keep him at a safe distance.

Scare off skunks

Tie bunches of blown-up latex birthday balloons (or congratulations balloons, or any other kind) around your house to ward off skunks. Be sure to place them wherever you suspect the skunks might lurk—on your patio, around the perimeter of your house, or near your trash. The rustling balloons will frighten them into leaving. A bonus: Raccoons are scared of balloons, too.

binder

Dollar stores sell plastic three-ring binders in a rainbow of colors. Designed to help students keep loose-leaf paper organized, they can be used for more than loose-leaf paper and for more than students. Check out the tips below.

Organize your garden

Devote an entire binder to keeping your garden organized. Make notes on what is planted where; when you planted seeds, bulbs, and seedlings; and the names of what you've planted. Make sure your binder has pockets for plant tags and receipts—even seed packets, as long as you won't forget you've stored them here.

Keep contacts under control

Make lists of contact information—phone numbers (including cell phones), addresses, e-mail addresses—of police and fire departments, gas and electric companies, doctors and dentists, and so on, and keep them handy in a binder. Organize the binder by type of contact: medical, home repair, financial, family, and more, and keep the binder where everyone in the family can find it.

Use regular old binder clips to seal bags of potato chips or cookies. The snacks will stay fresh longer.

Create a custom cookbook

It doesn't matter if you clip recipes or you write your own; insert plastic page protectors into the binder, organize by type of food or dish, and pop the recipes into the protectors. When you're cooking, just remove the whole page, which is now protected from splattering.

binder clips

Bigger and better than ordinary paper clips, binder clips also have bigger ambitions. They don't just hold pieces of paper together; they hold entire *pads* of paper together. And they can do so much more! Here are some big ideas for these big clips.

Mount a photo exhibit

String a piece of wire or rope from one wall to another nearby, and nail both ends into the walls. Put your photos in 8 1/2-by-11-inch clear document sleeves. Attach the photo holders to the line with binder clips, stand back, and admire your display.

Seal snacks for freshness

Forget about buying "chip clips" or using clothespins to keep bags of potato chips, tortilla chips, or cookies shut. Specially designed clips can be a waste of money, and clothespins don't really keep the air out of the bags. Instead, use regular old binder clips to seal them. The snacks will stay fresh longer.

Clip open a cookbook

Reading a recipe takes time, and your cookbook isn't giving you the time you need if it can't stay open to the page you want. Hold the pages open with two binder clips—one for each side of the book—and you can finally relax while you read and cook.

BINDER CLIPS

Louis E. Baltzley invented the binder clip in 1911 as a way to help his father, a writer, join his manuscript pages more easily. Prior to this springy clip, his dad held pages together by punching holes and using thread. Invention ran in Baltzley's family: He was a grandson of Elias Howe, the first American to hold a sewing machine patent.

Keep travel documents handy

You need your itinerary, your airplane ticket, your boarding pass, your photo ID, your passport (perhaps), your list of important phone numbers, and more when you travel by plane these days. Rather than scrounging around each time you need to produce a document, keep them together with a binder clip. Staying so organized will (hopefully!) get you through security and check-in much faster.

Organize your money

Keep your bills handy by making a money clip out of a binder clip. Place your paper money in a neat stack, fold the stack in half, and attach a binder clip. Your money will be right at hand the next time you need it.

boxes

Dollar stores generally carry a wide selection of decorative boxes, and they display them in the party supply aisle. They are the perfect solution for gift-givers who don't like to wrap gifts, and they can serve other purposes, too. Check them out below.

Use a box for a gift

Not an original idea? It is if you put the wrapped gift in a decorative box, then put that box in a larger

UP, UP, AND AWAY

AN UPLIFTING LOOK AT BALLOONS

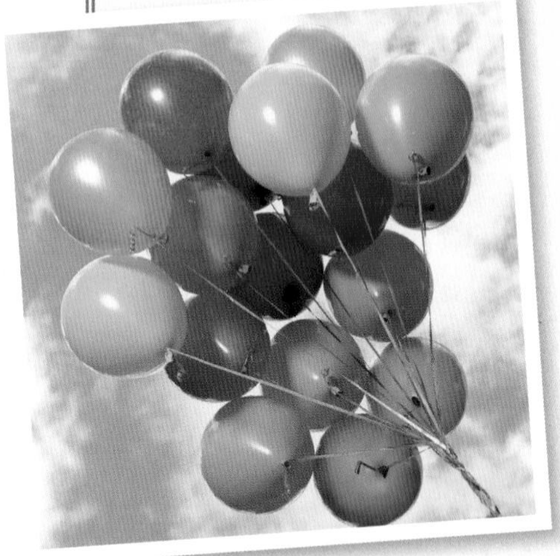

They're a necessity at children's parties; they're tied on the cars of brides and grooms; they're released into the air on special occasions. What did we do before we could float balloons? **The earliest toy balloons in this country were filled with hydrogen.**

This kept them aloft but it wasn't such a gas if they got anywhere near something flammable—like birthday candles. **Hydrogen is quite combustible.** So much so that in 1922, New York City officially banned hydrogen-filled toy balloons. This was done for safety and didn't deter or deflate the populace—helium was used for lifting power instead.

Greater safety allowed the use of balloons to expand. In the 1920s, Helen Warny founded the Toy Balloon Company in New York. She used balloons as a way to advertise. It's said she once **released 50,000 balloons at a time,** each bearing an advertiser's name.

The world's first novelty-shaped balloon is credited to Neil Tillotson. It was shaped with pointed ears to look like a cat's head. They were sold at a parade in Massachusetts in 1931 and children loved them. (Tillotson went on to become a celebrity of sorts, as **the first person in New Hampshire to vote in the presidential primaries.** He did this every four years until he died at age 102.)

Tillotson was on to something: cats, balloons, and parades. The Macy's Thanksgiving Day Parade is one of the

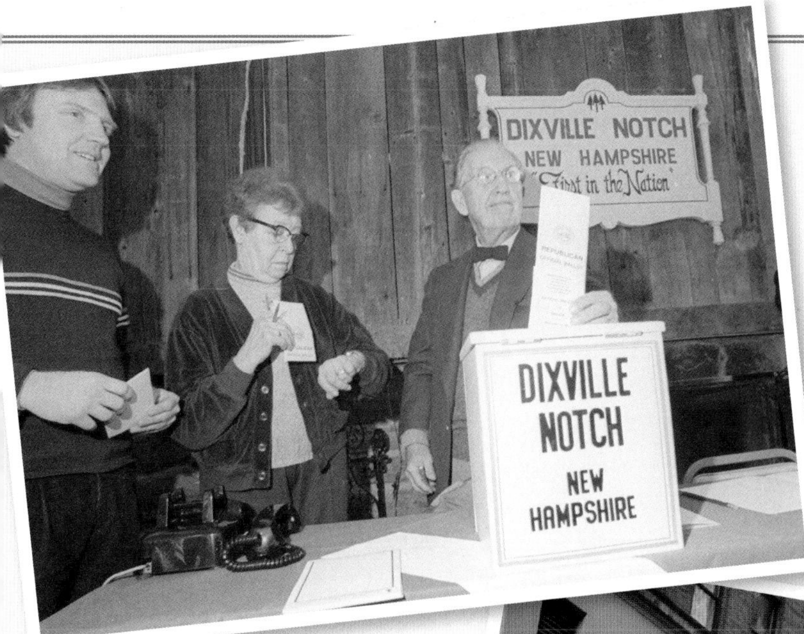

Neil Tillotson, Dixville Notch town moderator, prepares to cast the first primary vote in the Nation as Mrs. Cora Whitton, Supervisor of the Checklist, looks at her watch. This tiny New Hampshire town cast its 23 votes at exactly midnight February 26th 1980.

most-watched parades in this country. It started in 1924 and **featured floats and animals—including elephants!**—on loan from the Central Park Zoo. But Macy's wanted to garner a bigger audience, so they introduced balloons shaped like animals to replace the live ones. **In 1927, Felix the Cat was the first giant balloon to float down the streets of Manhattan.** After the parade, the helium-filled balloons (which had safety valves to keep them from popping) were cut loose and set free to float over the city. This tradition has been discontinued—but it must have been a sight to behold!

box, then place that box in a larger box still. You can leave the boxes unwrapped—they're decorative, after all—or you can have even more fun with the recipient by wrapping each box individually.

Think interior design

Stack three or four decorative boxes of descending size near a chair and place a small plant on top. The plant will cascade down the tiered boxes, creating a lovely focal point in the room.

Corral remotes

Stop losing your remote control—or several remotes, since so many electronics require so many remotes—by keeping them together in a decorative box. You'll clear up clutter, get organized, and add a touch of color to your TV stand.

Wrap it up

Store Christmas ribbons and bows, small pieces of wrapping paper, and scissors and tape in three different Christmas-themed boxes, and stack them in your living room. The holiday theme will enliven the room, and you'll have everything you need to wrap up another perfect Christmas.

Keep your appliances clean

Use an upside-down decorative box (without its top) to cover small kitchen appliances like mini food processors, blenders, and coffeemakers. It's a great way to keep them free of dust and dirt.

bubble wrap

Popping the bubbles in bubble wrap is entertaining, but not really the best use of the product. What's its best use? Most people use it to cushion items in packages they send. But they're not thinking of the glorious versatility of bubble wrap. Consider all the possibilities described here.

Take it shopping

Grocery shopping, that is. Particularly in summer, keep some bubble wrap in the trunk of your car so you can wrap up frozen foods to keep them from thawing out on the trip home. Even ice cream stays firm with an insulating layer of bubbles around it.

Protect your pants

Keep unwanted creases from imprinting themselves on the slacks you hang in your closet by wrapping the hangers in bubble wrap. Roll a layer of bubble wrap around the hanger bar, making sure that the smooth side of the wrap faces the pants and the bubbles face the bar. Keep the wrap in place with duct tape.

Plan a party on bubble wrap

Young kids like nothing better than to move and shake and make lots of noise. Fulfill all their wishes by holding a dance party on bubble wrap. Tape several sheets of bubble wrap together until you form a large square or rectangle, and make sure that the bubbles face up (so that the dancers will pop them as they boogie). You may want to duct tape the dance floor to your floor so that it doesn't move with the dancers. Freeze dancing is particularly fun on bubble wrap.

Shape up your shoes

Place a small piece of rolled-up bubble wrap in each of your shoes to help them maintain their shape. Roll up longer pieces to keep the calves of your boots standing upright—and to keep their shape.

Ride in comfort

Your car seat may be comfortable for short trips, but what about long ones? Make it dreamy by covering the seat and the back in a double layer of bubble wrap (with the bubbles facing out). The bubble wrap will support your body and provide a comfy ride over the long haul.

Sleep comfortably outside

Take a six-foot piece of bubble wrap with you the next time you go camping. Place it under your sleeping bag before you retire for the night. The bubble wrap will provide a cushion for your body and act as a tarp to keep your sleeping bag dry.

Protect tree trunks

Whether you mow your lawn or your lawn service mows for you, you'll want to protect small, fragile trees and tree seedlings. How? Wrap bubble wrap around their thin trunks. Keep the bubble wrap in place with masking tape. You can easily remove the bubble wrap when the lawn is done.

Insulate a doghouse

Bubble wrap is a safe, non-toxic option for insulating a doghouse to keep your pooch toasty in winter. And, unlike with fiberglass, if your pet gnaws at it, he'll merely get a surprise if a bubble pops!

Keep cold items cold

Heading out for a picnic? Wrap items you want to stay cold—cans of soft drinks, egg salad sandwiches, popsicles, and so on—in bubble wrap. Your picnic will be much more appetizing when you arrive at your destination.

Baby your tools

Protect your tools from each other and from the toolbox by lining the toolbox with bubble wrap. Hold the wrap in place with duct tape. The cushioning will help your tools last longer.

Make a perfect pillow

Pillows and camping don't mix, unless you make a pillow out of bubble wrap. Simply fold the bubble wrap a few times and place it inside a pillowcase. The bubble wrap won't get dirty and will provide a gentle cushion for your head.

Heading out for a picnic? Wrap items you want to stay cold in bubble wrap.

candy tins

Whether or not candy is part of the deal, candy tins are a good buy. They make nice decorative pieces and can also be used for assorted jobs around the house. Put them to work with the ideas below (and hope that they come with candy inside!).

Organize your workbench

Keep clutter to a minimum on your workbench by using several candy tins to hold small quantities of picture hangers, washers, nuts, and other pieces that don't have a logical home.

Corral quarters for your car

Keep a collection of quarters in a candy tin in your glove compartment. You'll be surprised how often you'll open the box—for parking, tolls, or even to buy a quick snack.

Create a mini-sewing kit

Store a few needles, thread, a thimble, straight pins, safety pins, and a button or two in a candy tin, and keep it in your suitcase as an emergency sewing kit. You'll have plenty of supplies to make quick repairs when you're on the road.

Round up a broken necklace

Don't let a broken necklace break your heart. Find as many pieces as you can, and store them in a candy tin. Take the tin with you the next time you visit the jewelry repair shop.

WAY BACK WHEN...

Schrafft's Candy Tins

Back in the day, companies like Schrafft's, near Boston, sold its sweets in fancy tins. These containers had panache, and you can still find them in antique shops and online. A typical tin was round with a tapered top. Schrafft's candy company was founded in the late 19th century and has the distinction of sponsoring the first annual telecast of *The Wizard of Oz.*

cap erasers

Pencils have a number of alternate uses, and surprisingly enough, pencil erasers do, too. Dollar stores sell pencil cap erasers in addition to pencils, and they work just as well as pencil erasers in their alternate universe.

Replace the back of your earring

The backs of pierced earrings seem to have a magical—and disturbing—way of disappearing, often at crucial times. As long as you have a pencil cap eraser (or even the eraser on a pencil) nearby, you can fix the situation pronto. Cut a small part off the eraser with a knife or scissors, and position it on the back of your ear. Place the earring in your ear as you normally would, and stick the eraser onto the earring shaft to keep it in place.

Erase marks on leather

Though scuff marks usually end up on a vinyl floor, they can show up on a leather couch or chair, too. Get rid of them by rubbing them with a pencil cap eraser. A regular pencil eraser will also work.

Get rid of grout grime

Cleaning bathroom tile grout can be difficult, especially in the corners of a tub and other tight places. Use a new pencil cap eraser (or a new eraser at the end of a pencil) to clean those hard-to-reach areas of grout grime.

chalk

Chalk isn't just for kids anymore. In fact, it can be used for very grown-up chores: filling holes, preventing rust, and even keeping ants out of your house. It has other uses, too (and you can always use it to draw on the driveway!).

Fill a hole

When you're filling a small hole with plaster, it's hard to keep the patch from sinking into the hole, however small. Break a few pieces of chalk and stuff them into the hole, wedging them against the sides, and then plaster over. The chalk both fills the hole and provides something for the fresh plaster to grab.

Set your screwdriver straight

Just as chalking a pool cue stops slippage when the cue hits the ball, chalking a screwdriver can stop slippage when the tool tightens a screw. Simply rub chalk on the tip of the screwdriver's blade before your next project for best results.

Keep a file functioning

Metal files tend to get their teeth filled up with debris from whatever you're filing. Run a piece of chalk back and forth over the file to leave a layer of chalk on it before starting work and the waste won't clog the file.

Draw a line in the sand

Actually, draw a line of chalk around windowsills and doorways to prevent ants from entering your house. Use the same tactic for protecting your outdoor plants from ants and slugs—scatter powdered chalk around the base of the plants.

Solve a sticking door mystery

If your door sticks but you don't know exactly where you should sand it, use chalk in your detective work. Open the door, and mark the sides of the door that touch the door frame with chalk. Shut the door, open it again, and take note of where the chalk is missing. Those are the areas that need to be sanded.

Prevent rust

Keep rust out of your toolbox—and stop your tools from pitting and rusting—by placing a few pieces of chalk in your toolbox. The chalk will absorb any moisture and keep your tools (and your toolbox) rust-free.

Place a few pieces of chalk in your toolbox to help keep rust out of it.

The Story Behind...

Liquid Paper

Bette Nesmith Graham was interested in art but had a child to support so she took a secretarial job. Meticulous, she developed a paint to match her office stationery; it hid typos better than erasing. Fellow typists wanted "Mistake Out," so Graham trademarked it as Liquid Paper. The Gillette Corporation bought her successful company in 1979 for $47.5 million plus royalties.

clipboard

Clipboards have such a singular purpose that it's hard to believe they can be used for anything other than holding a sheet of paper steady. But clipboards are surprisingly versatile, doing everything from hanging pants to holding maps while you drive. Here are some tips on how to use them differently.

Create a frame

Not all clipboards are dull and dark with a utilitarian metal clip on top. The latest generation of clipboards comes in a variety of materials, from plastic in neon colors to space-age aluminum. Hang one of these stylish clipboards on your wall and clip a photo to it. You can easily swap in a new photo whenever you like.

Corral school papers

Keep a clipboard designated for permission slips, school activity reminders, and tests that need to be signed in an agreed-on spot in your house. Your kids will know where to put important papers that you need to see, and you'll know where to look for them.

Keep your pants crease-free

If you don't have a hanger designed for pants and don't want to fold them over an ordinary hanger, use a clipboard to keep your pants looking sharp. Hang a clipboard from a hook on the inside of your bedroom door or your closet, and snap your cuffs to the clipboard. Your crease-free pants will be ready whenever you want them.

Map your route

Road maps are notoriously difficult to handle, even when you have two hands available for the job. And when you're driving, consulting a map can be impossible with all those folds and floppy paper. Attach your map to a clipboard—showing your current route—and you'll have no trouble seeing where you're headed.

Make a blackboard with a clip

Paint the clipboard with blackboard paint. Attach a piece of chalk to the hole at the top of the clip. Hang the clipboard by the phone or near the door. You can clip notes or bills to the top while scribbling messages on the board.

correction fluid

You'll find a lot of power in one little bottle of correction fluid. You can use it to fix tubs, cars, and decorative china—and that's not all! Make sure you keep a bottle of it on hand, because you'll find many unusual uses for it around the house.

Touch up your paint job

White moldings make any room look a little more elegant, but small marks and scrapes take away from that beauty. Return your room to its former glory by painting liquid correction fluid over any faults you find. To re-create the moldings' glossy look, cover the correction fluid with clear nail polish. (And don't forget that correction fluid works beautifully on small stains on walls and ceilings, too.)

Cover up a car's scratch

Don't despair if your nice white car gets a scratch; just get some correction fluid and paint it right on the mark. The scratch will be gone before the correction fluid even dries.

Fix a marred tub

Enamel bathtubs and other enamel surfaces can get scratched, no matter how carefully you care for them. The good news is that repairing a scratched tub is even easier than scratching it! Clean the affected area with a cotton ball moistened with rubbing alcohol, and let it dry. Simply brush on the correction fluid for a quick and easy fix.

Welcome winter on your windows

Paint white snowflakes on your windows with correction fluid to usher in the winter season. When the snow outside has melted and thoughts have turned to spring, remove the snowflakes using glass cleaner, vinegar and water, or nail polish remover. If the correction fluid is particularly stubborn, you can get rid of it with a painter's tool: a single razor blade in a holder (used for scraping paint off of glass).

Repair decorative china

Use correction fluid to cover small nicks and dark lines or stains in white decorative china. Do not use correction fluid on anything that is intended for eating and drinking.

Cover a stain on fabric

Your white blouse is perfect except for a dot of ink on the cuff, and you can't get that drip of red wine out of the tablecloth. Use a tiny dab of correction fluid to cover the stains.

crayons

Ah, to be young again—young enough to use crayons. But wait! You don't have to be under a certain age to use them, or even to use them for their original purpose. Check out the alternate ways you can use crayons, and use them to your (young) heart's content.

Fix furniture scratches

Whether your cat scratched your sofa's legs senseless or your young child scratched your coffee table with his scissors, you'll want to cover up the damage. How? Use a crayon. Find the crayon that matches the wood finish, and soften it with a hair dryer. Color in the scratches with the softened crayon, and then buff the repaired area with a clean rag.

Make a fire starter

A fire starter makes it easy to get a fire crackling in a fireplace. With crayons, making a chemical-free fire starter is easy. Melt crayons in a tin can set into a saucepan half-filled with water over medium heat. Wrap a pinecone loosely with string and roll it in the melted crayon, pulling out a tail of string to serve as a wick. Let the crayon soak into the pinecone, then let it cool and harden on waxed paper. To use, arrange twigs over the starter, add logs, and light.

Seal envelopes

Melt old crayons with a lighter over a cup lined with tin foil. Drip the wax from the cup over an envelope into pretty patterns before the wax hardens, or form a single spot and use a metal stamp to imprint a shape or initial you like.

Create colored candles

You don't have to be an experienced home candlemaker to get lovely results. Start with plain white candles. Melt a handful of crayons all the same color in tin can set in a pan half-filled with water over low heat. When the crayons melt, lift out the can onto a heatproof surface and dip the candles to coat them in a colorful way.

Decorate Easter eggs

Fancy Easter egg dye kits usually include a stick of wax for marking the egg before dipping it into the dye—the wax repels the dye and keeps the surface its original color. Forget about the stick of wax. Just use a crayon for a similar effect.

Color in the scratches on your wooden furniture with a softened crayon.

double-stick tape

Double-stick or double-sided tape can keep you organized, safe, and free from embarrassment. Who knew such a simple invention had so many important functions? You will, after you read this!

Repair a sagging hem

Staples and safety pins are good tools to use on a torn hem, but double-stick tape is even better because it won't show. Lay the pants or skirt on a table, counter, or desk, and cut a length of double-stick tape the width and length of the tear. Place the tape onto the hem, and then firmly press the two pieces of fabric together. Return to the world with confidence!

Secure throw rugs

Both people and pets can slip on a throw rug if it lacks a backing that keeps it in place. Don't put yourself, your family, and your dog or cat at risk of falling—just attach the rug to the floor with some double-sided tape.

Take a seat

Sliding off a chair during a dinner party would be considered very bad manners, so don't subject your guests to such a terrible faux pas. Stick the seat cushion to the chair with double-stick tape, and your guests will stay in one place.

Keep screws in place

Lay a few lines of double-stick tape on your workbench before you start a project. Stick nuts and bolts and screws to the tape as you work. You won't lose the pieces, and you'll know exactly where to find them.

envelopes

Envelopes have come a long way from just holding notes sent through the mail. No longer only plain white and a certain shape, envelopes come in all colors and sizes and have many more uses, too. Here are some of the best.

Feed the shredder faster

Whether you're disposing of ATM receipts, credit card receipts, or any other receipts that contain financial or personal information, you should shred them rather than toss them in the trash. And the fastest way to get rid of them is to put them in an envelope and shred the envelope, rather than individual receipts.

Get ready for the grocery store

Use an envelope as a shopping list—record what you need on the non-flap side—and keep coupons for items you plan to buy inside. When you go to the grocery store you'll have everything you need in one neat package.

Make a funnel

Refilling the salt and pepper shakers can be a messy job, unless you have a funnel. And don't despair if you don't have a funnel—you can make one quickly and easily out of a plain old envelope. Just seal it, cut it in half diagonally (suddenly you have two funnels), and cut a small corner off of each one. Now you have one funnel for salt and one for pepper!

Create family files

Need a place to hold gift cards after the holidays? Give each family member an envelope, and have them keep all gift cards in their designated envelope. You can keep all the envelopes or they can keep their own. Either way, the gift cards won't go to the wrong person. Use this system to keep other small family property divided, too.

THE Story Behind...

The Pink Pearl Eraser

When the F. W. Woolworth Co. arranged to have a pencil named "Pearl" sold exclusively in its stores, the company had no idea it was helping to birth an icon. The A. W. Faber Pencil Co. took a revolutionary step: They attached erasers directly to their products, and the Pearl got a pink one. Erasers (when sold separately) were named after the pencils they first adorned. The Pink Pearl eraser is recognized as classic, and is a staple on back-to-school lists.

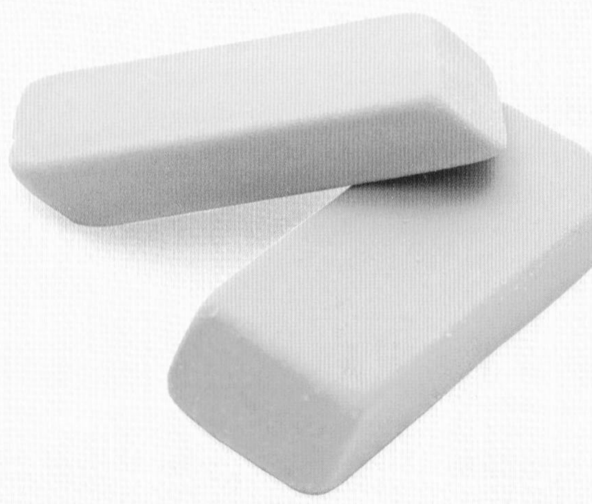

Secure teacher notes

Binders and backpacks are notorious black holes, particularly when it comes to notes sent home from teachers. Help your child keep those notes safe by punching three holes in one side of a manila envelope and placing it in the binder. Make sure notes are put in the envelope, and you'll never have to search for them again.

eraser

The main job of an eraser is to...erase. And erasers are generally used to remove pencil marks from paper. Here are a few completely different kinds of marks to remove, as well as jobs for an eraser that have nothing to do with erasing.

Rub away residue

Nothing destroys the joy of a new item more than the sticky residue left by the price tag. You scrub and you rub and you can't get rid of the gummy mess—unless you use a pencil eraser! Rub the goo with an eraser and get back to enjoying your purchase.

Clean a computer keyboard

When you've been pounding away on your computer keys for a while, you may notice dark grime building up on the curved face of the keys. It's risky to use water or cleaning products there, but you can rub the dirt gently away with an eraser, blowing to clear any eraser dust.

Clean spots off suede

Rub gently with an eraser not only to remove minor stains and marks from suede shoes and bags, but also to fluff up the suede fibers.

Erase the stain

If you find unidentifiable small smudges and spots on your walls, get rid of them with an art gum eraser. Rub the wall gently, and watch the stain disappear. You can also use an art gum eraser to rub fingerprints off wallpaper.

Make a pin cushion

Stop storing your straight pins in a box. They're too easy to spill and too hard to pick up, one at a time. Instead, stick them in a pencil eraser. You'll get exactly one when you want exactly one.

gift ribbon

When you tie ribbon around a gift, the ribbon serves only a decorative purpose—it's not really holding the package together. Why not give ribbon a real job to do? You can find one in the tips below.

Make stake ties

Use gift-wrapping ribbon to tie tall flowers like snapdragons and viny vegetables like tomatoes to their stakes. The ribbon is soft and flexible, so it won't hurt the plants.

Replace your lace

Shoelaces have a tendency to break at the worst possible time—usually as you tie them on your way out the door. If you don't have an extra on hand and have places to go and things to do, just replace your shoelace with a ribbon until you can buy another one.

Identify your luggage

Ever notice at baggage pickup how everyone on your flight has exactly the same suitcase you do? Set yours apart by tying a bright ribbon around the handle. You'll know it's yours, and if the ribbon is bright enough, you might even see it first!

grocery bags

Big paper bags—the kind your groceries are packed in—have multiple uses around the house. But the lunch-size paper bags you find at the dollar store have several uses, too, many of which having nothing to do with lunch. Here are big uses for these small bags.

Wrap small presents

Lunch bags are the perfect size to wrap CDs, DVDs, and small to medium-sized boxes. Cut the bag open, lay it flat, place the gift to be wrapped in the center, and wrap it as usual. Either tie a colorful ribbon around the plain brown wrap or decorate the paper with colored pencils, markers, or paint.

Gently rub suede shoes and bags with an eraser to remove minor stains and marks.

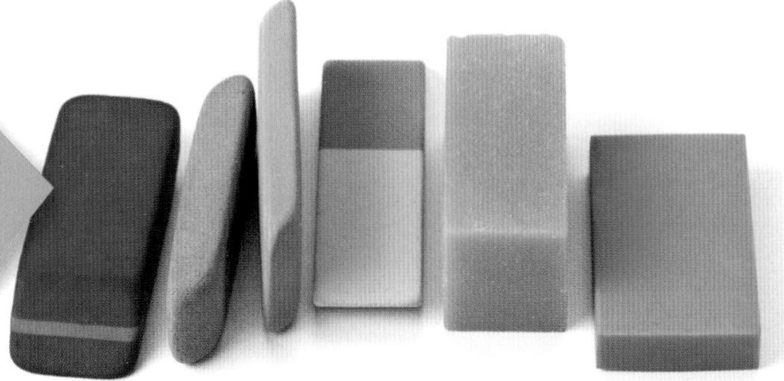

Keep your kitchen counter clean

Cut open a paper bag or two and place them on the kitchen counter the next time you peel carrots or potatoes or core an apple or pineapple. Use the bags to catch the mess. When you're done with your task, just roll up the bags and toss them into the garbage.

Make bread last longer

Transfer your bread from a plastic bag to a paper bag if you live in an area with high humidity. The bread will stay fresher longer—the crust will remain crisp and the center will stay soft.

Absorb cooking oils

Keep a couple of lunch bags on hand next Halloween when you prepare pumpkin seeds for eating. After you bake the seeds, put them on the lunch bags. The bags will absorb the oil or butter used in baking, and your seeds will be ready to eat.

Fill gift bags

Clean your paper shredder, then run a few lunch bags through it. Use the ribbons of brown paper as decorative filler in a gift bag. If you want to spice up the mix, shred a few pieces of construction paper and add those ribbons to the bag as well.

gum

Along with candy, dollar stores almost always stock chewing gum in or near the party and school supplies aisle, in addition to the grocery aisle. Gum makes a great addition to a goody bag that guests take away at the end of a party, but you might want to consider keeping some in the house—it fixes more than you might think. Chew on these additional ways to use gum.

Stop the wasps

If wasps have found a hole in your house and have decided to make a nest in the hole—and in your walls—bar them from entry by placing a wad of chewing gum over the hole. Plug the hole at night after you (or better yet, a professional) have killed the wasps. Wasps are least active between dusk and dawn, and you don't want to take the chance that any have survived.

Lunch bags are the perfect size to wrap CDs, DVDs, and small- to medium-sized boxes.

Fix clay pots

Don't toss a clay flowerpot or dog dish just because it sports a crack. Enjoy chewing a piece of gum, then use it to fill the crack. You'll save the pot and the bowl and a trip to the store.

Bid heartburn good-bye

Chew a stick of spearmint gum to relieve heartburn. The spearmint helps with digestion, and the act of chewing gum produces saliva, which in turn neutralizes stomach acid.

index cards

They're stronger than ordinary paper and a handier size. And they even have a life beyond recipes. Check out the other jobs index cards can do.

Shop strategically

Make several shopping lists on several different index cards depending on where you're shopping. Use one for the grocery store, one for the wholesale club, one for the dollar store, and so on. Using different colored cards for each store keeps you even more organized.

Make a handy reminder

Family members may claim they can't do the laundry because they don't know how. Tell them how, and then write simplified instructions on an index card, cover it with clear plastic (or transparent tape, if that's easier), and post it near the washing machine. No excuses now!

Toss your recipe book

Transfer your beloved ratty recipes to individual cards, slip them into index card protectors, and breathe life into them.

Level a table

Dinner table a bit wobbly? Fold an index card in half (or in thirds depending on how wobbly the table is) and slip it under the table leg. No more wobbles.

Make a bookmark

Why bother buying a bookmark when you can use an index card? Better still, you can write down favorite pages and passages, making it ideal for remembering the books that mean the most to you.

index card box

Chances are you fill an index card box with index cards. And chances are those index cards sport recipes. Consider taking a chance on using the index card box for something completely different!

File away your garden

Divide an index card box into sections, one for each part of your garden and yard: flowers, vegetables, shrubs, even your lawn. Make index cards for plant varieties you've tried and liked—and note how you've cared for them—and others for varieties you want to try in the future. You can even keep seed packets in the appropriate sections.

Ditch the address book

Using an index card box instead of an address book will keep you organized and on top of the paper tiger. Record the address, phone number, cell phone number, e-mail address, and any other pertinent contact information below the addressee's name on an index card. You can also add birth dates, anniversaries, spouse and children's names, and anything else you want to remember about that person.

Make a bookworm box

Big-time readers often have a tough time remembering what they've read. If you occasionally forget which books you've consumed, start a book file in an index box. Divide the cards by type of book—mysteries, novels, history, and so on—or by author.

Keep track of Christmas presents

Can't remember from one year to the next what you gave your loved ones? No problem. Assign each family member a card, write down their sizes and favorite colors, and each year write down what gift you gave them.

Buy it for this,
use it for that!

magnets

You learned about the poles of magnets in school and why they repel each other. (Do you remember why?) But you never learned how to use magnets in unusual and creative ways. Here is what you missed.

Decorate your refrigerator

Picture frames can display only a limited number of the photographs you've taken. Enjoy more photos by cutting around the subject(s), gluing a small magnet on the back, and posting them on the fridge. You'll see your friends and family every time you have a meal!

Keep office supplies in order

Place a small magnet in your desk drawer to corral paper clips. They'll be easier to find and a snap to use.

Mount small metal helpers

Attach a series of small magnets or one magnet strip on the wall in the bathroom to hold the metal tools you use there: nail scissors, tweezers, a nail file, and so on. Just be sure to keep them out of reach of children.

Keeps nails in jars

Even if you're not a klutz, you may knock over jars of nails or screws or washers when you're busy at your workbench. Add small round magnets to these jars. Why? So that the nails and screws and washers won't scatter all over your workbench if you happen to tip over the jars. The magnets will keep them contained.

Clean up a metal mess

Suppose you spilled a container of nails and nuts and other small metal objects, but didn't have a magnet inside the jar to stop from making a mess. Use a magnet now. Turn a ziplock bag inside out, and put a bar magnet inside. Pick up the nails with the bag—they'll stick to it—then turn it right side out to hold the metal pieces you've recovered.

Wear a brooch without a pin

Grandma's brooch may be beautiful, but do you really want to put holes in your favorite silk blouse to show it off? No you don't, and you don't have to. Take off the shaft of the brooch and superglue a magnet to the back. Once it dries completely, hold it where you want it on your blouse, and put the opposing magnet on the inside of the blouse. The magnets will hold the brooch just like a pin—but without the damage to your wardrobe.

Stop frozen locks

Cover your car door locks with magnets overnight in the dead of winter. They'll prevent the locks from freezing—and your hands from freezing as you try to defrost the locks!

Pick up pins and needles

Sewing hardly seems like a dangerous pastime, but it can be fraught with danger if you spill pins and needles on the floor. Before someone steps on them, use a magnet to pick them up. You'll spare your hands and their feet!

marbles

Marbles show up a lot as a standard party favor in 99 cent stores. They're inexpensive, fun to play with, and pretty. They can be more than window dressing, though. Here are several ways to put them to work. (Be sure to keep them out of the reach of small children because they are a choking hazard.)

Fix a fingertip

If you have a glove with a frayed fingertip, let a marble come to your rescue. Place it into the fingertip so that the fabric is stretched out and smooth—the way you want it when you sew.

Make a marble party game

Here's a way to occupy party guests at the beginning of a party while others arrive. Fill a jar with marbles—be sure to count them first—and set it out for everyone to see. Have each guest write down the number of marbles they think are in the jar. At the end of the party, give a prize for the closest guess—you can even give them the decorative jar of marbles to take home!

Prettify a vase

Clear glass vases are attractive, and they can be made even more so with the help of colorful marbles. Set a number of pretty marbles at the bottom of the vase, then fill the vase with water and flowers. You'll be amazed by the transformation.

HOW TO SHOOT A MARBLE

The tried and true method to keep your marbles is to shoot with skill. Here's how:

1 **With your dominant hand, fold your thumb into your palm and make a fist, keeping your thumb knuckle level with your index finger.**

2 **Stick out your index finger—the tip of your thumb will be held in place by your middle finger. Put your marble in the middle of your thumb knuckle, wrap your index finger around it tightly.**

3 **Kick out your thumb to shoot the marble from your hand!**

7 More Ways to Use MAGNETS

1 Find a Stud

A handsome man may be your goal but another stud (the metal kind) can be found by running a magnet along a wall. Before picking up your hammer, grab a magnet—and save yourself some fruitless pounding.

2 Child's Play

You can make a wall in a child's bedroom more fun by coating a wall with magnetized paint. Magnets—the flexible sheet kind—will stick to the painted area, allowing children to create a "magnetic" focal wall.

3 Seal a Vent

Reduce heating and air conditioning costs by preventing hot or cold air from entering unused rooms. Just cut some flexible sheet magnet to cover your metal registers. Your home will be more energy efficient and comfortable.

4 Book Marked

Advertising magnets can take over your fridge. If you are tired of looking at pizza and dry-cleaning mottos, cover one side of a magnet with colorful packing tape. Then trim the edges so they are flush and cut the magnet in half. Hinge the two pieces back together with another piece of tape. You can use the result as a bookmark.

5 Ear, Ear

What do you do with a single earring? If it's pretty and you don't want to let it go, glue it to a magnet and use it to stick photos on your refrigerator.

6 Magic Paper Clip

Drop a paper clip into a glass of water, and ask your friends if they can remove it without putting anything in the glass or dumping the water. Conceal a strong magnet between your fingers and touch the glass. After the paper clip attaches to the magnet, slowly move your hand up the glass. Your friends will be amazed at your "magic touch."

7 True North

If you have a straight pin, a piece of cork, a bowl of water, and a strong magnet, you can amaze your kids. Rub the pin across the magnet 50 times (in the same direction). Then push the pin through the cork and put it in the water. The pin will point north, no matter how you twist the bowl. Check it against a compass if your children don't believe you!

masking tape

Masking tape is another item that can be found in several aisles; it's main purpose is to mask off areas that shouldn't be covered with paint during a paint job. But it also has other roles when rooms are painted, and even more roles outside those rooms. Here are the many things masking tape can do.

Speed cleanup

Before you start your next paint job, cover the bottom of the brush bristles and the top of the brush handle with about two inches of masking tape. (Make sure that 1/2 inch of that tape covers the bristles.) When you're done, take the tape off the brush and throw it away. The bottoms of the bristles will be cleaner than usual, since you've prevented the paint from seeping into them. Cleanup will be a breeze!

Pick up spilled beads

Dropping a box of beads—or watching a beaded necklace break and spill onto the floor—can be upsetting and potentially dangerous. Get rid of the annoyance and the danger by picking up the beads quickly and easily. How? With masking tape. Simply wrap the tape around your hand, sticky side out, until most of your hand is covered. Now pat your hand on your floor repeatedly, until you've picked up lots of beads. Brush the beads off into a container, and continue to pat the floor until you've rescued all the beads.

Label cans with tape

Paint cans can get messy—and the labels on the cans unreadable—after you've painted a room or two. Since you need to know which paint can contains which color, label the can with a piece of masking tape and a permanent marker. Note the date you painted the room, which room(s) you painted, and the name and number of the color.

Tape diapers shut

It doesn't matter if the sticky tabs have failed on a disposable diaper because your child has learned how to undo them or because you pulled them off one time too many trying to get them just right—what matters is that you need a new way to attach them. Masking tape will hold them shut just fine.

Control pet hair, hands down

Wrap both your hands in masking tape—with the sticky side facing out—and run your hands over your hairy couch or chair. Use both sides of your hands for best results. This works on pet-hair-covered clothing, too.

Use masking tape to tape disposable diapers shut.

Avoid overfeeding fish

If your fish food container has too many big holes or is one big hole—which may result in overfeeding—cover half of the container's mouth or half of the holes with masking tape. You'll have better control over the amount you feed your fish.

Repair an umbrella

Fix a broken umbrella rib with masking tape and a coat hanger. Cut a length of wire from the coat hanger and attach it to the damaged rib with masking tape. You'll be ready for the next rainstorm.

Tape your locks shut

Prevent water from entering the locks on your car doors by taping over them with masking tape before you enter a car wash in winter. Why? So that the water doesn't turn to ice inside the locks and prevent you from locking or unlocking the doors. Take the tape off the door after you leave the car wash.

Keep a pen handy

You know how you can never find a pen when you need one in your car? Now you can—just tape a pen to the dashboard so you'll have it handy the next time you need to sign a receipt, jot down directions, or make a note of what you need on your next trip to the grocery store.

paper clips

Irons, eyeglasses, buttons, and CDs—what do they all have in common? Paper clips in general, and paper clips to the rescue in particular. Here are several alternate uses for the heroic little paper clip.

Repair your eyeglasses

When that delicate little screw disappears from the hinge of your glasses, it's easy to assume all is lost. But you can make a serviceable repair by using a small paper clip. Open one side and push it through the hinge. Gently fold the clip back down, and the glasses will hold very securely until you can get them fixed.

Attach a button

Don't hide in your office if you lose a button at work. You can fix it easily. Using the holes made by the original thread, push a straightened-out paper clip up through the garment, through one of the holes in the button, down through another hole, and back through the second original hole in the clothing. Twist the ends of the paper clip together, and bend them until the metal lies flat against your garment. Now get back to work!

Pick a lock

Not in a criminal way! Many of us have lost the tiny keys to diaries, jewelry boxes, or suitcases and despaired of ever getting the lock open again. Straighten out a paper clip and jiggle gently through the keyhole at the mechanism. It will likely spring open.

Rescue CDs and DVDs

CD and DVD players have been known to eat their discs. If your player refuses to return your disc, you'll have to rescue it without the help of the machine. Turn a paper clip into a hook, and place the hook over or under the tray. Jimmy the tray out enough that you can grasp it, then pull it out so you can take out your disc.

Lengthen a pull chain

Stop stretching or using a step stool to reach the chain on an overhead light or ceiling fan. Instead, attach a chain of paper clips to the end of the pull chain...and pull!

Mark the end of tape

If you've ever tried to find the beginning of a roll of transparent tape, you know that finding it is only half the battle—the other half is lifting the tape in one piece. Solve both problems by placing a paper clip under the end of the tape every time you use it. You'll never have either problem again.

Make a key chain

You always seem to have several key chains when you don't need them, and none when you do. If you need a key chain but don't have any on hand, thread several paper clips together into a chain and slip the key through the paper clip on the end. Instant key chain!

Remember your page

Beautiful paper bookmarks do an adequate job of keeping your place in a book, but an ordinary paper clip outperforms its paper competitor. A paper clip won't fall out and lose your spot if your book takes a tumble or gets upended in your book bag.

Unclog your iron

Minerals may be clogging the steam ports on the bottom of your iron if your iron doesn't emit steam the way it should. Unplug your iron, let it cool, and then try cleaning out the ports with the end of a straightened paper clip.

WAY BACK WHEN...

Straws

We welcome paper straws today as an alternative to plastic, but they're not new. The patent was issued in 1888 to Marvin Stone (a manufacturer of cigarette holders). The Stone Straw Corporation made paper straws by hand-winding them until 1906 when the process was mechanized.

party straws

What is a party drink without brightly colored straws? And what is a garden without multiple straws? You may know the answer to the first question but not the second one. Find the second answer—and many more straw tips—here.

Thaw with a straw

Ice can wreak havoc on cars—particularly on locks, which can freeze in the winter. If you can't insert your key into a frozen lock, try placing a straw on the lock and blowing into it. The warmth from your breath should melt the ice, and you should be able to then insert the key.

Help your flowers stand straight

Place a straw next to a bent or drooping flower stem in your garden, and attach the stem to the straw loosely with transparent tape. The straw will act as a splint.

Extend a caulk gun

Whether you need to seal a crack in an awkward space in the basement or caulk the top of the tiles in the shower, you may need to extend your caulk gun. Let an ordinary plastic straw help! Attach it to the nozzle of the caulk gun with duct tape, and use the tool as you normally would—with better results.

Prevent knots in chains

Use a straw as a jewelry chain protector. Just run your necklace through a straw, then close the clasp. The straw will keep the chain from getting knotted and tangled. Your necklaces will always be ready to go!

pencil

"Pencil pusher" is a derogatory term, but anyone who knows anything about pencils and all the jobs they can do would be thrilled to be called a pencil pusher. Here are a bunch of ways you can push pencils to your advantage.

A pencil marks the spot

A squirrel may be at the root of your missing bulb problem, and you can be sure a squirrel isn't going to fix it—but you can. Mark the spot where your flower didn't bloom with a pencil—push it firmly into the soil—so that come fall, you'll know where you need to replant the bulb.

Water plants the write way

Test the soil of your houseplant with a pencil to determine if it needs water. Push a pencil firmly into the soil and let it sit for half an hour. Pull it out and inspect the tip: If it's dry, you need to thoroughly water your plant. If the pencil comes up with dirt on the tip, the soil is moist enough.

Forget about a foot ache

Are your new shoes a little too tight? Did you walk a little too far? Did you stand in line a little too long? Ward off a foot ache—or stop one in its tracks—by doing a simple foot exercise. Place a few pencils on the floor, and pick them up one by one with your toes. You'll stretch your feet and feel relief.

Silence squeaky stairs

Don't let a noisy step keep you awake at night. Scrape some pencil lead into the seam where the flat part of the step and the riser—the back of the step—meet. The squeak will disappear. The pencil lead will eventually seep out of the joint, so be sure to reapply it when necessary.

Make a school picture frame

What could be more appropriate as a school picture frame than four pencils? Glue two sharpened pencils to the long sides of a frame and two shorter pencils (sharpen them down to size) to the shorter sides of the frame. The pencils and the picture will provide fond memories.

Lubricate your locks

Use pencil lead to "grease" your locks, rather than an oil-based lubricant, which may draw in dust and grime. Scrape the lead (which is usually a mix of graphite with a clay binder) of a No. 1 or No. 2 pencil onto a piece of wax paper with a knife, then rub the lead onto a key. Use the key to turn the lock a few times, and you're done. If you're pressed for time, just rub the point of the pencil against the key, then insert the key into the lock. Do this once or twice a year to keep your locks in tip-top shape.

Put the bite back into your zipper's teeth

If your zipper gets stuck moving up and down, lubricate the teeth by rubbing them on both sides with a lead pencil.

HERE'S THE POINT...

THE HISTORY OF THE #2 PENCIL

"Bring two sharpened #2 pencils." On the morning of an important exam many of us have rushed about in desperation looking for the "right" pencils and instead found ones stamped "HB" or "9H." If this is familiar, then then you've also had the simultaneous thoughts: "A *pencil is a pencil!*" and *"Am I doomed if this isn't a #2?"*

In ancient times, nobody cared about the lead in pencils. Scribes wrote with a rod called a stylus—a precursor to our pencil—and it left a mark of lead. The actual mark was light, but the figurative mark was indelible: To this day many people call the core of a pencil "lead" but it isn't, and it never has been (despite many a grammar school teacher promising direly, "If you keep chewing that pencil, you'll get lead poisoning!"). **Pencil cores are made of graphite,** a nontoxic form of carbon that came into wide use after **a large deposit was found in England in the 1500s.** Legend has it that a violent storm in the Borrowdale area of Cumberland (now known as Cumbria) uprooted trees and revealed a black material underneath. The substance was thought to be a form of lead and so was called *plumbago* (Latin for "lead ore"). **Shepherds used it to mark their sheep;** the graphite left a dark mark on the wool (though it was messy on the hands).

Wood-cased pencils were a great improvement, and William Munroe produced the first U.S.-made pencils in Concord, Massachusetts, around 1812. Another improvement in American pencils came in 1821, when **a different pencil factory in Massachusetts mixed the local graphite with clay** and created a superior product. John Thoreau & Co. had an employee named Henry David. Did you ever wonder how Thoreau wrote *Walden*? The answer is deliberately and with his own pencil!

Mass production of pencils began around 1870. Many **manufacturers started stamping their pencils with brand names.** The Joseph Dixon Crucible Company of Sturbridge, Massachusetts, the first to mass-produce its product, eventually became known as Dixon Ticonderoga. Does that ring any grammar school bells? **The Ticonderoga pencil was a popular one,** as were the Eagle and the Mongol.

If you didn't notice the names, you were likely fixated on the number. It is generally stamped after the name and before the metal that attaches the eraser to the body of the pencil (called a ferrule). This number denotes the hardness of a pencil's core; **the higher the number, the harder the graphite and the lighter the mark** left on the paper (and vice versa). In the United States, you will see numbers 1 through 4 on pencils. Outside the country, you will see letters. *H* indicates a hard pencil; *B* indicates a softer core. Theoretically you could use an *HB* and a #2 interchangeably, but why take that chance? **Pencil manufacturers set their own internal standards** for graphite hardness. So the sharp thing to do when someone directs you to be in possession of a #2 pencil is to make sure that is exactly what you have. If you must search madly on the morning of an exam, be cheered by the knowledge that when you finally find one, it will be covered in wood, clearly stamped...and you won't be using it to mark sheep.

Top: The Eagle Pencil Company, Cedar Keys, Florida, circa 1880. Bottom: American Lead Pencil Company's Manufactory in New York City, 1872.

Tighten a loose screw

Eyeglass frames are dependent on those tiny screws that don't seem to stay in place very long. Don't let a loose screw get the best of you—just turn a pencil upside down, press the eraser against the screw so that it engages the screw, and turn the pencil. You'll fix the frame and create a handy new tool at the same time!

Remove a cactus

If you want to replant a small cactus, let the soil dry out a bit first. Then put the eraser end of a pencil into the drainage hole through the bottom of the pot, and slowly push the cactus out through the top. The root ball should come out in one piece.

Accessorize your hair

Stick two pencils into your bun so that they form an *X*. The pencils will help keep your bun in place.

pencil case

Why is a pencil case called a pencil case when, in fact, it holds so many other items? Pens, erasers, mini staplers—those are just a few of the logical items pencil cases carry. If you think outside the box—or the pencil case—you'll find several other items you should keep in your pencil case. Here are a few.

Carry cosmetics

Pencil cases make excellent cosmetic cases—particularly if they're made of waterproof plastic—and they're an awful lot cheaper than their cosmetic case counterparts.

Make a first aid kit

There's no need to buy a premade first aid kit when you have an inexpensive pencil case. Just add adhesive bandages, antibiotic ointment, aspirin, an instant cold compress, and any other items you feel are necessary. Keep it in your house or your car or anywhere you might need it.

Protect your stockings

Don't let your suitcase or its contents make runs in your stockings. Roll them up and stash them in a pencil case when you travel. They'll remain safe and run-free.

rubber bands

They're good for shooting at friends and enemies and making into bouncy balls. But rubber bands have a number of more practical and uncommon uses. Once you see the uses, you'll wonder why they're not more common!

Prevent carpal tunnel syndrome

Computers can help you get organized, save time, and provide endless entertainment, but they can also cause trouble. Avoid the effects of repetitive hand motion—like carpal tunnel syndrome—by stretching your hands every couple of hours. Touch your fingertips to the tip of your thumb, then surround your hand with a rubber band just below your fingernails. Slowly open your hand, spreading your fingers, then close them. Do this 10 times for each hand.

Mark liquid content

Ever wonder how much liquid—like paint thinner, drain cleaner, or metal polish—is left in opaque containers? You can't tell by looking at the container—unless you wrap a rubber band around it to indicate how much remains. You'll never have to guess about the contents again.

Attach your tools to your stepladder

Making trips up and down your stepladder to get tools is a waste of time and potentially dangerous.

Wrap a rubber band around a container to help indicate how much remains.

Strap your tools onto your stepladder with large rubber bands. Stretch two rubbers bands around the folding tool shelf—or on the top step of the ladder, which you're not supposed to use anyway—and slip your tools under the rubber bands. They'll be at your fingertips the next time you need them.

Keep your cutting board in place

Stop your cutting board from sliding around the kitchen counter by wrapping a rubber band around each end. You'll have a much easier time cutting and chopping.

Protect your paint can

Want to keep the grooves in the top of your paint can from filling with paint every time you wipe your paintbrush on the side of the can? Place a rubber band around the can so that it stretches across the top of the can (and across the top of the paint). Wipe your brush on the rubber band rather than on the can to get rid of excess paint. You'll keep the grooves paint-free.

Organize your car

Get organized by wrapping two rubber bands around each sun visor in your car. You can use this newfound storage space for your garage door opener, maps, and directions.

Childproof your cabinets

Forget about buying expensive (and complicated) locks for cabinets that swing open. Simply secure them by tying rubber bands around the knobs.

Keep dresses on hangers

Dresses with spaghetti straps tend to fall off hangers. Keep your dresses where they belong by wrapping a rubber band around each end of a hanger. The dresses won't fall off.

rubber cement

People below a certain age don't even know what rubber cement is, but they should. It's a surprisingly versatile substance, even though it flies under the radar. Here are a few ways to use it that should put it back on the map.

Position a screw in a tight spot

If you can't reach the place where you need to insert a screw, you won't be able to hold the screw to start the job. How can you solve this problem? With a little rubber cement. Place a small amount of rubber cement on the slot of the screw, and put the tip of the screwdriver into the slot. Let the cement dry, then start work.

Place a small amount of rubber cement on the slot of the screw, to help position the tip of the screwdriver.

Cancel crayon marks

If your pint-sized Picasso got carried away and colored the (washable) wallpaper with crayon, don't worry that he's created a permanent masterpiece. Cover the offending marks with rubber cement, wait until it dries completely, then roll off the rubbery glue—and your budding young artist's work.

Fix a carpet burn

Don't despair if you find a hole burned in your carpet. Just cut the burned fibers out with scissors, then put rubber cement into the hole with a toothpick. Cover the ends of matching carpet fibers (that you've cut from a remnant or a hidden area of carpet) with rubber cement, and put them in the hole. Draw the tufts upright with a pin, then, when the patch is dry, blend the tufts into the carpet using the pin.

staples

You probably don't think of your clothing when you think of staples and staplers, but your life would be easier if you did. Check out how you can use staples on your clothes.

Hitch up your hem

Don't let a dragging hem get you down. If you don't have access to a sewing kit—or even a needle and thread—you can still repair your pants or skirt easily. Just staple the hem back where it belongs. You can even staple the hem from the inside of the garment so that very little of the staple will be seen on the outside. Best of all, the staples will come out easily when you have time to repair your garment properly.

Staple your pants shut

Splitting the seam of your pants is embarrassing in any circumstances and is particularly mortifying if you're at work and can't change them immediately. Save face by ducking into a restroom with a stapler. After you've removed your pants, line the seam up as it was previously sewn, making sure about half an inch of material remains on either side of the seam—and staple the seam shut.

Tame your cords

Your computer and stereo cords, that is. Glue or tape a piece of thick cardboard to the back of your desk or stereo cabinet, and then tack the cords into place. No more tangled mess!

tissue paper

Tissue paper is a lot tougher than it looks. It may appear fragile, but it knows how to protect cookies; whip clothes, hats, and purses into shape; and even keep tabs on your dryer. Here's how.

Keep cookies crisp

Soggy cookies take all the fun out of having cookies in the first place, so help your cookies stay crunchy with tissue paper. Crumple some up and keep it in the bottom of your cookie container. It will draw moisture away from the cookies and keep them fresh longer.

Shape your hat

Stuff the crown of your favorite hat with tissue paper—more than you think is necessary—so that the brim doesn't touch the shelf when you place the hat on it. By resting the hat on the tissue paper, you'll keep the brim in shape, along with the rest of the hat.

Check your dryer door

If you suspect the seal on your dryer leaks, try this experiment. Close the door and turn on the machine. Move a piece of tissue paper around the edge of the door. Is the paper drawn toward the door? If so, the seal of the door needs to be replaced.

Aim for a soft collar

Starched collars often look harsh. Give your blouse or shirt collar a softer look by placing a twisted piece of tissue paper underneath it.

Prevent creases

Garments made of very thin fabric are often very beautiful, but they are also very susceptible to creasing. Place a sheet or two of tissue paper in your favorite thin piece of clothing before folding it, and you'll minimize creases.

Keep your bags in shape

Stuff leather purses and briefcases with tissue paper to help maintain their shape when they're out of circulation. Plastic bags work well, too.

wrapping paper

Wrap up birthday and holiday celebrations in an environmentally friendly way by finding uses for all the wrapping paper you bought at the dollar store. Here are some ideas for that wrapping paper, whether new or used.

Protect your ornaments

Christmas is one of the biggest wrapping paper days of the year—and one of the biggest days of waste. Don't toss used wrapping paper just because it's ripped. Use it again to protect your ornaments when you store them for next year.

Pack your wrapping paper

Make your own packing material the next time you ship a package. Shred leftover wrapping paper and use it to protect whatever you're shipping.

Cover your book

Whether you have a title you want to keep to yourself or a textbook you want to protect, wrap the cover in wrapping paper. You'll end up with both privacy and a pretty cover.

Make pet bedding

Shred wrapping paper from birthday and holiday gifts and use it to create bedding for animals at a shelter or veterinarian's office. Be sure to ask if the shelter or the office needs bedding material before you drop it off.

9 More Ways to Use WRAPPING PAPER

1 Match a Matchbox

If you are giving a candle as a gift, a fun way to add to your present is to wrap a box of matches (the size you'd get at the supermarket) with wrapping paper that matches either the candle or the paper you've wrapped the candle in. This extra touch will delight the recipient.

2 Scrap to Keepsake

What can you do with wrapping paper left over from presents? If you have a pair of scissors and a wire coat hanger you can make a keepsake that can be reused each time the same occasion arises. Bend the hanger into a circle. Roll up a flattened piece of wrapping paper and cut it into 8-by-1-inch strips. Twist each strip around the coat hanger. Do this until your "wreath" is full and festive. If you have a leftover bow, pop it on!

3 Outside the Box

Do your kids have a lot of little toy figurines? Are you stepping on them because they're scattered all over? Box them up in a pretty way. Wrap an empty tissue box with paper that coordinates with your child's room. Now all of those toys that are outside the box have a home.

4 (Scrap) Book It

Some paper is just too pretty to throw away after you've opened a gift. Why not use some of it to decorate a scrapbook? You can create a page to commemorate the occasion the gift was received with the paper that it was wrapped in.

5 Holiday Theme

Take the mats from your framed pictures and wrap them in holiday-themed wrapping paper. This little decorating touch is inexpensive, but it will make a big impression on your guests. (This tip can work for birthday decorating, too!)

6 Cover a Corkboard

A corkboard is very useful but not particularly lovely to look at. If you want your corkboard to have some pizzazz, cover it with wrapping paper that matches your décor.

7 Book Wrap

Have you noticed how often high-end decorating magazines show monochromatic items on shelves? You can do this, too, by covering books of different sizes with solid-colored wrapping paper and then stacking them artfully.

8 Lovely Linens

Line the shelves of your linen closet with wrapping paper that makes you smile. Keeping sheets and towels washed and folded may not be your idea of fun, but seeing them all set on pretty paper can make finishing the chore more satisfying.

9 Framed

Beautiful wrapping paper can make very eye-catching (and inexpensive) art. Find a standard-sized frame and fill it with your favorite wrapping paper. This is also a good strategy if you are showing your home and want to "depersonalize" it without taking down all your framed photos. Simply slip attractive wrapping paper into your frames to hide photos during your open house.

AISLE 8

TOOLS

THERE ARE PLENTY OF USEFUL, PRACTICAL, and everyday tools available very cheaply at your local dollar store—more than you might think, when you peruse the tool aisle—and also a lot of things you can do with them beyond their obvious purposes. The tool aisle encompasses a huge variety of utilitarian items way beyond hammers, screwdrivers, and alligator clips. This is the place where you'll also find such items as bungee cords and duct tape, hacksaws and car wax, paint scrapers and screening, weather stripping and wire. When you add up all the fantastic uses beyond the basic, you'll find the tool aisle an utterly invaluable part of inexpensive domestic bliss.

PLEASE HELP
IDENTIFY ITEMS
STOCK NUMBER
5
6
23
16
10
2
25
4
20
3
17
21

alligator clips

Like their namesake reptile, these spring-loaded clips have powerful jaws that close with a vicious snap. Whether you're using them for their purpose of making temporary electrical connections or for something else, keep your fingers off their serrated edges!

Hang cards and photos

Christmas cards mount up quickly in December. Put them on display by stringing up some ribbon or twine between two tacks on a wall, and then use alligator clips to hang cards up by one corner. You'll get to enjoy each card *and* keep surfaces empty.

Mount photos

Use alligator clips in coordinating colors to clip photographs to a piece of mounting board, matting, or stiff poster board. The board should be trimmed only slightly larger than the picture. The clips have a clean, post-industrial look that makes a modern and attractive picture frame out of any color board you like.

Create jewelry

For earrings, use the smallest alligator clips you can find and thread the loops from a discarded pair of earrings through the hole in the base of the clip. Use the serrated teeth to grab anything you want to display, from dyed feathers to squares of sassy satin to braided leather strips. For bracelets or necklaces, thread a strip of wire or leather through the hole, string on beads or charms or tie on ribbons or feathers, and use the clip to grab the other end and hold the jewelry on.

Make hair bows for little girls

Use a glue gun to attach ribbon bows, rosettes, or streamers to a clip. The alligator clip holds tight to a lock of hair, so little girls won't lose these once they go out.

Decorate a Christmas tree

Out of wire hangers for your holiday tree, or can't find a way to string up decorations such as paper snowflakes or cranberry garlands? Alligator clips are secure and easy. Either clip the item directly to a branch, or string fishing line or thread through the hole in the base and attach it to the ornament so it can dangle off a branch.

box cutters

These ubiquitous cutting tools come in different shapes and styles. Some hold a traditional razor blade in place with screws, others have disposable blades that snap off to reveal a new sharp blade. Some have angled cutting edges, others are flat. Whatever type you buy, you can use them for more than cutting open a box.

Cut out a pattern

Trimming a paper pattern into pieces before you pin it to the fabric can be a tedious job using scissors. Speed the process by laying the paper over a safe cutting surface (either a work table or, better, a cardboard box opened and lying flat) and zip through it with a box cutter.

Trim pastry

When you're making a fancy pastry, such as strips for a lattice top or little decorations rolled from the scraps for the top of a double-crust pastry, a box cutter with an angled edge is just the tool for cutting out leaf or heart designs. Brush with beaten egg before baking and your pies will look beautifully professional.

Unstick painted-shut windows

A sharp box cutter is the best way to slice open windows that are stuck tight with paint. Run it firmly around the edges of the window, angling the blade to push it into the crack and past the paint that's gumming up the works. Don't forget to cut top and bottom. It may take several tries to get it open.

Clean gum off a floor

A piece of chewing gum can get really embedded in a floor with a slightly porous surface such as brick or cement. Use the edge of a box cutter to work the offending article off the floor, scraping gently to remove the gum and being careful not to mark the surface. If you run a piece of ice over the gum first to chill it, the blade may be able to pick the gum up in one piece.

Scrape paint off a window

Use an angled box cutter to remove paint from the glass when you've accidentally touched the pane while brushing. The sharp tip is good for trimming off excess paint right alongside the mullions or glazing bars, to give a clean line to the finished paint job.

bungee cords

Bungee cords are springy elastics covered with nylon and with a hook at either end. They come in different lengths and widths, and they're commonly used in shipping and hauling (not to mention extreme sports). But they can do a lot more than their industrial origins suggest.

Make a travel clothesline

Carry a length of bungee cord in your suitcase while traveling and you won't have to drape your freshly rinsed undies over the radiator in a hotel room. Just stretch it across a corner of your hotel room and drip dry.

Seal a suitcase

After you overstuff your suitcase with souvenirs and goodies, you can close it with bungee cords for extra support. If you've ever experienced the airlines bursting open your suitcase in transit and returning it to you in a taped-up plastic bag, you'll find this trick a no-brainer.

Use it as a yoga strap

Why spend money on pricey specialty yoga straps for stretching and exercising? There's nothing you can do with those flat lengths of rubber that you can't also do with a cloth-covered bungee cord.

Hold up your pants

A narrow length of bungee cord is discreet and extremely effective. Buy the lengths of bungee cord by the foot so you can get the size you need and attach the hook ends yourself.

Train branches on a tree

If you're trying to train a young tree to grow in a certain direction or into a certain shape, a bungee cord is a great tool for gardening. Use bungee cords to hold up the branches or tie them down until your tree looks just the way you want.

The Story Behind...

Turtle Wax

What would you do if you noticed a man shining one fender of your car? Benjamin Hirsch, a former magician and the inventor of Plastone, hoped you'd buy his homemade wax and finish the job! In 1953, while visiting Turtle Creek, Wisconsin, Hirsch had an epiphany. The word "turtle" represented his product exactly: a hard shell of protection. Plastone was renamed Super Hard Shell, and his company became Turtle Wax. Soon, the main office in Chicago sported a gigantic turtle on the roof. It told the time and temperature—and held a can of wax. Hirsch knew how to catch people's attention!

car wax

Liquid waxes for your car might give you a terrific shine, if all you want to do is shine your car. But to do more with your car wax than, well, wax your car, be sure to buy paste wax and try the tricks below.

Take a ring off a polished surface

It happens: Someone puts a glass down on your wooden coffee table and next thing you know there's a white ring from the condensation. Put a little paste wax on your finger and trace the ring. Let it dry, then buff with a soft cloth.

Keep fingerprints off appliances

Keep your stainless steel appliances shining. Put a thin layer of car wax on appliances such as refrigerator doors, and then buff vigorously with a soft, lint-free cloth. The next time the kids put their fingers all over the door, they won't leave any fingerprints behind to mar the surface.

Fight mildew in the bathroom

If you're tired of cleaning mildew off the bathroom tiles, give yourself a break by waxing the walls. First, clean any mildew and soap scum off the tile walls of the shower. Wipe the walls dry, then apply car wax (only to the vertical tiles, not the bathtub itself, or it will be dangerously slippery). Allow to dry, then buff to a shine with a lint-free cloth. Your tiles will stay clean and shiny for many months.

Clear snow with less effort

Rub a thick coating of car wax on the surface of your snow shovel, and the snow will slip off more easily. The extra effort you save each time you toss off a shovel-full will make the whole job easier. You can also wax the chute of a snow blower to stop it from clogging.

Help drawers and windows move smoothly

Don't let a sticking drawer or a stiff window slow you down. You can use car wax instead of brute strength. With a soft cloth, smooth a little car wax all the way along the tracks of the windows or drawers, polishing away any excess. You'll find that the moving parts slide along much more readily, with a lot less effort on your part.

caulk

Acrylic caulk is water-soluble and thus makes for easier cleanup for home projects. Silicone caulk is waterproof, so it's very messy to work with but once it dries, it's completely impermeable to moisture. Decide which type is best for these unconventional uses.

Repair aged grout

Regrouting tile is a big job. Instead, make a temporary but long-term repair with waterproof silicone caulk. Squeeze a little caulk over the surface of the cracking grout to keep it from falling out of vertical joints due to expansion and contraction in the shower.

Fill nail holes

Use opaque acrylic caulk to fill nail holes. Press a little caulk into the hole, then push it in with your finger and smooth the surface with a putty knife. Allow to dry completely before painting.

Keep out ants

Even in the cleanest kitchens, food has to be out on the countertops now and then, and it's like a siren call to any nearby ants, particularly in the warm months. When you've tried every trick in the book to no avail, try caulk. Put out something sweet, and when the ants come in, trace them back to their point of entry. Whatever it is, seal it with caulk—along the edge of the skirting boards, around the electrical outlets, anywhere ants might enter.

Seal cracks in plaster

Make a repair job that might well last for years by spreading a little opaque white caulk across hairline cracks in plaster. Press it in with your finger and then smooth with a putty knife. Let dry completely before painting.

Use as an adhesive

Most caulk is white, but you can also get clear caulk, which makes a good industrial type adhesive for home repair projects. You can use it to stick together wood, Plexiglas, ceramics, glass, and more.

Repair inflatable toys

Clear silicone caulk is a terrific adhesive and sealant for inflatable items such as a kid's pool toy or even a small inflatable kiddie pool. Locate the source of the leak as you deflate the toy, then cover it with clear caulk and seal it with a patch such as another piece of plastic or rubber. Let dry completely and reinflate—your patch will hold the rest of the summer!

charcoal briquettes

The dusty black chunks of charcoal that seem so messy to handle are in fact a great weapon in keeping all sorts of domestic places and items dry and clean. Be sure to buy plain charcoal briquettes, not the easy-lighting type that contain lighter or starter fluid.

Keep stored clothes dry

When you seal up seasonal clothes in plastic containers, any dampness inside (perhaps you put the clothes away on a humid day) can create an environment where mildew might grow. Keep clothes as dry as possible by wrapping charcoal briquettes in paper towels and storing a few of these moisture-sucking bundles in each container or sealed bag of clothes.

Remove mothball odors from an RV

Many people close up their RVs for the season with mothballs inside to protect against vermin. But when traveling time starts again, that mothball scent can be pervasive and lingering. Leave several bowls of charcoal briquettes (the plain type without lighter fluid) in the interior before you hit the road, and the odor will disappear.

Keep a cooler fresh

Before storing a cooler all winter, wrap a few briquettes in paper towels and put them inside. That way, even with the lid on, the cooler will still be dry and fresh inside when you open it for your first picnic the following summer.

Make a path

After burning charcoal in your grill, don't dump it in a garbage pile. Sprinkle the cooled ash along a garden path. Footsteps on the path will tamp it down into a lightweight, durable groundcover.

Keep flower water fresh

You've tried it all: bleach, aspirin, sugar. But the water in your flower vases still gets murky and foul-smelling in a day or two. Try a piece of charcoal and the water will stay fresher for days longer. Just don't use a clear glass vase and nobody will ever know!

clamps

C-clamps, so-called because of their shape, come in all sizes. Larger ones are generally used to hold two items tightly together while gluing. The smaller ones can have a host of other uses.

Crack nuts

Can't lay hands on your nutcracker, and a friend just dropped off an inviting bag of pecans in the shell? Use a C-clamp to crack them open.

Keep a cookbook open

Use a small C-clamp screwed onto each side so you can keep your place. That way, you won't swap from Irish stew to beef chili with the flick of a page mid-recipe.

Close a pet food bag

The thick, lined paper of some large, heavy-duty pet food bags can be difficult to keep closed. Use a couple of small C-clamps to hold the top rolled shut, and you can just slide them off each side when it's time to feed your pooch.

Hang holiday lights

The tiny C-clamps that look almost like toys are ideal for hanging a row of holiday lights in tricky places. You can attach them to the top edges of bookshelves or anywhere you can safely screw the clamp against an architectural feature, allowing the wire of the lights to hang off the "C," without needing tape or nails.

Before storing a cooler all winter,
wrap a few briquettes in
paper towels and put them inside.

contractor trash bags

Contractor bags are super heavy-duty bags that can hold building waste without breaking. The plastic is strong and sturdy and won't tear under the weight of broken wall-board or old tiles. That kind of strength makes it useful for other tasks as well.

Fashion a Halloween costume

Make a very convincing and extremely inexpensive black robe for your little trick-or-treater with a contractor bag. Cut a large semicircle from the bottom center of the bag for a neck hole, then two circles from the side for armholes. Cut a strip off the top edge (now the bottom of the robe) to make it the right length, then cut that circle in half to make a belt. You can snip a fringe around the bottom and even slice it open up the middle to make an open robe—add a witch hat and a candy bag and you're done!

Go sledding

Thick snow falling and you can't find the sled at the back of the downstairs closet? Don't let your child miss out on the fun. Hand over a contractor bag and let your kid "bum" down the hill with his bottom firmly planted on a tough plastic bag.

Store clothes

Contractor bags are sturdy enough to hold sweaters, heavy jeans, and winter coats for summer storage. Don't forget to add a charcoal briquette or two, wrapped in a paper towel or brown paper bag, to prevent humidity when you seal the bag.

Make a rain poncho

Need a hasty rain poncho to protect you in a downpour? Cut a neck hole and armholes in a contractor bag (they're big!) and keep your clothes totally dry.

cup hooks

These small metal hooks, usually with a screw tip at one end, are intended to fit under cabinets or shelves so you can hang a row of cups off them. Of course, they're also useful for lots of other things.

Hang keys

Never lose your keys again! Screw a row of cup hooks where you need it most—by the door. Whether you typically come in the front or back door, get in the habit of slinging your keys on the ring. When you're ready to go, there they are.

Hang toothbrushes

Take a lesson from nursery school and store your family's toothbrushes hanging upside down from a row of cup hooks mounted on the bathroom wall. When you hang toothbrushes upside down like this, they don't touch, preventing the spread of germs, and they dry quickly and efficiently after each use.

Create a necklace rack

If you're crafty, you can turn a strip of wood, a row of cup hooks, and some paint and glitter into a stylish and sophisticated necklace rack. Paint the wood in any design you like, then screw in the hooks at alternate levels across the strip. Mount on the wall and prevent your necklaces from ever again getting tangled up in a jewelry box.

Put up a hand towel

Got a work sink near the back door or in the basement? Make a handy towel rack by screwing in a cup hook nearby. Sling a hand towel over it and you'll have it ready to grab when your hands are wet.

drop cloths

Inexpensive, lightweight drop cloths are great for painting projects. They're disposable, so when you're done with the messy job, you can gather the whole thing up and throw it away. Cleanup doesn't get much easier. But there's plenty more to do with a drop cloth.

Cover furniture

Drop cloths are so inexpensive that you can buy several to protect your furniture during painting or renovation work. They're lightweight, so you can throw them on and off the sofa or chairs as needed.

Make a craft apron/paint poncho

Got a messy job? Protect yourself. Cut a neck hole in the center of a plastic drop cloth and pull it over you. It will fall in folds like a poncho, allowing you either to pull your arms out from underneath or cut slits to reach through. Either way, your clothing will emerge unscathed from dirty work.

Protect a tabletop

Whether you're trying to keep finger paints from getting out of hand, or you've invited your friends over for a shrimp boil, spread a lightweight drop cloth over the tabletop to catch all the drips. When you're done, gather it up and throw it away.

duct tape

Nowadays, more resilient space-age materials have replaced duct tape in the heating and air conditioning business—which frees up your roll of this silver miracle for other uses.

Prevent lockouts

Never get locked out of your car again! Tape a spare car key securely to the underside of your car with a couple strips of duct tape.

Line leaking gutters

The gutter might be mostly intact, but a few small cracks or holes here and there can leave leaks running down the side of the house. And replacing the gutters isn't in the cards right now. So let duct tape come to your rescue. Next time you're cleaning out the gutters in good weather, finish the job with a layer of duct tape stuck down the inside bottom of the gutter.

Remove lint and "pills" from clothes

Pat, don't rub, against the surface of coats and sweaters to remove lint and pet hair as well as those little "pills" of wool that tend to collect around the underarms and elbows.

Dissuade your cats from clawing a piece of furniture by temporarily wrapping the legs or base with inside-out duct tape.

Hem a pair of jeans

Sewing through thick denim is difficult—and it's frustrating when a child shoots up several inches the moment you finish the job! But you can make a sturdy, long-lasting hem with duct tape. It will last through several washes, and it will come off to reveal a few more inches of denim when that kid has another growth spurt.

Cover a blister

Breaking in a pair of shoes? A heel blister makes walking miserable, and most heel bandages rub as you go, worsening the pain. Put a gauze square over the actual sore, then cover your heel with a wide strip of duct tape and you'll be back on the road.

Hold a broken window together

If you have a lot of kids playing ball in your neighborhood, chances are you may have to replace a window sometime. Tape crisscrossing strips of duct tape over the broken glass before you lift it out of the window to prevent any (more) glass from falling.

Discourage a cat from clawing

Cats can be very determined when set on clawing a piece of furniture. Persuade them otherwise by temporarily wrapping the legs or base with inside-out duct tape. (As you spiral up the leg, the stickiness holds the next layer.) Cats will back off quickly!

Fix a plastic trash can

For something that simply sits behind the house, trash cans take a lot of wear and tear. If the plastic cracks down the side, you can make a long-term repair by sealing it with duct tape inside and out.

WHO KNEW?

THE TRUTH ABOUT DUCT TAPE

If it walks like a duck, talks like a duck... Johnson & Johnson manufactured the first duct tape to keep moisture out of ammunition cases during World War II. Army green in color, it was modeled after medical tape, made from cotton duck (woven cotton), and waterproof. Accordingly, people often called it "duck tape." However, during the post-war housing boom, it became indispensable for joining household ducts. The color was changed to silver (to blend in better) and the tape became known as "duct tape."

6 More Ways to Use DROP CLOTHS

1 Play Zone

Create a place where young children will play for hours. Cut a drop cloth to match the circumference of your dining (or kitchen) table. Include half an inch seam allowance. Then cut a piece equal to the height of your table and long enough to wrap all the way around it (again, add a one inch seam allowance on the top and bottom.) Sew the two pieces together and finish the edges. Leave an opening for a door! Let your kids paint on the details: windows, a doorbell.

2 Guard Pillows

The pillows on garden furniture will eventually get rained on, but that doesn't mean mildew if the cases are made from drop cloth with plastic backing. The backing keeps stuffing from getting wet and dries quickly. This type of drop cloth is sometimes called a "plastic laminated cotton dust sheet" and is easy to sew.

3 Sleep Longer

Drop cloths make fantastic blackout liners. Cut a heavy-weave drop cloth to the precise size of your expensive (but too sheer) drapes. Then hang the drop cloth behind the curtains (using clip-on hooks with rings—no sewing necessary!). You can darken any room you desire and sleep, sleep, sleep!

4 Dress Your Windows

If you have very tall windows, the thought of what curtains cost may fill you with dread. Not to fear: Drop cloths are here! They are cotton, a neutral color, and inexpensive. No sewing is necessary if you use clip-on rings to attach them to curtain rods. The clean lines and raw fabric will look very modern.

5 Stop Food Splatter

Who said drop cloths were only for paint? Babies in high chairs are mess-making machines! Put a canvas drop cloth underneath the chair and save your floor. The cloth can be tossed in the wash and reused.

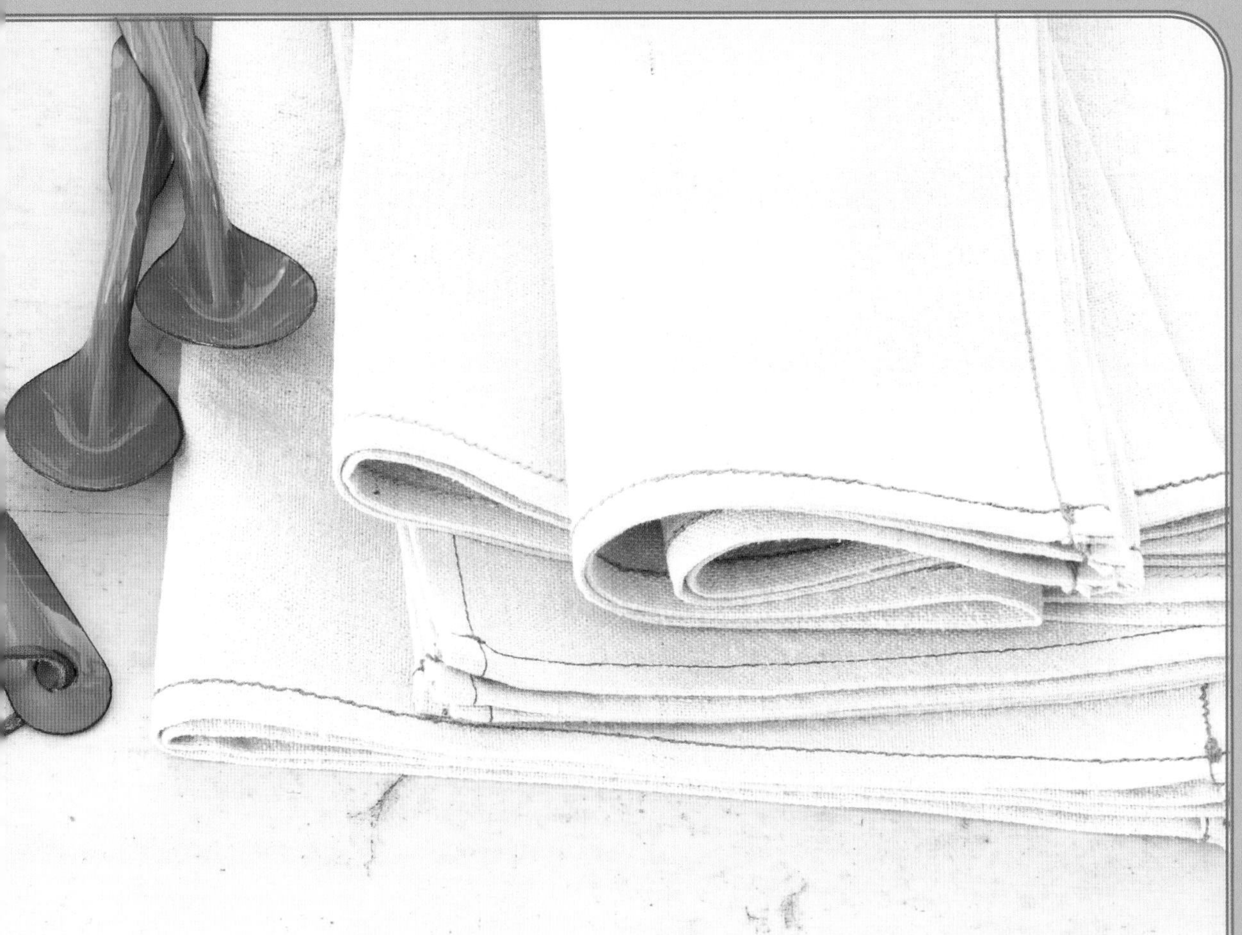

6 Everyday Napkins

A green alternative to paper napkins can be made from a light-weave drop cloth. They're not fancy, so you'll use them every day, not just on holidays! Create a pattern out of stiff paper, making it 1/2 inch larger on each side than the final desired size. Trace the pattern on a washed piece of drop cloth and cut out your napkin. Turn the fabric under 1/4 inch and press with an iron. Turn under another 1/4 inch and sew the hem all the way around.

Mend a metal screen

No time to take the door down and stretch a new screen? Make a repair that will last all summer by stretching some silver duct tape over the hole in the screen.

Seal your waterproof boots

Got a rip in your Wellingtons? There's no need to throw them away. Wrap them around and around with duct tape, overlapping the tape across the tear. You'll get the rest of the season out of them, at least.

face masks

Disposable face masks are handy for low-grade filtration, when you're sawing wood or spray-painting or perhaps cleaning out a dusty closet. But they have more uses than that.

Make a comforting inhaler

Camphor and mentholated rubs are great when you're congested, but some people find that the rubs burn when applied directly to the skin. Smear some on the inside of a disposable face mask and inhale in peace.

Cut onions

Add this to the folklore surrounding the ways to cut onions without tears. If you cover your nose and mouth with a face mask to avoid inhaling the fumes, the tears may never come. If it works for you, there's nothing to lose.

Create a cat toy

Drive your cat wild with this fabulous cat toy: Remove the elastic straps and put catnip in a mask. Top it with a second mask to make a hollow, rounded shape. Staple securely closed and toss it enticingly toward your kitty—it's more fun than a rubber mouse!

hacksaws

The narrow blades of a hacksaw have a jagged row of long teeth that are highly effective for sawing through tough substances. They are thin and flexible, which also means they wear out fast and are inexpensive to replace. Take one out of your workshop and into the house for tasks like these.

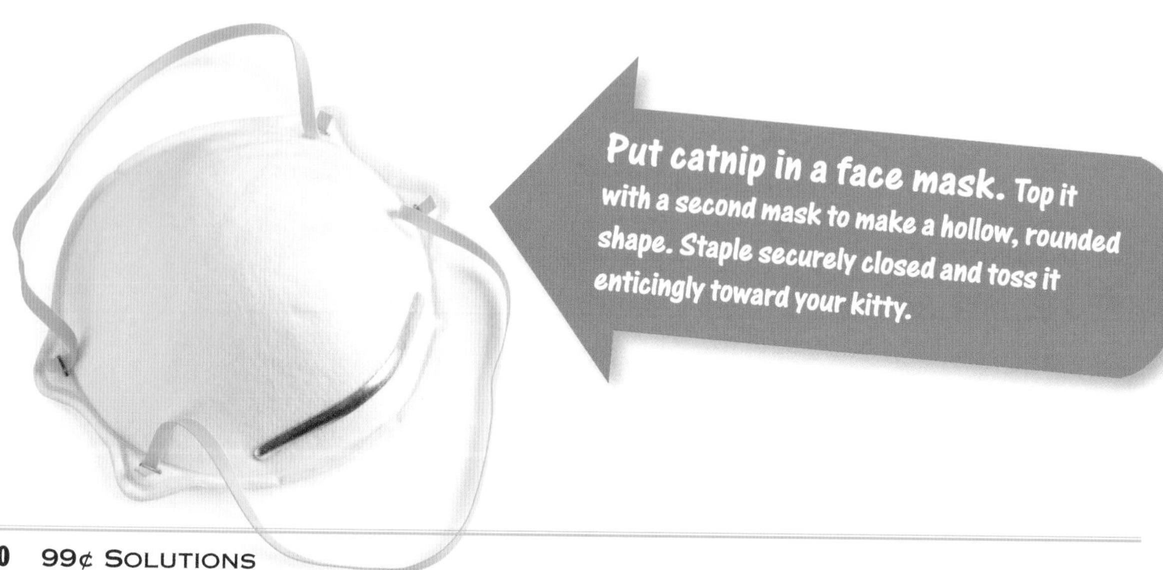
Put catnip in a face mask. Top it with a second mask to make a hollow, rounded shape. Staple securely closed and toss it enticingly toward your kitty.

Cut up bones for stock

Using a kitchen knife on bone is the fastest way to ruin a quality knife. Use a small hacksaw kept in your kitchen just for the purpose and trim bones for stock and soup.

Prune branches off a Christmas tree

Once your tree is in the door and in place in the living room, it's too late to start doing any major hatchet work on the branches. But if a few of them are ruining the look, use a small hacksaw to reach back and remove branches without a lot of mess.

Construct a camping knife

If you've got survivalist instincts, you'll appreciate this canny use of a very inexpensive item: Use tin snips to cut a fine-toothed hacksaw blade in half and rough it out into a knife blade shape, with a dent in the "handle" for a fingertip to rest on. Use the hacksaw's teeth as the "spine" of the knife, and use a file or belt sander to sharpen the opposite side.

hammers

Dollar store hammers and rubber mallets are likely to be moderately lightweight, which may not be so great if you're driving nails, but is in fact terrific if you want to attend to different domestic tasks.

Pound meat

A meat mallet is nothing more than a hammer with a large head. Lay a sheet of plastic wrap under the steak or chicken breast you want to beat out, then a second sheet on top. Beat away with a small hammer or mallet until it's thin and tender.

Crush ice

Put the ice in a ziplock bag, lay it on the floor or countertop, and pound away. The more ice in the bag, the better, because it won't skip and skitter away with each stroke.

Crack nuts

Can't lay hands on your nutcracker? Use a hammer instead. Put the nuts on a thick layer of newspaper, then aim to crack each nut open with one stroke—it's easier on the thumbs if you improve your aim so you don't have to hold each nut down with your fingers.

ladders

You won't find the sort of ladder that you can use to paint the outside of your house at a dollar store, but you may well find the sort of small, lightweight mini-stepladders that will let you reach the top of a cabinet with ease. But ladders can help you do more than climb heights.

Put light where you need it

A mini stepladder is ideal for moving a lamp to the task at hand. Whether you're cleaning in a dark part of a room or just reading in a chair and need more light, put a lamp on top of a short stepladder and you'll find light right at your elbow.

Build a tool caddy

Could you use an assistant to hand you tools? A short stepladder will do in a pinch. Set it up next to wherever you're working, and arrange your tools and supplies on the rungs. No more feeling around on the floor to see where you set down that hammer and no more clutching nails with your lips—just reach over to your materials ranged on the ladder.

Display knickknacks

Paint a wooden stepladder with bright, high-gloss enamel and use it to display teacups or figurines or any small knickknack that you fancy. It's an

HITTING THE NAIL ON THE HEAD

A BRIEF LOOK AT HAMMERS

When something needs pounding—usually a nail—you look for a hammer. The image that generally comes to mind is a steel-headed claw hammer. This is the type you'll likely find at a 99 cent store: the pounding side of the head is flat and the claw side is curved and split forming a "V." Yet there is a wide world of hammers, both past and present. **At the Hammer Museum in Haines, Alaska, more than 1,500 hammers are displayed.** Some are very odd looking. The difference is usually in the head rather than the handle. Viewing certain examples gives one the feeling of looking at a hammerhead shark: The body is recognizable, but the rest is extraordinary.

A hammer that was ordinary looking—yet still unusual—was issued in 1882. Gillett's Novelty Bluing Hammer contained tablets of laundry bluing in its handle. Why the combo of bleach and hardware? Advertising depicted men using the hammer to accomplish household tasks. **Choose to do the laundry with Gillett's tablets and your husband can simultaneously mend the house...**what a slick marketing move!

A hammer directly aimed at men (though women may have used them too) was patented in 1889. The hitching post hammer, designed by Reverdy B. Stewart of Warren, Pennsylvania, was a portable way to secure horses. The specialized spike head could be screwed securely into any piece of wood; the horse's reins were then tied to the handle.

As the country moved from horses to the automobile, roads became a concern. A Scotsman, John Loudon McAdam, invented a way to mix tar and gravel for paving material. The rocks used to make gravel were pounded down to size with macadamizing hammers. These hammers weighed about a pound and looked like a round piece of metal attached to a wooden stick.

As odd as a hammer with a completely round head may appear, what would you make of one with a head shaped like an "X"? **In its day this type of hammer was used to perforate checks indicating they'd been paid.** Banging down a banker's check-canceling hammer must have been satisfying. Today's soft stamps and electronic processing are much less dramatic.

A time you don't want drama is when you have an electrician working in your home. Electricians use hammers that—like the Gillett Novelty hammer—are distinguished by the handle more so than the head. The handle of an electrician's hammer is made of a high-density fiberglass, a material that, thankfully, does not conduct electricity.

The Hammer Museum may not have every hammer known, but it does have one of the largest sitting out front: at 19 feet tall it makes the building easy to find. **The world's largest hammer is in Eureka, California.** A claw variety, it stands in front of Pierson Building Center, is 26 feet tall, and serves as the store's signpost.

WAY BACK WHEN...

Steps to Safety

Fixing something you couldn't reach (though not changing a lightbulb) got easier after January 7, 1862. That's when the first U.S. patent for a safety stepladder was issued to John H. Balsley, a carpenter and a Dayton, Ohio, resident. Balsley ingeniously replaced round rungs with flat steps and placed hinges at the top of his ladder, allowing for easy folding and storage. Why was the stepladder not helpful in changing a bulb? The first public demonstration of Edison's lightbulb was still 17 years in the future!

excellent talking point in a room. For a festive air, crowd small vases and jars of flowers all over the rungs and top step of the ladder. It's like having a flower festival in one spot.

lighter fluid

Even if you don't smoke and have no intention of refilling a cigarette lighter, a tiny container of lighter fluid is a powerful solvent that has additional uses beyond the obvious.

Take oil stains off clothes

Cooking stains can be nearly impossible to remove from clothes. They might be invisible to the naked eye when the item goes in the wash, then become an indelible ring after a trip through the washer and dryer. Squirt greasy areas with a little lighter fluid and then wash as usual.

Get a sticker off a paper book jacket

It's annoying when price stickers threaten to tear the glossy book jacket of that new hardcover. Use a few drops of lighter fluid and the sticker will lift off, leaving the jacket intact.

Remove lipstick stains

Forgot a lipstick in your pocket when you ran that load of clothes through the washer? Or worse, when you turned on the dryer! But you don't have to throw every item away. Apply lighter fluid directly to the stains, then wash again.

Dissolve sticker residue

Lighter fluid is the easiest way to take stickers and labels off nearly any surface, from the bumper of your car to a glass bottle to a sticky sale tag on the jacket of a book. Drizzle a few drops directly from the bottle, then wait a few moments. Pull off any remaining sticker paper and use a paper towel to wipe off the glue residue.

magnets

Even a small magnet can be quite powerful, and they're enormously useful for cleanup around the house—they do a lot more than hold reminders and notices on the front of your fridge!

Hold paper clips

If you find that paper clips are scattered all over the surface of your desk or inside the drawers, don't use a magnet merely to pick them up but also to store them. Swing the magnet over the paper clips to gather them together, then put the magnet on the top of your desk as a sort of sculptural storage.

Clean up a workbench

Spilled a box of nails or screws over your work surface? Dropped a container full of washers or nuts? You need a magnet to do the pickup, quickly and easily.

Keep the car doors unfrozen

If you live in a northern clime, you have no doubt experienced the frustration of a frozen door lock in the morning. Use a wide, flat refrigerator magnet to protect the lock. Leave it over the locks overnight and in the morning, they will still open!

masking tape

Designed to help autoworkers mask off and paint a clean edge on a car body, masking tape quickly proved to be ideal for a much wider variety of domestic tasks.

Tape kitchen chair bottoms

In most homes, kitchen chairs end up getting more use than nearly any other chairs in the house. They're scooted in and out, in and out all day long for meals, homework, and other projects. It's not surprising that the bases eventually wear and start to leave dark scuffs on the floor. Tape them up thickly with masking tape, and you'll find that the chairs slide smoothly, scuff-free.

Wrap crayons

Children love a fresh box of brand-new crayons, but the next thing you know, they're all broken. Little fingers find the breaking point of a crayon with astonishing ease. Make a new box go a little longer by wrapping each crayon's middle with masking tape.

Make labels

It's ridiculous to spend money on a label maker or on fancy labels if you have a roll of masking tape and a pen. Masking tape is durable but easy to remove. Use a strip for labeling lunch boxes, food storage containers, snow boots, schoolbooks, and more.

Pick up broken glass

You've swept up the big pieces of glass, but it's hard to be sure that every one of the tiny shards is gone. Find them by pressing down the sticky side of a few strips of masking tape, before you find them with your bare feet.

Use a wide, flat refrigerator magnet to protect
a car lock from freezing overnight.

THE *Story Behind...*

Scotch Masking Tape

The monumental 3M company (formerly the Minnesota Mining and Manufacturing Co.) initially produced sandpaper. In 1925, employee Richard G. Drew noticed auto-body painters were aggravated with the tape they used for customizing. Drew decided to make a new product that didn't remove paint. A prototype combining cabinetmaker's glue and crepe paper didn't stick and earned the complaint: "Take this to those scotch (meaning cheap) bosses of yours and tell them to put on more adhesive!" Drew did, and Scotch masking tape, along with Drew's creativity, transformed 3M into an R&D-driven company.

microfiber car polishing cloths

The space-age synthetic microfiber material, sold in multipacks to wash and polish cars, is extremely absorbent and durable, making it ideal for lots of other things besides making your wheels shine.

Polish windows and mirrors

Instead of a paper towel, use a microfiber cloth when you're washing windows and mirrors around the house. It will absorb the window cleaner and impart a radiant shine, and one cloth will do dozens of windows.

Dust furniture

When used dry, the microfiber cloth attracts and clings to dust. Get a chemical-free shine and sparkle on your furniture when you dust with microfiber.

Wipe your specs

The synthetic fibers of a microfiber cloth are extremely delicate and won't scratch the lenses of your glasses. From a large cloth, cut out a small square to fold and fit into your glasses case and keep the cloth reserved for just this purpose.

Dry a child's hair

Most little ones hate having their hair blow-dried almost as much as they hate having you rub their heads with a towel! Wrap a clean large microfiber cloth around your child's hair, and you'll find that it sucks out the moisture like magic. Hair dries fast and nobody has to cry!

paintbrushes

You won't find real sable paintbrushes for high-end craft work at your dollar store, but you will find an astonishing range of shapes and sizes of inexpensive paintbrushes—just right for all sorts of tasks other than applying paint.

Clean a keyboard

A small brush will help you clean crumbs and dust out of the cracks and crevices of your keyboard. Hold the keyboard upside down over a workspace using one hand and brush it vigorously with the other.

Brush on kitchen glazes and sauces

Why spend money on a specialty food brush at a pricey culinary store? Buy a mid-size paintbrush and keep it exclusively with your kitchen utensils to brush on sauces or oils. Hand wash after each use.

Dust delicate items

A soft paintbrush is ideal for cleaning china figurines, chandeliers, lampshades—anything that you don't want to rub with a cloth. It's perfect for getting into the cracks and crevices of sculpted items, and it won't damage delicate parts.

Pretreat stains

A short stiff brush is perfect for working stain treatments into shirt collars or other dirty spots. Keep a brush near your laundry for just that purpose—there's no need to even rinse it out between uses.

paint scrapers

The thin, flexible blade of a paint scraper has a very straight, flat edge that makes it useful for a few things besides removing paint from glass, wood, and other surfaces.

Scrape off baked-on food

Keep a paint scraper in the kitchen solely dedicated to doing dishes. When you clean a glass or stoneware dish covered with baked-on food, it's much faster, easier, and neater to lightly scrape the surface with a paint scraper than to clog the fibers of a scrubbie.

A small brush will help you clean crumbs and dust out of the cracks and crevices of your keyboard.

Remove old drawer and cabinet liners

A paint scraper might have been made for this job. When you're replacing drawer and cabinet lining, whether paper or plastic, a paint scraper gets into the edges and lets you lift the liner along with any glue, as well as levering out tacks or small nails.

Use as a putty knife

A paint scraper is more flexible than most putty knives, allowing you to smooth spackle or even caulk into awkward spaces such as corners or curves.

Replace a spatula

A clean paint scraper kept solely for the purpose makes an ideal spatula for kitchen use. The thin metal makes it easy to prod and turn food while it's cooking, and the flexible blade makes it perfect for lifting out the first brownie or piece of pie from the pan.

WHO KNEW? DAWN DISHWASHING LIQUID CAN REPLACE A PLUNGER!

If you don't have a plunger handy, here's a trick: Use Dawn dishwashing liquid to unclog your toilet. Squirt a generous amount of soap into the clogged bowl. Wait until the water level goes down, fill a bucket with cool water (hot water could crack the bowl), and then pour it into your soaped toilet from waist high. Your clog should clear—though you may need to repeat the procedure a few times. This only works if the clog is paper or organic.

pliers

Used for grasping and turning nuts and bolts, among other things, pliers seem industrial, but once you take a pair of pliers out of the workshop, you'll find they're indispensable around the house.

Remove pin bones from fish

That filet of salmon is about to go under the broiler when you spot a tiny bone protruding from the surface. Pin bones in fish can be nearly impossible to see but you'll feel them quickly enough if you accidentally bite down on one. Remove them by running your fingertips against the grain of the fish and using a pair of needle-nose pliers to jerk the bone out in the opposite direction from which it's pointing.

Hold a tack or tiny nail

Don't risk your thumbs when you're hammering in tiny tacks or delicate nails for a craft project. Grasp the stem with a pair of needle-nosed pliers and then apply the hammer. You'll save your fingers and get a better view of the task at hand.

Crack nuts

Use a large tongue-and-groove pliers for cracking nuts. The adjustable head lets you open everything from walnuts in the shell to little filberts.

Skin a chicken

The recipe calls for skinless chicken thighs, but the darn things keep slipping out of your hands as you try to pull. Hold the bone or firmly grasp the meat with a pair of clean new pliers kept exclusively for kitchen use, and pull the skin back with the other hand (grasping it with a paper towel if you still can't get a grip). It's the fastest, most efficient way to get the job done.

plungers

That rubber cup on the end of a stick seems to have only one use: unblocking a clog in a drain or toilet. But even a dollar-store plunger has uses that are hidden to the naked eye.

Deter mosquitoes

At the end of the season, you can get a bargain on citronella candles, whose pungent scent discourages insects. Push the wooden handle of a new plunger into the ground, and put the candle in the upturned cup.

Fix a dent in your car

It's such a simple ding but the cost may be a shocker if you take it to a body shop. Save your money and try a plunger instead. Dip it in water to help create suction, then push it over the dent and pull out briskly. It might just work the first time.

rubber doorstops

These sturdy little triangles of rubber would seem to have a highly specific function—holding a door open but you can do more.

Prop a computer keyboard

Whether you want your keyboard to prop toward you or away from you—whichever position you find best for typing—two rubber doorstops will hold it securely and comfortably in place.

Put the brakes on rolling furniture

Having wheels on your bed or sofa is extremely handy for positioning it around the room wherever you want it. But once you've found the exact position, it can be extremely frustrating to make it stay there. Wedge rubber doorstops against each wheel on the bed or piece of furniture, turned inward to hide them, and your furniture won't move again until you're redecorating!

Shim a bookshelf

Bookshelves used to be a specialty item built by a carpenter, but fortunately, they're now easily available in all sizes to be constructed at home. Problem is, this type of flat-pack shelving can teeter, especially if your walls aren't flat. Use rubber doorstops for a secure shim to tilt the shelf very slightly back to the wall for a safe and secure fit. If the stops are pressed up under the kick at the floor, they'll be unobtrusive.

sandpaper

Available in a range of grits, from so fine you could smooth your skin to extremely coarse for industrial use, sandpaper is useful for more than rubbing wood surfaces.

Polish away mineral and lime stains

Instead of using harsh chemicals to remove stains from an old toilet, very gently polish them away with sandpaper. Clean the toilet first as usual with cleanser and a brush. Then turn off the water supply to the toilet, flush, and use the finest grit sandpaper you can find to rub gently in a circular motion at the stains at the water line.

7 More Ways to Use SANDPAPER

1 Sharpen Needles

Don't ditch dull needles. Instead, poke your old sewing needles through fine-grit sandpaper once or twice or twist them in a folded piece of sandpaper. They will be sharp and good-as-new in a jiffy. Point taken!

2 Save Shoes

Are your suede shoes feeling blue? Are they dirty and stained? Cheer them up! By very gently scuffing with sandpaper, you can revive the nap and take off some stains.

3 Smooth Nails

It never fails: You're in a hurry and a nail breaks. If you can't find your emery board, don't despair. A piece of fine-grit sandpaper will work just a well at smoothing the snag.

4 Create Keepsakes

Decorations made by hand become sentimental keepsakes. Seahorses, starfish, ginger–bread houses—draw a pattern and trace it onto the smooth side of a sheet of sandpaper. Do this twice and then cut out your ornament. Spread glue on the smooth sides of the sandpaper, fold some yarn in half, and sandwich it between the two pieces with a loop sticking out. After your creation dries, you may decorate as desired.

5 Outsmart Slugs

Sanding disks (round pieces of sandpaper) are perfectly sized to fit under your potted plants. Why would you place them there? To keep slugs out! No slug enjoys oozing across an abrasive surface. Make certain that the circumference of the sandpaper is wider than that of your planter.

6 Name Game

Cut the letters of your child's name out of sandpaper. Let your child feel the shapes and pick a favorite. Put a blank sheet of paper on top of the letter and let the little one rub over it with a crayon. The shape of the letter will appear like magic, prompting calls of "Let's do another!"

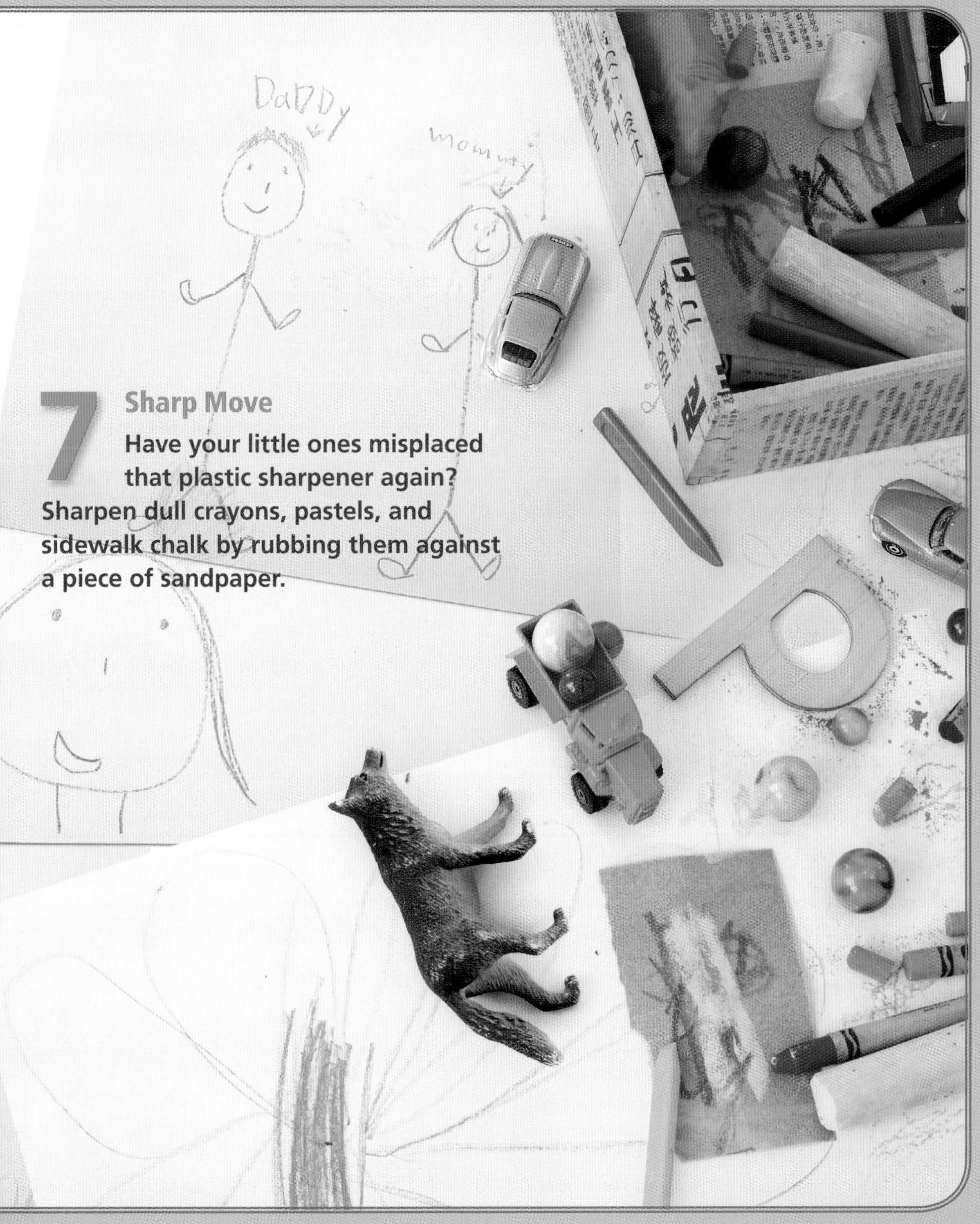

7 Sharp Move

Have your little ones misplaced that plastic sharpener again? Sharpen dull crayons, pastels, and sidewalk chalk by rubbing them against a piece of sandpaper.

Get out a little fine-grit sandpaper to help you remove stains from grout.

Smooth rough skin on your soles

No matter what you do, rough skin can build up on the soles of your feet, especially in summer when you might be wearing sandals or other open shoes. Experts warn against tools that shave off skin, and chemical smoothers can be harsh and abrasive. Instead, try a fine-grit sandpaper to buff off the rough edges and make your skin feel smooth and soft again. Be sure to slather on a rich foot lotion when you're done.

Sharpen tools

Quit using whetstones to sharpen chisels, axes and other tools. You can get an even sharper edge with sandpaper. Wet medium-grit sandpaper and lay it on a very flat and stable surface. The water will hold the sandpaper steady while you rub the edges of the tool in a regular circular motion, alternating sides. Hone the edge on a wet piece of super-fine grit paper.

Restore a ping-pong paddle

That old wooden ping-pong set in the basement offered hours of fun, before the paddles' covering wore out. All you need is some glue, medium-grit sandpaper, and a pair of scissors. Strip off the old covering and cut two new sides to fit. Use a scrap of sandpaper to rub off the old glue, and then attach the new coverings. Once you get some new ping-pong balls, you're ready for tournament play!

Open stubborn jars

Keep a piece of medium-grit sandpaper in the kitchen for opening stubborn jar lids. The sandpaper, grit side down, will let you get a grip on the lid to turn it.

Get back your edge on scissors

Favorite kitchen shears lost their edge? Sewing scissors snagging on the fabric? You can pay to have them sharpened by a professional—or you can get excellent results by slicing up a sheet of medium- to fine-grit sandpaper with your dull scissors.

screening

A roll of metal or plastic mesh screening may look like it's calling you to (finally) re-stretch that saggy panel on your back door. But it might be suggesting something else.

Sieve lumps out of paint

A can of paint that sits for awhile can get lumpy, even if you still need it to touch up a wall in the living room. Sure, you could stretch a width of screen over a bucket and pour the paint through. Or, you could cut a circle of screen the width of the can and push it carefully to the bottom with a stirring stick pressed to the center, to keep the screen level. The lumps will sink down with the screen, allowing you to stir up the remainder and start painting.

Cover picnic food

Nothing ruins a bowl of potato salad at a picnic like finding flies hovering over it. Cut several squares of screen to keep on hand for outdoor entertaining. Lay them directly over bowls and pitchers. They're unobtrusive and highly effective.

Keep seeds safe

When your seeds are newly planted in the ground, the local birds and wildlife thank you for the buffet. Make sure more of your seeds get a chance to sprout by laying screening over a row of newly planted seeds until the first tiny shoots come up.

screwdrivers

A screwdriver is such a simple item—a flat (or Phillips) piece of metal to turn a screw. It's also the *only* tool for the job. When you need one, nothing else will do. But once you have one, it will also do a wealth of other things.

Prop open a window

You finally got that painted-shut window open by dragging the edge of a flat-head screwdriver along the painted sill, and now the doggone thing won't stay open! Turn the screwdriver upside down and push it against one side of the window, with the handle propped against the sill, and the flat head nestled against the bottom of the window. It will hold securely, without slipping.

Open a letter

Reach for a flat-head screwdriver when the mail arrives. The angled tip makes it easy to slip the head into the flap and slit the letter open.

Scrape off paint

Use the flat side of the tip to scrape any remains of paint off glass when you're painting windows. You can also use the sharp edge of the tip to scrape paint out of tracks and edges of wood when you're stripping paint off furniture.

Make a sturdy lever for prying

The beauty of a lever is that it exerts a great deal of power on the lifting end (assuming the fulcrum is close to that end) relative to the amount of exertion you apply at the opposite end. With that in mind, don't forget about your sturdy flat-end screwdriver when you need to lift something. With a small piece of wood as a fulcrum, you could even lift the leg of a sofa so you could shove in or remove the edge of a rug.

Plant seeds

A screwdriver is an ideal "sowing stick" for planting seeds. Push it straight down into the ground, wiggle around to open the hole, and then drop in the seeds.

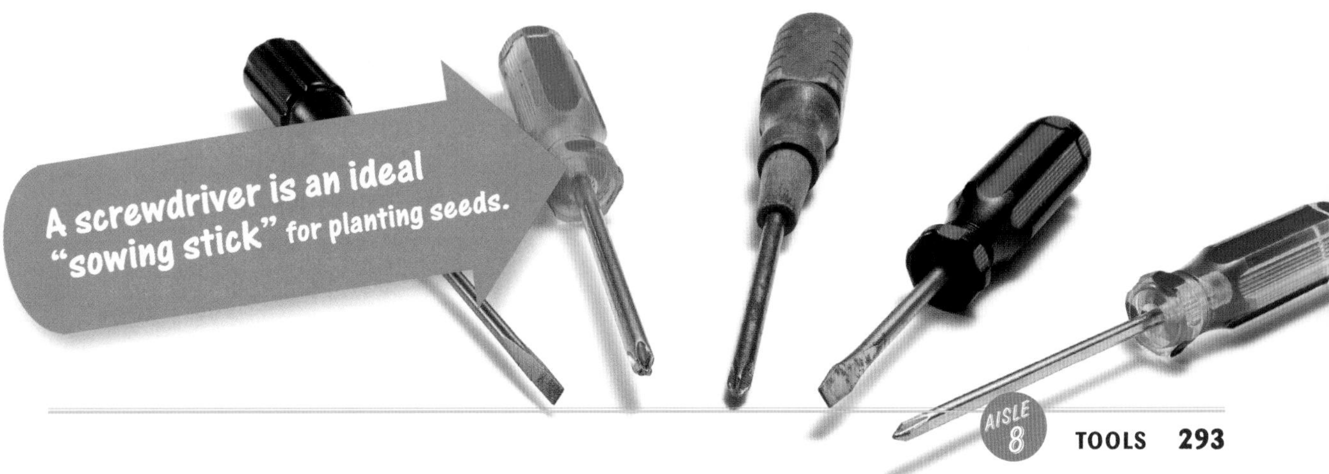
A screwdriver is an ideal
"sowing stick" for planting seeds.

Chip ice off the old block

If you've got a solid block of ice, as with store-bought ice that has thawed in the car and then refrozen into a hard mass in your home freezer, use your screwdriver like an ice pick, hitting the block with the flat head to break it up, and let the party start!

Remove staples

A flat-head screwdriver is as good as or better than a staple remover at prying out staples. Push it under the staple and lever it right out.

steel wool

When you're scrubbing crusted food off a cast-iron pan, steel wool is a lifesaver. It's tough and effective and can be used over and over. When it gets too rusty or dirty to use, just throw it out—it's very cheap. All of which makes it ideal for other uses in the home.

Give garden tools a rubdown

Give metal blades, tines, and shovels a blast of WD-40 and scrub off any dirt or rust stains with steel wool. Wipe the metal off with a dry cloth and put your tools away with a shine and a clean conscience!

Tell scuffs to get lost

Black heel marks on vinyl and linoleum floors are frustrating because they won't mop or wipe off, no matter how hard you scrub. A piece of steel wool will rub them away in a second. Scrub lightly, in small circles, and then wipe the area with a paper towel. Good as new!

Discourage rodents and other "boring" creatures

When it's cold outside, lots of little critters will expend lots of energy chewing through skirting boards. And carpenter bees don't care about the temperature while they're boring through the siding of your house. Outsmart the critters by stuffing holes and crevices with steel wool. It will give rodents something to chew on and quickly force carpenter bees to go looking for a new home.

Sharpen shears

Kitchen scissors, especially those you use for foodstuffs, can get dull quickly. Before you discard a well-used piece of steel wool, slice it to bits, directly into the garbage can, with your kitchen shears. Cutting through the fine metal threads will help bring the edge back to your scissors. Wipe the scissors with a damp sponge and then dry with a cloth before storing.

Rub crayon marks off walls

Little ones look at wallpaper and see a huge blank canvas. Parents look at the results of their handiwork ("But I only turned my back for a minute!") and see marks that seem like they can't possibly come clean. But before you repaper the hall, get a clean, new piece of unsoaped steel wool and scrub the crayon lightly, in one direction. You've got a good chance of returning the wall to its pristine state.

WD-40

Few homes are without the distinctive blue and yellow can of WD-40. It's the fastest and best way to stop hinges from squeaking, of course, but it's also a product that has inspired innovation among its users. You can find tales of WD-40 used for, among other things, uncoiling a python from a bus axle. Here are a few ways to start you thinking "outside the can."

Clean tough stains on clothes

WD-40 famously doesn't share its recipe, but it's easy enough to smell a petroleum product. Normally, that would suggest a potential grease stain if spilled on clothing, but, in fact, WD-40 is great at getting out a wide range of stains. As always, stains come cleaner when treated fresh, but if you can spray spots of tomato, tea, coffee, or blood with WD-40, then wash as usual, you may just get it out—with no grease spot remaining!

Remove spots from carpets and floors

Black scuffs and heel marks on linoleum, ink or wine on carpets and rugs, all can be difficult to remove to varying degrees. Spray with WD-40 and rub the floor or scrub the carpet, rinsing well with soap and warm water once the spot is gone.

Take dark stains off countertops

Spilled some blueberry jam? Let coffee or tea dry in? Dark colors can set into your countertops to stay, and no matter how you rub with a sponge or scrubbie, they won't budge. Try a spritz of WD-40 and they'll wipe right up. Be sure to wash it off and rinse well.

Make a blackboard look new

Wiping down a chalkboard with a wet sponge will certainly remove all the chalk, but it will leave a dusty residue over the board. Instead, clean a chalkboard with WD-40, and the whole thing will gleam like new.

Make a "dead" pen write again

Is your ballpoint truly out of ink, or is the tiny ball in the tip gunked up with dried ink? Before you toss it in the trash, find out by wiping the tip with a little WD-40 and a paper towel. There's a good chance your pen will live to write again.

Lubricate pins and needles

When you're sewing with a dense, heavy material, such as denim or tweed, it can be difficult to force the pins through the thick fabric. They'll slip through much more easily if you lubricate them first with WD-40. Dampen a cotton ball or crumpled paper towel with WD-40 and then wipe your pins on it.

Brighten lawn furniture

Faded plastic lawn chairs and tables may seem like a lost cause, but if you spray and buff them with WD-40, they'll not only look smoother and shiny, but the color actually appears to regain its luster.

Tell rabbits and rodents to bug off

If rabbits and other critters are digging and wriggling under your chain link fence to reach the tasty stuff in your garden, let them know their presence is highly unwelcome by spraying a generous amount of WD-40 along the base of the fence, directly on the metal.

Unstick gluey fingers

Accidentally sticking your fingers together with superglue can make anyone panic. Don't hop around in frustration, and don't slap your forehead with your gluey hand. Spray your sticky fingers with WD-40 and let them sit for a few minutes. They'll soon come unstuck. Use a bit more to remove any remaining residue—and be careful next time!

Spray and buff on faded plastic
lawn chairs and tables to bring back the shine.
WD-4

BLASTOFF!

THE HISTORY OF WD-40

Located in San Diego, California, the Rocket Chemical Company, founded by Norm Larsen in 1953, was created to develop a degreaser and rust preventer for the aerospace industry.

Developing a solvent was a tough nut to crack, but after 40 attempts, a petroleum-based lubricant worked. Larsen named it WD-40—**W**ater **D**isplacement, **40**th attempt. The first customer was an aerospace contractor: **WD-40 was used to protect the outer skin of the Atlas Missile.** The product worked so well that employees took some home. Based on this knowledge, Rocket Chemical decided to sell its product to the general public. Packaged in blue and yellow aerosol cans, it was sold locally to hardware and sporting goods stores.

Then, in 1961, Hurricane Carla, the largest and most intense hurricane seen in decades, hit the Gulf Coast. Severe damage was reported, caused by prolonged winds, high tides, and torrential rains. An order for a truckload of WD-40 was received. It was shipped from San Diego to the Gulf Coast to recondition flood- and rain-damaged vehicles and equipment. The spread of WD-40 had begun.

Sales continued to increase; yet the company didn't patent WD-40. Why? They didn't want to disclose the ingredients. In 1969, John S. Barry joined Rocket Chemical as president and CEO. One of his first acts was to change the company's name to the WD-40 Company. No one argued; the company only had one product, and it wasn't a rocket.

Barry focused on increasing distribution. Having served

in the military himself, he was adamant about sending free samples to soldiers in Vietnam to keep their weapons dry. The company shipped thousands and thousands of these each month! **Barry also worked toward getting WD-40 into supermarkets so that consumers could make "impulse purchases."** Under his leadership, the market for WD-40 grew exponentially.

The company went public in 1973 and since that time, WD-40 has grown by leaps and bounds. It reported sales of $292 million in 160 countries in fiscal year 2009!

To this day, the formula is a secret known to only a few. The product itself is so popular that customers write in to the company to reveal their favorite uses. With such an ardent following, the company started an official WD-40 fan club and has compiled a list of over 2,000 uses for WD-40 sent in by enthusiasts. **Some of the more unexpected uses: "keeps snake and reptile skins pliable in taxidermy"** and "lubricates bone joints of skeletons in laboratories."

Who would have imagined a solvent meant for space would be so thoroughly useful on earth?

The popularity and usage of WD-40 increased after Hurricane Carla hit the Gulf Coast in 1961. WD-40 was used to recondition flood- and rain-damaged vehicles and equipment.

Loosen up a vertical blind

Vertical blinds should swing easily open at the lightest touch of your fingertips on the plastic or wooden stick that attaches to the mechanism. If you find you're having to twist hard, spray WD-40 directly on the mechanism at the top of the stick (or on the roller that holds the chain).

Help doors run in their tracks

Sliding glass doors look beautiful leading out onto a patio or deck, but any homeowner who's ever dealt with sticking doors knows that it ruins the illusion of a glass wall if you always have to put your back into it and force the door back and forth. Use WD-40 to keep your doors freely moving. Spray it generously all along the tracks, being careful to stay within the metal grooves, and then push the doors vigorously back and forth several times to distribute the lubricant.

Lubricate locks and deadbolts

You may not realize how much effort it takes when you struggle with a sticky lock. Spritz your key and the inside of the lock with WD-40, then insert the key and jiggle it. Also spray WD-40 on bolts and hinges so that every time, your doors will open and swing smoothly.

Silence a bed

Does your bed frame squeak, jingle or rattle every time you roll over at night? Get a peaceful night's sleep with WD-40. Reach under the bed frame and spray all metal joints, screws or hinges, then lie on the bed and roll and bounce until the lubricant works its way through each joint.

Take marks off car paint

With a spray of WD-40, you can remove the paint smear where another car bumped against yours in a parking lot, and you can get rid of dead bugs and road tar, both of which can damage paint if left unattended.

Repel wasps and hornets

In the spring, mist the undersides of eaves and the corners of your porch roof with WD-40 so that wasps and hornets don't build nests there.

Polish a Formica backsplash

A spritz of WD-40 and a wipe with a soft cloth will remove stains or streaks from the Formica backsplash in your kitchen and help repel grime. (Don't spray directly on the countertop.)

Prevent silver from tarnishing

Once you have cleaned decorative silver, you can keep it gleaming much longer if you mist the surface with a fine spray of WD-40, then buff with a soft lint-free cloth. Do not use this on silver that you will use for eating; however, it's ideal for, say, a decorative silver tea set that you keep on display, rather than using for tea.

Untangle jewelry chains

When necklaces are stored together in a jewelry box, it can be hard to avoid a tangle and even harder to unpick the knot without breaking a chain. Spray the snarl with WD-40, and use your fingers to gently loosen and untangle it.

weather stripping

A roll of weather stripping is an inexpensive fix that can save you big money when you seal off drafty windows and doorjambs. Once you've done that, see what else you can do with this handy material.

Make a secure tool grip

Wrap an overlapping spiral of weather stripping around the handles of your favorite tools, from hammers and axes to wrenches and screwdrivers. You'll get a padded, more comfortable handle and a much better grip for tough jobs.

Add a nonstick base to appliances

Many countertop appliances such as coffeemakers and electric can openers can skid or slip easily. Help them stay put by affixing a few pieces of weather stripping to the base of each appliance.

Give footwear a grip

Waterproof footwear, such as smooth, one-piece Wellington boots, are great at keeping out snow and ice, but not so terrific for keeping your footing. Get a grip by using rubber cement or superglue to attach strips of flat weather stripping under the heels and toes. You can use this trick with hip waders, to help you get a better grip on slick rocks in rivers and streams.

wire

The tool aisle has many types of wire, from insulated varieties meant for electrical work to rolls of shiny naked metal. Whichever you choose, there's a lot you can do with a roll.

Design homemade jewelry

A length of bright copper or nickel wire is a necklace waiting to happen. String on beads or pendants, sequins or buttons, and create a piece of jewelry that expresses you.

Make a handle

Got a bucket with a broken handle? Want to decorate a jar of jam with a handle? Loop covered wire around the neck of the container, then weave wire back and forth, making a U-shape across the top and twisting wire all around the U to make a comfortable carrying handle.

Create a candleholder

Wrap glass jars of different shapes and sizes with metal wire of various colors and thicknesses to make exciting and unique candleholders. You can make several patterns and add glass beads for color and flair. Be sure not to wrap so thickly that the light can't shine through.

Hang photos and cards

A doubled length of wire swooping between two nails is an ideal way to display photos or holiday and birthday cards. Use paper clips or wooden clothes pegs to hang the pictures off the wire, and change your own personal art gallery as the mood strikes you.

Wrap an overlapping spiral of weather stripping around the handles of your favorite tools for a secure grip.

wire brush

Like an industrial scrubbing brush but made with stiff wire bristles, a wire brush is primarily used for removing paint and cleaning off rust. If you pick up a couple from the dollar store, you can use them for more.

Clean concrete and brick flooring

Use a wire brush and a mild soap solution to scrub dirt and grime off garage floors and brick patios. Work in a circular pattern and use a gentle touch.

Remove moss from flagstones

Pour white vinegar straight over mossy flags and scrub off the moss with a wire brush. The brush will remove the existing moss, and the vinegar will help kill off the spores. If the flags are set in a very damp, shady area, the moss will inevitably creep back, but if it has merely crept into an area where you don't want it, a wire brush and vinegar should do the trick.

WAY BACK WHEN...

Horse Hockey!

When you were young, did you ever ask for a pony and get handed a bottle of glue? Even if you didn't have a relative with a questionable sense of humor, you may have heard that "horses are sent to the glue factory." Glue made of rendered animal parts was once the most popular type of adhesive used in woodworking, but this is no longer the case. Today, synthetic glues dominate the market. Elmer's Glue does not use animals or animal parts to make its best-selling product.

Texturize paint for a custom look

Use a wire brush to create patterns and designs on wood or plaster. Depending on your artistic ability, you can make circles or long curving lines, feathered edges or waves. Apply a thick coat of paint to a portion of the wall or item you're decorating, and experiment with your wire brush. If you don't like your initial efforts, paint over them and start again.

wood glue

Based on resin, wood glue is specially designed to attach the porous, uneven surfaces of wood. A thick layer dries to form a weak bond, but a thin layer makes an extremely powerful, water-resistant bond.

Remove splinters

Got a splinter in your finger that won't come out? It's amazing how something so tiny can torture you. Instead of prodding your sore digit with needles and tweezers, put a thin layer of wood glue over it. When it dries, peel the glue off. The splinter will lift out with it.

Fill nail holes in wood

Holes in wooden paneling are a real problem to fill. You can't just put anything in there or it will show. But if you have wood glue, you can mix it with sawdust and use this mixture to fill the holes. If the wood has a very dark finish, you may want to tint the wood glue and sawdust with a few drops of stain to match.

Create a clear varnish

Wood glue dries clear, making it ideal for varnishing craft projects. Mix it half and half with water, and use this mixture to paint over decoupage or papier-mâché. If you tint it with a few drops of fabric dye, the resulting varnish will have a translucent color.

If you have a splinter in your finger, put a thin layer of wood glue over it. When it dries, peel the glue off. The splinter will lift out with it.

work gloves

The work gloves you're looking for in the tool aisle of the dollar store are the thick rubber kind, rather than the thin rubber dishwashing gloves you see in the cleaning aisle. While they're intended for industrial uses, they have other domestic purposes you may have never imagined.

Open jar lids

A durable rubber work glove is the best way to "get a grip" on a stubborn jar lid. Keep one in your utensil drawer and you'll never beat a jar of pickles in frustration on the countertop again.

Put a frozen "hand" in your punchbowl

Having a Halloween party? Here's what to drink: Fill a rubber glove with water, tie off the wrist, and freeze it solid. In a punchbowl or large mixing bowl, combine half cranberry juice, half ginger ale. Remove the hand from the freezer and snip the glove off with scissors. (Trying to tear it off will break the fingers.) Float the icy hand in the punch. Accept compliments.

Serve Thanksgiving dinner

Large birds are often too big and bulky to remove from roasting pans with tongs or a spatula. If you need to move a warm bird from pan to platter, slip on a pair of clean gloves and lift the bird from underneath. Your hands make the best tools.

Remove pet hair

A rubber glove is a pet-hair magnet. If you've gone through more vacuum bags (and vacuums!) than you care to count in cleaning pet hair off your sofas and chairs, all you need is a supply of dollar store rubber work gloves. Put them on and rub your hands all over the upholstery, and don't forget to fondle the throw pillows while you're at it. Pet hair will practically leap off your sofa and onto your gloves.

Sort recyclables

If you're like many of us, during the week you toss all your glass and cans and containers higgledy-piggledy into your recycling bin. Then you may have to hurriedly sort it out before pickup day. Make the job easier by keeping a sturdy pair of durable rubber work gloves right next to the recycling bin. Put them on each time you have to sort, to avoid nicks from open can lids and yucky drips from rinsed containers.

LUNCH COUNTER LEGENDS

IT DOESN'T MATTER WHERE YOU'RE FROM: The lunch counter at your local five-and-dime was not the place you went to eat fancy food. Instead, it's where you went to get a particular style of real cooking at its unvarnished best, which is why anyone who ever bellied up to the bar and ordered a meatloaf sandwich with a side of macaroni and cheese remembers it so fondly. And if you didn't want a whole meal, the lunch counter was where you took a break from the rigors of shopping to refresh yourself with those classic soda-fountain favorites: chocolate egg cream, lime rickey, or a foamy and delicious root beer float. And don't forget dessert! Whether you miss the lunch counters of your youth or you're just a fan of the classics, the recipes in this chapter are guaranteed to make you smile.

32

THE Story Behind...

Campbell's Chicken Noodle Soup

"Chicken with Noodles" soup was a variety introduced to the public by Campbell's in 1934. Despite the fact that it is now considered a mainstay comfort food, sales back then were slow—until the product's name was misread during an episode of the popular *Amos 'n' Andy* radio show. Once listeners heard the words "chicken noodle soup," consumer interest was captured. Folks began to call Campbell's to ask about this "new" soup. Wise to a good thing, the company quickly dropped the "with" and the "s" and renamed the soup to match the blooper that raised its sales.

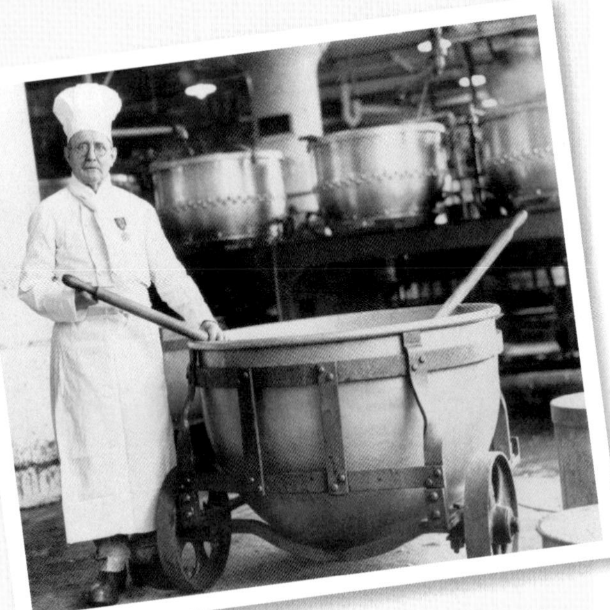

Bouis Charles Delisle, head of Campbell Soup Company, photographed in 1929.

soup of the day

Lunch counter soups are simple and hearty, serving as a meal in themselves or a side to a sandwich. Serve them up with a handful of saltines for authenticity.

Lip-Smacking Chili

Lunch counters aren't where you go for fancy regional chili. They're where you go for a simple, well-seasoned dish of meat and beans, with soda crackers on the side.

Serves: 6

- 1 tablespoon extra-virgin olive oil
- 1 pound lean ground beef
- 1 large onion, minced
- 2 garlic cloves, minced
- 1 can (28 ounces) diced tomatoes in juice
- 2 tablespoons chili powder
- 2 teaspoons ground cumin
- 1 teaspoon dried oregano leaves
- 1 can (28 ounces) red kidney beans, drained and rinsed
- Salt to taste
- Grated cheese and sour cream, to serve

1. In a large stew pot set over medium-high heat, warm the oil until rippling. Then brown the beef, spooning off excess fat. Push the meat to one side and add the onion and garlic. Cook until translucent, about 6 to 7 minutes.
2. Stir in the tomatoes and one tomato-can full of water. Bring to a boil, and stir in the chili powder, cumin, and oregano. Simmer for 30 minutes, until thickened.
3. Stir in the beans and heat through. Taste and add salt as needed. Serve with cheese and a dollop of sour cream.

Split Pea Soup with Ham

There's nothing more comforting on a cold, rainy day than a bowl of thick and hearty pea soup. You can easily make a delicious vegetarian version by leaving out the ham.

Serves: 6–8

1 pound dried split peas, picked over and rinsed

1 large onion, chopped

1 large carrot, peeled and diced

2 garlic cloves, minced

1 ham bone (or 1 1/2 cups cubed ham)

Salt and pepper, to taste

1. Place split peas, onion, carrot, garlic, and ham bone in a large soup pot and add 12 cups of water.
2. Bring to a boil, reduce heat, and simmer very gently for 1 1/2 hours, until the soup is thick and the peas are entirely dissolved. Season with salt to taste and a liberal amount of black pepper.

Cream of Tomato Soup

If you've only ever had tomato soup from a can, you'll love the fresh and sweet taste of this easy version. Be careful not to overdo the baking soda. A tiny pinch reduces the acidity and prevents the milk from curdling but too much makes the soup bland.

Serves: 4

1/4 cup (1/2 stick) unsalted butter

1 small onion, chopped

3 tablespoons all-purpose flour

2 teaspoons sugar

4 cups whole milk

1/2 teaspoon baking soda

1 can (28 ounces) whole tomatoes in juice, or 2 pounds fresh tomatoes, peeled, seeded and chopped (about 3 cups)

Salt and pepper, to taste

1. In a large saucepan, melt the butter and cook the onions gently until soft and translucent, not browned, about 7 to 8 minutes. Sprinkle the flour and sugar over the onions and stir, cooking 1 to 2 minutes.
2. Add the milk gradually, stirring continually to prevent lumps, and then bring the mixture to a simmer.
3. Stir the baking soda directly into the can of tomatoes (or your bowl of chopped tomatoes). They will foam. When the foaming subsides, pour the tomatoes into the milk. Simmer gently for 5 minutes if using canned tomatoes, or 10 minutes if using fresh.
4. Puree the mixture with an immersion blender or a blender or food processor. Return to the pot and reheat, seasoning to taste with salt and pepper.

Chicken Noodle Soup

One of the great things about homemade noodle soup is that you can use wide egg noodles, which are much tastier than the skinny little noodles in canned soup. You can make this speedy recipe with either canned or homemade broth. If you prefer rice to noodles, replace the noodles with 1 cup uncooked rice.

Serves: 6

2 quarts chicken broth

1 small onion, finely diced

1 medium carrot, finely diced

1 celery stalk, finely diced

2 cups uncooked wide egg noodles

Salt and pepper, to taste

1 Put the broth, onion, carrot, and celery in a large soup pot and bring to a boil. Reduce heat and simmer gently for 5 minutes to soften the vegetables.

2 Add the noodles and cook an additional 10 to 15 minutes, until the noodles are cooked and the vegetables are completely tender. Season to taste with salt and pepper.

Beef Vegetable Soup

The secret to a good version of beef vegetable soup is to load the pot with a big variety of veggies. To make that a little easier, whatever the season, feel free to use canned or frozen versions of the vegetables below.

Serves: 8

1 pound stew beef, cut in 1/2-inch cubes

3 medium potatoes, diced

1 large onion, chopped

1 large carrot, diced

1 can (28 ounces) diced tomatoes in juice

1 teaspoon salt, plus more for seasoning

1 teaspoon dried whole thyme leaves

1 package (10 ounces) frozen cut green beans

1 package (10 ounces) frozen shoepeg corn

2 tablespoons tomato paste

Black pepper, to taste

1 Put the beef cubes in a large stew pot and cover with 12 cups of water. Add the potatoes, onion, carrot, tomatoes, 1 teaspoon salt, and thyme. Bring to a boil, reduce heat, and simmer gently for 2 to 3 hours, until the meat and vegetables are so tender that they're nearly falling apart, adding a bit more water if needed.

2 Add the green beans and corn and stir in the tomato paste. Cook for another 30 to 45 minutes, until the soup is slightly thickened. Season to taste with more salt, if needed, and plenty of black pepper.

blue plate specials

The blue plate special, a term dating back to the 1930s and possibly earlier, originally referred to the daily all-in-one meal, generally consisting of meat, potato, one or two vegetables, and no substitutions. While some diners still advertise a blue plate special of the day, the term has also entered the culture to refer to the sorts of home-style and hearty main dishes you'll find here: meat loaf, pot roast, baked chicken, and more. Add a few sides and remind your family that with the blue plate special, there's no cooking to order!

Classic Meat Loaf

Soaking the bread crumbs in the beaten egg and milk until they swell results in a light and tender meat loaf the stays juicy to the last bite.

Serves: 8–10

2 eggs, beaten

3/4 cup milk

1 cup bread crumbs

1 tablespoon horseradish

1 medium carrot, shredded

2 teaspoons salt

Black pepper

1 small onion, minced

2 pounds lean ground beef

Ketchup, for topping and serving

1. Preheat the oven to 325°F. Line a rimmed baking sheet with foil.
2. In a large bowl, combine the eggs, milk, bread crumbs, horseradish, and carrot and stir to combine. Soak for 10 minutes until the crumbs have absorbed the liquid.
3. Add the salt, pepper, onion, and ground beef and combine well. (It helps to use your hands.) Form into a thick loaf about 4 x 10 inches on the foil-covered pan. Top with a generous amount of ketchup in a ribbon down the center, smoothing with a knife.
4. Bake for 1 1/2 hours, until browned and cooked through. An instant-read thermometer in the center will read 160°F. Serve with additional ketchup.

Perfect Pot Roast

Moist heat and long, slow cooking is required to make a pot roast that falls apart at the touch of a fork.

Serves: 6

- 4 pounds beef chuck roast
- 2 tablespoons all-purpose flour
- Salt and pepper, to taste
- 2 tablespoons cooking oil
- 3 large yellow onions, sliced
- 6 large potatoes, peeled and diced large
- 3 large carrots, peeled and cut into 1-inch rounds
- 4 cups beef stock

1. Preheat the oven to 300°F. Lay the chuck roast on a plate and dust both sides with flour, salt, and pepper. Heat the oil in a large Dutch oven and sear the beef, browning well on both sides, about 8 minutes altogether.
2. Add the onions, potatoes, and carrots, layering some under and over the meat. Pour in the stock and cover the pot.
3. Roast for 4 to 5 hours, until the meat and vegetables are so tender that they fall apart when poked with a fork. Check the roast every hour or so and add a bit more stock or water if needed.

Fish Cakes

Any leftover cooked fish can be used to make tasty fish cakes, but this simple preparation is nice with a whitefish such as cod.

Serves: 6

- 2 cups cooked fish, flaked
- 1 cup mashed potatoes
- 3 tablespoons finely minced onion
- 2 tablespoons chopped fresh parsley (optional)
- 1 egg, beaten
- 1/2 teaspoon salt
- 1/4 teaspoon ground black pepper
- All-purpose flour
- Vegetable oil

1. Combine the fish, potatoes, onion, parsley, egg, salt, and pepper, and form into 6 cakes about 3/4- to 1-inch thick. Put a little flour on a plate and roll the cakes lightly in the flour.
2. Film a nonstick skillet with a little vegetable oil and heat over medium-high heat. Add the fish cakes and fry 3 to 4 minutes per side, until golden brown.

Spaghetti and Meatballs

Using a food processor makes the sauce fast and easy, but if you don't have one, just chop the vegetables fine and proceed with the directions.

Serves: 6

For the sauce:

1 medium yellow onion, peeled

1 medium carrot, peeled

1 celery stalk

2 garlic cloves

2 tablespoons olive oil

1 can (28 ounces) whole tomatoes in juice

1 cup water

1 teaspoon sugar

1 teaspoon whole dried oregano

Salt and pepper, to taste

For the meatballs:

1 slice white bread

2 tablespoons milk

1 pound lean ground beef

1 garlic clove, minced

2 tablespoons Parmesan cheese

1 teaspoon whole dried oregano

1 teaspoon salt

1/2 teaspoon black pepper

To serve:

1 pound spaghetti, cooked according to package directions

Grated Parmesan cheese

1 To make the sauce, cut the onion, carrot, celery, and garlic into large chunks and put them in the bowl of a food processor fitted with a steel blade. Pulse until the vegetables are finely chopped.

2 In a large pot, heat the oil over medium heat and then add the vegetables. Cook, stirring frequently, until the vegetables are softened, about 10 minutes. Put the tomatoes in the food processor and pulse to break up the whole tomatoes. Pour them into the pot and add the water, sugar, oregano, salt, and pepper. Bring to a boil, then reduce heat and simmer for 10 minutes while you make the meatballs.

3 To make the meatballs, in a large bowl, break up the slice of bread and pour the milk over it. Let it soak for 2 minutes, then stir to break up the bread further. Add the beef, garlic, Parmesan, oregano, salt, and pepper and mix well to combine (it may be easiest to use your hands). Shape into meatballs about 1 inch in diameter and drop into the bubbling sauce. Partially cover and cook for 20 minutes.

4 Serve over cooked spaghetti, with additional Parmesan on the side.

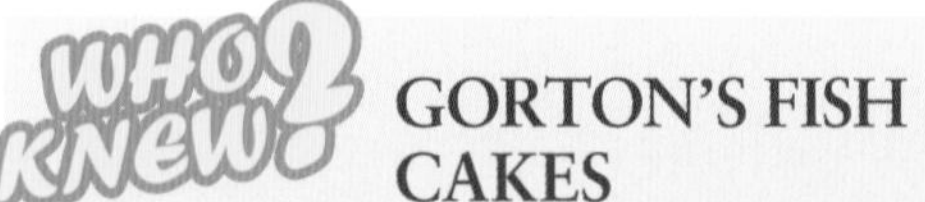

GORTON'S FISH CAKES

When you think of Gorton's Fish Cakes, you may conjure up an image of the Gorton's Fisherman, the company's trademark since 1905. Wearing a slicker, he's "the man behind the wheel" of a schooner—but did you know that in 1949 Gorton's (then known as Gorton-Pew) made headlines for a man behind the wheel of a truck? The company sent the first refrigerated trailer shipment of frozen fish across the country. Starting in Gloucester, Massachusetts, and arriving in San Francisco, California, the trip took a total of eight days!

Corned Beef Hash

The standard meat used in lunch-counter hash is corned beef, but you can use any leftovers you have—pot roast, ham, even chicken. Serve it with fried eggs for a hearty breakfast.

Serves: 6

- 3 tablespoons butter
- 1 large onion, finely diced
- 2 cups diced corned beef
- 4 cups diced cooked potato
- Salt and pepper, to taste

1. Melt the butter in a large nonstick skillet over medium-high heat. Add the onion and cook until translucent, 6 to 7 minutes.
2. Add the diced meat and potato and mix to combine. Press down with a spatula and cook until the bottom is browned. Cook 10 to 12 minutes, lifting and turning portions of the mixture, allowing the bottom to brown before turning it again. If necessary, add a bit more butter to prevent sticking.
3. Season with salt and pepper and serve hot.

sandwich classics

Back in the day, there was no seven-grain bread, no sourdough boules or ciabatta: It was white bread all the way, and the real classics such as tuna melt and egg salad still taste their most authentic like that. That said, any of the recipes here will be delicious on whatever bread you use, except for the All-American Reuben, which simply must be on rye.

Tuna Melt

A lunch-counter tuna melt is a very basic sandwich—tuna and mayo on bread, with a slice of American cheese melted over the top. You can add more seasonings to the tuna salad (a little diced onion is good) or vary the cheese to make a very different sandwich, but with this basic formula, it's hard to make a bad tuna melt! This recipe is for an open-faced sandwich, but if you want a closed one, toast 4 additional slices, spread on a little mayo, and top the broiled sandwiches before serving.

Makes 4 sandwiches

- 2 cans (6 ounces each) chunk light tuna
- 3 tablespoon mayonnaise
- 4 slices sandwich bread
- 4 slices ripe tomato
- 4 slices American or cheddar cheese

1. Preheat the broiler. Drain the tuna well and toss it with the mayonnaise, whipping with a fork to make the tuna fluffy.
2. Toast the bread in a toaster to give your sandwich more body. Lay the toast slices on the broiler pan. Mound the tuna high on each slice. Top each with a slice of tomato and a slice of cheese.
3. Broil the sandwiches for several minutes, until the cheese is melted and just starts to bubble.

Grilled Cheese

The best versions aren't grilled—they're fried, and there's no way around it. But the secret is pressing it in the pan, as in this recipe. The finest grilled cheese isn't very thick (the addition of crisp bacon or tomato is nice), and the cheese should be molten when it comes to the table. With a bowl of tomato soup, it's an ideal lunch: hot, easy, delicious.

Makes 1 sandwich

Softened butter

2 slices sandwich bread

Sliced cheese (American is standard and cheddar is always good, but any hard melting cheese will work)

1 Lightly butter the slices of bread on both sides. Preheat a dry cast-iron skillet over medium heat.

2 Put the cheese in the bread and top with the other slice. Lay in the skillet, pressing down firmly on top of the sandwich with a spatula.

3 After 3 to 4 minutes, when the bottom of the sandwich is golden brown, flip it and press down again with a spatula. Lay a plate on top of the sandwich and top with a heavy can (such as a large can of tomatoes) or a smaller skillet or saucepan to weigh down the plate. Press gently to flatten. Cook until the underside is golden brown and the cheese is molten, reducing the heat slightly if necessary to prevent burning.

BLT

Gourmet BLTs with thick-cut pepper bacon and homemade mayo on sourdough bread are not what you get at a lunch counter. The true BLT is a simple and basic rendition, the true classic.

Makes 1 sandwich

4 slices bacon

2 slices white bread

1 tablespoon mayonnaise

2–3 leaves crisp lettuce

3 slices fresh ripe tomato

1 In a skillet, cook the bacon until crisp. While it drains on a paper towel, toast the bread.

2 Slather the mayo on each slice and layer on the bacon, lettuce, and tomato in that order, so that the bacon touches the mayo on one side and the tomato touches it on top, with the crunchy lettuce in between.

All-the-Way Dog

The chili on an All-the-Way Dog is a thin dark red concoction of ground meat in a tangy sauce with no beans. Spicy brown or deli mustard is the way to go; no yellow mustard here.

Makes 1 hot dog

1 hot dog

1 hot dog bun

Spicy brown mustard

Chopped onion

Chili without beans

1 Cook the hot dog according to package directions and place in the bun. Slather spicy mustard on the dog. Shower with chopped onion.

2 Spoon on a generous amount of chili—it should drip.

North Carolina All-the-Way Dog

This well-filled dog is supposed to drip. If not, you didn't add enough toppings. The slaw is typically made of sliced cabbage, shredded carrot, mayonnaise, and a little lemon juice or vinegar.

Makes 1 hot dog

- 1 hot dog
- 1 hot dog bun
- Yellow mustard
- Chili with beans
- Chopped onions
- Coleslaw

1. Cook the hot dog according to package directions and place on the bun. Drizzle on yellow mustard—not too much. Spoon on chili liberally and sprinkle on some onions.
2. Add the coleslaw until it overflows the edges of the bun. Eat before your bun is too mushy to hold.

Egg Salad Sandwich

Egg salad should be a mild mixture—no herbs or spices, nothing more potent than perhaps a little onion and celery. If you prefer, it can be made of nothing more than egg, mayo, salt, and pepper. This recipe will make two well-filled sandwiches or four thin ones. The onion is up to you.

Makes 2–4 sandwiches

- 4 hard-boiled eggs
- 1 celery stalk, finely chopped (optional)
- 1 tablespoon finely chopped onion (optional)
- 1/4 cup mayonnaise
- Salt and pepper, to taste
- 4–8 slices white bread

1. Peel the eggs and dice them small, yolks and all. (If you like a fine-textured egg salad, use a fork to mash the eggs instead of chopping.)
2. Add the celery and onion, if using, and then blend in the mayonnaise. Season to taste with salt and pepper.
3. Toasting the bread is a matter of personal taste. Some prefer the crunch of toast against the egg salad, while others like soft bread surrounding the creamy filling. Either way, spoon the egg salad directly onto the bread. There is no need for additional mayonnaise.

WAY BACK WHEN...

Nathan's Famous Hot Dogs

In 1916, Nathan Handwerker started his own hot dog stand in Coney Island, using an all-beef recipe developed by his wife, Ida. He charged 5 cents because he wanted his product to be affordable. The public stayed away, reasoning that if it was so cheap maybe it was horse meat! Nathan devised a creative solution: He hired people to stand and eat in front of his place wearing lab coats and stethoscopes. He then posted a sign reading, "If doctors eat our hot dogs, you know they're good!" It was this type of moxie that enabled him to build his stand into a hot dog empire, and create a brand name that is recognized around the globe.

Hot Open-Faced Roast Beef Sandwich

A true lunch-counter classic, this open-faced sandwich makes the most of leftovers. Be sure to save some pot roast (page 307) and gravy, as well as mashed potatoes. A microwave makes short work of heating the meat, gravy, and potatoes, but heat them all separately before assembling the sandwich.

Makes 1 sandwich

Mashed potatoes

Sliced leftover pot roast

Beef gravy

1 slice white bread

1 Reheat the potatoes, roast, and gravy. (For ease, you can heat the meat in the gravy in a small saucepan while you reheat the potatoes in a microwave.)

2 Put the bread on a plate and add a scoop or two of mashed potatoes. Layer a few slices of meat on top of the potatoes, and then pour gravy over all. There should be enough to run down the sides and dampen the bread beneath. Serve at once.

variation: ***Hot Turkey Sandwich***
Replace the pot roast with sliced roast turkey and the gravy with turkey gravy. Serve with a dollop of cranberry sauce.

A Perfect Burger with Fried Onions

Nothing says supper like the scent of frying onions. A tangle of caramelized, golden onions elevates an ordinary burger to something special.

Serves: 4

2 tablespoons olive oil

2 medium yellow onions, thinly sliced

1 pound lean ground beef

Salt and pepper, to taste

4 buns

1 Heat the olive oil over medium heat in a large skillet. Add the onions and cook slowly, reducing heat if necessary to prevent burning, for about 20 minutes, until the onions are a softened, golden-brown mass.

2 While the onions are cooking, shape the meat into four patties and season with salt and pepper. Cook over medium-high heat in a dry skillet to the desired doneness (a medium burger should be 160°F on an instant-read thermometer stuck into the center).

3 Season the sautéed onions with salt and pepper. Place a burger on each bun and top with a tangle of onions.

sides

There are still plenty of parts of the country where mac and cheese is considered a "vegetable." That feeling stems from the typical roster of lunch counter sides, which often included a golden succulent square of baked mac and cheese as one of the options, along with the fluffy mashed potatoes, long-cooked green beans, and cinnamon-accented applesauce. And don't forget the French fries and onions rings—they *are* vegetables, after all.

Mac and Cheese

Most modern mac and cheese recipes pit one pound of pasta against one pound of cheese, but that's a little too rich for the lunch counter version, which has a little more white sauce and a little less cheese. The result is, in fact, creamier than the ultra-cheesy varieties, which tend to go a little greasy when reheating. When the casserole cools a little, you'll be able to cut and lift out solid squares of mac and cheese with a spatula, which was the typical way it was served at the lunch counter.

Serves: 8–10

1 pound elbow macaroni

1/4 cup (1/2 stick) butter

1/4 cup all-purpose flour

3 1/2 cups whole milk

2 cups grated cheddar cheese

1 tablespoon Dijon mustard

Salt and pepper, to taste

1 cup grated Parmesan cheese

1/2 cup bread crumbs

1 Preheat the oven to 375°F and grease a 2-quart baking dish. Cook macaroni according to package directions. Drain and rinse under cool water to stop the cooking.

2 In a large saucepan over medium heat, melt the butter and sprinkle in the flour, whisking to combine. Gradually whisk in the milk, stirring constantly to prevent lumps, and cook until bubbling and starting to thicken, 3 to 4 minutes.

3 Stir in the cheddar and mustard. Add salt and pepper to taste (you may not need any salt). Combine the sauce and macaroni and turn into the prepared casserole dish.

4 Mix together the Parmesan and bread crumbs and sprinkle over the surface. Bake for 25 minutes, until bubbling and lightly browned.

French Fries

Homemade fries are a real culinary pleasure. Even at a restaurant, it's hard to get fries as hot and fresh as when they come right out of the hot oil in your kitchen. The trick to making fries that aren't greasy is par-cooking them first, then finishing them with a quick second cooking in very hot oil. Sprinkle with salt and eat a few right away. It's the cook's privilege!

Serves: 6

4 cups vegetable oil, or more as needed

6 large russet potatoes, peeled and cut lengthwise into 1/4-inch strips

Salt, to taste

1 Pour enough oil into a large, heavy-bottomed pot to come about 2 1/2 inches up the side. Heat over medium heat to 250°F on a frying thermometer.

2 Cook the potato strips in batches for about 3 minutes, until softened and just starting to brown. Remove to a paper towel–lined platter. The potatoes can rest like this for up to an hour, or you can proceed at once with the second cooking.

3 Just before serving, bring the pot of oil to 350°F on a frying thermometer. Line a fresh platter or bowl with paper towels and cook the fries in batches in the hot oil until golden brown, about 2 more minutes. Drain on paper towels, sprinkle with salt, and serve at once.

Hash Browns

Most of us tend to think of hash browns as an accompaniment to a hearty breakfast, but they're equally good suppertime fare. A well-seasoned cast-iron skillet is the best pan for cooking these.

Serves: 6

- About 6 large russet potatoes
- 1 large yellow onion, finely chopped
- 1 medium green or red bell pepper, diced small (optional)
- 1/3 cup vegetable oil, or more as needed
- Salt and pepper, to taste

1 Grate the potatoes on the shredding blade of a food processor or with a hand grater. Mix the shredded potatoes with the chopped onion and bell pepper, if using. Heat the oil in a large cast-iron or nonstick skillet over medium heat. Add the potatoes and a sprinkle of salt and pepper.

APPLESAUCE

According to the United States Department of Health and Human Services, the recommended amount of fruit for children is 1 1/2 cups a day and for adults it is 1 1/2 to 2 cups per day. A one-cup serving of applesauce counts as a one-cup serving of fruit. It contains about 20 percent of the vitamin C you need daily and is naturally free of fat, cholesterol, and sodium. That's a snack you can feel good about!

2 Cook without stirring or moving the potatoes for 6 to 7 minutes, reducing the heat slightly if the potatoes seem to be browning too fast. Then use a spatula to lift and flip the potatoes by section, so that you're not stirring the potatoes but simply flipping it in portions. If the potatoes stick badly, add a bit more oil to the pan, lifting the edge of the potatoes with a spatula to pour the oil underneath.

3 Sprinkle with a little salt and pepper again and continue cooking for 7 to 8 minutes, until browned on the outside and cooked through inside. Serve at once.

Perfect Mashed Potatoes

Whether you like your potatoes fluffy and smooth or dense and lumpy—and we all have our preferences—you can make sure they're always delicious by never forgetting to heat the milk and butter before beating them in.

Serves: 6

- 1 1/2 pounds potatoes, peeled and quartered
- 1 teaspoon salt
- 1/2 cup whole milk
- 3–4 tablespoons butter
- Salt and black pepper, to taste

1 Put the potatoes into a saucepan and add cold water to cover and a teaspoon of salt. Bring to a boil, reduce heat and simmer 15 to 20 minutes, until they are tender throughout when prodded with a fork.

2 Heat the milk and butter together, either in the microwave or in a small saucepan. Drain the potatoes well and return them to the cooking pot. Put it over the heat for another moment or two to dry out the potatoes.

3 Use a potato masher to mash them as desired. Stir in the hot milk and butter, whipping with a fork to combine. If you like them dense, season with salt and pepper and serve at once. If you like them fluffy, add a little salt and pepper and then use a hand mixer to beat them for a minute or two until light.

Cole Slaw

Slaw is ubiquitous at lunch counters and diners, creeping into sandwiches or appearing in little metal or plastic pots next to many sandwiches and dinners. Make it at home for the freshest possible version.

Serves: 8–10

1/2 of a large head green cabbage, finely shredded (about 5 cups)

1 large carrot, grated

3/4 cup mayonnaise

2 tablespoons sour cream

2 tablespoons lemon juice

1 tablespoon dry mustard

Salt and pepper, to taste

1 Combine the shredded cabbage and carrots in a large bowl. Whisk together the mayo, sour cream, lemon, mustard, salt, and pepper and pour over the slaw. Stir to combine, and let rest, covered, in the refrigerator for at least an hour before serving.

2 Before serving, stir up from the bottom and taste to see if it needs a bit more salt or lemon.

Cinnamon Applesauce

Homemade applesauce is such a pleasure if you're only accustomed to the jarred kind. Use a cooking apple that dissolves into tenderness, such as a Macintosh, rather than an eating apple that stays crisp. This recipe is a basic guide—use as many apples as you like, and add as much or as little sugar or cinnamon as you prefer.

Serves: 4

4 large cooking apples

3/4 cup water

1/4 cup sugar

1/2 teaspoon ground cinnamon

2 teaspoons lemon juice (optional)

1 Peel, core, and chop the apples. Place in a medium saucepan with the water, sugar, and cinnamon. Cook over medium heat until the apples are tender and falling apart, 15 to 20 minutes. If you like, mash any large chunks of apple with a fork. (For a velvety smooth puree, cool the applesauce slightly and pulse in a blender or food processor.)

2 Taste to adjust seasonings. If the applesauce seems too sweet or bland, add a teaspoon or 2 of lemon juice to return tartness to the apples and brighten the flavor.

SNAPSHOT IN TIME...

THE HISTORY OF WOOLWORTH'S LUNCH COUNTER

There was a time before amazon.com and big box stores when small towns across America had shopping areas dominated by one general store—a Woolworth's. Frank Winfield Woolworth, a worker in a dry-goods store, opened his own shop in 1870 in Utica, New York. That store struggled, but his second store—opened in 1879 in Lancaster, Pennsylvania—thrived. Woolworth had an idea that revolutionized the way Americans shopped: **His establishment would be the first to allow shoppers to handle merchandise.** This seems like common sense, but the standing tradition in retail had been to keep all goods behind a counter and require customers to present their needs to a clerk. Woolworth had another groundbreaking thought: Everything should be affordable—priced at either 5 or 10 cents. The two ideas in combination made "five-and-dime stores" into destination shopping, places where you would go to spend time and browse. This could lead shoppers to develop an appetite—and as **Woolworth's stores spread across America, a solution to dining needs arose.**

F. W. Woolworth's five-and-dime store in Lancaster, Pennsylvania, opened on June 21, 1879.

At a time when most people ate at home, Woolworth's began opening lunch counters. They became something of a sensation: Suddenly, you could "eat on the go." For a child, a shopping trip with mom to buy housewares and a lipstick could now result in a quick peek at the **pet department (filled with goldfish, gerbils, and parakeets)** and end with a stop at the lunch counter. Sitting together on round red stools that could spin, you'd inhale the aroma of toasting white bread and brewing coffee. **You could hear the malteds being shaken by hand,** and you could see signs promising soda and dessert specials. Up until the 1950s, almost everything on the menu was less than 65 cents—so with no more than a dollar in her pocket your mother could order a toasted ham and cheese sandwich for 60 cents, a milkshake made with "two dippers of ice cream" for a quarter, and still **order a slice of apple pie for 15 cents,** and the two of you could eat dutch.

Lunches like these at Woolworth's are a treasured memory for many of us. For working people, a quick trip to the lunch counter was the way to eat well on a budget: You cold get hot dogs on buns that were buttered and toasted and wash them down with a lime rickey. If you were really hungry, you could order dessert: perhaps a lemon coconut cake or an icebox cheesecake. If you were a teenager, you might go on a date to Woolworth's and share an order of fries with two vanilla Cokes, made with syrup and seltzer. And if you were a doting grandparent, you treated your grandchildren to the sundaes or banana splits that were served with a fun tradition: **You had to pop a balloon to find out what the price was. Picking a "lucky balloon" could reveal a piece of paper that said 1 cent!** From chicken soup to warm nuts, until well into the 1960s, everything seemed to taste better when you ate it at a Woolworth's.

The counters themselves were something to behold. One, located on South Broadway in downtown Los Angeles, was 100 yards long and billed as "the longest lunch counter in the world in 1937."

THE Story Behind...

Chocolate Egg Cream

In the days when candy stores had soda fountains, you could buy a chocolate egg cream made fizzy with seltzer sprayed from a bottle. Today you can still order an egg cream at many diners, but the seltzer will likely come from a bottle. Besides seltzer, an authentic egg cream contains Fox's U-bet syrup and milk. Many people believe that Auster's soda fountain, located in New York City, is where the drink was born. Though this shop is long gone, Fox's U-bet syrup is still made in Brooklyn, New York, and has been for over 100 years.

soda jerk specials

Soda fountains and ice cream drinks were no small part of the lunch counter, but many of the classic drinks are now almost impossible to find. Fortunately, most are relatively simple to make at home, from a refreshing lime rickey, a sort of zingy limeade, to a purple cow, an ice cream float made with grape soda.

Lime Rickey

Fresh lime juice is terrific here, but you won't be sorry if you make your lime rickey with bottled lime juice. The simple syrup of water and sugar is important, so don't skip the first step or the sugar won't dissolve. This recipe can be easily doubled or tripled.

Serves: 2

- 1/4 cup water
- 1/4 cup sugar
- 1 cup fresh lime juice (from 4 large or 6 small limes)
- 1 1/2 cups (12 ounces) seltzer or club soda

1. In a small saucepan or microwavable cup, heat the sugar and water together and stir to dissolve the sugar completely. Allow to cool briefly.
2. Stir the lime juice into the simple syrup. Fill two tall glasses with ice and divide the lime and syrup mixture between the two. Top each glass with half the seltzer and stir gently.

Egg Cream

This addictive and deceptively simple drink gets its name because when the seltzer is added to the milk and chocolate syrup, it foams up like beaten egg. The result is light and frothy and yet richly chocolaty and deeply satisfying. If you've never tried one, it's time. Standard wisdom holds that you need whole milk for the drink to foam properly, and the traditional syrup is Fox's U-bet, a brand still available in some areas. Be sure that the milk and seltzer are very cold.

Serves: 1

1/4 cup whole milk
8 ounces (1 cup) seltzer or club soda
2 tablespoons chocolate syrup

1. Put the milk in a tall soda glass. Add the seltzer or club soda and stir vigorously with a long spoon, which will cause it to bubble and foam up.
2. Pour the chocolate syrup down the inside of the glass and use the spoon to stir it gently. There will still be streaks of chocolate at the bottom of the glass but the foamy head should remain white. Don't overmix or the foam will start to dissipate. Drink at once.

The Best Vanilla Milkshake

To make a good milkshake, it's important not to skimp on the ice cream. But to make one in a blender requires a bit more liquid than what's needed in the milkshake mixer of a soda fountain. This recipe gets the balance right, and the extra hit of vanilla makes it special.

Serves: 2–3

1 1/2 cups milk
1 tablespoon vanilla
3 scoops vanilla ice cream

1. Put the milk in the bottom of the blender container, then add the vanilla and top with the ice cream.
2. Blend until smooth, then immediately pour into glasses.

Vanilla Coke

Sure, you can buy commercially prepared variations on cola flavors, but it's not the same taste as the old-fashioned soda-fountain version where the cola was dressed up with a shot of simple syrup flavored with vanilla. This version gets it just right. Don't skip the salt; it helps balance the sweetness. Use chilled cola, and to avoid diluting the flavors, don't add ice.

Serves: 4

1/2 cup sugar
1/2 cup water
1/4 teaspoon salt
1 tablespoon vanilla
Chilled cola

1. Combine the sugar, water, and salt in a small saucepan. Bring to a boil and simmer for 3 to 4 minutes, until reduced by half. Remove from the heat and stir in the vanilla.
2. Cool the syrup completely in the refrigerator.
3. To make a vanilla coke, put several tablespoons of the vanilla syrup in the bottom of a tall glass. Slowly top with 1 1/2 cups (one 12-ounce can) chilled cola and stir very gently. Drink with a straw.

The Float Family

Whoever figured out that a scoop of ice cream was meant to float in a glass of fizzy soda did his fellow man a good turn. To make any of the versions here, first scoop the ice cream into the bottom of a tall soda glass, then slowly pour the well-chilled soda down the side. The scoop of ice cream will rise like a boat on the tide, and a reaction between the carbonation and ice cream will cause a dome of big creamy bubbles to rise over the top of the glass. There are many regional variations, but here are some of the classics.

Root Beer Float

1 bottle (12 ounces) root beer

1 scoop vanilla ice cream

Brown Cow

1 bottle (12 ounces) root beer

1 scoop chocolate ice cream

Coke Float

1 bottle (12 ounces) cola

1 scoop vanilla ice cream

Purple Cow

1 bottle (12 ounces) grape soda

1 scoop vanilla ice cream

Sherbet Float

1 bottle (12 ounces) ginger ale

1 scoop orange sherbet

Hot Cocoa

A steaming cup of hot cocoa is an unmatched treat on a wintry day. A Dutch-process cocoa powder will have a milder, more rounded chocolate flavor, while regular cocoa will have more intensity. The vanilla adds depth and richness. Top with a marshmallow, whipped cream, or a dollop of marshmallow fluff.

Serves: 1

1 cup whole milk

1 heaping tablespoon cocoa powder

1 tablespoon sugar

1 tablespoon cream

1/2 teaspoon vanilla (optional)

1 Heat the milk in a small saucepan or in the microwave. In the bottom of a mug, use a fork to blend the cocoa and sugar with the cream to make a paste.

2 Slowly stir in the hot milk, whisking with the fork to blend away any lumps. Stir in the vanilla, if using.

the last bite

"Save room for dessert!" It's the confident comment of a waitress who knows there's homemade pie on the countertop. And there was at many a lunch counter. Pie is the classic American dessert, and the recipes here cover many of the classics, along with a super-moist yellow cake with its traditional chocolate icing and a fistful of big, chewy cookies. You might just want to skip lunch and start with dessert.

Double-Crust Apple Pie

It's hard to beat homemade double-crust apple pie, even if you use a frozen piecrust. Commercial crusts tend to come in a two-pack, so assemble the pie in one crust, and then turn the other crust upside down on top and carefully lift off the foil pan (if it comes in a pan).

Makes one 9-inch pie

- 2 pounds cooking apples (about 6–8 apples), peeled and sliced
- 3/4 cup sugar
- 1/3 cup all-purpose flour
- 1 teaspoon cinnamon
- 1/8 teaspoon ground cloves
- 2 piecrusts (9 inches), or enough pastry for a double-crust pie, unbaked
- 2 tablespoons unsalted butter

1. Preheat the oven to 425°F. Put the sliced apples in a bowl and toss with the sugar, flour, cinnamon, and cloves. Spoon into the bottom crust and dot with the butter.
2. Cover the pie with the top crust, and poke with a fork or cut slits on the top, so the steam can escape.
3. Bake for 10 minutes, until top just starts to brown. Then reduce the heat to 400°F and bake an additional 40 minutes, until filling bubbles up through the slits and the crust is golden. If the crust starts to brown too much before the pie is done, cover it carefully with foil.
4. Cool the pie before serving.

Lemon Meringue Pie

To speed up a lemon meringue pie, don't let anything cool—spoon the hot filling into the hot crust. Then slather on the meringue and bake. Your pie can be ready in under half an hour, start to finish.

Makes one 9-inch pie

- 1 piecrust (9 inches)
- 4 eggs, separated
- 1 1/4 cup sugar
- 1/4 cup cornstarch
- 1/4 teaspoon salt
- 1 1/2 cups water
- 2 lemons, juiced and zested
- 2 tablespoons butter

1. Bake the empty crust according to package or recipe directions (leaving the oven on when you're done). Beat the egg yolks in a small bowl and set aside.
2. While the piecrust bakes, in a medium saucepan, whisk together 1 cup sugar, cornstarch, salt, and water over medium heat. Cook, stirring frequently, until it comes to a boil, then stir constantly for 2 minutes, until the mixture thickens. Set the pan off the heat for a moment. Whisk 1/2 cup of the hot sugar mixture into the egg yolks, then whisk the egg mixture back into the saucepan along with the lemon juice and zest. Return to a boil and continue to cook while stirring constantly until thick, 1 to 2 minutes. Remove from heat and stir in the butter. Spoon the hot filling directly into the hot piecrust.
3. Let the pie sit while you beat the egg whites with a mixer on high. When they become foamy, sprinkle in the remaining sugar and continue beating until glossy peaks form.
4. Spoon the meringue on the pie. Bake for 10 minutes in the preheated oven.

THE Story Behind...

Jell-O Pudding Mixes

Pudding was once thought of as fare for invalids—a high-calorie food for the sick. This began to change in 1934 when General Foods introduced a mix called "Walter Baker's Dessert." It was renamed "Jell-O Chocolate Pudding" in 1936, and within a few years vanilla and butterscotch flavors appeared. Advertised as "fabulously good desserts," the convenient little boxes of powder caught on, and "J-E-L-L-ooooh," as the jingle had it, is still a kitchen staple (the company is now owned by Kraft).

"ITS SO SIMPLE"
JELL-O
America's most famous dessert
THE great merit of Jell-O is that it is always ready. It is made as easily as a cup of tea is brewed. Write for a free booklet describing a wide variety of uses.
The GENESEE PURE FOOD COMPANY. LE ROY. NEW YORK
Canadian Factory at Bridgeburg, Ontario
JELL-O
STRAWBERRY

Coconut Cream Pie

You can top this pie with meringue according to the directions in the Lemon Meringue Pie, or you can set the whites aside for another use and top the pie with whipped cream, as in the directions below.

Makes one 9-inch pie

- 1 piecrust (9 inches)
- 4 eggs, separated
- 1 cup + 2–3 tablespoons sugar
- 1/2 cup all-purpose flour
- 1/4 teaspoon salt
- 3 cups whole milk
- 3 tablespoons butter
- 2 teaspoons vanilla
- 1 cup flaked coconut
- 1 cup whipping cream

1. Bake the empty crust according to package or recipe directions. Beat the egg yolks in a small bowl and set aside.
2. In a saucepan over medium heat, whisk together 1 cup sugar, flour, and salt, then gradually whisk in the milk. Bring to a boil, stirring frequently, and cook for 3 to 4 minutes until the filling thickens and bubbles. Remove from the heat for a moment and whisk 1/2 cup of the mixture into the egg yolks.
3. Return the egg yolk mixture to the saucepan and bring the filling to a gentle boil. Cook, stirring constantly, for 2 minutes. Remove from the heat and stir the butter, vanilla, and coconut into the hot mixture. Pour the hot filling into the baked crust and cool completely.
4. When the pie is cool, beat the cream and remaining sugar until stiff peaks form. Smooth over the surface of the pie and serve at once, refrigerating any leftovers.

Butterscotch Pudding

Making butterscotch pudding from scratch is just as easy as making it from a mix that requires cooking, but the difference in flavor is exponential. It's tempting to eat it up while the pudding is hot, but if you let it cool a bit, the butterscotch flavor is more pronounced.

Serves: 4

3/4 cup brown sugar

2 tablespoons cornstarch

1/4 teaspoon salt

2 cups milk

3 tablespoons butter

1 1/2 teaspoons vanilla

1. In a medium saucepan over medium heat, whisk together the sugar, cornstarch, and salt. Slowly pour in the milk, whisking constantly to avoid lumps.
2. Bring to a boil, stirring frequently, and then cook, stirring constantly, until the pudding boils and thickens, 3 to 4 minutes.
3. Remove from heat and stir in the butter and vanilla, mixing until the butter melts. Cool before serving. Store any leftovers in the refrigerator.

Yellow Cake with Chocolate Frosting

The moist and tender yellow cake is perfectly good and could even be eaten on its own, perhaps with a sprinkle of confectioners' sugar. But what really sets this dessert apart, the gilding on the lily—the icing on the cake, in fact—is the rich, dark chocolate frosting. It may seem like extra effort to mix the yolks and eggs in separately, but the extra effort results in a cake that's exceptionally light-textured.

Serves: 12

For the cake:

2 1/2 cups all-purpose flour, plus more for dusting

1 1/2 teaspoons baking powder

1 teaspoon salt

1/4 teaspoon baking soda

3/4 cup (1 1/2 sticks) butter, softened

1 3/4 cups sugar

2 teaspoons vanilla

3 egg yolks

3 whole eggs

1 cup milk

For the frosting:

1/2 cup (1 stick) butter, softened

4 cups (1 pound) confectioners' sugar

1 teaspoon vanilla

1 1/2 ounces (1 1/2 squares) bittersweet chocolate, melted

1. To make the cake, preheat the oven to 350°F and grease a 9 x 13-inch metal baking pan. Lightly coat the pan with flour, tapping out any excess. Mix together the flour, baking powder, salt, and baking soda in a small bowl and set aside.
2. Beat the butter and sugar with a mixer on medium speed until light and fluffy. Beat in the vanilla, and then the egg yolks, one at a time, followed by the whole eggs, each time

letting them be fully incorporated before adding the next.

3 With the mixer on low, add half the flour and mix just to blend, followed by half the milk. Repeat with remaining flour and milk. Turn the batter into the pan and bake until the edges are set and pull slightly away from the pan, about 35 minutes. Cool completely on a wire rack.

4 To make the frosting, beat the butter, confectioners' sugar, vanilla, and chocolate together in a mixer, continuing to beat for 3 to 4 minutes until light and fluffy. Spread thickly over the cake in the pan, and serve in large squares.

Chewy Peanut Butter Cookies

If you like peanut butter cookies that are chewy, not crunchy and crumbly, these are for you. To avoid overbaking, stay nearby while they bake and remove them from the oven when you smell the scent of "baked cookie," even if there is still a minute or two left on the timer.

Makes about 12 cookies

1/2 cup smooth peanut butter
1/2 cup (1 stick) butter, softened
1/2 cup granulated sugar, with extra for dipping
1/2 cup light brown sugar
1 egg
1 teaspoon vanilla
1 1/4 cups all-purpose flour
1/2 teaspoon baking powder
3/4 teaspoon baking soda
1/4 teaspoon salt

1 Preheat the oven to 325°F and grease two cookie sheets.

2 With a mixer set on medium, cream the peanut butter, butter, and sugars in a medium bowl. Beat in the egg and vanilla.

3 Stir in the flour, baking powder, baking soda, and salt. Use an ice cream scoop to place dough 3 inches apart on the cookie sheets. Dip a fork in sugar and press each ball down, making crisscross hatch marks.

4 Bake for 10 minutes, until the edges are just turning golden. Cool completely on wire racks.

Lunch Counter Lingo

A Quick Guide to Understanding Short-Order Language

It's happened to all of us: We're sitting at the counter, we order a toasted English muffin and a glass of milk, and the waitress calls back to the cook, "One burn the British and a moo juice." Over the years, lunch counter (and diner) cooks have developed their own terms for commonly ordered dishes. Here's what they're really saying:

LINGO	DISH
Adam and Eve on a raft	Two poached eggs on toast
Adam's ale	Plain water
Axle grease	Butter
Cow (or moo) juice	Milk
Belch water	Seltzer
Birdseed (or twigs)	Cereal
Bossy in a bowl	Beef stew
Bow-wow	Hot dog
Breath	Onion
Bridge party	Four of anything
Bun pup	Hot dog
Burn one	Hamburger on the grill
Burn the British	A toasted English muffin
Cat's eye	Tapioca pudding
Chopper	A table knife
City juice	Water
Clean up the kitchen	Hash
Coney Island	Hot dog
Cowboy	Western omelette
Cow feed	Salad
Crowd	Three of anything
Deadeye	Poached egg
Dog biscuit	Crackers
Draw one	Coffee
Eighty-six	Sold out
Eve with a lid	Apple pie
GAC	Grilled American cheese
High and dry	Plain sandwich without mayo
Houseboat	Banana split
In the alley	Serve as a side dish
Lumber	A toothpick
Mike and Ike	Salt and pepper
On the hoof	Meat cooked rare
Put out the lights and cry	Liver and onions
Sinkers and suds	Doughnuts and coffee
With wheels	To go
Wreck 'em	Scrambled eggs

A

B

C

F

G

H

I

J

K

L

M

P

S

U

V

W

Photo credits

16, 41 (bottom), 46, 49, 50, 92, 103 (top), 118, 145, 163, 250, 290-291 (drawings), 301, Dan Lipow

18-19, 20, 23, 24, 30, 35, 37, 42, 44, 48, 52-53, 55, 57, 58, 61, 64, 68, 71, 72-73, 74, 78, 81, 83, 88-89, 91, 95, 97, 103 (bottom), 106-107, 109 (top), 114, 111, 119, 121, 122, 124-125, 126, 129, 133, 134, 136, 138-139, 146-147, 148, 151, 151, 155, 157 (bottom), 161, 173, 178-179, 181, 183, 184-185, 187, 189, 196, 199, 201, 204, 208, 210-211, 215, 220-221, 223, 224, 227, 230, 233, 235, 236, 243, 240, 246, 249, 245-255, 256, 259, 262, 264, 266-267, 269, 278, 277, 278-279, 280, 285, 287, 289, 290-291, 290-291 (background), 292, 295, 299, 303, 311 Ellen Silverman

9 (top), Library of Congress; 9 (middle), Library of Congress; 9 (Bottom), Library of Congress; 11 (top), Getty Images; 11 (middle), Wikipedia; 11 (bottom left), Getty Images; 11 (bottom right), Wikipedia; 14 (top), Arm & Hammer; 14 (bottom), Library of Congress; 21, The Associated Press; 22, © Swim Ink 2, LLC/Corbis; 28, King Arthur Flour; 29 (top), King Arthur Flour; 29 (bottom), King Arthur Flour; 31, © Sean O. S. Barley, 2010, Used under license from Shutterstock.com; 32, Adolph's Meat Tenderizer; 40, Wise Snacks; 41 (top), Library of Congress; 47, Wikipedia; 62, SSPL via Getty Images; 63, public domain, graphic-design.tjs-labs.com; 66, public domain, graphic-design.tjs-labs.com; 70, © Valery Potapova, 2010, Used under license from Shutterstock.com; 76, © Olga Sapegina, 2010, Used under license from Shutterstock.com; 77 (top, center), © farres, 2010, Used under license from Shutterstock.com; 77 (right), U.S. Geological Survey Photographic Library; 80, © Sebastian Duda, 2010, Used under license from Shutterstock.com; 84, © H. Armstrong Roberts/ClassicStock/Corbis; 85, Getty Images; 86 (top), Getty Images; 86 (bottom), © Bettmann/Corbis;100 (top), © Daniel Krylov, 2010, Used under license from Shutterstock.com; 100 (bottom), © Amy Walters, 2010, Used under license from Shutterstock.com; 104 (top), Time & Life Pictures/Getty Images; 104 (bottom), © Bettmann/Corbis; 109 (bottom), © FloridaStock, 2010, Used under license from Shutterstock.com; 112, © Philip Dyer, iStockphoto; 113 (bottom), Library of Congress; 113 (top), Library of Congress; 116, National Geographic/Getty Images; 117 (bottom), Time & Life Pictures/Getty Images; 117 (top), © GWImages, 2010, Used under license from Shutterstock.com; 132 (top), public domain, graphic-design.tjs-labs.com; 132 (bottom), public domain, graphic-design.tjs-labs.com; 142, Wikipedia; 149, © slobo mitic, iStockphoto; 150, Getty Images; 156, © VIPDesignUSA, 2010, Used under license from Shutterstock.com; 157 (top), © Kevin Fleming/Corbis; 164, © amfoto, 2010, Used under license from Shutterstock.com; 168, Wikipedia; 170, © Bloch Lainé/photocuisine/Corbis; 171, © Bob Sacha/Corbis; 174, © DNY59, iStockphoto; 177, Corbis; 188, public domain, graphic-design.tjs-labs.com; 191, © Joe_Potato, iStockphoto; 192, public domain, graphic-design.tjs-labs.com; 193 (center), public domain, graphic-design.tjs-labs.com; 193 (right), public domain, graphic-design.tjs-labs.com; 202, © Anita Patterson Peppers, 2010, Used under license from Shutterstock.com; 206 (top), Library of Congress; 206 (bottom) Library of Congress; 207, © marymary, 2010, Used under license from Shutterstock.com; 212, public domain, graphic-design.tjs-labs.com; 216, © Jitalia17, iStockphoto; 218, Getty images; 228, © Norbert Bieberstein, iStockphoto; 229 (top and bottom), © caleb sheridan, iStockphoto; 229 (center), © stocksnapp, 2010, Used under license from Shutterstock.com; 238, Masterfile; 239 (top), © Bettmann/Corbis; 239 (bottom), © Iourii Tcheka, 2010, Used under license from Shutterstock.com; 242, Time & Life Pictures/Getty Images; 244 (top), © Patrick Duffy, iStockphoto; 244 (bottom). © Dick Stada, iStockphoto; 248 (top), © DNY59, iStockphoto; 248 (bottom), © JR Trice, 2010, Used under license from Shutterstock.com; 258, Sheri L Giblin, FoodPix; 260 (top), Library of Congress; 260 (bottom), Getty Images; 261 (top), The New York Public Library Digital Gallery; 261 (bottom), The New York Public Library Digital Gallery; 272 (top), City Of Beloit,WI; 272 (bottom), © worldinmyeyes.pl, 2010, Used under license from Shutterstock.com; 281, © Jump Photography, 2010, Used under license from Shutterstock.com; 282, © DNY59, iStockphoto; 283 (top), unknown/Blue Lantern Studio/Corbis; 283, © BrainOnAShelf, iStockphoto; 284 (top), © STILLFX, 2010, Used under license from Shutterstock.com; 284 (bottom), © jsemeniuk, iStockphoto; 296, Wikipedia/US Air Force; 297 (top), Time & Life Pictures/Getty Images; 297 (bottom), WD-40; 300, © morganl, iStockphoto; 304, © Bettmann/Corbis; 309, Masterfile; 312, Masterfile; 315, Masterfile; 316, Corbis; 317, Corbis; 318, Tom Grill, Getty Images; 322 (top), © Tobik, 2010, Used under license from Shutterstock.com; 322 (bottom), © Bettmann/Corbis; 323 © Jill Chen, iStockphoto; 324 © David Smith, iStockphoto

SAVE energy SAVE money!

201 Do-It-Yourself Projects, Tips, and Ideas

From the Editors of The Family Handyman®

Reader's digest
The Reader's Digest Association, Inc.
New York, NY | Montreal

Introduction

Congratulations on making one of the smartest investments of your life—this book. Smart, because between these two covers you'll find more than 250 pages of energy-saving and money-saving ideas you can put to work TODAY.

When it comes to saving money, there are lots of areas where the situation is out of your control. If you need a gallon of milk, a postage stamp, or a ticket to a baseball game, you pretty much have to pay the going rate. You could drink less milk, deliver your letter by hand, or buy a cheaper seat, but in all those cases there's a downside.

But the energy zone is an area where you can save money *and* wind up with an upside. With a small initial investment of time or money, there are hundreds of ways you can lower your energy bills and reap side benefits to boot. A compact fluorescent lightbulb doesn't only save you $36 over its lifetime, it lasts 5 to 10 times as long. A well-insulated house isn't only cheaper to heat, it's quieter and more comfortable. Fixing a drippy faucet leads to both a lower utility bill and a better night's sleep. And on a broader scale, saving energy helps save natural resources and the environment.

Let's not completely sugarcoat things. Sometimes there are tradeoffs. Using a programmable thermostat may mean a cooler trip to the kitchen for that midnight snack. Installing insulation means putting up with the scratchy stuff for a day or two. Purchasing a high-efficiency furnace may mean not recouping your initial additional investment for five years or more. But, for the most part, these are small prices to pay for a lower utility bill and a cleaner world.

This book isn't just filled with ideas for saving energy; it's filled with simple step-by-step instructions on how to implement those ideas. Whether it's tuning-up an air conditioner, weatherstripping a window, or installing a storm door, *Save Energy, Save Money!* will give you the hands-on information you need to do just what the title promises.

So read on and save!

Contents

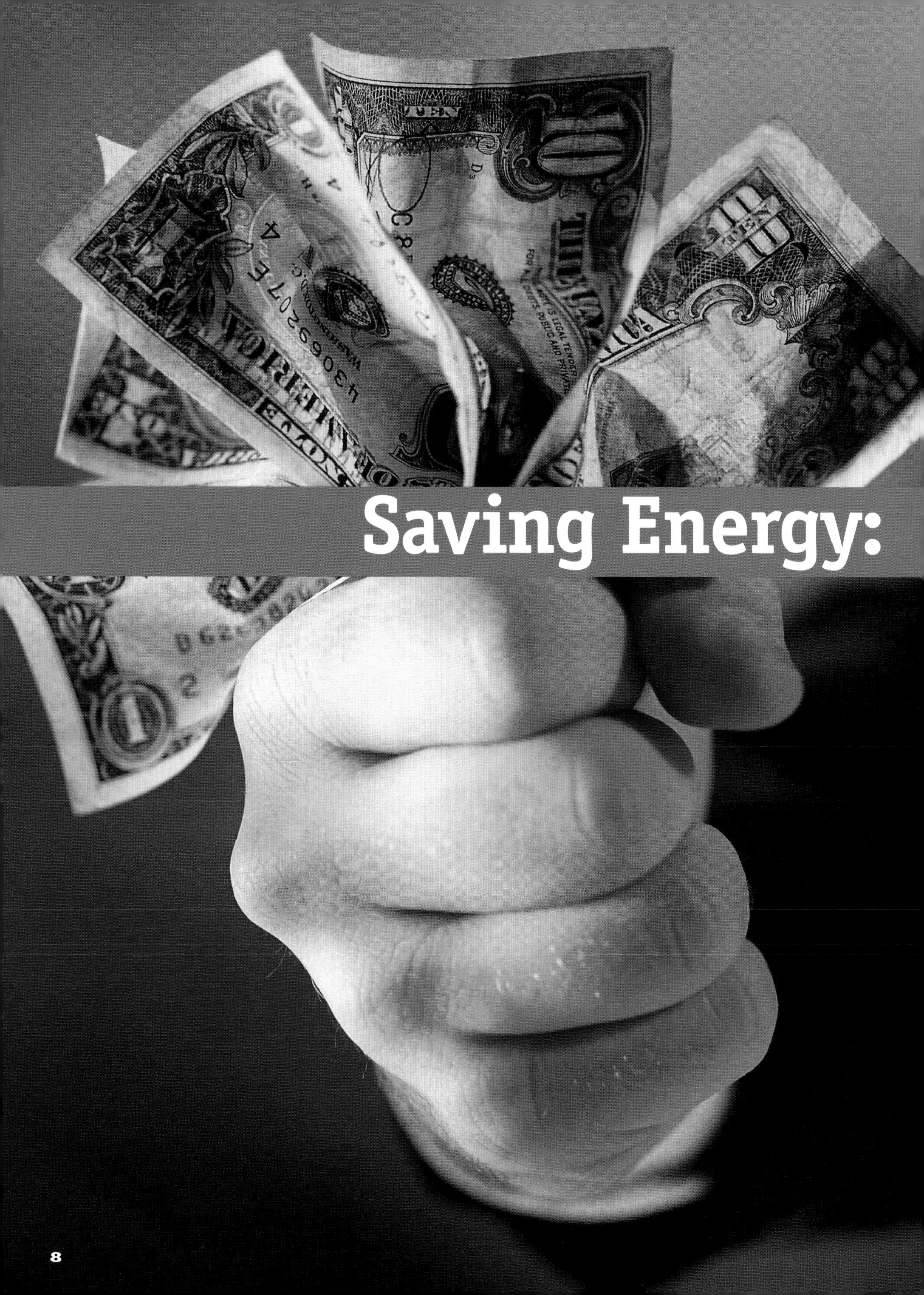

Saving Energy:

The Big Picture

Making your home more energy efficient without a game plan is like taking a trip without a road map: You'll eventually reach your destination, but it will take you longer, be more of a hassle and cost you more.

Having the big picture in mind is important. It will help you prioritize what to do first based on which projects have the biggest impact and quickest payback. Having a game plan will not only help you lower your utility bills faster but also help you maximize your comfort level, increase the safety of your home and leave more cash in your checkbook at the end of the day.

This first section will help you set your priorities based on the condition and location of your home, your budget and your skill level. Those with a $100 budget will have a different approach to saving energy than those with a $10,000 budget. Those living in Miami will be more interested in energy-efficient cooling strategies than those living in blustery Minneapolis. And those who are do-it-yourselfers will look at things a little differently than those who are more comfortable with "point and pay."

Whoever you are and wherever your house is, make sure to pay close attention to the section on carbon monoxide poisoning starting on p. 22. Sealing up your home changes the way it breathes. You want a house that's not only energy efficient but safe as well.

An 8-step energy-savings strategy

If you wince every time a gas or electric bill arrives in your mailbox, take heart. You can easily reduce energy use in your home. And we don't mean by wearing three sweaters, taking cold showers and shuttering the windows. Energy efficiency and a pleasant indoor environment work hand in hand. You'll not only reduce the drain on your bank account but also find your home more comfortable.

Here, we'll give you the BIG picture on how to evaluate your home's energy performance, determine where the biggest savings lie and maintain a healthy indoor environment. Other articles in this book deal with the specific simple steps you can take to save energy and money.

We'll tell you right off that big energy savings aren't as easy to get today as they were 30 years ago. During the energy crunch of the 1970s, many homeowners added insulation and caulked around windows and doors to capture the biggest savings. And since then, new homes have been built to higher energy-efficiency standards. Still, if you follow these simple steps, you'll find plenty of savings out there.

Figure A How energy is lost

The biggest culprits are air leaks (infiltration) and poor-performing windows. But every home is unique. An energy auditor will tell you where the biggest savings lie in your home.

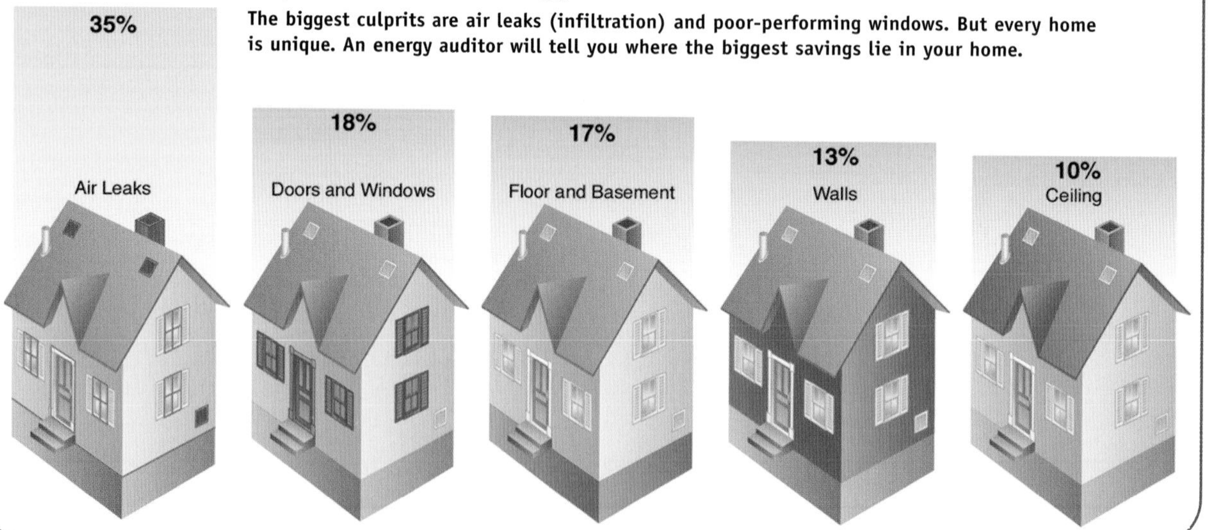

35% Air Leaks

18% Doors and Windows

17% Floor and Basement

13% Walls

10% Ceiling

1

Hire an energy auditor

It's worth hiring a pro to evaluate your home and help you sort out the many possible energy-saving strategies. Call your local utility company to find energy auditors. It may supply this service for free or recommend an auditor.

An energy audit typically costs $250 to $400, but sometimes community programs subsidize the bill. The energy auditor will inspect your home and rate its current performance in terms of insulation levels, air leakage, condition of heating or cooling equipment and other criteria. (You can also conduct a somewhat crude energy audit yourself by going to www.homeenergysaver.lbl.gov.)

> **tip** **Schedule a time when you can walk through your home with the auditor. Ask lots of questions. You can learn a ton about your home and how it works.**

The auditor can then tell you which upgrades are cost-effective and estimate your energy savings. Cost-effectiveness is the key. You can spend thousands of dollars for upgrades that won't save you much, and a good auditor will steer you away from those. For an improvement to be worthwhile, the estimated savings should cover the cost of the improvement in about seven years. For example, adding $200 of insulation to your attic will be worth it if the estimated savings are about $30 per year ($210 after seven years). But installing a new efficient window for $200 won't be worth the cost if you save only $10 per year ($70 after seven years). The auditor's report should clearly specify the estimated savings.

> **tip** **Have the auditor tell you which improvements you can do yourself. That eliminates the labor cost and makes many more upgrades cost effective.**

Keep in mind that as energy costs go up, more retrofit ideas become cost-effective.

Quick tip

SAVE BIG BY WASHING COLD. When you use your washing machine, 90 percent of the total amount of energy used goes into heating the water and only 10 percent into operating the actual appliance. Use cold water and cold-water detergents whenever you can.

2

Reduce air leakage

Think of the warm air leaking out through gaps, cracks and holes in your home's walls and ceilings as your energy dollars floating away (Figure A). Sealing these openings is one of the most cost-effective ways to save energy.

Stopping air leaks in the attic is usually enough. You don't have to work your way through every room caulking every crack, inside and out. Just get the largest and worst offenders, which are almost always in the attic.

For do-it-yourself information on sealing attic bypasses, see p. 54.

You'll notice that your house feels more comfortable too, because you'll have fewer drafts. The less warm air that leaks out, the less cold air that leaks in to replace it.

*Sealing air leaks is one of the most effective ways to save energy **and** money.*

3

Conserve energy

There are hundreds of energy-saving steps that cost little or nothing. Some ideas involve a small investment of time and money—for example, installing a programmable thermostat or caulking around windows. Others involve a small investment of energy—yours. These simple steps include lowering the temperature setting on your water heater and closing the curtains.

See pp. 30-33 for simple energy-saving tips

4

Buy high-efficiency windows

(when it's time to replace them)

Windows are the weakest link in your home's outer defenses against heat loss, accounting for about 18 percent of the heat loss in the typical home. But windows are also expensive, so it isn't cost effective to replace them just to save energy. If they're worn out, however, it's cost effective in all but the southernmost regions to upgrade to double-pane windows with low-E coatings. Your window specialist will help you choose the type of coating that works best, depending on whether you mostly need to slow heat loss or reduce solar gain.

See "Saving Energy: Windows & Doors," starting on p. 114, for more complete information.

Windows are the weakest link in your home's outer defenses against heat loss.

Quick tip

WHAT'S U-VALUE? The National Fenestration Rating Council tests all new windows and assigns each a "U-Value." The lower the U-Value, the more energy efficient the window.

5

Add insulation

Add 6 in. of insulation to an uninsulated attic and you'll reap substantial energy savings. Add 6 in. more and you'll get additional energy savings, but to a lesser degree. To find the point of diminishing returns, consult the Department of Energy charts at www.owenscorning.com or www.certainteed.com. The recommended values are based on climate, fuel costs and other factors. Adding more than the suggested amounts will result in a longer payback period for your investment.

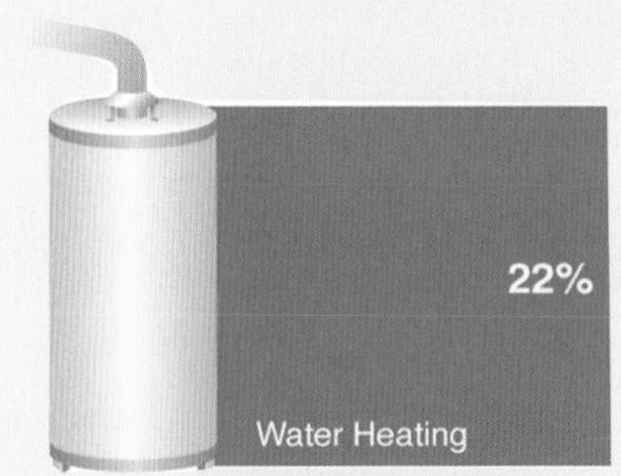

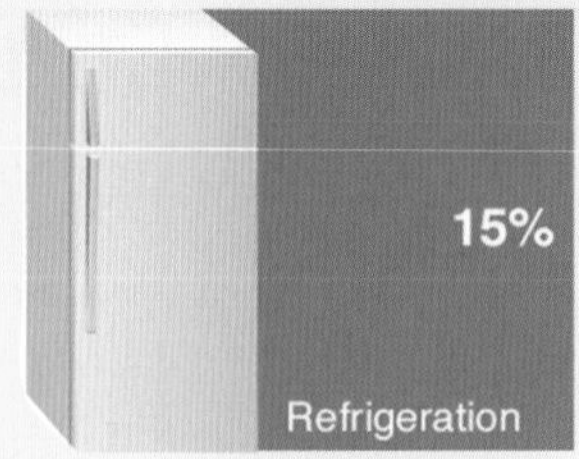

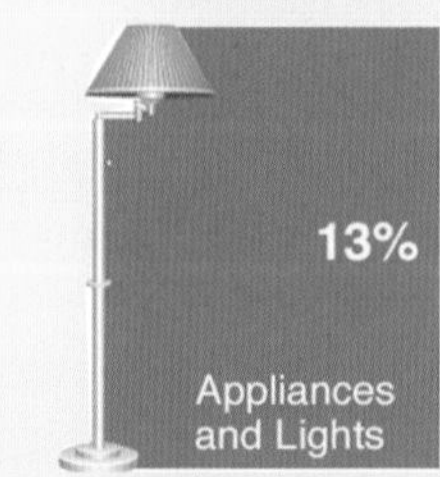

Figure B Where energy goes

About half of the energy consumed in the average home goes to space heating and/or air-conditioning. But all areas are targets for energy improvements as energy costs rise.

6

Shade your home

Shading is the best way you can save energy dollars in the summertime with your own sweat equity. Shading saves energy because it blocks out direct sunlight, which is responsible for about 50 percent of the heat gain in your home. Most of it strikes the roof and works its way through the attic, then down through the ceiling; the rest comes in mainly through windows. If you upgrade your attic insulation to at least 12 in. thick (about R-36) and make sure to buy light-colored roofing next time you reroof, you'll stop most of that roof heat. And steps like planting trees, attaching awnings and extending roof overhangs will shade the most vulnerable south-facing windows as well as those facing east and west. Most of these are low-cost, do-it-yourself strategies.

See "Cooling with shade," p. 86, for more on cooling strategies.

Shading saves energy because it blocks out direct sunlight, which is responsible for about 50 percent of the heat gain in your home.

7

Stop air conditioner duct leakage

Studies have shown that an average duct system loses 10 to 40 percent of the cool air through gaps in the duct joints. This cooling is wasted when the ducts run outside the interior conditioned space, in an attic or a crawlspace. While sealing ducts is a common practice now, few air-conditioned homes have had this done. Sealing ducts is difficult. You'll have to rely on professional services (see "Air-Conditioning" in your yellow pages) to test the ducts for leakage and to retest to show the effectiveness of their work.

Quick tip

LIGHT-COLORED SHINGLES SAVE ENERGY. Installing white shingles (which reflect heat back into the sky) instead of dark shingles (which absorb heat) can reduce the cooling load in a home by up to 20 percent.

8

Protect your health and the health of your home

Energy-efficiency improvements can increase the risk of carbon monoxide (CO) poisoning. This can occur in homes with devices that burn gas, oil or wood and in homes with attached garages. At a minimum, install a CO alarm.

Watch your windows for excessive condensation. Most energy-saving measures reduce air leakage, allowing excessive moisture to build up inside. This moisture can cause mold and rot and an unhealthy indoor environment. Condensation on windows is common at the beginning of the heating season but should largely disappear except during cold snaps. Usually the best prevention strategy is to find the moisture sources (some of the worst culprits are improperly vented dryers, bath fans and the rooms they're in) and eliminate them or improve ventilation.

See "Prevent carbon monoxide poisoning" on p. 22 for information on alarms and placement.

Save $$ with an energy audit

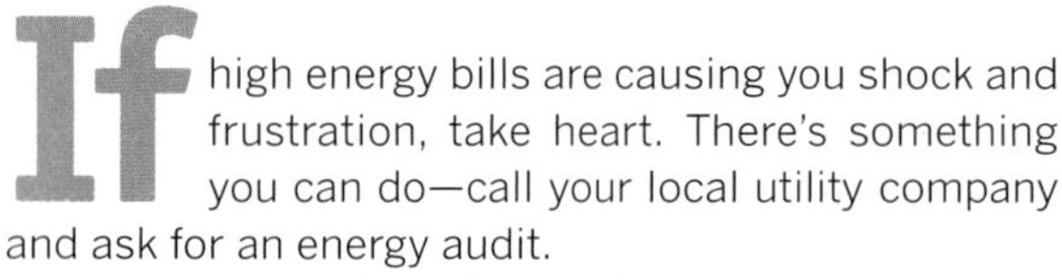

If high energy bills are causing you shock and frustration, take heart. There's something you can do—call your local utility company and ask for an energy audit.

An energy auditor will come to your home and conduct a series of tests to provide detailed information about your home's energy usage and energy loss. A report, generated at the conclusion of the two- to three-hour audit, will detail:

- The condition and efficiency of your heating and cooling system
- The overall efficiency of your home, including the primary areas of air leakage in your exterior walls and ceilings
- Low-cost ways you can improve energy efficiency and save energy
- Larger upgrades that will pay back their cost with energy savings within a relatively short period.

Here, you'll walk through a professional energy audit with Erik Lindberg, a Minnesota state-certified energy auditor, whose company, Enervision, has performed more than 12,000 audits. An audit typically costs $250 to $400, but most utility companies offer a rebate to reduce the cost to you. The house shown here was built in 1979.

"An energy audit addresses five priorities:

First is home safety. If your house isn't safe, energy efficiency doesn't matter. Second is durability. Finding and fixing moisture problems and rot helps the house last longer. Third is comfort. The audit identifies drafts and cold spots. Fourth is to set up the best action plan to make your home more efficient, especially things you can do yourself. Fifth is cost benefit, which tells you what it'll cost to make improvements, and how long it'll take for the savings to pay off those costs."

Erik Lindberg, Certified Energy Auditor >

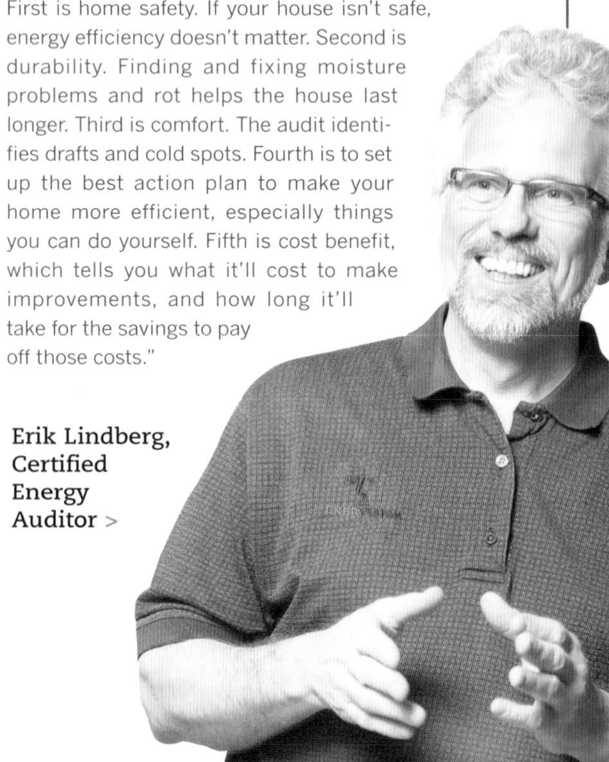

Checking heating and hot-water systems

The audit starts with a furnace combustion efficiency test. With the furnace running, Erik inserts a gas analyzer in the furnace's draft diverter (Photo 1). If there's no draft diverter, he drills a small hole in the flue for the wand, then later patches it. The analyzer provides an immediate reading. Our furnace had a 76.9 percent combustion efficiency—not bad considering furnaces at least 15 years old are usually 55 to 68 percent efficient and this unit is 27 years old (typical lifespan is 15 to 20 years).

This test also measures:

- The amount of carbon monoxide in the flue gases
- The draft pressure in the flue to determine if gases could leak into the house.

These are safety issues. If waste gases aren't being drawn up the chimney, then moisture, carbon monoxide and other pollutants could be flowing into your home. Common causes of vent problems (allowing gases to "backdraft" into the home) are birds' nests in the vent pipes and vents that have come apart. Erik often finds these problems. He notes one common clue: "If you have moisture on your windows, the first thing to check for is backdrafting in the furnace and water heater flues."

Erik tests for backdrafting in the water heater flue as well by holding a flame or a smoke stick next to the draft diverter (Photo 2).

1 FURNACE EFFICIENCY TEST: The auditor tests the furnace exhaust with an electrical gas analyzer, which gives a combustion efficiency reading. It also measures draft pressure to determine if flue gases might leak into the house.

The check of the heating and hot-water systems concludes with a visual inspection. Rust particles (called "scaling") inside the furnace heat exchanger indicate corrosion, which will eventually lead to holes and combustion gas leakage. Scaling may also be visible on top of the water heater around the draft diverter.

Erik looks to see if the furnace filter is clean and installed correctly. "Clogged filters can cause a moderate increase in heating costs, but more significantly, cause the heat exchanger to overheat and fail, and cause the fan motor to heat up, increase electric consumption and reduce the life of the motor." He also looks for combustibles stored near the furnace or water heater, because the flame could cause an explosion.

Other common problems Erik has found include disconnected flue pipes, leaky ductwork, clogged condensation pipes, dirty burners and dirty fan blades. "I've found many furnaces missing the cover for the filter slot, and major leaks in the return-air ductwork. This causes depressurization in the furnace room and can draw dangerous exhaust gases out of the flue pipe and distribute these gases throughout the house," he says.

"Old boilers, originally designed for coal, then converted to oil and then to natural gas, can be as low as 55 percent efficient—that's 45 percent waste! The best furnace designs feature variable-speed fan motors and modulating or multi-stage burners, which enable the furnace to match its Btu output to the home's temperature needs, thereby increasing the system's efficiency."

2 BACKDRAFT TEST: With all doors and windows closed and all combustion appliances turned on, the auditor tests for backdrafting at a natural-draft gas water heater. The flame, held next to the draft diverter, should be drawn up into the flue.

Testing for air leakage

Part two of the audit entails a "blower door" test, which measures the home's "tightness," or air infiltration rate. Erik first closes all doors and windows, then he sets an adjustable panel with a variable-speed fan in a doorway, completely sealing it. He turns on the fan to blow air out of the house, which reduces the indoor air pressure, and then measures airflow through the fan at predetermined pressure points (Photos 3 and 4). Outside air then enters through cracks and gaps in walls and ceilings.

With the fan running, you can feel air come in with your hand, especially around leaky windows and doors. Gauges connected to the fan measure the airflow rate needed to maintain a constant pressure, allowing the auditor to calculate the leakage rate.

Newer homes are built tighter under the most recent Minnesota building code. (Most other state codes have tighter rules too.) It even requires special ventilation fans to ensure adequate fresh air. Still, their leakage rate is often equivalent to a 6 x 6-in. hole in a wall. Older homes weren't built nearly as tight. They often have a leakage rate equivalent to a 19 x 19-in. hole, which is like having a window wide open all the time! The house we tested had leaks totaling .77 sq. ft. (about an 11 x 11-in. hole). Erik estimates that sealing air leaks alone will save 10 to 20 percent on this home's annual heating bills.

tip Have the audit performed in the spring, summer or fall. Auditors are usually busier in the winter, when homeowners see a spike in energy bills, and the wait for an audit can be two months or more.

Erik pointed out several signs of air leaks: stains around exhaust fans and dirt on insulation. A batt of insulation between joists in the basement was dirty, meaning the insulation was serving as a filter for air leaking in through the foundation. "You can't fix these leaks with insulation because it won't stop the airflow," Erik says. "You have to seal them with caulk, expanding foam or some other sealant."

"In my opinion, there's no limit to how tight you can make the ceiling. The less air that goes out the ceiling, the less that will come in around doors, windows and other leaky areas. When you're carrying water in a bucket, it doesn't matter if the top leaks, because no water is going to get out. What matters is the bottom. Think of your house like an upside-down bucket holding heat."

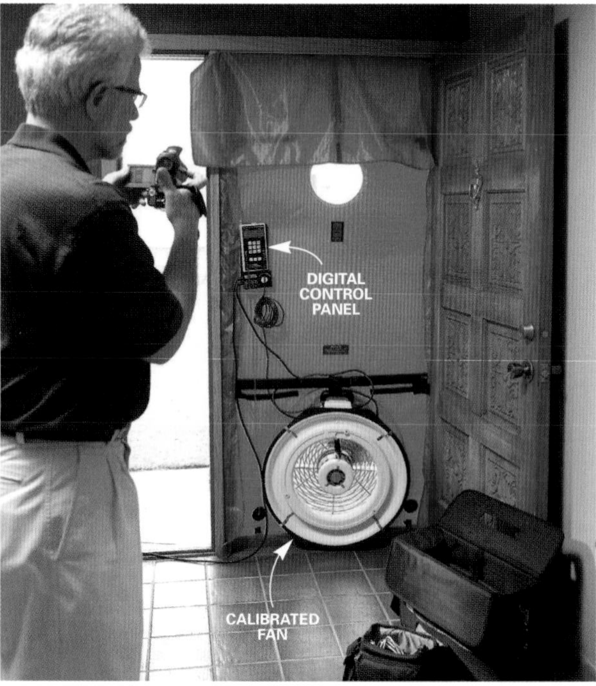

3 BLOWER DOOR TEST: With all doors and windows closed, the auditor inserts a blower door in the front or back doorway and starts the fan.

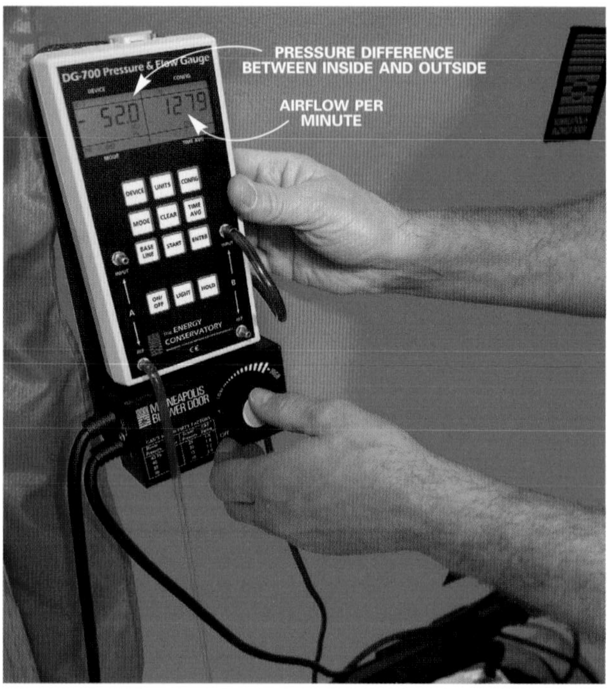

4 THE GAUGE shows the pressure difference between the inside and the outside and the airflow per minute. From these, the auditor calculates the leakage rate.

Pinpointing sources of energy loss

While the blower door test measures the overall leakiness of the house, infrared scanning (technically called "thermography") graphically identifies the precise locations of those leaks. Erik keeps the blower door fan running to draw in outside air. Then, using an infrared camera, he scans the walls and ceilings, photographing surface areas that show up as cooler (Photo 5).

Cold areas show up as blue, and warm areas as yellow (Photos 6 – 8). Today (a chilly day in March), the framing members showed up as blue, since they're cooler than the insulated portion of the walls. (The opposite would be true on a hot day when the indoors is air conditioned and the outside air is warmer.)

Air leaks in the ceiling typically cause the greatest energy losses. Openings made for light fixtures, plumbing vents, exhaust fans, attic access and smoke alarms will leak if the builder didn't make an extra effort to seal them. In this house, the area around the attic access panel and the exhaust fan in the upstairs bathroom showed extensive leaking (Photo 6), while a ceiling light fixture, which must have been sealed better, leaked very little.

Electrical outlets and light switches on outside walls also usually leak, unless the builder took extra pains to seal them. The infrared scan showed that four of these in the north kitchen wall leaked profusely (Photo 7). The homeowner confirmed this, noting that she often felt cold drafts when standing by this wall.

While some of these problems are easy to fix—foam weatherstripping on the attic access panel, spray foam or caulk around the exhaust fans, and foam seals under the outlet and switch cover plates—others are difficult to seal and may not be practical to go after. Leaks around exterior wall top plates and inadequate insulation in some wall cavities are common (Photo 8), but hard to access and therefore expensive to remedy.

Expect some air leakage around windows, sliding patio doors and exterior doors. "All doors will leak, especially since people step on the threshold as they enter and leave the house, wearing a gap between the door and sill," Erik explains. "The only doors that don't leak are the ones on submarines."

Infrared scanning can identify other hidden problems. It'll show cold spots where insulation is poor or missing. Erik has even found double-pane windows that have failed. Condensation between the layers of glass, which is the usual sign of failure, hadn't shown up yet. Yet the infrared image showed that the centers of the panes were cooler than the sides, which meant the special argon gas they had been filled with was completely gone.

Since infrared scanning works by identifying heat differences, it can also detect water leaks (not to mention warm-blooded critters in the walls). Erik once found an area in a basement floor that was inordinately warm. Turns out a hot water pipe was leaking under the concrete, which explained the homeowner's high energy bill.

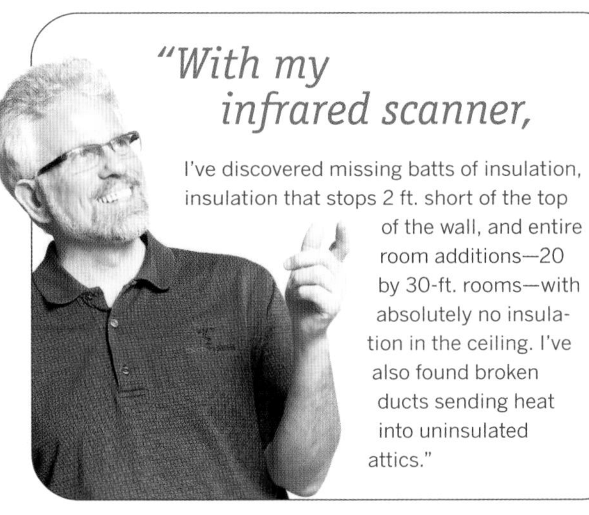

"With my infrared scanner,

I've discovered missing batts of insulation, insulation that stops 2 ft. short of the top of the wall, and entire room additions—20 by 30-ft. rooms—with absolutely no insulation in the ceiling. I've also found broken ducts sending heat into uninsulated attics."

5 THERMOGRAPHY: The auditor uses an infrared camera to scan walls and ceilings. The camera detects temperature differences and can pinpoint cold spots and air leaks.

Photos and infrared scans

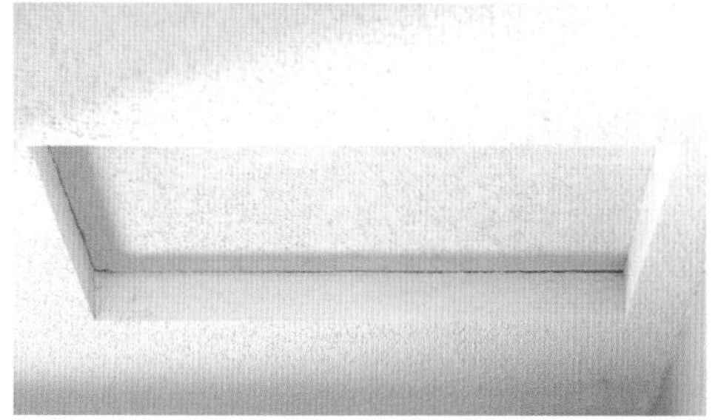

6 **DARK BLUE AREAS** around the perimeter of the attic access panel indicate air leakage. The overall blue tinge indicates poor insulation.

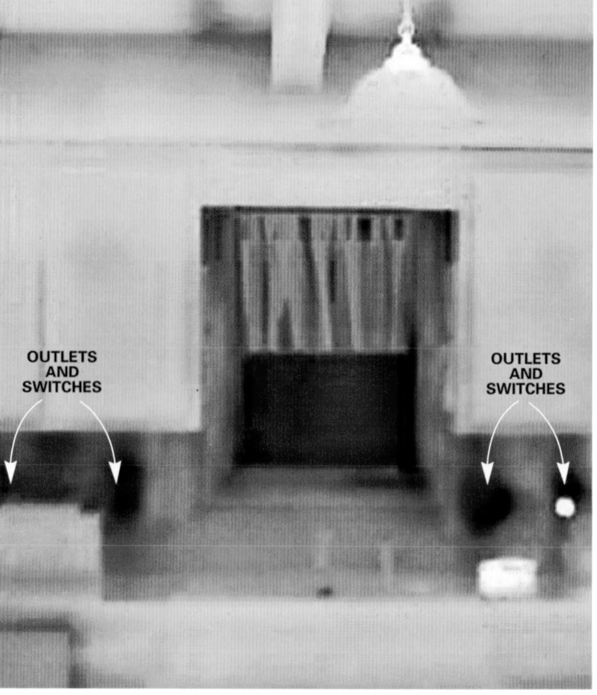

7 **ELECTRICAL OUTLETS AND SWITCHES** typically leak, but this is excessive. This kitchen wall feels cold and drafty in the winter.

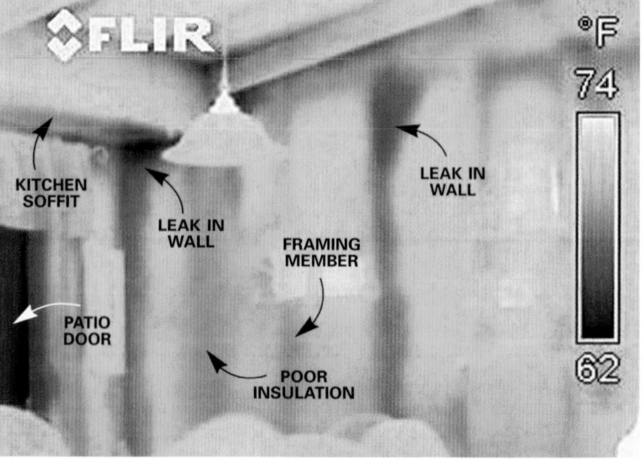

8 **INADEQUATE INSULATION** in a wall cavity and gaps in the top plates (wall framing) cause most of the air leaks in this dining room.

Final report—what you can save

Once the testing is complete, the auditor prepares a comprehensive report detailing the amount of leakage, ways to improve efficiency, the cost of specific improvements and the time frame for recouping those investments (see below).

The report lists specific low-cost steps for reducing energy usage that you can usually do yourself. For this house, they include insulating the attic access panel, weatherstripping it with closed-cell foam tape, sealing ceiling penetrations at electrical fixtures, insulating kitchen soffits, adding attic insulation, insulating the rim joists and caulking around windows, doors and base trim. Erik estimates that these upgrades will cut annual energy bills by 15 to 20 percent. Adding insulation to exterior walls isn't worth the cost.

The furnace, installed when the house was built in 1979, had an "annual fuel utilization efficiency" (AFUE) of about 68 percent. This furnace is operating well below the current minimum standard specified by the building code and far below the efficiencies currently available. (ENERGY STAR furnaces must have at least a 90 percent AFUE. See p. 26 for more on ENERGY STAR.) Erik recommends replacing any old furnace (in Minnesota's cold climate) that's not at least 80 percent efficient since newer models use less energy and eventually pay for themselves (in this case, in nine years). Your energy auditor will make these calculations and recommendations based on your local climate. Furnaces that are at least 95 percent efficient may qualify for a federal tax credit.

Installing a programmable thermostat in this home will pay for itself in just two to three years. A new high-efficiency air conditioner isn't a priority, but it's likely to be a priority in warmer climates. You want to recoup your investment through predicted energy savings within seven to 10 years.

Recommended energy-saving tips

- Seal leaks in ductwork
- Clear space in front of heating units, registers and radiators
- Reduce water usage by using low-flow showerheads
- Insulate the water heater tank and water pipes
- Wash clothes in cold or warm water and rinse with cold
- Dry laundry loads consecutively to maximize dryer efficiency
- Replace incandescent bulbs with efficient compact fluorescent bulbs
- Use timers or motion detectors to turn off lights when not needed
- Install air-sealing gaskets behind switch/outlet cover plates
- Lock windows to create a better seal
- Add weatherstripping and caulking around doors and windows
- Seal around pipes and ducts that penetrate outer walls

Page 4

FINAL REPORT

Home performance and building diagnostic services

		CONTRACTOR		DIY		
COMPONENT		Cost	Payback (years)	Cost	Payback (years)	1st Year Savings
Exterior walls	OK	—	—	$2,024	46	$44
Attic floor/ceiling	Re insulate to R44 after attic bypass sealing is done	—	—	$300	10	$30
Knee wall	Not applicable					
Side attic floor	Not applicable					
Slant walls	Not applicable					
Basement walls	Build 2x4 stud wall, R-15 fiberglass	$2,640	13	$845	4	$203
Foundation	Not applicable					
Rim Joist	Install Icynene or spray polyurethane insulation	$385	7	$275	5	$58
Windows	Seal with 3M weatherizing tape and install plastic window insulator			$8	1	$13
Doors	Weather strip doors with Q-Lon; see examples in audit's extra folder	$90	*	$40	*	
Attic bypass	Seal plumbing, wiring, top plates and other air leaks into attic	$375	*	$75	*	
Attic access panel	Insulate and weather strip attic access panel; see examples in audit's extra folder	$55	*	$25	*	
Air sealing	Caulk window, door and base trim	$140	*	$28	*	
Programmable thermostat	Install programmable thermostat; use 10° setback for 8 hours	$120	3	$60	2	$39
APPLIANCES						
Furnace/boiler	Install 95% AFUE "sealed combustion" furnace. Get $200 tax credit, plus rebates!	$2,500	8	—		$317
Water heater	Install high-efficiency/direct vent water heater	$600	8	—		$74
Air conditioner	Replace with 14 SEER model	$1,800	12	—		$150
Cost/benefit analysis notes	*Cost/benefit amounts are difficult to specify for small items, but savings are significant. Additional benefits are reducing drafts, reducing moisture intrusion into wall and ceiling cavities, and avoiding ice dams and other costly problems.					

< The final report lists energy-efficient upgrades, their cost (hiring a contractor vs. doing it yourself) and estimated annual savings. Upgrades that pay back in seven to 10 years are considered good investments.

Energy-saving projects and payback

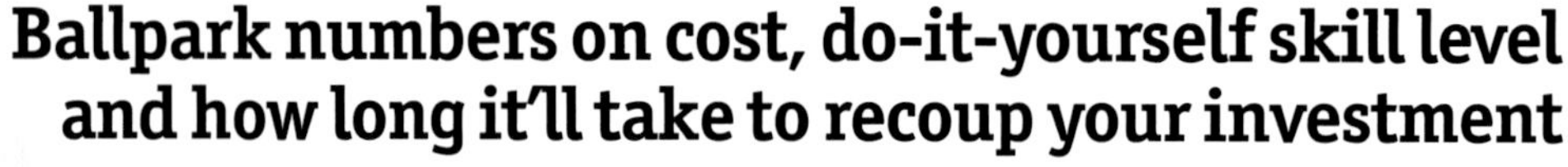

Ballpark numbers on cost, do-it-yourself skill level and how long it'll take to recoup your investment

Deciding which energy-saving home improvements to make first (or at all) can be a daunting task. But knowing a few facts—especially regarding payback—can help uncomplicate matters.

The term *payback* refers to how many years it typically takes to recoup your investment in a product or project by way of utility bill savings. For instance, if a new energy-efficient water heater costs $200 more than a standard model, and saves you $20 per year, it will take you 10 years to recoup your investment. If it saves you $50 per year, that payback period drops to four years. After the payback period, you pocket the savings.

Inflation, utility costs, house age, living habits and other factors can greatly affect payback—but in general terms, the shorter the payback period, the smarter the investment.

Here are 15 of the top energy-saving home improvements, along with typical cost, payback period and skill level needed to tackle the job. The list is arranged from those with the shortest payback period to those with the longest. Best of all, we show you how to tackle nearly every project listed here in other parts of this book.

Rank: #1

Project: Install compact fluorescent bulbs
Difficulty level: Easy
Typical cost: $3 per bulb
Typical payback: 1/2 to 1 year

Rank: #2
Project: Install a programmable thermostat
Difficulty level: Intermediate
Typical cost: $30 to $100
Typical payback: 1/2 to 2 years

Rank: #3
Project: Seal large and small ceiling air leaks
Difficulty level: Easy to intermediate
Typical cost: less than $200
Typical payback: 1 to 2 years

Rank: #4
Project: Seal air duct leaks
Difficulty level: Easy
Typical cost: less than $25
Typical payback: 1 to 2 years

Rank: #5
Project: Install a water-saving showerhead
Difficulty level: Easy
Typical cost: $10 and up
Typical payback: 1 to 2 years

Rank: #6
Project: Insulate water heater
Difficulty level: Easy
Typical cost: $8 to $20
Typical payback: 1 to 2 years

Rank: #7
Project: Weatherstrip windows and doors
Difficulty level: Easy to intermediate
Typical cost: $10 to $20 per opening
Typical payback: 1 to 3 years

Rank: #8
Project: Tune up furnace or other heating equipment
Difficulty level: Professional
Typical cost: $100 and up
Typical payback: 1 to 3 years

Rank: #9
Project: Install ceiling insulation
Difficulty level: Intermediate
Typical cost: $.30 to .50/sq. ft. (based on 6-in. fiberglass batts)
Typical payback: 2 to 5 years

SOURCE: Data compiled from www.xcelenergy.com, www.energystar.gov and U.S. Department of Energy (www.energy.gov).

Rank: #10
Project: Install floor insulation (when space below floor is unheated)
Difficulty level: Intermediate
Typical cost: $.30 to .50/sq. ft. (based on 6-in. fiberglass batts)
Typical payback: 2 to 5 years

Rank: #11
Project: Install storm windows
Difficulty level: Intermediate
Typical cost: $30 per window and up
Typical payback: 4 to 10 years

Rank: #12
Project: Replace heating system
Difficulty level: Professional
Typical cost: varies greatly
Typical payback: 5 to 20 years

Rank: #13
Project: Blown-in wall insulation
Difficulty level: Advanced or professional
Typical cost: $1 to $2/sq. ft. of wall (includes material and labor)
Typical payback: 6 to 12 years

Rank: #14
Project: Landscaping (trees for windbreaks and sun screening)
Difficulty level: Intermediate
Typical cost: $30 and up per tree
Typical payback: 5 to 10 years (varies greatly)

Rank: #15
Project: Window replacement
Difficulty level: Advanced
Typical cost: $300 to $800 per window; higher for professional installation
Typical payback: 15 to 30 years

Keep your energy-efficient home safe

Prevent carbon monoxide poisoning

Follow these two steps to keep this silent killer at bay

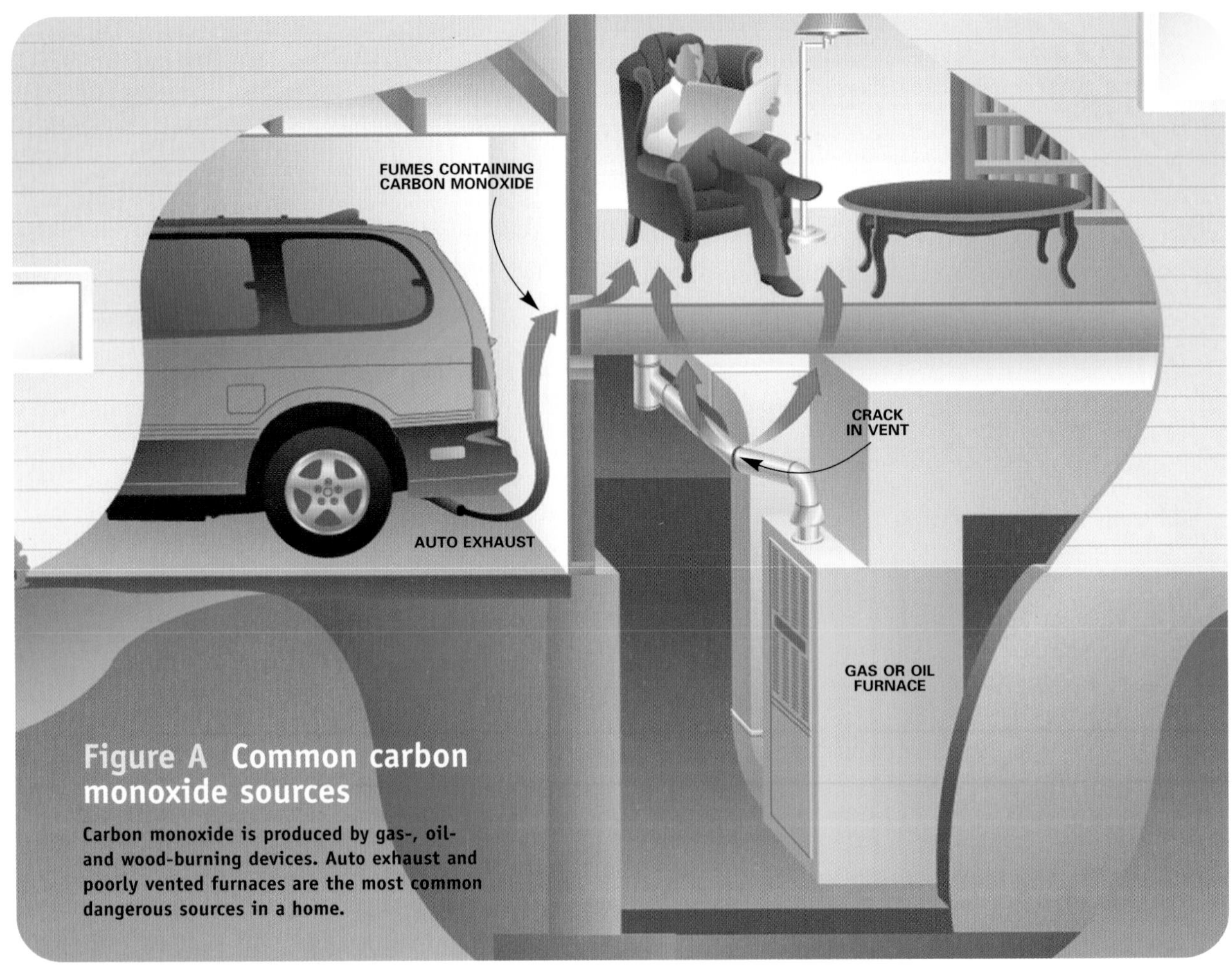

Figure A Common carbon monoxide sources

Carbon monoxide is produced by gas-, oil- and wood-burning devices. Auto exhaust and poorly vented furnaces are the most common dangerous sources in a home.

1 Install carbon monoxide (CO) alarms

What is CO?

CO is an invisible, odorless gas that's produced by fireplaces, furnaces, stoves, water heaters and heaters that burn natural gas, propane, oil or wood. Usually chimneys and flues safely carry these combustion by-products up and out of your home. But not always. Flue blockage, poor natural drafting, leaks and other problems sometimes cause CO and other combustion gases to spill out into your living space and pollute the air you breathe (Figure A). The CO is gradually absorbed into the bloodstream. Light doses cause flulike symptoms, and larger doses lead to unconsciousness and death.

Cars, lawn mowers and snow blowers also produce a lot of CO, especially at start-up. If you have an attached garage, natural drafts tend to pull that CO into your home, even if you have the garage door open! As a rule, never let a car engine idle in a garage.

Plug-in alarm with digital display (about $45)

Battery-powered alarm (about $20)

Both types of CO alarms sound an alarm when hazardous levels of CO are present. The type with a digital display will also show the peak CO level in your home when you push the peak level button. It will not record very low levels.

Is the CO threat greater in an energy-efficient home?

Sometimes. Reducing air leaks in your home is one of the best ways to make your home more energy efficient. Air tightening includes such things as closing up attic bypasses, weatherstripping, caulking around doors and windows, and installing new windows. But as your home gets tighter, flues and chimneys can't vent CO and other combustion gases to the outside as easily, because they don't have as much makeup air (see Step 2, p. 24). CO alarms are simple, inexpensive insurance to warn you if CO spillage reaches a hazardous level ... even if your home is new or you haven't taken steps to improve energy efficiency.

How dangerous is CO?

Accidental carbon monoxide (CO) poisoning accounts for several hundred deaths in the United States every year. The deaths are particularly tragic because most could have been easily prevented with a warning from a $20 to $45 CO alarm.

Where do I put the alarms?

At a minimum, put an alarm near the sleeping rooms on each level in your home. CO accumulates in the bloodstream, and you're most vulnerable during long periods of sleep. Position alarms on ceilings or walls, away from drafts and solvents. (Read the directions that come with each alarm for more details.)

What's the best CO alarm to buy?

Look for a CO alarm with a UL (Underwriters Laboratories) listing on the package. It can be either battery-powered or a plug-in type (often with a battery backup; photos above). All alarms have a test/reset button that you should push weekly to make sure the alarm is operating.

We recommend the plug-in type with a digital readout that tells you the peak CO concentration whenever you push the peak level button. The CO level might not be high enough to trigger the alarm. But detecting a low level can alert you to a potential problem so you can trace the source before the CO reaches a higher level. This is particularly important if you have more vulnerable folks in your home such as young children, the elderly and those with certain illnesses.

What should I do if an alarm goes off?

Here are general guidelines taken from the more detailed instructions that come with your alarm:

1. Push the test/reset button. (This is easier with a wall-mounted CO alarm.)

2. Call an emergency number, such as 911 or your fire department in most areas.

3. Go outside or move to a well-ventilated area, like next to an open window or door. Make sure all family members are accounted for. Wait for emergency services to arrive; they'll make sure your house is well aired out.

4. If the alarm goes off again within 24 hours, follow steps 1 – 3 above and call in a qualified technician to test your fuel-burning equipment and find the problem. Be aware that furnace start-ups can set off the alarm under some conditions, as can starting cars in an attached garage.

WARNING: If an alarm sounds, you have a potentially lethal amount of CO in your home! Take the alarm seriously. Make every effort to find an explanation. You don't want any level of CO in your home, much less a lethal level. Unfortunately, CO sources can be difficult to pinpoint. Don't hesitate to call in a heating and ventilating technician experienced in CO issues to search out the probable causes and recommend corrections.

Also be aware of the symptoms of CO poisoning: slight headache, nausea, vomiting and fatigue (all flu-like symptoms) from mild exposures, and throbbing headache, drowsiness, confusion, fast heart rate or unconsciousness from heavier exposures.

2 Ask a heating service technician to conduct a complete backdrafting test at your annual heating equipment checkup

Backdrafting occurs when the combustion gases can't go up and out flues and chimneys because outdoor air is already flowing down them (Figure B). This often occurs when you run a clothes dryer, powerful range fan or any combination of venting fans. All suck air out of your home. If your house can't get enough makeup air leaking in around windows and doors and through cracks and gaps in walls, the makeup air may come down the flues or chimney. Then your furnace, water heater or wood-burning fireplace may not vent properly, and combustion gases, including CO, will spill into your living space. (Studies have shown that backdrafting is common even in homes that are not energy efficient or airtight, so this test is worthwhile regardless of any energy-efficiency improvements you've made.)

A complete backdraft test only takes about 10 minutes. The service technician should close all doors and windows and turn on your ventilating fans, creating a worst-case situation. The technician will then turn on your water heater and test it for combustion gas spillage, and test the furnace as well.

If you have significant spillage, the technician should inspect your venting system and recommend solutions.

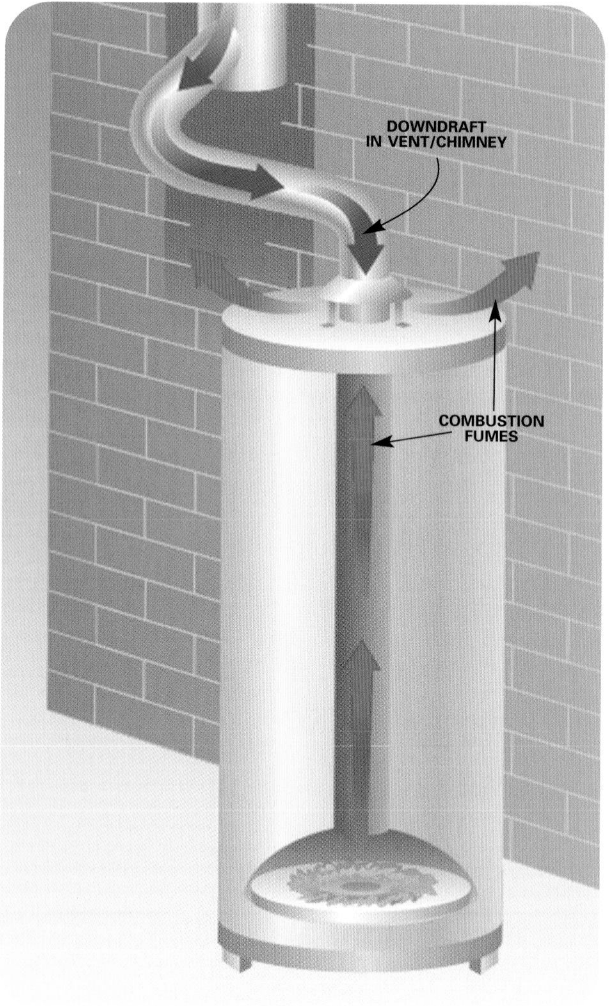

Figure B Backdrafting

Backdrafting is a condition in which air flows down a flue or chimney rather than up, and combustion fumes can't flow out. The fumes spill into your living spaces.

Permits, inspections and contractors

Permits

Many energy-saving home-improvement projects require you, or your contractor, to obtain a permit. Obtaining permits can be a hassle, but getting caught doing work without one, or using substandard building practices, can be much worse.

FREQUENTLY REQUIRED PERMITS

Permit requirements vary greatly from one community to the next. Some common projects requiring permits include:

- Projects involving structural alterations to your house, such as adding a larger window or removing a wall.
- Installing a deck, fence, outbuilding or pool.
- Finishing a basement or attic space.
- Adding an electrical branch circuit, outlet or fixture.
- Installing or replacing a water heater, furnace, air conditioner or fireplace.

Depending on the project, you may or may not be required to submit a blueprint or plan.

Inspections

Some small projects may require a single inspection, while larger ones may require a dozen or more. Make certain you know when and where inspections are required. Also remember you may not be able to move to the next step of your project until the inspection has been completed. Plan and schedule ahead.

FREQUENTLY REQUIRED INSPECTIONS

- Footing inspections (after the footings are formed, but before the concrete is poured).
- Framing inspections (after the framing materials and sheathing are in place).
- Rough plumbing/gas line inspection (while pipes are exposed).
- Final plumbing inspection (supply and drain-waste-vent pipes are pressure tested for leaks).
- Insulation inspection (sometimes after the vapor barrier is installed).
- Drywall inspection (often after drywall has been fastened, but before taping begins).
- Rough-in electrical inspection (rough wiring completed in electrical boxes but devices such as switches, outlets and light fixtures not installed).
- Final electrical inspection (all switches, outlets and lights in place and wiring at circuit panel complete).
- Final inspection (final check to make sure all codes have been followed).

Working with contractors

Though horror stories of unscrupulous contractors abound, most in the business are honest, hardworking folks. Most live and die by their reputations. Those who take the money and run or do substandard work don't stay in business long. Yet, there are things you should check out.

QUESTIONS TO ASK, THINGS TO CHECK

1. **Legal matters.** Do they have the proper licenses and insurance to work in your community? Ask to see the actual documents.
2. **Contract.** The more specific, the better. Specify the exact materials to be used, right down to the manufacturer, when necessary.
3. **References.** Will they provide names and contact information for their most recent clients? If the references are old or few-and-far-between, ask why. How long have they been in business? Check with the Better Business Bureau to see if any complaints have been filed.
4. **Down payment and money matters.** Determine at what points in the project payments will be made. One-third down for materials is common.
5. **Work schedule.** What date will the project start and what is a realistic date to expect completion?
6. **Changes.** Commonly, a change order spelling out the design and financial implications is drawn up and signed by the homeowner and contractor when there is a change in the initial contract.
7. **On the job.** Determine whom you'll speak with regarding the day-to-day operations. Who handles questions? How early in the day would work start and how long would it go on in the evening? What about a bathroom, smoking and eating? Who cleans up and when?

Understanding ENERGY STAR

Shop smart, save energy, save money

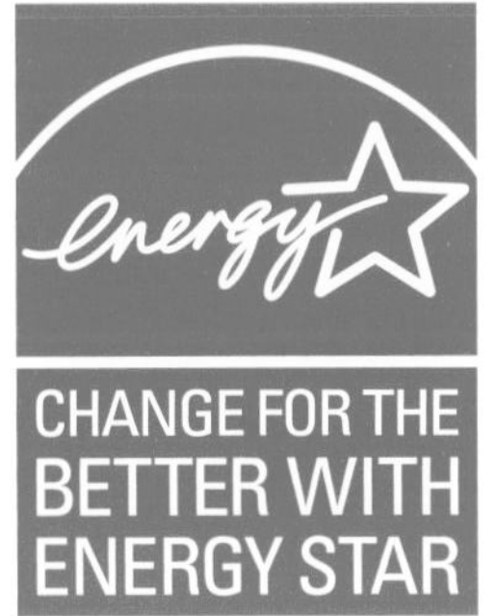

energy
CHANGE FOR THE BETTER WITH ENERGY STAR

As you can see, you don't have to sacrifice beauty and comfort for energy efficiency.

PHOTO COURTESY OF PELLA WINDOW

If you've been shopping recently for appliances, home electronics or building materials, chances are you've run across the blue ENERGY STAR logo. So just what does it mean?

Products that have earned the ENERGY STAR logo meet strict energy guidelines set by the U.S. Department of Energy and the U.S. Environmental Protection Agency. Products in over 50 categories are eligible for the rating. Items include the expected—furnaces, air conditioners and windows—as well as the unexpected—televisions, laptops, cordless tool chargers, vending machines, even entire new homes. The designation means you don't need to wade through all the complicated specifications and abbreviations to find the most energy-efficient product; the legwork has been done for you. ENERGY STAR standards and products are also often used by manufacturers, utility companies and government agencies to grant rebates and tax credits.

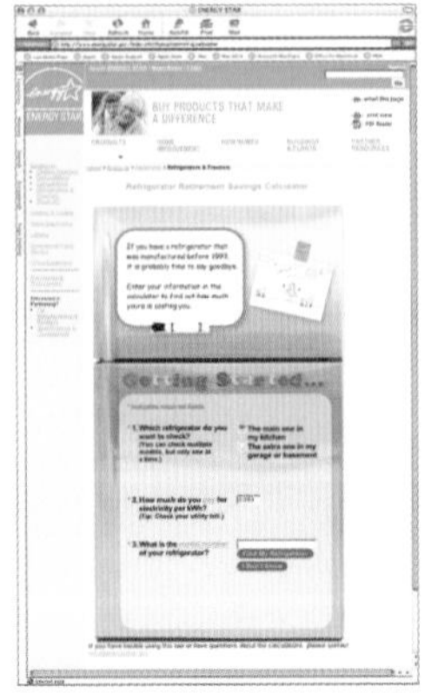

Examples of ENERGY STAR products and qualifiers include:

- Televisions must consume 3 watts or less when switched off (most standard TVs consume 6 watts).
- Washing machines must use 50 percent less energy than standard washers.
- Furnaces must have an efficiency rating of 90 percent or greater.
- Computer monitors must consume 2 watts or less in SLEEP mode and 1 watt or less in OFF mode.

Descriptions of what it takes for a product to gain the ENERGY STAR, along with a manufacturer-by-manufacturer breakdown of qualifying products can be found at the ENERGY STAR Web site at www.energystar.gov. Other information on how to make your home more energy efficient, including interactive features such as the "Refrigerator Retirement Savings Calculator," the "Home Energy Yardstick" and store locators can also be found on the Web site. The ENERGY STAR Web site is refreshingly easy to navigate, and packed full of specific product and how-to information.

And is it working? You bet. Through the ENERGY STAR program, Americans saved $12 billion on their utility bill in one year alone.

Here are some general ENERGY STAR product categories, along with examples of the savings you might expect to see.

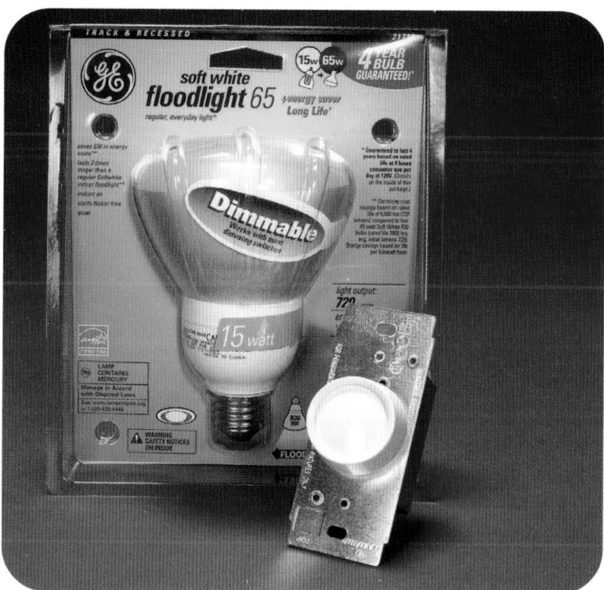

Lighting

ENERGY STAR-qualified bulbs—primarily compact fluorescent lights or CFLs—use two-thirds less energy than incandescent bulbs, while generating 70 percent less heat and lasting up to 10 times longer. ENERGY STAR light fixtures have been designed to easily accommodate energy-efficient bulbs and distribute light more efficiently, while using 33 percent less energy than standard fixtures. Many also contain extra energy-saving features, such as built-in dimmers, motion sensors and automatic daylight shutoffs.

When replacing bulbs and fixtures, start with the five most frequently used fixtures. Often they're the kitchen ceiling light, living-room table and floor lamps, bathroom vanity and outdoor porch or post lamps.

You can save $20 to $30 in energy costs over the lifetime of a single CFL. Save $60 per year by replacing your five most frequently used fixtures and/or the bulbs with ENERGY STAR-qualified models.

Appliances

When shopping for a new appliance, there are actually two price tags to look at: the one attached to the appliance and the one attached to your utility bill each month. In many cases, what initially looks like an expensive product can start looking like a smart investment when the utility bills roll in. ENERGY STAR-qualified appliances use anywhere from 10 to 50 percent less energy and/or water than standard models.

Here are laundry room and kitchen appliances that currently qualify for the ENERGY STAR:

Dishwashers. Heating the water is the most expensive part of running a dishwasher. Most ENERGY STAR-qualified units have built-in water temperature boosters that allow you to keep your water heater set at a lower temperature. Most also use less water. To qualify for the ENERGY STAR, a dishwasher must use 41 percent less energy than the federal minimum standards—which boils down to a savings of about $90 over the dishwasher's lifetime.

You can reduce the amount of energy your refrigerator uses by positioning it away from heat-producing sources such as ovens, dishwashers or direct sunlight.

Refrigerators and freezers. In most homes, the refrigerator consumes more energy than any other kitchen appliance. ENERGY STAR-qualified models are better

insulated and have higher-efficiency compressors—the workhorse of any refrigerator. Qualifying refrigerators use 40 percent less energy than standard models sold in 2001, while freezers consume at least 10 percent less energy than federal standards. Check out the "Refrigerator Retirement Saving Calculator" on the ENERGY STAR Web site for a real eye opener. If your refrigerator was made prior to 1993, you may be able to save $100 or more a year by switching to a more energy-efficient model.

Clothes washers. Compared to a pre-1994 unit, an ENERGY STAR-qualified washer can save up to $110 per year on your utility bill. To qualify, a machine must use 50 percent less energy than a standard model. Most use half the amount of water as conventional older machines.

Ventilation and clean air

Clean, fresh air is something everyone appreciates—and using ENERGY STAR-qualified dehumidifiers, fans and ventilation fans can help save money at the same time.

Dehumidifiers. The lower the humidity, the cooler a body feels—meaning a dehumidifier may allow you to run your air conditioner less often. ENERGY STAR-qualified units use 10 to 20 percent less energy than conventional models, and in doing so, can save up to $20 per year in electricity costs.

Ceiling fans. Air movement from a ceiling fan can help make a room (and those in it) feel 2 to 8 degrees cooler, leading to lower air conditioning bills. ENERGY STAR-qualified ceiling fan/light units are 50 percent more efficient than standard units, which means you can save another $15-20 per year on utility bills by installing one.

Ventilating fans. Kitchen range hoods, as well as bathroom and other types of fans not only use 65 percent less energy than standard models, but are 50 percent quieter to boot.

Windows, doors, skylights and roofing

ENERGY STAR-qualified **windows, doors and skylights** are designed using new technologies to help keep your home warmer in winter and cooler in summer. Qualifying units also help reduce condensation and fading. Units qualify based on the climates in four geographic zones. Go to www.energystar.gov for more specific information. The Web site also includes tons of great information on purchasing products and on insulating and sealing your home.

Certain ENERGY STAR-qualified **reflective roofing materials** reflect more of the sun's rays, helping to lower roof surface temperature by as much as 100 degrees F. These lower temperatures mean cooling bills that are 10 to 15 percent lower.

Heating and cooling

Up to half your utility bill dollars go to heating and cooling your home. The older and less energy efficient your existing heating and cooling equipment, the greater your long-term savings with ENERGY STAR products. **Room and central air conditioners, furnaces, boilers, heat pumps and programmable thermostats** can all qualify for the ENERGY STAR. Qualifying furnaces are up to 15 percent more efficient than standard models.

One of the smartest places to put your money is in a programmable thermostat that can save you $150 or more per year depending on your utility costs, usage habits and house.

You can also save up to $25 per year by replacing a 10-year-old room air conditioner with an ENERGY STAR-qualified model.

The ENERGY STAR site also contains information on locating and hiring a dependable heating and cooling contractor.

Rebates, tax credits and incentives

Shop around for "free" money before you go shopping

Buying energy-efficient products can cost more initially, but save you money in the long run. In order to encourage people to make that bigger initial investment, government agencies, utility companies and, sometimes, even manufacturers and retailers offer rebates, assistance programs and tax incentives to help defray those upfront costs.

What, when, where, from whom and how much these incentives are worth varies greatly, but they're worth looking into. Here are a few tools to help you in your initial search.

Government incentives

One good starting place to look for both state and federal tax credits is the U.S. Department of Energy's Web site at www.energy.gov. Any current federal tax incentives will be prominently shown on the "Consumer" portion of the Web site.

For state incentives, click on the name of the state where you live, then look for relevant information and links. You may find listings under headings like "Incentives for Renewable Energy" or "Energy Assistance Programs." Or conduct a Web search by typing in "energy rebates" or "energy tax credits" along with the name of your state.

Utility company incentives

Utility companies often offer rebates or incentives to their customers for purchasing energy-efficient products; many use ENERGY STAR ratings as qualifiers. To find out about incentives, check the inserts that come with your monthly bill, call your utility companies or visit their Web sites.

A quick check of one Midwest utility company's Web site showed rebates of up to $100 to those installing tankless water heaters, and of more than $300 for those installing high-efficiency heat pumps.

While you're at it, check into "peak demand" energy conservation programs. One type involves the installation of a remote-controlled switch on your central air conditioner that the utility company can activate for brief periods during hot summer days when demand for electricity peaks. As an incentive, you'll receive some type of discount on your total electric bill; often in the 10 to 20 percent range.

Manufacturer and retailer incentives

When shopping for appliances, heating and cooling equipment or other products, check to see if manufacturers offer rebates. Some rebates are linked to energy efficiency, while others are linked to "package deals" or other scenarios.

Check manufacturers' individual Web sites, or check general information on Web sites such as www.rebates.com for more information. The ENERGY STAR Web site at www.energystar.gov also lists special rebates and offers from thousands of their ENERGY STAR partners.

40 low-cost energy-saving tips

Save fuel, electricity and cold hard cash

ENERGY-SAVING COMPACT FLUORESCENT BULB

Install and use an automatic setback thermostat

You can reduce your heating and cooling costs by 5 to 15 percent.

Replace worn-out thresholds

and weatherstripping around windows and doors.

Replace lightbulbs

used more than two to three hours per day with compact fluorescent bulbs. Fluorescent bulbs last longer and use only one-third as much energy as standard bulbs.

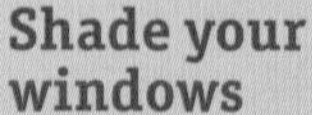

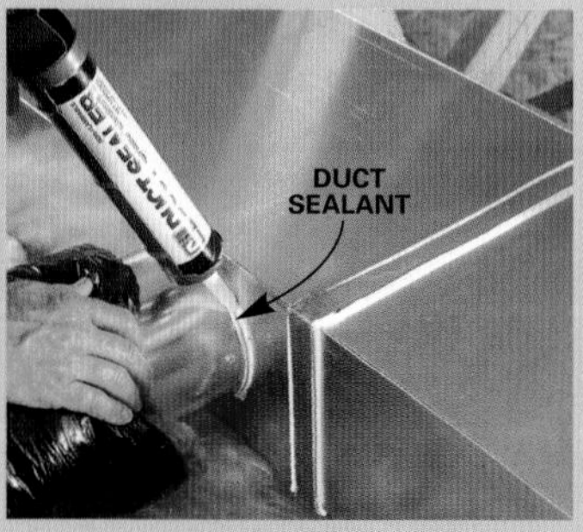

Seal the joints

of heating and cooling ducts that run through attics and basements, and save 10 percent on your heating and cooling bills.

Shade your windows

with trees, awnings, overhangs, shutters or other devices to keep direct sunlight from entering your home. Add window tint film.

Wrap the tank of your gas-burning water heater in a special fiberglass blanket to decrease heat loss. Check your owner's manual to make sure that a blanket is a viable option for your model.

Change furnace filters every month, more often if needed.

MOTION SENSOR

Install light controls like motion sensors, photocell switches and timers to shut off lights automatically when they're not needed.

Clean the air conditioner condenser coils and fins when you see grass and airborne debris collected on them.

Insulate pipes, especially if they pass through an area you don't want heated or cooled.

More tips

- Reduce hot water usage by replacing high-volume shower-heads with low-flow heads (2 to 3 gallons per minute). Save up to $40 per year.
- Have a furnace tune-up to clean and adjust burners and improve fuel-burning efficiency.
- Fix leaky faucets; dripping hot water can cost $35 per year.
- Buy gas stoves with electronic ignition rather than pilot lights.
- Replace recessed light fixtures with air-tight models when you remodel.
- Install a reflector (shiny aluminum foil over cardboard will do) behind radiators to reduce heat driven into and through the wall. Save 5 percent.
- Have your air conditioner serviced to clean hard-to-reach evaporator coils and adjust coolant pressure to achieve maximum efficiency.

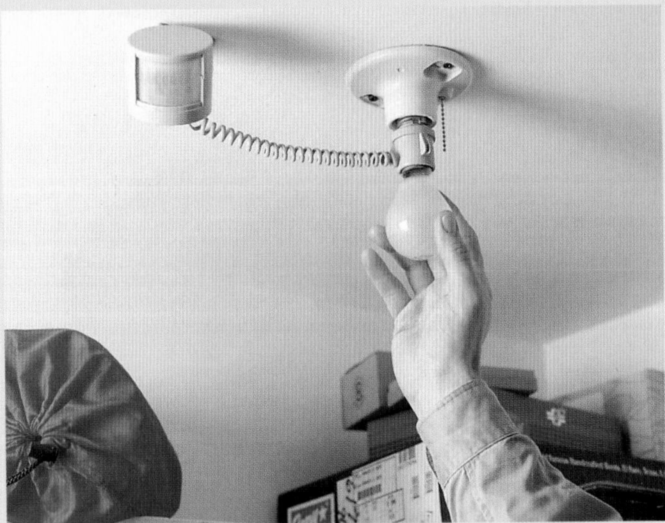

Finally—a light that turns itself off

Are your kids are always switching on the lights in the laundry room, storage room and pantry and never turning them off? Sometimes the lights burn all night, even for days, before you discover the light streaming under the closed doors. Here's a solution: buy a wireless motion-sensing light adapter ($20 at home centers) and aim the sensing unit straight down the wall inside the top of the door. The light automatically turns on when it senses that someone is after a can of tuna or wants that special T-shirt out of the wash, and then turns off.

Furnace filter reminder

Whenever you buy a new box of furnace filters, write the months of the year on the individual filters (and change them monthly). That way, you'll always know when you last changed the filter.

1 Lower the indoor temperature a few degrees in winter (you'll save about 2 percent per degree). Set it even lower at night and a full 10 degrees lower when you're on vacation.

2 Close the fireplace damper when the fireplace isn't in use. If it's never used, seal the flue with a plastic bag stuffed with insulation.

3 Open shades and blinds to let in sunlight during the day and close them to reduce heat loss at night. For cooling, close them during the day.

4 Close off unused rooms and lower the temperatures by adjusting the registers and dampers. You'll save up to $50 per year.

5 Clean your furnace's blower fan with a soft brush and vacuum cleaner.

6 Ventilate and cool your home with window or whole-house fans during the cooler hours of the day.

7 Fill clothes washers and dishwashers for more efficient energy use, rather than cleaning partial loads.

8 Skip the dishwasher's drying cycle (and cut the energy use by about half!).

9 Wash clothes in cool rather than hot water.

21 money- and energy-saving ideas that don't cost a dime

10 Clean clothes washer and dryer lint screens after every use.

11 Turn off lights not in use. Reduce bulb wattage and use dimmers.

12 Clean refrigerator coils with a soft brush annually, or more often if you have pets that shed.

13 Run major appliances late in the evening or early in the morning when electric loads are less (off peak).

14 Flush your garbage disposer with cold water rather than hot. Grease solidifies in cold water and will wash away.

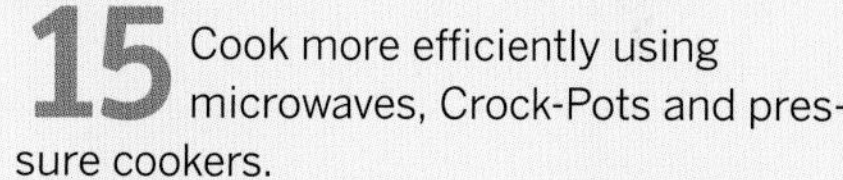

15 Cook more efficiently using microwaves, Crock-Pots and pressure cookers.

16 Turn off room air conditioners when you leave for an hour or more. You can quickly cool the room later.

17 Recycle. Reuse. Take your bike instead of your car.

18 In warm weather, set the thermostat higher (75 to 78 degrees F) and rely more on ceiling and table fans for cooling, even when the air conditioner is running.

19 Reduce humidity in bathrooms and kitchens with exhaust fans. When dehumidifying a basement, keep basement doors and windows closed.

20 Consider higher-efficiency appliances when purchasing new refrigerators, freezers and dishwashers. The energy savings usually pays back the extra costs within a few years. The same goes for furnaces and water heaters.

21 Lower your water heater setting to 120 degrees F for both energy savings and safety. (Measure hot water temperature at a faucet with a cooking thermometer if the water heater setting isn't calibrated in degrees.)

Energy-savings

Window film can be installed in about 30 minutes. The hazy appearance will disappear after 10 days.

Heat-reducing window film

Q My son's west-facing bedroom gets very hot in the spring and summer. Will a window film help, and if so, can I install it myself?

A A heat-control window film will help keep your son's room cooler, and yes, you can install it yourself. These films reflect the sun's heat and ultraviolet rays, and reduce glare without obscuring the view. Applying the film takes about 30 minutes per window. The film should last about 10 years. Prices vary with film size. A 3 x 15-ft. film (which can cover two to three windows) costs $30. The film is sold at home centers and hardware stores. Gila is one company that makes heat-control film (800-528-4481, www.gilafilms.com).

Different types of film are available, so get the one designed for heat control. The film can be applied to any window, including double-pane low-e windows, although they already reduce radiant heat loss and gain.

One drawback is that the film may void the manufacturer's warranty for the seal on double-pane windows. If the window warranty has already expired or reducing excessive heat is more important to you than a warranty, apply the film. Otherwise, consider options such as installing shades, awnings or shutters, or even planting a tree on the west side to block the sun.

Too-hot water heater

Q If I set my gas water heater temperature to 120 degrees F, it's often not hot enough. The water dispensed has been as low as 90 degrees. That's a 30-degree temperature swing. I don't want to raise the temperature setting, because the water at times will be scalding hot. Is this normal?

A No, the temperature range you're experiencing is not typical. A 17-degree swing is considered standard. The swing often occurs because the thermostat won't switch the heater on until the water cools a certain amount.

In an opposite situation, a water heater heats water beyond its temperature setting. This is usually caused by "stacking," which occurs when you use just enough water to switch on the burner but draw little off. Doing this repeatedly causes overheated water to rise to the top of the tank, where it could be drawn off extra hot.

Since you've tried adjusting your thermostat setting and you still get too large a temperature swing, you probably have a bad thermostat. Call a plumber. If you have a standard water heater that's more than five years old, buy a new unit. Gas water heaters cost about $400, and it would cost at least half that to have a plumber diagnose the problem and more for the fix.

Q&A

Straight scoop on triple glazing

Q I'd like to replace the drafty single-pane windows in my house. Is upgrading to triple-pane windows a good idea in cold climates where it's often below zero in the winter?

A In cold regions, triple-glazed windows can save 2 to 3 percent of your heating bill, compared with double-glazed windows. From a cost standpoint, it'll take a few decades to recoup the 10 to 15 percent upcharge to go from low-e double-glazed windows to triple-glazed. For example, if you pay $1,000 per year in energy bills, have 20 windows in your house, and 22 percent of your energy is lost through your windows (which is average), then each window is losing $11 worth of energy per year. A triple-glazed window will reduce that loss by about $1, so it'll take 35 years to cover a $35 upcharge for triple-glazing. Of course, if your energy bills and energy loss are greater, you'll recoup the cost sooner.

However, the investment may be worth the cost in terms of comfort. Triple glazing will reduce condensation, which will allow you to maintain a higher indoor relative humidity in cold weather. These windows also reduce cold drafts. If you don't want to pay for triple-pane windows throughout the house, get them for the north- and east-facing rooms, where you'll get the biggest payoff.

Most of the major window manufacturers in the United States don't offer triple glazing. But here are two that do: Marvin (888-537-7828; www.marvin.com) and Weather Shield (800-222-2995; www.weathershield.com). Many Canadian window manufacturers offer triple glazing.

PHOTO COURTESY OF MARVIN

Marvin's triple-glazed window consists of three panes of glass, two of which have a low-e coating. The space between the panes is filled with krypton gas.

Duct booster for cold rooms

Q Our son's bedroom, located at the end of a long hallway, stays about 10 degrees cooler than the rest of the house. How can we direct more heat to just that room? We have forced-air heat.

A First check to make sure all the dampers controlling heat to that area are open; there can be as many as three. The damper in the floor- or wall-mounted register can be seen using a flashlight and can be adjusted by moving a lever or wheel on the register. Often there's another damper in the branch duct leading to the register. This is controlled by a wing nut on the side or bottom of the duct; when the wing nut is aligned parallel to the duct, the damper's open. In some cases there can even be a damper in the main trunk line, usually controlled by an L-shaped lever on the side of the vent.

If all the vents are wide open, consider installing an in-duct air boosting fan. This $25 part won't create more heat, but will pull more air to the trouble spot.

If you install the air-boosting fan, bear in mind:

- Install it as near as possible to the cold room.
- You can wire it to a manually controlled switch or to the furnace's blower fan, so the booster fan turns on every time the furnace blower fan kicks in. Follow the manufacturer's instructions and all applicable codes.
- Installing it can be a pain. It's usually easiest to remove a few duct support brackets, drop down and remove one or two sections of round duct, install the booster fan, then reinstall the whole works.
- These fans can also be used to improve the circulation of a gravity-type warm-air furnace.

Saving Energy:

Four out of every five homes built before 1980 have a less-than-recommended amount of insulation. Back when oil cost only a few dollars per barrel neither builders nor homeowners gave much thought to installing the stuff.

But insulating your home today can easily reduce both your heating and cooling bills by 20 percent to 40 percent. And with heating and cooling often accounting for nearly half the utility bill, insulating your home makes good economic sense. Adding attic insulation is by far the easiest and most cost-effective step you can take. Insulating walls with blown-in insulation will also save money in the long run, but it's nearly always a messier, more expensive proposition.

It is critical to remember that sealing up air leaks and insulating go hand in hand. For starters, it's much easier to seal attic air leaks before insulating. Secondly, your insulation will be much more effective when it doesn't have to fight air infiltration; after all, insulation is simply thousands of little pockets that trap air.

Insulation

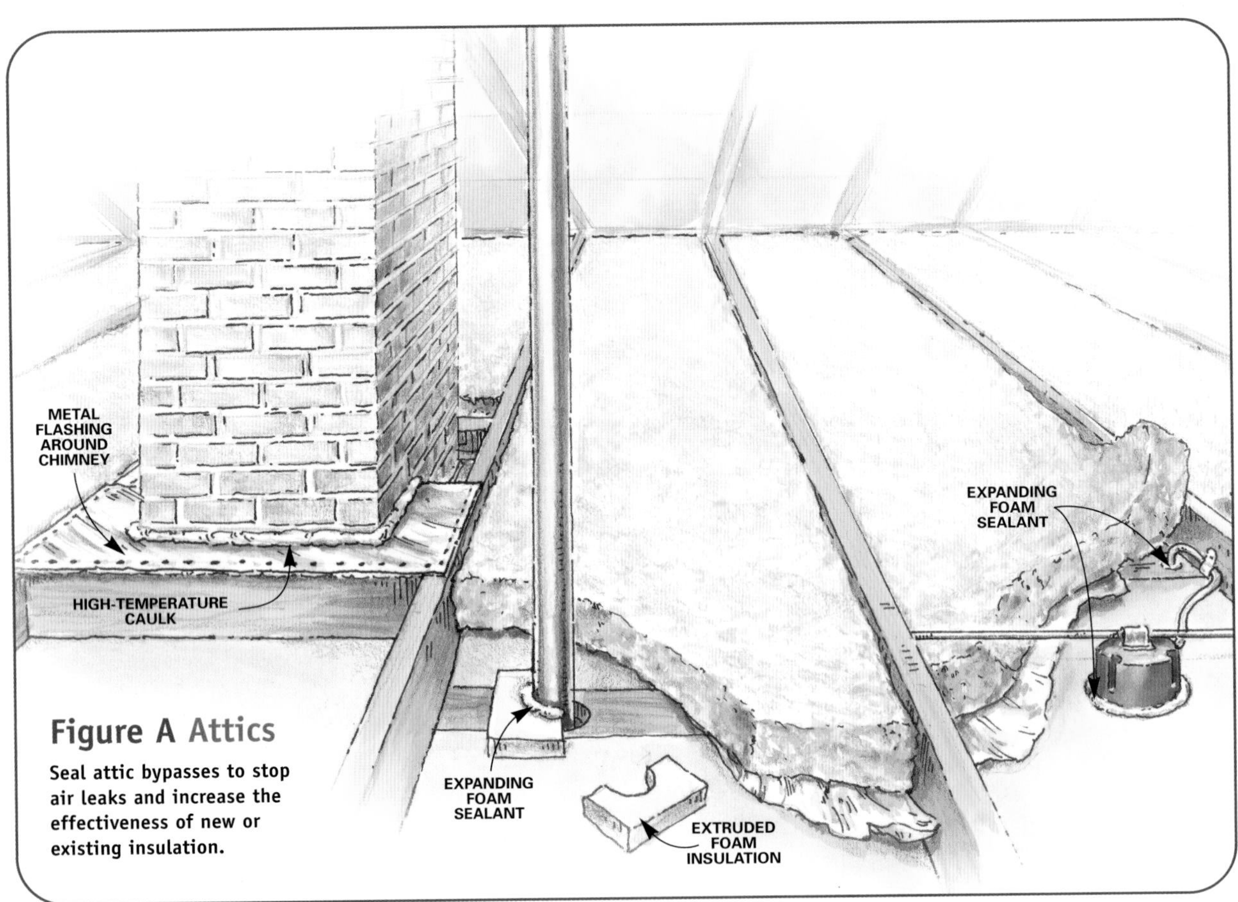

Figure A Attics

Seal attic bypasses to stop air leaks and increase the effectiveness of new or existing insulation.

Insulating

Do it right to save $$, save energy and stay warm

Insulation—silently hidden in your walls, no moving parts to fix—is a material you probably spend precious little time thinking about. Then along comes subzero (or sweltering!) weather, a three-digit utility bill or chilly drafts, and you start thinking about it a lot! At home, you ponder whether it's worth the time and expense to add it to your ceilings, walls and basement. At the store, you ponder which type, thickness, width and density to buy. And when you install it, you wonder just how good is "good enough."

We asked insulation manufacturers and installers which questions they field most—and which blunders they see most. Following are six things they (and we) think you should know.

1 Seal up air bypasses before adding attic insulation (or you'll be wasting money).

Attics are one of the easiest and most cost-effective places to add insulation. But you'll increase the effectiveness of insulation substantially if you first seal up air bypasses (Figure A) around chimneys, plumbing vents, wires, interior walls and exhaust fans—places where warm, moist interior air escapes into the attic.

Heat has a natural inclination to both rise and migrate to colder areas. Combine these two tendencies and you can see why air bypasses can reduce the effectiveness of attic insulation by 30 to 70 percent. You can track down bypasses by lifting existing attic insulation and checking for dark patches of moisture or dust. Or head to the attic on a cold day and feel for pockets of warm air or use a stick of incense to check for drafts.

Before installing (or adding) attic insulation, take these steps:

- Use caulk and expanding foam sealant to close air gaps around pipes, ducts and electrical wires where they enter the attic.
- Cut and fit strips of 24-gauge sheet metal between the masonry chimney and the surrounding wood framing. Use high-temperature caulk to seal the flashing where it meets the chimney.
- Install weatherstripping around the perimeter of the attic access opening, then use screw hooks to pull the hatch tight against the weatherstripping. Glue rigid extruded foam insulation to the top of the hatch.

NOTE: After air-tightening your home, always test your carbon monoxide detectors, or install them if you don't have them ($20 to $40 at home centers and hardware stores).

2 Careful installation increases the insulation's R-value by over 20 percent.

Leaving 5 percent of a wall uninsulated will reduce the entire wall's R-value (resistance to heat flow) by 20 percent. It doesn't take much more time to install fiberglass insulation properly (Figure B). The most important steps you can take:

- Fill the stud cavity from top to bottom and side to side. To avoid guesswork when insulating walls built from standard 92-5/8-in.-long studs, purchase and install precut fiberglass batts that are 93 in. long and 15 in. wide. When you have to custom-cut batts at wall corners and other places, cut the batts 1 in. higher and wider than the cavity you're filling.
- Split your insulation so half goes in front of and half goes behind electrical wires. Compressing insulation reduces its R-value.
- Around electrical boxes, notch, rather than compress, the batt—then tuck the cutout behind the box. To help prevent frozen pipes, insulate only on the cold side.

3 You probably don't need kraft-faced insulation.

Kraft paper—the asphalt-impregnated brown paper facing available on insulation—is rarely called for these days. When insulation was first developed, it was only an inch or two thick and the attached kraft facing was stapled to studs to keep it from sagging. Insulation today is so "full-bodied" and fills stud and joist cavities so completely that it resists settling—even when walls have been purposely vibrated in tests.

Kraft paper does act as a vapor retarder to slow the movement of interior moisture through the wall cavity and insulation. But for a thorough job, especially in bathrooms and other high-moisture areas, a continuous 6-mil plastic sheeting vapor barrier is much more effective. Kraft paper still serves the purpose of temporarily holding insulation in place on horizontal or sloped surfaces. And when you're retrofitting insulation in the floor of a crawlspace (Figure D), installing the kraft-faced insulation paper-side-up provides an adequate vapor retarder. Kraft paper and its underlying asphalt adhesive are flammable and should always be covered with drywall or other fire-resistant material.

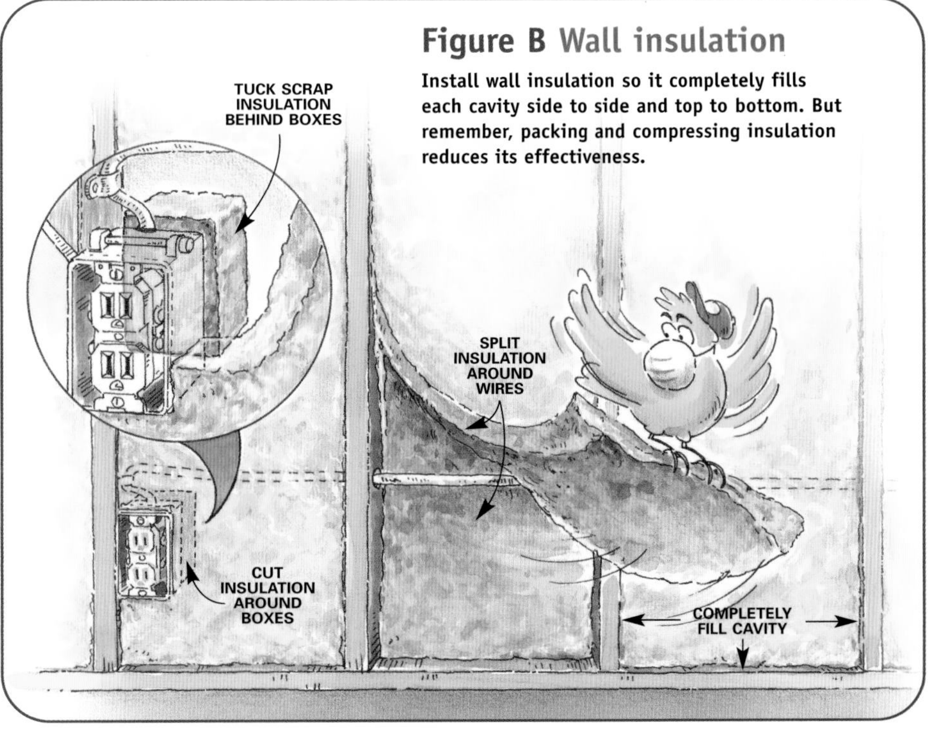

Figure B Wall insulation

Install wall insulation so it completely fills each cavity side to side and top to bottom. But remember, packing and compressing insulation reduces its effectiveness.

Another important point: Except in hot coastal regions, insulation should be installed with the kraft paper (or plastic vapor barrier) on the interior side of the wall. In hot regions, vapor barriers are often eliminated or positioned toward the outside of the stud wall. If in doubt, consult a local building inspector.

4 High-density insulation can pay off.

Insulation is rated according to its R-value, or resistance to heat loss: the higher the R-value, the higher the insulating value. Standard fiberglass insulation has an R-value of about 3.5 per inch of thickness (Figure C); this provides an insulating value of R-11 for 2x4 walls and R-19 for 2x6 walls. But if you're serious about energy savings, you can buy better-performing products. High-density types of fiberglass insulation, with more fibers and air spaces per square inch, offer R-values of up to 4.25 per inch. Some provide R-15 for 2x4 walls and R-21 for 2x6 walls. There's also high-density insulation for ceilings and attics. You'll wind up paying more, and in many cases you'll need to special-order it, but high-density insulation delivers up to 35 percent more insulating value per inch.

You can also pack 5-1/2-in.-thick insulation into a 3-1/2-in.-thick wall to increase its R-value, but the compressed R-19 batt will only yield an R-value of about 17.

Energy-Saving Hint

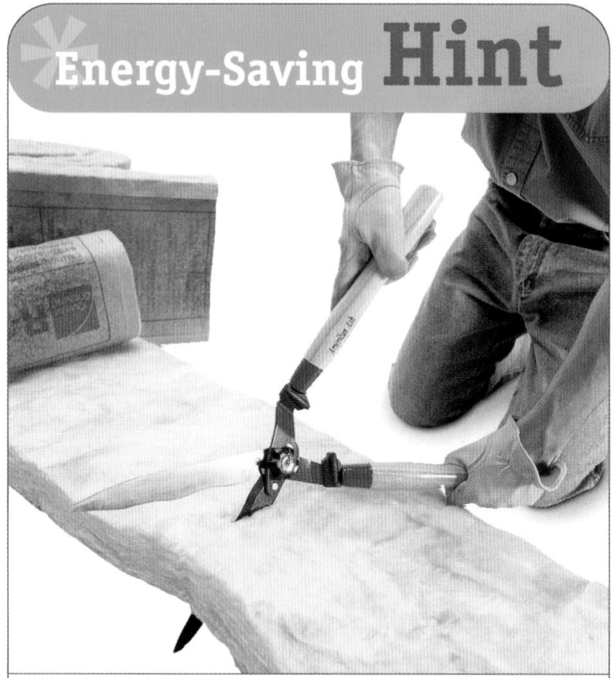

Insulation trimmer

Here's a faster, cleaner way to cut fiberglass insulation. Use a hedge shears to slice through the insulation. Unlike a utility knife, the shears won't spread loose tufts of insulation all over, and the best part is, you stay itch free.

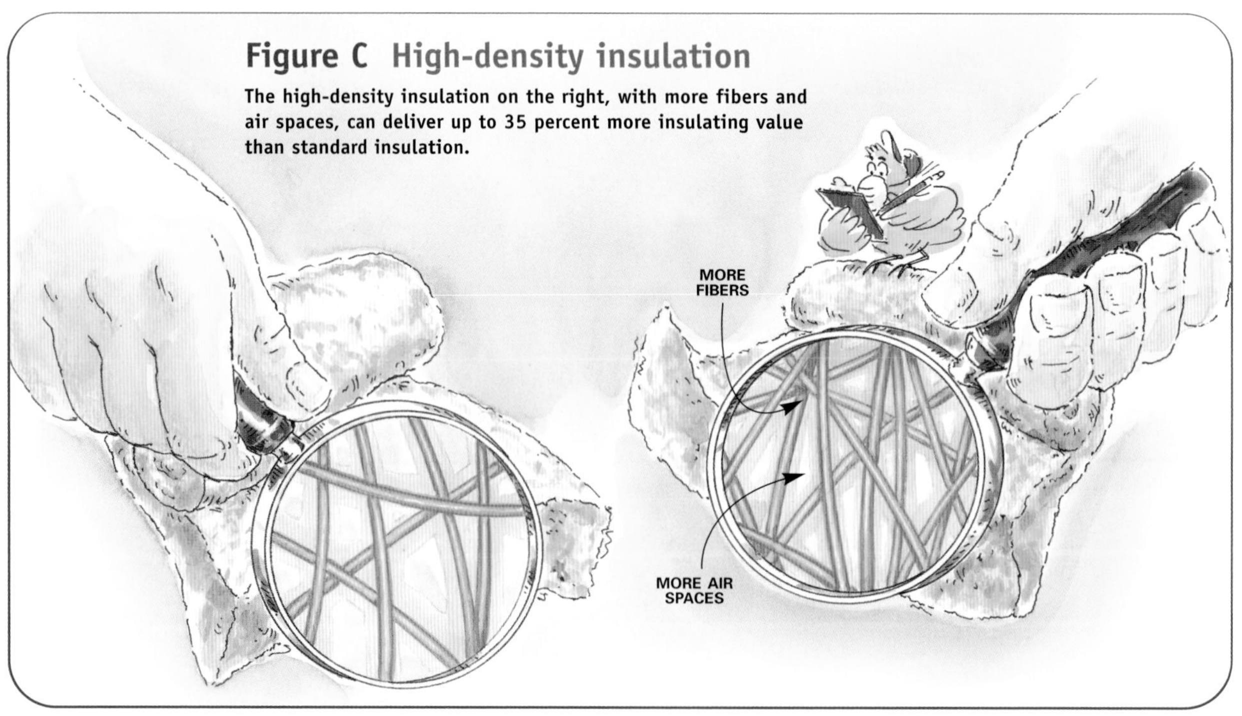

Figure C High-density insulation

The high-density insulation on the right, with more fibers and air spaces, can deliver up to 35 percent more insulating value than standard insulation.

Figure D Attic and crawlspace insulation

VENTING ATTICS AND CRAWLSPACES is critical to reduce moisture problems and allow the insulation to perform right.

RIDGE VENT

CHUTES TO MAINTAIN 1" AIR SPACE

SOFFIT VENT

5 How much insulation is enough?

The first 3 in. of insulation you add to a bare ceiling or wall will yield huge savings. Adding another 3 in. will increase energy savings, but not to as great a degree. For charts showing the Department of Energy's optimal amounts of insulation to install, go to www.certainteed.com or www.owenscorning.com. Their recommendations are based on climate, fuel costs and other factors. Adding more will give you a diminishing return on your investment.

The payback period for retrofitting insulation varies greatly, but studies show that added insulation usually pays for itself in saved energy costs within five to 10 years. One typical two-story Minnesota home was fitted with blown-in wall insulation, additional ceiling insulation and rim joist insulation at a cost of $1,890. The result was a $325 savings in yearly heating costs, which represents a payback period of slightly less than six years. Payback in more temperate areas takes longer, but remember that insulation reduces air-conditioning costs too.

6 When you insulate attics and crawlspaces, you've got to vent them too.

Since insulation changes the way attics and crawlspaces "breathe," it's critical that you maintain or install proper ventilation (Figure D). At first, it seems odd to add insulation for warmth and then purposely create ventilation "holes" for cold air to enter. But if you don't do this, you're setting yourself up for moisture problems.

When you add insulation to **attic rafters** and **attic floors**, it's important to maintain at least a 1-in. continuous air space between insulation and roof sheathing, from eaves to ridge. This air space flushes out moisture. It also helps maintain a "cold roof," which prevents ice dams from forming in the winter and excessive heat from damaging shingles and increasing cooling costs in the summer. The biggest mistake homeowners make with installation is to install it so it blocks the flow of air at the eaves. The best way to avoid this problem is to install inexpensive air chutes to keep the space open. See "Improve Attic Ventilation," p. 108.

Newly insulated **crawlspaces** also need proper ventilation. The standard procedure is to insulate the ceilings of unheated crawlspaces and the walls of heated crawlspaces. To reduce moisture migration if there's no slab, a 6-mil polyethylene vapor barrier should be laid on the ground in both cases. At least 1 sq. ft. of ventilation should be installed for each 1,500 sq. ft. of floor area.

There are regional differences and various codes and interpretations for insulating crawlspaces and attics. Contact a local building official to make sure your house stays code-compliant.

What is R-value?

The key to understanding insulation

The capacity of an insulating material to resist heat flow is called its R-value. The higher the material's R-value, the better it insulates. Recommended R-values differ for various parts of your home and vary by region. Check with your local utility company or read the insulation manufacturer's literature.

Type	R-Value per Inch	Cost	Pros & Cons
Fiberglass	R-3.0 to R-3.8	Low	**Pros:** Easy-to-install batts press into place; made in standard stud and joist widths; available with Kraft paper facing attached. **Cons:** Can be irritating to installer's skin and lungs; susceptible to air gaps during installation.
Loose fill	R-2.2 to R-4.0	Low	**Pros:** Better coverage in irregular spaces and over trusses; can be poured or blown into walls. **Cons:** Messy to work with; quality can vary; lower R-value; can shift or settle; may need to rent insulation blower.
Extruded foam	R-5.2	High	**Pros:** High compressive strength; great performance underground. **Cons:** Cover with drywall or other fireproof material.
Expanded foam	R-3.8 to R-4.3	Medium	**Pros:** Lowest cost among foams. **Cons:** Not for underground. Cover with drywall or fireproof material.
Sprayed urethane foam	R-6.0 to R-7.3	High	**Pros:** Makes a tough, seamless thermal and vapor barrier; covers irregular surfaces; adds structural strength. **Cons:** Must be professionally applied. Very expensive. Cover with drywall or other fireproof material.

Energy-Saving Hint

Easier fiberglass cutting

For easier cutting, temporarily flatten unruly fiberglass insulation with a piece of scrap plywood. Just cut a 1-1/2-in.-wide slot in the center of a 16 x 30-in. board, use the slot as a straightedge and get a clean cut every time.

Installing fiberglass batts

You have only one chance to do it right! Here's how.

Filling stud spaces with fiberglass batts is the cheapest, easiest way for you to insulate new walls. It's also the best way to upgrade wall insulation during remodeling. Installing the batts doesn't require any special skills, but it's slow, tedious, itchy work. It's often done poorly, and even small gaps can reduce efficiency as much as 25 percent. Here you'll discover how to cut and fit fiberglass batts and how to work around electrical outlets and cables to get the best job with the least hassle.

Push batts all the way to the back of each stud space and then pull out the front edges until they're flush with the face of the studs.

Fill all voids

The key to a quality insulating job is tight-fitting batts that completely fill the stud cavity with no voids or gaps. You can do top-quality work with only a few basic tools. You'll need a utility knife with a good supply of sharp blades, a tape measure and a straightedge, and a 3- or 4-in. putty knife for stuffing insulation around doors and windows. Fiberglass can irritate your throat and skin, so wear protective gear. Buy a two-strap mask rated for fiberglass insulation (3M No. 8210 is one example) and wear a hat, gloves, a long-sleeve shirt and goggles to keep fibers out of your eyes.

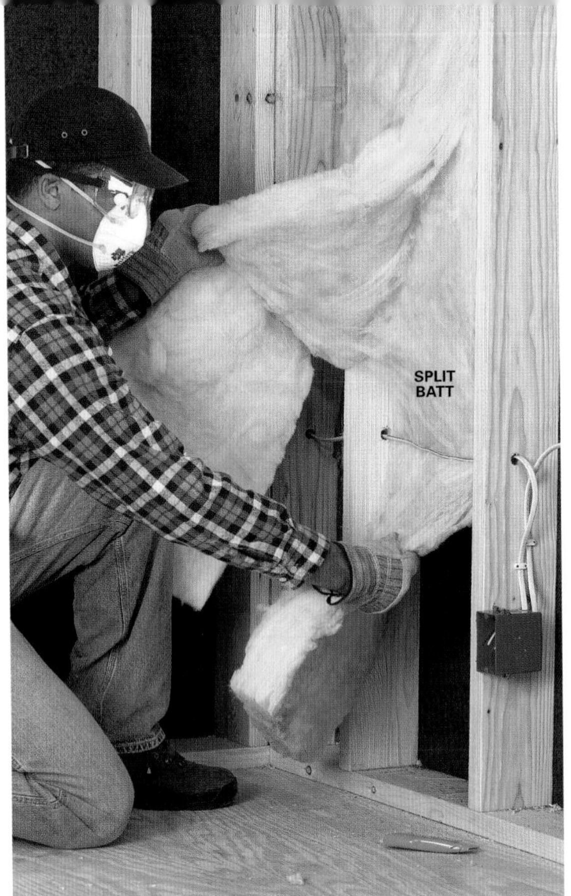

Fit batts tightly around electrical cables and boxes

Running a full batt in front of electrical cables leaves an uninsulated space behind. Avoid this by splitting the batt as shown. Then when you come to an electrical box, trim the insulation to fit snugly around it. Run your knife blade against the outside of the box to guide the cut. But don't cut too deep or you risk nicking the wires. If you have plumbing pipes on an outside wall, insulate behind them, but leave the side facing the interior uncovered to allow heat from the house to keep the pipes warm.

Split batts to fit around electrical cables. Tear the batt in half, starting from the bottom. Slide one half behind the cable and lay the other half over the top.

Split and cut batts to fit behind and around electrical boxes. Slide half the batt behind the box. Then cut the front half to fit tightly around the box.

Fit first, then cut to length

We're using unfaced batts that are sized to friction-fit into standard stud spaces (either 16-in. or 24-in. on-center studs). They're also available precut to lengths that fit standard 8-ft. and 9-ft. walls. Buying precut batts eliminates some work, but you'll still have to cut some batts to length. You could measure the space and cut the batt to fit, but a quicker method that's just as accurate is shown below. Leave an extra 1/2 in. of length for a snug fit.

We're using unfaced batts because they're easier to cut and install. In most climates, you'll have to staple 4-mil plastic sheeting over the batts to form a vapor barrier. Check with your local building inspector for the recommended practice in your area.

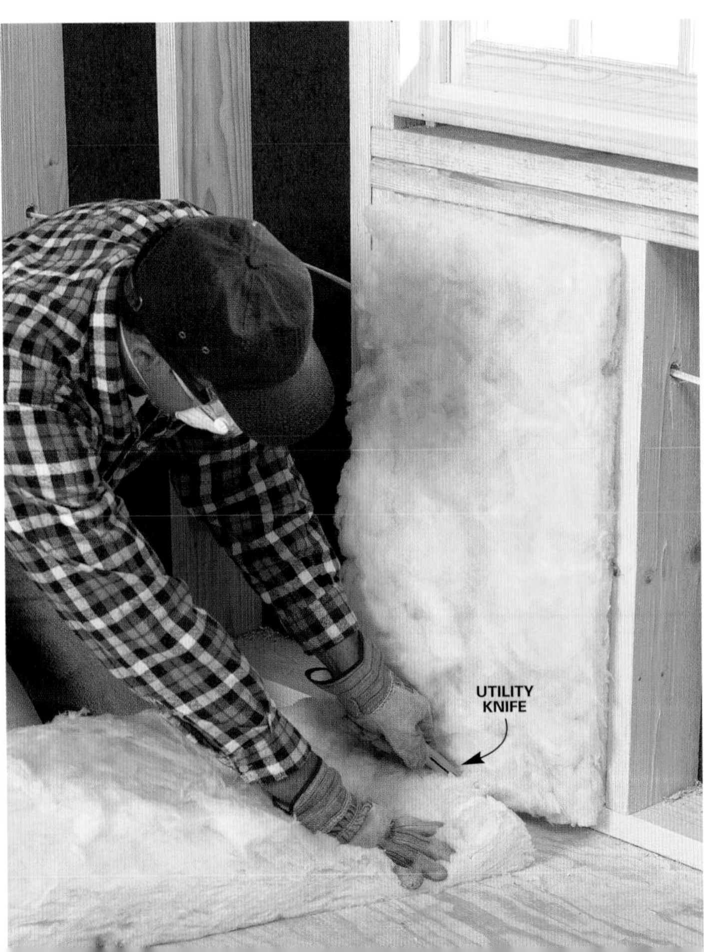

Cut batts to length by setting the top of the batt into the space and cutting against the bottom plate with a sharp utility knife. Leave an extra 1/2 in. of length for a tighter fit.

Trim batts in place

Accurate cutting is essential (actually, slightly oversized batts are best). A batt cut too small leaves gaps, and one cut too large bunches up and leaves voids.

The photos show two methods of cutting batts to width. If you're having trouble getting an accurate cut with the "eyeballing" technique, measure the width of the stud space and use the straightedge method instead. Add about 1/2 in. to the width to ensure a tight fit. It's better to compress the batts a little than to leave gaps. Don't worry if the batts bulge out a bit. The drywall will compress them tightly.

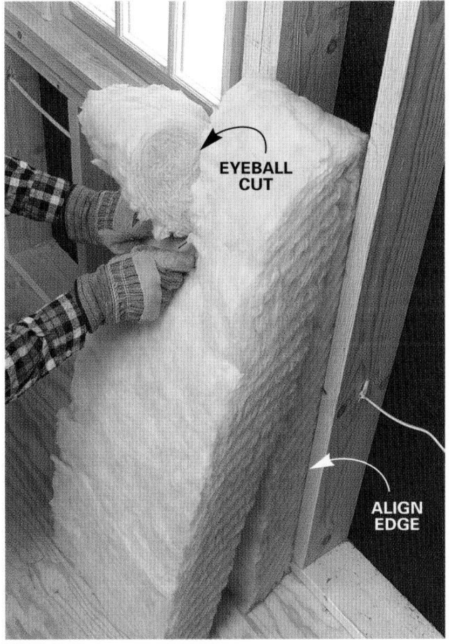

Leave the batt folded in half and hold one edge against the edge of the stud. Slice down the length while holding the top of the batt. Cut against the stud face.

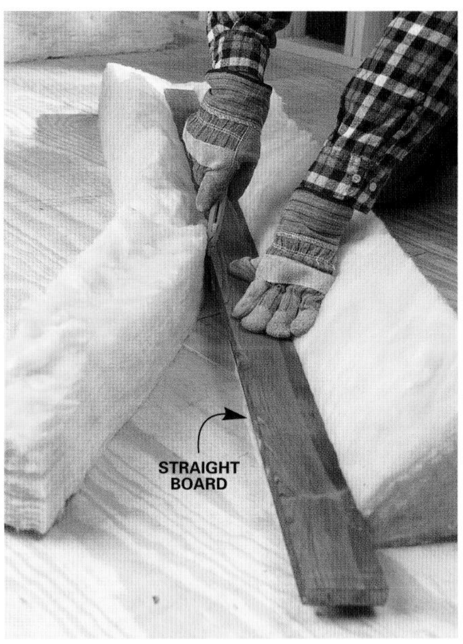

Alternate method: Press a straightedge down on the batt at the desired width and use it as a guide for the utility knife.

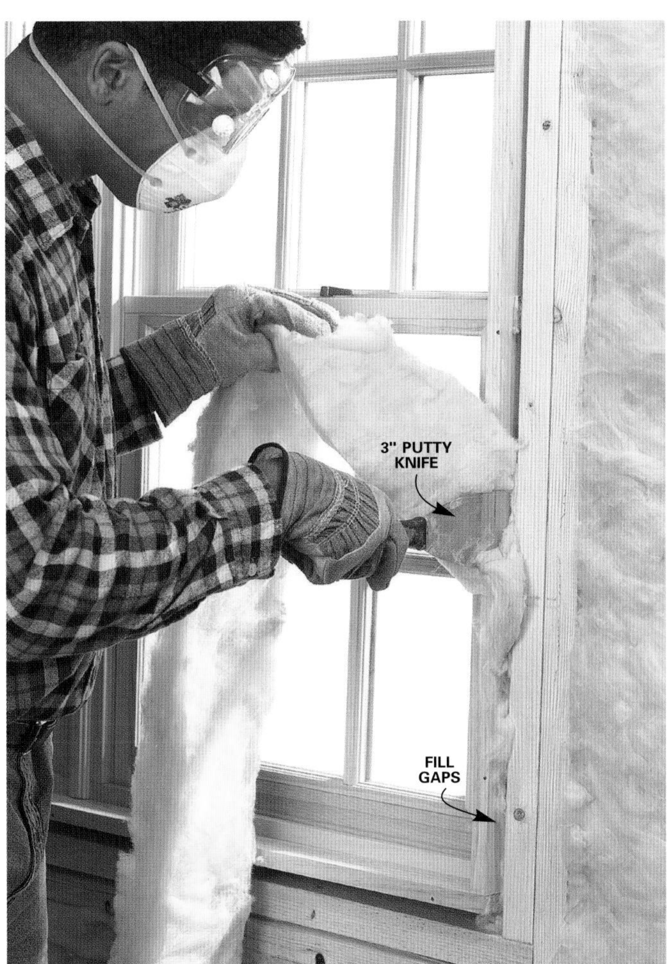

Fill gaps around windows and doors

The shim space around windows and doors is a prime spot for air leakage. Stop these leaks by reaching to the back of this space with the straw-type nozzle included with a can of expanding foam insulation and applying a bead around the perimeter. Let it cure at least an hour before stuffing the remaining space with a thin strip of fiberglass. Don't pack the fiberglass too tight or it will bow the jambs and cause trouble with the operation of the window.

Stuff skinny strips of batting into spaces around windows and doors with a 3-in.-wide putty knife. The insulation should fit snugly, but don't pack it.

Quick tip

INSULATE RIGHT! When you insulate, do it right. Compressing fiberglass batts or leaving even small gaps can cut the efficiency of your new insulation in half.

Batt insulation

Buying the right stuff now helps you save big

Fiberglass insulation has a reputation for being itchy and irritating, but when it comes to convenience, price and installation ease, it can't be beat. You can buy it at almost any home center, toss it in your car and install it in a jiffy.

But it can be confusing to pick out the best type for your project. Fiberglass insulation varies not only in size, thickness and length but also in efficiency, type of vapor barrier and potential for skin irritation.

The following four steps show you how to sort through the many types of fiberglass insulation and choose the one that works best. Once you decide, call lumberyards and home centers to locate the product. And check for substitutes in case you can't find the type with the exact features you want.

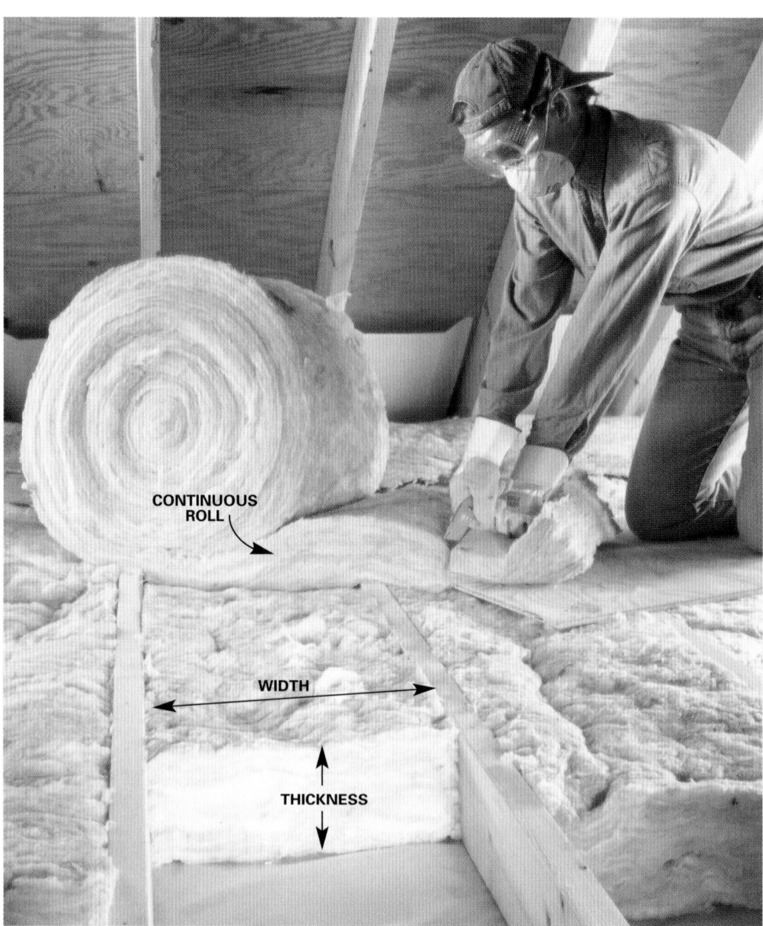

1 Begin by selecting batts that completely fill the joist, rafter or stud space.

- **Width.** Buy 15-in. widths for studs or joists 16 in. on center, or 23-in. widths for spacing 24 in. on center.
- **Thickness.** Buy 3-1/2-in.-thick insulation to go between 2x4s, 6-in.-thick insulation (actual range between 5-1/2 and 6-1/4 in.) to go between 2x6s. (You can compress a 6-in. batt into a 3-1/2-in. space, but you won't gain much insulation value compared with a 3-1/2-in. batt.) Batts 8, 10 and 12 in. thick are also available for attics and deeper framing members.
- **Length.** If installing insulation between studs at a standard wall height, buy batts precut in lengths that fit (usually about 93 in.). If the height isn't standard, buy whatever is readily available, from continuous rolls to standard precut 4-ft. lengths.
- **Amount.** Measure and multiply to find the number of square feet you need to cover. The packaging for each bag, bundle or roll of insulation lists the square footage it covers.

2 Buy "faced" or "unfaced" depending on your installation method.

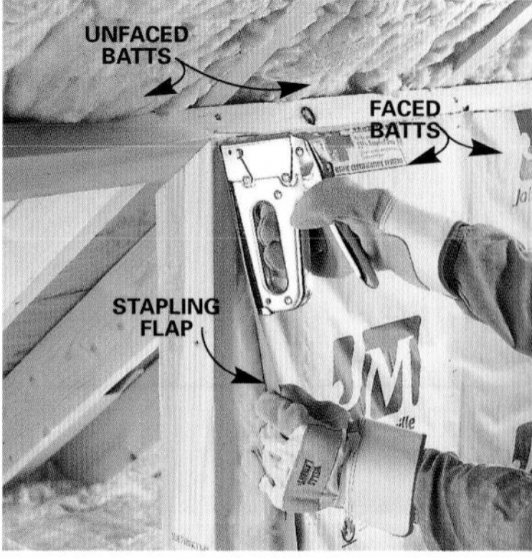

Faced batts have a brown kraft or shiny facing paper glued to one side. This special paper serves as a vapor barrier and has flaps so that you can staple the batt to studs and joists to keep it in place. The vapor barrier isn't necessary if you intend to cover the wall or ceiling with plastic. However, you'll need the paper facing for stud or joist spaces where unfaced batts might fall out. Faced batts cost about 2¢ more per sq. ft.

The vapor barrier should face the inside of the wall, except in hot coastal regions. If in doubt, call your local building inspector.

basics

bucks in the long run.

3 Select the thermal resistance value (R-11, for example) according to the insulation requirements of your region.

Manufacturers now produce batts with higher fiberglass densities, so you can buy 3-1/2-in.-thick batts with R-11, R-13 or R-15 thermal resistance values. The higher the number, the better the insulation. The high-density R-15 batts are best, but they cost more than twice as much as R-11 batts. (They also contain three times as much fiberglass!)

Balance the price with the insulation requirements of your local building codes. If you have to cram more insulation into a minimal wall space, high-density batts might be worth the price. But in most cases, low- or medium-density insulation is adequate. And where you have plenty of space, like in an attic, buy the least expensive. You can easily achieve adequate thermal resistance by piling it higher.

Because batts are sold in bundles of various sizes, cost comparisons are difficult. The best approach is to compare the cost per square foot for batts of the same thickness. You'll need a pocket calculator to do the math!

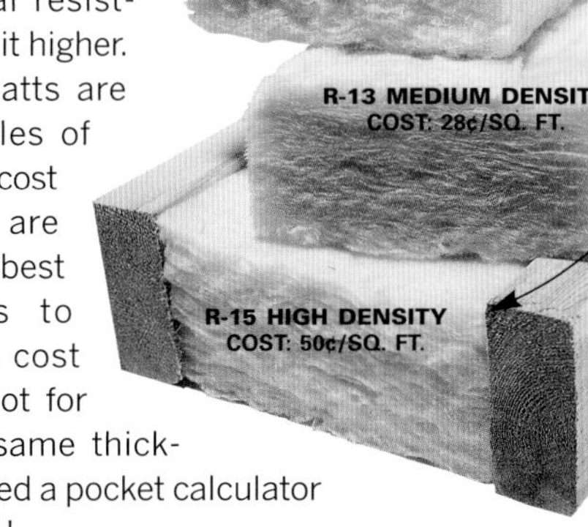

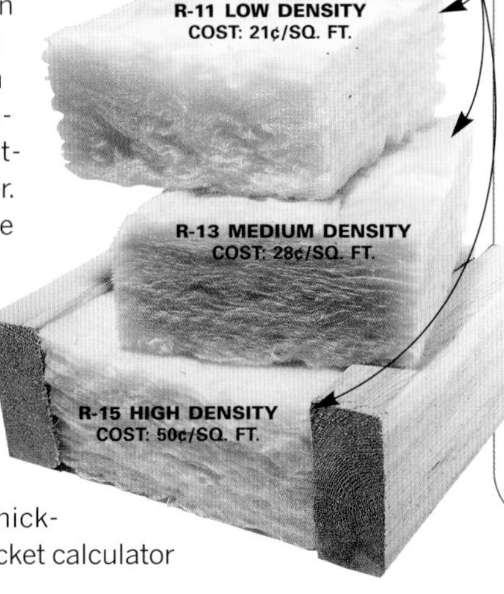

Energy-Saving Hint

Stop a draft in 60 seconds

In exterior walls, electrical boxes that hold switches or outlets can let in a lot of cold air. Worse, they can let warm, moist indoor air into walls, causing problems like wood rot or peeling exterior paint. One way to stop the airflow is to seal the gaps around them and the holes inside them with caulk—messy and time consuming. But there's a much easier way: With foam gaskets, all you have to do is unscrew the cover plate, stick the gasket in place and put the plate back on. A pack of a dozen gaskets costs about $3 at home centers and hardware stores.

4 Look for wrapped or low-itch batts if the glass fibers cause skin irritation, coughing or any other discomfort.

Fiberglass dust is an irritant, so wear eye protection and a dust mask, as well as gloves and long sleeves and pants, when installing it (see top photo, opposite). Batts wrapped with perforated plastic or other materials reduce the dust and irritation while still letting moisture through. One brand, Miraflex (Owens Corning), is virtually dust-free.

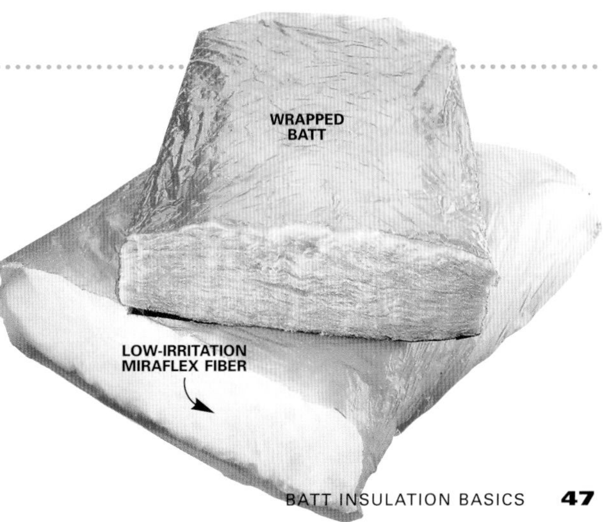

Blowing in wall

Save energy, save money and feel more comfortable

About 65 percent of a home's heat loss occurs through the attic. Insulating and sealing up that, along with caulking around windows and doors, costs far less, saves far more, and is much easier than insulating the walls.

Serious DIYers can buy insulation and rent the blowing machine, but you need special tools and know-how to do the job right—and for a task you'll most likely undertake once in a lifetime, it may not be worth the hassle. Pros can often finish the job in a day. Some larger companies also provide before-and-after infrared pictures of your walls to show they did a complete job.

Installing blown-in insulation creates a huge mess, so most pros prefer to work from the outside. The procedure is to drill 2-1/2-in. holes in each stud cavity, fill the cavity with insulation, then plug the holes with tapered plugs. If the house has its original lap siding or has been re-sided, pros will remove rows of siding, do the work, then reinstall the siding. Some contractors (as in our example) remove a single strip of siding in the middle of each wall, blow the top half of the cavity first (the cellulose will stay put), then blow the bottom half. Others bore holes at the top or both midway and top, then blow insulation down through the holes. Odd-size cavities and spaces below

insulation

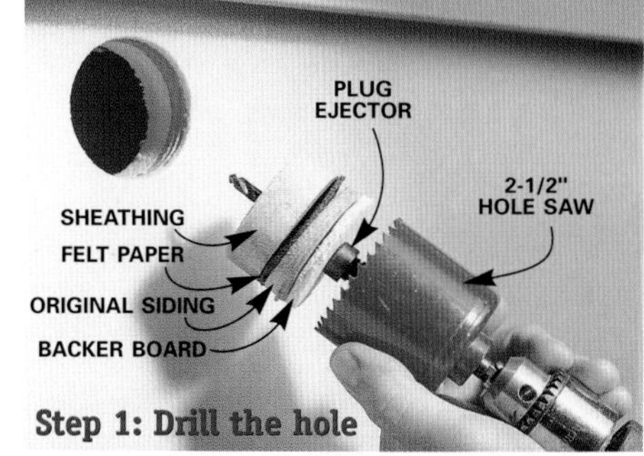

Step 1: Drill the hole

Step 2: Fill the cavity

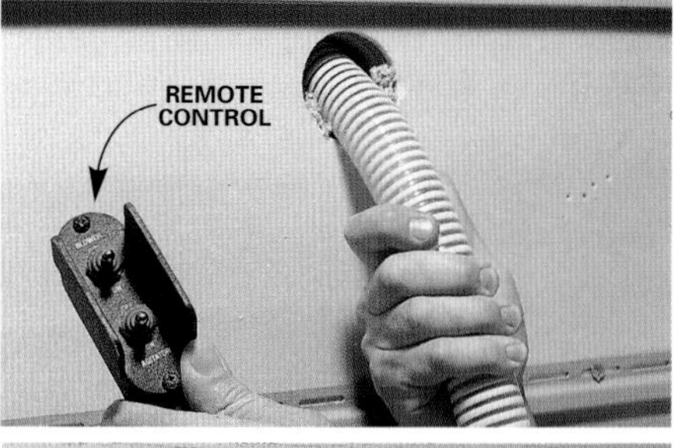

Step 3: Install the plug

CELLULOSE INSULATION

WOOD PLUG

windows should also be insulated, though sometimes it's not cost effective to insulate every little nook and cranny.

Houses with brick exteriors must be insulated from the inside. Stucco homes can be insulated from the outside, but the dozens of plug holes can be an eyesore if the patches don't match perfectly. This is a challenge even for stucco experts. Working from the inside makes sense if the house is vacant or if remodeling is under way and the insulating holes will be painted, wallpapered, drywalled or paneled over.

Cellulose insulation is a popular choice because it's inexpensive, easy to blow, minimally irritating and good for packing around ducts, electrical boxes and wires. Fiberglass, mineral wool and foam insulation are also available.

Is it worth it? Many contractors charge $1 or more per sq. ft. of wall. The $1,500 job that saves $250 yearly on heating and cooling bills has a six-year payback. But there are other payoffs: Your house will be less drafty, the walls will feel warmer, your furnace and air conditioner won't work as hard, and you'll conserve natural resources.

Our advice? Get an energy audit that breaks out how much money each energy improvement will cost you—and save you—then make your decision. Also check with your utility company to see if it offers any special financing or testing programs. *[ALWAYS check your combustion appliances, especially the water heater and furnace, for backdrafting after making any energy improvement.]*

Energy-Saving Goof

Insulation frustration

My wife and I rented an insulation blower to add insulation in our attic. When I got the unit home, I noticed it had remnants of tape on the hose connection. I checked it out, and it seemed to work fine. With my wife feeding bags into the hopper and me up in the attic with the hose, we proceeded to get the nasty job done. Working my way around the attic, I noticed that the hose seemed to be caught, so I gave it a tug. Then nothing was coming out, and finally I heard the machine stop. I squeezed back downstairs to discover the downstairs covered in insulation. After a whole day of cleaning, I figured out what all the tape was for!

The best way to insulate a foundation

Before beginning any work, you must determine whether your basement has any moisture problems. If your foundation walls are only damp on humid summer days, fine—you're good to go with the methods we recommend. But if you have any problems with standing or leaking water in the spring or during heavy rains, you've got some "prework" to do.

Fixes usually are as simple as adding or repairing gutters and downspouts or adjusting the grade to direct runoff water away from the house. But serious water problems may call for drastic measures, like interior or exterior drain tiling, or exterior waterproofing, which could mean digging around the house or tearing up part of the slab. You must solve all water problems or you'll risk boxing future water in behind a finished wall, thereby ruining it. You'll end up spending hundreds of bucks re-remodeling a recently finished lower level.

Just about every carpenter or building inspector has a different opinion on how to finish walls against masonry. The methods we'll demonstrate work well in most conditions, but consult with your building inspector before beginning any work to make sure you're meeting building codes in your area.

There are two methods of finishing against masonry: fiberglass-insulated 2x4 walls and foam-filled 2x2 walls. Both methods include a 3/4-in. foam moisture barrier between the framing and the foundation wall to eliminate condensation from interior humidity and to protect the walls from exterior moisture. Tack the foam to the foundation wall with a few blobs of foam construction adhesive to hold it while you frame the walls.

2x4 framing method

Fast to build; lots of room for wiring and plumbing

Gobbles up 38 sq. ft. of space in a 20 x 36-ft. basement

3" DRYWALL SCREWS

TOP PLATE SCREWED TO CEILING JOISTS

3-1/2" FIBERGLASS

3/4" RIGID INSULATION

2x4

PRESSURE-TREATED 2X4 BOTTOM PLATE

Method 1

Method 1: A conventional wall (R-16)

The easy finishing method is to simply frame conventional 2x4 stud walls with pressure-treated bottom plates (the 2x4s the wall rests on) and fill the walls with fiberglass insulation. Hands down, it's the way to go—if you have oodles of space in the room you're finishing. Two-by-four walls are quick to install, and there's plenty of space for electrical work. Plus, you don't have to hassle with fastening furring strips to concrete, and it's easier to cut fiberglass insulation than to fit foam. The downside is that each wall steals nearly 6 in. of floor space from the perimeter of the room.

Look at the photo above to see the details. Note that the wall is pushed against the foam and then anchored to the slab with concrete screws and to the ceiling with 3-in. drywall screws. Don't install a vapor barrier between the fiberglass and drywall, because moisture will be trapped in the wall.

wall Two options for a warmer, more energy-efficient basement

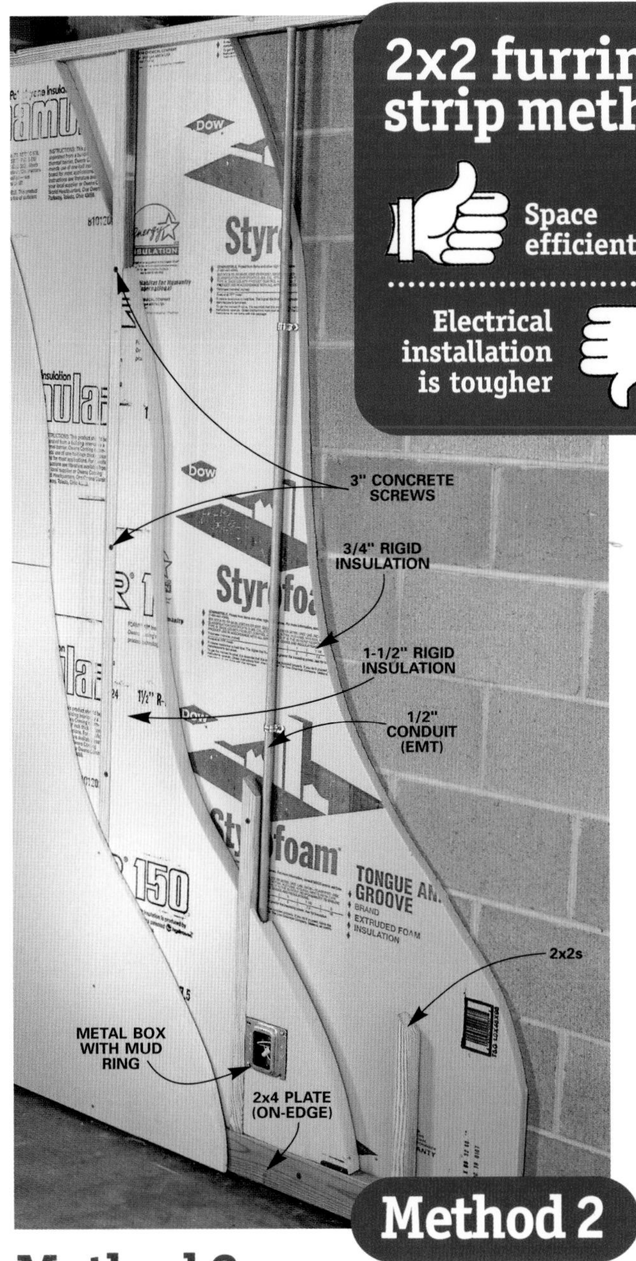

Method 2: 2x2 furring strips and foam (R-12)

To save precious floor space, use a thinner wall composed of 2x2s and foam insulation attached directly to the wall. Nail or screw a 2x2 to the bottom of the floor joists at the top of the wall, and screw a treated 2x4 flat against the bottom of the wall through the foam and into the concrete with 3-in. concrete screws. Then lay out the stud positions on the plates. Screw the treated 2x2s to the wall with three evenly spaced screws and fill in between with foam insulation ripped to fit. Hang the drywall with 1-1/4-in. drywall screws.

The downside is that electrical outlets and switches have special installation requirements. Cables must be at least 1-1/4 in. behind the front of the wood framing to prevent fasteners from accidentally piercing and damaging the cable. Use 1-1/4 in.-deep steel boxes and run cable through EMT (electrical metallic tubing) between the furring strips to the boxes. Boxes and conduit straps are screwed through the foam and into the masonry with 1-1/2-in. concrete screws.

Energy-Saving Q&A

Winterizing crawlspace vents

Q The crawlspace under my house has a vapor barrier and quite a few vents, so I don't have any moisture buildup. But the floor of my house is uninsulated. So, should I close off the crawlspace vents during the winter to save energy? I live in Georgia.

A In the South, where you're located, moisture in the crawlspace is a year-round problem, so the vents should stay open. To save energy, a better solution is to spend the money to add unfaced R-19 insulation between the floor joists. For the occasional freeze, you should also insulate any exposed pipes in the crawlspace.

In states where winters are moderate to hard, winter air tends to be much drier. So, closing crawlspace vents during the winter months is less likely to cause moisture problems and may slightly lower your energy bills. However, the walls of the crawlspace should be insulated (also with R-19), or closing the vents won't make much difference.

AIR
CHUTE
R-13 BATT
INSULATION
RAFTER
BAY
2" R-10
RIGID FOAM
STAPLER

Insulating a finished attic

The BEST way to save energy and headroom

If you need to insulate and ventilate your attic but don't want to lose headroom, use a combination of dense batt insulation, rigid foam sheeting and air chutes.

Most codes require a specified minimum amount of headroom, and it's tough to meet this requirement when insulating a finished attic, especially since most codes require insulation equal to R-38 or more. However, most inspectors we've spoken with will lower the insulation requirement if it means that the finished space won't otherwise have the required headroom. To get the most R-value with the least thickness, use batt insulation with a higher R-value per inch in combination with rigid foam insulation.

Rigid foam sheeting has an R-value ranging from R-5 to R-10 per inch of thickness. This means you can have a combined R-value ranging from R-23 to R-31 with only 5-1/2 in. of combined fiberglass and foam insulation.

RIDGE VENT

CONTINUOUS SOFFIT VENT

AIR ENTERS the soffit vents, travels along the underside of the roof boards, then exits through the ridge vents to maintain a "healthy" roof.

Energy-Saving Hint

Duct tape wristbands

When you're working with fiberglass insulation, tape the cuffs of your long-sleeve shirts to gloves with duct tape. It'll keep the glass fibers from getting under sleeves and irritating your skin. Your wrists will thank you.

To effectively ventilate your roof, create a 1-in. airspace from the soffit to the ridge by installing a continuous air chute in each rafter bay. To install the air chutes, staple them directly to the roof decking.

Air chutes, when combined with soffit vents and a ridge vent, will help prevent problems with condensation and ice dams. They come in 4-ft. lengths and 14-1/2 and 22-1/2-in. widths. They're readily available at home centers and cost 75¢ to $2 apiece.

(Air chutes work only when the rafter spaces run from the soffit to the ridge. This method won't work where rafter spaces stop short, such as in a valley or in the corner of a hip roof.)

Sealing attic air leaks

Sure, it's dusty, dirty work, but it's the quickest, cheapest way to save money on your energy bills

Chances are, your ceiling has the equivalent of a 2-ft.-square hole that's acting like a chimney, drafting expensive heated air into your attic and sucking cold air in around your windows and doors. You can't see the hole because it's the sum of many smaller openings. These gaps around plumbing pipes, light fixtures, chimneys and other attic bypasses are hidden under your insulation.

For less than $100 in materials and a day's labor, you can save lots of money on heating every year by sealing these holes. We'll show you where to find the bypasses in your attic and simple techniques for plugging and sealing them.

You'll find everything you need at any full-service hardware store, home center or lumberyard. If you can't find the reflective foil insulation (Photo 3, p. 56), substitute drywall or pieces cut from 4 x 8-ft. sheets of rigid foil-faced insulation. Fitting rigid material requires more precise measuring, but the result is the same.

1 Get your bearings from below

Before you crawl into the attic, make a quick sketch of the floor plan. Make note of dropped soffits over kitchen cabinets or bath vanities, slanted ceilings over stairways, and any other dropped-ceiling areas. These areas usually have open stud cavities leading directly into the attic that are huge sources of air leaks (Photos 1 – 3, p. 56). Locate the main plumbing stack, furnace flue or chimney and note this on your sketch for a reference point once you get into the attic.

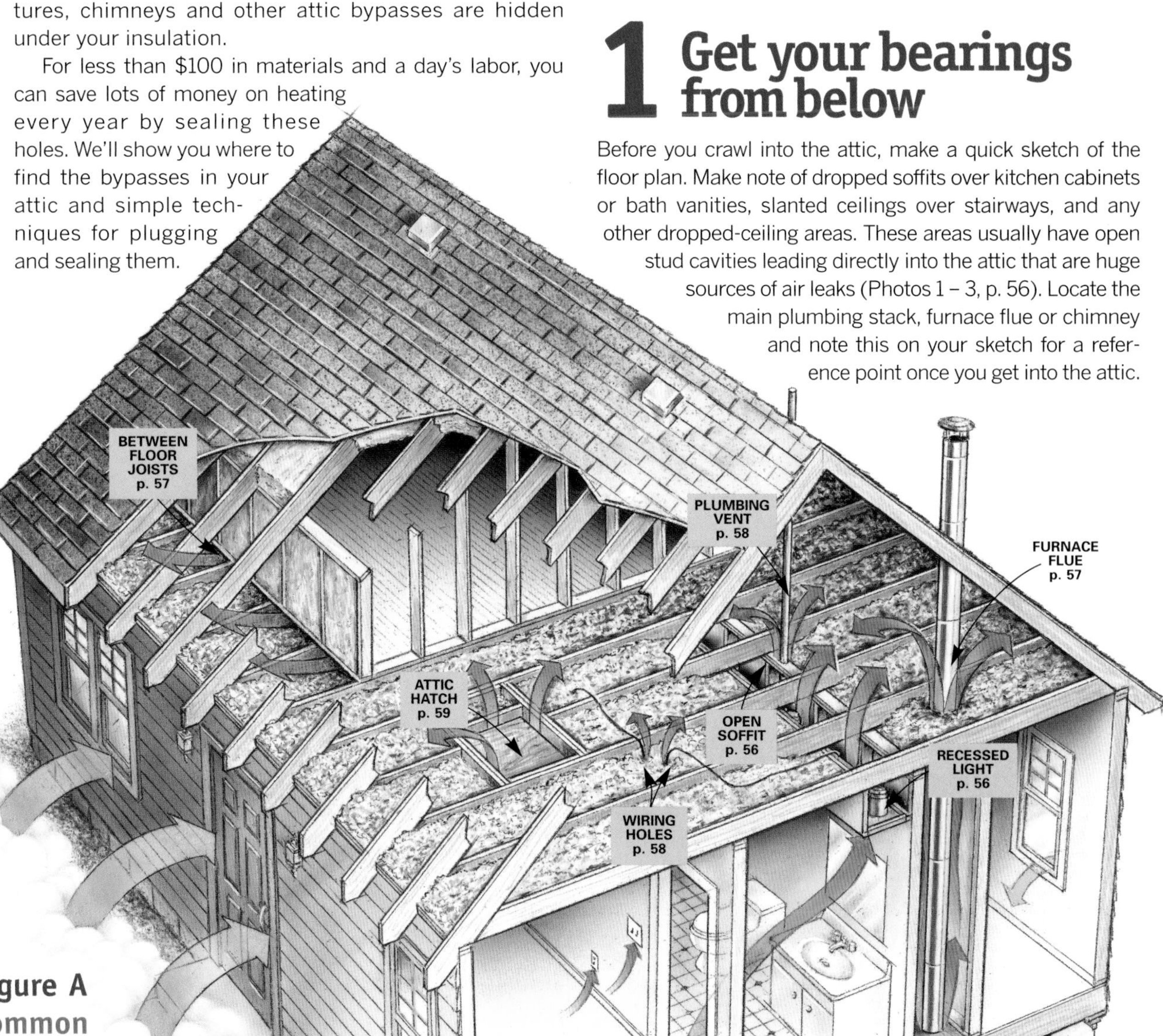

Figure A Common attic air leaks

2 Pressurize your house

Before you crawl into the attic, place a box fan in a window so it's blowing air into the house and close all the remaining windows and doors. Tape cardboard around the fan to cover large gaps. When you turn the fan on high, the house will be pressurized, like an inflated balloon. And just as you can feel the air from a leaky balloon, you'll be able to confirm leaks in the attic by feeling the draft with your hand. You may even be able to locate bypasses visually by looking for insulation being blown about. Close the attic access door or hatch behind you to maximize the effect.

Gather your supplies and suit up. Attics are miserable places to work. Be sure to read the tips on p. 58 before you start.

3 Plug the big holes first

It's tempting to grab a can of expanding foam and squirt it into all the little holes, but your biggest savings will come from plugging the large holes. Find the plumbing stack or flue for a reference point. Then use your sketch to locate the soffits, stairwells or other dropped-ceiling areas. You'll probably have to dig around in the insulation to uncover them. Soffits may be filled with insulation or covered with cardboard or fiberglass batts. Push back the insulation and scoop it out of the soffits. Now plug the open stud spaces (Photos 1 and 2) and seal the top of the cavities with reflective foil (Photo 3). Cover the area with insulation again when you're done.

Caution:
Some attics have vermiculite insulation, which may contain asbestos, a health hazard. Vermiculite is a lightweight, pea-size, flaky gray mineral. Don't disturb vermiculite insulation unless you've had it tested by an approved lab to be sure it doesn't contain asbestos. Contact your local health department for the name of an approved lab.

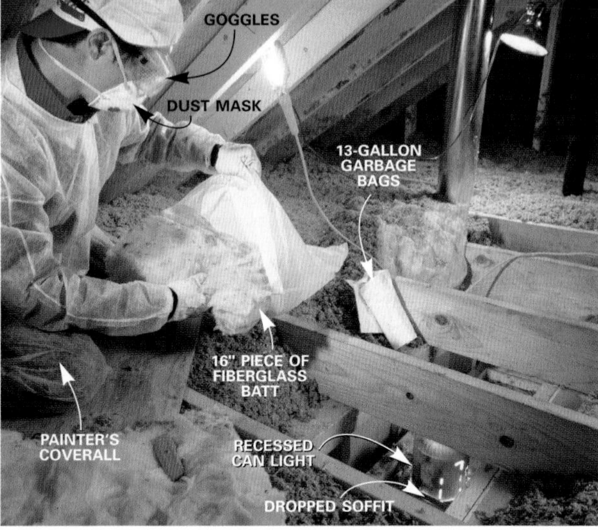

1 CUT a 16-in.-long piece from a batt of unfaced fiberglass insulation and fold it at the bottom of a 13-gallon plastic garbage bag.

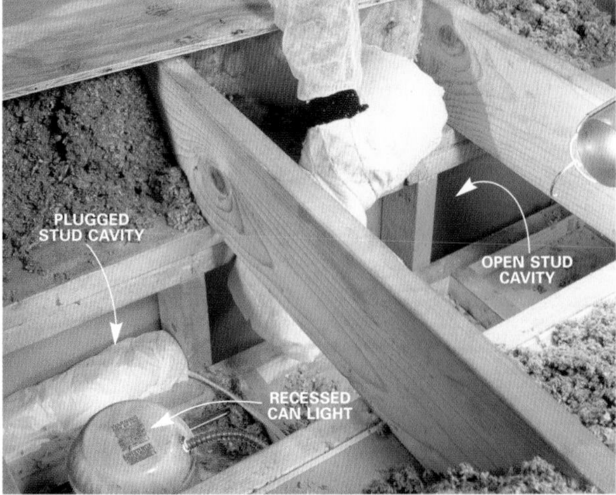

2 FOLD the bag over once and stuff it into the open stud cavity. Make sure there's enough insulation in the bag to form a tight fit in the cavity.

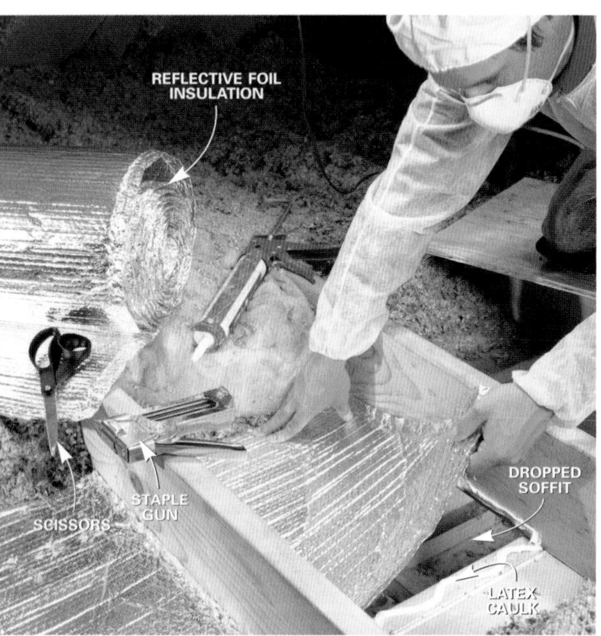

3 WITH a scissors, cut a length of foil insulation about 6 in. longer than the opening to be covered. Apply a bead of latex caulk around the opening. Embed the foil in the caulk and staple it in place.

4 Stuffed bags seal joist spaces too

Heated rooms built into attics often have open cavities in the floor framing under the walls. Even though insulation may be piled against or stuffed into these spaces, they can still leak air. Photo 4 shows how to stuff these spaces with the same type of garbage-bag plug we used to seal stud cavities.

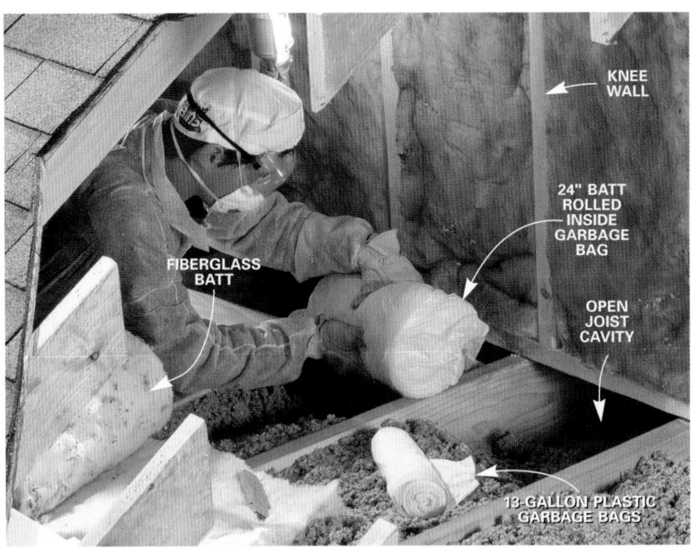

4 PLUG all open joist spaces under insulated side walls. Cut a 24-in.-long piece from a batt of fiberglass insulation and place it at the bottom of a 13-gallon plastic garbage bag. Fold the bag over and stuff it into the joist space under the wall.

5 CUT aluminum flashing to fit around the flue. For round flues like ours, cut half circles out of two pieces so they overlap about 3 in. in the middle. Press the flashing metal into a bead of latex caulk and staple it into place. If there's no wood, staple it right to the drywall.

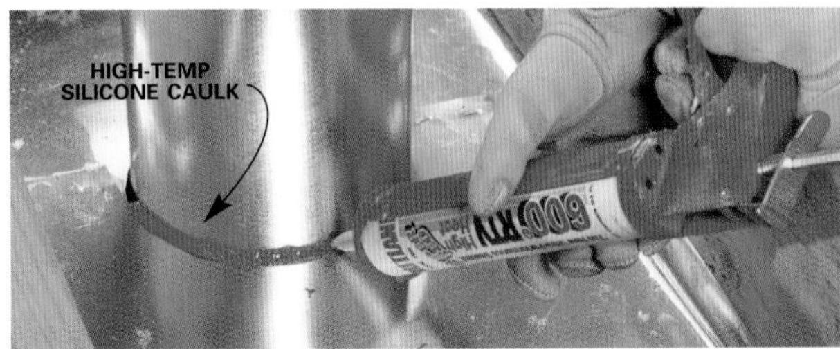

6 SEAL the gap between the flue and metal flashing with special high-temperature silicone caulk. Don't use spray foam here.

5 Furnace flues require special techniques

The opening around a furnace or water heater flue is a major source of warm air into the attic (Photo 5). Because the pipe gets hot, building codes require 1 in. of clearance from Class B flues (2 in. from masonry chimneys) to any combustible material, including insulation. Photos 5 and 6 show how to seal this gap with lightweight aluminum flashing and special high-temperature silicone caulk ($12 per tube). Before you push the insulation back into place, build a metal dam (Photo 7) to keep it away from the pipe. Use this same technique for masonry chimneys.

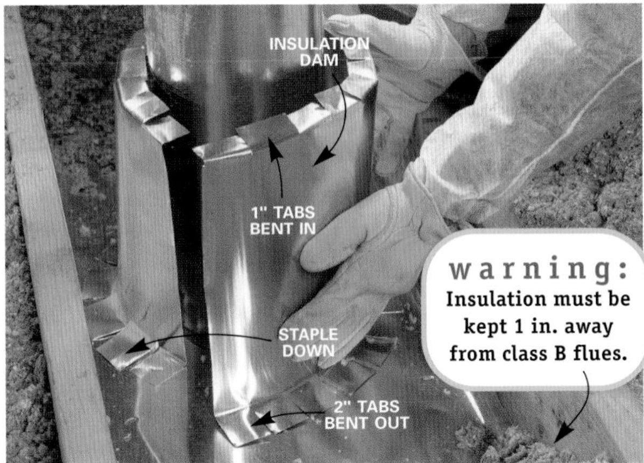

7 FORM an insulation dam to prevent insulation from contacting the flue pipe. Cut enough aluminum from the coil to wrap around the flue plus 6 in. Cut slots 1 in. deep and a few inches apart along the top and bend the tabs in. Cut slots about 2 in. deep along the bottom and bend out the tabs. Wrap the dam around the flue and secure the bottom by stapling through the tabs.

6 Use foam and caulk to seal small holes

Seal openings around plumbing vents and electrical wires with expanding foam (Photos 8 and 9). Be careful, though; this stuff is super sticky and almost impossible to get off your clothes and skin. Wear disposable gloves and eye protection. Seal around electrical boxes with caulk (Photo 9).

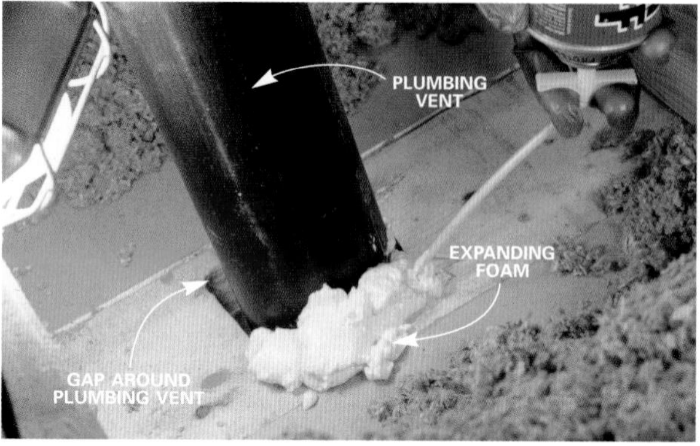

8 **STUFF a small piece of fiberglass batt insulation into the space around the plumbing vent pipe as a backer for the expanding foam. Then follow the directions on the can to fill the space around the pipe with expanding foam insulation.**

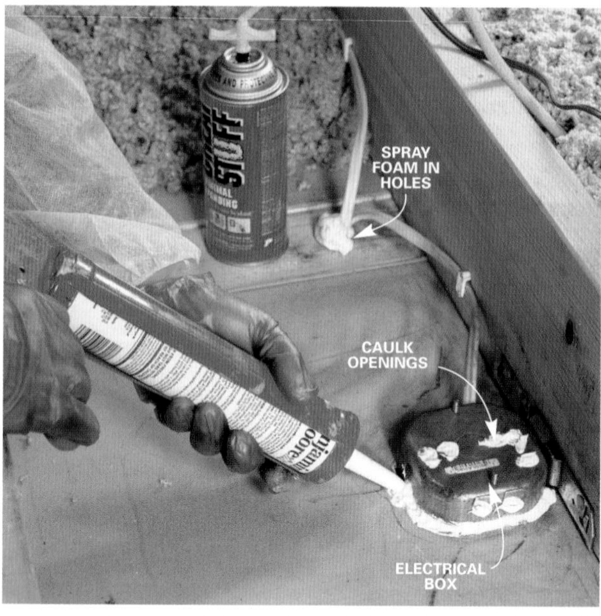

9 **FILL wiring and plumbing holes with expanding foam. Caulk around electrical junction boxes and fill holes in the box with caulk.**

tip Telltale signs–finding attic bypasses

Even though most of the gaps spilling warm air into your attic are buried in insulation, you'll still see evidence of the escaping air. While in your attic, look for areas where the insulation is darkened (see photo), a result of filtering dusty air from the house. In cold weather, you may see frosty areas in the insulation caused by warm, moist air condensing and freezing as it hits the cold attic air. In warmer weather, you'll find water staining in these same areas. If you pressurize the house with a window fan (see "Pressurize your house," p. 56), you may be able to feel the leaks with your hand as the air finds its way into the attic.

Materials checklist

- Roll of reflective foil insulation
- Bundle or roll of unfaced fiberglass batt insulation
- Acrylic latex caulk
- Special high-temperature silicone caulk
- Roll of 14-in.-wide aluminum flashing
- Roll of 13-gallon plastic garbage bags
- Can of expanding spray foam insulation

Tips for working in the attic

- Start in the morning when it's cool. Pick a cool, cloudy day if possible. Don't spend more than 15 or 20 minutes in a hot attic.
- Wear a lightweight disposable coverall (available in paint departments), gloves and a hat to keep itchy insulation off your clothes and skin.
- Always wear a double-strap dust mask or an OSHA-approved particulate respirator.
- Wear knee pads if you have them. Crawling around on joists gets painful. Use scraps of plywood to kneel on and as a platform for your supplies.
- Buy a rough-service lightbulb ($2.50) and a clamp-on light ($6), both available at hardware stores. Have a flashlight handy just in case.
- Minimize trips in and out of the attic by collecting all of your tools and supplies and placing them in the attic before you go up.
- Look out where you step. You must walk on ceiling joists or truss chords and carry a small piece of plywood to work from. Don't step on the ceiling drywall.

10 **WEATHERSTRIP the attic access hatch or door. Cut 1x3 boards to fit the perimeter of the opening and nail them on with 6d finish nails. Apply self-adhesive foam weatherstrip tape to the top edge of the stop.**

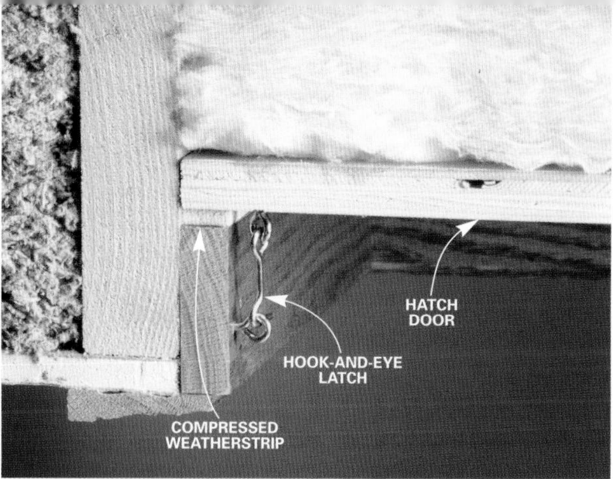

11 **ATTACH hook-and-eye fasteners to the door and stops. Position the eyes so that the weatherstrip is compressed when you latch the hooks.**

7 Complete the job by sealing the hatch

When you're done sealing your attic bypasses, push the insulation back into place with an old broom handle or stick as you back out of the attic. Then finish up by sealing the access hatch with self-sticking foam weatherstrip (Photos 10 and 11). If your hatch rests directly on the moldings like ours did, add 2-1/2-in.-wide stops around the opening. The stops provide a wider surface for attaching the weatherstrip and a space to mount hook-and-eye fasteners. Position the screw eyes so the weatherstrip is slightly compressed when the hooks are latched.

Check for backdrafting

Whenever you make energy improvements—like sealing attic bypasses—that result in a tighter house, install carbon monoxide (CO) alarms if you don't already have them. Allow one per floor. Also have a pro check your combustion appliances for backdrafting at the next servicing.

Recessed can lights—no easy solution

Cut a 6-in. hole in your ceiling and add a 100-watt bulb—enough heat to bake cookies—and you have a recipe for huge heat loss as well as a major contributor to ice dams. That's what a recessed light does. Here are the solutions we recommend if you have recessed can lights protruding into your attic:

- Replace incandescent bulbs with cooler-operating compact fluorescent bulbs.
- Replace your old recessed lights with new airtight models available at some home centers and lighting stores. This is the best solution for those with electrical skills. New cans are relatively inexpensive—about $20 apiece plus decorative trim and bulb—and can usually be installed in a few hours each.

Energy-Saving Goof

Insulation surprise attack

After moving into our new/old house, I decided to add 6 in. of insulation to our attic. Our attic is accessed through a small closet (36 x 30 in.) with a 30 x 14-in. opening at the top. I figured the best way to insulate the attic and keep the mess of fiberglass insulation out of the house would be to squeeze the tightly packaged rolls through the closet opening and open them in the attic.

Intending to pull them up after me, I climbed into the attic and proceeded to pull on the first roll of insulation. I found out very quickly that it wasn't going to fit. So rather than getting down from the attic, I decided to reach down and cut the plastic wrapping with the roll sitting on the closet shelf and pull up the pieces individually.

The roll exploded open and engulfed the small closet with insulation, leaving me trapped in the attic. (Attics sure are quiet and HOT.) The insulation was so tightly bound in the closet that I couldn't push it out of the closet or pull it up. I finally had to use a utility knife to cut the insulation into smaller pieces so I could make my itchy, scratchy escape!

Saving Energy:

Just as tuning up your car will help you save at the gas pump, tuning up your furnace or boiler and fireplace before winter will help you save on your monthly utility bill. Some tasks—like tuning up your furnace or boiler—can be complex enough to require professional help. But there are simple steps anyone can take. Just replacing the dirty filter on your forced-air furnace can reduce your gas or electric bill by 10 percent. Sealing up leaky air ducts can reduce it by another 10 percent. And installing (and actually using) a $50 setback thermostat can save you hundreds of dollars over the course of a winter.

Don't overlook the obvious. Make sure the glass panels of your storm windows and storm doors are shut tight. Keep south-facing shades open during the day to harvest free solar heat. Make sure your fireplace damper is closed when not in use. And when it does come time to replace that old 60 percent-efficient furnace or boiler, look into one of the high-efficiency units available; some of the newer, ENERGY STAR-qualified furnaces and boilers are 90 percent or more efficient.

3 Heating Season

Warm up a cold room

16 common problems & 16 (sometimes) simple solutions

Bugged by a chilly room in the winter? If you have to wear an extra pair of heavy socks in the family room or huddle under the covers at night, you're not alone. A chilly room is as common as, well, a common cold.

It's not always easy or cheap, but there's always a way to chase those chills. Here you'll find the causes (Figure A) and the solutions (Figure B, p. 65). Plus, you'll discover the least expensive options, what you can do yourself and when to call in a heating expert. The focus here is on homes with forced-air heating systems—that is, homes with blowers and ductwork. However, many of these solutions will work in homes heated by other systems.

Problems in the duct system

Obstructions. It may seem obvious, but you might have forgotten that you closed the register during the cooling season (**1**). Embarrassing! But more often the culprit is at the furnace in the form of a clogged filter or dirty air-conditioning coil that's blocking the airflow (**2**). It's easy to change the filter, but you can't clean the coil yourself, and on many furnaces you can't see it well enough to tell if it's dirty. Rely on professional service every year or two to detect a dirty coil.

Sofas, desks and chairs as well as drapes can block the airflow at registers (**3**). Plastic deflectors or registers with different "throw" patterns aren't always attractive, but they offer partial solutions. Or move the furniture; it's simpler than moving the register.

Sometimes construction debris falls into the ducts, and the builders forget to fish it out (**4**). Unscrew the register and look down with a flashlight, or reach into the duct with a gloved hand to retrieve anything you can feel. With any luck, it won't have fur or feathers!

Badly balanced dampers. Every duct system is supposed to have dampers to balance the heat flow to each room (**5**). In fact, some systems require that you adjust the dampers twice a year, when you go from

Figure A Common causes of cold rooms

Energy-Saving Goof

Insulation inflation

My husband and I bought a big bundle of insulation to insulate our shop. The huge bundle was actually five bundles wrapped together. I could barely lift it into the truck, so we decided to cut the bundle and load the individual bundles one at a time onto the truck bed. As soon as we cut it, it expanded to about four times its original size, much too large to fit into the truck. We had to buy some rope and spend a half hour wrestling the stuff into a manageable size.

PROBLEMS

1. Closed register
2. Furnace filter or air-conditioning coil dirty and clogged
3. Drapes and furniture block heat flow
4. Clogged ducts
5. Dampers closed down
6. Thermostat located in a warm area
7. Duct has too many bends or is too small
8. No cool-air return
9. Drafty windows
10. Addition has many windows
11. Poor attic or wall insulation
12. Cold floor over crawlspace
13. Cold basement
14. No air chutes or poorly installed chutes
15. Heat loss due to leaks
16. Uninsulated floor

air-conditioning mode to the heating mode and back again. Look for the dampers near the main trunk lines. Contractors usually label the correct position. But not always. Open the damper farther for the duct serving the cold room. Unfortunately, dampers are often covered during remodeling, or hidden under insulation in the attic. You might have to call in a heating contractor to help out.

"Hot" thermostat. If the thermostat area heats up fast, it'll shut off the furnace before other rooms warm up (**6**). Close nearby registers to lessen the warm airflow near the thermostat, and adjust the register louvers in other rooms to help balance the heat flow. A $3 room thermometer is handy for comparing temperatures from room to room.

Bad duct design. Design problems can include too many bends in a run (**7**) and inadequate cool-air returns (**8**). While Figure B suggests design solutions, be sure to consult a heating contractor for advice on the best methods and materials. But go through the rest of this list first. You might find a simpler, less expensive solution.

Bad windows

Leaky, inefficient windows are notorious heat drains, especially in older homes (**9**). Stop drafts with caulk and weatherstripping and add heavy drapes if necessary. Replacing worn-out windows with new, energy-efficient windows often solves the cold room problem.

But even good windows can't always make up for the heat loss in a room with a lot of glass (**10**). For these rooms, you may have to consider additional ducts, or an additional heater with a separate thermostat. Both are expensive and require the advice of a heating pro.

Bad insulation

Finding out you have poor insulation is frustrating, because insulation was easy to install when your house was built, but it's difficult and expensive to add it now (**11**). Attic insulation is an exception. If your attic has 6 in. or less, add at least another 6 in. of fiberglass or cellulose to warm up cold rooms directly below. Other exceptions include crawlspace or floor insulation for cold floors over a crawlspace (**12**), and rim joist insulation for basements (**13**).

While you're up in your attic, make sure you have vent chutes and that they're properly positioned (**14**). Cold air blowing through the insulation can chill the ceiling of the room below.

Insulation installers often fail to close up ceiling gaps, and warm air leaks out (**15**). Seal areas around light

Figure B Ways to warm up a cold room

Quick tip

FEEL WARMER WITH HIGHER HUMIDITY. By increasing the amount of humidity in your home during the colder seasons, you'll feel warmer. Additional interior moisture can make a room set at 68 degrees F feel 5 to 8 degrees warmer.

fixtures, plumbing pipes, ducts and other gaps into attics with caulk or expanding foam. Usually you can reach these only from the attic.

Bad mixing & cold slabs

Without good mixing, warm air rises and cool air falls, chilling your feet, especially in rooms with tall ceilings and on uninsulated concrete floors (**16**). If the airflow from the registers doesn't do the job, slow-moving ceiling fans can get the warm air down to the floor where you need it.

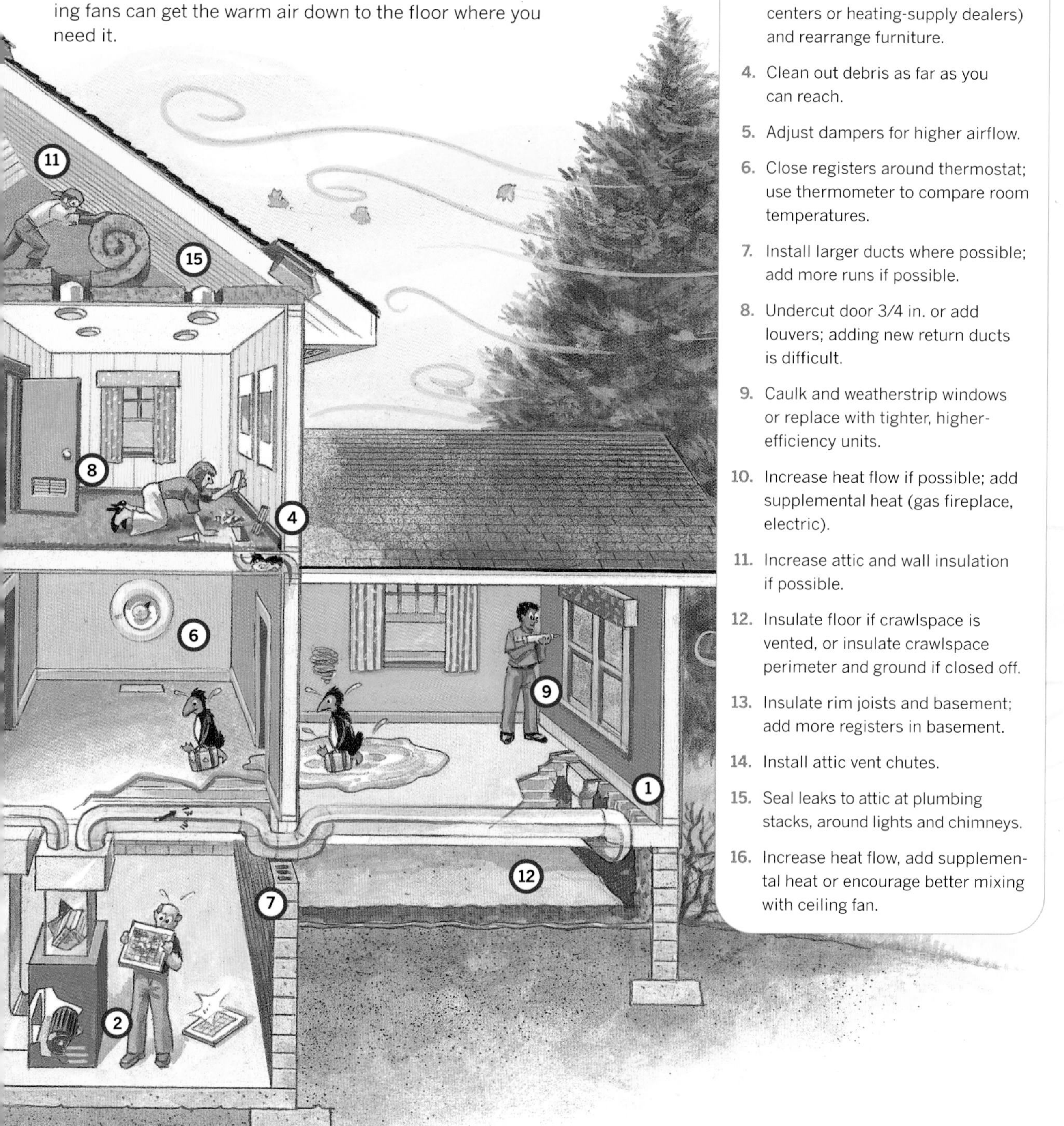

SOLUTIONS

1. Open the register.
2. Change furnace filter and check for dirty air-conditioning coil with flashlight; call a pro to clean the coil.
3. Add plastic deflector ($5 at home centers or heating-supply dealers) and rearrange furniture.
4. Clean out debris as far as you can reach.
5. Adjust dampers for higher airflow.
6. Close registers around thermostat; use thermometer to compare room temperatures.
7. Install larger ducts where possible; add more runs if possible.
8. Undercut door 3/4 in. or add louvers; adding new return ducts is difficult.
9. Caulk and weatherstrip windows or replace with tighter, higher-efficiency units.
10. Increase heat flow if possible; add supplemental heat (gas fireplace, electric).
11. Increase attic and wall insulation if possible.
12. Insulate floor if crawlspace is vented, or insulate crawlspace perimeter and ground if closed off.
13. Insulate rim joists and basement; add more registers in basement.
14. Install attic vent chutes.
15. Seal leaks to attic at plumbing stacks, around lights and chimneys.
16. Increase heat flow, add supplemental heat or encourage better mixing with ceiling fan.

Save energy with a programmable

Invest $75 now and save hundreds

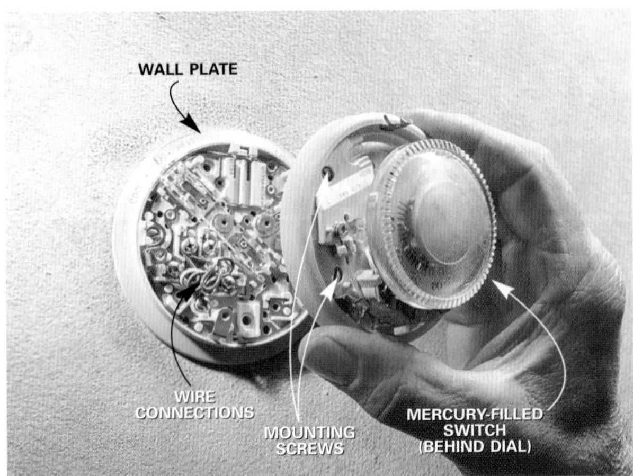

1 TURN OFF power to heating/cooling systems at the main panel. Mark wires with a tab (or tape) and letter that represents the terminal; unscrew them. Remove and discard the old thermostat.

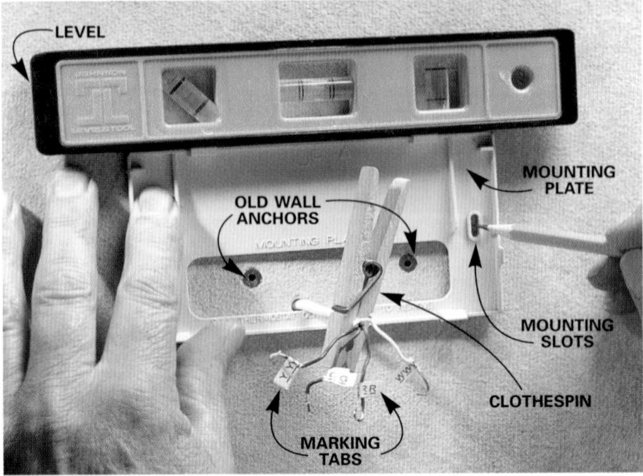

2 LEVEL the new mounting plate in position and mark the mounting screw holes. Drill 3/16-in. holes, insert drywall anchors and screw the plate to the wall.

You can reduce your home's heating and cooling costs by about 15 percent with a programmable thermostat. It automatically keeps the temperature at a comfortable level when you're home, but switches to an energy-saving level when you're away or asleep. Programmable thermostats are available from home centers and hardware stores for $25 to $100. The higher-priced models provide more programming options.

Programmable thermostats will work with most gas or oil furnaces, and central air conditioners. However, heat pumps, electric baseboards and a few other systems require special features. Read the package to make sure the programmable thermostat you buy is compatible with your heating and cooling system. If you're unsure, call your local utility or a heating and cooling contractor listed in your yellow pages.

Quick tip

PROGRAMMABLE THERMOSTAT OPTIONS. When shopping for a programmable thermostat, select one with the options that are right for you. Some contain a time-to-change-the-filter light or low-battery indicator. Others have keypad lock features to prevent tampering, or contain mechanisms that automatically reset your temperature settings when moving between heating and cooling seasons.

Energy-Saving Q&A

Setback thermostats save money

Q We've always used a setback thermostat to lower the temperature at night and during the day while we're gone. My son-in-law says we're not saving anything, claiming the amount of energy used to reheat the house is far greater than if we left the thermostat set at a constant temperature. Who's right?

A You're right. Your son-in-law holds a common misconception, which has been dispelled by years of research and numerous studies. The fuel required to reheat a building to a comfortable temperature is roughly equal to the fuel saved as the building temperature drops to the lower setting. You save fuel between the time that the temperature stabilizes at the lower level and the next time the heat is needed. So, the longer your house remains at the lower temperature, the more energy you save.

Studies show you can cut costs by as much as 20 percent by lowering your thermostat 5 degrees F at night and 10 degrees during the day when no one is home. The same goes for raising the temperatures by that same amount when using air-conditioning in warmer climates.

thermostat
in the years to come

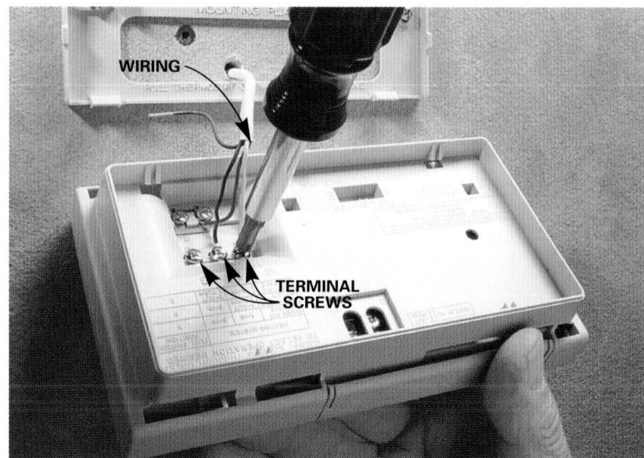

3 SCREW wiring to terminals on new thermostat using labels as reference (strip wires back if needed). Hook wires up to same terminals on new thermostat. Snap thermostat to mounting plate.

Quick tip

DON'T USE DUCT TAPE ON DUCTS. Studies have shown that cloth-backed duct tape is one of the worst materials you can use for sealing leaky ducts; it degrades quickly. Use aluminum tape, mastic or other adhesive specially approved for sealing ducts.

Remove the old thermostat as shown in Photo 1. If your old thermostat contains mercury, you'll see a small glass tube with a shiny silver ball inside. Mercury is toxic. Take this type of thermostat to a hazardous-waste disposal site.

There will be anywhere from two to five wires hooked up to the old thermostat. Label the thermostat wiring with marking tabs using the letters on the old screw terminals as reference. If your new thermostat doesn't come with marking tabs, use masking tape.

Clip a clothespin to the cable so it doesn't slide down inside the wall cavity, and mount the new wall plate (Photo 2). If the thermostat has back-up batteries, insert them before wiring the new thermostat (Photo 3).

The thermostat may need to be configured to your heating system. It may come preprogrammed, but to maximize savings, set it up according to your schedule. Consult the instructions that come with the thermostat for system adjustments and programming. You won't save energy if the thermostat isn't programmed correctly.

Energy-Saving Q&A

Duct tape: not for ducts

Q What's the best way to seal leaks in my ductwork? Duct tape seems to deteriorate pretty quickly.

A It's one of those goofy ironies that duct tape really doesn't work well on ducts. In fact, the Model Energy Code bans the use of duct tape for sealing ducts. Instead, use the aluminum tape you'll find with the vents and ducting at home centers. This tape, which costs about $20 for a large roll, works on most ductwork connections as long as the metal is fairly clean.

Aluminum tape won't work where a round trunk line connects to rectangular ductwork. For these joints, use either pure silicone ($3 to $4 a tube) or a sealant specifically designed for ducts.

Aluminum tape for straight seams

Silicone for curved seams

Fall furnace tune-up

Simple maintenance pays big dividends for comfort, efficiency and safety

1 FLIP the electrical power switch to OFF. Remove the combustion chamber door by lifting up and pulling it out, and remove the burner cover (if you have one). It's usually held in place by two screws.

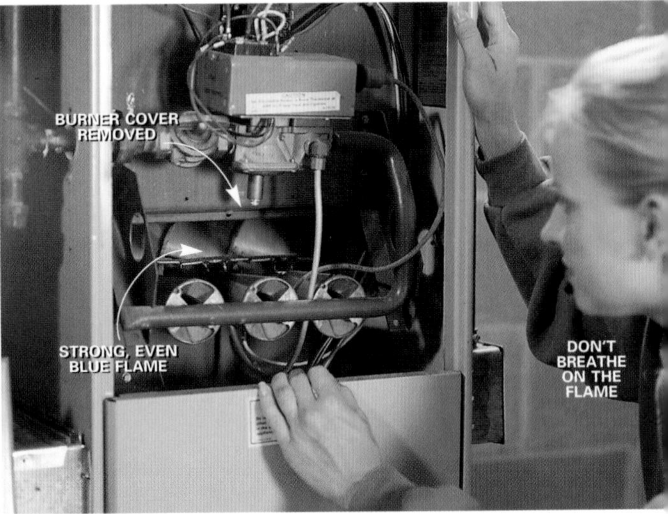

2 TURN the power switch on and activate the burners by turning up your thermostat. Inspect the burner flames. The flames should be fairly even and blue. Yellow flames indicate dirty burners. (Don't breathe on the flames because the extra oxygen will also make them turn yellow.) Don't adjust the burners yourself. Call in a pro.

When it comes to furnaces, an ounce of prevention truly is worth a pound of cure. To help you avert the hassle of your furnace dying or simply not putting out enough heat—just when you need it most—we'll walk you through a series of simple steps that will keep it in tip-top shape. The entire maintenance operation takes less than three hours and costs only a few dollars—pretty cheap insurance.

Here, the focus is on natural gas and propane-fueled furnaces. The maintenance tasks involving the blower chamber also apply to oil furnaces; however, oil furnace combustion chambers are very different and should only be worked on by professionals.

(Heat pumps, on the other hand, work more like a central air conditioner than like a furnace, so we won't deal with them here.)

Routine furnace maintenance and cleaning don't require special skills. If you're handy with a few basic

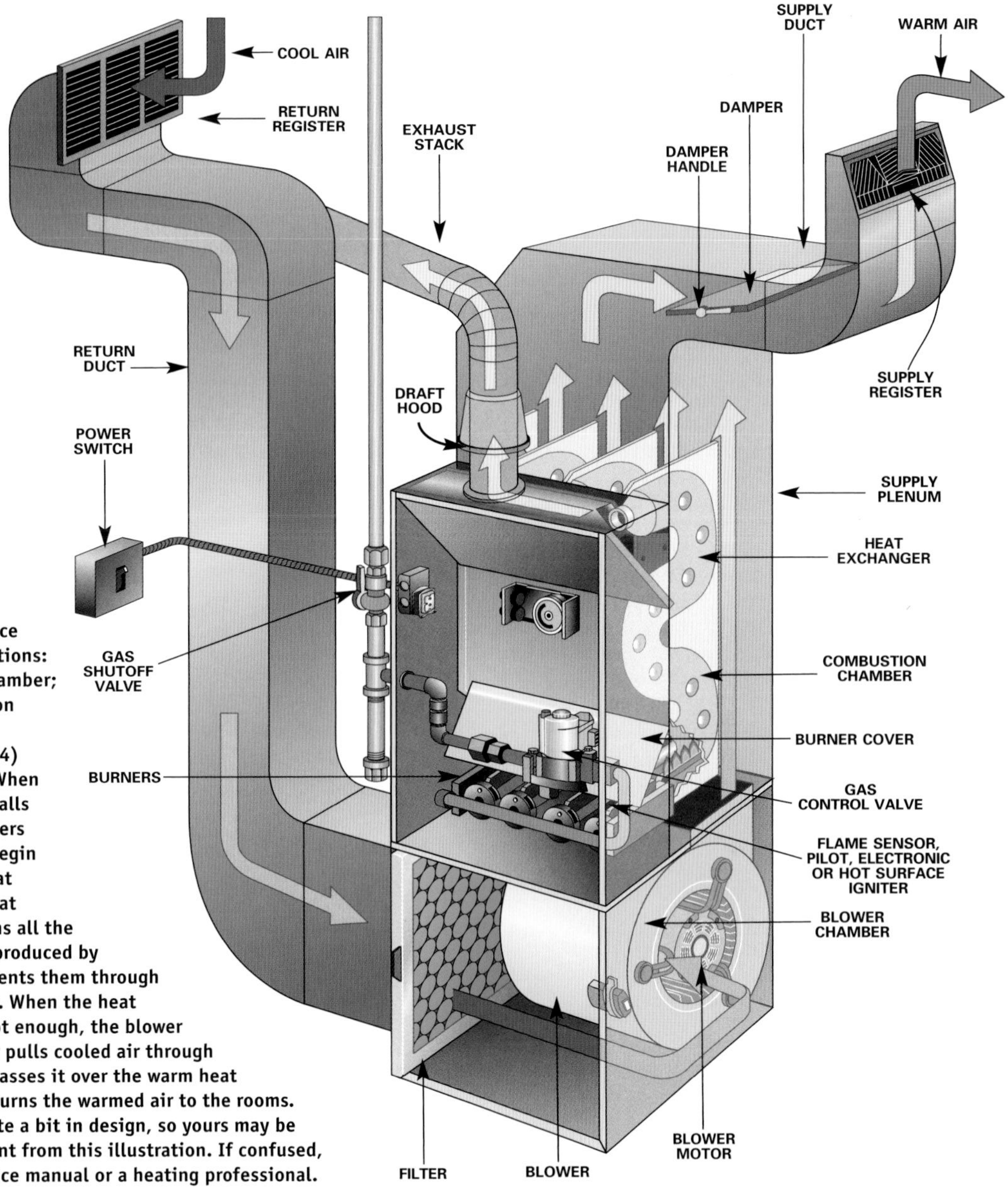

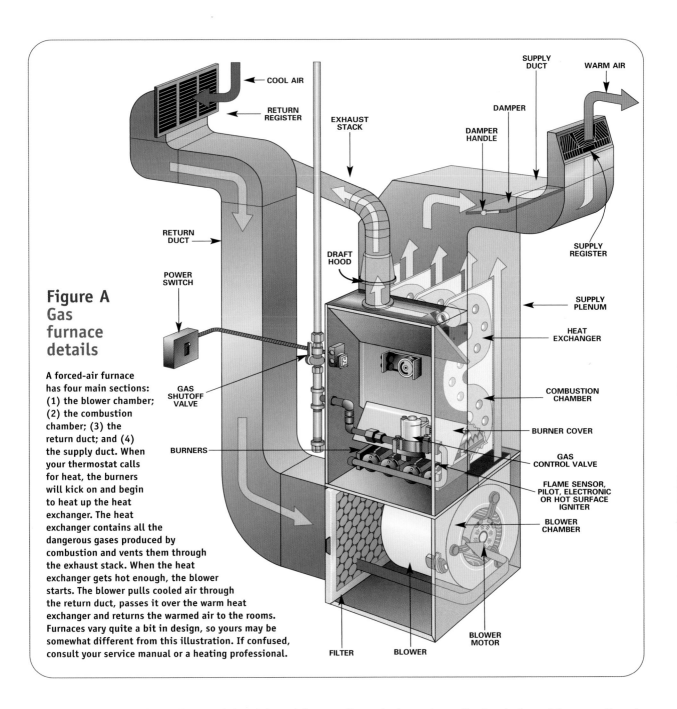

COOL AIR
RETURN REGISTER
EXHAUST STACK
SUPPLY DUCT
WARM AIR
DAMPER
DAMPER HANDLE
RETURN DUCT
DRAFT HOOD
SUPPLY REGISTER
POWER SWITCH
SUPPLY PLENUM
HEAT EXCHANGER
GAS SHUTOFF VALVE
COMBUSTION CHAMBER
BURNER COVER
BURNERS
GAS CONTROL VALVE
FLAME SENSOR, PILOT, ELECTRONIC OR HOT SURFACE IGNITER
BLOWER CHAMBER
BLOWER MOTOR
FILTER
BLOWER

Figure A Gas furnace details

A forced-air furnace has four main sections: (1) the blower chamber; (2) the combustion chamber; (3) the return duct; and (4) the supply duct. When your thermostat calls for heat, the burners will kick on and begin to heat up the heat exchanger. The heat exchanger contains all the dangerous gases produced by combustion and vents them through the exhaust stack. When the heat exchanger gets hot enough, the blower starts. The blower pulls cooled air through the return duct, passes it over the warm heat exchanger and returns the warmed air to the rooms. Furnaces vary quite a bit in design, so yours may be somewhat different from this illustration. If confused, consult your service manual or a heating professional.

hand tools, you can do it. You won't be doing tricky or potentially dangerous stuff like adjusting the gas burners. Leave that for a pro. See "Symptoms That Call for a Heating Professional," p. 72, for more details.

We should warn you that your furnace may look somewhat different than the one we show here. If you don't feel confident about taking some of the steps shown, skip them. And pay close attention to the safety precautions in this article, in your furnace service manual (if you can find it!) and posted on your furnace.

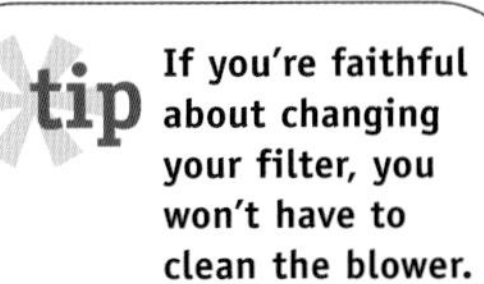

If you're faithful about changing your filter, you won't have to clean the blower.

Even if you follow our maintenance steps, call in a heating professional for a thorough furnace checkup at least every three years. (Look under "Heating" in your yellow pages.)

3 **TURN OFF** the power switch again and shut off the gas by giving the valve a one-quarter turn (see Figure A for approximate gas shutoff valve location). Vacuum the burners and the furnace base. To get at the back of the burners, tape a 20-in. length of 1/2-in. drain line to your vacuum hose. Vacuum everywhere you see dust. While everything is open, use a flashlight to look for signs of soot (fine black powder), which often indicates poor combustion (see Symptom 5, p. 72). Lift off the lower door (blower door) and vacuum the blower compartment.

4 **REMOVE** the blower (also called a squirrel cage) in order to clean it. If you have a control panel in front of the blower, two screws will loosen it and you can let it hang. Next, using a 7/16-in. socket and ratchet, remove the two bolts that hold the blower in place, then gently lift it out.

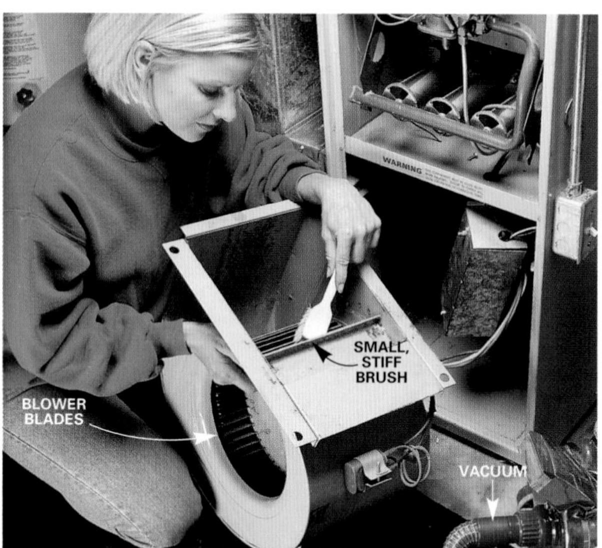

5 **CLEAN** the blower blades thoroughly with a vacuum and small brush. Take care not to stress the wiring or disturb the counterweights that will be on the fan blades. If you can't clean the blower thoroughly, don't clean it at all; you could throw it off balance.

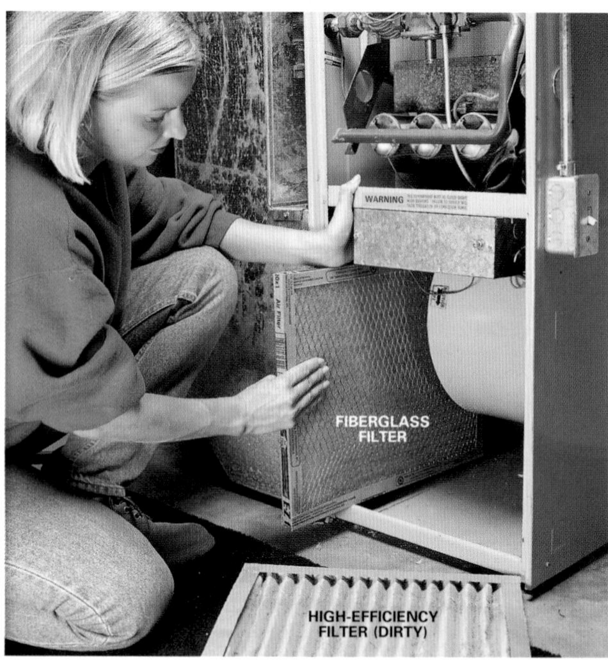

6 **CHANGE** the furnace filter every one to three months. A $1 fiberglass filter will adequately protect the blower and blower motor. If you want to install a more expensive, high-efficiency filter, check the owner's manual for the manufacturer recommendations. High-efficiency filters can restrict the airflow, strain the blower motor and make your furnace less efficient. If you want cleaner air, the best option is a separate air-cleaning system.

Carbon monoxide alarm

INSTALL A CARBON MONOXIDE ALARM on each floor. If you already have these alarms, test them. Carbon monoxide is an odorless, colorless gas sometimes produced by oil-, gas- and wood-burning appliances (furnaces, stoves, fireplaces, etc.). If this gas spills into your home in high enough concentrations, it can be fatal. Plug carbon monoxide alarms into electrical outlets or directly wire them to the electrical system. They cost about $40. Do not install them in utility rooms, garages, kitchens or bathrooms.

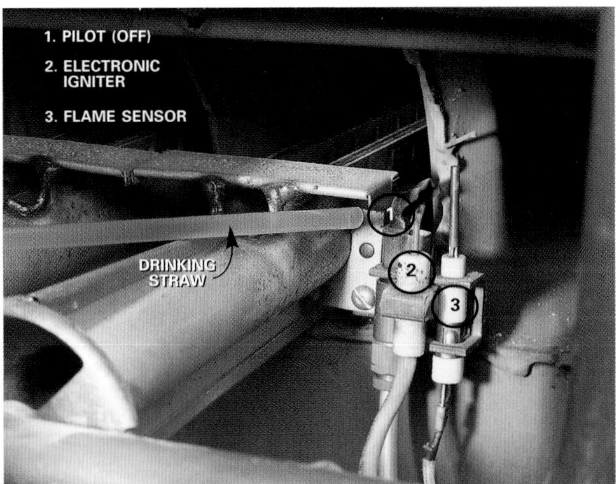

7 BLOW dust off the pilot. Direct air to the exact spot by blowing through a drinking straw. A dirty pilot can cause the flame sensor (or thermocouple) to get a false reading that the pilot isn't lit. Some newer furnaces have hot surface igniters instead of pilots and electronic igniters (Photo 9). (Note: One burner was removed for clarity.)

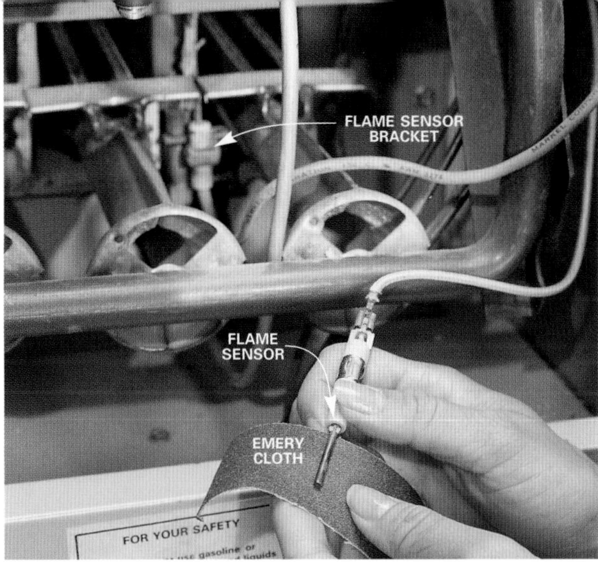

8 THE FLAME SENSOR occasionally becomes coated with residue and will prevent your furnace from lighting. Remove it by pulling it down out of its bracket. Lightly clean the surface with fine emery cloth and slip the sensor back into its bracket.

Caution:

While working on your furnace, do not remove burners, stick anything into the pilot orifice or make adjustments. Misaligned burners can pose a serious hazard by allowing gas to build up before the burner ignites, causing a flash fire. Poking a sharp object into a pilot can widen the orifice, turning the pilot into a flamethrower.

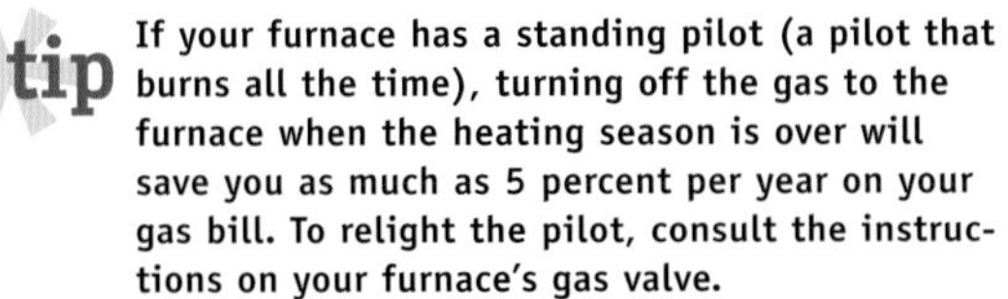

tip If your furnace has a standing pilot (a pilot that burns all the time), turning off the gas to the furnace when the heating season is over will save you as much as 5 percent per year on your gas bill. To relight the pilot, consult the instructions on your furnace's gas valve.

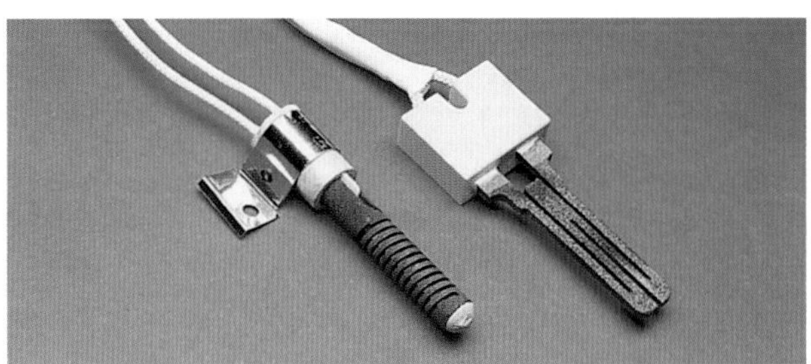

9 HOT SURFACE IGNITERS are the most common ignition system on furnaces being manufactured today. They take the place of standing pilot lights and electronic igniters. Clean the dust off the hot surface igniter by leaving the igniter in place and blowing air through a straw. This part breaks very easily; don't even touch it. In fact, when you replace the furnace doors, do so gently to avoid breaking the igniter.

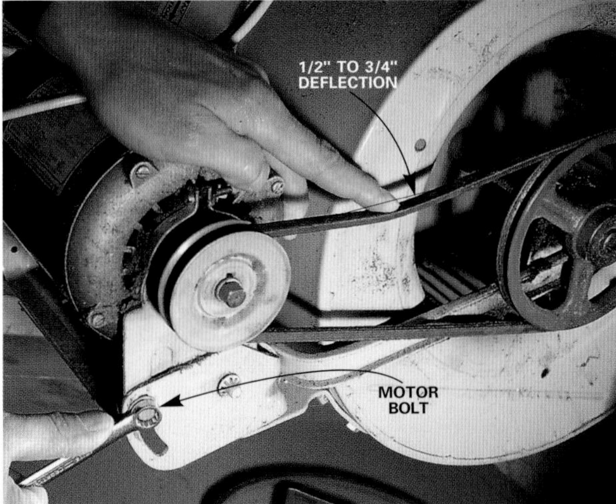

10 THE BELTS on belt-driven blowers need occasional adjustment or replacement. Inspect the drive belt for cracks or frayed areas. A new belt costs about $5. When you install the new belt, tension it so it deflects 1/2 to 3/4 in.

11 SOME OLDER FURNACES have two motor bearings and two blower shaft bearings that require annual oiling. Clean around the oil caps and remove the caps. Apply two to three drops of lightweight machine oil and replace the caps. Don't overlubricate!

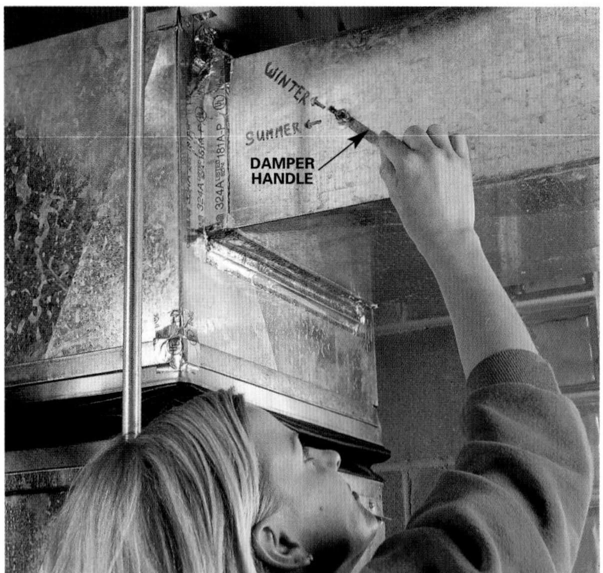

12 **IF YOUR FURNACE heating ducts also serve as air-conditioning ducts, they may have dampers that require adjusting for seasonal changes. The seasonal settings should be marked. Two-story homes often have separate supply trunks to serve the upstairs and downstairs. To send more warm air downstairs (winter setting) or more cold air upstairs (summer setting), adjust the damper handle on each supply trunk.**

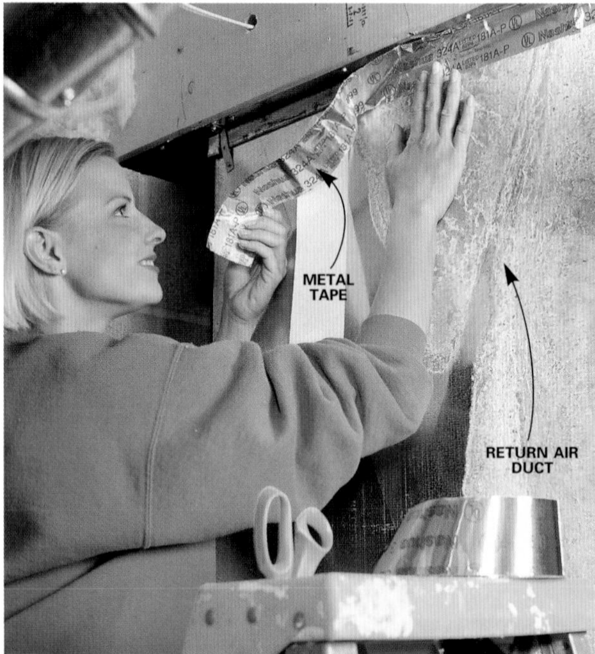

13 **SEAL leaky ducts, especially return-air ducts, with special metal tape (available at home centers for $12) or high-temperature silicone. Then conduct the following backdrafting test to make sure the combustion gases go up the flue: Adjust the thermostat so the burners come on. Hold a smoking stick of incense beside the draft hood (Photo 14). The smoke should be drawn into the hood. Also inspect the exhaust vent pipes on your furnace and water heater (while they're cool). White powdery residue can indicate corrosion. Gently squeeze the exhaust stack with your hand. It should be firm but slightly flexible. Call a heating professional or plumber to fix all these types of problems.**

Symptoms that call for a heating professional

Symptom 1: Short cycling

When your furnace runs for only short periods (less than three minutes) before shutting off, the problem is called short cycling. This happens when the thermostat is out of adjustment or when the heat exchanger overheats and the burner automatically shuts off to prevent damage.

Symptom 2: Irregular flame

Properly functioning burners have fairly even rows of flames. If the flames are uneven or lean toward the back of the furnace, call in a pro. It could be a sign of dirty burners or a cracked heat exchanger.

Symptom 3: Odd noises or rumbling

While rumbling and popping aren't cause for concern in a hot water or steam heating system, they shouldn't be present if you have forced-air heat.

Symptom 4: Chronic illness

Frequent headaches or flulike symptoms can be a sign of combustion gases leaking from a cracked heat exchanger or carbon monoxide leaking from an exhaust stack. With these symptoms, have your heating system checked out even if your carbon monoxide alarm remains silent.

Symptom 5: Soot deposits

Soot is a fine black powder that collects when combustion is incomplete. Its presence may indicate that your burners need adjusting or that you have a cracked heat exchanger that needs replacing.

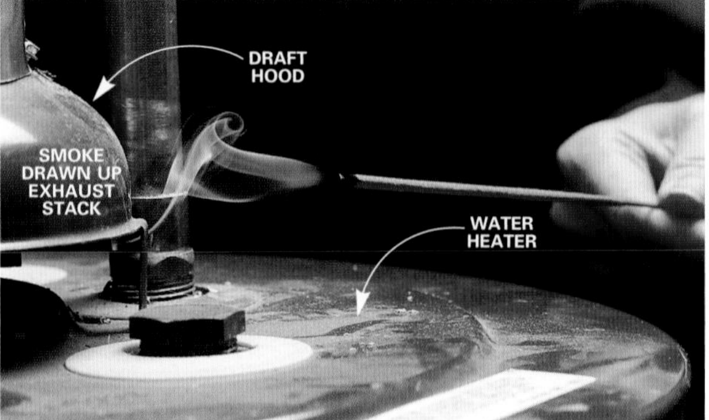

14 **TEST your gas water heater for backdrafting while your furnace is off. Turn up the water heater thermostat until the water heater burner comes on. After a minute or more, hold a smoking stick of incense or match up to the exhaust stack. The smoke should be pulled into the stack. Conduct the test with all exterior doors and windows closed and bath and kitchen fans running. If the vent doesn't draw, call in a heating specialist or plumber to find the problem. Turn the thermostat back down.**

Cheap vs. expensive furnace filters

When you purchase higher-cost filters, you're getting a filter that requires less changing and captures more, and smaller, particles. The $1 woven fiberglass filters do one thing—screen out dirt and debris that could damage your furnace blower motor, though they do take out some pollen and mold spores. If you can remember to swap them out every month and air quality isn't an issue, these will do the job.

But if you're the kind of person who forgets to change the oil in your car, buy $4 pleated filters, which require changing only every three months. If you stretched out the accordion-like material in these filters, you'd find two, three or four times the amount of surface area. This means they can capture smaller particles for longer periods of time without impeding the airflow of your furnace.

If members of your household smoke or have allergies or asthma, or if you have pets, look into the more expensive, high-efficiency electrostatic filters—ones that both filter and magnetically attract contaminants. Some are effective for up to a year. They can filter out bacteria, dander, odors and smoke particles. But health experts warn that you may be wasting your money on these $20 to $40 filters unless you take the following steps: Use them in conjunction with a high-efficiency vacuum cleaner, install a dedicated air purifier, wash or vacuum the filter monthly and take other steps to clean up your air and house as well.

Many filters carry a MERV (minimum efficiency reporting value) rating, which indicates their effectiveness. The higher the MERV rating, the more effective. Most spun filters have a MERV rating of 4. Standard pleated filters average MERV 6. Electrostatic pleated versions start at MERV 8, with the highest quality ones hitting MERV 12.

Bleed a hot-water radiator

If some fins on your radiator stay cold while others are hot, don't despair! The only thing that's clogging your hot-water radiator is trapped air, and getting rid of it is simple. At the top or bottom of your radiator, look for a small valve like the one shown. Use a radiator key, 1/4-in. 12-point socket, or a flat screwdriver (depending on your valve type) and slowly turn the valve counterclockwise until water starts dripping out. This will release trapped air and let hot water into the cold fins. While you're at it, you should repeat the process with your other radiators.

Bleeding the radiators will lower the pressure in your system, so you might have to slowly add water to increase the pressure. Do this by opening, then closing, the valve on the water pipe above the boiler. In fact, you may need to add water while bleeding the radiator in order to purge the air from the system. This is where a helper will save on trips up and down the stairs. If you're unfamiliar with your system, call a pro.

How much pressure you need depends on how high the water has to rise. The basic rule is 1 lb. of pressure for every 2 ft. of rise. Your gauge may read in pounds, feet or both. A basic two-story house, with the boiler and expansion tank in the basement, needs 12 to 15 lbs., or 25 to 30 ft., of pressure.

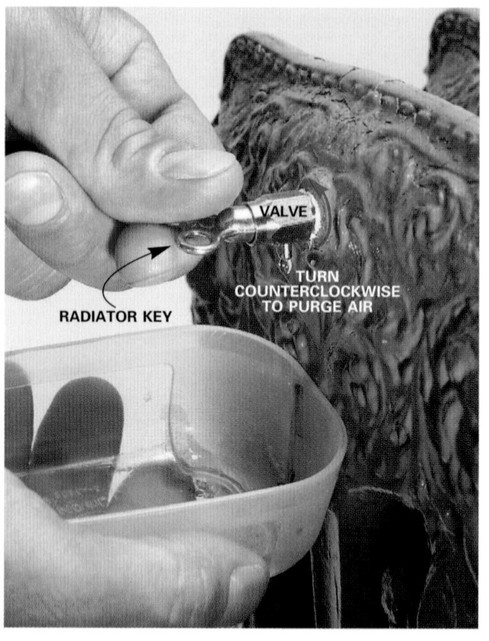

Clear a steam-radiator vent

Don't confuse a hot-water system with a steam system. Steam radiators have an air vent, like the one shown, about halfway down the side. Unfortunately, many of these air vents get painted over, plugging the air hole. Clear the air hole in the top of the vent with a small wire or a sewing needle. If you're still worried about the air vents working, consult a hot-water/steam-heat specialist. Replacing these vents costs $16 to $20 per radiator.

Flip a Switch, Save $200

Look for simple solutions first

A furnace can be intimidating—especially when it's not working. However, there is good news from furnace repair pros. Roughly a quarter of all service calls could be avoided with easy fixes that cost little or nothing.

Here, you'll learn about the common culprits and what to do about them.

> **Caution:**
> **Always turn off the shutoff switch (see No. 2 on p. 77) and turn the thermostat off or all the way down before changing the filter or working on the thermostat or furnace.**

8 quick furnace fixes you can do yourself

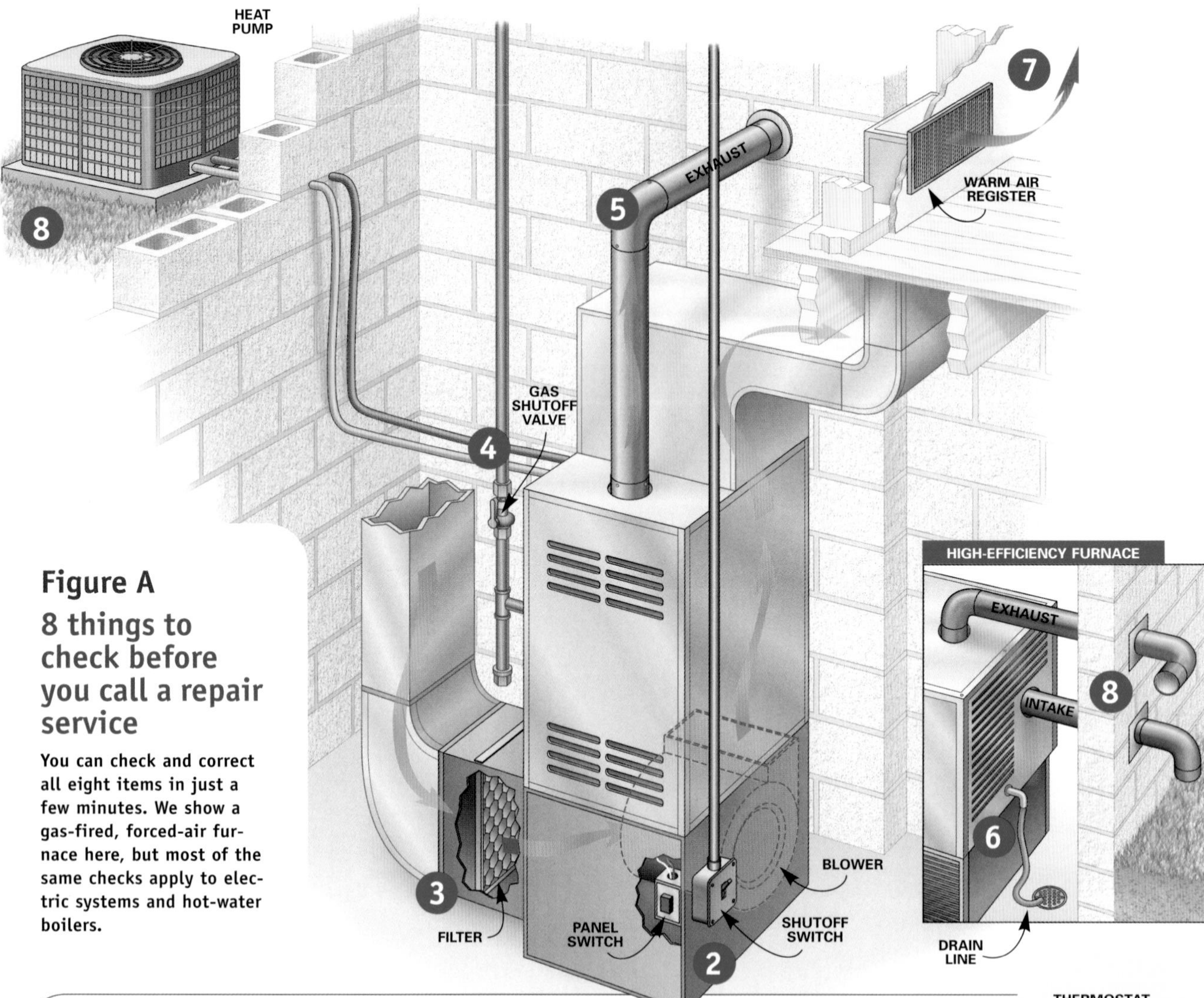

Figure A

8 things to check before you call a repair service

You can check and correct all eight items in just a few minutes. We show a gas-fired, forced-air furnace here, but most of the same checks apply to electric systems and hot-water boilers.

1 Check the thermostat to make sure it's on

THERMOSTAT

Before you assume you have a furnace problem, check the thermostat to make sure it's actually telling the furnace to turn on. Thermostats, especially programmable ones, can be complicated, and the more options a thermostat has, the more that can go wrong.

- Make sure the switch is on "Heat" rather than on "Cool."
- Check the temperature setting.
- Compare the temperature setting to the room temperature. Set the temperature five degrees higher than the room temperature and see if the furnace kicks on.
- Make sure the program is displaying the right day and time, as well as A.M. and P.M. settings.

> **tip** **Lost your owner's manual? Most major-brand manuals are listed on the Web—just go to the manufacturer's Web site.**

- Trace the thermostat wires back to the furnace to check for breaks, especially if you've done any remodeling recently. If you find a break in one of the thin wires, splice the line back together and wrap it with electrical tape.
- Replace the battery. If you have a power outage with a dead battery, you'll lose your settings and the thermostat will revert to the default program.
- Open the thermostat and gently blow out any dust or debris. Make sure it's level and firmly attached on the wall, and that none of the wires coming into it are loose.
- If you can't make the program settings work, you can bypass them altogether. Simply punch in the temperature you want with the up/down control and then press the "Hold" button. That will switch on the furnace if the thermostat programming is the problem.

2 Check shutoff switches and breakers

It sounds unbelievable, but furnace technicians often find that the only "repair" a furnace needs is to be turned on. Look for a standard wall switch on or near the furnace—all furnaces, no matter what age or type, have one somewhere. Check the circuit breaker or fuse for the furnace as well. Make sure the front panel covering the blower motor is securely fastened—there's a push-in switch under it that must be fully depressed for the furnace to operate.

3 Change filters

Dirty filters are the most common cause of furnace problems. Dust and dirt restrict airflow—and if the filter gets too clogged, the heat exchanger will overheat and shut off too quickly, and your house won't warm up. If the blower is running but no heat is coming out, replace the filter. A dirty filter also causes soot buildup on the heat exchanger, reducing the efficiency of the furnace and shortening its life.

The owner's manual shows where the filter is and how to remove it. Change inexpensive flat filters at least once a month. Make sure that the arrow points toward the furnace. Inspect pleated filters once a month. Hold them up to the light, and if you can't see the light clearly through them, replace them. Manufacturers say pleated filters are good for three months, but change them more frequently if you have pets, kids or generate lots of dust.

NEW FURNACE FILTERS

4 Make sure the gas is on

Just as with switches, someone may have turned off a gas valve and then forgotten to turn it back on. Trace the gas line back from the furnace to the meter, and if you see a handle that's perpendicular to the gas pipe, turn it so it's parallel.

If you have an old furnace or boiler, you may have a pilot light. Remove the front panel and the burner cover and check to make sure it's lit.

5 Make sure the chimney exhaust flue is clear

Drawn by the warmth, birds sometimes fall into the chimney exhaust flue. Turn the furnace off and the thermostat all the way down, then dismantle the duct where it exits the furnace and check for debris. Be sure to reassemble the sections in the same order and direction that you took them out.

6 Flush out drain lines

High-efficiency furnaces can drain off several gallons of water a day in heating season. If the drain lines become restricted by sediment or mold growth, the furnace will shut down. If the drain hose looks dirty, remove the hose, fill it with a mixture of bleach and water (25 percent bleach), then flush it after several minutes.

7 Look for blocked or leaky ducts that can restrict airflow

If your furnace comes on but one or two rooms are cold, first make sure all the room registers are open. Then examine any ductwork you can get access to and look for gaps between sections or branching points. Seal any gaps between sections of duct with special metal duct tape. Don't use standard cloth duct tape—it quickly deteriorates, and it may also cause ducts to leak if it was used to seal sections in the past.

Also check for handles protruding from the ductwork. These are dampers or air-conditioner bypasses—make sure they're open.

8 Clean away leaves and debris from heat pumps or intake and exhaust vents

If you have a furnace that vents out the side of the house, make sure nothing is blocking the intake or exhaust. If either of the pipes is covered with screen mesh (like window screen), replace it with 1/2-in.-mesh hardware cloth. If ice is clogging one of the pipes, you have a bigger problem somewhere in the system. Clear it off and call a technician to find out why it's happening.

If you have a heat pump, clear away grass and leaves from the fins of the outdoor compressor unit. Before heating season starts, hose it down gently from the top to rinse dirt and debris out of the housing.

Warming up fireplaces

Dampers, glass fronts, inserts & "good habits" make for better efficiency

Many people have a love-hate relationship with their fireplace. There are an estimated 35 million fireplaces in the United States, which means nearly 1 billion fireplace fires burn each year. Most of your neighbors have fireplaces. And if your home lacked a fireplace and you installed one, you'd recoup more than 75 percent of your investment at resale.

All of this, despite the fact that your fireplace is by far the least efficient piece of equipment in your home; 90 percent of the heat it creates goes—literally—up the chimney. It pulls four to 10 times more air out of a room than what's required to keep the fire going. Even when the fireplace is not operating, the chimney sucks warm air from your home. Furthermore, the smoke from your fireplace contains methane, carcinogens, carbon monoxide and other toxic gases. When conditions aren't right, the fireplace backdrafts, sending that sooty smoke into your house, blackening a wall and stinking up the place for days. Plus you have to cut, split, haul and store all that wood.

Still, you wouldn't give up your fireplace for anything. Why this twisted love affair?

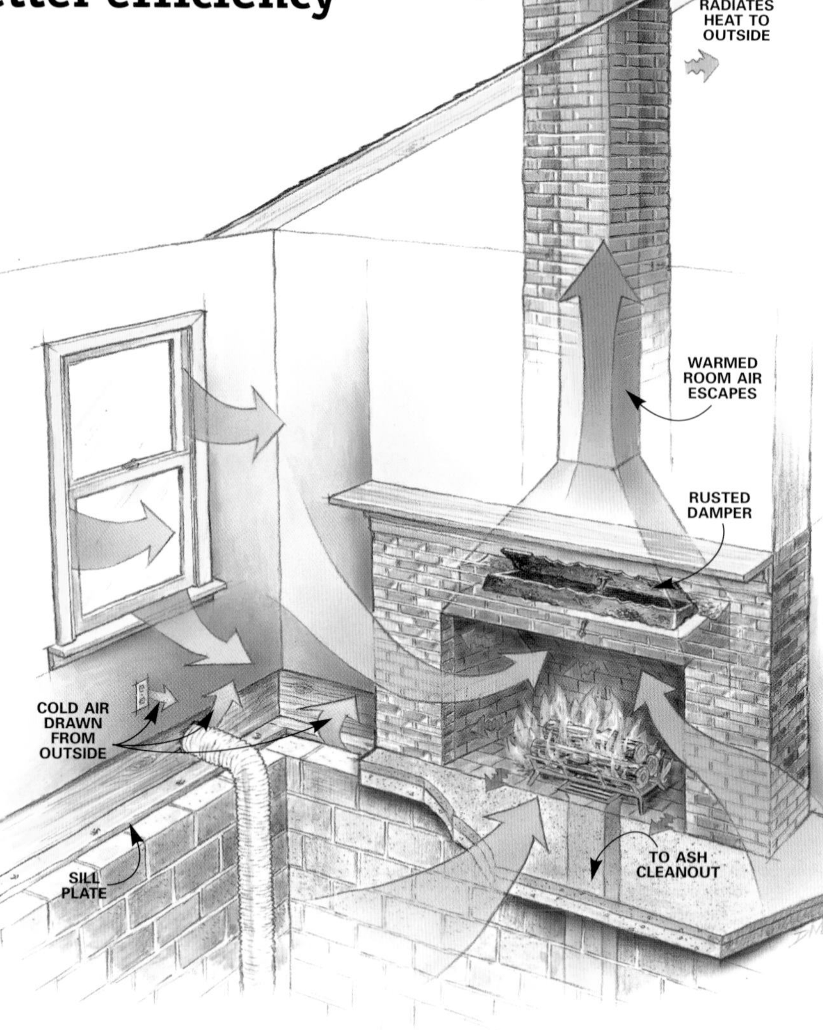

Figure A Standard masonry fireplace

Fireplaces provide "heat highways" for the warm air of your home to escape. When the fire is burning, cold air drawn in from around windows, doors, vents and outlets is heated and then propelled up and out the chimney. When not in use, rusted or loose-fitting dampers still allow warm air to escape.

Quick tip

CLOSE THAT DAMPER. Keep the flue damper tightly closed when the fireplace isn't in use. An open damper is an open escape path for warm air—whether it's generated by your fireplace or furnace.

A brief history of the fireplace

By the 1200s, fireplaces roughly resembling yours were being built. These fireplaces, grossly inefficient, would warm the front sides of those huddled about them—while their back sides and the rest of the room froze.

Despite the fireplace's crucial role in both cooking and heating, improvements came slowly. In the 1400s, firebacks—metal sheets that reflected heat back into the room—came into use. In the 1600s, metal doors were added to prevent room air from escaping up the chimney, baffles for circulating heated air into the room were experimented with, and coal came into use. In the early 1700s, someone by the name of Count Rumford designed a fireplace with a sloping back, angled sides and an improved chimney that greatly increased efficiency. Still, in the mid-1700s Ben Franklin bemoaned, "In common chimneys the strongest heat from the fire, which is upwards, goes directly up the chimney and is lost—five-sixths of the heat is wasted."

And truth be told, your 20th-century masonry fireplace still burns at about the same efficiency as one built 200 years ago.

Why are fireplaces such losers?

Let's look at what happens when you fire up your fireplace on a winter night that's a brisk 10 degrees F.

Place crumpled newspaper, kindling and logs on the grate. As you open the damper, heavy, cold outside air pushes its way down the chimney and into the room—creating a reverse draft. You light the newspaper and stand back. One of two things may happen: The fire could create a strong enough updraft and pull smoke up the chimney. But not only is your house built fairly tight, your daughter is cooking in the kitchen with the range hood on, your son just finished a shower and left the bath fan running; and the gas furnace and water heater are sucking up air for combustion. There's simply not enough air to go around, and the house becomes a vacuum. The fireplace loses this air tug-of-war, and smoke is pulled into the room. You crack a window to let in more air. (If your house was built in the '70s or later, building codes require a fresh-air intake for combustion air to the fireplace.)

Eventually a strong draft is created. Your fire begins pulling and exhausting air from the surrounding room at a rate of about 450 cubic feet per minute. The house, still unable to provide enough air, sucks in air from around windows and doors, through dryer vents and electrical outlets and along sill plates. This 10-degree-F outside air mixes with heated room air, is drawn past the fire, and then is exhausted up the chimney.

When the fire is well established, you—if you remember—will close that open window and partially shut the damper to slow the rate of burn. Now is when your fire will burn most efficiently, returning a whopping 20 percent of the heat it generates back into the room. However, if you place a spark screen in front of the opening, this number will drop to about 12 percent.

As the fire dies down, you turn in for the night. As you sleep, the dying fire generates little heat—but the draft up the chimney creates a virtual freeway for heated house air to escape. The net result? You reached your main objective of spending a comfy hour or two reading in front of the fire. But all in all, the fire drew more heat out of your house than it generated. A working knowledge of why your fireplace performs so poorly offers clues as to how to make it perform better.

Good fire-building habits

You can improve the efficiency of your fireplace by simply improving your habits. You should burn hot, blazing fires because the combustion of wood and gases is more complete and the fire and surrounding bricks radiate more heat more efficiently. You should also get rid of your raised grate and use good old-fashioned andirons. These metal stands allow the burning logs to fall into the hot bed of coals, where they burn more efficiently.

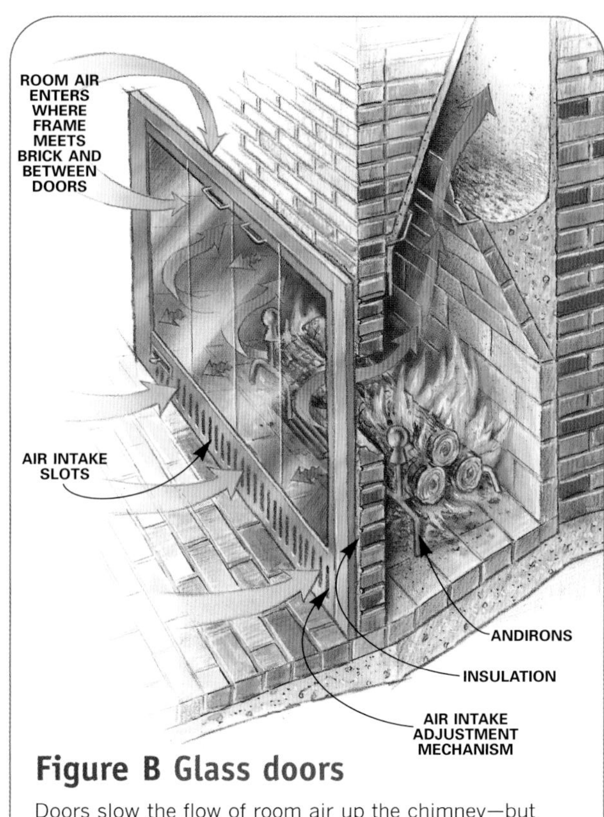

Figure B Glass doors

Doors slow the flow of room air up the chimney—but also block the fire's heat from entering the room. For best results, keep the doors open while the fire is burning hot; close them in the waning stages of the fire.

Energy-Saving Goof

Caution: Highly foolhardy

I came home early one spring afternoon to find it was a bit cool in the house, so I decided to build a fire in the fireplace. I hate to admit it, but sometimes we use a little charcoal lighter fluid to get the fire started. This time, however, the can was empty. I went to the garage to find a substitute and spotted a can of starting fluid that said "highly flammable." Just what I wanted, or so I thought. I brought it into the house and sprayed some onto the logs. Big mistake. I lit a match, and before I could even get it into the kindling, there was a thunderous explosion. Blue flames shot out of the lower vent, hitting my shins just above my shoes and scorching my socks. Luckily I escaped without injury or any major damage to my house. I never told anyone, not until now. My advice: Start your kindling only with a little newspaper and a match!

Dampers and glass fronts

When a fire is burning, adjust your damper to the smallest opening that's possible without smoke spilling back into the house. And shut it completely when the fireplace isn't in use. Still, your built-in damper—like most—is notoriously leaky. If the masons who built your fireplace never put a cap over it, years of rain and condensation may have rusted and pitted the damper. And high heat may have slightly distorted it. To fix this, you could install a chimney-top damper—a spring-loaded cap that seals off the top of the chimney to block air leakage when the fireplace isn't in use. It can be opened to varying degrees when the fireplace is in use.

You could also install tempered glass doors (around $500) with adjustable air intake slots (Figure B). They'll help prevent room air from escaping up the chimney when the fireplace isn't in use, and slow the mass exodus of room air up the chimney in the waning stages of a fire. But if you leave the doors closed during a fire, they'll block over half the heat from entering the room.

Wood-burning inserts

You can increase the output of your fireplace up to five-fold with a wood-burning insert (Figure C). This metal unit sits inside the fireplace and uses the old chimney as a chase for a new metal liner. Faceplates cover the space between the insert and fireplace opening. The unit's heat-exchange chamber, which warms and circulates room air, is part of what makes these so efficient. Their other advantage is you can adjust the air intakes to closely control the amount of room air allowed into the fire chamber during combustion and close it off completely when not in use. Some inserts come with glass doors for fire viewing; others have metal doors.

If you go this route, you'll need to go through some

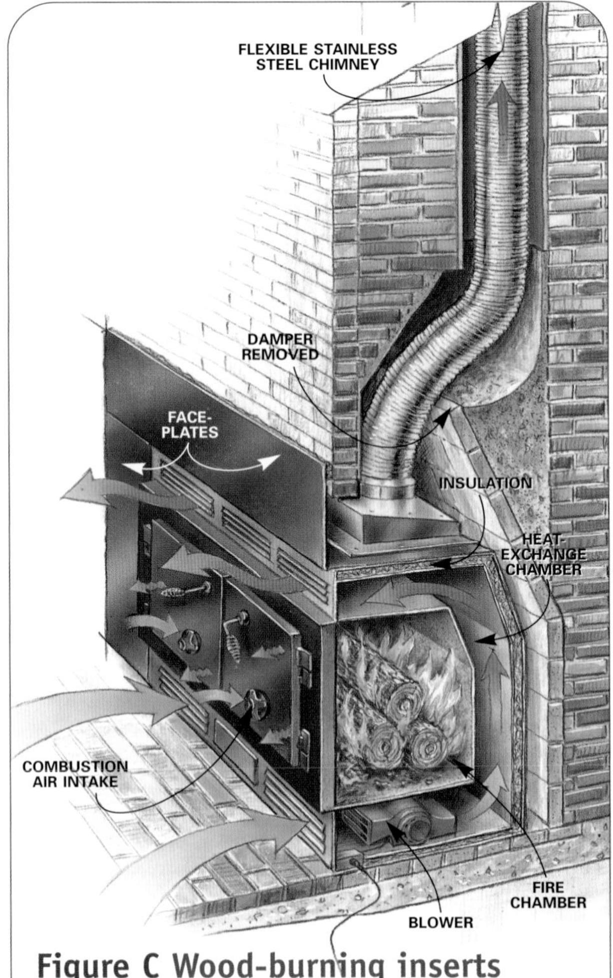

Figure C Wood-burning inserts

These inserts allow you to control the amount of room air entering the fire chamber. Air circulated and warmed through the outer heat-exchange chamber makes efficient use of the fire's heat.

serious contortions, snaking the 25-ft., flexible stainless steel liner through the existing chimney and attaching it to the insert. Most damper openings are only about 6 in. wide, so you may need to use several different connectors and elbows.

A less complicated insert you could install is a tubular grate/glass door variety. C-shaped hollow tubes, the ends of each protruding above and below the glass doors, sit in the firebox. Room air enters the bottom of the C, is heated as it flows past the fire, then exits through the top of the C as heated air. Tubular grates alone—not used in conjunction with glass doors or blowers—won't appreciably increase the efficiency of a fireplace. The warmed air is apparently sucked back into the fireplace and up the chimney.

Gas-fired inserts

If you were building a house today, you'd have the option of installing an enclosed, gas fireplace (Figure D). These sealed units are airtight, meaning combustion air is brought in, heat is created, and exhaust gas is exhausted, all within the confines of the firebox. Blowers circulate air up and around the units, expelling warmed air into the room. No room air is used for combustion or escapes up the chimney.

True, you couldn't burn wood or roast marshmallows in your gas fireplace, but neither would you have to haul in wood, haul out ashes or lose massive amounts of heat. If you installed a direct vent unit—one that vents directly through the wall behind the unit—your gas fireplace could be 75 percent efficient. If you really wanted to go first class, you could operate it by remote control.

But even with your existing house and masonry fireplace, you can make use of this technology. You can slide a top-venting gas fireplace insert into your old fireplace—and still have the brick hearth, mantel and fairly natural-looking flame—and 50 percent efficiency. The fresh-air intake and exhaust pipes would run up through your existing chimney.

You would pay at least $1,500 for the insert and pipes. You'd have to remove the existing damper or permanently clamp it in place for safety. And you'd be wise to hire a licensed plumber to install the gas line to the unit and tie into the existing gas lines—but the rest of the installation you could do yourself.

Making sure

Before you get too excited about any changes, have a professional chimney sweep come out to clean and inspect your fireplace. Some chimneys are so encrusted with creosote deposits, they present a fire danger.

Also, consult your local building inspector. He or she may require the installation of an outside air intake near your wood-burning insert. Or, if you go the gas insert route, you'll have to abide by the many regulations regarding the distance between the outside vents and windows, the ground and the gas meter.

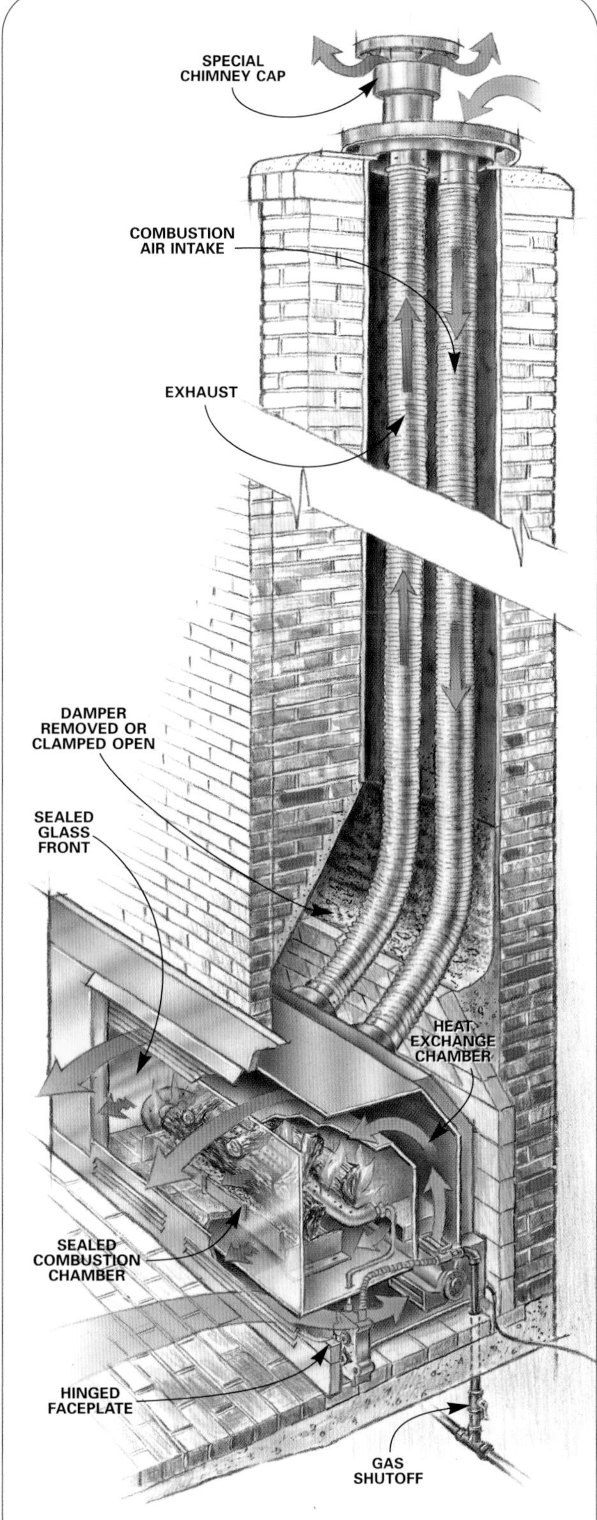

Figure D Gas-fired inserts

These inserts use the existing chimney to draw in fresh air and exhaust spent gases. The combustion chamber is sealed off from the room, and the outer heat-exchange chamber makes these units up to 75 percent efficient.

Understanding

Escaping heat creates higher energy bills

A picturesque array of icicles might make a nice image for a holiday card, but there's nothing charming about the damage that built-up roof ice can do to your home, especially the continuous chunks called ice dams. Several conditions are required for their formation (see "How ice dams form," below), but the factors you can control are heat loss through your roof and proper ventilation to maintain a cold roof.

Spot problem roofs by observing them during the few days following a snowfall. If significant heat loss occurs, the blanket of snow will rapidly develop thin areas or holes from melting. Icicles will soon appear at the eaves, then thicker layers of ice will form above them.

The only effective strategy against ice dams is this: Keep the attic cold by preventing upward heat loss from the living areas of the house, and keep the roof cold by providing a clear path for cold air to move from eave to ridge. Attic insulation between and above the ceiling joists is essential; most modern codes specify as much as 1 ft. of insulation with a heat retention value above R-32. Equally critical is sealing off ceiling penetrations—from a small electrical box to a large access hatch—that allow warm air to leak past the insulation.

How ice dams form

Ice dams can't form from snow and cold weather alone; they need a warm roof too. This is how they're created:

1. Heat rises through ceiling penetrations and into an attic.
2. The snow on the shingles melts, and the water runoff travels down the roof slope until it gets to the edges.
3. Because the heat loss stops at the eaves, they are typically cold enough to refreeze the melted water, forming icicles and ice dams. Gutters magnify the problem by providing a platform for the ice to accumulate on and are often damaged by the added weight.
4. As the dams accumulate ice, they form an obstacle to the melted water that's still making its way down the roof.
5. With nowhere else to go, the water backs up under the shingles and eventually finds its way through the sheathing and into the house.

Quick tip*

FREE HEAT FROM THE SUN. During the winter and other cold months, keep the curtains on the south side of your house open during the day to let in free solar heat. Close those curtains at night to help prevent heat loss.

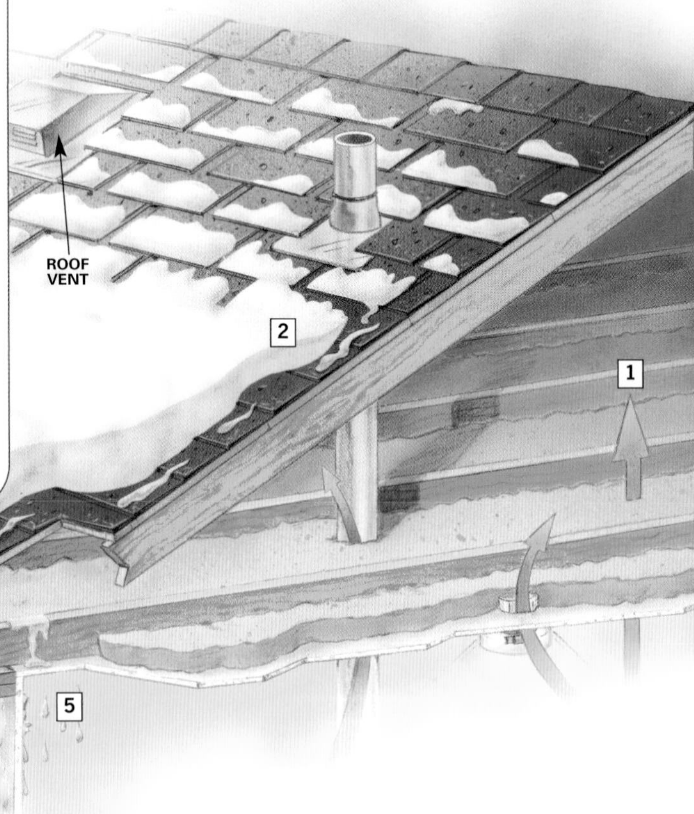

ice dams

and harmful ice dams

Ice dam solutions

When ice dams occur on a roof, it's usually not long before the symptoms move inside. Rust spots from drywall fasteners might show up on the ceilings, paint will peel and water stains will appear around windows and exterior doors. Even under the best conditions, some ice dam formation is often unavoidable; the daytime sun can melt snow on sections of a roof, but as night falls, temperatures drop and the water refreezes. You can't prevent this melting-refreezing cycle completely, but you can reduce the attic heat loss that aggravates it, and you can also protect your roof sheathing and house from the inevitable ice dams that will form from normal climatic changes.

Above all, stop or at least minimize the heat loss through your attic. Air leaks can occur wherever a ceiling or wall penetration isn't sealed properly. Light fixture boxes, access hatches and open pipe or duct chases can all be routes for warm air to migrate up into your attic, so use caulk, expanding foam insulation or other sealants to close them. This requires a trip to the attic to pull away the insulation and apply a sealant from the top side of the drywall or plaster, so this is a good project to tackle in the fall, when the attic will be reasonably cool. Aside from reducing the ice dams' severity, these measures should lower your energy bills. Upgrading insulation also helps; it's likely the attic already has some—probably fiberglass batting nested between the joists—but additional blown-in cellulose or fiberglass helps seal gaps and improve the R-rating.

Also important is maintaining a cold roof by installing or improving ventilation with soffit vents and roof or ridge vents that keep cold air circulating freely. Even with some attic heat loss, this will reduce the melting rate. Also, the next time you reroof, install a self-sealing membrane along the roof edges.

Keeping a cold roof

Insulate and seal every ceiling penetration so heat intended for living areas can't migrate into the attic and warm the roof. Add an extra layer of insulation across the entire attic, if necessary. Make sure there's adequate vent area along the soffits and eaves so cold air from outside can flow freely under the roof sheathing and out through vents on or near the ridge.

Installing ice-and-water barrier

Even if ice dams do form, you can prevent damage to the roof sheathing and interior by installing an ice-and-water membrane along the roof edges before shingling or reshingling. These 3-ft.-wide adhesive membranes are waterproof and self-seal around nail and staple holes. The membrane should run at least 2 to 3 ft. up the roof beyond the exterior wall plane.

Using secondary measures

If there's no snow on the roof, it can't melt to form ice dams at the edge. You can remove snow manually using a snow rake on an extension handle, although you'll have some cleanup to do on the ground afterward. Beware of overhead power lines. For a surefire preventive measure, place heating cable intended for this purpose along the roof edges and all the way out the downspout to melt the ice and snow. Always follow all manufacturer's instructions.

Keeping a Cold Roof

Installing Ice-and-Water Barrier

Using Secondary Measures

Saving Energy:

Y ou can take a clue from the chapter on saving energy during heating season to help you save energy during cooling season, too. Clean furnace filters, well-sealed air ducts and programmable thermostats can go a long way in lowering your cooling bill. And other things, like insulating, caulking and sealing up attic bypasses—things normally associated with keeping cold air out in the winter—will also help lower your cooling bill by keeping warm air out in the summer.

Keeping your ceiling fans on and air conditioner tuned up will obviously help save on your electric bill, but one of the smartest ways to save energy during the summer is to keep the heat out to begin with. Trees, window shades, tint film and awnings are all passive forms of cooling that will deliver active forms of savings.

4 Cooling Season

Figure A
Natural Cooling

Cool your home with shade to supplement or eliminate air-conditioning. Window shading devices include awnings, interior and exterior shades, shade screens, dark films and tinted glass. Other shading features, like roof overhangs, covered porches, arbors, trellises and trees, shade the roof and walls of your house as well as the windows.

Cooling with shade

Use Mother Nature and window shading to lower your energy bill

Summer heat. It makes tomato plants droop, barefoot kids hotfoot it across paved sidewalks, and your ice-cream cone drip before you can give it a lick.

It's hard to imagine that only two generations ago, before air-conditioning, shade was the best defense against summertime heat. In those days, everyone worked inside if they could, near open windows. After work, they headed for the nearest covered porch, where they sat and fanned themselves, waiting for a cool breeze or simply sweating it out. Indoors, electric fans worked overtime. And once commercial air-conditioning arrived, they escaped to the air-conditioned theater for the afternoon matinee or shopped in an air-conditioned department store on weekends.

Today, about 60 years later, shade has taken a back seat to air-conditioning, which has become standard in homes, workplaces and cars. But don't dismiss shading strategies as outdated. Although porches are no longer so common, good shading still provides comfort and energy savings. Shade can reduce your air-conditioning bill by as much as a third. And it will make your yard cooler and more pleasant too.

Here you'll see how shading can help you and your house escape the sun's heat. If other front-line cooling strategies, like insulation and ventilation, are already in place, consider shading as a secondary strategy.

To begin, we'll follow the sun through a typical summer day and describe how it heats your house.

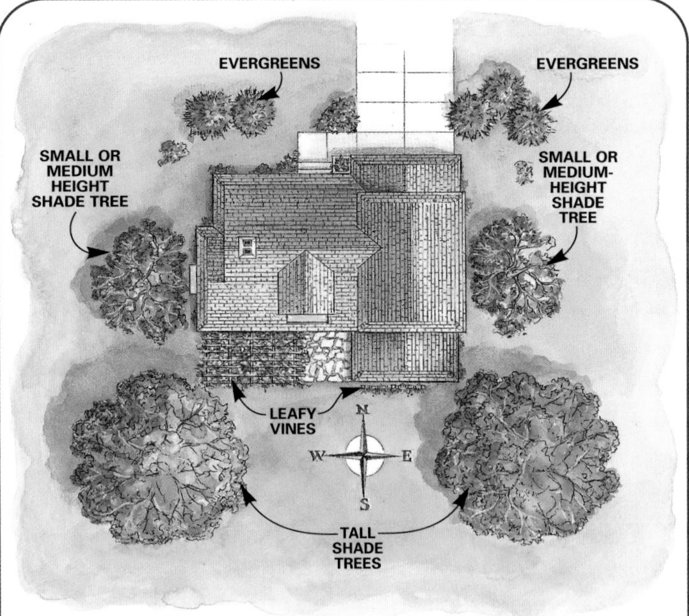

Figure B Shade

Shade with foliage by planting trees to shade the east- and west-facing walls of your home. Leave the south side open to receive the sun's warmth in winter. In regions with cold winters, plant dense evergreens on the north side to block the wind.

Following the sun's path

Morning

As every gardener, construction worker and farmer knows, sunrise is the coolest time of the day and the best time to get heavy work done. All night long, while the sun bakes folks on the other side of the globe, air temperatures drop around your home. At sunrise, the process reverses and the air begins to heat up again.

While the heat might not bother you, it does affect your house. Morning sunlight directly strikes the east wall of your house and begins a daylong warming process. The massive walls and roof slowly but steadily absorb the sun's rays on the outside, then warm up and radiate heat to the inside. Houses don't sweat, so once this heating begins, there's almost no way to reverse the process until sundown, except by turning on an air conditioner.

In most homes, good wall and attic insulation provides at least one built-in defense against heat buildup. The same insulation that keeps your home warm in winter keeps it cool in summer, trapping most of the heat in the exterior part of a wall. As long as the interior surfaces of the walls and ceilings remain cool, your house will feel cool. However, even a well-insulated house has weak spots—the windows. Morning sunlight that pours through the eastern windows bypasses the insulation and rapidly accelerates the heat buildup inside. To keep cool without turning on the air conditioner, it's critical that you shade these east-facing windows. (See more on shading methods on p. 88.)

Noon

By noontime, the sun's rays reach maximum intensity, beating down from directly overhead. Your roof and attic catch the brunt of the noontime heat. Roof temperatures can soar beyond 160 degrees F (egg-frying temperatures!), and attics become ovens. Fortunately, most homes have a thick blanket of insulation on the attic floor, usually twice as much as in walls. Good attic ventilation helps too, but insulation is the main defense to keep the heat from reaching the rooms below. Before the widespread use of ceiling insulation, hot weather sometimes forced entire families to cook, eat and sleep on the covered back porch so they could escape the stifling heat indoors.

The walls and windows of your house absorb much less heat during this period because the sun hits them at such a sharp angle during the summer months (Figure C, p. 88). Actually, the noontime sun perches slightly to the south side of your house. Good roof design should include overhangs or porch roofs to shade the south walls and windows during the middle of the day.

Afternoon

The sun continues to heat the roof and begins to hit the west walls. On most hot summer days, your air conditioner will switch on by now to counteract the heat buildup from the morning and noon hours. The outside air temperature usually peaks about 4 p.m., then begins to drop.

Evening

In most regions, a summer day feels hottest about 6 p.m. By now, the air temperature has dropped slightly, but rising humidity in the early evening intensifies the sensation of heat. So the evening sun can feel especially hot. If your kids are going to grumble, they'll probably do it now, and you can

In most regions, a summer day feels hottest about 6 P.M.

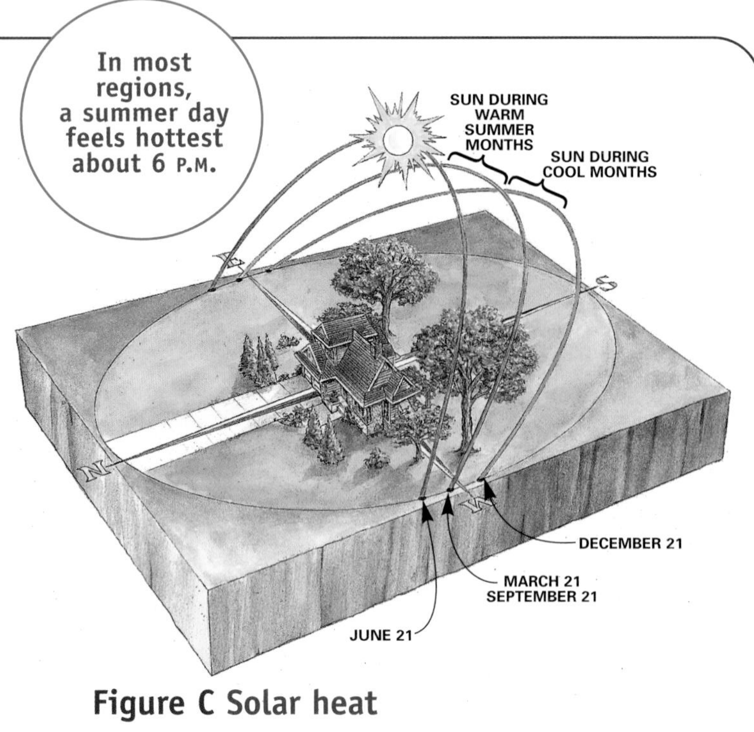

Figure C Solar heat

The sun's path changes from summer to winter. For the best cooling, landscape to shade your house from the path of the summer sun.

bet that the evening shade will feel especially welcome.

The evening sun heats your home just like the morning sun, except that it strikes the west wall instead of the east wall. However, its effect feels hotter than the morning sun's because the inside of your house has been heating up all day. In fact, unless your air conditioner is running, the inside temperature will continue to rise even after sunset, because the heat already absorbed by the exterior walls and ceiling slowly continues to work its way inside, where it radiates off the walls. You can sweat it out inside, but it's more pleasant to relax outdoors or on a screened porch in the evening and into the night.

After sunset, your house slowly cools down until morning, when sunrise begins the process all over again.

Window-shading devices

The path of the sun dictates the best placement for shading devices. Figure A, on p. 86, shows a variety of ways to shade windows, especially those east- and west-facing windows that catch direct sunlight. Blinds and curtains are perhaps the most popular because they also provide privacy. The side facing out should be light-colored so it reflects heat away from the window. Dark-colored shades absorb heat and draw it inside. Outside blinds work better than inside blinds because they block the heat before it gets into the house. But few people use them because it's so inconvenient to run outside every time you want to raise and lower them. On the downside, blinds, curtains and shades block your view as well as the cooling breezes if you keep your windows open.

One shading product particularly popular in the South is a densely woven insect screening, sometimes called shade cloth. This screening, made from fiberglass or aluminum, blocks up to 75 percent of sunlight. Another option is tinted plastic film in various densities that you apply to your window glass to reflect or filter out some of the heat. These films are particularly useful if you want to prevent rugs and upholstery from fading. Don't apply these films to double-pane windows, however, because they can cause a temperature imbalance that could crack the glass.

If you have to replace your windows, buy double-pane glass with tinted or "low-E" coatings. Low-E windows, which are specifically designed for cooling, block much of the sun's heat without darkening the view through the window (a weakness of tinted glass). These are good choices for east-, west- and south-facing windows if you spend more for air-conditioning than for heating.

All of these shading methods (except buying new windows) are relatively inexpensive and can do a good job. You can install most of them yourself, using materials from well-stocked lumberyards and home centers.

Awnings are a good alternative if you want to catch cooling breezes, because they shade without blocking the wind. And they only partially block the view. They're semipermanent, you don't have to open and close them, and you can leave them up until cooler weather arrives in the fall. If you have a good sewing machine, you can make them yourself from canvas or reinforced nylon and inexpensive hardware parts purchased from an awning dealer. Awnings should extend about halfway down the window and have fabric sides to block the sun at all but extremely low angles.

No matter which ideas you use, remember to shade your east-facing windows to block the morning sun, and your west-facing windows to block the evening sun. Shading can also be effective over south-facing windows. In all regions except Florida and the extreme southern United States, you'll save on heating costs if you remove the shading devices during cold winter weather to allow maximum heat gain from the sun.

Shading with landscaping

Landscape shading blocks the sun before it ever hits your house. So it's a great house-cooling strategy, plus it'll make your yard cooler and more attractive too.

For maximum energy savings, place trees and other foliage so that the house is shaded in summer but not in winter. Figures A, B and C show low foliage positioned on the east and west sides to block the early morning and late evening sun. Moderate-size trees block late morning and early evening sun, and tall trees placed fairly close to the house cast shade over the roof during midday hours. These are all broadleaf deciduous trees, which conveniently lose their leaves in winter, allowing more sunlight to hit the house when you welcome the heat. (In stormy areas with frequent high winds, you might not want to plant trees close to your house. Ask experts at your local nursery for advice about which trees to plant and where to plant them.)

However, even the branches of leafless trees can block 30 to 40 percent of the sunlight. Because the winter sun hangs so low in the southern sky (Figure C), the south-facing windows are by far the most important to keep as unobstructed as possible for winter heating.

Landscaping with trees is a long-term proposition, and an ideal plan might run afoul of other hazards. Large, south-facing exposures are ideal, but your house might face the east or west. Electrical and underground utility lines might limit tree positioning. Your yard might be too small, and established trees might be growing in the wrong spot. You won't want to cut down a beautiful tree just because it's in the wrong place. So use Figures A and B as models and pick the parts that apply to your situation.

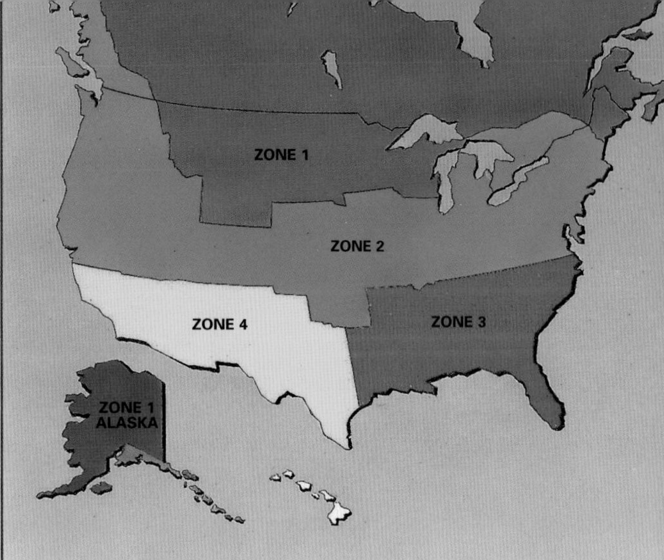

Figure D Zones

Climates vary, so plan shading strategy according to local conditions. Zone 1 has warm summers but cold winters. Zone 2 has hot summers, cold winters and sometimes high humidity. Zone 3 has hot summers, mild winters and high humidity. Zone 4 has clear, hot, dry summers and mild winters. Hawaii's climate is moderate year-round.

Landscaping by region

A good shading strategy has to take account of the local climate. (Suitable shade trees and plants vary too, so rely on your local nursery to help you choose.) Figure D illustrates four zones, all of which have somewhat different cooling requirements.

In Zone 1, summer cooling isn't nearly as important, or as expensive, as winter heating. If you live in this zone, gear your landscaping plan to winter rather than to summer. Position trees and evergreens on the northwest side, the direction of cold north winds, and keep the south side completely clear to gain as much heat through the windows as possible in winter. Even broadleaf shade trees that lose their leaves block considerable sun in the winter. You'll also want to shift the shading arbor out into the yard away from the south wall and build your screen porch on a different wall as well. In Figure A, both shade the south wall.

Without modifications, the landscape plan in Figure A works best in Zone 2. This zone is a region of hot and cold extremes, so the cooling shade of the arbor against the house makes sense. The arbor also shades the patio, which would otherwise reflect sunlight and heat into the house. Closely spaced trees and shrubs on the north side still block the cold north wind, but foliage on the other three sides should be open enough to channel cooling summer breezes around the house.

The design in Figure A also works well in Zone 3, except that you don't have to worry about blocking a cold north wind. Shade trees with high canopies (leaves and branches) work best here because they allow the breezes to circulate easily beneath them. (Obviously you can't grow tall trees overnight, so keep them if you have them and get them started if you don't!)

The high humidity in this zone will make you feel hotter and stickier. Since dense foliage produces a lot of humidity, move vines and arbors away from the house and rely more on awnings, porches, roof overhangs and other architectural devices for window shading.

In Zone 4, the hot, arid region, you can plant the shading vines, arbors and other foliage right near the house, because the extra moisture these plants produce helps cool the air in this dry region. Your plant choice will be more limited in an arid climate, so you might have to rely on awnings, window shades, porches and other architectural features to shade the east, west and south walls and windows.

Quick tip*

PASSIVE COOLING = ENERGY SAVINGS

Shading your home with trees, awnings and shades can lower the indoor temperature by as much as 20 degrees F on a hot day.

The payoff

No one shading device or landscaping idea is best for every home. But basic shading principles will help you choose what fits your home's style, your local climate (sometimes different from the regional climate) and certainly your budget. The main payoff is the comfort of not having to rely on your air-conditioning as much. The bonus is that your home will look better and be more energy-efficient.

How to plant a shade tree

A natural way to lower your summer utility bills

Fall is the ideal time of year to plant a shade tree—or any other tree, for that matter. The cool weather of fall gives roots a chance to grow, develop and get established without the stress of developing new leaves or fruit. Don't be surprised to find that you'll have to wait for a whole growing season to see significant growth. In fact, with fruit trees, it's a good idea to pinch off any blossoms or fruit the first year so the tree can channel its energy into establishing its root system instead of developing fruit.

The basic planting techniques are the same for all trees. For starters, pick a well-drained area (one where water doesn't pond after rain) in a sunny location so the tree will get the light it needs to thrive. Keep in mind the mature size of the species you're planting and consider whether nearby trees, buildings and power lines could cause problems later.

When you've picked your planting spot, first dig a 1-ft.-square, 1-ft.-deep drainage test hole, fill it with water and go have a cup of coffee. If there's still water in the hole after about an hour, you have heavy, poorly drained soil. If so, use the same directions as for well-drained areas, but dig the hole only as deep as two-thirds the height of the root ball. Then heap dirt over the root ball before mulching. That way, some water is directed away from the hole so the root ball won't drown in trapped water.

For well-drained areas, dig a hole 1 to 2 ft. wider than the root ball and as deep as the height of the root ball of the tree. Your tree will be sold either in a plastic container or bundled in burlap. Rough up the sides of the hole with the tip of the shovel, especially when planting in heavy soil. It'll make it easier for roots to penetrate the surrounding soil. Carry the tree by picking up the container or the burlapped root ball. Never carry the tree by the trunk; you could damage delicate roots.

If you have a burlapped tree, lower the burlapped root ball into the hole. Burlapped trees have a wire basket to hold the root ball together. You can leave the wire basket in place; the roots will grow through it and the rotting burlap. If your tree has synthetic burlap, or if you're planting in heavy clay or sand, remove the wire and burlap first. If you have a container-grown tree, cut away the sides of the container and peel them back to expose the root ball. Lift the ball from the container and lower it into the hole.

Hold the tree straight while you fill the hole with soil. Tamp the soil down around the ball with the end of a 4x4 until the soil level is about three-fourths the depth of the hole (but be careful not to damage roots). Cut away the exposed burlap in the top one-fourth of the hole. Fill the hole with water to allow the soil to settle and to remove trapped air. After the water drains, finish filling the hole with soil and lay a 3- to 6-in. bed of mulch around the base of the trunk to help retain soil moisture.

Always use native soil to fill around the root ball. Filling with enriched soil will pamper the roots and they'll refuse to penetrate poorer surrounding soil to establish a good root base.

Don't fertilize your tree right after planting. Instead, apply a 10-10-10 fertilizer the following spring and every year thereafter.

CUT OFF TOP QUARTER OF BURLAP

3" TO 6" DEEP MULCH

ABRADE SIDES OF HOLE WITH SHOVEL

HOLE SAME DEPTH AS ROOT BALL

LEAVE ON WIRE AND BURLAP

HOLE 1' TO 2' WIDER THAN ROOT BALL

Window air conditioner spring cleaning

Easy steps to make it work more efficiently

Follow these steps to get a window-mounted air conditioner ready for summer.

The secret is simply a good cleaning. Room air conditioners, like central air conditioners, have two sets of coils (a "coil" is an arrangement of fins and tubes for efficient heat transfer). The condenser coil is on the outside and the evaporator coil on the inside (Figure A). Keeping them clean is 90 percent of the battle in keeping your air conditioner operating efficiently.

The most important maintenance steps are easy, but if this is the first time you've cleaned the unit, allow about a half day to pull things apart and put them back together. A professional (look under "Heating and Air-Conditioning" or "Air-Conditioning Service" in your yellow pages) will service an air conditioner for about $75. But don't expect quick service in the spring when everyone has the same idea.

You really can't clean your window air conditioner unless you unplug it and remove it from the window. Hold on to it when you remove the window support. It can weigh 100 lbs. or more. Have a strong helper standing

Figure A Window Air Conditioner

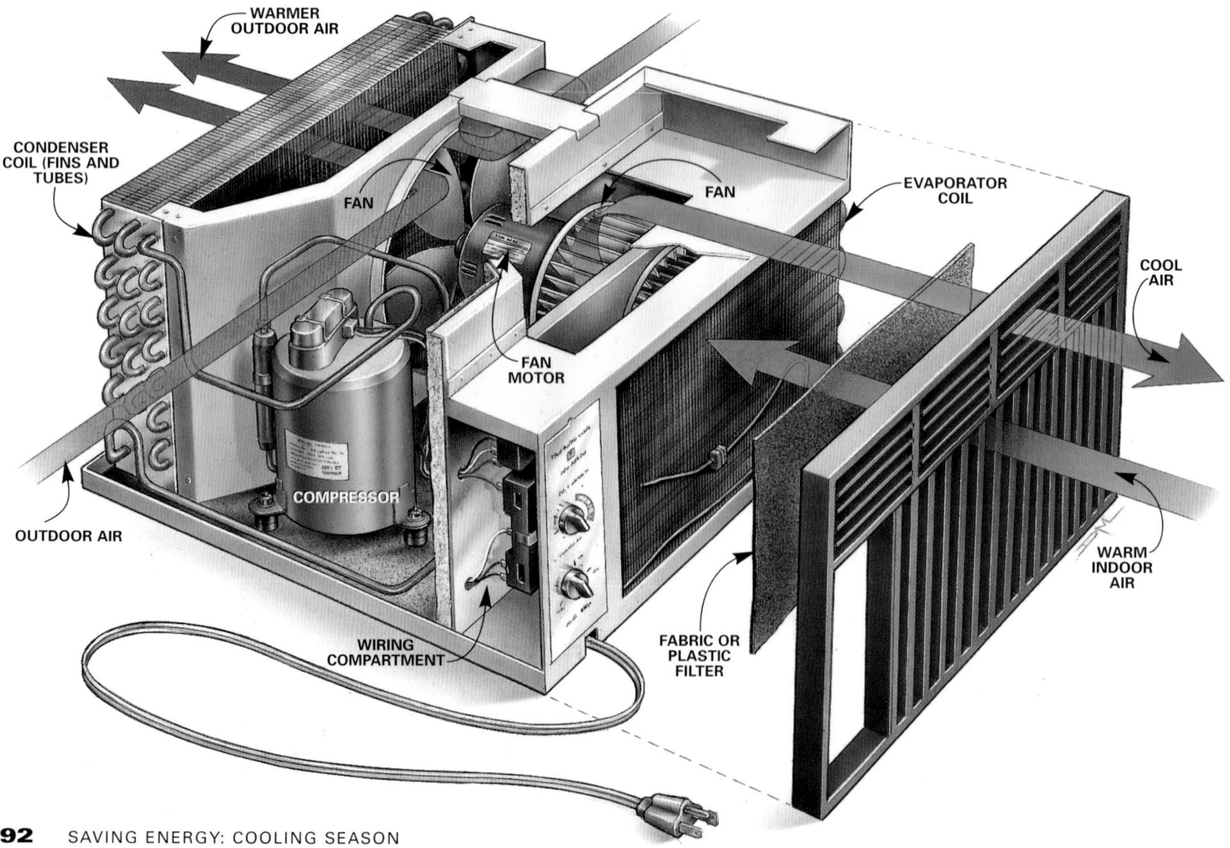

SAVE $$$ BY INSTALLING YOUR AC UNIT IN THE SHADE

A window or central air conditioner located in the shade can use up to 10 percent less energy than one located in the sun. Install units on the north side of your house or shield them with shrubbery (but don't block the airflow).

by to help you lift it out. The cleaning process shown in the photos applies to most air conditioners, but refer to your owner's manual for more details about your brand and model.

When the air conditioner doesn't seem to cool well, most folks assume that the coolant needs recharging (a job for pros only). But most often the culprit is dirt, a problem solved by cleaning the coils. The evaporator coil (Photo 2) is protected by a filter. Rinse it out or replace it ($1 from appliance stores), and vacuum the fins if they're dusty.

The dirtiest side of the condenser coil, the fan side, is harder to get at (Figure A). Since you usually can't vacuum the fins from the fan side, spray water back through the fins from the outside (Photo 5). Do this outdoors or inside near a floor drain. Wrap plastic around the fan motor to protect it and keep the wiring compartment dry (Figure A). Let the unit dry for 24 hours before setting it in the window and plugging it in again.

It's important to use the correct oil for fan motor lubrication. Don't use all-purpose or penetrating oils. Buy oil made specifically for electric motors (usually nondetergent SAE 20 motor oil) unless otherwise specified in

1 UNPLUG the unit and lift it from the window. Remove the front cover, then unscrew and lift off the case to expose the compressor, fan motor and evaporator coils.

Quick tip*

COOL TIPS FOR BUYING AN AIR CONDITIONER

Central air-conditioning systems carry a SEER rating (Seasonal Energy Efficiency Rating), which typically ranges from 10 to 17. The higher the SEER rating, the more efficient the unit. Before you go air-conditioner shopping, check with your utility company to see if it offers rebates for AC units with a high SEER rating.

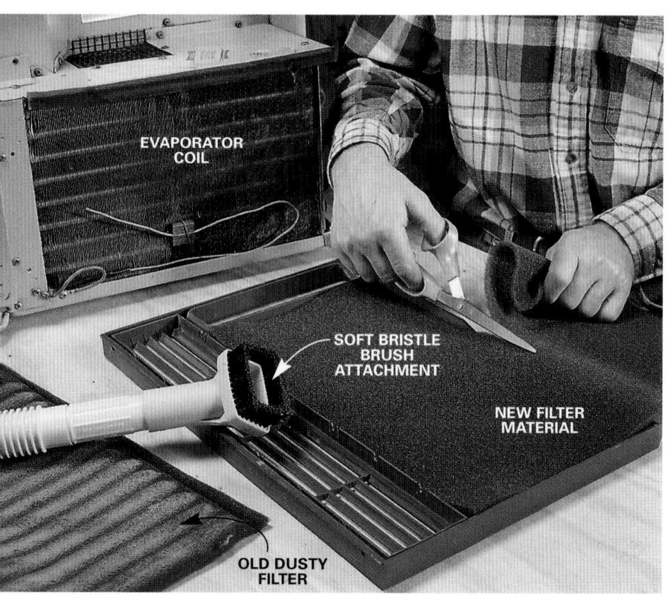

2 VACUUM the evaporator fins (the inside coil) with a soft brush attachment. Replace the filter or wash and reuse the old one.

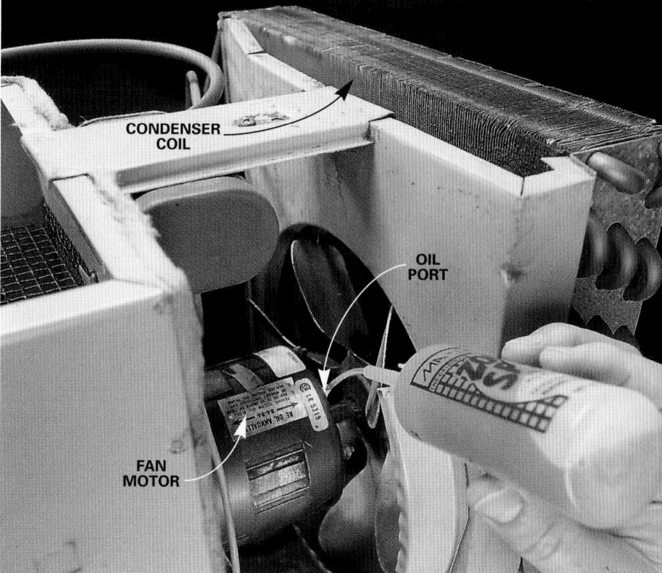

3 LUBRICATE the fan motor with five drops of electric motor oil if you can find oil ports. Check the owner's manual for help. Don't apply too much oil—more is not better.

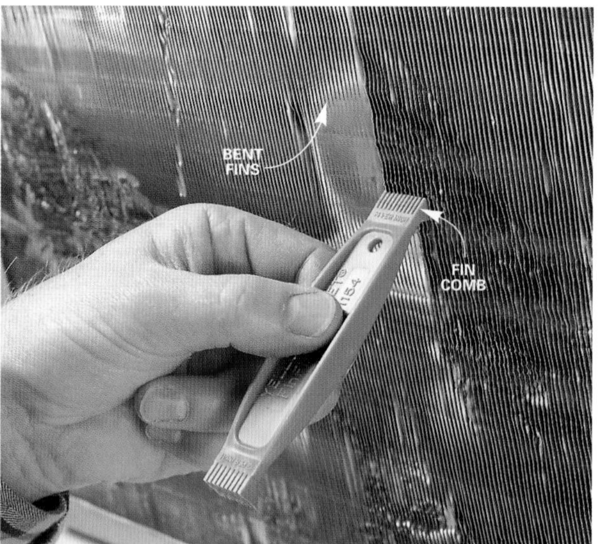

4 STRAIGHTEN bent fins with a special plastic fin comb to improve air circulation.

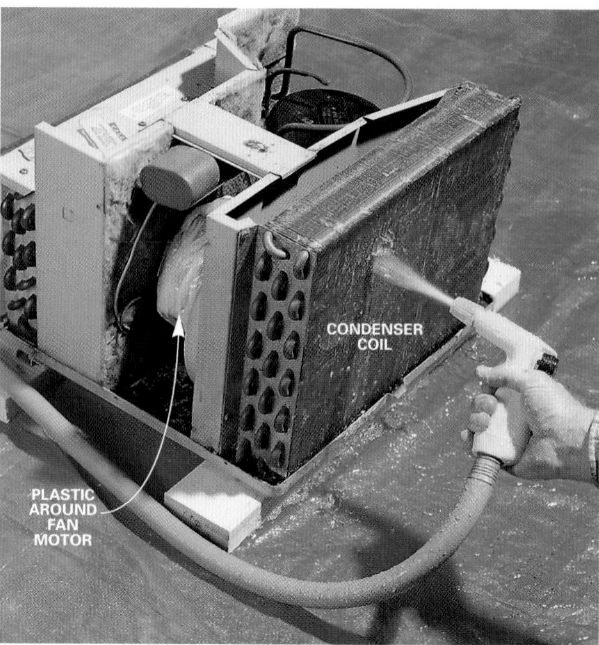

5 WASH the condenser coil with a spray of water from the outside inward. Cover the fan motor with plastic to keep it dry. Then rinse and wipe up as much dirt and crud as possible from the bottom pan, making sure drain holes and overflows are open.

your owner's manual. The oil bottle in Photo 3 has a handy plastic tube that reaches fittings in tight areas. It costs $1.50 at appliance parts or repair dealers.

Another handy tool is the fin comb we show in Photo 4. Fins are delicate and can easily bend when you're handling the unit. You'll be amazed at how fast and easily a fin comb can straighten them. It costs only $3–$5, but you might have to buy a whole set to get the right size. You can use them on the outdoor units of central air conditioners too. Finally, inspect the cord for cracks in the insulation, especially around the plug. Replace the entire cord if it's damaged.

Energy-Saving Goof

A/C on the loose

At the end of the summer, I decided to beat the fall to-do list and remove the window air-conditioner units at my law office. I proceeded to remove the screws from the window sash of the first unit and muscle it out myself. Well, it slipped and fell out the window a few feet into a mulched flower bed. My secretary asked if I could use some help with the next one. Stubbornly I forged ahead by myself. The second unit was much larger, and my plan of attack failed even more miserably as the unit slipped from my hands and went crashing to the sidewalk 10 ft. below. Luckily, no one was in its path. I promised my secretary that next time I'd ask for help!

Central air conditioner tune-up

Stay cooler and save energy with these simple steps

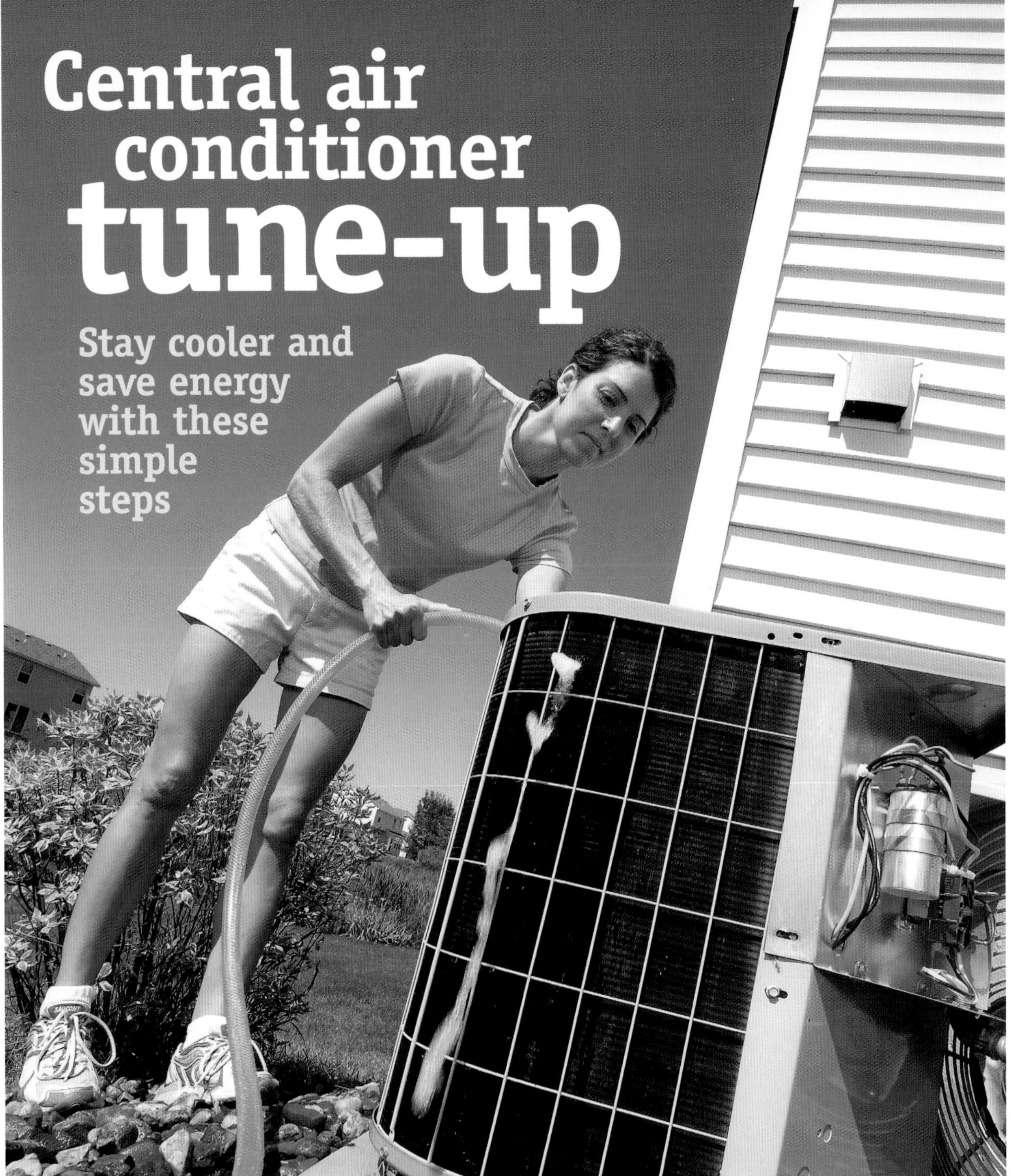

Chances are that if you've neglected a spring checkup, your air conditioner isn't cooling nearly as well as it could. A year's worth of dirt and debris clogging the cooling fins, a low coolant level, a dirty blower fan filter and a number of other simple problems can significantly reduce the efficiency of your air conditioner and wear it out faster.

You can't do everything; only a pro can check the coolant level. But you can easily handle most of the routine cleaning chores and save the extra $120 that it would cost to have a pro do them.

Here you'll see how to clean the outdoor unit (called the condenser) and the accessible parts of the indoor unit (called the evaporator). All the steps are simple and straightforward and will take you only a few hours, total. You don't need any special skills, tools or experience. If you aren't familiar with air conditioners and furnaces/blowers, don't worry. See Figure A "Parts of a central air conditioner,"

1 **TURN OFF the electrical power to the condenser unit at the outdoor shutoff. Either pull out a block or move a switch to the "Off" position. If uncertain, turn off the power to the AC at the main electrical panel.**

2 **VACUUM grass clippings, leaves and other debris from the exterior fins with a soft brush attachment. Clear away all bushes, weeds and grass within 2 ft. of the condenser.**

3 **REALIGN bent or crushed fins with gentle pressure from a dinner knife. Don't insert the knife more than 1/2 in.**

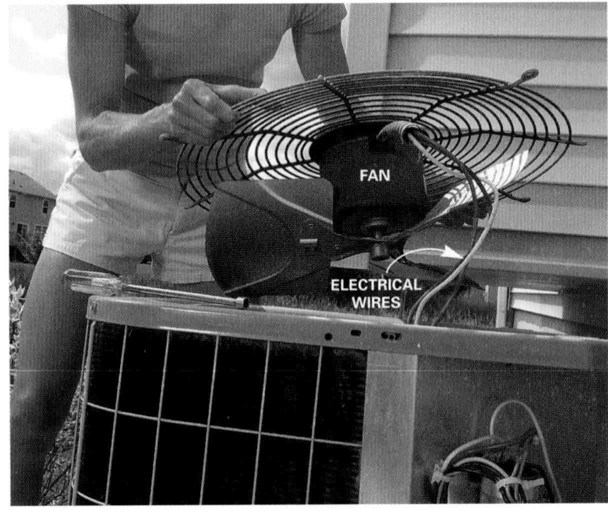

4 **UNSCREW the top grille. Lift out the fan and carefully set it aside without stressing the electrical wires. Pull out any leaves and wipe the interior surfaces clean with a damp cloth.**

p. 97, to become familiar with how an air conditioner works and the parts of the system.

You may have a different type of central air conditioner than we show here—a heat pump system, for example, or a unit mounted horizontally in the attic. However, you can still carry out most maintenance procedures because each system will have a condenser outside and an evaporator inside. Use the owner's manual for your particular model to help navigate around any differences from the one shown in our photos. And call in a pro every two or three years to check electrical parts and the coolant level ($150).

tip **Call for service before the first heat wave, when the pros become swamped with repair calls!**

Cleaning the condenser

Clean your outdoor unit on a day that's at least 60 degrees F. That's about the minimum temperature at which you can test your air conditioner to make sure it's working. The condenser usually sits in an inconspicuous spot next to your house. You'll see two copper tubes running to it, one bare and the other encased in a foam sleeve. If you have a heat pump, both tubes will be covered by foam sleeves.

Your primary job here is to clean the condenser fins, which are fine metallic blades that surround the unit. They get dirty because a central fan sucks air through them, pulling in dust, dead leaves, dead grass and the worst culprit—floating

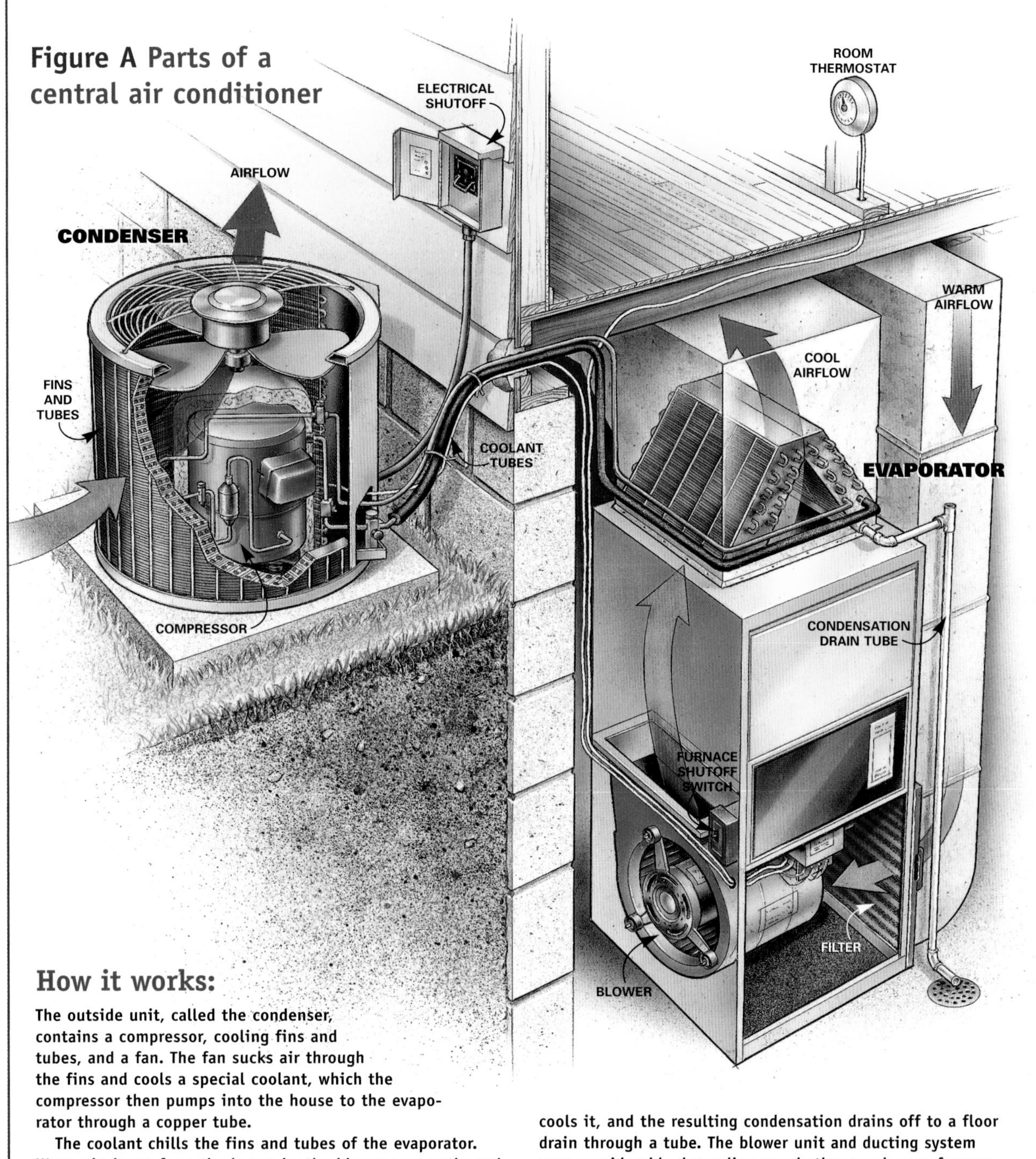

Figure A Parts of a central air conditioner

How it works:

The outside unit, called the condenser, contains a compressor, cooling fins and tubes, and a fan. The fan sucks air through the fins and cools a special coolant, which the compressor then pumps into the house to the evaporator through a copper tube.

The coolant chills the fins and tubes of the evaporator. Warm air drawn from the house by the blower passes through the evaporator and is cooled and blown through ducts to the rooms in the house. The evaporator dehumidifies the air as it cools it, and the resulting condensation drains off to a floor drain through a tube. The blower unit and ducting system vary considerably depending on whether you have a furnace (shown), a heat pump or some other arrangement. It may be located in the basement, garage, furnace room or attic.

"cotton" from cottonwood trees and dandelions. The debris blocks the airflow and reduces the unit's cooling ability.

Always begin by shutting off the electrical power to the unit. Normally you'll find a shutoff nearby. It may be a switch in a box, a pull lever or a fuse block that you pull out (Photo 1). Look for the "On-Off" markings.

Vacuum the fins clean with a soft brush (Photo 2); they're fragile and cann be easily bent or crushed. On many units you'll have to unscrew and lift off a metal box to get at them. Check your owner's manual for directions and lift off the box carefully to avoid bumping the fins. Occasionally you'll find fins that have been bent. You can buy a special set of fin combs ($10 at an appliance parts store) to straighten them. Minor straightening can be done with a blunt dinner knife (Photo 3). If large areas of fins are crushed, have a pro straighten them during a routine serv-

5 SPRAY the fins using moderate water pressure from a hose nozzle. Direct the spray from the inside out. Reinstall the fan.

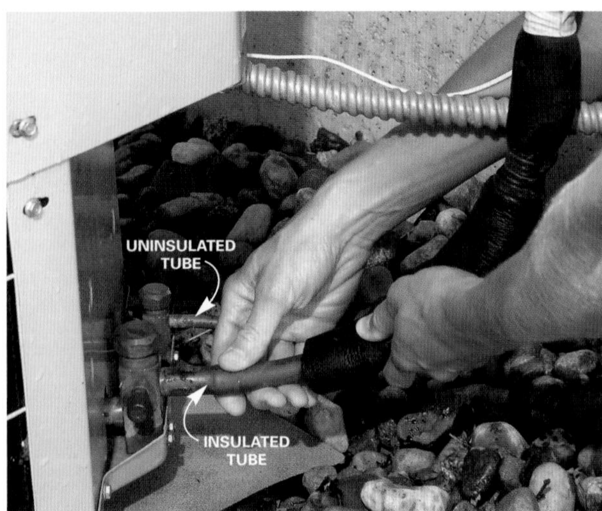

6 TURN the power back on, then set the house thermostat to "Cool" so the compressor comes on. After 10 minutes, feel the insulated tube. It should feel cool. The uninsulated tube should feel warm.

7 TURN OFF the power to the furnace at a nearby switch or at the main panel. Then pull out the furnace filter and check it for dirt buildup. Change it if necessary.

8 OPEN the blower compartment and vacuum up the dust. Check the motor for lubrication ports. If it has them, squeeze five drops of electric motor oil into each.

ice call.

Then unscrew the fan to gain access to the interior of the condenser. You can't completely remove it because its wiring is connected to the unit. Depending on how much play the wires give you, you might need a helper to hold it while you vacuum debris from the inside. (Sometimes mice like to overwinter there!)

After you hose off the fins (Photo 5), check the fan motor for lubrication ports. Most newer motors have sealed bearings (the one shown does) and can't be lubricated. Check your owner's manual to be sure. If you find ports, add five drops of electric motor oil ($5 at hardware stores or appliance parts stores). Don't use penetrating oil or all-purpose oil. They're not designed for long-term lubrication and can actually harm the bearings.

If you have an old air conditioner, you might have a belt-driven compressor in the bottom of the unit. Look for lubrication ports on this as well. The compressors on newer air conditioners are completely enclosed and won't need lubrication (Figure A, p. 97).

Restarting procedure

In most cases, you can simply restore power to the outside unit and move inside to finish the maintenance. However, the compressors are surprisingly fragile and some require special start-up procedures under two conditions. (Others have built-in electronic controls that handle the start-up, but unless you know that yours has these controls, follow these procedures.)

1. If the power to your unit has been off for more than four hours:
   - Move the switch from "Cool" to "Off" at your inside thermostat.
   - Turn the power back on and let the unit sit for 24 hours. (The compressor has a heating element that warms the internal lubricant.)
   - Switch the thermostat back to "Cool."
2. If you switched the unit off while the compressor was running:
   - Wait at least five minutes before switching it back on. (The compressor needs to decompress before restarting.)

With the air conditioner running, make sure it's actually working by touching the coolant tubes (Photo 6). This is a crude test. Only a pro with proper instruments can tell if the coolant is at the level for peak efficiency. But keep a sharp eye out for dark drip marks on the bottom of the case and beneath the tube joints. This indicates an oil leak and a potential coolant leak as well. Call in a pro if you spot this problem. Don't tighten a joint to try to stop a leak yourself. Overtightening can make the problem worse.

Clean the indoor unit

The evaporator usually sits in an inaccessible spot inside a metal duct downstream from the blower (Figure A). If you can get to it, gently vacuum its fins (from the blower side) with a soft brush as you did with the condenser. However, the best way to keep it clean is to keep the airstream from the blower clean. This means annually vacuuming out the blower compartment and changing the filter whenever it's dirty (Photos 7 and 8).

Begin by turning off the power to the furnace or blower. Usually you'll find a simple toggle switch nearby in a metal box (Photo 7); otherwise turn the power off at the main panel. If you have trouble opening the blower unit or finding the filter, check your owner's manual for help. The manual will also list the filter type, but if it's your first time, take the old one with you when buying a new one to make sure you get the right size. Be sure to keep the power to the blower off whenever you remove the filter. Otherwise you'll blow dust into the evaporator fins.

The manual will also tell you where to find the oil ports on the blower, if it has any. The blower compartments on newer furnaces and heat pumps are so tight that you often can't lubricate the blower without removing it. If that's the case, have a pro do it during a routine maintenance checkup.

The evaporator fins dehumidify the air as they cool it, so you'll find a tube to drain the condensation. The water collects in a pan and drains out the side (Figure A). Most tubes are flexible plastic and are easy to pull off and clean (Photos 9 and 10). But if they're rigid plastic, you'll probably have to unscrew or cut off with a saw to check. Reglue rigid tubes

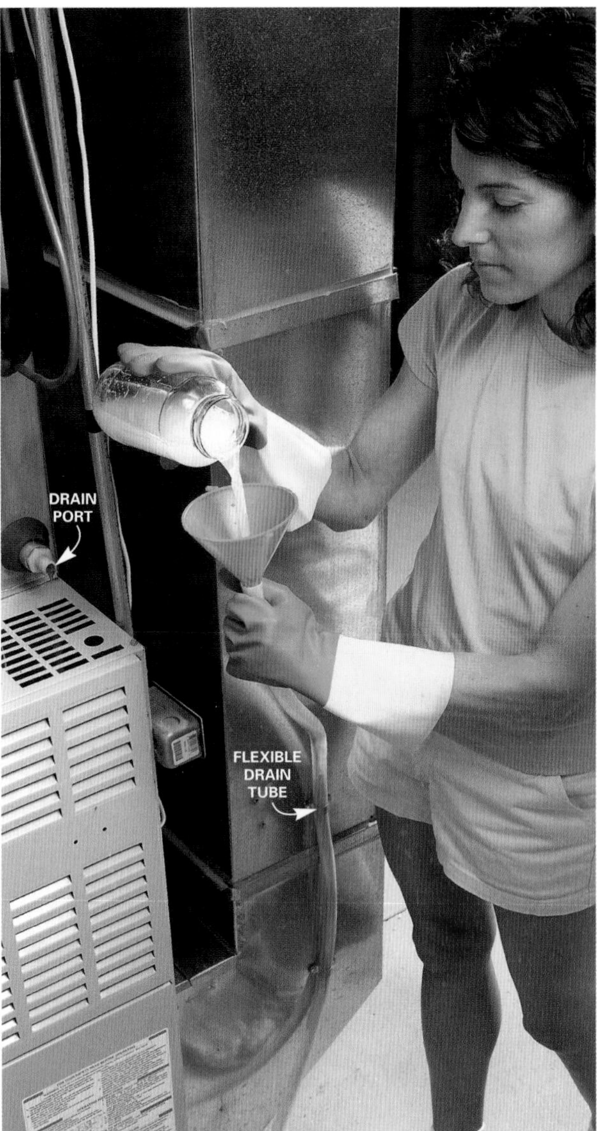

9 PULL OFF the plastic condensation drain tube and check it for algae growth. Clean it by pouring a bleach/water solution (1:16 ratio) through the tube to flush the line. Or simply replace the tube.

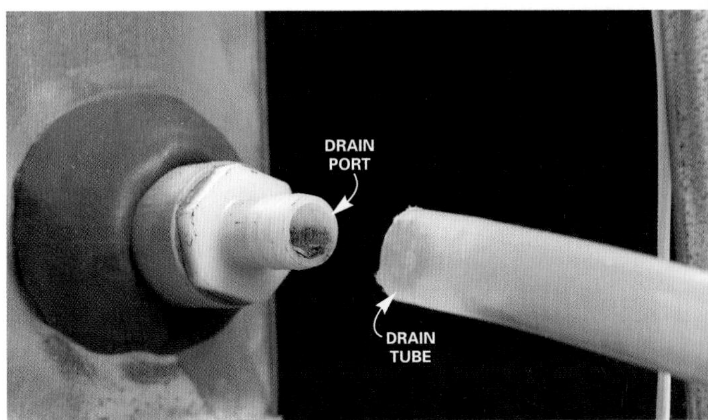

10 POKE a pipe cleaner into the drain port and clean out any debris. Reinstall the drain tube and turn the power back on.

More to top-

Strategies for

If your upper floors are too hot and lower floors too cold in the summer, try this: In the summer, almost completely close down the first-floor heating and cooling vents (there's usually a lever on the grate) and completely open the ones on the second floor. That may force more cool air upstairs. The cool air will sink to the lower floor naturally. Reverse the procedure during the heating season.

If that doesn't work, contact an air-conditioning company to have a pro look over your home and see if it's possible to convert your heating and cooling system to a "zone"-type system. Each floor is then treated as an independent zone—complete with its own thermostat and helper fans that force heated or cooled air to where it's needed. Depending on the existing ductwork and structural considerations, it may be next to impossible to convert an existing home, but a pro can help you decide.

If a zone system isn't feasible, ask the company about installing a "split," or "ductless," air conditioner that will be solely dedicated to cooling the upper floor. A split air conditioner is similar to a conventional window air conditioner except that it's split in half. The unit that contains the

SPLIT AIR-CONDITIONING REMOTE CONTROL

cool air floor bedrooms

efficient and quieter whole-house cooling

noisy compressor is usually on the ground outside the house. Refrigerant lines connect it to an indoor air handler that's typically mounted to a wall or ceiling in the area you wish to cool. A very quiet fan blows room air over cool coils to distribute the conditioned air. Installation costs start at $2,000, including parts and labor.

RAISE YOUR THERMOSTAT, SAVE $$. You can save up to $100 in a summer by raising your air conditioner's thermostat to 78 degrees F.

Energy-Saving Product

Portable air conditioner for cool rooms

When you want to stay cool without the expense of firing up your central air and cooling the entire house, plug in a portable air conditioner. They cool up to 400 sq. ft., and you can roll them from room to room—wherever you want to cool. We tried a $500 unit (DeLonghi, www.delonghi.com) and were impressed. It made little noise when running and quickly cooled the room.

Most portable air conditioners have an exhaust hose that goes out the window. The exhaust also drains condensation water, so there's no drip pan to empty. Air intake can come from the room (for higher efficiency) or from outside through an intake hose (for fresher air).

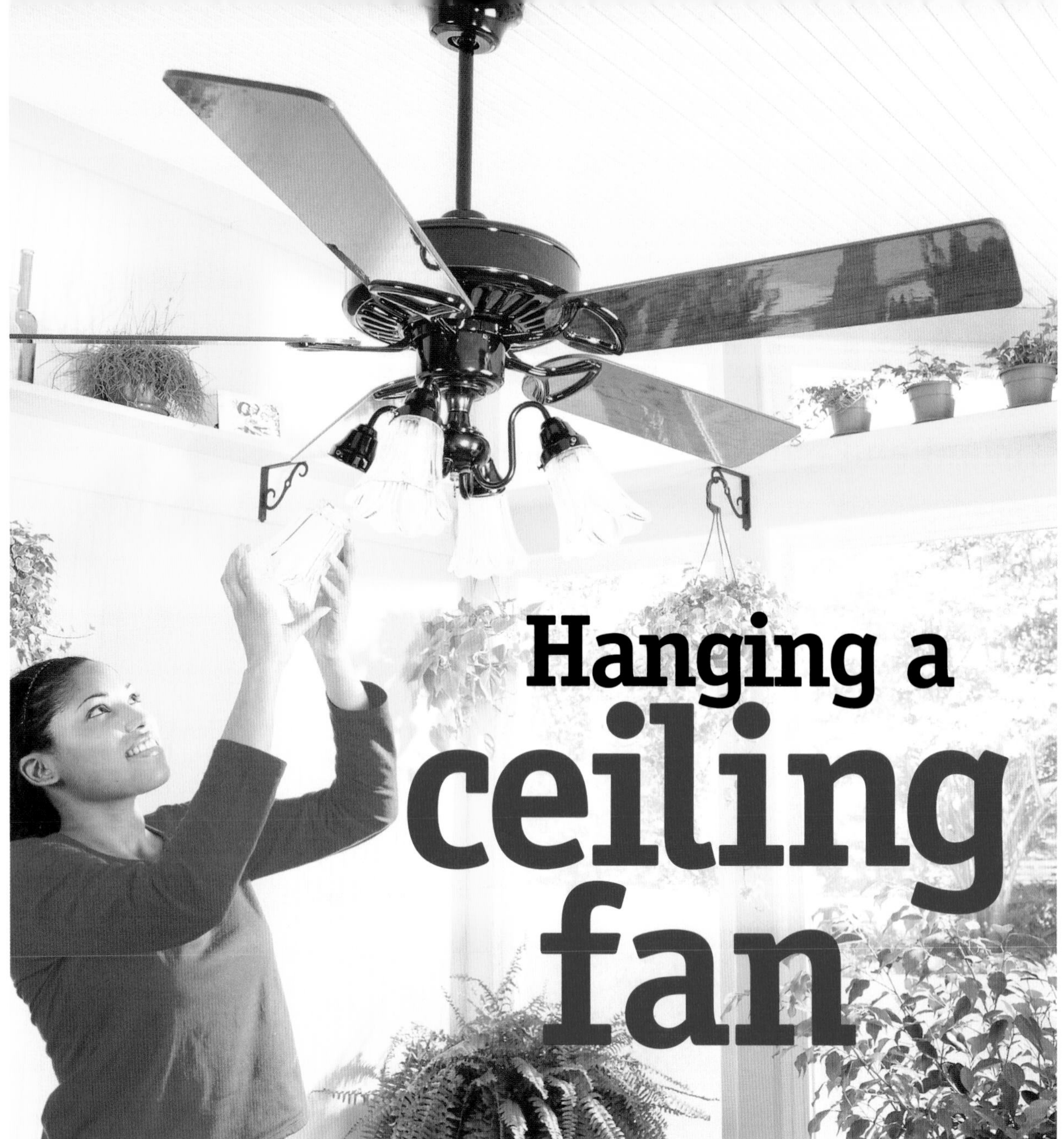

Hanging a ceiling fan

Ceiling fans keep you cool for a few cents a day

A high-efficiency ceiling fan can cost as little as $1 a month when run eight hours a day; a window air conditioner can cost 50 times as much to run. And you can enjoy a fan all year long, as it circulates warm air in the winter.

Ceiling fans (technically called "paddle fans") used to be frustrating to install, to say the least. Most of the time you had to wing it because specialty hanging systems were poorly developed or nonexistent. Now, most manufacturers have designed versatile mounting systems that take the hassle out of installation. When you add in the improved, stronger ceiling boxes, you'll find that just about any ceiling fan can go up quick and easy on any ceiling, sloped or flat.

Here you'll find crystal-clear instructions that go beyond the basic set included with the fan. Also, see how to avoid common pitfalls like putting on parts in the wrong order and forgetting to slip shrouds on ahead of time. Some mistakes are more serious than these. Standard electrical boxes or blades hung too low can be downright dangerous.

Expect to spend at least $150 for a high-quality fan (see "Buying a ceiling fan," opposite) and a bit more for accessories like electronic controls, fancy light packages and furniture-grade paddles.

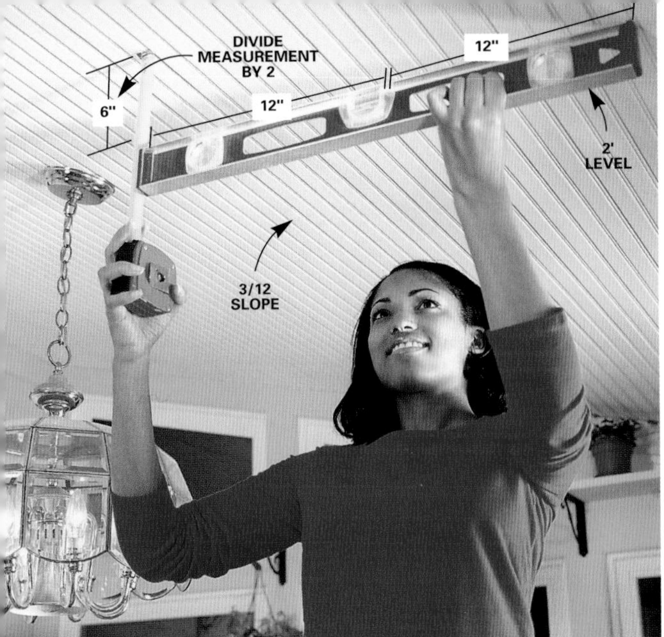

1 DETERMINE the ceiling slope by holding a 2-ft. level against the ceiling and measuring the vertical distance from the level to the ceiling. Divide that number by 2 to get the drop over 12 in. of horizontal run, 3/12 slope in our case. See the chart on p. 107 to determine the minimum downrod length for the blade diameter you'd like.

2 SHUT OFF the power at the main panel and remove the light fixture. Knock the existing electrical box free of the framing with a hammer and a block of wood, then pull the electrical cable free of the old box and through the ceiling hole. Leave the old box in the ceiling cavity unless you can easily remove it through the hole.

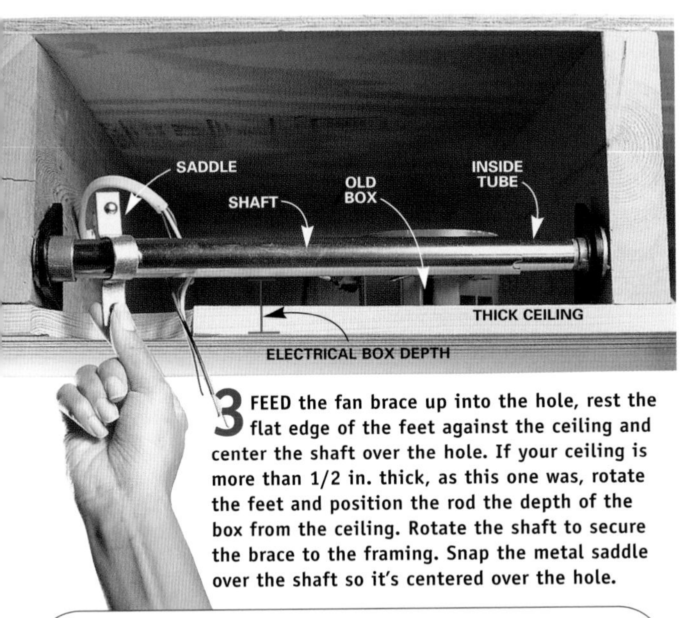

3 FEED the fan brace up into the hole, rest the flat edge of the feet against the ceiling and center the shaft over the hole. If your ceiling is more than 1/2 in. thick, as this one was, rotate the feet and position the rod the depth of the box from the ceiling. Rotate the shaft to secure the brace to the framing. Snap the metal saddle over the shaft so it's centered over the hole.

tip Before you knock the existing electrical box free (Photo 2), bend back the plastic clamps or loosen the metal cable clamps so it'll be easier to pull the electrical cable free after the box is loosened.

Put up a new fan in a leisurely Saturday afternoon

If everything goes well, you can put up a ceiling fan in a couple of hours, including cleanup. In most cases, the whole job will take only a hammer, a screwdriver, a 3/8-in. nut driver and a wire stripper.

Buying a ceiling fan

IF YOU HAVEN'T WALKED UNDER A LARGE FAN display yet, hold on to your hat. You'll be overwhelmed by the selection of colors, styles and accessories, especially if you visit a ceiling fan store. If you intend to use your fan regularly, invest in a model in the $150-plus category. You'll get a quieter, more efficient, more durable unit. If you spend beyond that amount, you're usually paying for light packages, radio-actuated remote and wall controls, style and design (fancier motor castings, inlays, blade adornments or glasswork). If you spend less, you're likely to get a less efficient, less durable, noisier unit with fewer color, blade and electronic choices.

Choose the blade diameter that best suits the room visually and make sure the unit will fit under the ceiling without jeopardizing the foreheads of your tallest friends. (See p. 107 for height requirements.) Bigger rooms call for wider fan blade diameters. The bigger fan will not only look better but also move more air.

Most ceiling fans are designed for heated, enclosed spaces. If you're putting a fan in a screen room, a gazebo or other damp area, the building code requires you to use a "damp-rated" fan. These fans have corrosion-resistant stainless steel or plastic parts that can stand up to high humidity and condensation. If you live in a coastal area with corrosive sea air, or if you're putting a fan in a particularly wet environment like a greenhouse or an enclosed pool area, you should choose a "wet-rated" fan.

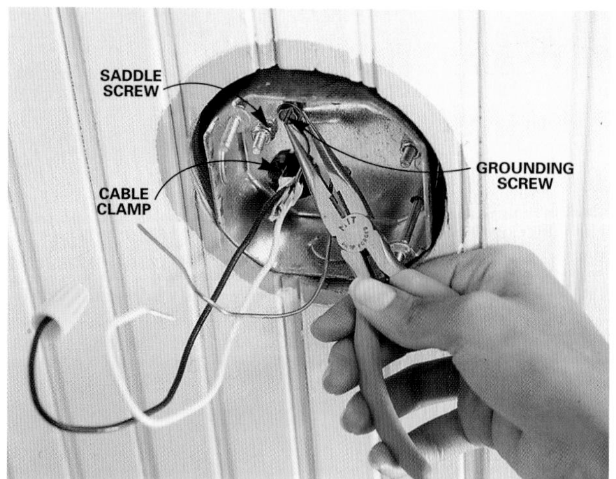

4 **FEED the existing wire through the cable clamp in the top of the new metal box, slip the box over the saddle screws, and tighten the nuts to clamp the box to the shaft with a nut driver or a deep-well socket. Crimp a loop of grounding wire three-quarters around the grounding screw and tighten the screw.**

5 **POSITION the hanger bracket so that the opening in the bracket is on the uphill side of the sloped ceiling. Then screw it into the box with the special screws provided with the fan brace.**

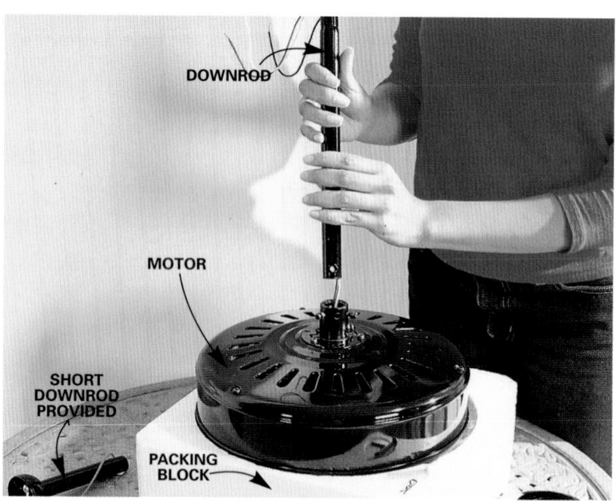

6 **PLACE the motor right side up, thread the wire through the downrod and insert the downrod into the mounting collar.**

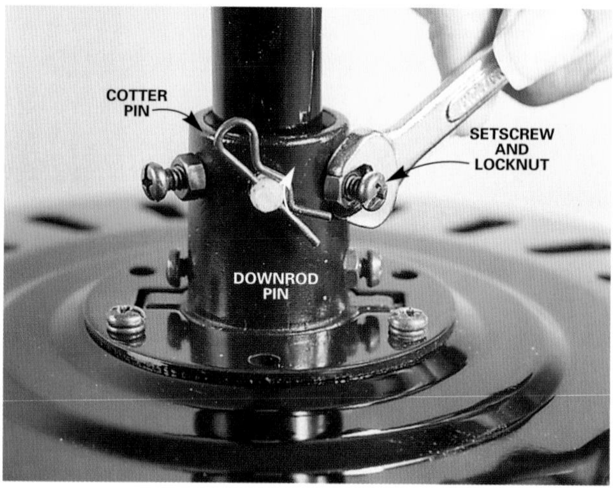

7 **SLIP the downrod pin through the collar and tube, lock it into place with the cotter pin, and tighten the screws and locknuts.**

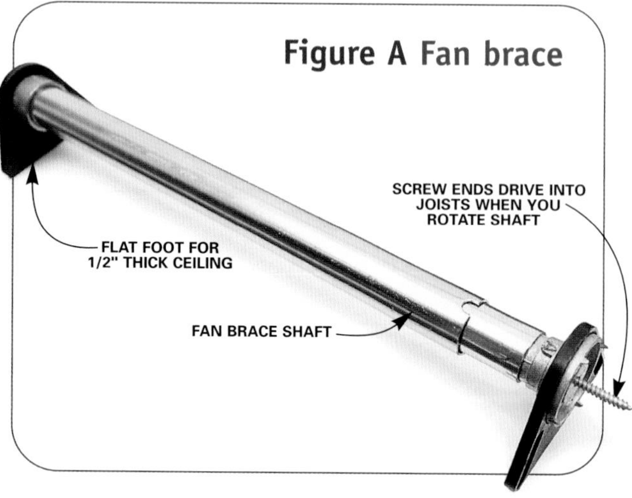

tip Tighten the locknuts firmly. Loose locknuts are the most common cause of wobbly fans.

Most of the time, the wires that fed a previous ceiling light fixture are adequate for hooking up a new fan. If you have a wiring arrangement that's different from the one shown here and you are unfamiliar with wiring techniques, consult an electrician or building inspector for help.

Follow the photo series for basic installation steps that apply to more than 95 percent of all fans. There may be small variations, particularly when it comes to the light and blade mountings, so you'll still need to consult the instructions provided with your fan. As with any other electrical work, you may need an electrical permit from your local building department before starting the job. The inspector will tell you when to call for an inspection.

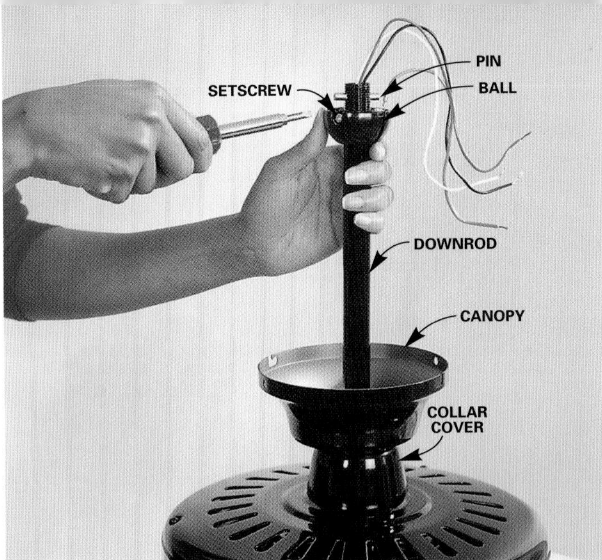

8 **SLIP the collar cover, then the canopy, over the downrod. Slide the ball over the downrod and push the pin through both sets of holes, then lift the ball over the pin and tighten the setscrew.**

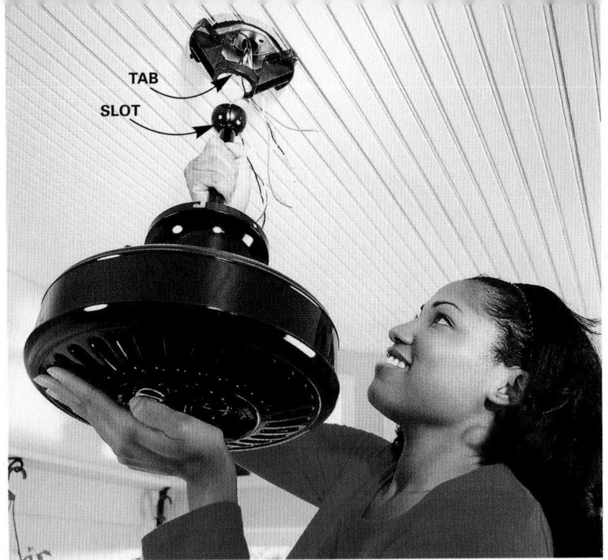

9 **LIFT the assembly over the open side of the bracket and lower it into place. Rotate the motor until the ball slot locks into place over the tab on the bracket.**

10 **CONNECT the bare ground wire from the box to the green ground wire on the bracket with a wire connector. Connect the white neutral wire from the motor to the neutral wire from the box. Connect the blue and black wires from the motor to the black hot wire from the box and neatly fold them into the box.**

Energy-Saving Q&A

Sizing a ceiling fan

Q **I understand ceiling fans can save energy and money for heating and cooling. Is there a rule of thumb for what size fan I need?**

A Yes, a quick rule of thumb matches the diameter of the fan with the largest dimension of a room. For 12 ft. or less, use a 36-in. fan. For 12 to 16 ft., use a 48-in. fan. For 16 to 18 ft., use a 52-in. fan. And for dimensions larger than 18 ft., install two fans.

Placement of a ceiling fan for adequate air circulation is 7 ft. above the floor with the blades 8 to 10 in. from the ceiling. And to move more air at low speed, a fan with five blades is best.

Regarding energy savings, research has proven that ceiling fans can save energy during the cooling season by creating a gentle breeze. You get your savings then by raising your thermostat by a minimum of 2 degrees. This decreases air conditioning energy used by 10 to 15 percent, or 5 to 8 percent per degree.

By reversing your fan (so it runs clockwise) during winter, you pull heat from the ceiling and push it down to the floor for more even heating.

Replace electrical boxes with specially designed paddle fan braces

Before starting any work, shut off the circuit breaker that feeds the switch and light fixture. If there's a working bulb in the fixture, turn it on. Then you'll know you have the right breaker when the bulb goes out. Check the wires with a voltage tester to make sure they're off after removing the fixture and when changing the wall switch.

The next step is to remove the existing plastic or metal electrical box and install a "fan brace" that's designed to hold ceiling fans. Few conventional boxes are strong enough to support a ceiling fan, so don't even think about trying to hang your fan from an existing box. Instead, buy a fan brace (about $15) when you purchase your fan. You can choose braces that fasten with screws if the framing is accessible from the attic or if it's new construction. Otherwise, pick a brace that's designed to slip through the ceiling hole and through the electrical box.

11 **SCREW the fan blades to their brackets and screw the brackets to the bottom of the motor. It's easiest to hold the screw in the bracket with the screwdriver while you lift the blade assembly into position. Then drive in the screw.**

12 **PLACE the radio receiver into the switch housing/light pod assembly and connect the light pod wires according to the manufacturer's instructions. Note the settings on the receiver's code toggles so you can dial in the same settings on the electronic controls at the wall switch. Now loosen the screws in the switch-housing hub halfway. Plug the motor wiring into the receptacle on the receiver and twist the switch housing into place on the hub. Retighten the screws.**

These braces (Photo 3) adjust to fit between the framing members in your ceiling; you simply rotate the shaft to anchor them to the framing.

Most existing electrical boxes are fastened to the framing with nails, making them easy to pound out with a hammer and a block of wood (Photo 2). After you free the cable, just leave the old box in the cavity (Photo 3) rather than struggling to work the box through the ceiling hole. Then pull the cable through the hole and slip the fan brace through the opening and secure it, following the directions that came with the brace. Little feet on the ends of braces keep them the correct distance from the back side of 1/2-in.- thick ceilings so the new electrical box will be flush with the surface. If you have a thicker ceiling, rotate the ends to achieve the correct spacing.

New electronic controls save you from running additional wiring

Since most fan installations are retrofits into existing electrical boxes, there's usually a single electrical cable connecting the fixture to a single wall switch. You can leave the switch and use it to turn the fan on and off, then use the pull chains on the fan to control fan speed and lights. A second option is to install electronic controls. Higher-quality fans give you the option of adding a radio receiver kit for about $75. The receiver accepts signals from a special wall switch (included in the kit) to control the fan and light separately without additional wiring. The receiver also accepts signals from a handheld remote, so you can operate multiple fans and fine-tune fan speed and light intensity from your easy chair. Electronic switches are matched to fans by flipping code toggles in the controls and the fan, just like with your garage door opener. Installing an electronic switch (Photo 12) is a snap. The receiver drops right into the fan housing and plugs into the bottom of the motor.

If the old light is fed by two three-way switches instead of a single switch, the control options are a little more complicated. You have three choices:

1. Leave the existing switches in place and turn one of them on. Then use a remote (see photo, opposite) to control the fan and lights.
2. Use the existing switches and control the fan and lights independently with pull chains.
3. Disable one of the three-way switches and rewire the other one to receive a wall-mounted electronic control. Sorting out all the wires is complex. You'll need an electrician's help for this.

Fan height requirements

Manufacturers generally require that fan blades be at least 7 ft. above the floor. Since most fan and motor assemblies are less than 12 in. high, they'll fit under a standard 8-ft. ceiling with the proper clearance.

13 **CHECK and reset (if necessary) the code toggles on the wall-mounted electronic switch to match the ones on the receiver. Remove the existing wall switch and connect the two black wires on the new switch to the ones that were connected to the old switch with wire connectors. Screw the switch into the box and install the cover plate.**

Quick tip*

CEILING FANS HELP ALL YEAR LONG

In the summer, set your fan so the blades are pushing air downward to create a breezy, cooling effect. In the winter, reverse the direction so the blades push hot air that accumulates near the ceiling out toward the edges of the room, then down the walls.

Angled ceilings require that you install "downrods" (also called extension tubes or downtubes) that will lower the motor and fan blades so they'll clear a sloped ceiling surface. The more space between the ceiling and the fan, the better. The fan will have more air to draw from, and you'll feel more air movement because the blades are closer to you.

Most fans come with a short downrod designed for mounting on 8-ft. ceilings. If your ceiling's less than 8 ft., you'll need to remove the rod provided and flush-mount the fan. But if you have a higher or sloped ceiling, purchase a longer downrod.

Minimum downrod length (in inches) for angled ceilings

Blade Dia.	Ceiling Slope 3/12	4/12	5/12	6/12	8/12*	10/12*	12/12*
27 in.	6	6	6	12	18	24	36
36 in.	6	6	6	12	18	24	36
44 in.	6	6	12	12	24	30	42
52 in.	6	12	18	18	24	30	42
56 in.	12	12	18	24	30	36	48

* Also requires slope adapting kit.

*Energy-Saving Goof

Fan-tabulous job!

When my son turned seven, I decided to build a special bed/shelving/desk project to fit into his small bedroom. Having read previous goofs in your magazine, I was careful to use knockdown hardware so I could get this sizable project in and out of the room. When the big day arrived to install this 6-ft.-high beauty, my son climbed up the ladder to the bunk. My wife turned on the light to admire the project and the ceiling fan nearly took my son's head off. I'd completely forgotten about the fan in the middle of the room. We moved the project into every conceivable configuration and still the fan spun over the bed. The fan just wasn't in the plan!

Improving attic ventilation

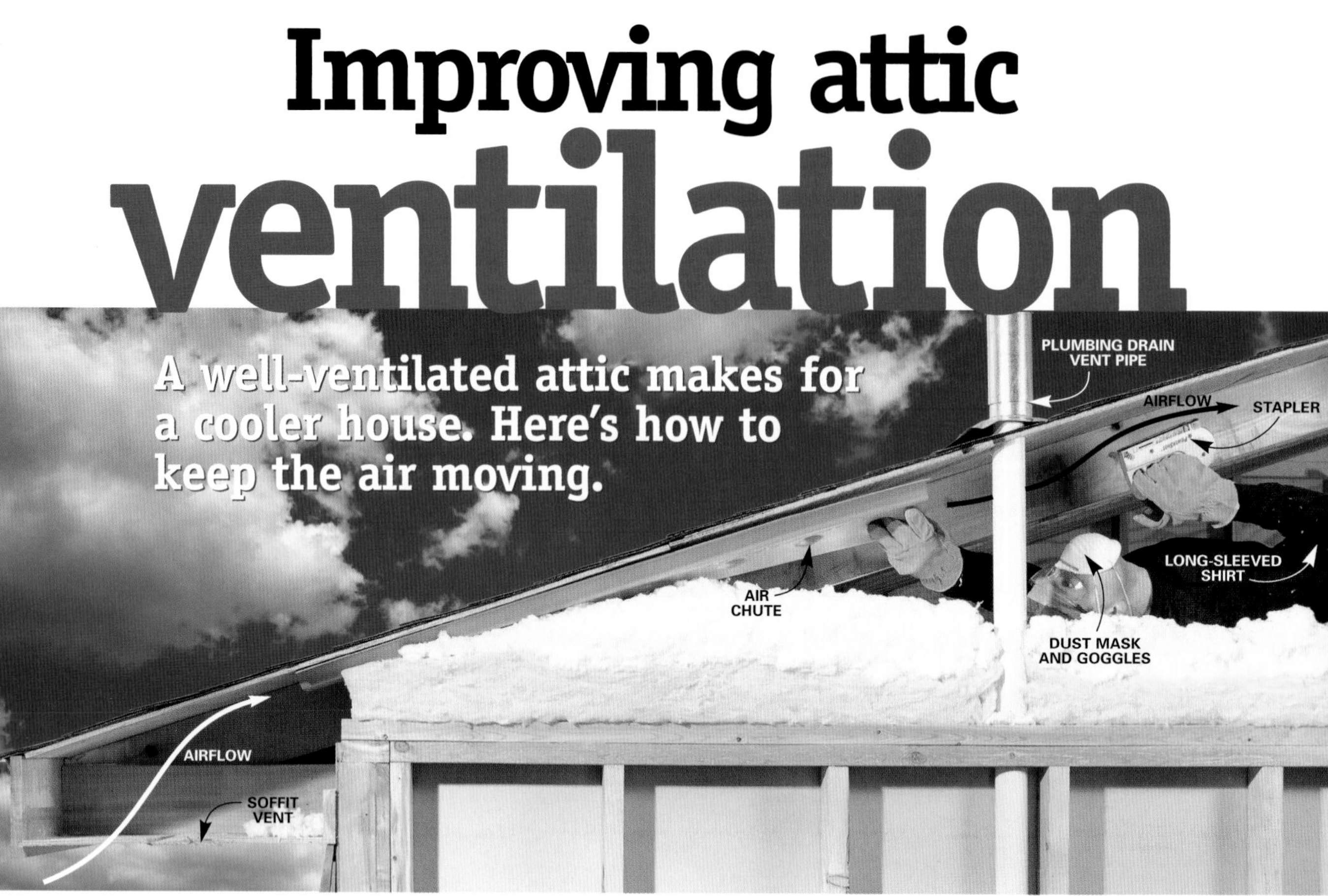

1 INSTALL air chutes ($1 each at home centers) in each rafter space to keep the air path clear between the rafters and the roof sheathing. Staple the chutes in place. Be sure to wear long sleeves, goggles and a dust mask. Tip: Coat your arms, face and neck with talcum powder to reduce the itching from insulation.

A well-ventilated attic offers four benefits:

1. It reduces cooling costs in the warm season. The savings will be slight if you have a well-insulated attic space, greater if you have little insulation.
2. It prevents mildew growth and rot on your roof's framing and sheathing by reducing moisture buildup.
3. It helps prevent ice dams in winter by keeping your roof colder. (See p. 82 for details on ice dams.)
4. It extends the life of your shingles by keeping the roof cooler in hot weather. (The manufacturer's shingle warranty requires ventilation.)

Here you'll learn when to add ventilation, how to install several types of passive roof vents and soffit (eave) vents, and how to keep your ventilation system working. We won't cover fan-powered ventilation, since this type is usually not necessary.

As you will see, improving attic ventilation isn't expensive, time-consuming or difficult, even for the novice. You only need basic hand and power tools. However, when you climb up on your roof, be sure to follow safety precautions. If your roof is steep or you don't feel confident up there, hire a pro. (Look under "Roofing" in your yellow pages.)

Does your house need more vents?

Before you go out and start poking holes in your roof and soffits, check to see if you have the type of problem that attic ventilation can solve.

One common problem is caused by ice buildup along the edges of a roof. These ice dams form when warm attic air melts the snow on the roof and the water refreezes along the colder edge of the roof. The ice traps water behind it, allowing the water to seep back under the shingles and leak through the roof. Increased ventilation will make the entire roof cold and reduce or eliminate ice dams. (For more details, see "Understanding ice dams," p. 82.)

Another common problem is moisture buildup. After cold weather arrives, grab a flashlight and inspect your attic. Cover all your skin to protect it from the itchy insulation, and wear a dust mask. If your attic doesn't have a walkway, take two small (2 x 4-ft.) sheets of 1/2-in. plywood to move around on. Here are the signs to look for:

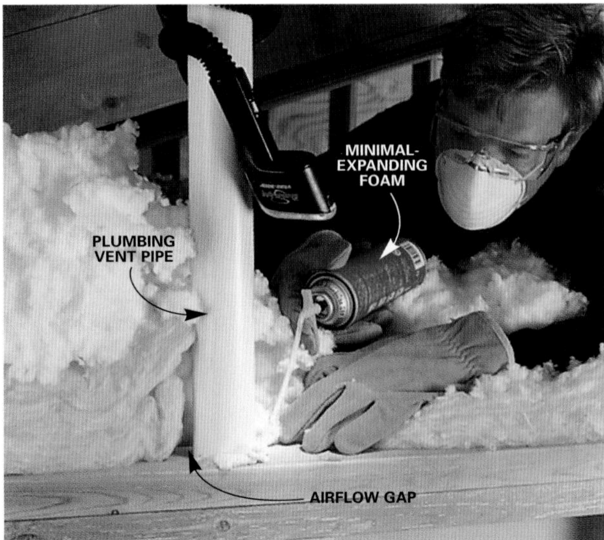

2 **SEAL gaps around plumbing drain vent pipes, ductwork and electrical boxes with minimal-expanding foam or caulk. This helps keep warm, moist air out of the attic.**

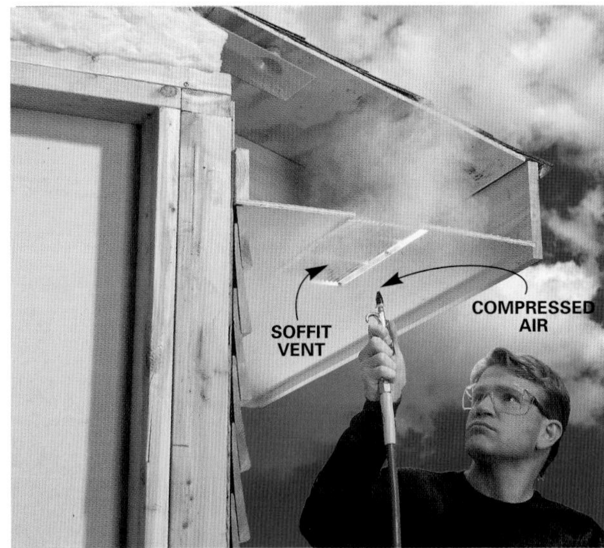

3 **CLEAR your soffit vents every few years with blasts of compressed air. Always do this after you install air chutes because you'll probably knock insulation down into the soffit.**

Roof safety tips

TIP 1: Use a safety harness (see Photo 9), especially if your roof has a slope steeper than 6:12.
TIP 2: Work only when the roof is dry. Wet shingles can be slippery.
TIP 3: Keep your shoe soles flat on the roof, rather than digging in with the edges.
TIP 4: After making cuts with your circular saw, sweep away the sawdust to avoid slipping.
TIP 5: Don't step on power cords or ropes. They'll roll under your feet and cause a fall.

1. Frost on the underside of the roof or rafters. Warm, moist air trapped in the attic condenses and freezes on the wood.
2. Water-stained or blackened wood. A sign of mildew or rot. You can also spot this in the summer.
3. Heavily rusted nails. A sign that condensation is forming on metal surfaces.
4. Matted-down insulation. A sign of roof leaks from ice damming or other causes.

If you have either ice dams or moisture buildup, improve your attic ventilation. Begin by making sure your existing system works (Photos 1 and 3), plugging major air leaks into the attic (Photo 2) and correcting any other of the "Five common causes of poor attic venting" (at right). If those steps don't solve the problem, add more vents, following the techniques shown in Photos 4 – 17. For help figuring how much venting you need, see "Minimum venting requirements," p. 110.

Even if you aren't having problems, bring your attic venting up to code when (1) you install new shingles and (2) you add attic insulation.

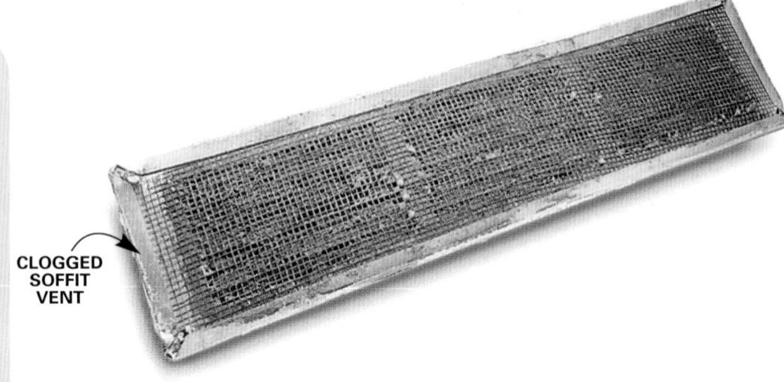

Five common causes of poor attic venting

PROBLEM 1 Insulation often clogs the space between the rafters, blocking air from traveling to and from the soffit area. **Solution:** Install air chutes or clear them if they're clogged (Photo 1).
PROBLEM 2 Aluminum or vinyl soffits (eaves) installed over plywood soffits that don't have venting holes. **Solution:** Cut holes in plywood soffits as needed.
PROBLEM 3 Gaps to the attic around plumbing pipes, ducting and electrical boxes. Many experts consider plugging these holes to be more important than ventilation. **Solution:** See Photo 2.
PROBLEM 4 Rectangular roof vents installed on one side of the roof only. Rectangular roof vents work best when the wind blows over the top of them, rather than into them. **Solution:** Install rectangular roof vents on both sides of the roof.
PROBLEM 5 Kitchen and bath fans vented into the attic. **Solution:** Vent these fans through the roof or soffit.

Rectangular Soffit Vents

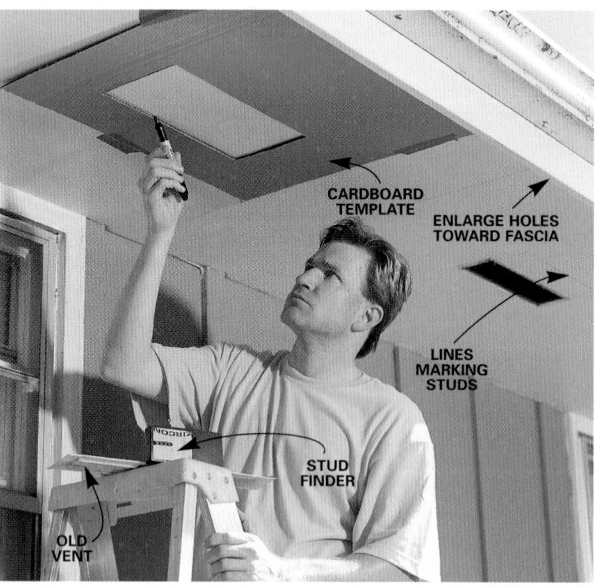

4 ADHERE template against fascia and mark soffit hole locations. Make vent hole 1/2 in. smaller on each side than the new vent. If you widen existing holes, widen them toward the fascia, but no closer than 3 in. from the fascia to avoid ripples in the soffit plywood. Position holes between rafters at equal intervals. You can find rafters by locating nailheads or using a stud finder.

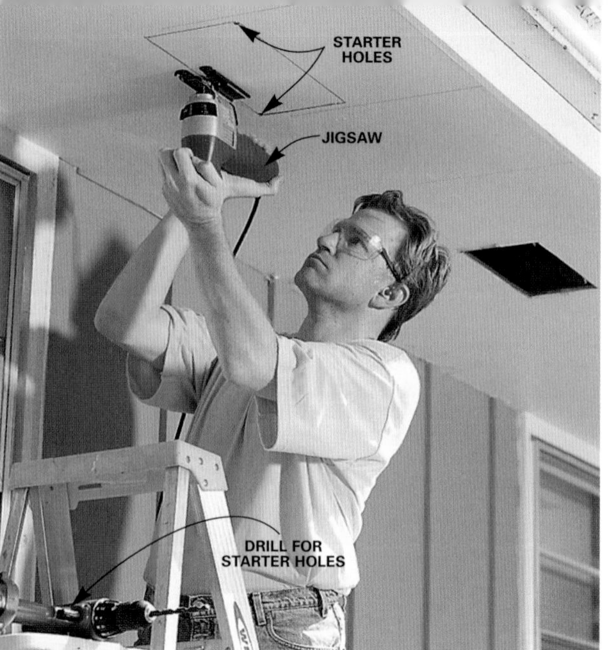

5 DRILL 3/8-in. starter holes at opposite corners of the vent hole. Then cut out the hole with a jigsaw. If the soffit plywood begins to tear and splinter in the crosscut, use a utility knife to score the cutting line.

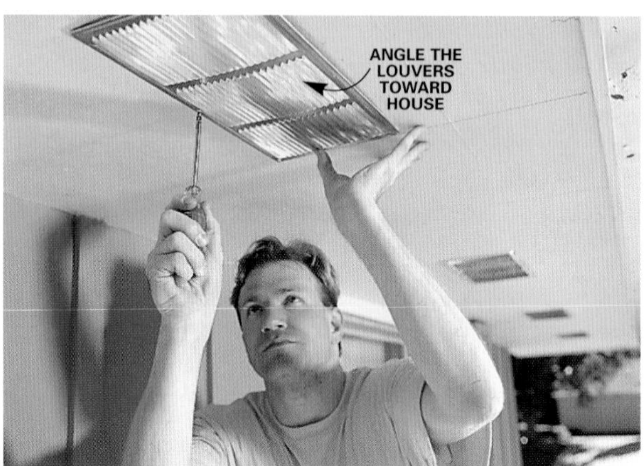

6 INSTALL the soffit vent with self-tapping screws. Angle the vent louvers toward the house wall. (This prevents blowing snow from entering the vent, and it looks better from the ground.)

Add soffit vents first

You can gain the most airflow with the least amount of trouble by installing soffit vents. The two most common are rectangular vents (Photo 9) and continuous strip vents (Photo 7). Continuous strip vents allow perfectly even ventilation along the eaves (Photos 7 and 8), but they're difficult to retrofit in an existing soffit.

Rectangular vents are easiest to install (Photos 4 – 6). Here all 4 x 16-in. vents (28 sq. in. of net free vent area, or NFVA) with 8 x 16-in. vents (56 sq. in. NFVA) were replaced and more were added. This increased soffit ventilation almost five times. An 8 x 16-in. vent costs less than $2 and takes less than 10 minutes to install.

Minimum venting requirements

MOST BUILDING CODES REQUIRE 1 sq. ft. of venting (technically, "net free vent area," or NFVA) for each 150 sq. ft. of attic. In some circumstances you can have less, but we recommend the 1:150 ratio. So a house with a 1,500-sq.-ft. attic will need 10 sq. ft. of venting, ideally about half placed high on the roof and half in the soffits. Look for the NFVA of each vent you buy stamped somewhere on the metal.

Caution:

Asbestos has been found in some types of vermiculite insulation. Vermiculite, a lightweight material resembling gravel, was used as attic insulation in perhaps as many as a million homes. If you have vermiculite in your attic, don't disturb it unless you have a sample checked by an accredited laboratory. Disturbing it can release the asbestos fibers, which, once airborne, can enter your lungs and eventually cause lung disease. For a list of accredited testing labs, call your local department of public health. For more vermiculite details, go to www2.epa.gov/asbestos and click on "Learn about vermiculite insulation" or call your regional EPA office.

Soffit Strip Vents

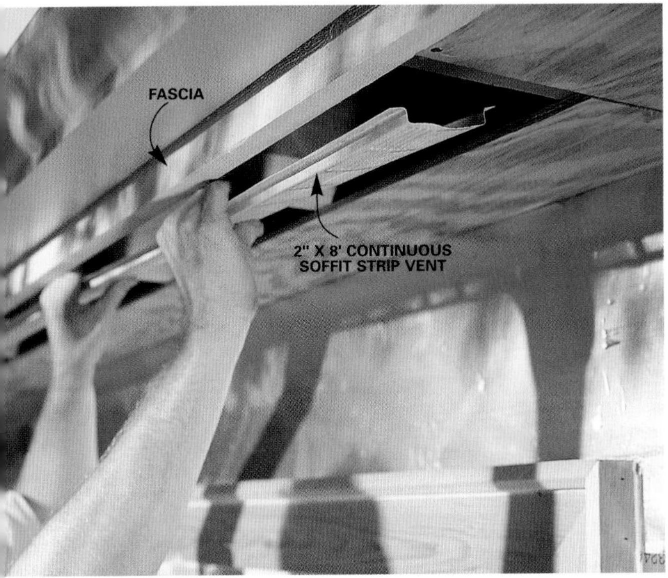

7 INSTALL a 2-in. continuous-strip soffit vent so that it's closer to the fascia than to the house wall. Loosely nail one side of the soffit, then slide the strip vent's flange underneath the plywood.

8 FINISH nailing up the strips. The narrowest soffit plywood strip should be at least 3 in. wide.

Energy-Saving Q&A

Flat roof vents vs. wind-driven turbine vents

Q I've hired a roofer to replace my shingles. He's planning to tear off all the shingles and replace all the roof vents and flashing. Here's my question. He wants to replace the wind-driven whirligig-style roof vents with flat roof vents, saying they'll handle the venting just as well and look better. Am I getting taken? (I know the flat ones are cheaper.) If they're just as good, I'm happy since I'm sick of hearing the old ones squeak all the time.

A All things being equal, wind-driven turbine vents do move more air than flat vents (but only when the wind blows). The question: How much air must be moved? A largely arbitrary rule of thumb that's been adopted into most building codes calls for 1 sq. ft. of vented area for every 300 sq. ft. of attic space. So a 1,500-sq.-ft. attic must have 5 sq. ft. of vent space—half dedicated for air intake in the soffits and the other half for exhaust on the roof. (These can be ridge vents, wind turbines or the flat vents your roofer wants to install.)

In cold climates, good attic ventilation is important for preventing ice dams. It also keeps your home cooler in the summer, vents moisture that finds its way from the living spaces of your home into the attic and helps shingles last longer. The fact is, it's hard to overventilate an attic—generally, more is better.

If you don't like the looks of wind turbines, don't be afraid to use the flat vents; just be sure to follow the 300-sq.-ft. rule. But if you want to use wind turbines, buy high-quality ones that have permanently lubricated ball bearings or plastic bushings in the spinning mechanisms. Usually, it's the cheaper units with metal bushings that will squeak and eventually drive you (and your neighbors) out of your mind on windy nights.

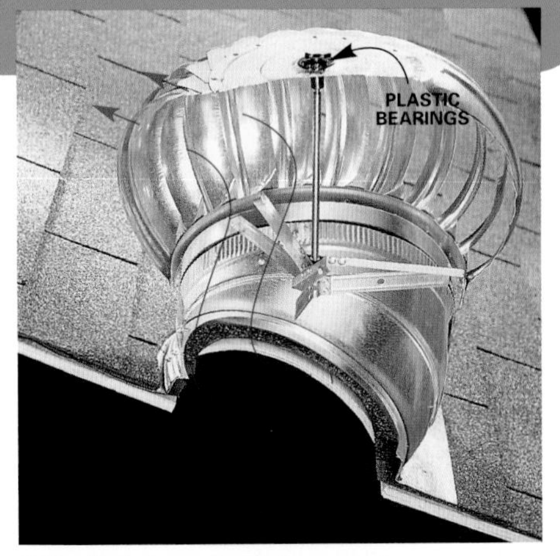

Wind-driven turbine vent

Flat roof vent

Rectangular Roof Vents

9 CUT a square hole in the roof the same size as the hole in the base of the vent you're installing. Locate the top of the hole about 15 in. below the peak of the roof. Mark the hole with chalk and set your saw depth to cut through the shingles and the roof sheathing only. Don't cut into any rafters. For a roof with a single layer of shingles, start with a depth of 3/4 in. Use an old carbide blade for cutting, and wear safety goggles and hearing protection because you will hit nails.

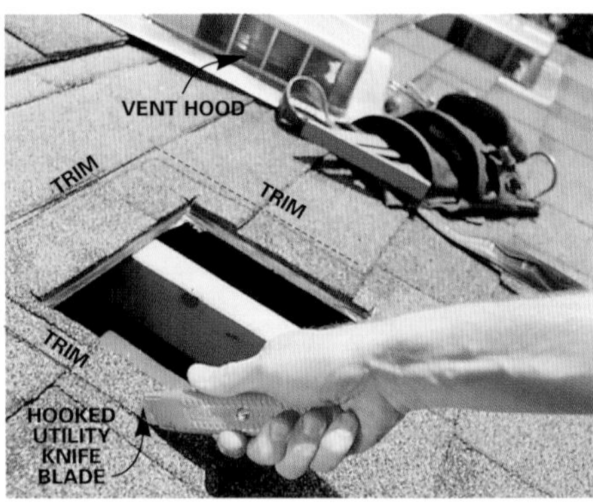

10 MEASURE the vent hood size and trim the topmost shingles with a hooked knife blade so they will butt against the vent hood on the top and the sides. You'll have to trim two or three rows of shingles (see Photo 12).

11 PULL nails as necessary so the vent's flange can slide into place. The best time to do this is when the shingles are cool (early morning). Use your flat pry bar to carefully separate the shingles from one another. Apply roofing cement around the perimeter of the hole.

12 HOLD the vent up at an angle and slide it into place. Then set it down into the roofing cement.

13 NAIL the flange to the roof on the front edge. Finish sealing the vent by applying cement to the areas where the shingles overlap one another and where they overlap the flange.

How to choose roof vents

We recommend two types of roof vents: heavy-gauge rectangular metal vents (Photo 13) and plastic shingle-over ridge vents with baffles (Photo 16).

tip Work in cool weather so you don't mar the shingles.

Ridge vents with baffles have several advantages: Their low profile and shingle cover make them blend into the roof, and they distribute ventilation evenly along the ridge. You're also less likely to damage the shingles when you install them.

Ridge vents cost about $10 per 4-ft. section and are available from roofing dealers and many home centers. Follow Photos 14 – 17 for installation tips.

Rectangular metal roof vents work best on hip or pyramid roofs that have a short ridge line. Look for galvanized steel vents. (They cost $6 to $10 and are available at roofing supply stores and some home centers.) Follow Photos 9 – 13 for installation tips. Consult a roofing supply store for special installation instructions if you have a metal, slate, cedar or tile roof.

Ridge Vents

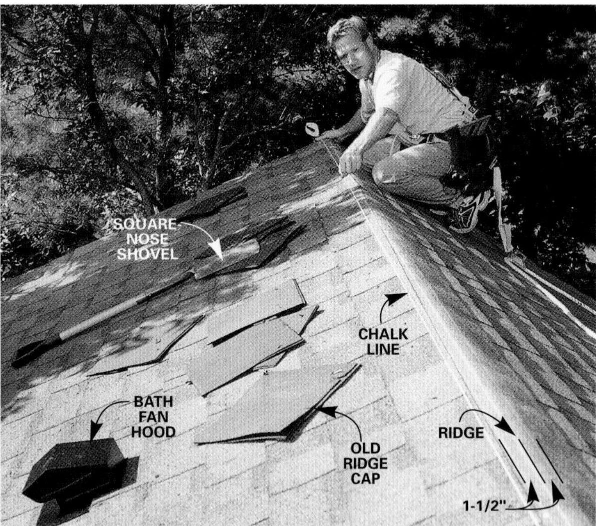

14 **REMOVE the old ridge cap with a flat pry bar or square-nose shovel. Pull out any nails left behind. Use a chalk line to mark your cutting line. First, pop a line along the very top of the ridge. Then pop a line 1-1/2 in. down from your ridge line on both sides of it. These will be your cutting lines.**

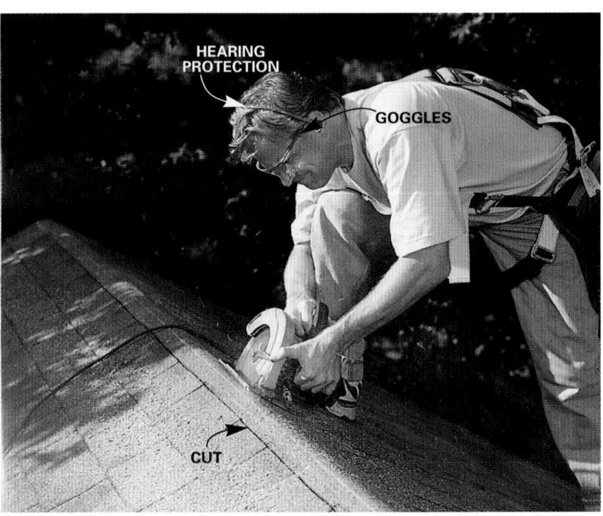

15 **CUT OUT a slot in the shingles and the sheathing with a circular saw equipped with an old carbide blade. For a single shingle layer, start with a blade depth of 3/4 in. and make sure it doesn't cut into the rafters. If you have an overhang, stop the slot short so the opening is only over the attic space, not the overhang. If you have a hip roof (no gabled ends), stop the slot 6 in. short of the beginning of the hip. Wear your goggles and hearing protection because you WILL hit nails. Sweep off the sawdust and open the slot with a flat pry bar.**

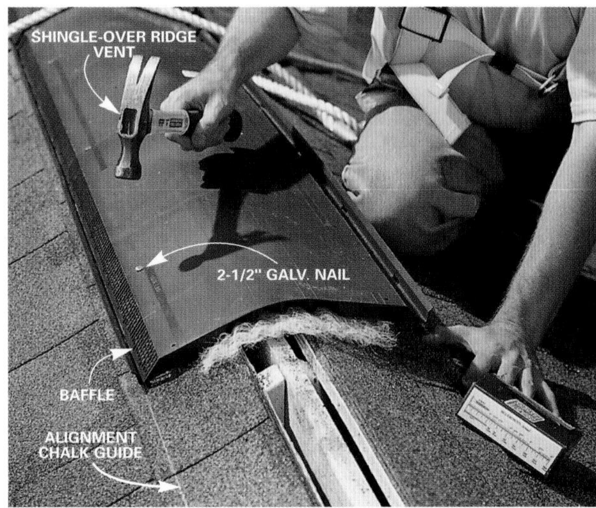

16 **TO INSTALL a ridge vent, first pop a chalk line down from your ridge line equal to half the width of the ridge vent. Align ridge vent pieces. Nail one side of vent in place with 2-1/2-in. galvanized nails. To keep the line straight, finish nailing the side you aligned with your chalk line before nailing the other side.**

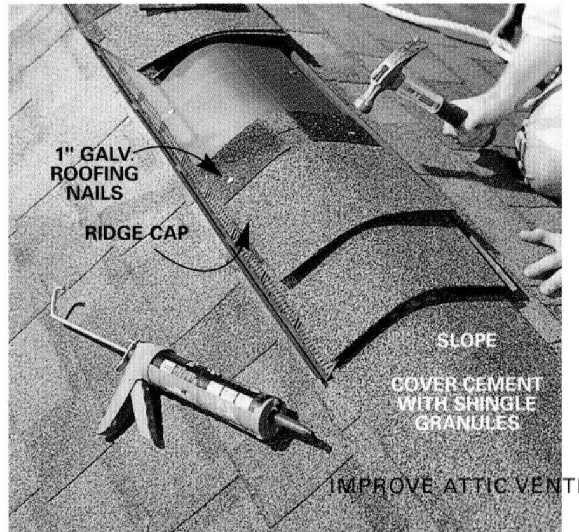

17 **COVER the vent with ridge cap shingles using 1-in. galvanized roofing nails. The vent will have a nail line marked on it. You can buy special ridge cap shingles for laminated shingles (shown here), or cut your own ridge cap from three-tab shingles (the shingle packaging will have directions). If you have to stop the ridge vent short of the end of the ridge, install the remaining ridge cap so that it slopes away from the vent.**

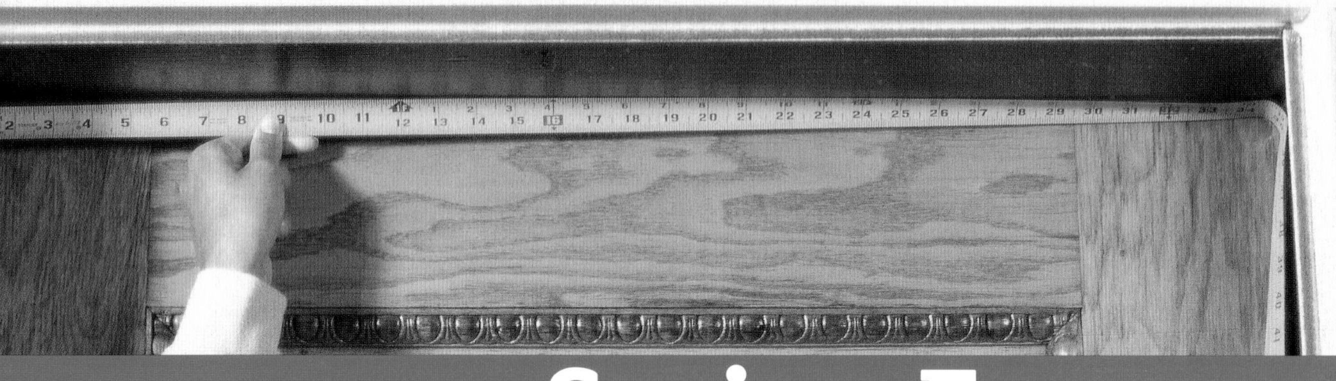

Saving Energy:

Windows and doors are the weakest link of all of the other components—ceilings, walls and floors—that work together to create your home's "energy envelope." The insulating qualities of even the best-built high-tech windows and doors pale in comparison to that of the walls and ceilings that surround them. In short, these "holes in the wall" need all the help they can get. That "help" can range from installing new weatherstripping to installing caulk and replacement windows and doors.

Like so many other energy-saving projects, improving windows and doors offers collateral benefits. New windows usually mean lower maintenance and a quieter house. New storm doors usually mean not only fewer drafts in winter but fewer bugs in summer. Caulking windows, doors and siding can help your house look better and last longer. When you ponder the costs of improving your windows and doors, consider these added benefits as well.

5 Windows & Doors

Window tint films

Instant, affordable energy efficiency—winter and summer

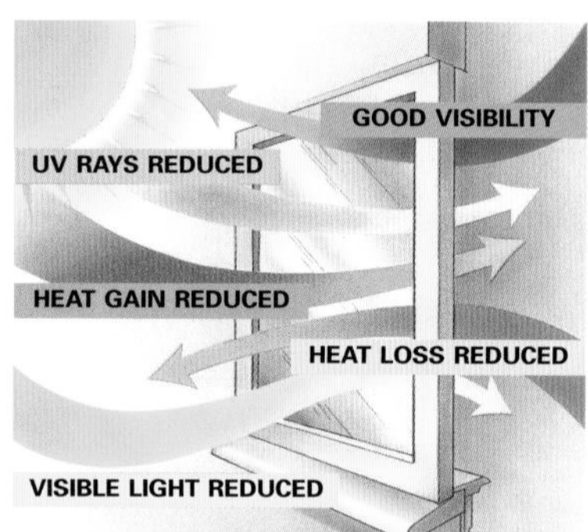

Low-E films reflect both outside summer heat and inside winter heat and offer fade protection.

If your windows let in too much heat in the summer and too much cold in the winter, a simple, affordable option to improve their efficiency is to apply low-E or tinting film. Low-E films offer these major benefits:

- Like reflective and nonreflective films, low-E films virtually eliminate the ultraviolet ray penetration, helping to reduce fading problems while doing little to affect window visibility.
- They reduce heat gain from the outside in the summer.
- During the winter, they reduce heat loss by 60 percent.
- Glare is reduced by filtering 50 to 60 percent of the incoming light.
- In the case of a broken window, the film helps hold the pieces of glass together.
- Most tint films come with complete directions. Follow them for best results.

Quick tip*

PLASTIC-FILM STORM WINDOWS MAKE SENSE. You can reduce heat loss through older and single pane windows by 25 to 50 percent by installing special clear plastic film on the interior. Most install with tape and a hair dryer and cost as little as $4 per window.

1 CLEAN windows thoroughly. Spray window with wetting solution following manufacturer's directions.

2 POSITION film on dampened window, making sure it overlaps sash on all sides.

3 SPRAY film surface with wetting solution. Make a single squeegee pass across the top, then use vertical passes down.

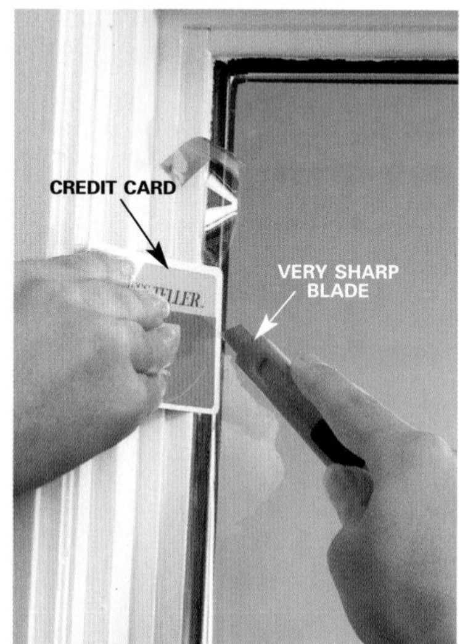

4 TRIM excess film using a credit card shield and very sharp utility knife. After trimming, wet and squeegee a second time.

Installing combination storm windows

Add warmth, quiet and an extra layer of protection

Combination storm windows offer many benefits. They improve a window's thermal efficiency, improve security by adding a layer of protection, help protect primary windows against rain and hail, and act as a screen to allow ventilation. Some standard-size units are available at home centers; others must be special-ordered.

1 MEASURE existing window at inside edges of brick molding and order windows. Predrill holes along outer edges of storm window frame 2 in. from each corner and every 12 in. between.

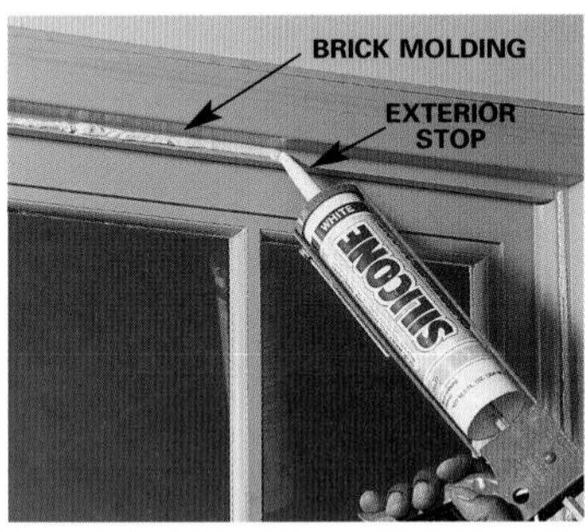

2 TEST-FIT the storm window. Use a belt sander to trim its lip, if necessary. Don't twist the window out of square to make it fit or it won't operate properly. Now apply a bead of silicone along the openings' top and sides but not the bottom.

3 POSITION storm windows in openings. Lift window as high as possible, then lower expansion seal at bottom. Attach window with screws. Make sure moisture can pass freely through weep holes at the bottom.

Energy-Saving Goof

Thar she blows!

One fine fall day I was caulking around my garage doors. I went through one cartridge, loaded another, clipped off the tip, then went back to work again. But I noticed that the caulk wasn't flowing and the trigger was getting harder and harder to pull. Suddenly the caulk tube burst open like a can of refrigerator biscuits, covering the garage door, my arms and my face with blobs of gooey caulk. It was then I realized I had forgotten to puncture the inner seal of the cartridge before squeezing the trigger of the gun.

Replacing double-pane windows

Fix 'em for maximum energy efficiency

Insulated glass can get broken or lose the seal between the panes and permanently fog. Start by taking the entire sash to a shop that repairs windows. They'll measure the size and thickness of the insulating unit, help you identify the manufacturer, determine whether a window is still under warranty and discuss energy-efficient replacement options. Manufacturers recommend one of three methods for installing the sealed units. Savvy do-it-yourselfers can repair the units themselves. Sometimes it's easier and cheaper to replace the entire sash.

GASKET METHOD. With sash removed, take out screws that hold horizontal rails and vertical stiles together. Tap frame loose from gasket and glass with wooden block and hammer. Remove old gasket from faulty pane and install it on a new glass double-pane unit. Push two frame pieces together around the gasket and fasten the frame back together. Seal any gaps in corners using clear silicone.

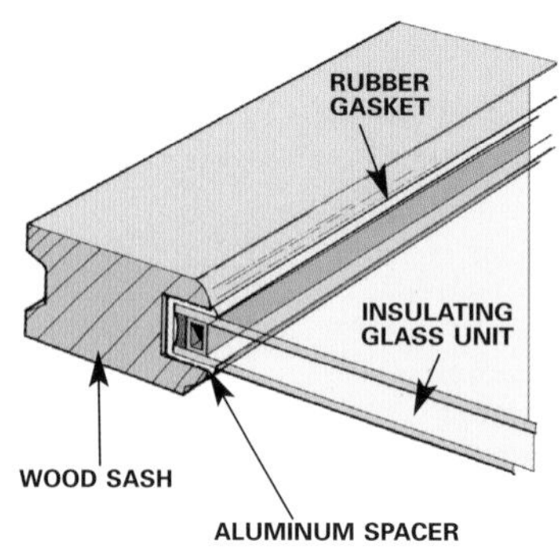

ADHESIVE TAPE METHOD. Pry out stops using a putty knife. Flip window over and slice through tape bond with a utility knife blade. Scrape old tape and clean lip with adhesive solvent. Lay new setting tape in place. Position spacing blocks against one side of frame, position glass against blocks and carefully drop it in place. Replace stops and seal gaps with clear silicone.

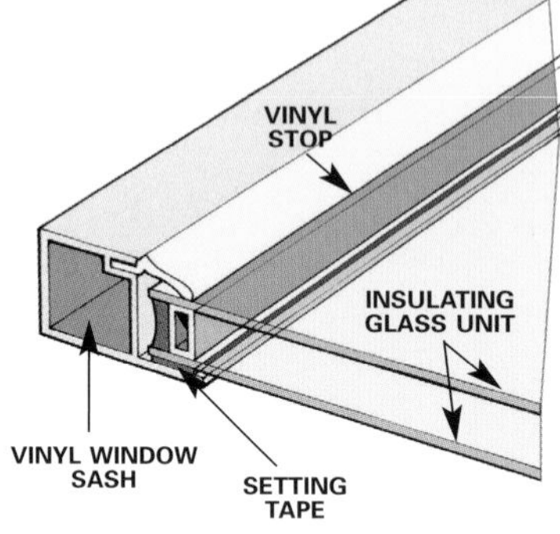

CAULK METHOD. Carefully pry off wood stops. Flip window over and cut caulk with a utility knife. If necessary, break window after covering it with carpet. Soften adhesive using a heat gun, and then scrape and clean edges. Position spacing blocks, apply bead of neutral-cure silicone to frame and drop in new glass unit. Apply silicone to glass's stop side and reinstall stops.

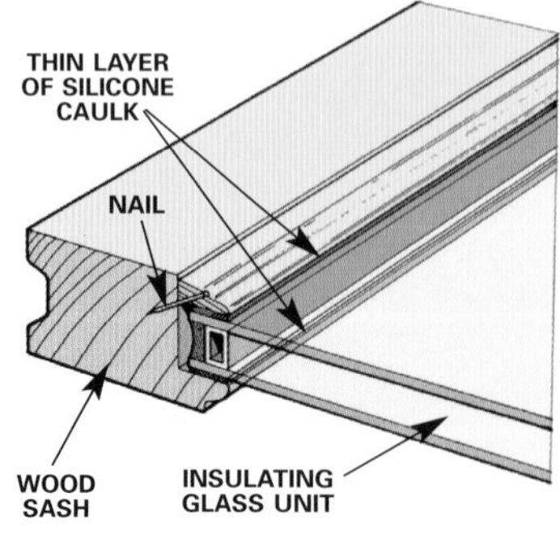

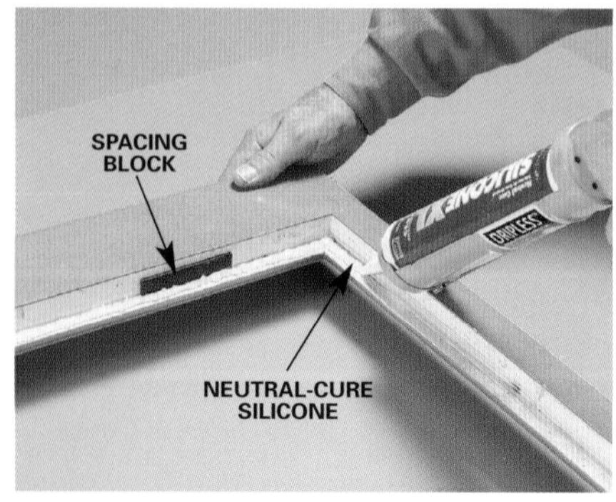

Weatherstrip a wooden entry door

Simple-to-install kits make it easy to stop annoying, energy-wasting drafts

Feeling a winter chill? If you run your hand around the perimeter of your closed door and feel a cool draft, your weatherstripping is probably worn, cracked or deformed.

Maintaining an airtight seal on your doors and windows usually won't save a lot of energy and money, but it's essential for stopping cold drafts and keeping your home comfortable. And in older, leaky homes, it actually can be a good money-saving strategy.

Replacing weatherstripping on newer windows and doors (less than about 35 years old) is fairly easy. You can usually slide out the old weatherstripping and push or slide new vinyl or foam into the grooves in the door or the surrounding frame. The biggest hassle is finding replacement

Project facts

COST
$10 to $20 per three-piece weatherstripping kit; $3 to $6 per door sweep (see p. 121 for details)

TIME
1 – 2 hours per door

SKILLS
Novice carpentry

SPECIAL TOOLS
Coping saw or hacksaw, depending on weatherstripping type

1 **LIFT the door by the doorknob to check for loose hinges. If the door moves upward, tighten the top hinge screws. That might solve the draft problem!**

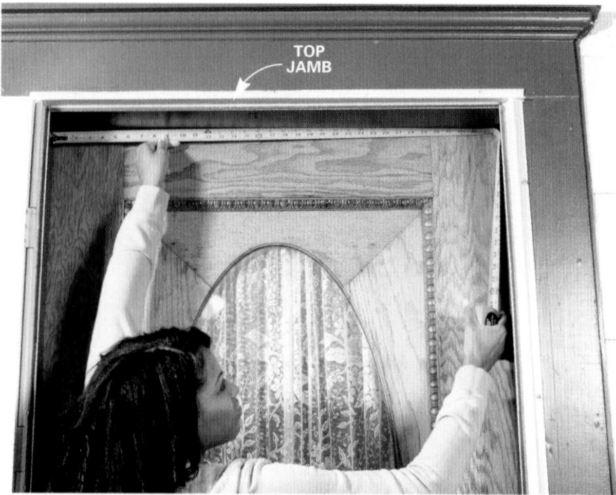

2 **CLOSE the door and measure the top of the frame from side to side. Mark the length on the short section of your purchased weatherstripping with a clear, sharp line.**

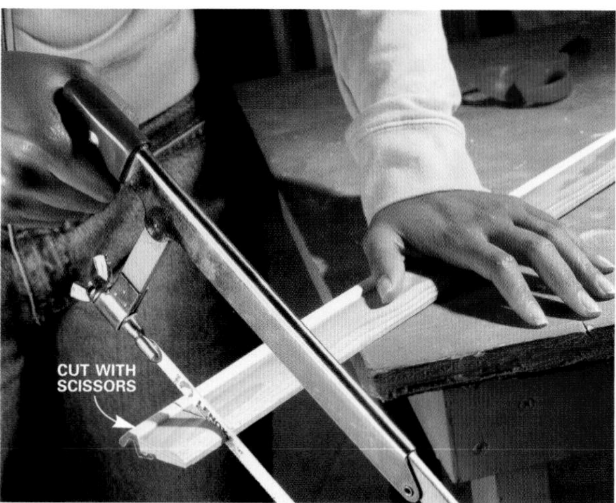

3 **CUT the foam part of the weatherstripping with sharp scissors. Then cut the wood flange with a hacksaw or other fine-tooth saw.**

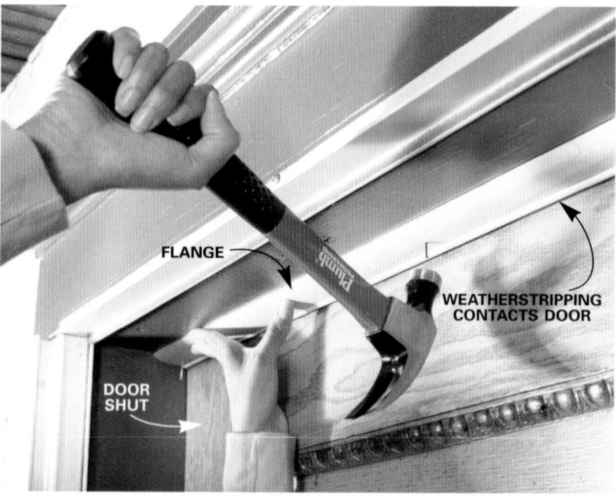

4 **TAP 1-1/2-in. nails into the wood flange and position the weatherstripping so the entire length of the foam seals against the door. Tack the weatherstripping in place but don't drive the nails home yet. Then measure the length of the sides of the frame.**

weatherstripping that exactly matches the old. See "How to buy weatherstripping," opposite, for advice.

Older windows, especially double-hung windows, are difficult to weatherstrip. If they're in bad shape, consider replacement windows.

Installing new weatherstripping on older doors (and doors for which you can't find replacement weatherstripping) is fairly easy, and we'll show you how to do it here. Weatherstripping kits are available at most full-service hardware stores and home centers ($10 to $20; see photos, opposite). They include two side strips, a top strip and fasteners.

We'll also show you how to install a door sweep ($6) to stop drafts from coming under the door. A wide variety of these are usually available on the hardware store or home center shelf alongside weatherstripping.

Quick tip

THE TWO-INCH HOLE IN YOUR WALL A 1/16-in. gap between the bottom of an exterior door and the threshold is equivalent to cutting a 2-in. square hole in your wall. When you apply weatherstripping, be meticulous.

Size up your leaky door

On the door shown here, the old, worn bronze weatherstripping was not replaced with new bronze because the project is difficult, especially around the latch plates. (You can still find several types of replacement bronze

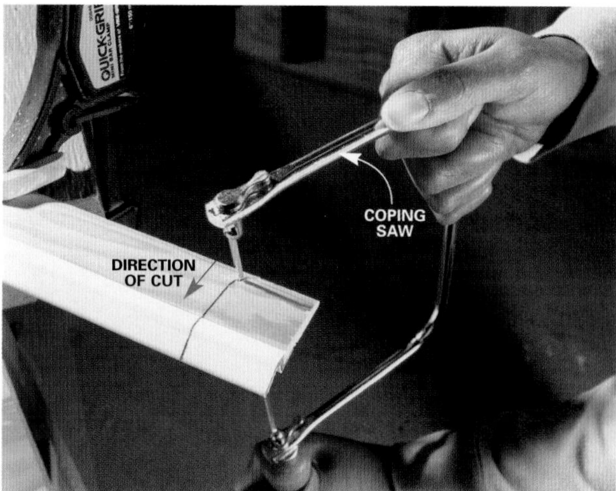

5 **CUT one end of each side weatherstripping to fit the profile of the top piece. Mark the profile using a scrap for a guide, cut the foam with scissors and cut the profile with a coping saw.**

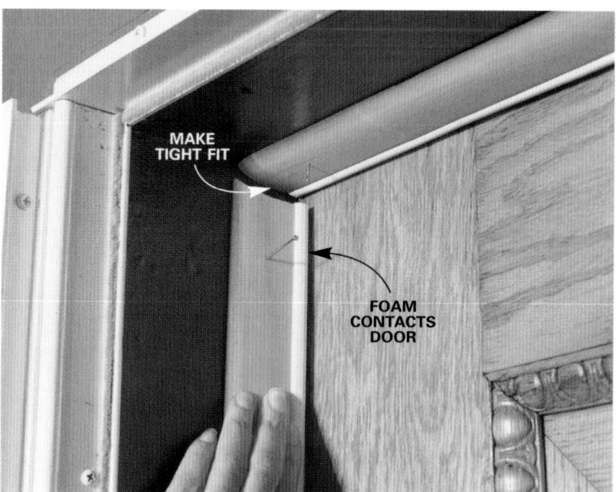

6 **FILE or sand your cut for a tight fit. Then measure and cut the bottom to length (Photo 3). Position the weatherstripping so that the entire length seals to the door and tack it in place.**

at full-service hardware stores.) The wrapped foam type shown is easier to install and more effective. Later you can paint the wood flange to blend with the frame.

Before you go out to buy your materials, check the door to make sure the draft isn't caused by loose hinge screws (Photo 1). If the screws no longer bite, you may have to glue wood plugs in the holes and redrive the screws.

Cut and nail—this stuff goes up fast

The weatherstripping kit will come with two long pieces for the side jambs and a short piece for the top jamb. Begin with the top and follow Photos 2 – 7 for the basics. Make precise measurements and cuts so you get a nice,

How to buy weatherstripping

You can usually find the types of weatherstripping shown below at well-stocked hardware stores and home centers. Many other types are available, but you'll probably have to order them from a catalog. Ask to see a catalog at your local hardware store and order through the store if possible. (An online catalog is available at www.mdteam.com.)

We like the wrapped foam type (A and B below and shown in our story). It's durable, retains its shape, withstands abrasions and conforms to a wide range of gaps. The metal flange with slots for screws (B) is a bit more adjustable than the nail-on wood flange type (A).

The vinyl or silicone bulb type (C) won't cover wide gaps as well as wrapped foam, but it has a smaller profile with a cleaner look.

Finding new weatherstripping to match the exact profile of the old can be difficult. If you know the door manufacturer or where the door was purchased, try there first. (Check the door and frame for a label.) Otherwise, call a local door or window repair service. (Look under "Doors, Repair" or "Windows, Repair" in your yellow pages.) They may stock the materials or tell you where to call. Replacement kits for the wrapped foam and magnetic (for steel doors) types are sometimes available at hardware stores and home centers.

A good Internet source for weatherstripping is the Energy Federation Inc. at www.efi.org.

Common weatherstripping types

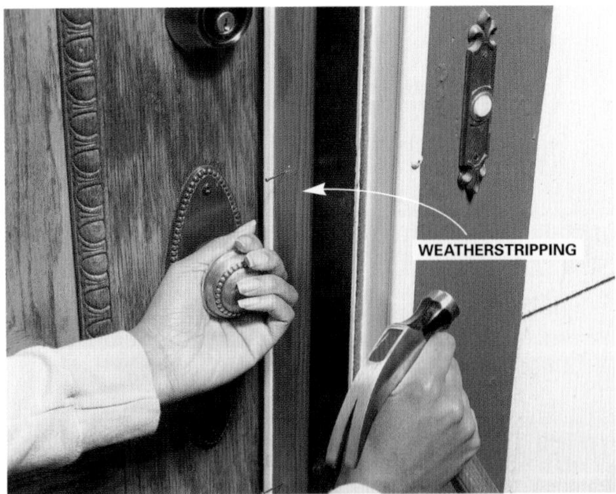

7 **OPEN and close the door several times to make sure the weatherstripping seals against the door and the door latches and locks. Adjust the weatherstripping as needed. Drive the finish nails home.**

tip **Follow the old carpenter's rule: Measure twice, cut once.**

8 **MEASURE the width of the door from inside and mark the length on your new sweep.**

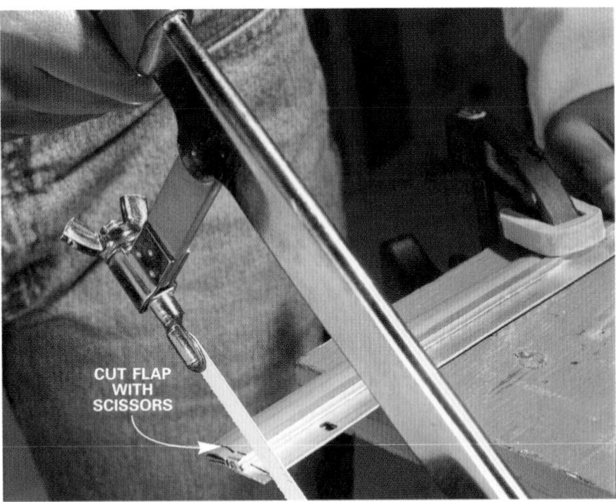

9 **CUT the flexible flap with sharp scissors or sharp utility knife. Then cut the flange with a hacksaw.**

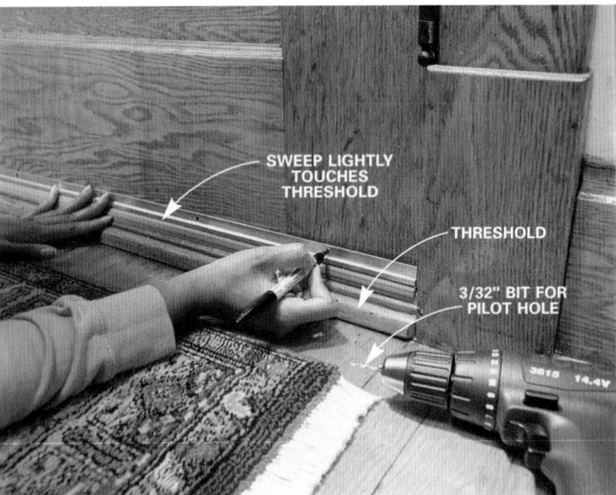

10 **POSITION the door sweep with the flexible portion lightly touching the top of the threshold. Then mark the screw positions and drill the pilot holes.**

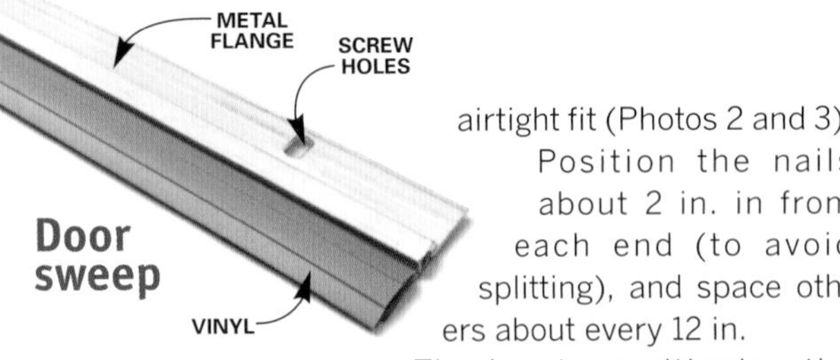

Door sweep

airtight fit (Photos 2 and 3). Position the nails about 2 in. in from each end (to avoid splitting), and space others about every 12 in.

The key to positioning the new weatherstripping is to shove it against the door so it compresses slightly along its entire length (Photo 4). If you compress it too much, the door won't latch when you close it, a common rookie mistake.

The "coped" cuts on the side jambs make a clean, tight joint (Photo 6). Make this cut first, leaving plenty of length for the bottom cut.

It's critical to make sure that the door shuts and latches easily before you drive the nails home (Photo 7). However, the weatherstripping also needs to fit snug to the door over its full length. For small adjustments, pull the nails and start them in a new spot.

tip **When you paint the wood flange, keep the paint off the foam.**

Install a door sweep

Shut the door, then look for daylight and feel for a draft coming under the door. If you see a lot of light or feel a draft, install a new door sweep.

The door shown here had old bulb-type weatherstripping attached to the threshold. While these types can be effective, you have to replace them every few years because foot traffic wears and crushes them.

Door sweeps last longer but won't always work if they brush or rub against the floor or carpet when you

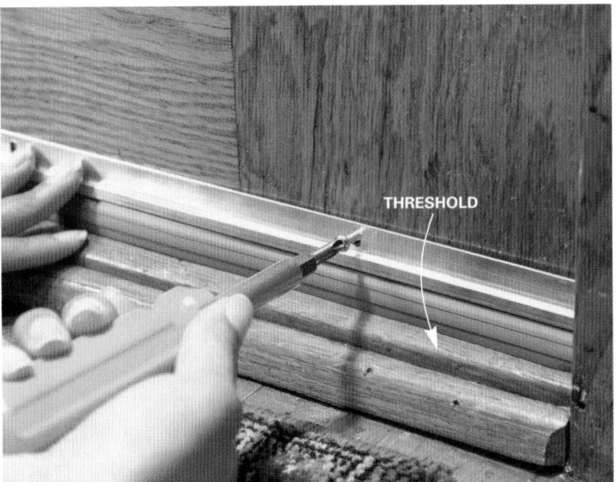

11 **PUSH the sweep down against the threshold and drive the screws. Open and close the door to test the seal.**

12 **CUT two 2 x 1-3/4-in. pads from 1/8-in.-thick felt. Nail the pads at the bottom of each side frame as shown. Open and shut the door and adjust the pads if necessary.**

open the door. If the floor, carpet or rug is even with or higher than your threshold (the bottom of the door frame; Photos 8 and 11), you can't use a sweep.

For a replacement, choose a simple face-mount door sweep with a flexible vinyl flap because it's easy to mount and adjust. Photos 8 – 11 show you how to measure, cut and screw it to the door.

You'll be left with a pair of small gaps between the weatherstripping on the frame and the sweep, at the bottom corners of the door. Unless you want a perfectly airtight, draft-free door, don't worry about these gaps. However, Photo 12 shows one way to close them. It's not precise; use whatever thickness of felt (or combination of layers) fits between the door and frame without hindering the door operation.

Good work! You can look forward to a more comfortable winter.

Replacing a U-shaped astragal on a steel garage door

The hollow rubber weather seal on the bottom of steel doors is called a U-shaped astragal, and its job is to keep both cold winds and mice out of your garage. U-shaped astragals are sized according to their width as they lie flat. Choose the width that best fits your situation. Use a larger seal if you need to fill a wider gap between the door and the garage floor. The best source for U-shaped astragals is a garage door dealer.

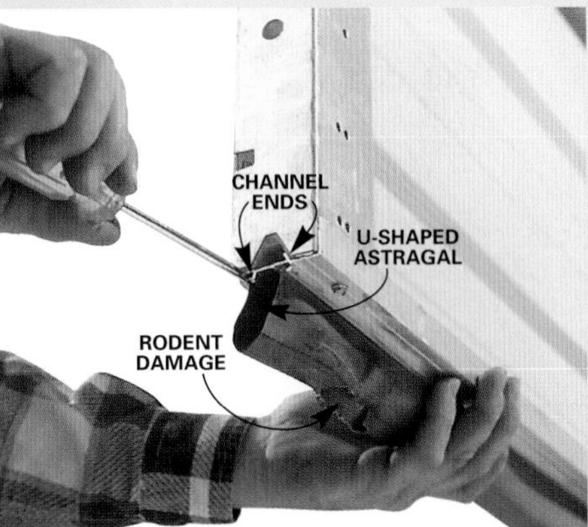

USE a flat-blade screwdriver to open the ends of the channels that hold the old seal on both ends of the door. Then pull out the old seal.

SLIDE the new seal into the channels. To make the job easier, lubricate the channels with silicone spray or rubbing alcohol. After the seal is in place, crimp the channel ends on both ends of the door with pliers.

Hang a new storm door

Add an extra layer of protection from the cold with a storm door.

You no longer have to put up with a rusty old storm door that bangs shut every time the kids go out. Modern storm doors are stronger, smoother and a heck of a lot more handsome than older doors. In fact, installing a new one is one of the least expensive ways to dress up an entry and improve energy efficiency.

Replacing an old storm door is easier than you might think. Manufacturers have made installation more DIY friendly by providing standard sizes that'll fit almost any door opening and simpler installation kits. Still, you'll find some sticking points. The following step-by-step directions walk you through some tricks and techniques you won't find in any instruction manual.

If you have a hacksaw, screw gun, a short level and a pair of side cutters and two to three hours, you're on your way to saving the $100-plus cost of a professional installation. Replacing an old storm door or installing a new one is a perfect Saturday morning project, even if you have limited carpentry skills. Choose a storm door that fits the style of your home. Prices range from $100 to $500.

Selecting the door

To find the size of the storm door you need, simply measure the height and width of the main door. Most front entry doors are 36 in. wide and require a 36-in. storm door.

Shown here is a "full-view" storm door (opening photo). This door has removable screen and glass panels that you interchange each season. The other common type, a "ventilating" storm door, has glass panels that slide open or closed over the screen, much like a double-hung window.

Nearly every storm door sold is reversible. That is, you can install it with the hinge on either side. The manufacturer's directions tell you how to do it. When you buy it, you don't have to specify which way the door must swing.

You typically mount storm doors to the exterior door trim using "Z-bars." The hinge-side Z-bar may already be screwed to the door (ours was), or you may have to mount it once you determine the door swing direction. On some doors, you'll also have to drill holes for the latch.

Getting started

Begin the project by folding open the box and removing the glass storm panel. Set it and the screen panel in a safe place out of the wind. Then check for damaged or missing parts by comparing the contents with the parts list in the instruction manual. (The one shown had been returned, repackaged and sold as new. One of the parts had already been cut to length and the mounting screws were missing.) Use the cardboard as a work surface to prevent scratching the parts while you work on the door.

Then determine the door swing. In general, hinge the storm door on the same side as the main door. However, consider these exceptions:

- **Adjoining walls.** If there's an adjoining wall or rail, it's best to have the door swing against it; otherwise entry can be awkward, especially if you're carrying groceries.
- **Electrical.** Will the door open against any light fixtures? Will the doorbell or light switch wind up on the latch side where they belong?
- **Wind.** If there's a strong prevailing wind, it's best to have the door hinge side face the wind direction. That way, sudden gusts can't fling it open and break it.

Out with the old storm door

Taking off an old aluminum door is usually just a case of unscrewing the mounting screws on the door, closer and safety chain. But sometimes there's caulk around the frame. You can usually cut through the caulk with a utility knife. But worse yet, you could find old caulk between the frame and the door casing. If so, you'll have to pry the frame away with an old chisel and scrape the trim surfaces clean. A heat gun may help soften the caulk. Get rid of an old door by throwing the glass panel in the trash, and then cut up the aluminum frame and door with a circular saw and a carbide-tipped blade. Toss the pieces into the recycling bin.

Wooden storm doors generally have hinges that are mortised (notched into the wood) and screwed to the door casing. Don't worry about the hinge or latch recesses. When you install your new storm door, they'll be hidden behind the new door frame.

Why a storm door?

A traditional storm door was a real workhorse. It protected the handsome but vulnerable wooden main door from harsh weather and helped to insulate it.

Today's better insulated and protected main doors have little need for a storm door and are often eliminated from new homes, showing off fancy front doors. However, the "full-view" storm door (like the one shown here) still showcases the main door and, when screened, allows you to take advantage of those cooling summer breezes too.

1 FIND a flat area near the entry door, lay the box flat on the ground, fold it open and check to make sure you have all the parts.

2 ADD a trim extension if needed to doors with sidelights. Prime and paint the new trim, position it with a reveal equal to the other trim and then nail it into place.

> **tip** If your entry door trim needs paint, do it now. It's a pain in the neck painting around a new door, and you'll have a neater-looking job.

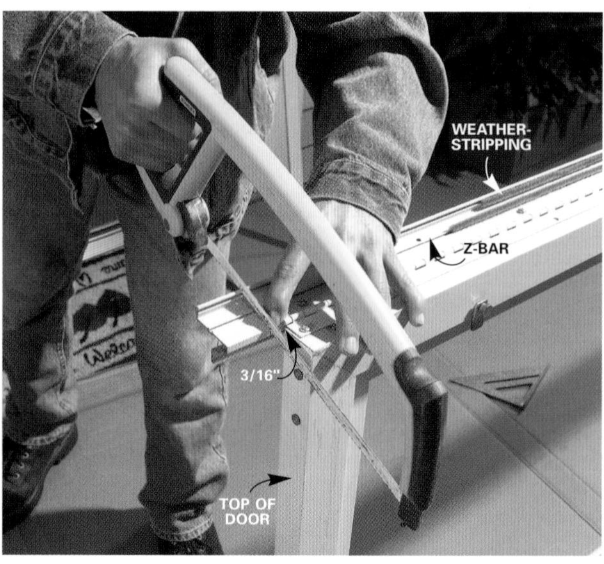

3 CONFIRM the door swing direction and fasten the hinge-side Z-bar to the correct side (if necessary). Mark a cutting line on the Z-bar 3/16 in. above the top of the door with a square. Slide the weatherstripping aside and cut the Z-bar with a hacksaw.

> **tip** Use an 18- to 22-tooth-per-in. hacksaw blade for smoother, easier cuts.

4 MEASURE from the outside lip of the threshold to the top door casing. Transfer the measurement to the bottom of the hinge-side Z-bar and cut it to length, matching the angle on the threshold.

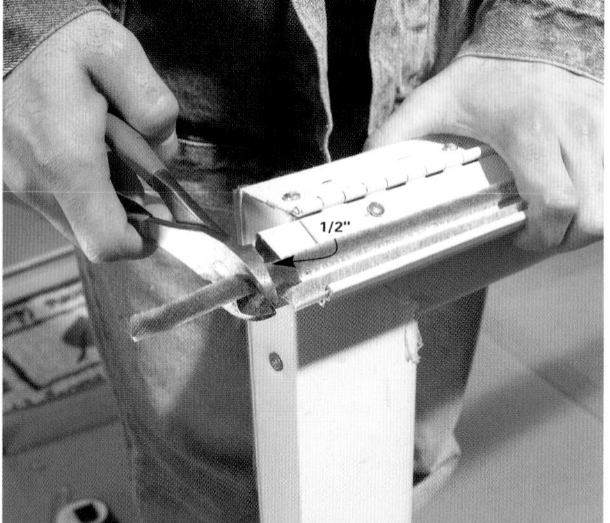

5 CENTER the weatherstripping in the Z-bar, then snip off the ends, leaving it 1/2 in. extra long at each end.

Prep the opening

Storm doors hang from the door trim, technically called "exterior casing." If the door has never had a storm door (as in our situation), you may have to extend the trim between the door and a sidelight (Photo 2). This is the most difficult situation you're likely to encounter. You have to rip a new trim piece to match the thickness of the other trim (usually 1-1/8 in. thick).

Manufacturers make storm doors a bit narrower than standard openings to make sure they'll fit. If your opening is typical, you'll have to "fur out" the sides to center

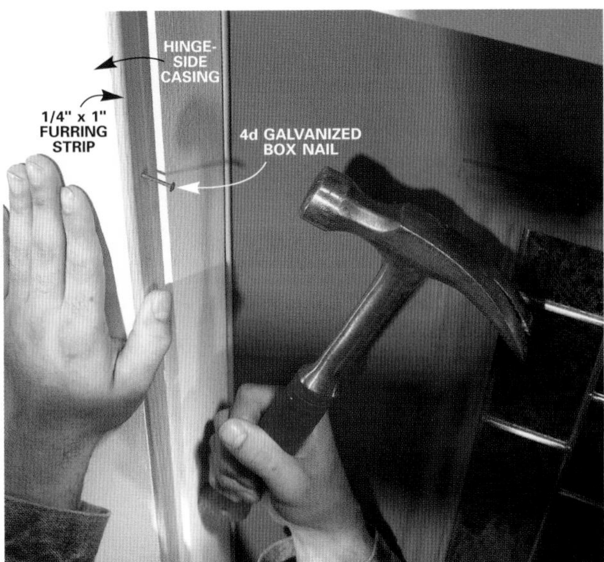

6 MEASURE the opening width and determine the furring strip thickness (see text). Cut a furring strip to length, then nail it to the inside edge of the hinge-side casing with four evenly spaced 4d galvanized box nails.

7 LIFT the door into the opening and pry it against the hinge-side casing with a twist from rubber-handled pliers on the latch side. Screw the hinge Z-bar into the door casing side.

> **tip** An 8-ft. furring strip made from 1/4-in.-thick pine "screen moldings" usually works fine. Find them in the millwork section at the home center.

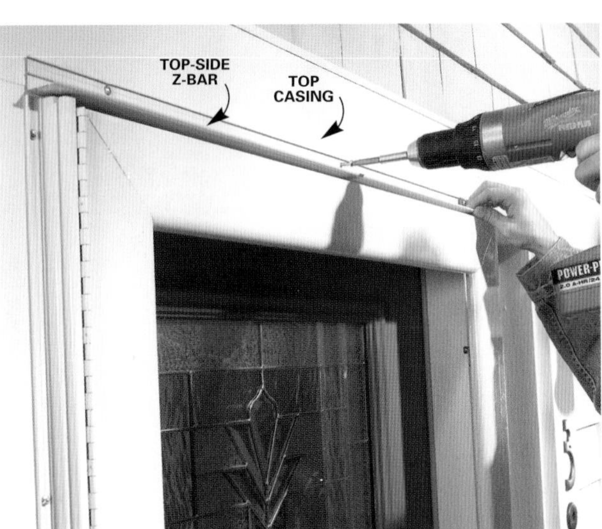

8 SWING the door open, slip the top-side Z-bar into place and close the door to hold it. Adjust the gap between the Z-bar and the top of the door until it's even and screw it into the top casing.

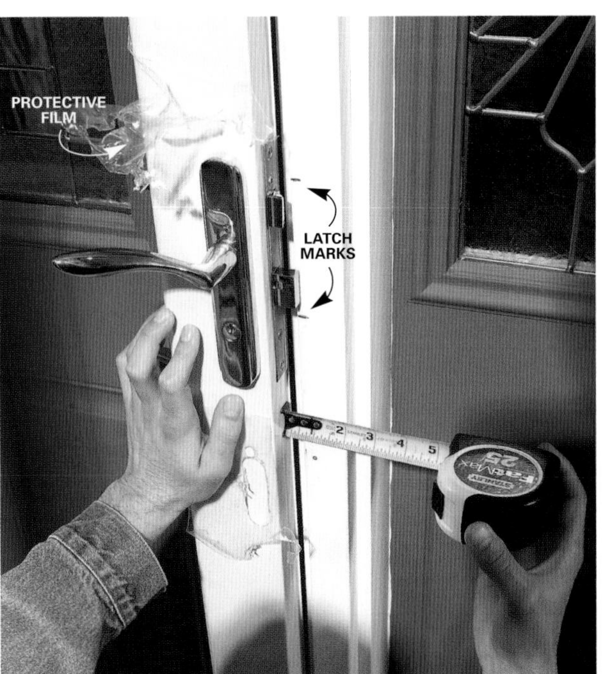

9 MOUNT the latch mechanism, then mark the position of the top and bottom of the latch on the door casing. If the space between the door and the casing is over 5/8 in., nail two 1/4-in.-thick furring strips to the inside of the casing, one above and one below the marks (see Photo 11).

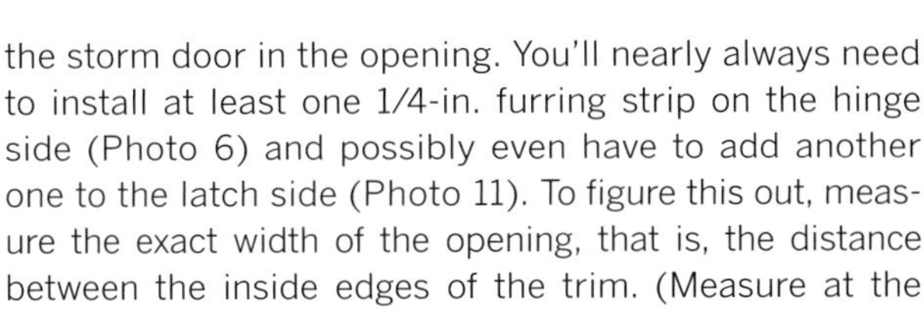

the storm door in the opening. You'll nearly always need to install at least one 1/4-in. furring strip on the hinge side (Photo 6) and possibly even have to add another one to the latch side (Photo 11). To figure this out, measure the exact width of the opening, that is, the distance between the inside edges of the trim. (Measure at the

> **tip** Your door may come with a protective plastic film. Only peel off those areas needed for installing hardware during installation (Photos 9 and 13). That way the door will be protected from scratches. After installation is complete, peel away the plastic.

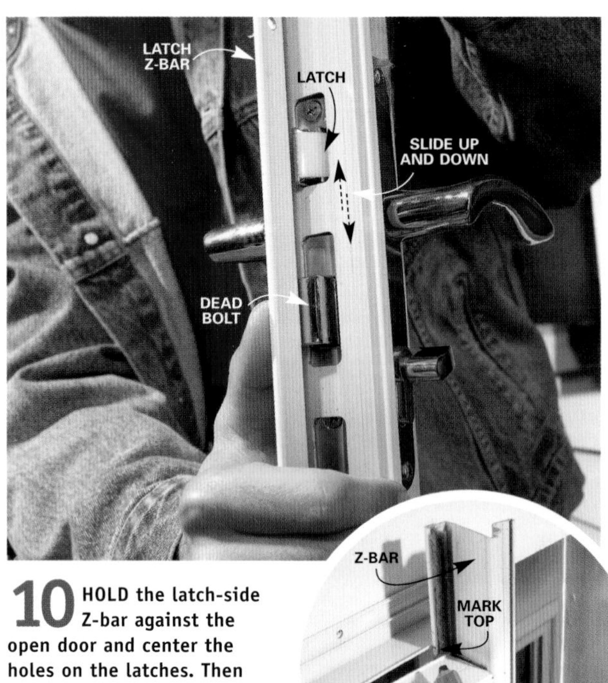

10 **HOLD the latch-side Z-bar against the open door and center the holes on the latches. Then push the door and Z-bar against the doorframe and mark and cut the bottom at the angle of the threshold. Then mark the top (inset) and cut it.**

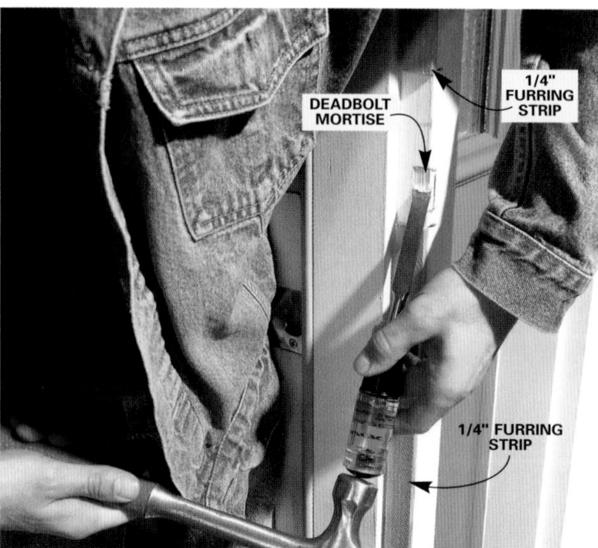

11 **CLOSE the door against the casing with the deadbolt extended and chisel out the wood where the deadbolt hits. Slip the latch-side Z-bar into place, close the door against it and screw it to the casing, keeping a consistent 1/8-in. gap with the door.**

12 **SLIDE the rubber weatherstripping into the door sweep and crimp the ends. Slide the sweep over the door bottom and tap it down to snug it to the threshold. Drill 1/8-in. holes through the adjustment slots and add the screws.**

13 **POSITION the closer bracket and screw it to the jamb. Attach the closer, level it and mark the screw positions on the door. Drill 1/8-in. pilot holes and screw the closer to the door. Repeat for the top closer.**

middle, top and bottom.) The manufacturer's instructions will usually list the minimum width required. Subtract that width from your measurement and make the furring strip thickness along the hinge side about half the difference.

It's important to mount the door tightly to the hinge-side trim. Pry against the latch side to make sure it snugs up tight (Photo 7).

Follow the photos with your instructions for the rest of the installation steps. Door latch and Z-bar systems vary. Cutting the latch-side Z-bar is a bit fussy. The idea is to

Adjust a storm door for a perfect close

IF YOUR STORM DOOR SLAMS SHUT or won't close hard enough to latch, try a few simple adjustments to make it close just right.

First, change the mounting position of the closer's connecting pin (Photo 1). To remove the pin, you have to first lock the door open with the hold-open washer to release the tension on the pin. But there's a good chance that your hold-open washer won't work. In that case, open the door and snap locking pliers (such as Vise-Grip pliers) onto the closer shaft to hold the door open. To repair the washer, slip it off the shaft, put it in a vise and make a sharper bend in it using a hammer. Or you can take the entire closer to a home center or hardware store and find a similar replacement for about $10. Some closers mount a little differently from the one shown here. For example, you may find that the door bracket, rather than the closer, has two pin holes.

If moving the pin makes matters worse, return it to its original position and try the adjustment screw (Photo 2). Turn it clockwise for a softer close, counterclockwise for harder. If your door has two closers, treat them exactly alike. Adjust both screws equally and make sure their pins are in the same position.

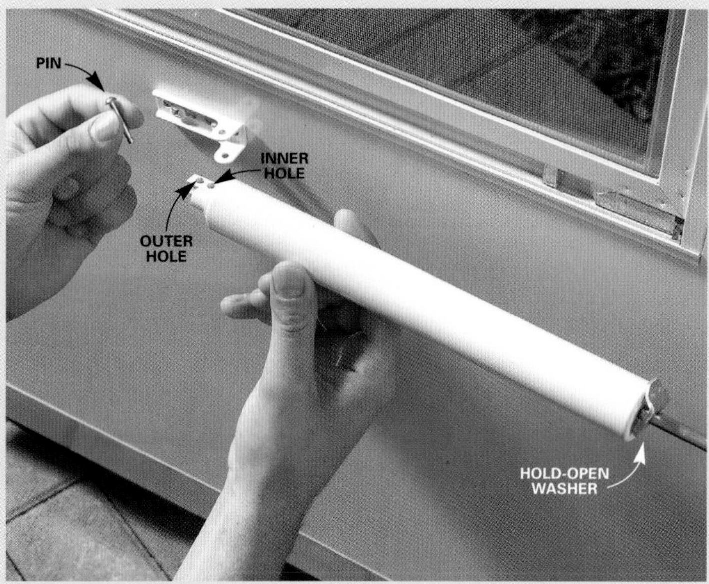

1 LOCK the door open and remove the pin. Connect the closer at the inner hole to make the door close harder. For a softer close, use the outer hole.

2 TURN the adjustment screw to make the door close harder or softer. Make a quarter turn, test the door and continue making quarter turns until the door closes just right.

center it on the latch and lock (Photo 10). Observe where it strikes the sill and cut the bottom at an angle that matches the sill. Then cut the top so it fits against the top Z-bar. Don't worry if the latch and lock bolt end up a bit off-center, as long as they work smoothly.

You may need to chisel out the latch or deadbolt pocket as shown (Photo 11). It all depends on the door latch style.

After installing the door sweep and closers, adjust the closer tension. Begin with the window panel rather than the screen in place. The closers should be set with the door at its heaviest. You may want to reset a gentler setting for the screen panel.

Finally, it's a good idea to save the boxes for the window and screen panel for off-season storage. Under a bed is a great safe storage location.

Install a new

Front door

We'll show you the techniques that will result in a perfect weathertight installation

It's not often that you can complete a project in a weekend that will save you money and dramatically improve the looks of your house. But that's what will happen when you replace a worn, drafty front door with a stylish, energy-efficient new one. And since modern doors come prehung in a weatherstripped frame, you don't have to be a master carpenter to do a first-class job.

Here you'll learn how to order a door that'll fit like a glove. Then you'll see, step by step, how to get your old door out and the new one in.

If you can handle basic carpentry tasks, you'll have no trouble installing a new prehung door in a day. Figure on another day to finish the details and start painting the door. You can complete most of the job with basic hand tools. You'll need a hammer, pry bar, tape measure, level, utility knife, nail set and saw. If you decide to install new interior trim, you'll also need a miter saw.

Shown here is a top-quality prehung wood door (Simpson Bungalow No. 7228) from a lumberyard. Including the special 2-1/2-in. wide exterior trim (casing), the total cost was $1,100. You could purchase a steel or fiberglass door for much less, but the style and crisp detailing of the wood door matched this house perfectly. The door arrived about two weeks after the order was placed.

4216

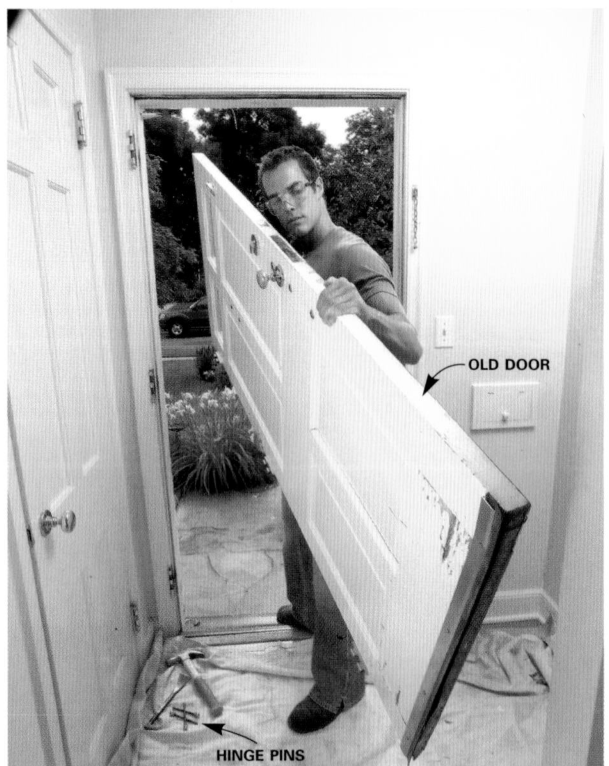

1 **TAP the hinge pins loose with a hammer and nail set. Then swing the door open and lift it off. Protect the floor with a dropcloth. The old door will be heavy.**

2 **PRY the interior trim loose from the doorframe. Protect the wall with a wide putty knife. If you plan to reuse the trim, first score the intersection between the molding and jamb with a utility knife.**

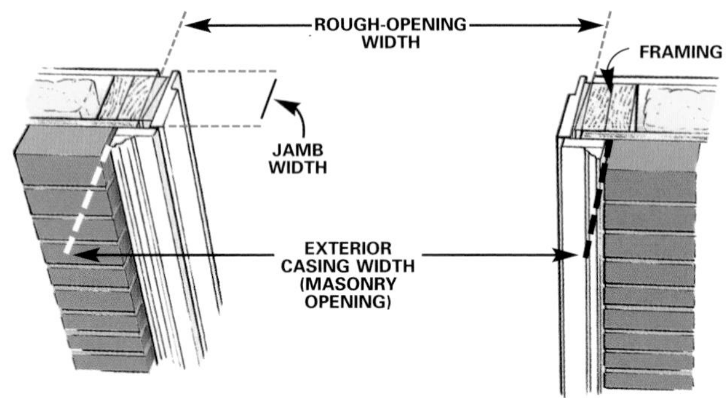

Figure A Measuring

Measure your old door

In most cases, simply order a new door the same size as the old one. If you alter the size or add sidelights, you'll have to reframe the opening and alter many details. This usually doubles or triples the size of the job. Here are the four sets of measurements you'll need to order a door (refer to Figure A, above, for extra details):

- **Door size.** Measure the width and height of your old door. Round these up to full inches to find the size of the replacement door you'll need. If, for example, your door measures 35-3/4 in. wide and 79-1/2 in. tall, you'll order a 36 x 80-in. door.
- **Jamb width.** Measure from the back side of the interior trim to the back side of the exterior trim (Figure A). Specify this jamb width when you order your new prehung door. This guarantees that the interior trim will fit flush to the wall without adding "jamb extensions."
- **Rough opening.** You'll have to remove the interior trim to get accurate measurements of the rough opening. Measure the opening width between framing members and from the bottom of the sill to the top of the opening. Compare these measurements to the rough opening requirements of your new door to make sure it will fit.
- **Exterior opening** (or "masonry opening" if you have a brick or stone door surround). Measure to the outsides of the exterior casing and then from the bottom of the sill to the top of the trim.

Compare these measurements with those of a prehung door that has standard 2-in.-wide "brick molding" trim. If the framed door with standard trim is too small to completely fill the space or if you want a different trim style, you have three options. The best solution is to order a door with wider, flat casing to fit the opening. You can always add a piece of decorative molding to approximate the style of your existing exterior trim. (For this project, 2-1/2-in. flat

3 **SLICE the caulk joint between the siding (brick) and exterior trim and pry the trim from the doorjamb with a pry bar.**

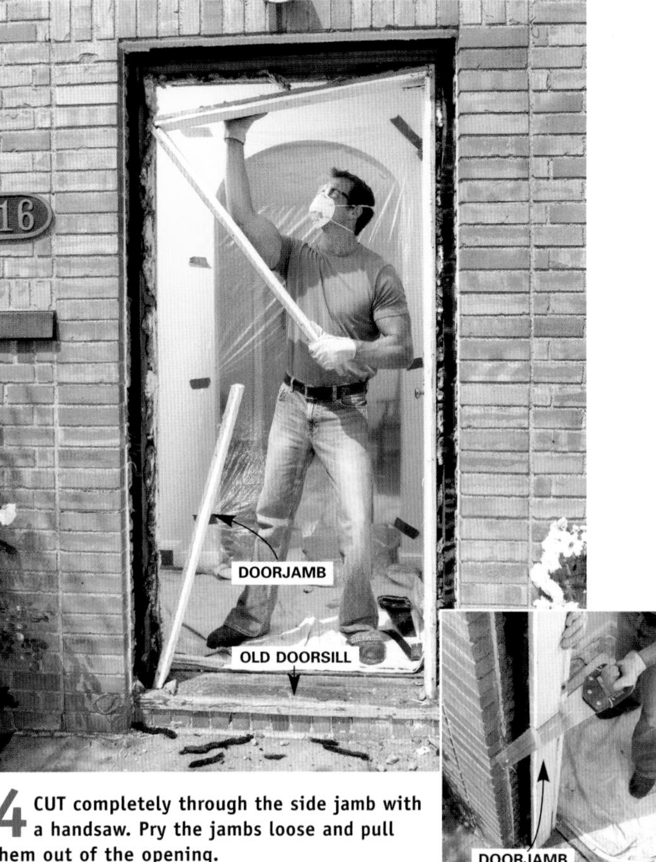

4 **CUT completely through the side jamb with a handsaw. Pry the jambs loose and pull them out of the opening.**

casing was ordered and the existing decorative molding was reinstalled.) Second, you can order your door with standard molding and fill the gap with additional strips of wood. The last option is to order the door without exterior molding and make your own to fit.

Start by tearing out your old door and preparing the opening

Photos 1 – 4 show how to take out the old door and frame. If you plan to reuse the interior moldings, pull the nails through the back side with pliers or a nipper to avoid damaging the face. Cutting through one side jamb makes it easy to tear out the entire frame (Photo 4).

After the doorframe is out, check the condition of the framing and subflooring in the sill area. Cut out and replace any rotted wood. If the sill on your new door is thinner than the one you removed, you may have to build up the sill area as shown in Photo 5. Set the sill height so the door just clears carpeting or rugs when it swings inward.

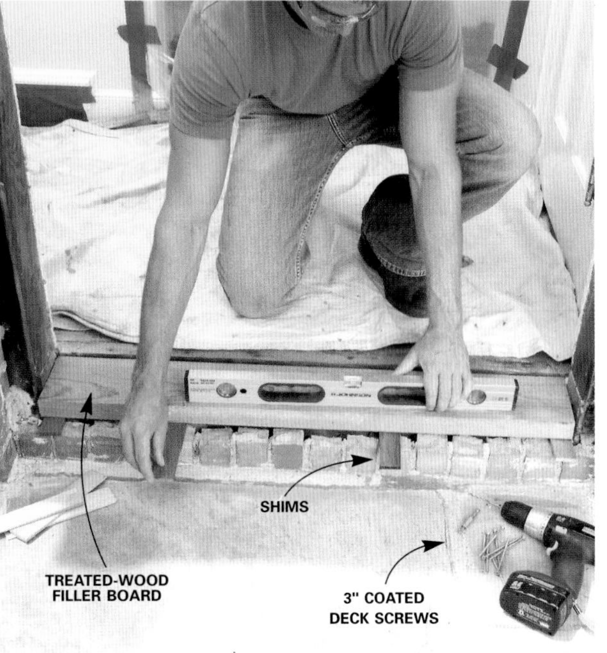

5 **BUILD up the sill area to the proper height with treated lumber. Add shims to level it. Fasten it with coated deck screws.**

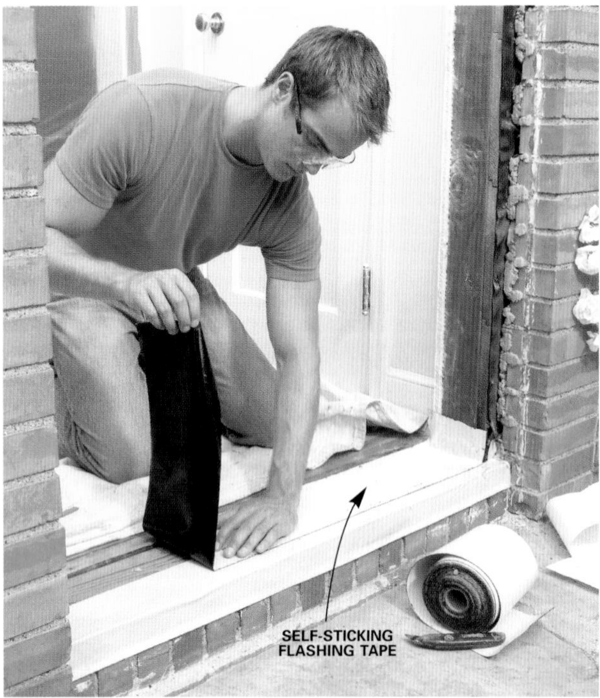

6 **COVER** the rough sill area with self-sticking flashing tape. Wrap it up the sides of the opening and over the front edge. Set the door in the opening, plumb it and check the fit.

7 **APPLY** a bead of caulk along the sides and top of the door opening and at the sill according to the manufacturer's instructions.

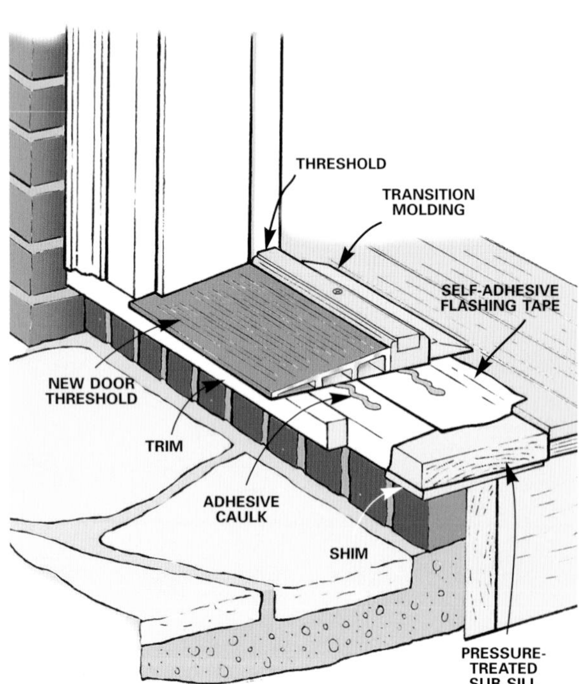

Figure B Sill detail

8 **MAKE SURE** the doorsill is level. Then center the top of the door in the opening and tack it into place with galvanized casing nails. Plumb the hinge-side jamb and tack the bottom corners.

9 **SHIM behind each hinge. For large spaces, start with small squares of plywood. Then finish with pairs of shims. Make sure the hinge-side jamb remains plumb.**

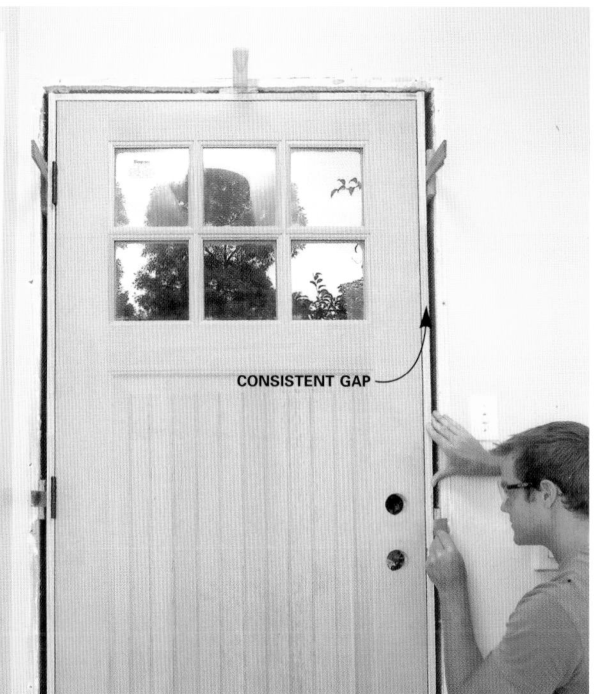

10 **SHIM at the top, middle and bottom of the latch-side jamb and at the top until the gap between the door and the doorjamb is consistent. Score the shims with a utility knife and break them off.**

Photo 6 shows how to protect the sill from water intrusion. Buy the flashing tape at a lumberyard. If you're installing a door in a newly constructed wall, you can buy a special plastic sill flashing kit instead. One brand is Jamsill (www.jamsill.com; call 800-526-7455 for ordering information). Details will vary depending on the doorway situation. The idea is to channel water away from the wood. If your home is built on a concrete slab, the doorframe will probably rest directly on the slab.

If your door is exposed to the weather, direct water away from the door with a metal drip cap (Figure C). Brick openings like this, and doors protected by porches with roofs, don't require a drip cap. You'll find drip caps at home centers and lumberyards. If the drip cap is damaged or missing, install a new one before you set the door frame in the opening. Cut the metal drip cap to fit and slide it under the siding and building paper (Figure C). If nails are in the way, slip a hacksaw blade under the siding and cut them.

Quick tip*

SEAL A DRAFTY DOOR Big screws heads in the threshold of newer entry doors can raise or lower the built-in narrow strip. If you can see light between the threshold and the door, raise the threshold where the light enters by turning the nearest screw counterclockwise.

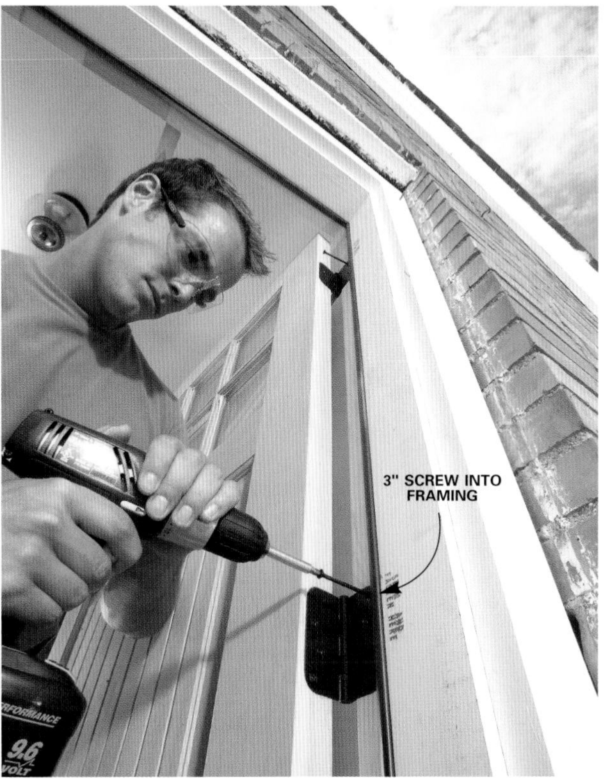

11 **REPLACE a screw in each hinge with a 3-in. screw driven into the framing. Drive additional casing nails every 16 in. along the sides and top of the exterior trim.**

12 FILL the space between the doorjamb and the framing with minimal expanding foam insulation. After the foam has expanded and skinned over, loosely stuff any remaining space with strips of fiberglass insulation.

13 CUT and install new interior trim or reinstall the old trim. If there's a gap between the new sill and the existing flooring, cover it with a beveled transition molding.

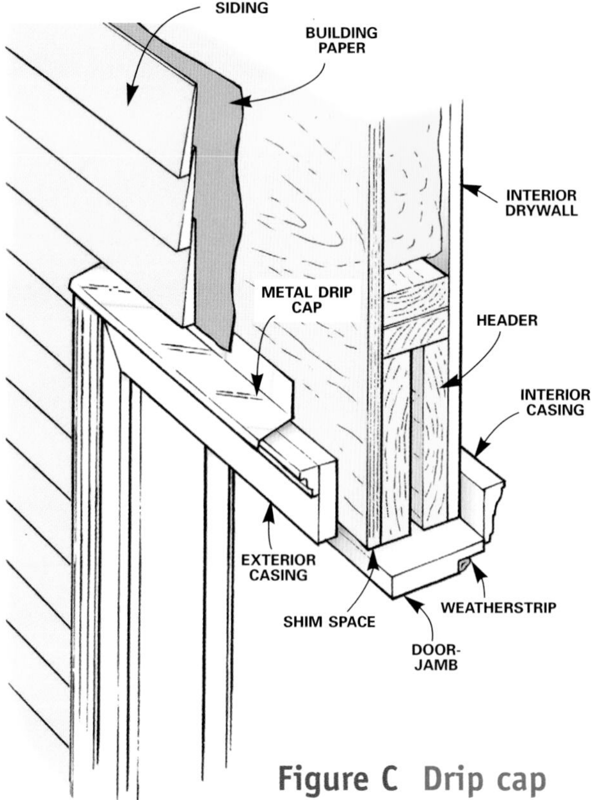

Figure C Drip cap

14 PRESS foam caulk backer into the siding/trim gap. Apply a neat bead of caulk between the siding and the door trim. Cut a trim board to fit under the sill and screw it to the framing.

Solid shimming is the key to long-lasting, trouble-free operation

The brick opening shown here was level and plumb, but this isn't always the case. Start by checking the sill area with a 2-ft. level. If you're building it up as shown in Photo 5, it's easy to level it with shims at the same time. Otherwise, level the sill area with pairs of shims spaced about 4 in. apart.

Then set the door in the opening for a test fit. Hold a level against the hinge jamb and adjust the door and frame until the jamb is plumb. Check to see how the casing fits against the siding. If the siding is so far out of plumb that the doorframe and casing don't fit in, you either cut back the siding or trim the casing. It looks better if you can cut the siding, but it's usually more practical and easier to trim the casing. Mark the casing in areas that need trimming. Then take the door out and trim the casing with a belt sander or circular saw.

Make sure the building paper is intact around the frame edges. If not, slide strips of No. 15 felt behind the siding and tack it to the framing with staples. When you're sure the door will fit, caulk along the sill and behind the casing and tip the door into the opening. Photos 8 – 10 show how to shim and nail the door. The goal is to center the door in the opening and shim the sides until they're plumb and straight. Adjust the pairs of shims until the gap between the door and the jamb is consistent on the sides and top of the door. When you're happy with the fit, nail through the jamb into the framing at each shim location. Then replace one screw closest to the inside in each hinge with one long enough to reach the framing. This will keep the door from sagging over time (Photo 11).

After insulating the space around the door (Photo 12), install the interior trim. Photo 13 shows how to cover a gap between the doorsill and flooring. Complete the job by caulking the exterior (Photo 14). For gaps wider than 3/16 in., insert a foam backer (available at home centers, hardware stores and lumberyards) and apply caulk over it. Most doors require an additional trim board under the sill to support its outer edge. Finally, remove the door and paint or stain and varnish the door, jamb and trim.

Materials List

- Treated lumber to build up the sill (optional)
- Roll of flexible self-sticking flashing membrane
- Two tubes of polyurethane caulk
- Three packages of shims
- Two cans of minimal expanding foam
- Roll of foam caulk backing (optional)
- Transition molding (optional; Photo 13)
- One pound each of 12d and 16d galvanized casing nails
- One pound of 3-in. coated deck screws
- 4d, 6d and 10d finish nails

Buying a new door

Most home centers stock prehung exterior doors in a limited number of styles. Common jamb widths for stock doors are 4-9/16 in. and 6-9/16 in., and they usually include 2-in.-wide brick molding for exterior trim. These doors work great for newly constructed walls and for replacing doors in newer homes. But if, after measuring the jamb width and opening sizes for your existing door, you discover that you need a different size jamb or that your exterior trim is wider, then you'll save a lot of headaches by ordering a door to your exact specifications.

There are three types of doors to choose from. Steel doors ($150 to $300) are popular because they're inexpensive and require little maintenance. Fiberglass doors ($250 to $1,200) won't warp or rot, and the more expensive models are hard to tell apart from real wood. You'll find the widest selection of styles in wood doors ($300 to $1,500), but be prepared to spend extra time maintaining the finish.

Prehung exterior doors are available at home centers and lumberyards. If you can't find what you're looking for in stock, you can order it. Take along your measurements and a sketch showing which way the door swings.

If you plan to install a new entry knob and deadbolt, pick them out before you order the door. Then ask the salesperson to have the door drilled to accept your hardware. It'll cost a little extra, but it's well worth it to avoid the nerve-racking job of drilling into a new door. Don't forget to order hinges that will match the finish of your hardware.

Stop window and door drafts

Make your home more comfortable, and cut energy bills

1 SLICE through paint where the trim meets the wall and jamb. Put a new blade in your utility knife and make several passes over heavy paint buildup.

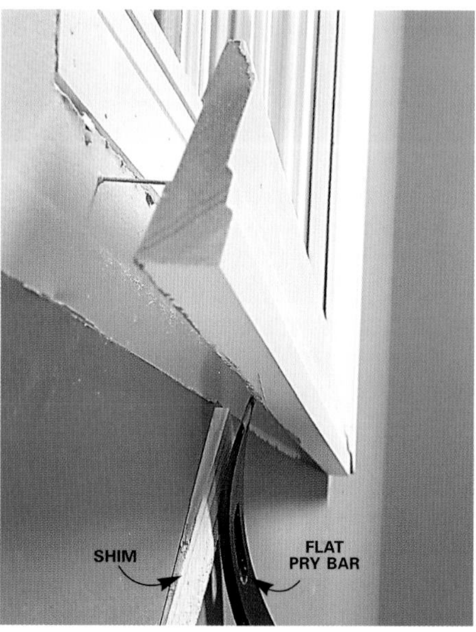

2 PRY away the trim gently with a flat pry bar. Protect walls with a shim or a scrap of wood as you gradually work the trim away from the wall.

If your windows or doors are a source of chilly drafts all winter long, the problem could be worn-out seals, weatherstripping or thresholds. Then again, sloppy installation might be to blame. When cold weather arrives, hold the back of your hand near the edges of windows or doors to track down the source of leaks. If you feel cold air flowing out from behind the trim, chances are the spaces around the window and doorjambs weren't properly sealed.

Plugging these leaks is a time-consuming job: You have to pull off the interior trim, seal around the jambs and then reinstall the trim. But if your doors and windows are otherwise fairly airtight, the payoff can be big too. Stopping drafts not only makes your home more comfortable but also cuts energy bills (air leaks are a major source of heat loss in most homes).

First investigate further: Remove one piece of trim from a window or a door. To prevent chipping or tearing paint, cut through the paint first (Photo 1). Slip a stiff putty knife under the trim and lift it enough to insert a flat pry bar. Don't simply force up one end of the piece. Instead, work along the length of the piece, moving your pry bar and lifting the trim off gradually (Photo 2). At mitered corners, watch for nails driven through the joint. To prevent these nails from splitting mitered ends, pry up both mitered

Caution:
Lead paint chips are hazardous. If your home was built before 1978, call your local health department for information on testing and handling lead paint safely.

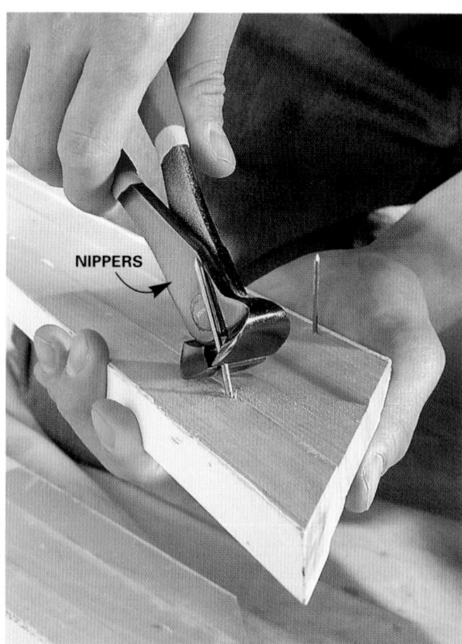

3 PULL nails out through the back side of trim with nippers or pliers. Also write the location of each piece of trim on the back side.

4 PULL insulation from between the jamb and the wall framing. Seal the gap around the jamb with foam sealant. Be careful not to overfill and bow the jamb.

5 TACK each section of trim exactly in its original position with a couple of nails. Ridges in the wall paint can help you align each piece perfectly. Make sure the parts fit together tightly at the corners before you add more nails.

pieces together. Then pull them apart. When you're removing nails from the trim, pull them through the back side to avoid damaging the face of the trim (Photo 3).

With one piece removed, examine the space between the jamb and the wall framing. If the drywall covers the space, trim it back with a utility knife. If you see only a few loose wads of fiberglass insulation or no insulation at all between the jamb and framing, it's likely that all your windows and doors are poorly sealed.

To seal the gap, remove the remaining trim and inject foam sealant (Photo 4). Some sealants will push jambs inward as they expand, so be sure to use one that's intended for windows and doors (check the label). DAP Tex Plus was used here because it's easy to clean up with a damp rag. Most expanding foams are nearly impossible to clean up before they harden.

Let the foam harden and trim off any excess foam with a knife before you reinstall the trim. Position each piece exactly as it was originally and tack each one up with only two nails (Photo 5). When all the pieces are in place, check their fit. With only a couple of nails in each piece, you can make small adjustments by holding a block against the trim and tapping it with a hammer. Then add more nails.

If your trim has a clear finish, fill the nail holes with a matching colored filler such as Color Putty or DAP Finishing Putty. With painted trim, it's best to fill the holes with spackle and repaint.

Energy-Saving Q&A

Icy windows

Q Our winter temps reach minus 30 degrees F. We have low-E double-pane windows and maintain a low humidity level in our house (35 to 40 percent), but we still get ice on all of our windows. The only way I've found to defrost my windows is to aim fans at them. What can we do to remedy this situation?

A Double-pane windows with a low-E coating have an insulation R-value of about 3. Theoretically, they can sustain an indoor relative humidity of about 70 percent at 30 degrees F and 60 percent at 0 degrees F. With any higher relative humidity, condensation will form on the glass.

The glass edges of double-pane windows, the area you see wet and frosted, get considerably colder than the center of the glass. Depending on the sealing method, the edges can only sustain 45 to 55 percent relative humidity at 30 degrees F, and 25 to 35 percent at 0 degrees F before condensation begins. If you sustain a relative humidity at 40 percent or higher, your windows will be continually wet.

In your case, the simplest solution for controlling condensation is to reduce moisture sources. That means covering crawlspaces, sealing basement walls and floors, covering aquariums, reducing the number of houseplants, running ventilating fans during showers and while cooking, and making sure combustion devices are venting properly. Allowing more heat to get to the windows by keeping drapes open and circulating air with room fans will also help. Installing an air exchanger (an expensive option) will also lower indoor humidity.

When you shop for new windows, buy a type with higher-performance edge seals or consider triple-pane glass. Either will allow you to sustain a higher, more comfortable relative humidity in zero and subzero temperatures.

Exterior caulking that lasts

Here's how to make caulk do its job and look good at the same time

With prepackaged tubes and slick caulk guns, caulking has become so quick and easy that it's almost fun. A squirt here, a squirt there.

But don't rush through this step. A good caulking job ensures that you've sealed up all those energy-wasting gaps and cracks on the exterior of your home. It plugs the cracks where water can seep in and lift the paint. And it smooths over ugly gaps that make your home look shabby.

Here you'll find out what types of caulks and guns to buy to deliver fast and smooth results, yet still provide lasting protection. You'll also learn caulking techniques that'll result in an effective, long-term moisture barrier. Finally, you'll learn what caulk can't do and where you can go wrong when you apply it.

Better caulking guns are sturdy and have smooth ratcheting actions and releases. Larger handles are easier to squeeze. The bent end of the rod hooks over ladder rungs. An attached wire conveniently pokes a hole in the tube seal.

Buy a good caulking gun

Professional caulking guns begin at about $25, but even as little as six or seven bucks buys you a decent one (photo at left). The quality is all in the action. Better guns (even priced as low as $6) have smoother-operating, no-slip ratcheting mechanisms, easier-to-squeeze handles, and better pressure control, so you can deliver just the right amount of caulk where you need it. Look for one that's also "dripless," which means that it releases pressure when you relax your grip so you don't have that 2-in. bead of slop-over dribbling onto your shirt and shoes. A stiff wire attached to some guns comes in handy for puncturing the foil seal inside the nozzle.

If you have small hands, buy the longer-handled variety of gun, which is easier to squeeze. The trick is to compress the handle to a comfortable position with the mechanism released, then apply the caulk with a shorter handle movement.

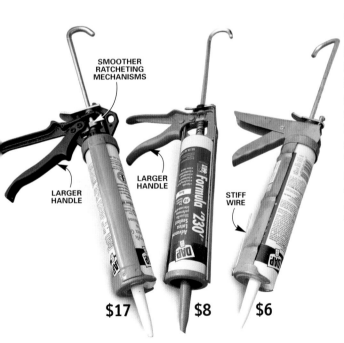

AVOID $2 CHEAPIES

A good gun is twice as fast and half as tiring.

Caulk to stop water and improve appearance

CAULK ALL EXTERIOR JOINTS that are vulnerable to water. Moisture is your home's worst enemy, so caulk around doors, windows, decks and other penetrations where water or wind-driven rain could get into the walls and rot the framing (Photo 2).

Caulk also protects wood siding and trim (Photo 4). Water soaking in through joints can cause paint to peel and siding to rot.

And finally, caulk gaps and cracks to improve your home's appearance (Photo 3). Stand back and look at each wall of your home. Then simply caulk distracting dark lines that you think will mar a neat paint job.

Four reasons to caulk:

1. To improve energy efficiency
2. To prevent rain and moisture from entering walls
3. To protect siding and trim
4. To improve appearance

DOOR-JAMB

EXTERIOR TRIM

DARK CRACK

Seal the joints between trim pieces to block water and erase distracting dark lines. Otherwise, the paint will crack at these joints. Acrylic caulk works well for most joints.

Caulk decorative trim to improve its appearance. Apply and smooth a thin bead here to keep the corners crisp. A good caulking gun pays off to speed up this slow, painstaking job.

Follow the three-step caulking rule

Step 1: Prepare a solid base

Dig out old, loose caulk with a putty knife or sharp-pointed tool (Photo 1). Caulk hardens and cracks as it ages, usually breaking away from the wood, leaving it exposed to moisture. Clean loose caulk from cracks and gaps, but leave the caulk that still adheres well. (Poke at it with your putty knife. If it readily breaks away, dig it out.)

Then work primer back into the gaps. (Normally you'd do this during the paint scraping and priming stages, but if you missed spots, get them now.) Because primer adheres better to bare wood, it's the best base for caulk. This isn't the case with concrete, brick and other masonry surfaces. With these materials, use polyurethane caulk, which is sometimes called "self-priming" because it adheres so well.

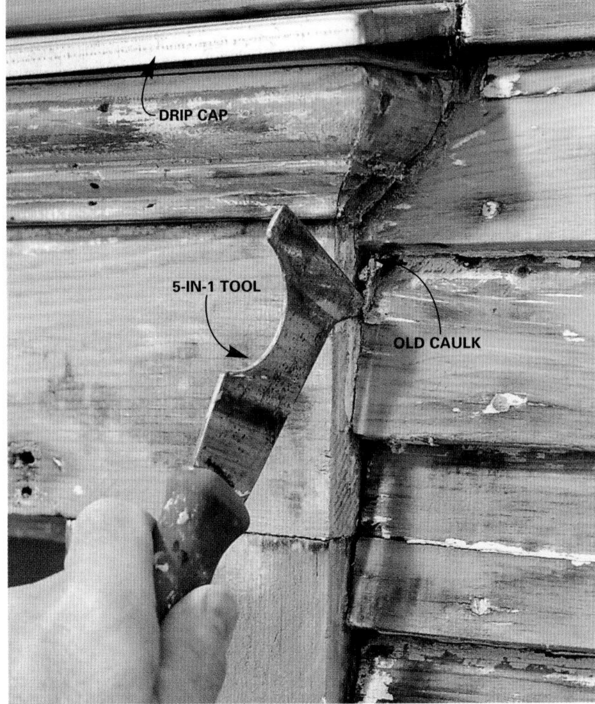

1 CLEAN the joints by digging out old, loose caulk with a 5-in-1 tool or a stiff putty knife. Prime all bare wood, working the primer as far back into the joints as possible.

Step 2: Lay a ribbon of caulk

Rest the tip of the tube on the joint and squeeze on a ribbon that just covers the gap (Photo 2). Technique pays off here. Pull the tip of the tube along the joint, concentrating on covering the gap with a layer rather than completely filling it with a thick bead. The idea is to bridge the gap with caulk, not to fill it. A thick bead will crack and pull away from the wood when it hardens. A ribbon will stretch with the normal expansion and contraction of the wood (Figure A, below right).

For smoother caulking, cut the tip of the tube at a 45- to 60-degree angle so the hole is slightly smaller than the size of the gap you want to caulk (photo, bottom). It's much easier to squeeze out additional caulk than to clean up the mess caused by too much.

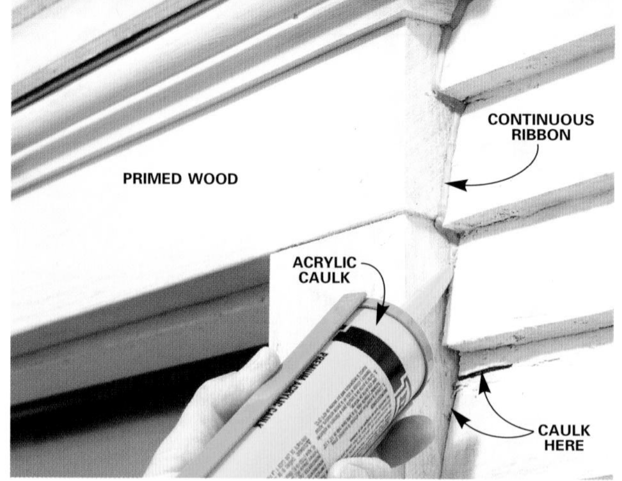

2 **SQUEEZE a smooth, even ribbon of caulk over the joint, completely covering it. Squeeze steadily, resting the tip of the tube on the wood and dragging it along at an even pace to get an even flow.**

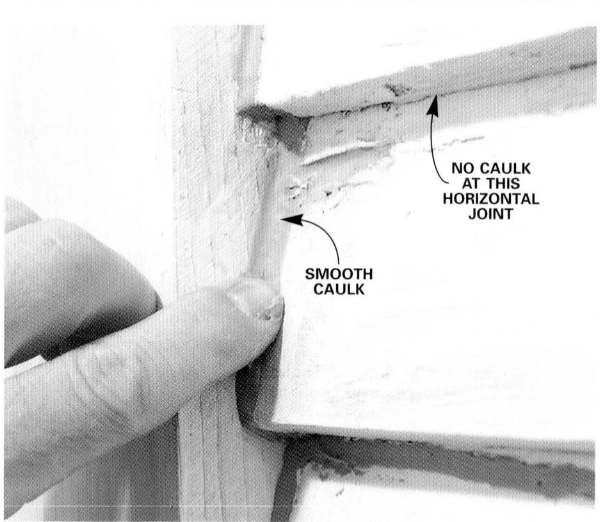

3 **MOISTEN a finger and press the caulk against both sides of the joint to ensure good adhesion, smoothing it as you go. Wipe away excess along the sides with a damp cloth. Don't caulk the horizontal joints between wood siding; your wall needs enough cracks to be able to "breathe."**

FOR BIG PROJECTS, cut open two tubes with a sharp utility knife, making one hole slightly larger than the other. Switch tubes to match the joint size.

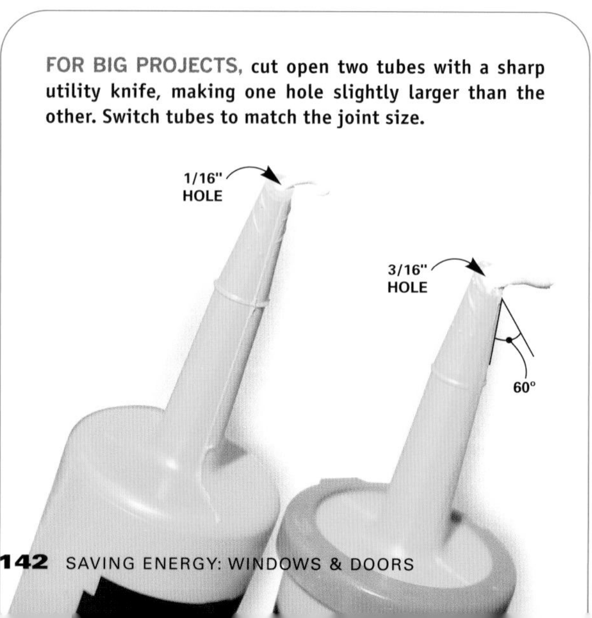

Step 3: 'Tool' the caulk to ensure good adhesion and to smooth it

Dampen your finger (with water for acrylic, paint thinner for polyurethane) and run it along the joint, pressing the caulk against the sides and flattening and smoothing the surface (Photo 3), a process called tooling. The key to a durable caulk joint is to get good adhesion on each side of the joint (Figure A). Your finger will leave the joint slightly concave, but don't press the caulk tightly into corners trying to make them sharp. Acrylics and polyurethanes shrink 20 to 30 percent when they dry, so you can expect the concavity to increase.

THE IDEA IS TO BRIDGE the gap with caulk, not to completely fill it.

Keep a wet cloth on hand to clean acrylic caulk from your hands and to wipe away excess. Work about 2 ft. of joint at a time, stopping to smooth each section. Otherwise, acrylic caulk will begin to skin over and won't smooth easily.

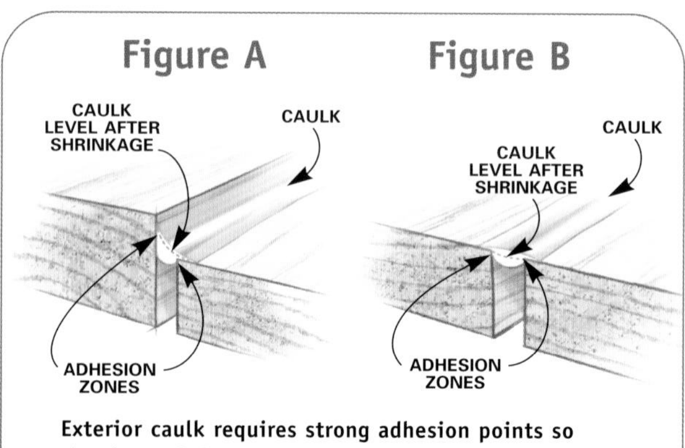

Exterior caulk requires strong adhesion points so that it won't break loose when the wood expands and contracts.

You need only two types of caulk

DESPITE THE VAST, CONFUSING ARRAY OF CAULKS on the home center shelf, you need only two types for your home's exterior—acrylic and polyurethane. Both types stick solidly to wood and most other building materials, accept paint well and retain their flexibility for years.

Acrylic

Use acrylic (sometimes called acrylic latex) as an all-purpose caulk (Photos 2 and 5). It's water-based, so you can smooth it and clean it off your hands and tools easily. Once spread, it skins over within minutes, so you can paint it almost immediately with an acrylic latex paint. Buy the highest-quality premium acrylic caulk available. Price is a good indicator—the more expensive, the better. Better acrylics typically cost $2 to $4 per standard 10-oz. tube.

Acrylic is an all-purpose, water-based caulk.

Silicone acrylic is more flexible, a good feature, but if you buy it, make sure the label states that it's paintable.

Polyurethane

Polyurethane performs better than acrylic in all ways, but it's stickier and much harder to apply. You'll see how to use it in Photos 1 – 4 on pp. 144 and 145. You have to use mineral spirits or paint thinner for cleanup. Use it when you caulk concrete, stucco or other masonry and when you want extra-strong adhesion, for example, in areas especially vulnerable to water (Photo 2, p. 144). It costs $4 to $5 per tube.

Polyurethane caulk has extra-strong adhesion.

Use backer rods to caulk wide joints

For a durable caulk joint wider than about 1/4 in., insert a special foam backer rod to fill the bulk of the gap. If you fill the entire gap with caulk, it'll soon harden and crack. To retain flexibility, your ribbon of caulk shouldn't be more than 1/8 in. to 3/16 in. thick (Figure C). Many home centers and full-service hardware stores carry foam backer rods in several sizes (photo at right). Otherwise, call a concrete products dealer.

Photos 1 – 4 on pp. 144 and 145 show the basic caulking steps for a wide gap. Shown is polyurethane caulk because it adheres better to stone than acrylic does. But it's tough to handle because it's super sticky. Keep a rag and paint thinner nearby for cleaning it off your hands and tools. If you're doing extensive caulking, wear plastic gloves to limit your skin exposure to paint thinner. Apply polyurethane sparingly; excess is difficult to clean off.

You can file an old putty knife to a round profile to use as a shaping tool (Photo 3, p. 145). Smoothing a wide joint so it looks nice takes practice, so begin with less-prominent joints.

Backer rods in a variety of sizes help seal large cracks.

Quick tip

CHOOSE A CAULK COLOR that'll blend with concrete or other masonry. Then leave the caulk unpainted.

Figure C

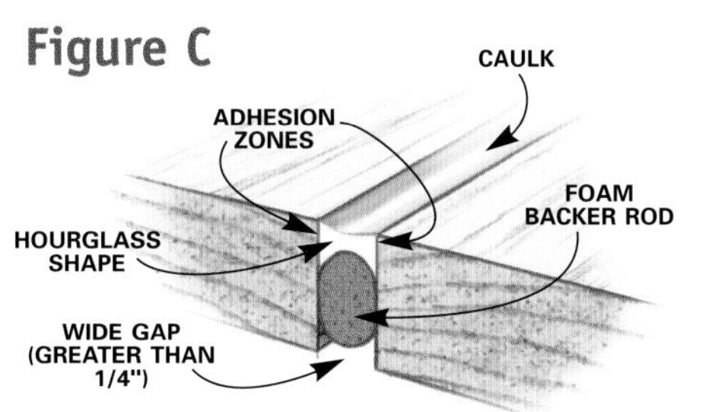

The hourglass shape is ideal for a caulked joint. The caulk flexes in the middle yet remains solidly anchored to the sides.

1 **PRESS foam backer rod into gaps larger than about 1/4 in. using a putty knife or other blunt tool. Buy various sizes so you won't have to compress large rods into small gaps.**

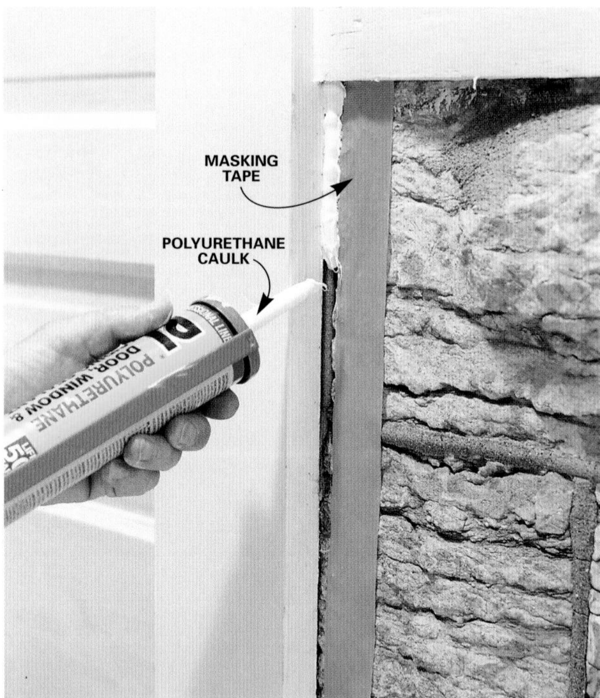

2 **LAY masking tape along the stone to ensure a crisp, even edge on the rough surface. Then spread caulk over the remaining gap.**

Energy-Saving Hint

Mini caulk gun for tight areas

An ordinary caulk gun is just too big and bulky for working in tight spots, such as behind a sink or at the back of a tub faucet. For these places, a 20-cc plastic syringe (without a needle) makes an ideal mini caulk gun. Just cut the syringe tip at a slight angle, pull out the plunger and load it with caulk. Syringes are available at pharmacies and farm supply stores.

A final step: Test for backdrafting

Exterior caulking on a large painting project has the side effect of making your house more airtight. Although increasing airtightness saves energy, it can have negative consequences too. (See "Where *not* to caulk," below.)

Where *not* to caulk

DON'T CAULK JOINTS THAT AREN'T AFFECTED BY WATER and won't mar the appearance of the final paint job. Two examples are horizontal joints under lap siding (Photo 3, p. 142) and the tops of drip caps over windows and doors where flashing carries water to the exterior. Joints protected by roof overhangs don't need caulk either.

Moisture generated inside must have ways to get out. If you seal your home in an airtight skin, you'll trap that moisture in the walls, especially in cold weather, and it'll soak the wood, cause rot and lift the exterior paint.

Still, a good caulking job will make your home more airtight. So afterward, check your gas- or oil-burning appliances to make sure they continue to vent waste gases properly.

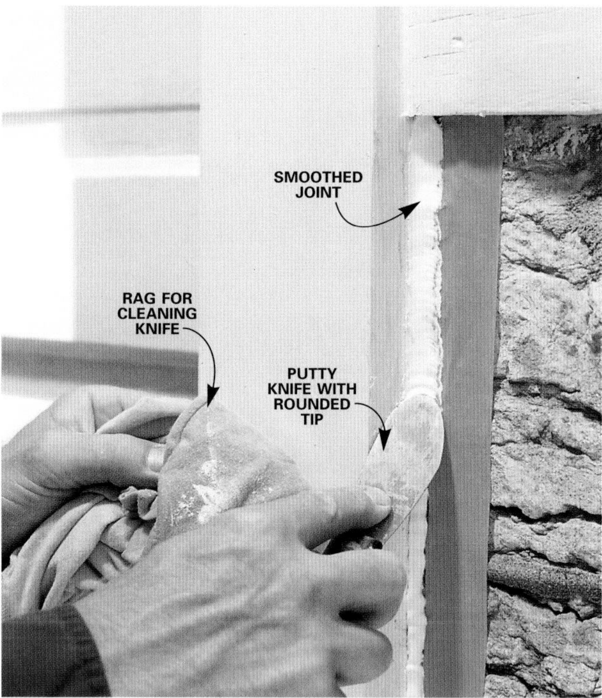

3 SMOOTH the caulk with a round-end tool to shape the joint and ensure good adhesion on the edges. Using a finger won't work on wider joints like this, especially with this sticky type of caulk. Keep a cloth dampened with thinner handy to clean off excess polyurethane caulk.

4 PULL OFF the tape before the caulk begins to harden. Otherwise, the caulk will stick to it and you'll have to cut it off.

A tighter house can cause potentially hazardous exhaust fumes from gas-, oil- or wood-burning devices to spill into the house rather than flow out a chimney or vent. This phenomenon is called backdrafting. Test your water heater for backdrafting (it's the most likely candidate) by closing all your doors and windows and running hot water until the water heater comes on. After about a minute, check the vent hood with a smoking match to make sure the exhaust pulls the smoke up the vent. If the vent isn't drawing properly, call in a heating contractor to find and correct the problem.

Quick tip

A FEW TRICKS TO REMEMBER WHEN CAULKING:

- Use expanding foam to seal large gaps, especially around dryer vents, electrical service entry points and other places where utilities enter your home.
- Caulking inside is often more effective than caulking outside. Before repainting a room, caulk around "leaky" moldings.
- As a rule of thumb, you'll use 1/2 tube of caulk per door, 1/4 tube of caulk per window.

Energy-Saving Hint

Caulking extender

If you have to get caulk into a tight spot, just tape a flexible drinking straw to the tip of your caulking gun and you'll be ready to caulk into any nook the straw will reach.

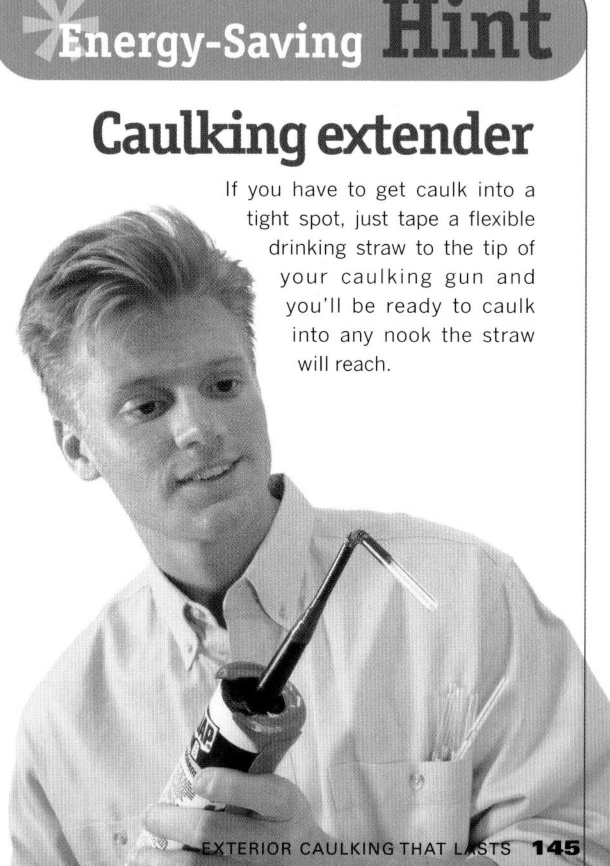

Energy-saving replacement windows

Out with the old and cold. In with the new and warm.

Are you ready to replace your drafty old windows with new energy-efficient units? You'll be glad to know that you don't have to tear off interior moldings or disturb exterior trim and siding.

Here you'll learn, step by step, how to remove the old sash from double-hung windows and mount either a new sash kit or a wood or vinyl replacement insert inside your existing window jamb. Even a beginner can do it.

Both the sash replacement kit and the wood or vinyl replacement insert fit in the space between the outside stop, called the blind stop, and the removable interior stop (see Figure A, opposite). The sash replacement kit is designed to replace the sash in double-hung windows only. Wood or vinyl replacement inserts, on the other hand, are self-contained units with their own jamb and sash and can therefore be slid into almost any type of window jamb. They are available as double-hung, sliding or casement-style windows.

CAUTION:

Houses built before 1978 may contain lead paint. Before disturbing any surface, get a lab analysis of paint chips from it (about $10 - 15 per sample). Contact your public health department for information on how to collect samples and where to send them.

Option 1

Wood or vinyl replacement inserts

For a maintenance-free window that doesn't require any painting or staining, consider vinyl replacement windows. Some companies even make a simulated wood grain interior. Since wood or vinyl replacement inserts have their own jamb, they can be installed in window jambs that are slightly out of square. Ask your window dealer for help measuring, though, since you'll have to downsize the window slightly to fit.

Shopping for replacement windows is a little trickier than buying sash kits because the quality of the windows varies dramatically and many are available only to contractors. The window we ordered cost $275 and arrived in about three weeks. Make sure to inspect and operate an actual working model of the window before you order. Look closely at details like the locking system, weatherstripping, and sash and frame joints. Then consider the overall appearance. Some windows, like ours, have narrow vinyl sash parts that allow more light and a better view than windows with wide sash frames.

Buyer's Guide

The following companies manufacture vinyl replacement windows. Call for the retailer nearest you.

CRESTLINE WINDOWS AND DOORS: (800) 826-5509. www.crestlinewindows.com

MARVIN WINDOWS & DOORS: (888) 537-7828. www.marvin.com

PELLA WINDOWS: (877) 473-5527. www.pella.com

Option 2

Double-hung sash replacement kits

If you want to retain the authentic wood look of your old double-hung windows, sash replacement kits are the best option. You can order the sashes with grilles to match the rest of the windows in your house and paint or stain the wood. (You can choose grilles that either snap in or are glued to the glass.) But your old window jamb must be square and rot-free. Measure diagonally. If the diagonal measurements differ by more than 1/2 in., the new sash won't seal properly and you should replace the window or use a vinyl replacement window instead.

Double-hung sash replacement kits consist of two new wood window sashes, two vinyl jamb liners and installation hardware. They range in price from about $200 for a basic window with a snap-in grid to more than $400 for windows like ours with simulated divided panes. Features like energy-efficient low-E glass and maintenance-free exterior cladding are available for an extra cost. Contact one of the manufacturers listed at right for more information and to find out where to order windows in your area.

Figure A
Window parts

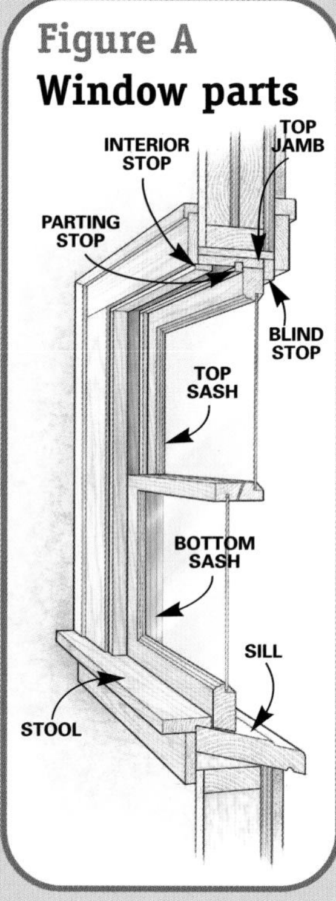

Buyer's Guide

Here are a few companies that sell double-hung sash replacement kits. Check your local lumberyard or home center for other sources.

JELD-WEN: (800) 535-3936. www.jeld-wen.com

KOLBE & KOLBE MILLWORK INC.: (800) 955-8177. www.kolbe-kolbe.com

MARVIN WINDOWS AND DOORS: (888) 537-8266. www.marvin.com

Option 1

Wood or vinyl replacement inserts

Start your replacement insert installation by removing the interior stop, sash and parting stop. The parting stop is usually caked with paint and difficult to remove. Use pliers to break out the lower section. If the upper sash is stuck, pry or break out the upper section of parting stop with a chisel. If your windows have spring balances or metal jamb liners rather than sash weights like ours, start by removing the interior stops (Photo 1). Then look for the screws or nails that secure the sash hardware and remove them. The goal is to remove all hardware back to the blind stops (Photo 2). You don't have to worry about dinging up the jamb and sill, because they'll be covered. If your window has a sash weight cavity, stuff it with insulation.

Make sure your window insert is square

Your wood or vinyl replacement insert will be slightly smaller than the window jamb opening to allow for shimming. The key to a window that operates smoothly and seals properly is getting the frame perfectly square and the sides straight. Photos 5 and 6 show how. Don't be afraid to remove the screws and readjust the window in the opening if necessary. In addition to checking the window by measuring the diagonals (Photo 5), open and close the sashes to make sure the tops and bottoms are parallel with the sill and top jamb and that the top and bottom sashes are parallel to each other where they meet in the middle. Keep tweaking the shims until everything is square and lined up. Then snug but don't overtighten the screws. Complete the installation by reinstalling the interior stops (Photo 7) and sealing up the exterior (Photos 8 and 9). You can also install wood or vinyl replacement inserts in casement and sliding window jambs. We won't talk about them in detail here. Be sure to read the installation instructions that come with each window.

1 GENTLY PRY off the interior stops. Pry against a stiff putty knife to protect the wood. To minimize paint chipping on painted windows, score the joint between the window frame and stop with a utility knife before prying off the stop. Pull the nails through the back side of the stop with a nail nipper or pliers. Complete the window prep by following Photos 2 and 3.

2 **SLIP** the new window insert into place to make sure it fits. Then remove it and lay a bead of polyurethane caulk along the inside of the blind stop and the back side of the window stool.

3 **REST** the bottom of the replacement window on the sill and tilt the window into place against the blind stop. If your window includes a head expander, position it over the top of the jamb first. Press the window tight against the caulked blind stop.

4 **LOOSELY FASTEN** the window into the frame with partially driven screws in the lower left and upper right corners. Close and lock the sash.

5 **MEASURE** diagonally across the new window. Slide shims behind the screw holes in the four corners and adjust them until the diagonal measurements from opposite corners are equal. Drive screws through the upper left and lower right screw holes.

6 **HOLD** a level against the side jamb and slide wood shims behind each remaining screw hole until the side jamb is straight. Snug up all screws and check that the sashes slide easily and align perfectly where they meet in the middle. Be careful; overtightening screws could warp the vinyl jamb.

7 **CUT OFF** the shims with a sharp utility knife and then replace the interior stops and nail them in place with 4d finish nails.

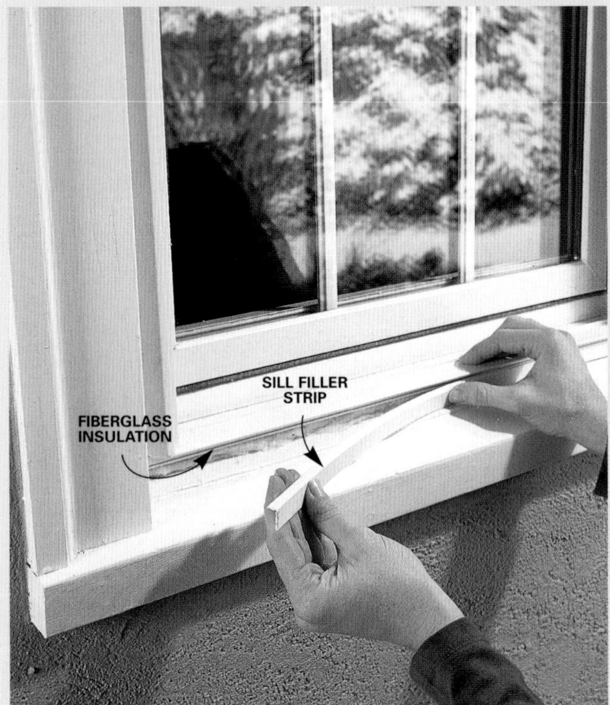

8 **STUFF** fiberglass insulation in the gap under the sill of the new vinyl window. Measure the size of the gap and cut the vinyl filler strip to fit. Use a sharp utility knife and straightedge or tin snips to cut the vinyl. Press the filler into place.

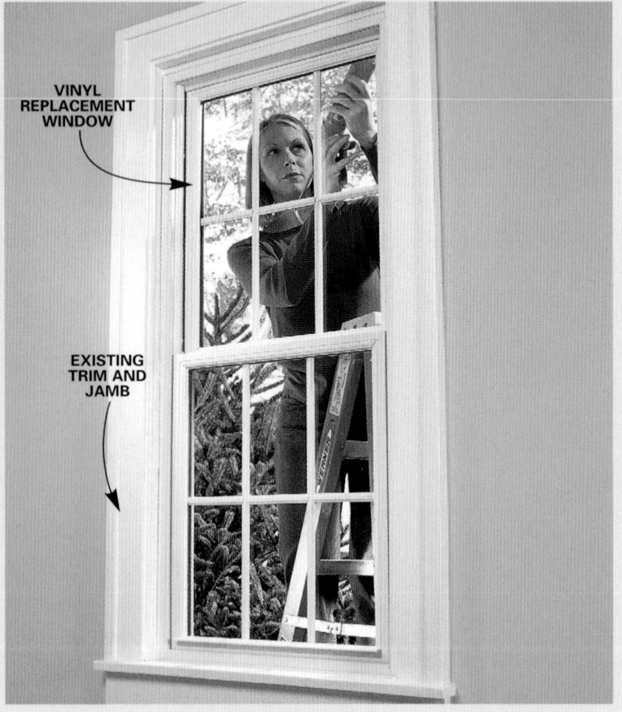

9 **CAULK** the joint between the new window and the blind stop and between the windowsill and the filler strip.

Option 2

Double-hung sash kits

The toughest part of sash replacement is tearing out the old window. You have to pry off the stop (carefully for reuse) and the parting stop (which you can discard; see Photo 3, p. 152). You can either nail or screw the new liner clips in place (Photo 4). We chose screws because driving nails can be difficult in old window jambs. Be sure to leave a 1/16-in. space between the clip and the blind stop or the jamb liner won't snap in (Photo 4). Then replace the interior stops and top parting stop (Photo 5). Read the instructions included with your window for the exact procedure to use for lowering the sash lifts (Photo 6) and tilting the sash into place. If you have trouble pushing in the sash after you tilt it up, try working with one side at a time. Compress the jamb liner with one hand while you ease one top corner of the sash in with the other. Then repeat the process on the other side. Also position the top of the sash toward the center of the opening.

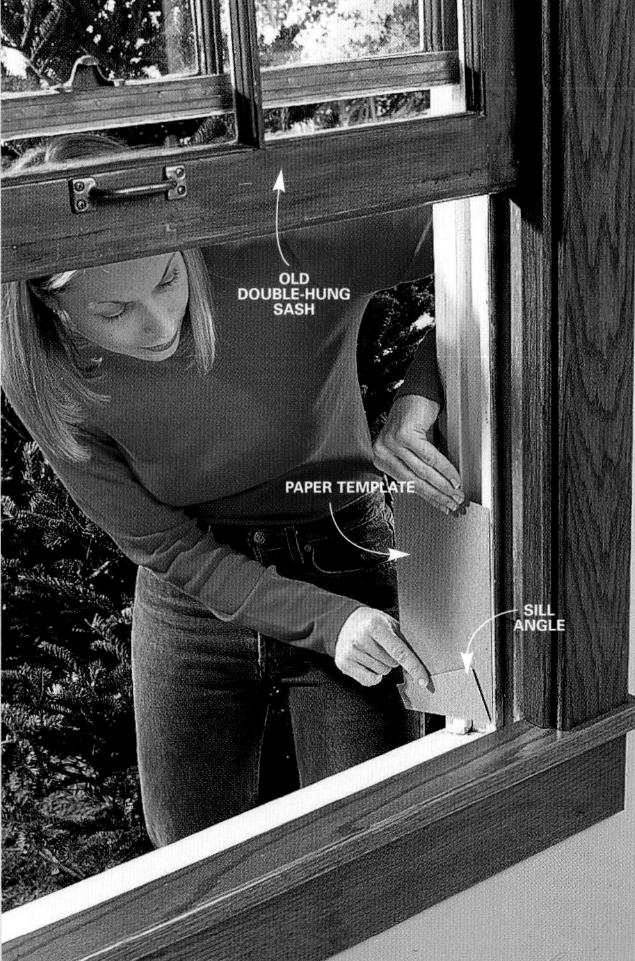

1 **ALIGN the edge of a heavy piece of paper with the window stop and fold the bottom to match the angle of the sill. Lay a protractor (Figure B) on the folded paper to determine the angle. Then measure the interior height and width of the window frame. Use these measurements to order your sash replacement kit.**

Figure B
Find the sill angle

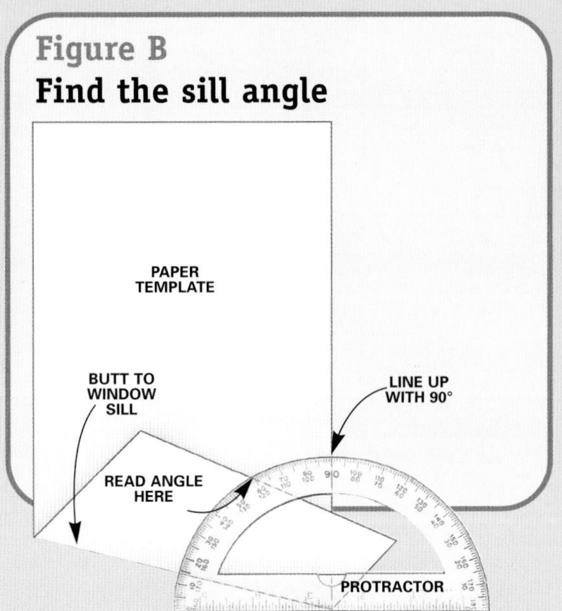

Your old jamb must be solid

The window replacements we show must be installed in a solid, rot-free jamb. Inspect your old window frame carefully for signs of water damage. Pay particular attention to the sill. Probe with a screwdriver to uncover hidden soft spots. Normal exposure to rain and snow often causes the exposed parts of poorly maintained windowsills or the lower sections of the exterior trim to rot. An experienced carpenter can usually repair these areas with sections of new wood or you can use an epoxy repair system. Rot along the top or interior parts of windows, including the window jamb, is more difficult to repair and often signals a bigger problem. Don't mess with repairs. Plan on tearing out the entire window and installing a new one.

Measure carefully

There's nothing worse than discovering that your nonreturnable custom-sized window doesn't fit. Measure the width between the side jambs at the top, middle and bottom and record the smallest measurement. Measure all the way to the jamb, not the blind stop or parting stop (see Figure A). Now measure the height from the top jamb to the sill (see Figure A). Measure both sides and the middle and record the smallest measurement. Finally, determine the sill angle (Photo 1, p. 151) and specify this when you order a sash replacement kit to make sure the jamb liners fit tight to the sill. This step isn't necessary for ordering wood or vinyl replacement inserts. Keep a record of all correspondence with your window supplier and ask for written confirmation before the windows are ordered so you can double-check the sizes.

If your house was built before about 1940, you'll likely have double-hung windows with sash weights and cords like the ones shown here. Newer double-hungs may have springs or jamb liners instead, but once these are removed, the installation process is the same.

2 **REMOVE the lower sash and cut the sash cords. If your window has weatherstripping or hardware other than sash cords, pry out or unscrew these to remove the sash.**

3 **PULL or pry the parting stop from the groove in the window frame and discard it. Remove the top sash, cut the sash cords and take out the sash weight pulleys, sash weight cover and weights. Stuff the cavity with fiberglass insulation. Screw the jamb liner clips to the jamb with No. 6 x 3/4-in. pan head screws (inset). Position clips 4 in. from the top and bottom and space the remaining clips evenly between them. Leave a 1/16-in. space between the clips and the blind stop to allow space for the jamb liner to slide in.**

4 SNAP jamb liners over the metal clips after installing the sash stops and gaskets according to the instructions included with your window. Align the jamb liner so its outside edge fits between the blind stop and the metal clips. If your jamb liner has a vinyl flap facing the outside, make sure it lies over the blind stop. Press firmly over each clip location until you hear or feel the liner snap onto the clips.

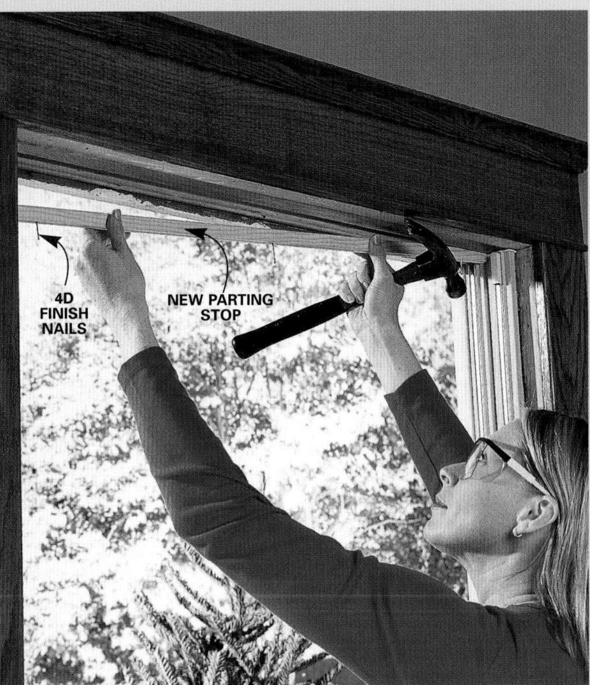

5 SLIP the new parting stop into the groove in the top jamb with the weatherstripped edge facing the outside. Drill 1/16-in. pilot holes and nail the stop in place with three 4d finish nails. Replace the wood interior stops on the sides and top of the window and nail them in place with 4d finish nails.

6 SLIDE the sash lifts down to within about 10 in. of the windowsill. Press down firmly with a flat-blade screwdriver. Twist the screwdriver slightly from horizontal to slide the lifts. Then twist back to horizontal to engage the lifts in their new locations.

CAUTION: Release pressure very slowly to make sure the clips are engaged before you remove the screwdriver completely.

7 HOLD the top sash with the exterior facing up and the metal cams away from you. Tilt the sash and align the metal pivots with the slots in the jamb liner closest to the exterior. Make sure the pivots are above the sash lifts. Tilt up the sash and press outward on the jamb liner while you snap the top of the sash into place between the jamb liners. Slide the sash down until the metal cams contact the sash lifts. Repeat the process on the lower sash.

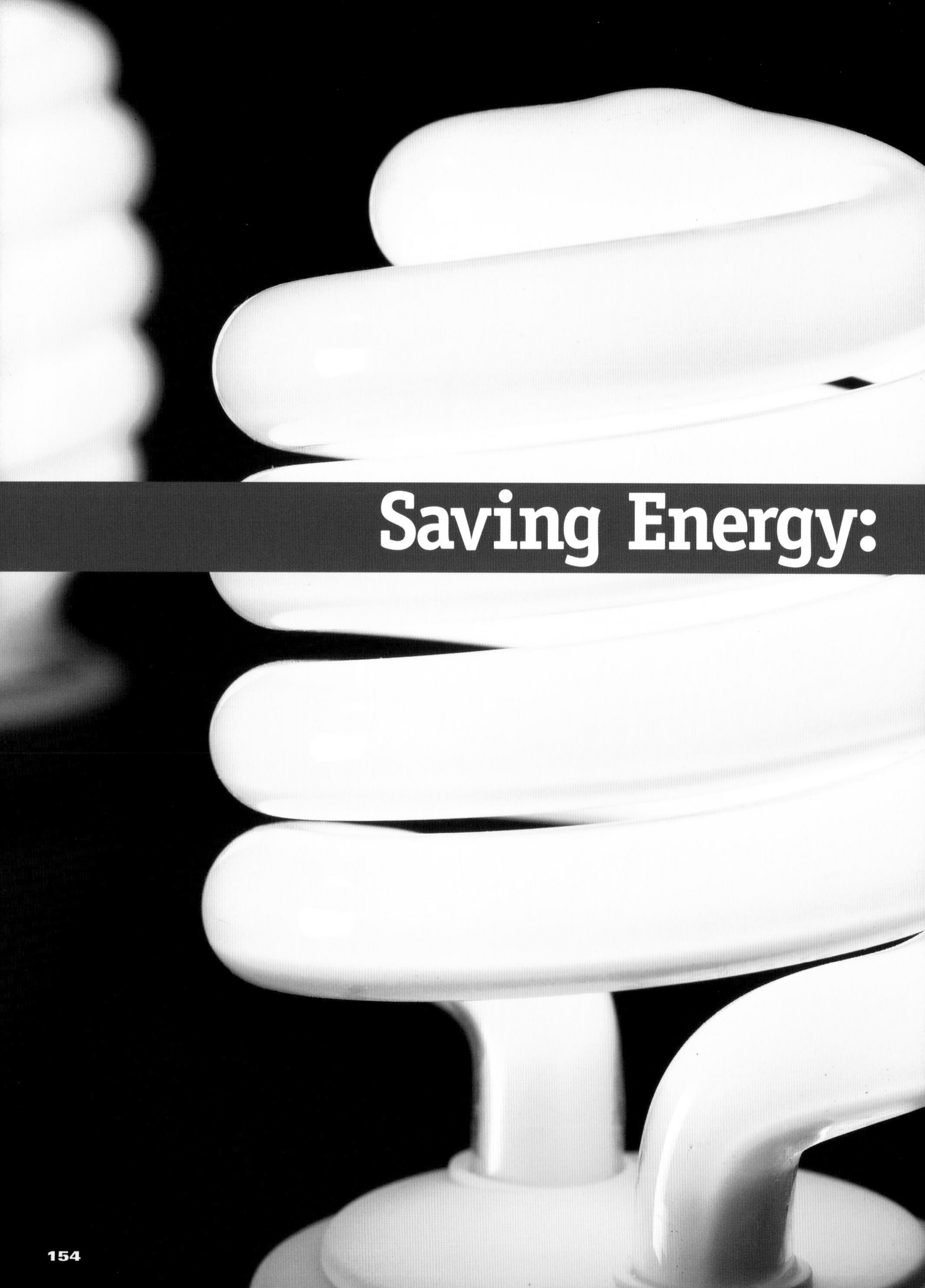

Saving Energy:

Installing energy-efficient light bulbs and using them, and other lights, wisely is perhaps the simplest and most easily accomplished form of energy conservation of all. It can be as simple as flicking a switch or screwing in a new bulb.

Compact fluorescent bulbs (CFLs) have come a long way since first being introduced two decades ago. Originally expensive, CFLs can now be purchased for as little as $3 apiece. That may be five times the cost of an incandescent bulb, but a single CFL can save $30 to $40 in electricity over the course of its lifetime, and last five to 10 times longer than its incandescent cousin.

Motion-activated lights, dimmers and homeowner habits can also greatly reduce lighting bills. Energy-efficient lighting is a good place to begin your energy saving plans.

6 Smarter Lighting

Compact fluorescent bulbs

10 common questions; 10 commonsense answers.

Compact fluorescent bulbs—usually referred to by the initials, CFL—traveled the rocky path of most new products. Initially they were expensive (as much as $15 apiece) and fraught with problems (they appeared "dim," flickered, didn't come on instantly and burned out sooner than promised).

But that was then. New technology has solved most of the old problems. Today CFLs are one of the easiest and most effective ways of saving money on energy. It's as easy as screwing in a bulb and flipping a switch. Many CFLs can be purchased for around $3 and some utility companies offer discounts or rebates to customers who buy them.

That said, buying and using CFLs can still be confusing. The answers to these common questions will help you put these great energy-saving bulbs to best use.

1

CFLs vs. incandescent bulbs

Q How do compact fluorescent lights work and how do they differ from standard bulbs?

A Standard incandescent bulbs work by using electricity to heat up a thin filament inside the bulb. As the filament heats up, it glows, producing light. The drawback to standard bulbs is that most of the energy consumed—over 80%—goes into creating heat, not light.

CFLs work on a totally different principle. They consist of two basic parts: a gas-filled tube (what many of us would call the "bulb") and a ballast that contains the electronics. In simple terms, electricity from the ballast excites phosphors on the inside surface of the bulb; these phosphates in turn glow, producing light. Since CFLs don't waste as much energy creating heat, they're much more energy efficient. You see the savings when you compare the wattages; a 15-watt CFL provides about as much light as a 60-watt incandescent bulb.

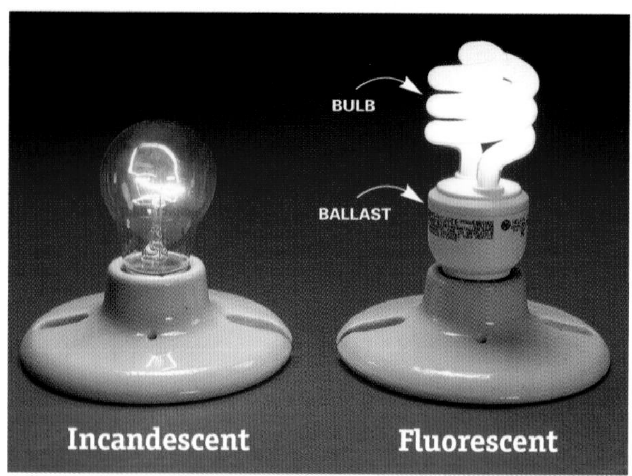

CFL bulb
Purchase price: $2.50
Energy usage cost: $12.00
TOTAL COST: $14.50
Incandescent bulb
Purchase price: $.50
Energy usage cost: $48.00
TOTAL COST: $48.50

2

Payback: How long? How come?

Q **CFLs cost five or six times as much as regular bulbs. How long do I need to use them before I recoup my investment?**

A Although CFL bulbs have come down dramatically in price, their electronic ballast and other features do make them more expensive to manufacture than incandescent bulbs. The payback period will vary based on how much electricity costs in your area. However, based on a cost of 10¢ per kWh, a 15-watt CFL will cost about $12 to operate over its 8,000-hour projected life span. Burning a 60-watt incandescent bulb with equivalent light output for the same length of time will cost about $48; a cost difference of $36 (and you'll need to buy four to eight bulbs since they have a much shorter lifespan). Based on those numbers, a CFL will pay for itself in about 500 hours (in about four months if the bulb is used four hours per day).

COOLER YET. Since CFLs generate less heat than standard incandescent bulbs, your air conditioner won't have to work quite as hard in the summer.

3

Dim the lights

Q **Can I install CFL bulbs in fixtures that operate on a dimmer switch?**

A Yes—but only if you buy the right ones. Look for CFLs that are labeled "dimmable" on the package; they have special ballasts that allow them to be operated using a standard incandescent dimmer switch. Expect to pay $3 to $4 more for a dimmable CFL than a regular CFL. Dimmable CFLs are available at most discount department stores, but they're relatively new, so you may have to search around town (or the Internet) to find them.

Quick tip

PLUGGING ELECTRICAL LEAKS. Even when your appliances and electrical equipment are turned "Off," the truth is, they're still "On." One-fifth the energy used by televisions, stereo equipment, computers and even answering machines is consumed while they're in standby mode. One solution to the leaking electricity problem is to physically unplug appliances or turn them off via a power strip when they're not in use.

4

Outside in the cold

Q **Can I use CFLs outside and in my garage during the long, cold winter?**

A Yes, they're great energy savers outdoors, but beware. Older fluorescent lights—both compact and tubular—are powered using magnetic ballasts. The lower the temperature, the more difficult it is for these bulbs to "get up to speed" and operate evenly. However, most CFLs made today have electronic ballasts that are much less sensitive to the cold.

If you're planning to use a CFL in an area exposed to the elements, purchase one designated for "exterior" or "outside" use. These usually have an extra translucent shell surrounding the fluorescent bulb to offer additional protection. Specialty bulbs like the "bug light" (above) and exterior floodlights are also available.

5

Best (and worst) places to use them

Q **Are there some places where using a CFL makes more sense than others? Are there situations to avoid?**

A Two scenarios make particular sense: 1. Since many CFLs have projected life spans of 8,000 hours or more, consider placing them in difficult-to-reach fixtures. It may mean climbing the ladder once every five years instead of once every year; 2. It also makes sense to use CFLs in light fixtures that are continuously "On" more than three to four hours per day.

Situations to avoid? Frequently switching a CFL "On" and "Off" and excess jostling can shorten its lifespan. Also, electronic ballasts are very sensitive to heat. Using CFLs that are not rated for use in enclosed fixtures can shorten the lifespan of a ballast (or bring about its demise altogether).

6

Lumens or watts?

Q **Is there a formula or rule of thumb for determining fluorescent bulb wattage in order to get the same amount of light as that cast from an incandescent bulb?**

A Generally speaking, if you divide the wattage of an incandescent bulb by 4 you'll come up with the equivalent wattage needed in a fluorescent. In other words, you'd replace a 60-watt incandescent bulb with a 15-watt fluorescent (60 divided by 4 equals 15), a 25- to 30-watt fluorescent to replace a 100-watt incandescent and a 35- to 40-watt CFL to replace a 150-watt incandescent.

But actual light output varies among brands. The most accurate way of comparing light output is to compare the lumens listed on the package of an incandescent bulb against that of a CFL. Be wary of CFLs that don't list the lumens on their packages, but only the "equivalent to" number. Sometimes the claims that their light output matches a certain incandescent wattage are misleading or wrong.

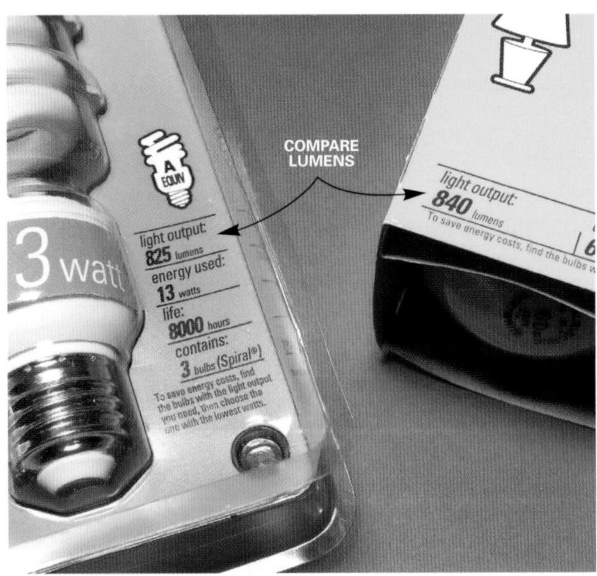

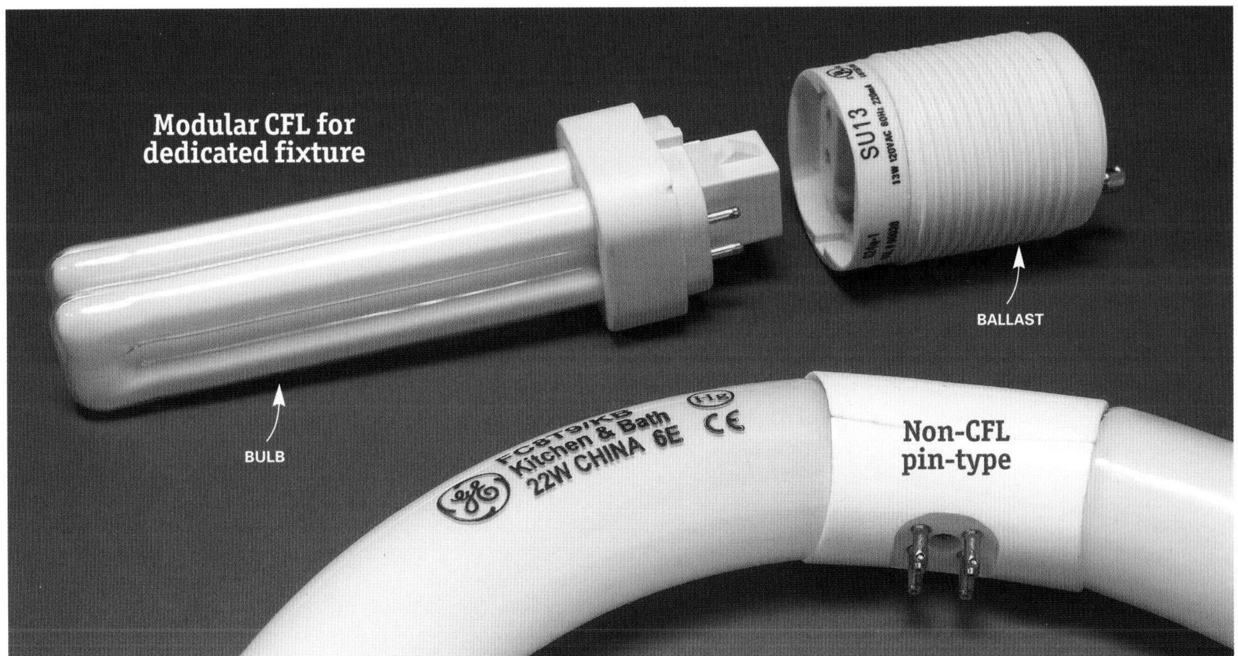

7

New CFLs on the block

Q **I've seen smaller fluorescent bulbs that don't screw in. What's the story on pin-type fluorescent bulbs?**

A The pin-type fluorescent bulb familiar to most of us is the classic circular kitchen bulb (above). These aren't considered true CFLs since the ballast is in the fixture itself, not built into the bulb.

But there is a new generation of pin-type bulbs, like the bulb shown at the top of the page. These are true CFLs, but they have a base designed to fit only into fixtures made specifically for these pin-type bulbs. Another unique feature of these bulbs is that the ballasts and tubes are separate. One of the reasons behind this modular design is that a typical ballast can last 30,000 hours, while a typical CFL bulb lasts 10,000. By making the parts independent, one only needs to change the bulb part that fails. These bulbs also meet the strict energy code in California.

Quick tip

RULE OF THUMB
There is a small power surge and a small spike in electrical usage when most lights are turned on, but as a rule of thumb, you'll save money by turning off lights that will not be used for more than five minutes.

8

Three-way bulbs

Q **Are there three-way CFL bulbs, and if so, do they require a special lamp or light fixture?**

A Yes, three-way CFLs are available, and no, you don't need a special lamp—usually. The three-way bulbs that ramp up to the equivalent of a 150-watt incandescent can be either circular or spiral in shape. Either way, they're quite large. For bulbs in that range, check to be sure they'll fit the harp and shade of your lamp.

Also make certain your three-way bulb is screwed in snugly. Unless the contacts on the bottom of the bulb make solid contact, your three-way bulb may work like a single-output bulb.

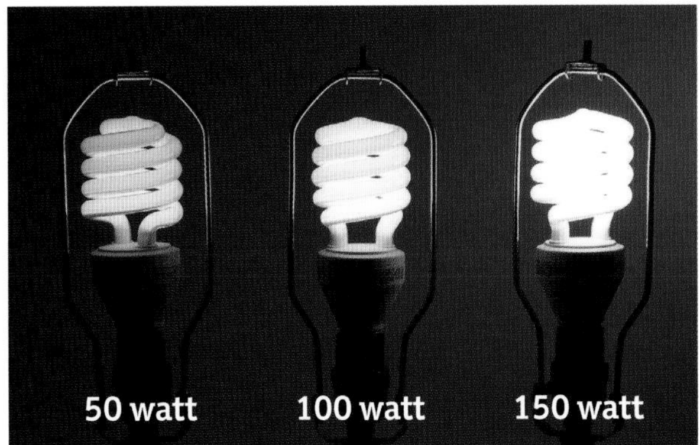

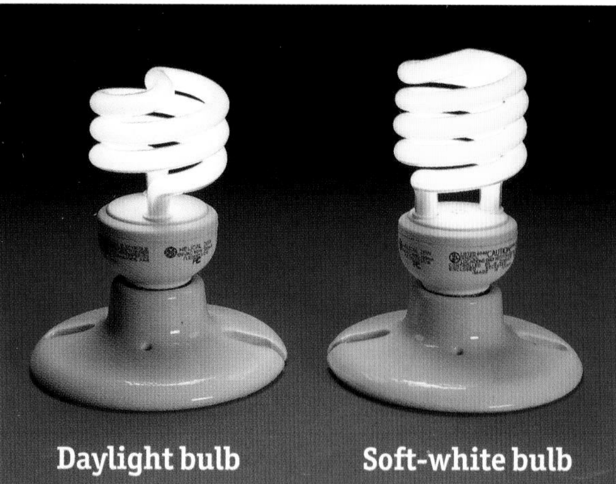
Daylight bulb Soft-white bulb

9

The "quality of light" factor

Q I stopped buying CFLs because the first few I bought years ago seemed dim and the color of the light was weird. Are CFLs more like "normal" incandescent bulbs these days?

A The longevity of CFLs has been a double-edged sword. Since they last so long, some of the first generation bulbs—that indeed had problems—are still burning and giving people the wrong impression of the newer CFLs.

The newer bulbs and electronic ballasts flicker less, make less noise, start up faster and emit light very similar to that of the standard "Type-A" incandescent bulbs we're used to seeing. The spiral shape, which is often used in CFLs, casts light more like a standard incandescent bulb. The color of the light has improved dramatically. If you couldn't see the bulb, you wouldn't know whether the light was incandescent or fluorescent. "Daylight" bulbs (left in photo above), which broadcast a whiter light, are available for those desiring a cooler light with less of a yellowish cast.

Quick tip

WHAT A WATT COSTS

The cost of electricity in the United States ranges from under 10 cents per kilo-watt hour to nearly 40 cents per kilo-watt hour. The more expensive your electricity, the faster you'll recoup the extra money you pay for CFLs.

10

Disposing of CFLs

Q What's the best way to dispose of a spent or broken CFL bulb?

A Manufacturers have taken steps to reduce the amount of mercury in CFLs, but they still contain a small amount—on the average, about 5 milligrams (roughly equivalent to the tip of a ballpoint pen). Special steps should be taken when disposing of CFLs. Recycling options include:

- Many municipalities have hazardous waste facilities that accept broken or spent CFLs. You can find information on sites near you by visiting www.earth911.org. Type your zip code into the "location" box, then click on "Household Hazardous Waste" and "Fluorescent bulbs" to find facilities in your area. Note that most facilities accept hazardous waste only during certain business hours and/or on certain days.
- Some retail stores offer a fluorescent bulb collection service. You may find some in your area by visiting the Web site listed above, then scrolling down to find the "Local Commercial Locations" section. Some ACE and other hardware stores serve as collection sites. Many IKEA stores also take back spent CFLs.
- There are a number of national organizations that can help. The U.S. Environmental Recycling Hotline (877-327-8491) can help you find local collection centers. Additional information for businesses and homeowners can also be found at www.lamprecycle.org.

NEVER send a CFL or other mercury-containing product to an incinerator. If a CFL breaks, sweep up the glass fragments and place them in a sealed plastic bag, along with the wet paper towel you use to pick up stray shards. Don't use a vacuum. Open windows to air out the house.

Quick tip

HOT AND COLD

Most CFLs sold today will operate effectively in temperatures ranging from 20 to 140 degrees F. In temperatures lower than 20, CFLs may take longer to start up and have reduced light output. In temperatures higher than 140, CFLs may also have reduced light output and have reduced ballast life.

Special CFLs for special uses

If every American household replaced just one standard incandescent bulb with one high-efficiency compact fluorescent light bulb, enough energy would be saved to light over 2-1/2 million homes for an entire year! There used to be a limited number of compact fluorescent options, but now there are dozens. Here are a few:

TUBE CFLs have one of the smallest overall sizes and are available in a wide range of wattages. Some have a rated life of up to 15,000 hours.

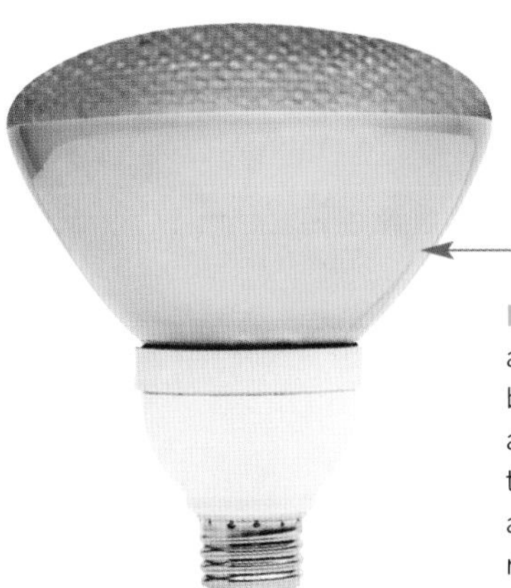

REFLECTOR CFLs are available in a variety of beam spreads for indoor and track lighting applications. Some are dimmable and/or rated for use in recessed light fixtures.

DECORATIVE CFLs are available for fixtures where bulbs are exposed, such as bathroom strip lights or chandeliers. They're available in "candle," "globe," "bullet" and other shapes.

LARGE LOOP CFLs are ideal for ceiling fixtures and torchiere lamps. Many are modular with independent ballasts and bulbs.

PRODUCT PHOTOS COURTESY OF GE

Energy-Saving Q&A

How to choose CFL bulbs

Q **I've looked at compact fluorescent bulbs at the home center, but I'm not sure what to buy. How do I know which provides as much light as a regular 60- or 100-watt bulb?**

A First, look at the lumen rating, not the bulb wattage, to compare real light output. Then buy a compact fluorescent bulb (CFL) with 20 percent more lumens than the incandescent bulb you want to replace. For example, if a 60-watt incandescent bulb has 870 lumens, buy a CFL with at least 1,050 lumens. If you follow wattage guidelines on the package (such as a 13- to 17-watt CFL equals a 60-watt incandescent; a 25- to 27-watt CFL equals a 100-watt incandescent), you may not be satisfied with the light output. This is especially true if you're over 50, because older eyes take in only half as much light as 20-year-old eyes.

Another reason you need more lumens is that the CFL will dim over time. It will lose 20 to 25 percent lumen power after 4,000 hours (40 percent of a CFL's 10,000-hour-rated life). Incandescent bulbs lose minimal lumens, but their life is extremely short compared with that of CFLs.

Finally, while CFLs can last up to 10 times longer than incandescent bulbs, certain circumstances can shorten their life:

- Frequent on-off switching (it's best to use CFLs only in lights that are on more than three hours per day).
- Excessive vibration or impact (you may not want to install CFLs near doors).
- High humidity levels.

SCREW-ON COVER (750 LUMENS WITH COVER)

15 WATTS (900 LUMENS WITHOUT COVER)

New styles in Fluorescent Lighting

Energy-efficient fluorescent lighting will look great in any room—and you'll save on your electric bills

Large pendant light

Wall sconce

What you get

STYLE: These fixtures feature handsome glass shades, not plastic. Many other styles are available through lighting stores and catalogs (see the Buyer's Guide, p. 164).

ENERGY SAVINGS: Fluorescent bulbs consume about one-third as much electricity as a standard incandescent bulb to produce the same amount of light. Choose a fluorescent bulb in the 13- to 17-watt range to replace a 60-watt incandescent, an 18- to 24-watt fluorescent to replace a 75-watt incandescent and a 25-to 28-watt fluorescent to replace a 100-watt incandescent.

NICE LIGHT: The light looks identical to the light from an incandescent bulb. You can't tell the difference if you can't see the bulb.

LONG-TERM SAVINGS: These fixtures use only fluorescent bulbs. The bulbs last 8,000 to 10,000 hours compared with about 1,000 hours for incandescent bulbs. You can expect to save $10 to $40 per bulb before they wear out. The list prices quoted here include the bulb. Retail prices are often lower—sometimes much lower.

Small pendant light

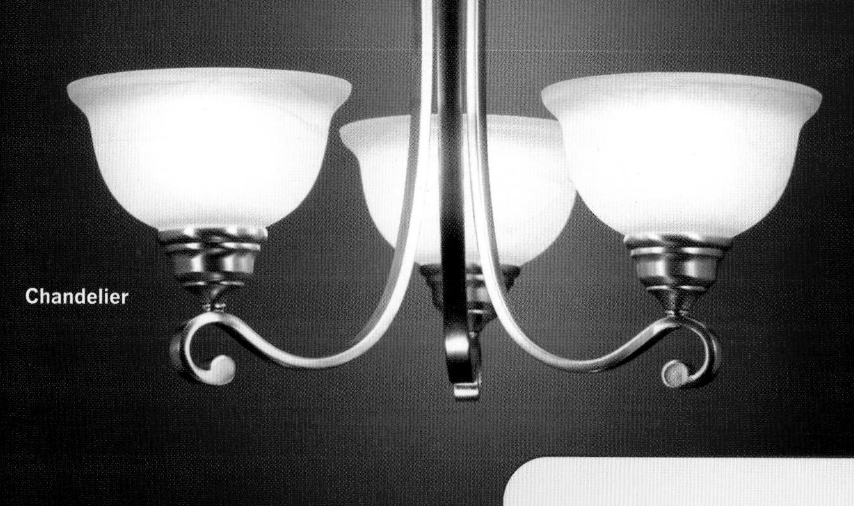

Chandelier

Ceiling light fixture

Shade-style wall sconce

Double wall sconce

Buying tips

For the **biggest savings**, buy fluorescent fixtures for lights that you use at least **two hours a day**. The electricity saved adds up quickly for lights you keep on that long. The electrical savings on heavily used lights will soon make up for the higher purchase price of a fluorescent bulb.

Estimate the amount of light you need, then **go for a brighter fixture.** Fluorescent bulbs dim somewhat over their long (10,000 hours) life span.

You can't put a dimmer switch on most fluorescent fixtures . . . yet. The manufacturers are working on this, but for now, if you want to dim your lights, stick to special screw-in compact fluorescents or incandescent bulbs.

When you're buying an **outdoor fixture**, make sure the fluorescent bulb will **start in cold weather**. Most of these start at temperatures as low as 0 degrees F or lower. However, in cold weather, the bulb will require a few minutes to reach full brightness.

Unless you're highlighting a workbench, countertop or other work space, **buy "warm white"** bulbs (labeled as either 2,700 or 3,000 degrees K) for interior use. "Cool white" light (labeled as 4,000 degrees K) creates a more commercial atmosphere.

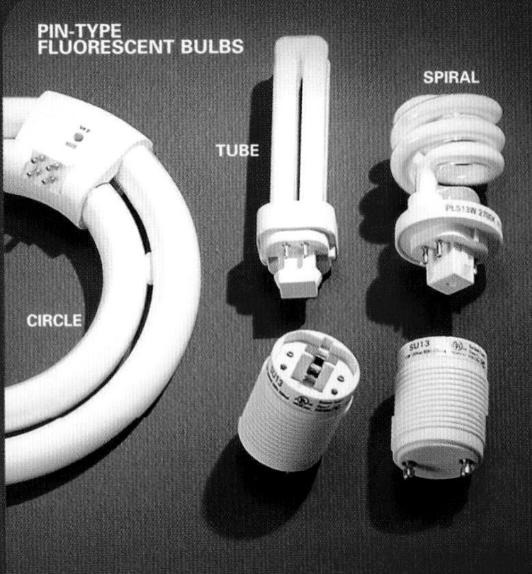

Globe-style outdoor light

Sconce-style outdoor light

Enclosed-style outdoor light

Fixtures, bulbs and ballasts

The fixtures shown here have a ballast and a pin-type fluorescent bulb that plugs into it (photo above). You can't screw in a standard incandescent bulb or even a screw-base compact fluorescent. The small ballast shown here is used in many of these fixtures. It accepts either spiral- or tube-shape bulbs. However, a ballast accepts bulbs of only one wattage level. You can't switch from a 13-watt bulb to an 18-watt bulb without switching ballasts.

Fixtures with higher light output utilize several small bulbs or one of several circle-type bulbs. These circle bulbs also have pin mounts.

Typically, the bulbs last 10,000 hours and the ballasts about 30,000 hours. At three hours per day, that's almost 10 years for the bulb and 30 years for the ballast! Sometimes you can find replacement bulbs ($5 to $10) at home centers and lighting stores. Pin configurations vary. Take the old bulb with you when you go to buy a replacement to make sure you get the exact same base. You can also order them through a lighting store or from an Internet source. (See the Buyer's Guide.) New ballasts cost $15 to $40. The ones shown above cost about $16. Order them through lighting stores.

Buyer's Guide

FIXTURE MANUFACTURERS

American Fluorescent: (847) 249-5970. www.americanfluorescent.com
Kichler Lighting: (866) 558-5706. www.kichler.com
Sea Gull Lighting: (800) 347-5483. www.SeaGullLighting.com

FLUORESCENT BULBS ONLINE

One online retailer of fluorescent bulbs is www.efi.org, which sells replacement pin-type bulbs as well as screw-base compact fluorescents, including dimmable bulbs. For other sources, type "compact fluorescent bulbs" into a search engine.

Bonus: lighting handy hints

Fluorescent bulb storage

Safely store extra fluorescent bulbs in jumbo-sized vinyl-clad storage hooks in a handy location near your fixture in the shop, garage or basement. Cut the hooks off one end of a couple of mini bungee cords and use zip ties to attach the severed ends to the top of two vinyl-clad steel storage hooks. Store several fresh bulbs and mark your bad bulbs with a marker and store them until it's time to recycle.

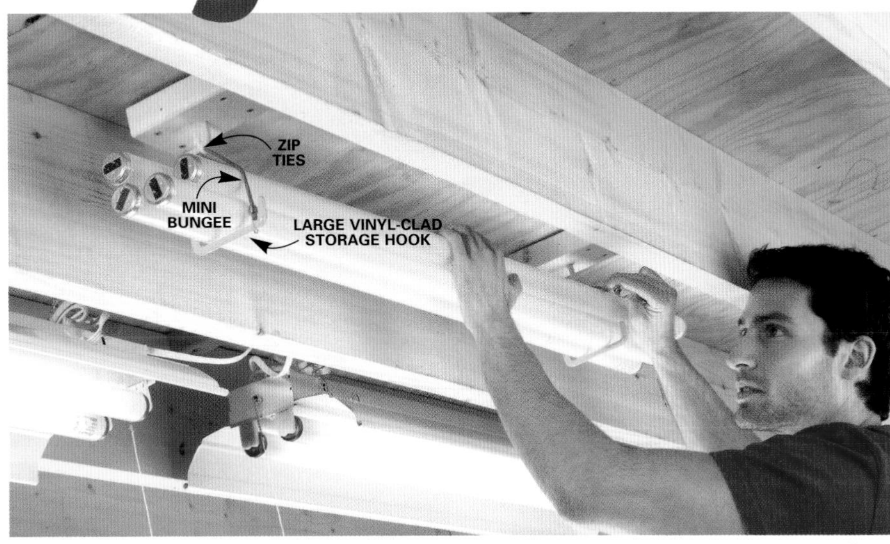

Longer-lasting light for garage door openers

Standard light bulbs can't take much vibration, so they may not survive long in garage door openers. For light that lasts, use a bulb designed to withstand hard knocks. "Rough-use" bulbs cost about $4 at home centers.

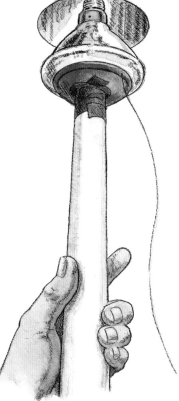

Bulb changer

Use this handy gizmo to get light bulbs out of high ceiling fixtures. It's a length of PVC pipe with a hardware store suction cup taped to the end. Just wet the rim of the suction cup, stick it to the bulb, and turn. The trick: make a small hole near the rim with a string attached. This makes it easier to get the suction cup off the bulb once it's in place.

Mark fluorescent bulbs for easy install

Fluorescent light bulbs can be a real hassle to install. You can't see where the prongs are, so you twist this way and that until it feels right. But if the prongs aren't locked in, the bulb can fall out, even though it lights up as usual. The solution is simple: Mark the orientation of the prongs on the bulb with a felt-tip pen.

ELECTRONIC DIMMER

Install a dimmer switch

Dimming a light decreases energy consumption and increases bulb longevity.

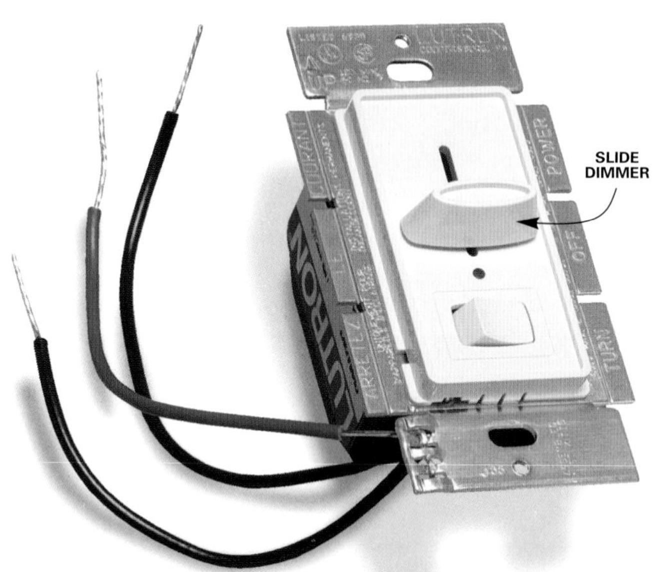

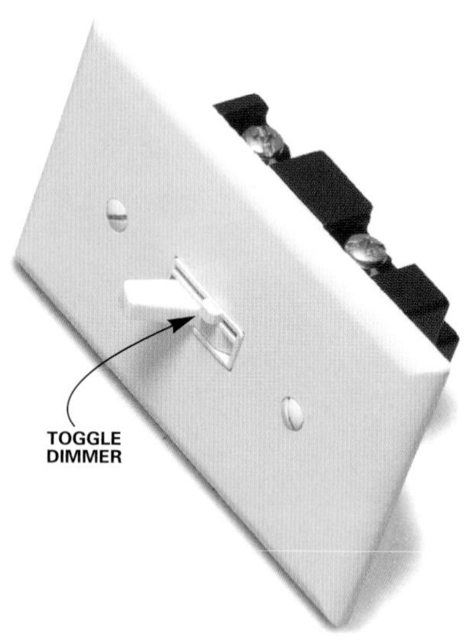

It doesn't take long to replace an ordinary light switch with a full-feature dimmer. But while you're at it, to make your home safer, you should upgrade the wiring to meet the latest requirements of the National Electrical Code. The step-by-step instructions here will show you how to install the dimmer, concentrating on details that will guarantee a safe installation.

The tools you'll need are inexpensive and will come in handy for all your electrical projects. You'll need a screwdriver, wire stripper, inexpensive voltage tester and needle-nose pliers to install a dimmer.

Double-check for hot wires in the box

Turn on the light and have a helper watch as you switch off the circuit breakers, or unscrew the fuses one at a time until the light goes out. Leave this circuit turned off while you work.

In Photo 1, we're using a non-contact voltage detector to double-check for voltage before removing the switch. These detectors are available at hardware stores and home centers for about $12. This type of tester is recommended because it'll detect voltage without direct contact with the metal conductor. That's huge—it means you can check potentially hot wires before you handle them. After you unscrew the switch and pull it away from the box, probe around inside the

WIRE WISDOM. If the circuit breaker is labeled "15 amp," the wires are probably 14-gauge, if it's "20 amp," the wires are likely 12-gauge.

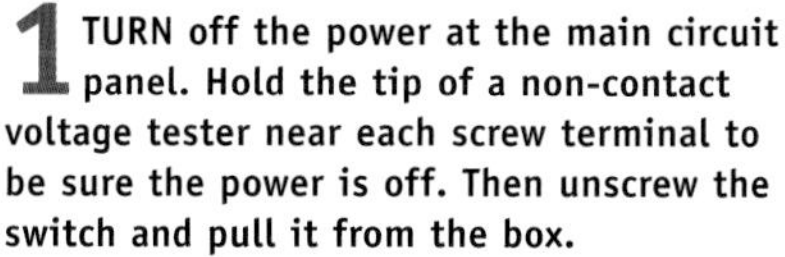
1 **TURN off the power at the main circuit panel. Hold the tip of a non-contact voltage tester near each screw terminal to be sure the power is off. Then unscrew the switch and pull it from the box.**

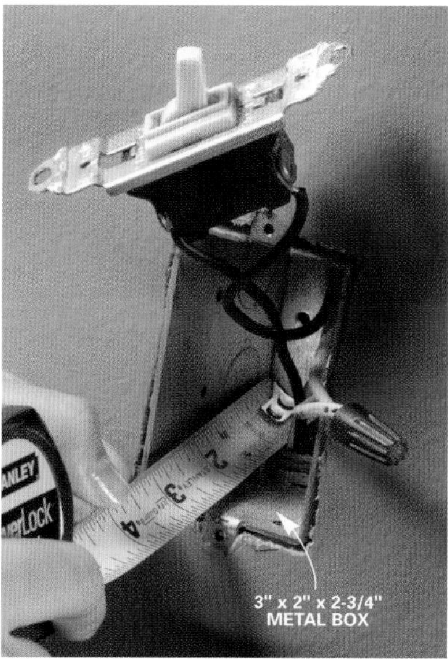

2 **MEASURE the height, width and depth of metal boxes and refer to Figure A below to determine the box volume. Plastic boxes have their volume stamped inside.**

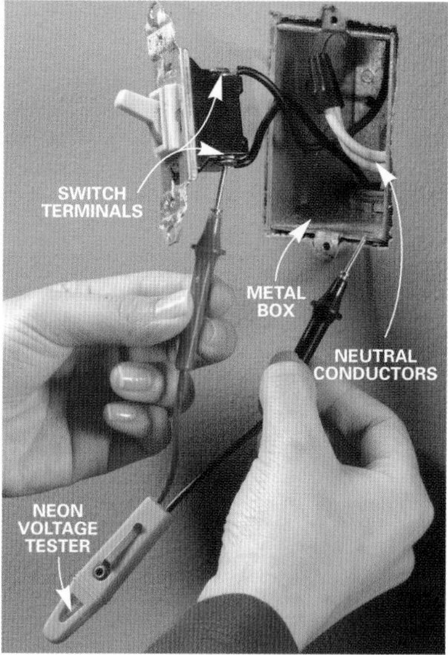

3 **TEST for a ground. Turn the power back on. Then place the leads of a voltage tester between each screw terminal and the metal box. If the tester lights, the box is grounded.** Caution: Turn off the power again before proceeding.

box with the detector to make sure there are no other hot wires from another circuit.

Make sure the box is large enough

Too many wires and devices stuffed into a box can cause dangerous overheating, short-circuiting and fires. The National Electrical Code specifies minimum box sizes to reduce this risk.

To figure the minimum box size required by the electrical code, add: 1 for each hot and neutral wire entering the box, 1 for all the ground wires combined, 1 for all the clamps combined, and 2 for each device (switch or receptacle) installed in the box. Multiply this figure by 2 for 14-gauge wire and 2.25 for 12-gauge wire to get the minimum box volume in cubic inches.

To help determine the gauge of the wire in your switch box, look at the amperage of the circuit breaker or fuse in the main electrical panel. Fifteen-amp circuits are usually wired with 14-gauge wire and 20-amp circuits require 12-gauge or heavier wire.

Figure A Common metal box sizes

Height/width/depth (inches)	**Volume** (cubic inches)
3 x 2 x 2-1/4	10.5
3 x 2 x 2-1/2	12.5
3 x 2 x 2-3/4	14.0

Compare the figure you get with the volume of your existing box. Plastic boxes have the volume stamped inside, usually on the back. Steel box capacities are listed in the electrical code. Listed in Figure A is the volume of the most common steel boxes. If you have a steel box, measure it (Photo 2) and consult the chart to see if it's large enough. If your box is too small, replace it with a larger one. It's possible to replace a box without cutting away the wall, but it's a tricky job. It's better to just remove about a 16-in. square of drywall or plaster and patch it after the new, larger box is installed.

Test your ground before you connect it

New dimmers have either a green grounding wire or a green ground screw that you'll have to connect to a grounding source if one is available. Houses wired with plastic-sheathed cable almost always have bare copper ground wires that you'll connect to the dimmer. But test first using the procedure shown in Photo 3 to verify that the wire is connected to a ground.

Some wiring systems, like the one shown, rely on metal conduit for the ground. If you have one of these systems, Photo 3 shows how to test the metal box to verify that it's grounded. If it is, attach a short ground wire to the metal box with either a metal grounding clip

Caution:
If you have aluminum wiring, don't mess with it! Call in a licensed pro who's certified to work with it. This wiring is dull gray, not the dull orange that's characteristic of copper.

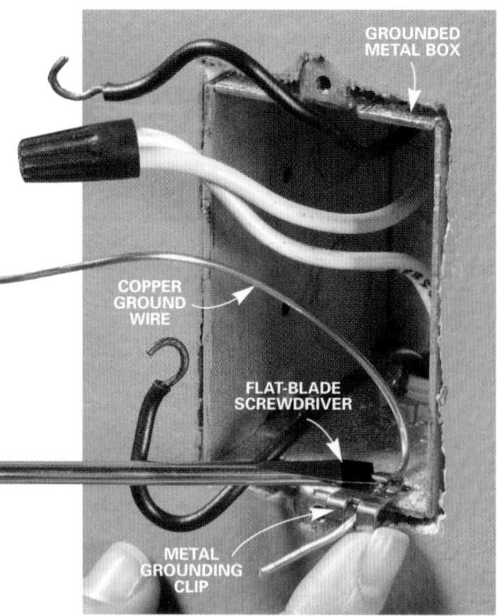

4 PRESS a grounding clip and 6-in. length of bare copper wire onto the metal box with a screwdriver. Cut away a little bit of drywall under the box to provide clearance for the clip.

5 BEND the ground wire back onto the clip and squeeze it down tight so it won't interfere with the dimmer switch.

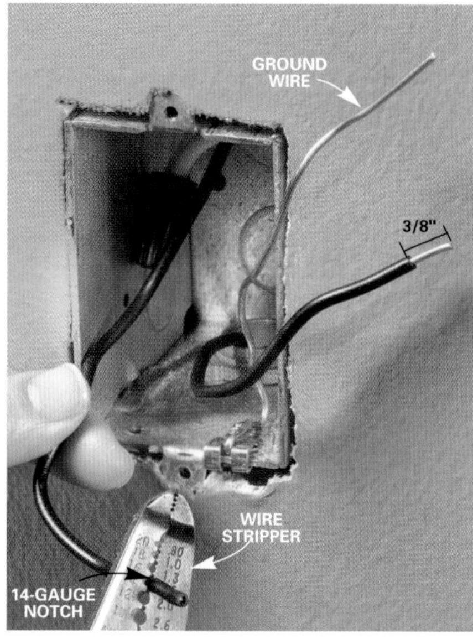

6 CLIP off the bent end of each wire with the wire cutter. Strip 3/8 in. of insulation from the end of the wires.

as shown in Photos 4 and 5 or a green grounding screw screwed into the threaded hole in the back of the box. Then connect it to the dimmer.

If testing reveals your box isn't grounded, you can still install the dimmer, but you must use a plastic cover plate and make sure no bare metal parts are exposed.

The easy part is installing the dimmer

Some dimmers, like the one shown, have stranded wires attached. Photos 7 and 8 show how to install this type of dimmer. Others have screw terminals instead. For these, strip 3/4 in. of the insulated covering from the wires in the box and bend a loop in each with a needle-nose pliers. Place the loop clockwise around the screw terminals and close the loop around the screws with the needle-nose pliers. Then tighten the screws.

Caution:
Call an electrician if the original switch is connected to two white wires. This may indicate a dangerous switched neutral.

It doesn't matter if you reverse the two switch wires to a single-pole dimmer. But if you're replacing a three-way switch with a three-way dimmer, label the "common" wire (it'll be labeled on the old switch) when you remove the old switch so you can connect it to the "common" terminal on the dimmer.

In most cases, the two switch wires will be some color other than green or white, usually black. But one of the wires may be white if your house is wired with plastic-sheathed cable (like Romex). Put a wrap of black tape around the white conductor to label it as a hot wire.

Buying dimmers

IF THE SWITCH YOU'RE REPLACING is the only switch controlling the light, buy a standard single-pole dimmer ($5 to $30). If the light can be switched on and off from two or more switches, buy a three-way dimmer switch. But you won't be able to dim the lights from every switch location unless you buy a set of special dimmers (about $70 per pair) with advanced electronics and install one at each switch location.

MOST DIMMERS ARE DESIGNED to handle 600 watts. Add up the wattage of all the light bulbs you'll be dimming. Then read the dimmer package to make sure it can handle the load. Heavy-duty 1,000- and 1,500-watt dimmers are also readily available. Read the package if you'll be installing dimmers side by side in the same electrical box because the wattage rating is reduced to compensate for extra heat buildup.

FINALLY, you have to use a special device, not a dimmer, to control the speed of ceiling fans and motors. Some fluorescent lights can't be dimmed without altering the fixture.

7 HOLD the wires together with the stranded wire protruding about 1/8 in. beyond the solid wire. Match the size of the wire connector you're using to the size and number of wires being connected. Check the manufacturer's specifications on the package to be sure. Twist a plastic wire connector clockwise onto the wires to connect them. Stop twisting when the connector is snug.

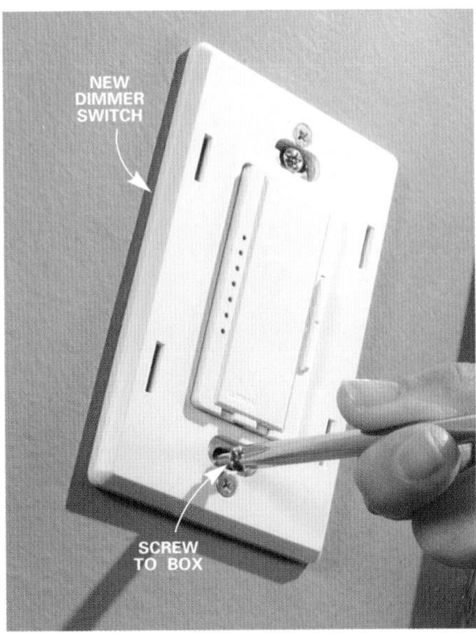

8 FOLD the wires neatly into the box. Screw the dimmer to the box with the screws provided. Finish the job by installing the cover plate and turning on the power to test the new dimmer.

Energy-Saving Q&A

Instant garage light

Q We would like more light in the garage when we arrive home after dark. The bulb in the garage door opener isn't enough. What's a good solution?

A For more light, simply replace your existing light switch near the door leading to the house (in an attached garage) with a motion-activated switch that works by detecting a moving object that emits heat (such as a person or a car). Not only will this provide automatic instant light when the car arrives home, it also will light up the garage when entering from the house, and then shut off automatically.

The motion-activated switch shown (about $16) allows you to adjust the length of time the lights stay on from 5 seconds to 20 minutes. It also features an adjustable photo cell that can switch the lights on only when it's dark or when it's daylight, too. It also allows for manual on/off switching. Coverage area of the sensor is a 150-degree-wide pattern that senses 15 ft. on the edges of the pattern and 30 ft. dead ahead of the sensor.

When buying the switch, make sure you don't exceed the switch's maximum wattage rating or volt amperage (VA) rating. To calculate it, simply add up the total wattage of all bulbs, and multiply that total by 1.25.

Halogen bulbs –

They burn brighter and are up to 20% more energy efficient. Here's where to use them.

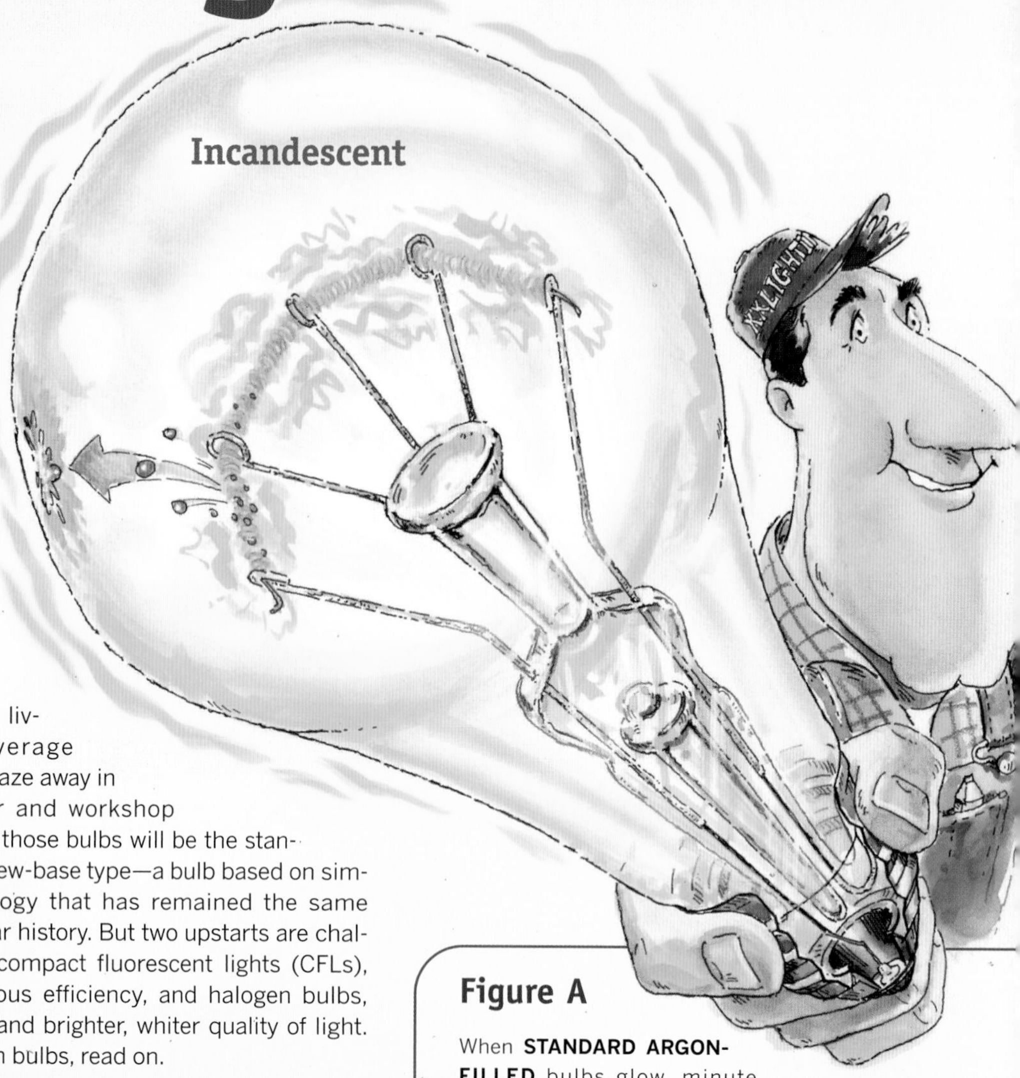

Incandescent

If you're an average homeowner living in the average house, 32 light bulbs will blaze away in your hallway, refrigerator and workshop tonight. The lion's share of those bulbs will be the standard 50¢ incandescent, screw-base type—a bulb based on simple yet ingenious technology that has remained the same throughout its 100-plus year history. But two upstarts are challenging this old standby: compact fluorescent lights (CFLs), because of their tremendous efficiency, and halogen bulbs, because of their longevity and brighter, whiter quality of light. For the lowdown on halogen bulbs, read on.

How halogens are different

Standard incandescent bulbs (Figure A) work on a very simple principle: Electric current passes through a thin tungsten filament inside a gas-filled bulb. The resistance that the filament puts up causes it to heat up and glow. The gas inside the bulb—traditionally, argon—prevents the filament from combining with oxygen and burning out. As the filament glows, microscopic amounts of tungsten burn or evaporate from the filament and are deposited as "soot" on the bulb wall. When enough tungsten has evaporated, the weakened filament finally breaks (usually from the shock of being clicked on) and POOF, you've got a burned-out light bulb.

Halogen bulbs (like the one shown in Figure B) function similarly, but with a few key differences: They're composed of a small, pressurized, peanut-size bulb inside a larger outer shell.

Figure A

When **STANDARD ARGON-FILLED** bulbs glow, minute amounts of tungsten evaporate from the filament and are deposited as "soot" on the inner shell of the bulb. This burned-off tungsten has two drawbacks: The "soot" gradually reduces light output, and it slowly weakens the filament until it becomes thin and breaks and the bulb "burns out."

COST: About 50¢ for a 75-watt bulb
LIFE SPAN: 750 to 1,250 hours
LIGHT OUTPUT: 1,180 lumens for a 75-watt bulb
BEST USES: The best and most affordable all-purpose bulb around. Good for general lighting in bedrooms and other living spaces where you want "soft" light and for fixtures with bulbs that are in the line of sight.

– a brilliant idea

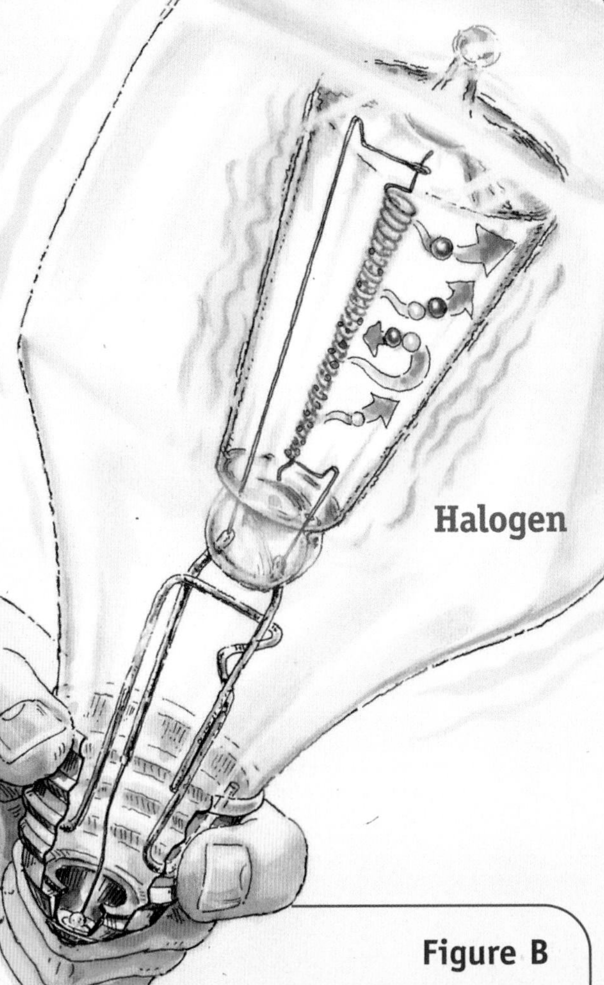

The gas inside this inner bulb is halogen. When tungsten evaporates from the filaments of these bulbs, the halogen combines with it, escorts it back to the filament where it's redeposited, then heads out to round up more escaped tungsten particles. Since there's less soot on the bulb's shell, light output remains strong, and since filaments are constantly being rebuilt, the bulbs last longer. But the key difference—and the quality that makes them useful and unique—is they emit a whiter, brighter and more easily focused beam of light, almost like real sunshine.

Figure B

When high-tech **HALOGEN-FILLED** bulbs glow, small amounts of tungsten burn off the filament, but instead of being deposited on the bulb shell, they combine with argon, which redeposits the tungsten back onto the filament. This has two advantages: The globe isn't darkened by soot, and the filament lasts longer, since it's continuously being "rebuilt."

COST: About $4 for a 75-watt bulb

LIFE SPAN: 2,000 to 2,500 hours (some manufacturers guarantee lights for two years or more)

LIGHT OUTPUT: 1,300 lumens for a 75-watt bulb

BEST USES: In track and recessed fixtures that you want to focus light on a particular area or object; in desktop, reading or other work-area lights where you want bright, focused light; in fixtures that are tough to reach; in banks of light where you want all the bulbs (new or old) to glow at the same intensity.

Bright benefits of halogen lights

The pure white light halogens emit makes them ideal for certain fixtures and situations.

- For reading and other exacting tasks, the bright light reduces eyestrain.
- For display lighting, where you want to highlight artwork, photos, crystal or architectural features, the white focused light makes colors appear more vibrant. Halogen spotlights allow pinpoint focus. Using standard bulbs for general lighting in the same room heightens the effect of halogens even more.
- For outdoor use, halogen floodlights cast a brighter, easier-to-see-by light. And since they last twice as long as standard bulbs, you won't need to struggle to reach hard-to-access outdoor fixtures as often. They have other benefits too. They're 10 to 20 percent more energy efficient and cheaper to operate. They burn brighter longer (a halogen bulb will still be cranking out 94 percent of its original light output near the end of its life, while a standard bulb diminishes to a measly 82 percent).

Of course, not everyone or every place loves halogen. They cost at least four times as much and don't give off that warm glow of a standard bulb we're accustomed to. And they have an intense glare; they need to be shaded, shielded or directed so the filament isn't in your line of sight.

Halogen bulbs burn hotter

Halogen bulbs burn hotter than standard incandescents, so care must be taken in their use. It's possible for the protective outer shell to break and for the inner bulb to continue working (though the outer shells are incredibly durable). This can pose a hazard, as the hot inner bulb can explode if moisture hits it. Dispose of any damaged bulbs just like you would an incandescent bulb. And, as you should do before replacing any bulb, check the light fixture label to make sure a halogen bulb is compatible and within the fixture's listed limits.

Tame a hyperactive motion detector

Save you—and your neighbors—from unwanted "trips"

An outdoor motion detector light can save electricity and scare off intruders. But if passing cars or the neighbor's dog constantly triggers the light, you don't get either benefit. To stop unwanted "trips," you have to limit the "detection zone," the area where the sensor can see moving objects.

First, aim the detector. Turn the sensor head right or left and up or down so that its field of vision is roughly centered on the area you want to cover. To make the head stay put, you may have to tighten screws or ring nuts (Photo 2) on the arm that supports the head. Next, set the "on-time" switch to "test" (Photo 1). This will let you determine the detection zone by walking across the detector's field of vision. When it sees you, the light will go on for a couple of seconds. (Your detector may need a one- or two-minute warm-up period before it starts to work.)

If the detection zone in front of the detector is too long, aim the head down slightly. If the zone is too short, raise the head, but keep it at least 1 in. from lightbulbs and lamp covers. When the range is about right, make finer adjustments using the range dial (Photo 1). It may be labeled "range" or "sensitivity." Start with the dial set at the maximum range and turn it down to shorten the zone.

If the zone is still too wide, narrow the lens opening with electrical tape (Photo 2). This is a trial-and-error process that can take a few minutes. Normally, you need to apply narrow blinders only to the right or left ends of the lens, but you can cover as much of the lens as you like. When the length and width of the zone are just right, reset the on-time switch.

1 SHORTEN the sensor's detection zone by adjusting the "range" dial. Start with the dial set to "max" and turn down until the range is correct.

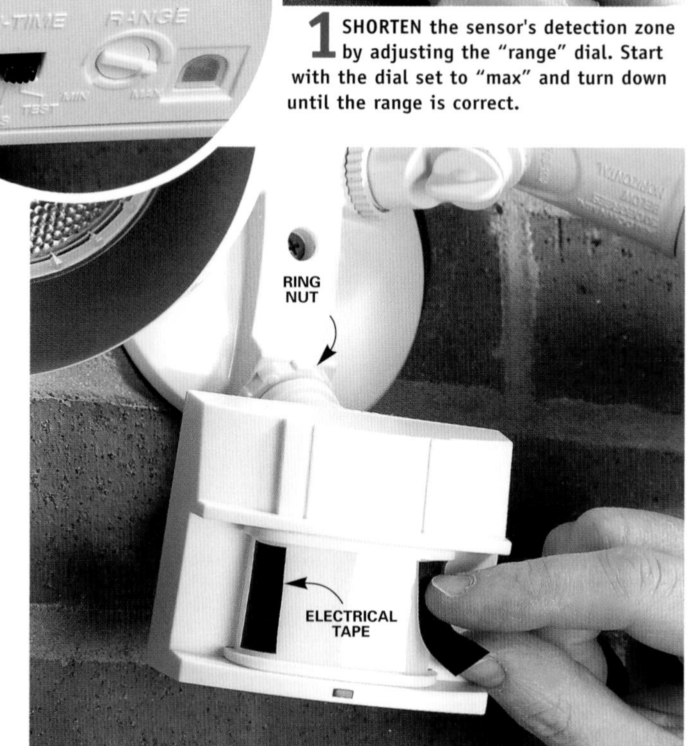

2 NARROW the detection zone by sticking electrical tape blinders on one or both sides of the sensor's lens.

Energy-Saving Products

Three cool, energy-saving light devices

1. Program a light to turn on and off automatically

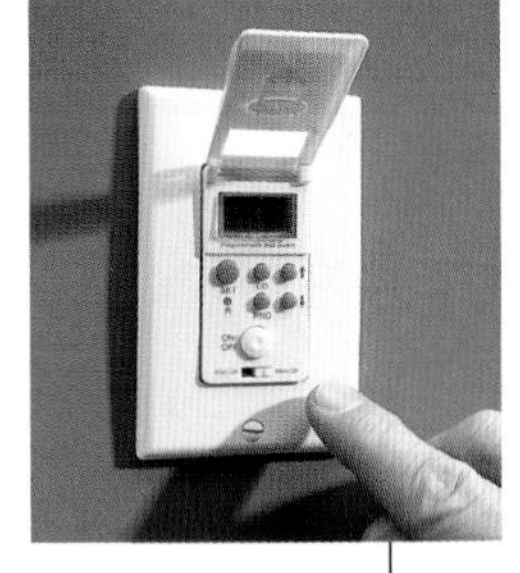

Replace a light switch with the Programmable Wall Switch Timer and forget it. This device turns all of the lights controlled by a particular switch on and off automatically. Light stairwells during the night for bathroom runs, turn the lamp on and off to fool cat burglars while you're on vacation, or maybe control the front porch light during prime visiting times. Very cool lighting controller for around $30 plus shipping.

Sporty's Tool Shop, (800) 776-7897, www.sportys.com/shoptool

2. Switching switched lights to motion activated

Wanna have the lights turn on automatically when you walk into a room? It's easy. Just replace the light switch with a motion detector light switch. They're especially useful for rooms where you have to grope in the dark for the switch (think garage) or dangerous areas where good light is imperative (think stairwells). They also have conventional on/off switch positions. You'll find a version in any well-stocked electrical department at home centers or hardware stores. Expect to pay $20 to $50 depending on amperage and quality. If you're just controlling a light, buy a cheap one. If you're switching several lights or lights and an exhaust fan, choose one with higher amperage.

3. Motion-activated porcelain lights

If one of your hobbies is shutting off the storage closet light, take heart. You can install the Automatic Light Socket. It's as easy as unscrewing the light bulb, screwing in the Light Socket and then screwing the bulb back into the unit. It contains a motion detector that detects movement up to 12 ft. away and turns on the light, which stays on for four minutes and then shuts itself off. Around $40 plus shipping.

Sporty's Tool Shop, (800) 776-7897. www.sportys.com/shoptool

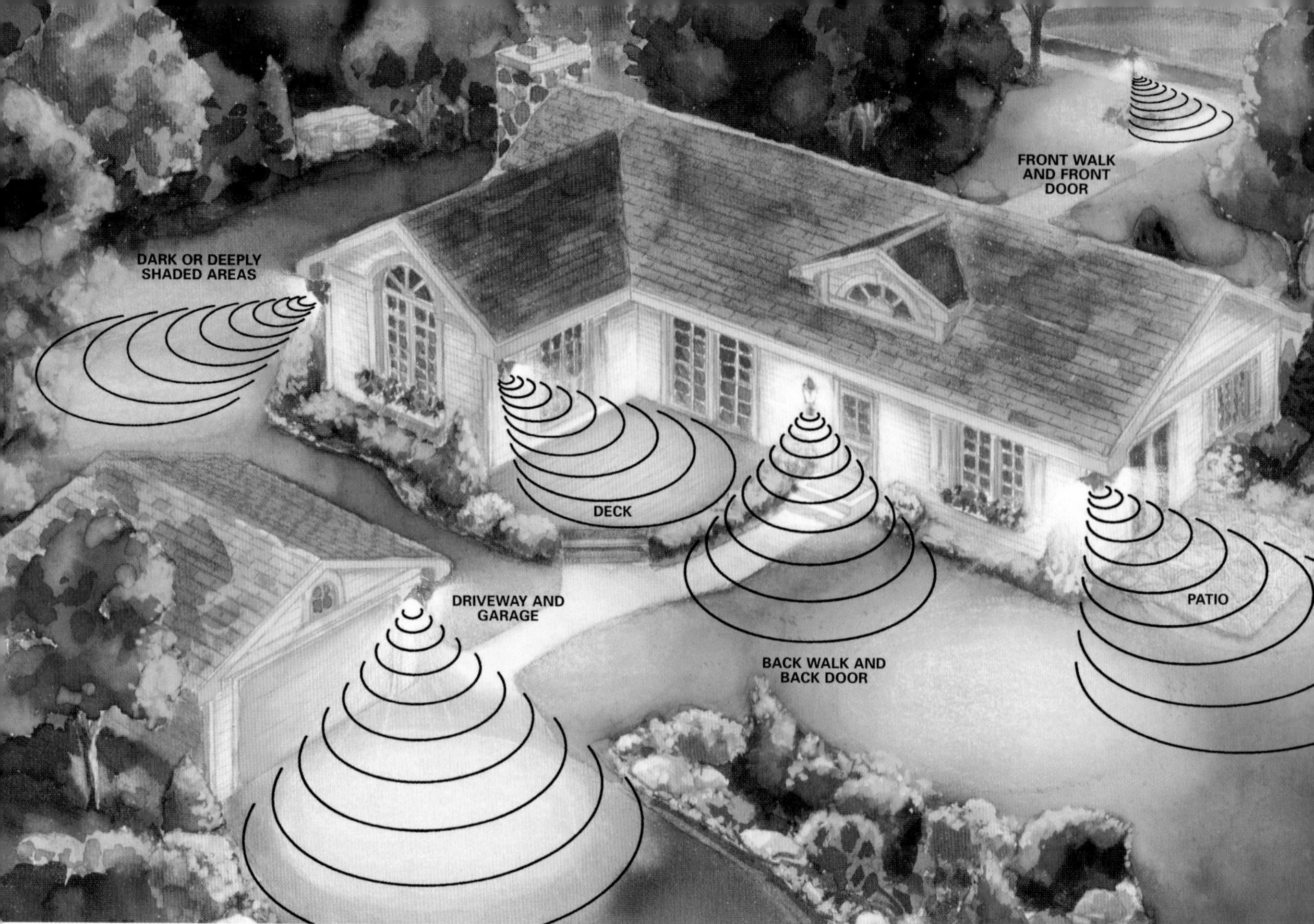

Motion detector lighting

Automatic night lighting when and where you need it.

Why come home at night to a dark door? Or try to walk an icy sidewalk you can't see? Or pay to leave a light on all night when you only need it for a minute or two?

Outdoor lights that are automatically activated by motion detectors can solve all these problems—and others. They'll automatically come on to light up the kids who cut through the yard or the intruder on the deck, and they'll even expose the furry critter that's been raiding your garbage can.

In most cases, motion detector lights are easy to install if you're simply replacing an existing outside light fixture. And they won't cost you a fortune: Prices range from about $25 for a basic two-bulb floodlight—like the one shown here—to about $60 for a decent-quality front door light.

Here you'll learn how motion detector lights work, the best places to put them, and the how tos for a safe and trouble-free installation.

Figure A Motion detector and light styles

1. Flood 2. Decorative 3. Remote

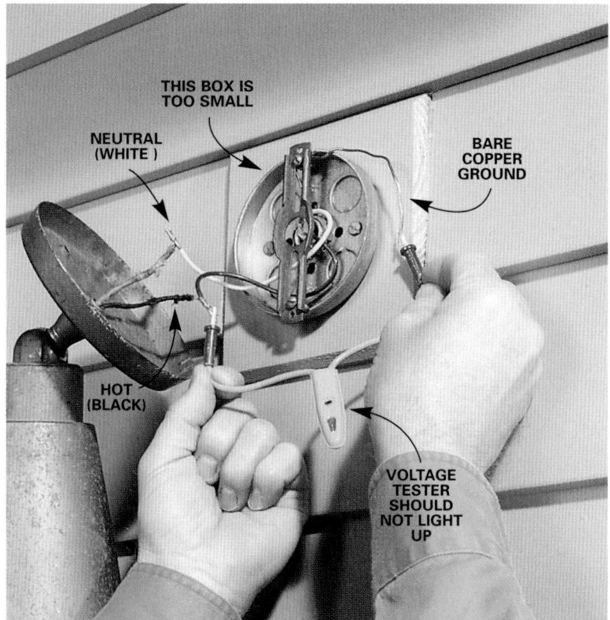

1 TURN OFF the power to the fixture at the main panel, then test the wires to make sure the current is off. Rub one lead of a voltage tester ($3 at hardware stores or home centers) against the ground wire and rub the other lead first against the hot wire (black), then the neutral wire (white). If the tester lights up in either case, the power is still on. Shut off the correct circuit at the main panel.

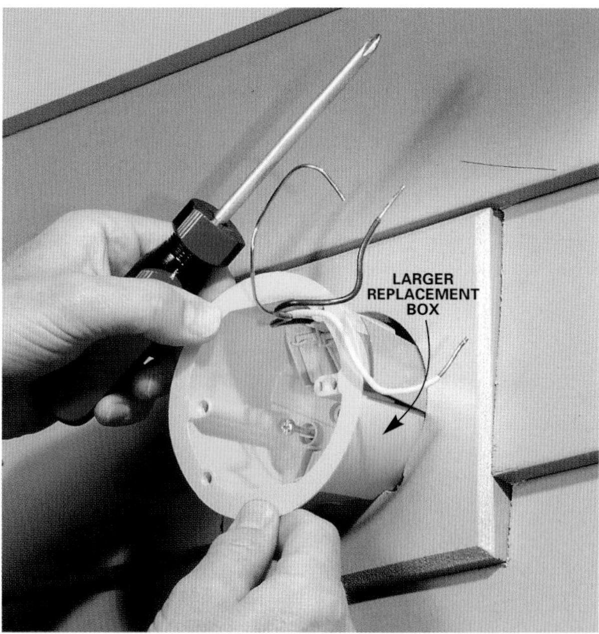

2 INSTALL a replacement electrical box if your existing box is too small (see "Size Requirements of Electrical Boxes," p. 176). Plastic boxes have the size in cubic inches stamped on them.

How motion detectors work

Motion detectors are small electronic eyes that detect infrared waves—heat waves that radiate from moving objects. When the detector senses an object moving across its field of view—especially warmer objects such as people, animals and cars—it electronically turns on the lights. The light stays on anywhere from 1 to 20 minutes, depending on how you preset the timer. Then the detector automatically shuts the light off unless it continues to sense movement. A photocell deactivates the light during daylight hours.

Most motion detectors have a semicircular field of view of up to 240 degrees and a distance range, adjustable on most detectors, that extends to 70 ft. or more. The detector will react to the movement of your dog, an approaching person, a passing car or sometimes even wind-blown leaves.

Nuisance "trips," such as blowing leaves or a passing car, can fool the detector and turn the lights on when you don't want them. These can be annoying to both you and your neighbors, and in fact, some homeowners won't install motion detector lights for this reason.

However, you can solve most unwanted switching-on by adjusting the distance-range setting and by carefully aiming the sensor to limit its field of view. You can also narrow the field of view even more by applying tape to the sensor, as shown in Photo 7. If nuisance trips concern you, be sure to buy a light that has an adjustable distance-range setting, and an aimable detector unit as shown in Figure A, Nos. 1 and 3.

Motion detectors allow you to operate the light in the conventional, manual way, usually by flipping the switch off for a second, then back on. This allows you to keep the light on at night when you want to, even when there's no motion. By double-flipping a second time, you return to automatic.

Where to put them

For best effectiveness, position motion detector sensors to cover the walks leading to your front and back doors and the driveway (see large illustration, p. 174). That way the lights will come on when you come home at night. You can also use them to light up decks, patios and any potentially hazardous locations such as around stairways and swimming pools.

If improved security is a priority, position the lights to cover all the approaches to your house, including fence gates, the patio door, the darker areas of your yard, and around trees and bushes. Good lighting can't guarantee security, of course, but it's one of the best low-cost ways to get unwanted intruders to back away.

Ideally, it's best to mount motion detector lights 6 to 10

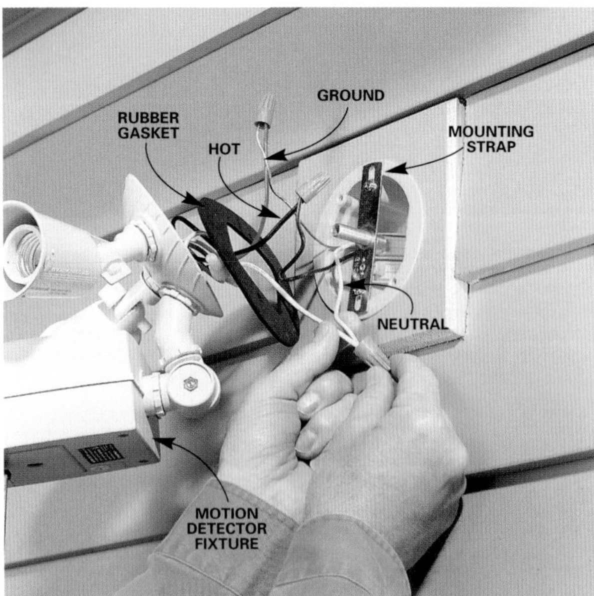

3 MOUNT the light fixture according to the manufacturer's instructions. Run the wires through the rubber gasket. Then connect the neutral wires (white), hot wires (black) and ground wires (green or bare copper) with wire connectors.

4 SCREW the fixture in place. Make sure the rubber gasket seals the edges of the box so moisture can't get in. Apply a bead of clear silicone caulk around the edges if necessary.

Computation table for electrical box size

Wires entering box (neutral and hot)	2
Ground wires (combined total count as 1)	1
Clamps	1
Fixture itself	2
Total	**6**

- 14-gauge wire requires 2 cu. in. space per wire.
- 2 cu. in. wire x 6 wires = 12 cu. in.
- New box = 16 cu. in., so it's large enough.

ft. above the ground and position them so that most movement will occur across the sensitivity zone rather than directly toward the detector.

Obviously you can't always do that if you use existing light locations. One solution is to buy a remote motion sensor unit that you can mount some distance away from the light itself. Remote sensors cost $15 to $25. The wires connecting them to the light are low-voltage and not dangerous, so you don't have to enclose them in metal or plastic conduit.

Installing motion detector lights

Motion detector lights are easy to install, but each brand has a few different details, so read the instructions. You'll find the basic information printed on the outside of the box. Read the box before you buy the unit so you know what you're getting. You'll find more detailed instructions inside the box.

The step-by-step photos and tips here provide a general guide of how to do the job. In most cases, you'll simply replace an existing fixture with the new one, as shown. Make sure to turn off the power to the fixture at the main panel before removing it.

However, if you have to run a new electrical line and install a switch, the job can get much more complex. Outdoor electrical lines must be encased in approved conduit and weatherproof electrical boxes. If you're not familiar with conduit or the rules for running new electrical circuits, call in a licensed electrician.

Working with old electrical boxes can be tricky too. Sometimes they don't contain a ground wire (bare wire or one with green insulation) or other grounding means such as metal conduit. The National Electrical Code requires all electrical boxes and fixtures to be grounded. If you're not sure yours is, check with your electrical inspector to determine if you have to run a new ground wire.

Size requirements of electrical boxes

You also need to check out the size of your electrical box. A shallow box like the one shown in Photo 1 no longer meets code requirements, and must be replaced with a larger box, as shown in Photos 2 and 3.

The computation table, above left, gives the method for calculating minimum box-size requirements. To do the calculation, count the number of wires coming into the

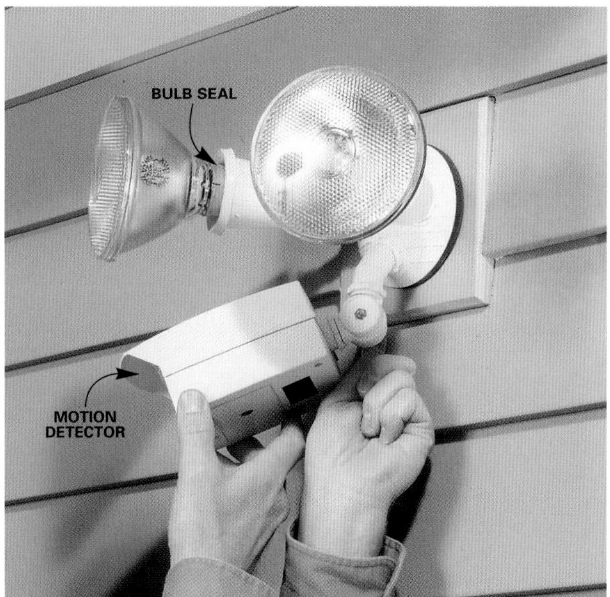

5 AIM the motion detector at the field of view you want covered. (Later, you can aim the detector lower to reduce the field of view if nuisance trips are a problem.) Point the light bulbs to the area you want lit. Keep the bulbs as far away from the detector as possible.

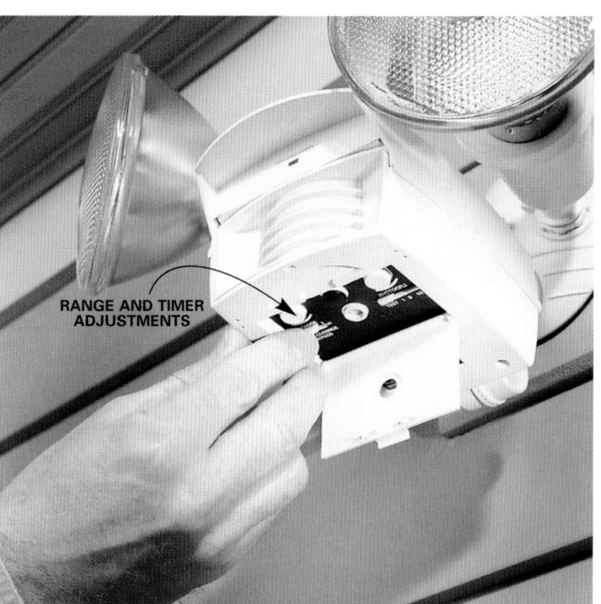

6 SET the detector's distance range as desired. You can also reduce this later, if necessary, to eliminate nuisance trips. Also set the timer shutoff control. On most units you can choose automatic shutoff after either 1, 5 or 20 minutes.

box. However, some other things besides wires are counted as "wires" for computation purposes. For example, all the cable clamps used count for one wire, and always count the fixture as two wires. Then multiply this total wire number by 2 cu. in. for 14-gauge wire (or 2.25 cu. in. for 12-gauge wire, even if there's just one of the heavier wires in the box).

The computation method given here sometimes overestimates the minimum box size required by code, but it simplifies the calculation.

Additional installation tips

- The cover of an outdoor electrical box must be waterproof. Seat the rubber gasket carefully (Photo 4). And if you are placing it against a rough surface, caulk it as well.
- Moisture can seep into the detector and light sockets and ruin them. To prevent this, either locate the fixture under an eave or other protected area or buy one that has bulb seals (Photo 5) and angle the bulbs downward so water can't run into the socket.
- Heat from the light bulb itself can confuse the detector. Keep the bulb and detector as far apart as possible (Photo 5).
- Adjust the field-of-view angle and set the distance range of your motion detector to avoid nuisance trips from normal passing traffic, animals, pools of water, air conditioners, heating vents and wind-blown trees and shrubs (Photos 5 – 7).
- Get an electrical permit from your local department of inspections. Check for special local rules and have your work inspected when finished.
- CAUTION: Don't let your ladder or your body touch lethal overhead power lines while you're working.
- CAUTION: Aluminum wiring requires special handling. If you have aluminum wiring, call in a licensed pro who's certified to work with it. This wiring is dull gray, not the dull orange that's characteristic of copper.

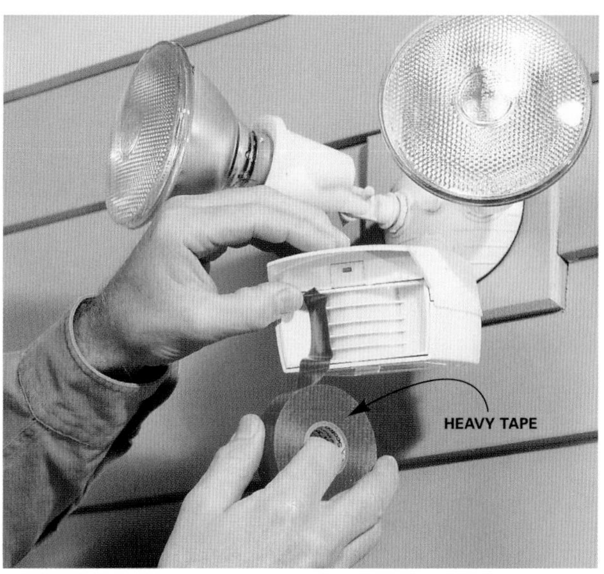

7 COVER a portion of the detector lens with plastic tape if it becomes necessary to narrow its side-to-side field of view more than the adjustments will allow.

Recessed lights

Insulating to prevent heat loss.

Recessed light fixtures that are rated IC (insulation contact) are designed so that insulation can be installed in direct contact with them. These fixtures have a high-temperature cutoff switch that turns off the lamp if excessive heat builds up. If they cycle on and off, that's the reason.

To resolve the problem: First, check the information on the fixture label (p. 179) to make sure the bulb is an acceptable type and wattage. Second, check the fixture label to make sure the trim is compatible with the housing (p. 179) The wrong trim can trap too much heat inside the fixture housing. Look for a part number on both the housing and the trim and call a supplier to confirm their compatibility. Third, if the housing allows the bulb to be adjusted up and down, move the bulb down. Fourth, the thermal protector might be defective and require replacement. This is a tough one to diagnose. If you have several lights turning on and off, the protectors are probably OK. A single problem light might well have a faulty protector. Call in a licensed electrician to fix it.

If you've tried these fixes and the light is still cycling off and on, build an airtight box around the problem light, as shown. You have to do it from within the attic (not a pleasant working environment!). Cut the box from 2-in.-thick rigid extruded foam board, then glue and screw the joints. Caulk all seams and penetrations from either inside or outside the box. It's important to make the box airtight to keep warm air from escaping into the attic. It provides air space around the fixture to help prevent overheating, yet interior air cannot get into the attic, and your insulation is still intact.

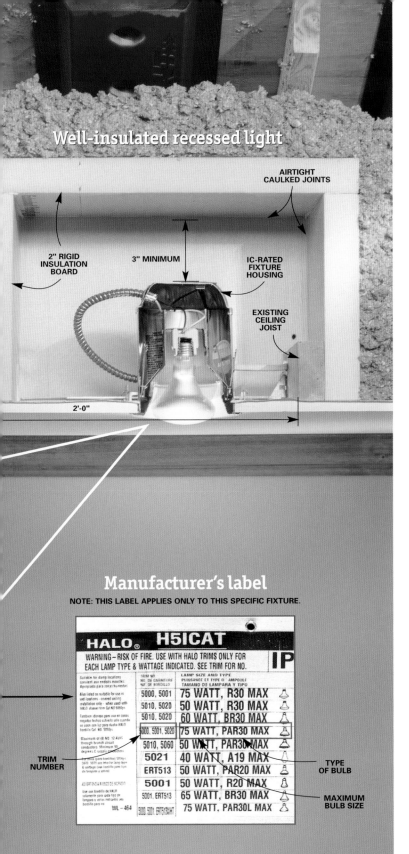

Well-insulated recessed light

AIRTIGHT CAULKED JOINTS

2" RIGID INSULATION BOARD

3" MINIMUM

IC-RATED FIXTURE HOUSING

EXISTING CEILING JOIST

2'-0"

Manufacturer's label

NOTE: THIS LABEL APPLIES ONLY TO THIS SPECIFIC FIXTURE.

HALO® H5ICAT

WARNING – RISK OF FIRE. USE WITH HALO TRIMS ONLY FOR EACH LAMP TYPE & WATTAGE INDICATED. SEE TRIM FOR NO.

IP

TRIM NO. / NO. DE GARNITURE / NO. DE BORDILLO	LAMP SIZE AND TYPE / PUISSANCE ET TYPE D'AMPOULE / TAMANO DE LAMPARA Y TIPO
5000, 5001	75 WATT, R30 MAX
5010, 5020	50 WATT, R30 MAX
5010, 5020	60 WATT, BR30 MAX
5000, 5001, 5020	75 WATT, PAR30 MAX
5010, 5060	50 WATT, PAR30 MAX
5021	40 WATT, A19 MAX
ERT513	50 WATT, PAR20 MAX
5001	50 WATT, R20 MAX
5001, ERT513	65 WATT, BR30 MAX
5000, 5001, ERT513WHT	75 WATT, PAR30L MAX

WL – 464

TRIM NUMBER

TYPE OF BULB

MAXIMUM BULB SIZE

Energy-Saving Products

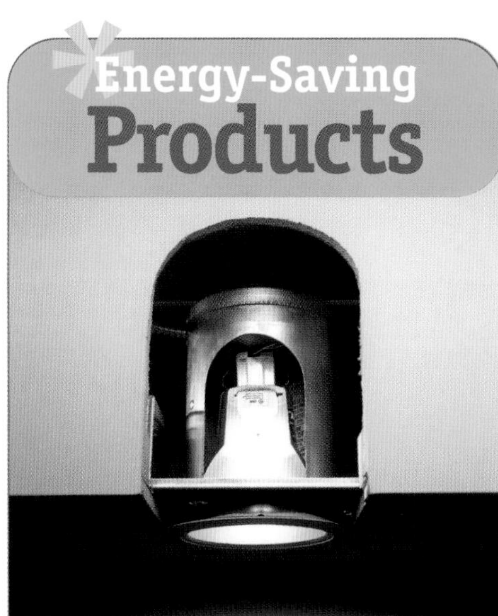

Recessed CFLs

The trend toward energy-efficient lighting has recently expanded to recessed lights. Rather than installing conventional recessed fixtures, you can now install fixtures for fluorescent lights only. Each fixture comes with a built-in ballast and accepts a pin-based compact fluorescent bulb. You'll get the same amount of light using only about one-third the electricity.

The housing, cone trim and light (each sold separately) cost a total of $110 and are available (usually by special order) at lighting stores.

Juno, (847) 827-9880. www.junolighting.com

Long-lasting bulbs for recessed lights

You can save energy by using standard compact fluorescent light bulbs (CFLs) specially designed for use in standard recessed light fixtures. Bulbs with different beam spreads are available to suit a variety of situations, and some are dimmable. And like most other CFLs, they'll last three times as long as their incandescent counterpart. Offered by GE and other bulb manufacturers.

Saving Energy:

Saving water may, at first glance, seem to be an oddball inclusion in a book on saving energy, but let's take a second glance. Even a slowly dripping faucet can waste 2,000 to 3,000 gallons of water per year. And if that faucet is dripping hot water, it's wasting the energy used to heat that water as well.

As you can conserve coal, oil and electricity through maintaining and upgrading your heating and cooling systems, you can conserve water—another precious commodity—by maintaining your plumbing systems.

Finally, you can put a stop to the "mental energy" that's wasted while you listen to the annoying drip, drip, drip of an ailing faucet or showerhead.

Conserving Water

Repair drippy faucets

Leaky faucets waste water and the energy that heats it

Usually the hardest part of repairing a faucet is finding the right replacement parts. Hardware and plumbing supply stores normally carry parts for common models, but if you have a faucet from a small manufacturer, you may have to special-order replacement parts. (Sometimes it's easier to simply replace the whole darn faucet.) Most repair kits include thorough instructions and some of the specialized tools you'll need.

Examine the faucet closely to determine where the leak is coming from. Leaks around the base of a spout require a different repair than a drip from the end of a spout. After you turn off the water supply, open the valve in the center position to relieve water pressure.

Pay close attention to the order and orientation of the parts as you remove them. A digital camera is handy for recording each step in case you forget later. Set the parts aside in the order you removed them. When all the

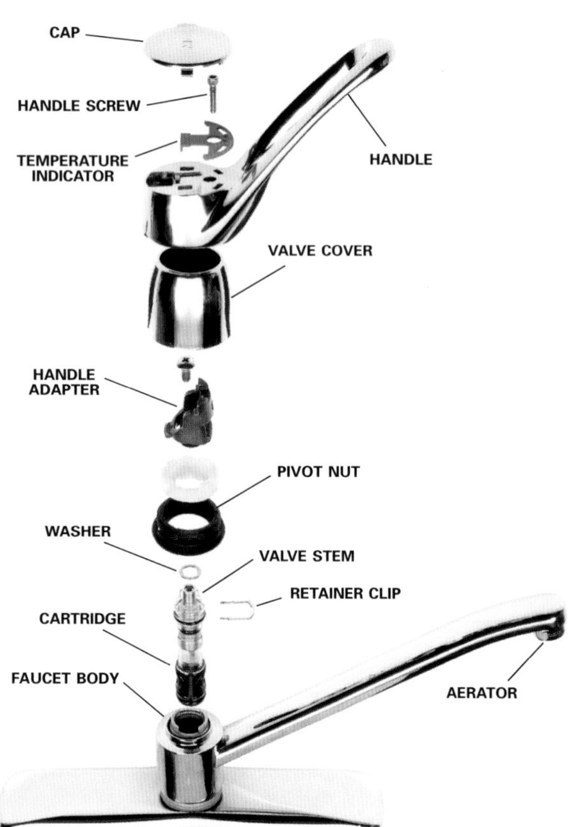

1

Cartridge-type faucet

Cartridges are used in both single- and double-handled faucets. If the levers or knobs on your two-handled faucet turn only 90 to 180 degrees, you most likely have a cartridge-type faucet. On a cartridge faucet, the handle is secured to the faucet by a screw that's hidden under a cap.

To stop drips at the spout or correct problems with hot and cold mixing, remove the cartridge and replace either the O-rings on the cartridge if they're damaged or the entire cartridge.

Don't be surprised if the cartridge seems stuck. It may take considerable force to pull it out. Really stubborn cartridges require the use of a special cartridge-pulling tool.

Quick tip

PLAN AHEAD

If you don't find shutoff valves under the sink, you may have to turn off the main valve to your entire home. Let your family know ahead of time when you're going to make your repair.

parts are out, inspect the interior of the valve for bits of deteriorated gaskets or mineral deposits. To clean these surfaces, use a cloth or fine-abrasive nylon pad.

Slow water flow can be caused by plugged holes in the faucet body. Use a small screwdriver to clean them out. Before you replace worn parts and reassemble the faucet, hold a rag over the faucet and open the water shutoff valve slightly to flush out loosened debris, catching it in the rag. Here are other tips to remember when you repair a faucet of any type:

- Always take old faucet parts with you to the store to get an exact match.
- Plug or cover drains and strainer baskets to avoid losing small parts.
- Line sink with a towel to prevent dropped tools from damaging it.
- Slow flow is frequently caused by a plugged aerator. Simply remove it, clean it and return it to its place. If it still works poorly, replace it.
- Always pay attention to alignment of parts as you reassemble the faucet.
- Many faucet manufacturers offer a lifetime guarantee. Take them up on it if yours drips or malfunctions.

A faucet dripping at the rate of one drop per second can waste nearly 2,000 gallons of water per year.

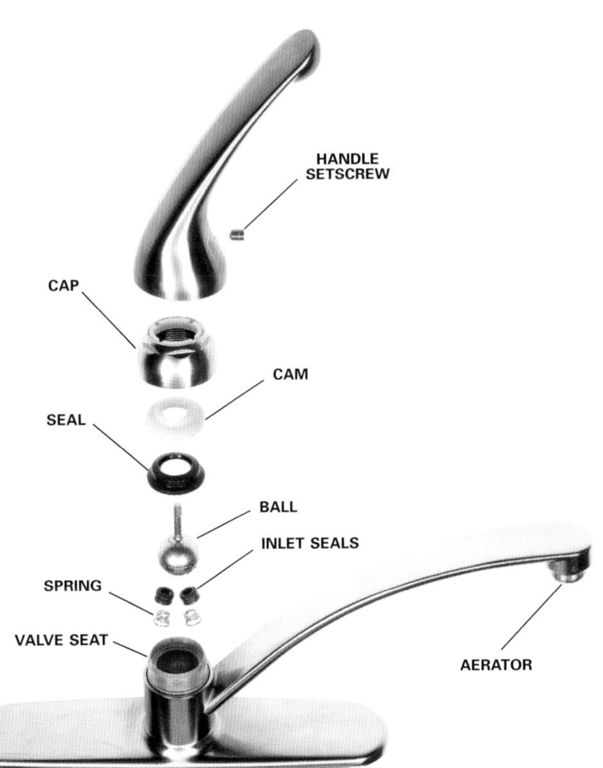

2

Ball-type faucet

Water flow and temperature in a rotary-ball faucet are controlled by a hollow plastic or steel ball that rotates in a socket.

If water is leaking around the base of the handle, you may be able to fix it by removing the handle and simply tightening the cap. If it still leaks, replace the O-rings around the faucet body. If the faucet drips from the end of the spout, replace the seats and springs.

Plastic or brass balls are softer than stainless steel balls and can become scratched by debris. Inspect the ball and, if you see damage, replace it with a stainless steel ball. Be sure to align all the parts properly as you reassemble the faucet.

TOTAL RECALL

Pay close attention to the order and orientation of parts as you remove them. A digital camera comes in handy in case you forget.

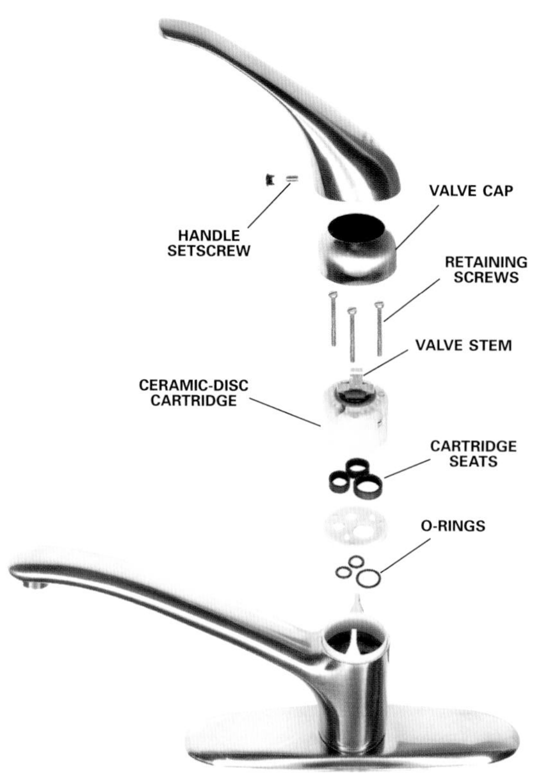

3

Ceramic disc-type faucet

Ceramic-disc faucets are like cartridge faucets, except discs inside the cartridge control the water flow. This type of valve is sturdy and reliable and rarely needs fixing. In fact, many manufacturers offer a lifetime warranty on the cartridge. Leaks can result from faulty rubber seals or a cracked disc inside the cartridge. Since replacement cartridges are expensive, start by replacing the seals and reassembling the faucet. If it still leaks, replace the cartridge.

TRACKING DOWN PARTS. Look for the brand name stamped on the faucet. Knowing that will help if you need to order new parts.

4

Outdoor-type faucet

Most outdoor faucets, including the freeze-proof one shown, have a washer at the end of the valve stem. Freeze-proof faucets are particularly prone to worn washers because, when the faucet is turned off, it continues to drain for a few seconds; consequently, people tend to turn the faucet tighter, damaging the rubber washer. Before beginning your repair, turn off the faucet's water supply.

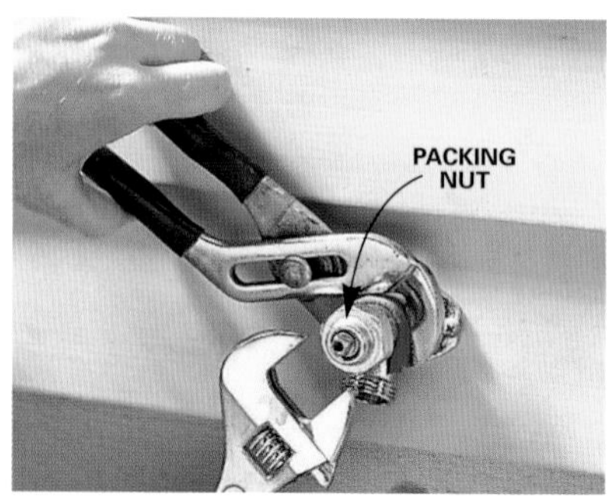

1 UNSCREW the handle and remove the packing nut. Hold the faucet steady while loosening the nut to avoid twisting the interior pipe. Even hard copper pipe can be twisted.

2 PULL stem out of faucet. For removal, some stems have to be turned so a key lines up with a slot; reattach handle to turn and pull stem.

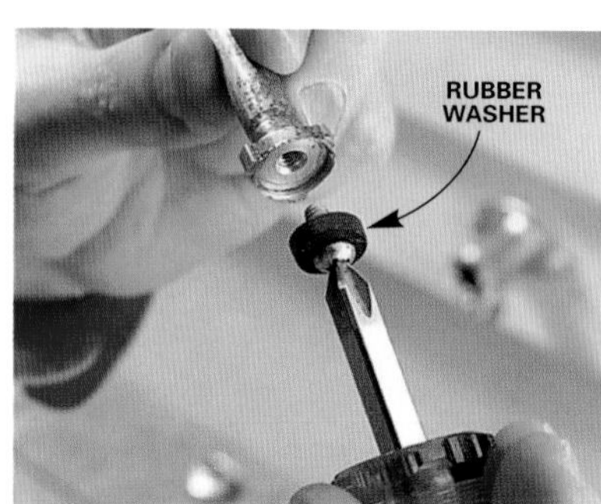

3 REMOVE and replace rubber washer on the stem end. If there are rubber O-rings on the stem, replace these as well.

5
Washer-type faucet

A leaky faucet has a torturous way of wearing on nerves and water resources. Even a slow drip can waste hundreds of gallons per month. Luckily, most dripping washer-type faucets can be cured in 30 minutes for less than a dollar.

To repair a washer-type faucet, you'll need to replace the washer on the bottom of the valve stem and sometimes the valve seat as well. Replace washers for both the hot and cold water while you're at it, not just the one that's leaking. Before you begin, turn off the water-supply valves and close the sink stopper so small parts won't disappear down the drain.

Most faucet handles are secured by a screw, which is sometimes covered by a snap-on cap or button. You may need to tap, wiggle or pry the handle a bit to remove it. The washer on the end of the valve stem may be flat or beveled. The new washer should be the same profile and fit snugly inside the circular lip without having to be forced.

With your finger, feel down inside the area where the stem assembly enters the faucet to determine whether the valve seat is rough or grooved. If it is, replace it with a new valve seat that exactly matches the old in diameter, height and threads.

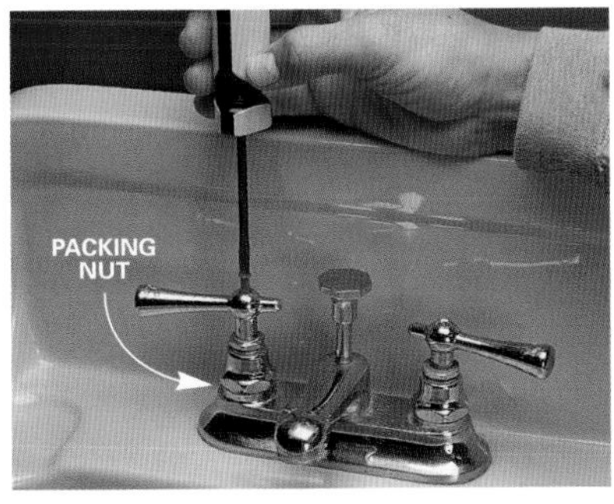

1 REMOVE the screw holding the handle, then loosen and remove the packing nut. Remove the stem assembly.

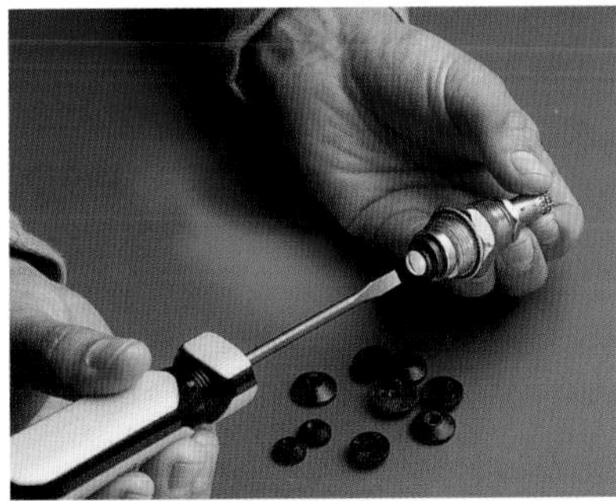

2 REMOVE the worn washer and replace it with the correct type: flat or beveled. The new washer should fit snugly without being forced.

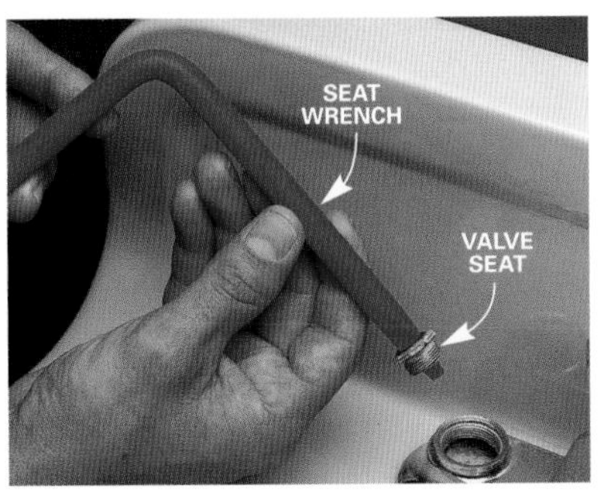

3 USE a seat wrench to remove the worn valve seat. The new seat must match the old one exactly in diameter, height and number of threads.

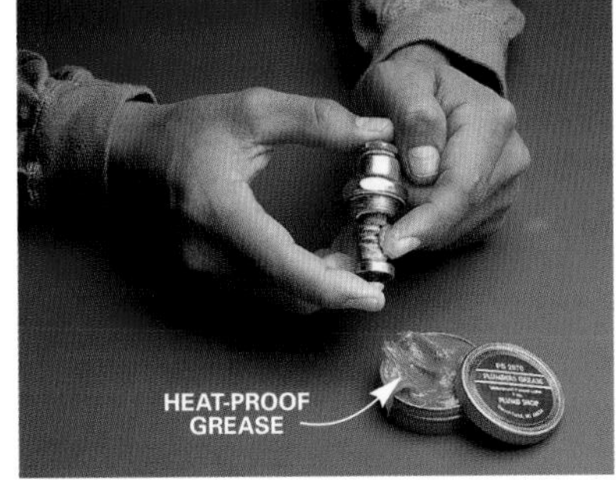

4 LUBRICATE the working parts of the stem assembly with heat-proof faucet grease. Reassemble faucet.

Energy-Saving Goof

Strike one, you're out!

I needed to replace the ballcock assembly on our running toilet. Once all the nuts were loosened, I tried to remove the assembly, but it wouldn't budge. I decided to give it a little help by gently hitting it with a hammer. Unfortunately, one of my gentle swings missed and hit the side of the tank, splitting it. Now I know to keep my hammer away from the toilet. I also know how to install a new one!

Fix a running toilet

A toilet that runs is both annoying and wasteful

A toilet that won't stop running can drive you crazy, and can waste more than 20,000 gallons of water per year. But there is good news: You can put an end to this water wasting yourself, even if you have no plumbing know-how. You may be able to solve the problem in just a few minutes without spending a dime. At worst, this fix will cost a few hours and $20 in toilet parts.

Finding the problem is usually simple

A toilet runs constantly because the fill valve that lets water into the tank isn't closing completely. A toilet runs intermittently because the valve opens slightly for a few minutes. In either case, you have to figure out why that valve isn't stopping the incoming water flow.

First, look for leaks. A leak in the tank can make a toilet run constantly or intermittently. If your toilet is leaking, you've probably noticed it already. But take a look just to be sure. If you find leaks coming from the tank bolts or flush valve, you'll most likely have to remove the tank from the bowl so you can replace the tank bolts, the rubber washers and the gaskets on the flush valve. If there are leaks around the fill valve, tighten the locknut (see Photo 6, p. 189). Leaks can come from cracks in the tank, too. In that case, the only reliable solution is a new toilet.

If you don't find any leaks, lift off the tank cover. At first glance, the array of submerged thingamajigs inside may look intimidating. But don't let them scare you. There are really only two main parts: the flush valve, which lets water gush into the bowl during the flush; and the fill valve, which lets water refill the tank after the flush. When a toilet runs constantly or intermittently, one of these valves is usually at fault.

To determine which valve is causing the trouble, look at the overflow tube. If water is overflowing into the tube, there's a problem with the fill valve. Fill valve fixes are shown on the next page. If the water level is below the top of the tube, the flush valve is leaking, allowing water to trickle into the bowl. That slow, constant outflow of water prevents the fill valve from closing completely. To fix a flush valve, see pp. 190 and 191.

For these photos, the fronts and backs of new toilets were cut away to show you how to replace these parts. Your toilet won't look so pristine inside. You'll find scummy surfaces, water stains and corrosion. But don't be squeamish—the water is as clean as the stuff that comes out of your faucets.

Figure A
Toilet cutaway

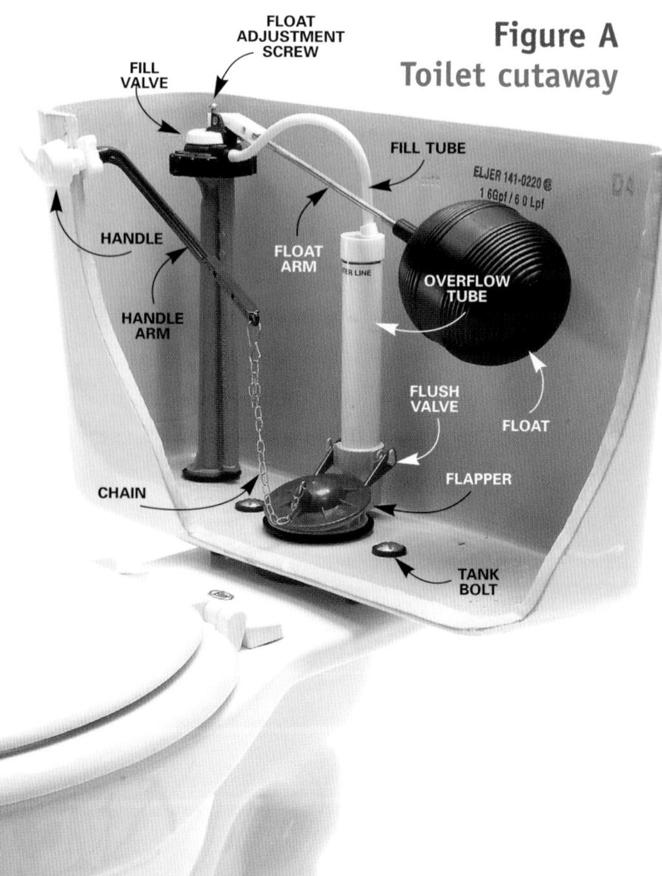

1
Repair the fill valve

You may have to replace the fill valve, but these three fixes are worth a try first.

Fix 1: Adjust the float

If your valve has a ball that floats at the end of a rod, gently lift the rod and listen. If the water shuts off, you may be able to stop the running by adjusting the float. Some fill valves have a float adjustment screw on top (see Figure A). If there is no adjustment screw, bend the float arm (photo below). If you have a Fluidmaster-style fill valve, make sure it's adjusted properly (Photo 8, p. 189.) You don't have to empty the tank to make these adjustments.

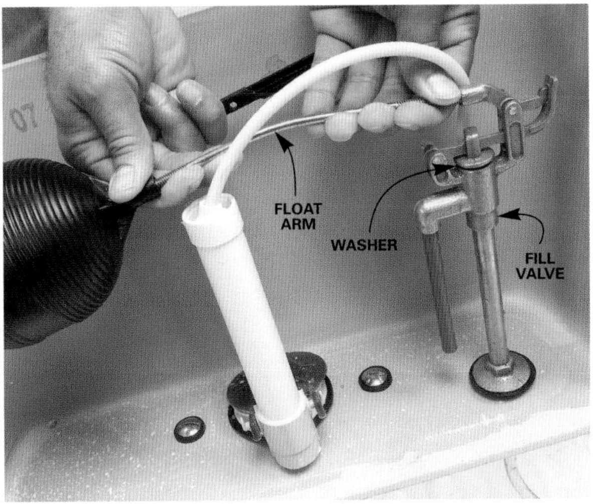

Gently bend the float arm down to put extra pressure on the valve. (To adjust a float that doesn't have an arm, see Photo 8.) Then flush the toilet to see if it works.

Fix 3: Replace the washer

When you remove the cap to flush out the valve, inspect the washer for wear or cracks. Replacing a bad washer is cheap ($1) and easy (photo below). But finding the right washer may not be. The most common washers are often available at home centers and hardware stores. Other styles can be hard to find. If you decide to hunt for a washer, remove it and take it to the store to find a match. Plumbers usually replace the whole fill valve rather than hunt for a replacement washer.

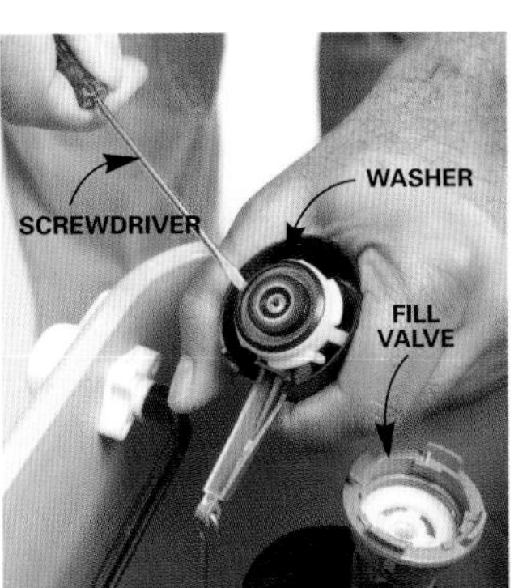

REPLACE a worn, cracked valve washer by prying the old washer out of the cap with a small screwdriver. Press the new one into place.

Fix 2: Flush the valve

Hard water, debris from old pipes or particles from a break in a city water line can prevent a flush valve from closing completely. Running water through it from the supply line will clear the debris. Photos 1 and 2 show you how to do this on one common type of valve. Even though other valves will look different, the clearing process is similar. However, you may have to remove a few screws on top of the fill valve to remove the cap.

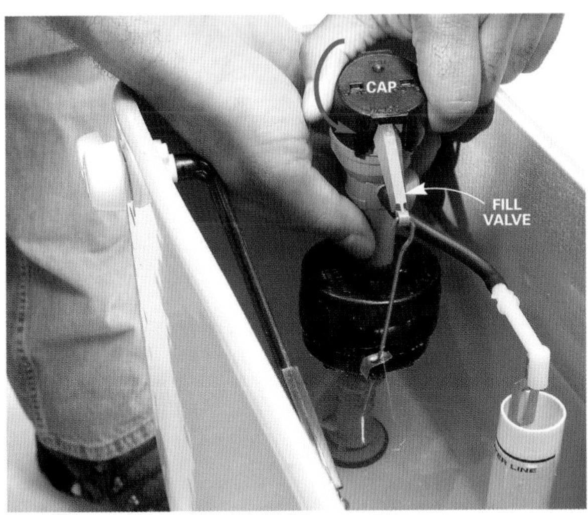

1 REMOVE the fill valve cap. On this type of valve, press down and turn counterclockwise. Remove screws on other types of valves.

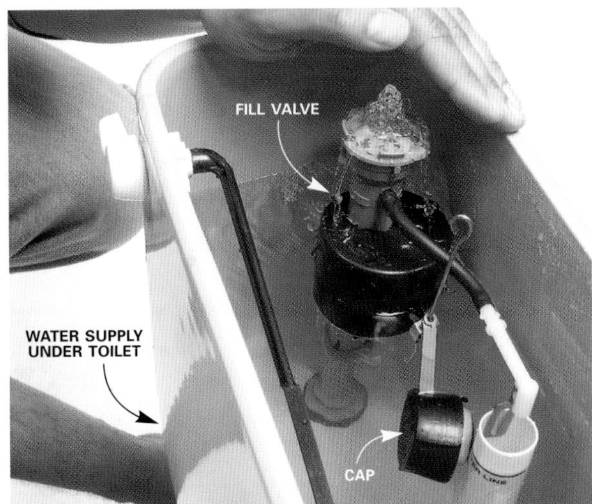

2 COVER the valve with your hand. Turn on the water (cautiously, so you don't get a cold shower!) and let it flush out the valve for a few seconds.

Fix 4: If you can't fix the fill valve, replace it

Replacing a fill valve requires only a few basic tools (adjustable pliers and a pair of scissors) and an hour of your time. A kit containing the type of valve shown here and everything else you need costs about $12 at home centers and hardware stores.

Your first step is to shut off the water. In most cases, you'll have a shutoff valve right next to the toilet coming either through the floor or out of the wall. If you don't have a shutoff, turn off the water supply at the main shutoff valve, where water enters your home. This is a good time to add a shutoff valve next to the toilet or replace one that leaks. This is also a good time to replace the supply line that feeds your toilet (Photo 6). A flexible supply line reinforced with a metal sleeve costs about $7 at home centers and hardware stores. Photos 1 – 8 show how to replace the valve. If the height of your valve is adjustable, set the height before you install the valve (Photo 5). If your valve is a different style from the

1 REPLACE the fill valve. Turn off the water at the shutoff valve. Flush the toilet and hold the flush valve open to drain the tank. Sponge out the remaining water or vacuum it up with a wet/dry vacuum.

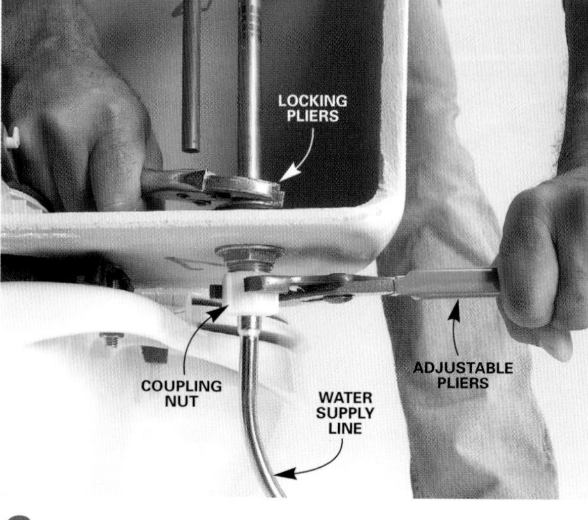

2 UNSCREW the coupling nut that connects the supply line. If the valve turns inside the tank, hold its base with locking pliers. Tip: Throw a towel on the floor underneath to catch water that will drain from the line.

3 REMOVE the locknut that holds the valve to the tank. Push down gently on the valve as you unscrew the nut. Pull out the old valve.

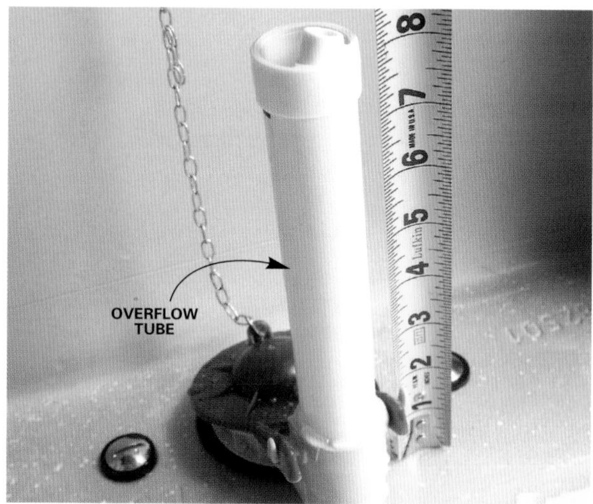

4 MEASURE the height of the overflow tube. Measure to the top of the tube, not to any water level label on the tube.

one shown, check the directions. After mounting the valve (Photo 6), connect the fill tube (Photo 7). The fill tube squirts water into the overflow tube to refill the toilet bowl. The water that refills the tank gushes from the bottom of the fill valve. When you install the valve and supply lines, turn the nuts finger-tight. Then give each another one-half turn with pliers. When you turn the water supply back on, immediately check for leaks and tighten the nuts a bit more if necessary.

Quick tip

WASTE NOT, WANT NOT. A leaking toilet can waste 55 gallons of water per day or more. It pays to fix it fast! And don't worry about putting your hand in the tank. The water is the same as what comes out of the tap.

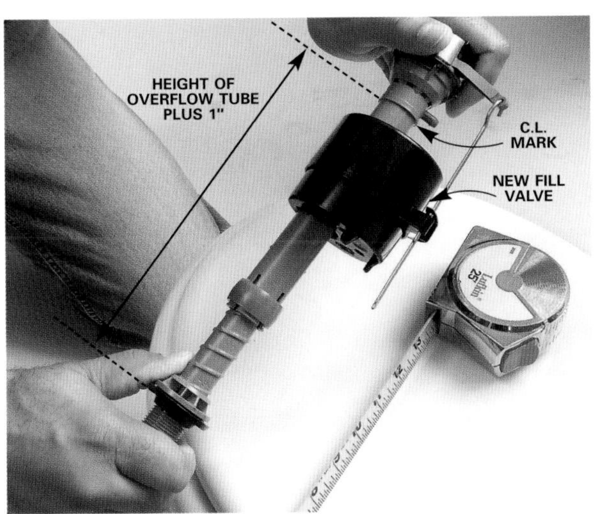

5 ADJUST the height of the new fill valve by holding the base and twisting the top. The height from the base to the CL (critical level) mark should be the height of the overflow tube plus 1 in.

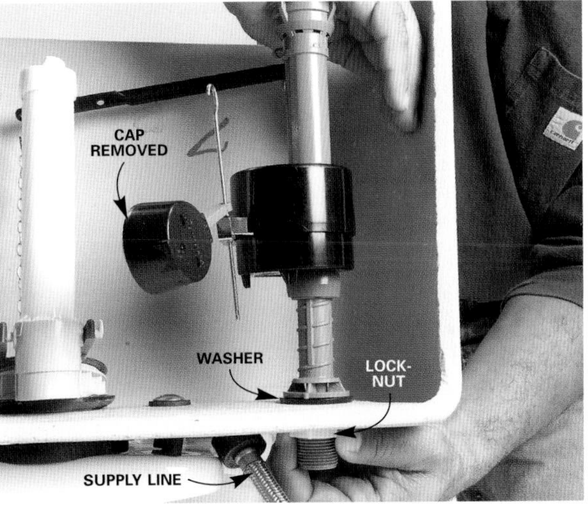

6 REMOVE the cap, press down to compress the washer and screw on the locknut. Connect the supply line and flush the valve as shown in Photo 2, p. 187. Reset the cap and check for leaks.

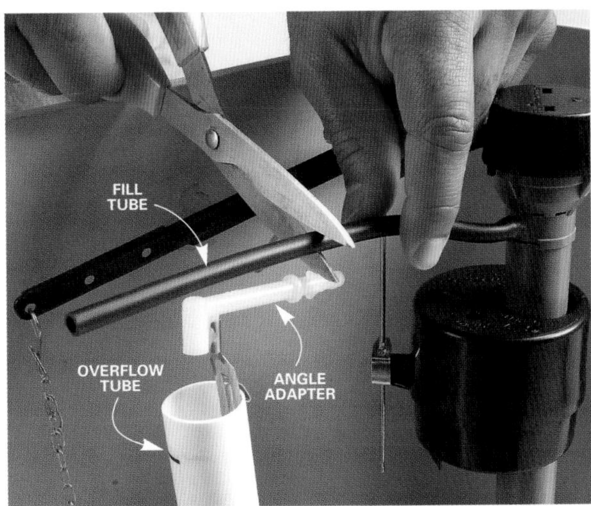

7 SLIP the fill tube onto the fill valve. Clip the angle adapter onto the overflow tube. Then cut the tube to fit and slip it onto the angle adapter.

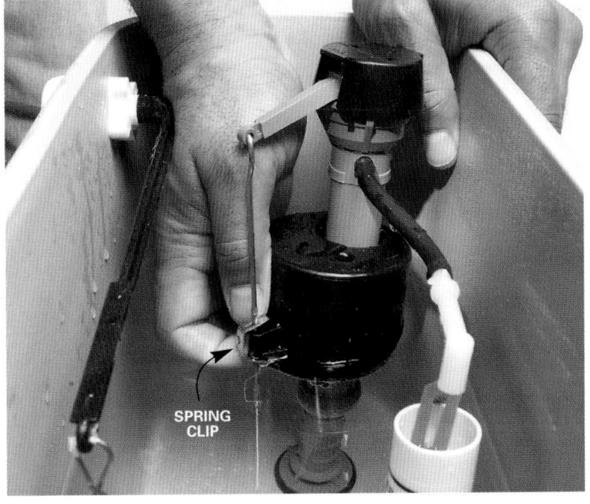

8 TURN on the water to fill the tank. Pinch the spring clip and slide the float up or down to set the water level 1 in. below the top of the overflow tube or to the water line marked on the tank.

2
Fix the flush valve

When a flush valve causes a toilet to run, a worn flapper is usually the culprit. But not always. First, look at the chain that raises the flapper. If there's too much slack in the chain, it can tangle up and prevent the flapper from closing firmly. A chain with too little slack can cause trouble too. Photo 3 on p. 191 shows how to set the slack just right.

Next, test the flapper as shown in Photo 1. If extra pressure on the flapper doesn't stop the running-water noise, water is likely escaping through a cracked or corroded overflow tube. In that case, you have to detach the tank from the bowl and replace the whole flush valve. Since the overflow tube is rarely the cause of a running toilet, that repair is not shown here.

If pressing down on the flapper stops the noise, the flapper isn't sealing under normal pressure. Turn off the water, flush the toilet to empty the tank and then run your finger around the rim of the flush valve seat. If you feel mineral deposits, clean the flush valve seat with an abrasive sponge or ScotchBrite pad. Don't use anything that might roughen it. If cleaning the flush valve seat doesn't solve the problem, you need to replace the flapper.

Replacing your flapper may require slightly different steps than we show (Photos 2 and 3). Your flapper may screw onto a threaded rod or have a ring that slips over the overflow tube. If you have an unusual flush valve, finding a replacement flapper may be the hardest part of the job. To find a suitable replacement, turn off the

1 PUSH down on the flapper with a yardstick and listen. If the sound of running water stops, the flapper needs replacing.

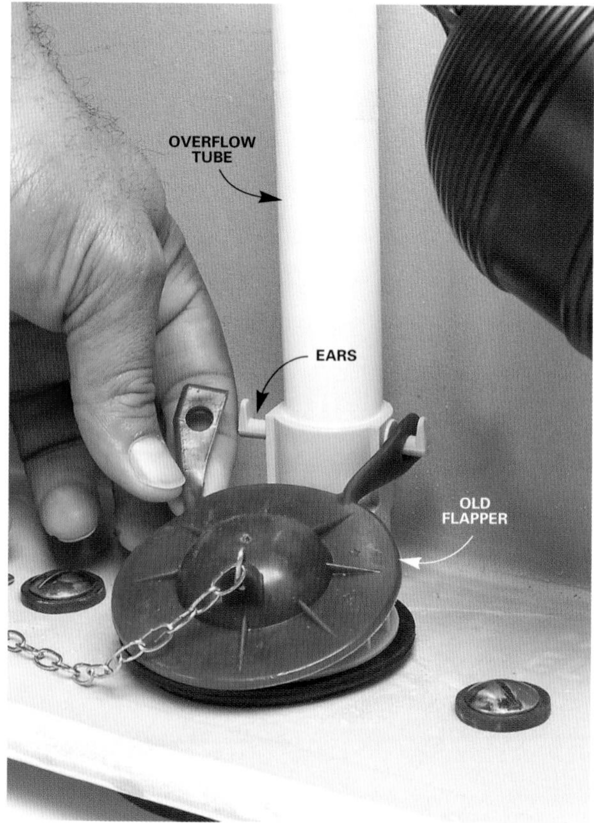

2 REMOVE the old flapper from the ears of the overflow tube and detach the chain from the handle arm.

water, take the old one with you to the home center or hardware store. (Turn off the water before removing the flapper.) You may not find an identical match, but chances are you'll locate one of the same shape and diameter. If not, try a plumbing supply store (in the yellow pages under "Plumbing Supplies") or search online (a good source is www.doplumb.com). It helps to know the brand and model of your toilet. The brand name is usually on the bowl behind the seat. In some cases, the model or number will be on the underside of the lid or inside the tank. Matching an unusual flapper can become a trial-and-error process. Even professional plumbers sometimes try two or three flappers before they find one that works well.

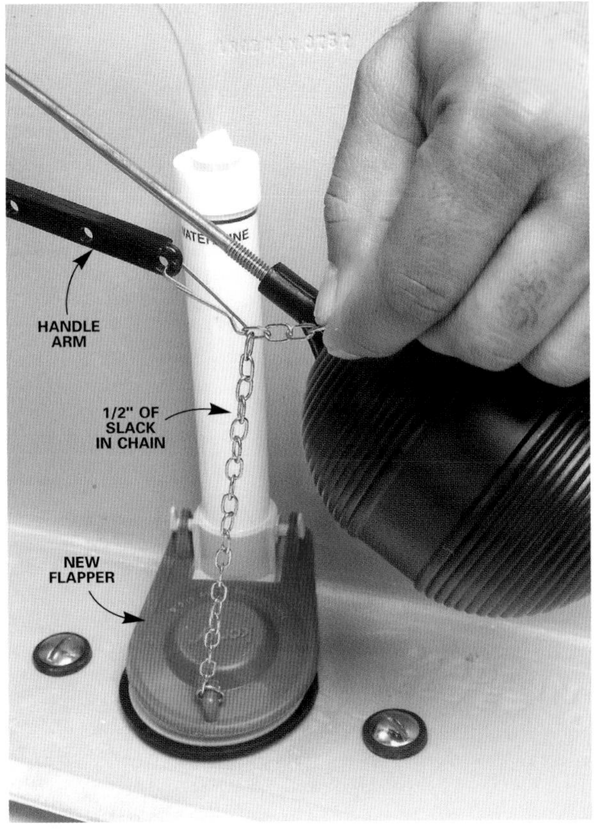

3 ATTACH the new flapper to the overflow tube and hook the chain to the handle arm. Leave 1/2 in. of slack in the chain. Turn the water back on and test-flush the toilet.

Energy-Saving Product

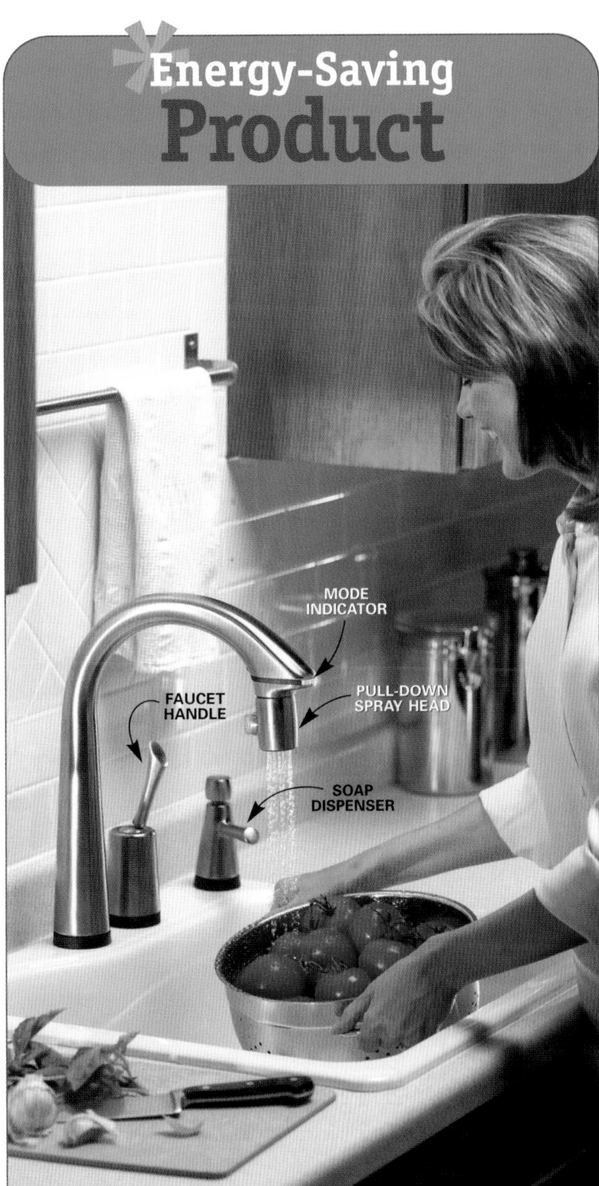

Hands-free kitchen faucet

When your hands are full, you don't want to set down your load to turn on the kitchen faucet. With a hand-free faucet like this one from Brizo (www.brizo.com), you don't have to. Water starts and stops when you lightly tap the faucet or use the hands-free feature. Pulling out the spray head also turns on the water.

The "Smart Technology" on/off switch distinguishes between the pan sitting in the sink and a pan placed under the faucet to be rinsed. You can also turn the faucet on conventionally with the handle.

In search of the perfect flush

Toilet technology puts an end to wasted water

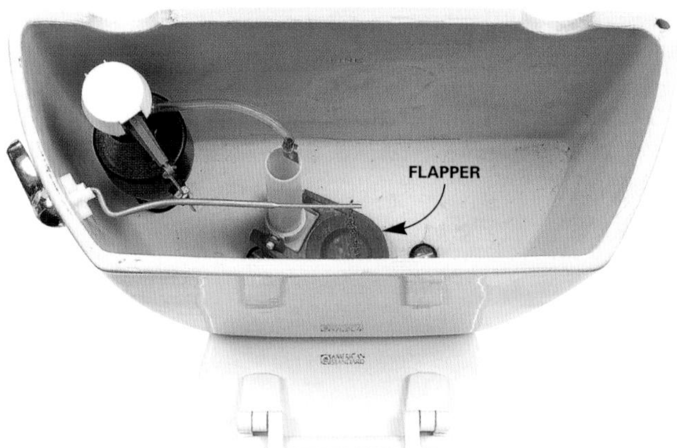

In 1994 Congress decided to conserve water by requiring toilets to use no more than 1.6 gallons per flush. It was a good idea, but when manufacturers came out with their first water-saving models, they hadn't yet figured out how to make toilets perform as well as before (most toilets at that time used 3.5 gallons or more). So homeowners got stuck with toilets that required two or even three flushes to clear and clean the bowl. These wimpy toilets plug up more often too. Their design is poor, and there isn't much you can do to improve them. The only real solution is a new toilet.

Manufacturers have refined old designs and developed entirely new systems to make water-saving toilets work better. But there are still some weak flushers out there, so do some research before you buy (see below). When you're shopping, you'll find three types of flushing systems:

TO SEE HOW WELL 80 TOILET MODELS CLEARED SOLID WASTE in a recent laboratory test, see "Maximum Performance Testing of Popular Toilet Models" at www.cwwa.ca/freepub_e.asp.

FOR REAL-WORLD EXPERIENCE AND OPINIONS on various models from plumbers and homeowners, click on "Terry Love's Report on low-flow toilets" at www.terrylove.com.

Gravity flush

This is the system toilets have used for over a century: The flush valve (flapper) opens and water rushes down through the bowl. Manufacturers have steadily improved tank and bowl designs to create a more powerful flush with less water. One of the most effective improvements was to simply enlarge the flush valve from 2 in. to 3 in. or more.

Pros:

- **Cost.** Some of the models that perform well in lab tests cost as little as $150.
- **Easy to maintain.** Diagnosing problems and finding replacement parts is relatively easy.

Cons:

- **Tanks can sweat.** If condensation forms on the tank of your current toilet, the same problem will likely occur with any gravity toilet.
- **Big differences in performance.** There are still a lot of wimpy flushers out there. You have to do your homework to find a model that performs well (see "Quick Tip," at left).

Quick tip*

PUT IT TO THE TEST. Pressure-assist toilets are common in public restrooms, so you can take one for a test drive at an office or business. Just lift the tank lid and look for the pressure tank to see if it's a pressure-assist model.

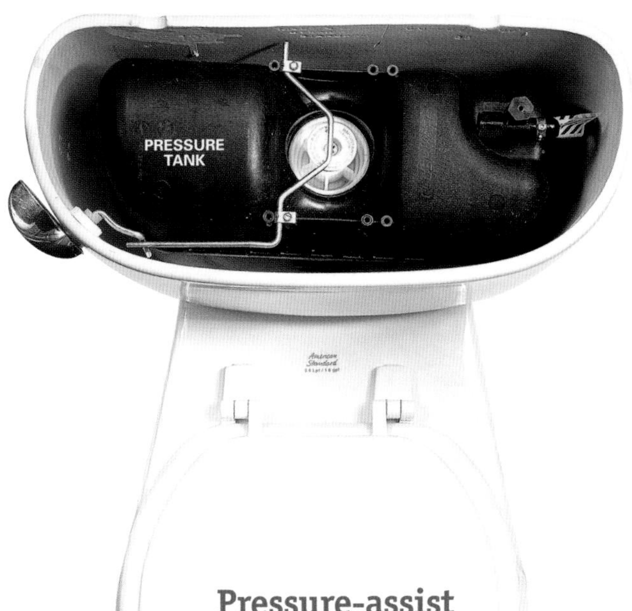

Pressure-assist

These toilets have a pressure tank inside that works like a big water balloon. Water fills the tank and is held there under pressure. When the flush valve opens, pressure and gravity combine for an explosive flush.

Pros:

- **Powerful flush.** When it comes to clearing the bowl of solid waste, pressure-assist models generally outperform other types.
- **No sweat.** Because water is held inside a pressure tank rather than the porcelain tank, condensation won't occur on the outside of the toilet.

Cons:

- **Cost.** Starting at about $240, pressure-assist models cost more than some of their cousins.
- **Repairs.** Diagnosing problems, finding parts and making repairs can be a headache.
- **Noise.** Pressure-assist toilets create a loud flush.

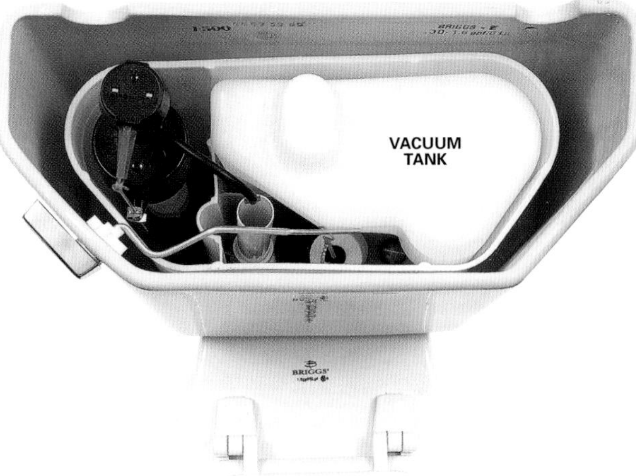

Vacuum-assist

This is the latest flush innovation. The porcelain tank contains a vacuum tank that's connected to the trapway (the large tube that carries water out of the bowl). When the toilet is flushed, water flowing out of the tank creates suction in the vacuum tank and trapway to help suck waste out of the bowl.

Pros:

- **Easy repairs.** Vacuum-assist toilets use the same type of fill and flush valves as gravity models, so they're simple to repair.
- **Strong flush.** Vacuum-assist toilets do well in lab tests. In clearing solid waste, they outperform most gravity types but don't do as well as many pressure-assist models.
- **No sweat.** Like pressure-assist models, vacuum-assist toilets store water in an inner tank, so condensation won't form outside the porcelain tank.

Cons:

- **Cost.** Starting around $180, vacuum-assist models cost slightly more than some gravity models.
- **Limited choices.** There are currently only two vacuum-assist toilets from major manufacturers: Briggs' Vacuity (www.briggsplumbing.com) and Crane's VIP Flush (www.craneplumbing.com).

Water-conserving sprinklers

Lower your water bill by watering smart

When it comes to saving water when watering a square garden, you have two great choices: a rotary sprinkler with a fairly square pattern that matches your garden size, and a rotary impact sprinkler with a circular pattern larger than your square garden (see photos below and p. 195).

Oscillating sprinklers (not shown) aren't water efficient. Any sprinkler that produces a fine mist or launches water skyward will cause water to evaporate as well as be blown off target. Oscillating sprinklers also lack uniform coverage because the water delivery rate tends to be much heavier at the sides than at the center of the pattern.

A good rotary sprinkler will deliver a fairly square pattern and water a square garden evenly. Check the box to determine its maximum coverage area. This sprinkler type will be suitable for more soil types as well. You can reduce the water volume for slower watering of poorly absorbing, heavy clay soils, or increase the volume for faster-absorbing sand or loam soils. The goal is to make sure all the water is absorbed, not running away from the garden. While reducing water volume does reduce coverage, it adds versatility beyond your garden. Your sprinkler will fit smaller flower beds or limited landscaped areas. Wheels on the sprinkler help when you're moving it.

Rotary Sprinklers

- Uniform water coverage
- Irrigation speed adapts to soil types

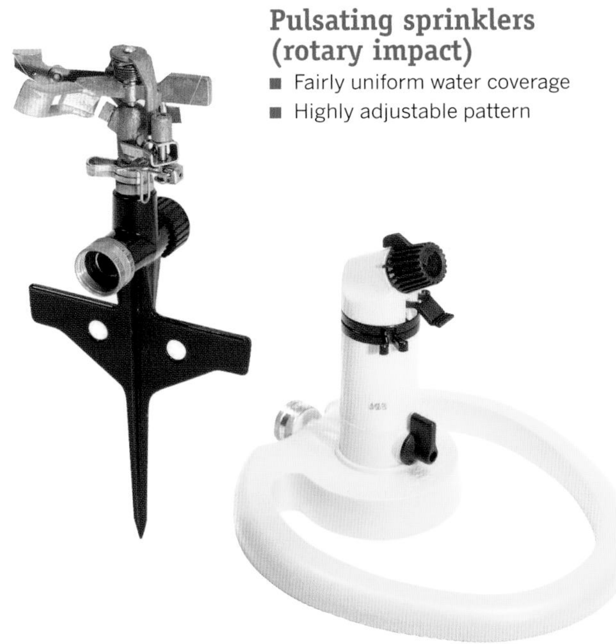

Pulsating sprinklers (rotary impact)

- Fairly uniform water coverage
- Highly adjustable pattern

The second choice is a rotary impact (or pulsating) sprinkler (shown above). It uses a water-driven flapper that hits an anvil and drives the nozzles in a circular pattern. Most models are highly adjustable, from changing the circle diameter to watering a portion of a circle and to changing droplet size. You'll have some water waste covering a square garden with a larger circle, and coverage isn't as uniform as it is with the rotary sprinkler. However, they do a good job of keeping water close to the ground to minimize drift and reduce evaporation.

A 72-in.-tall pulsating sprinkler (not shown) is very useful for large gardens as plants grow and become tall enough to interfere with sprinkler patterns. An elevated sprinkler is more costly, but you can always build a platform or use a bucket to elevate your sprinkler above your tall tomatoes.

Finally, it's smart to measure the amount of water you apply. A good rule of thumb is to make sure your garden gets an inch of rainfall or irrigation per week, wetting the top 3 to 5 in. of soil. And it's always best to water in the morning, giving plants the rest of the day to dry so leaf diseases won't develop.

Energy-Saving Q&A

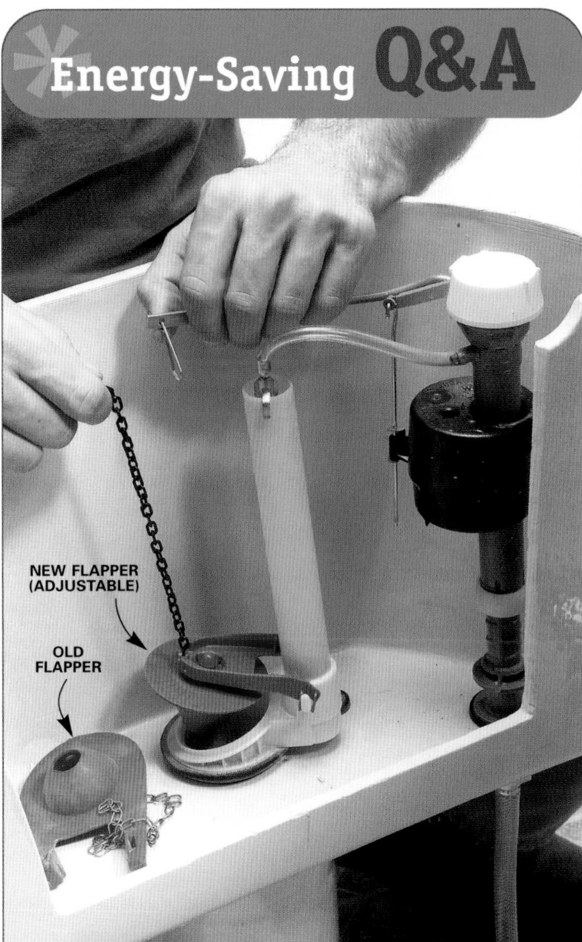

Two flush fine; one doesn't

Q **I recently installed three identical toilets in my home. Two flush fine, but the flapper on the third falls back and stops the flush too soon. I wind up flushing it two or three times, which wastes water. I've tried adjusting the chain length and water level, but nothing has helped. What else can I do?**

A Most likely the problem toilet developed a manufacturing defect in the bowl or passages during the casting process. Defects can occur on any toilet but are more often found in lower-priced types. The easiest solution is to experiment with different flappers. You can usually find a variety of them at home centers and hardware stores. Start with one that's similar to the original. Then try one of the adjustable types, which you can set to stay open longer. Keep in mind that any flapper that solves the problem will probably increase the flush volume, from the standard 1.6 gallons to the 2- to 3-gallon range, but you'll still save water in the long run. As a last resort, take the toilet out and return it.

Micro Irrigation

Use less water and spend less time watering

Whether you're growing roses to win prizes or just trying to keep a few flower beds looking good, you know that keeping your plants well-watered is critical. Micro irrigation—a network of plastic tubing and low-volume drippers and sprinklers that reach every part of the garden you want to water—takes the hassle out of watering and keeps your water utility bill to a minimum by putting water only where it's needed.

The materials are inexpensive (you can get started for less than $100) and easy to install, using nothing more than a pruning shears and a special hole punch tool. Once you lay out the tubing and connect the drippers, sprinklers or sprayers, you'll be able to water your plants by simply turning on the water and letting it run for an hour or two. Add a battery-operated controller for about $40 more and you won't even have to remember to turn on the water. It'll turn the water on and off automatically at the times you select.

Micro irrigation saves more than time and energy; it saves water by distributing it more efficiently. Because you use dozens of watering devices to replace one regular sprinkler, you have much greater control over where the water goes and how much is supplied to each plant. Instead of flooding the ground all at once, micro irrigation lets you apply a small amount over longer periods, allowing it to soak into the plants' root zone for maximum benefit. And since runoff and evaporation are kept to a minimum, micro irrigation uses less water.

Here you'll learn the basics of micro irrigation, including planning tips and step-by-step installation instructions. For more details, especially in the planning phase, read through one of the manufacturers' free planning guides or browse the Internet sites we've listed (see Buyer's Guide on p. 200).

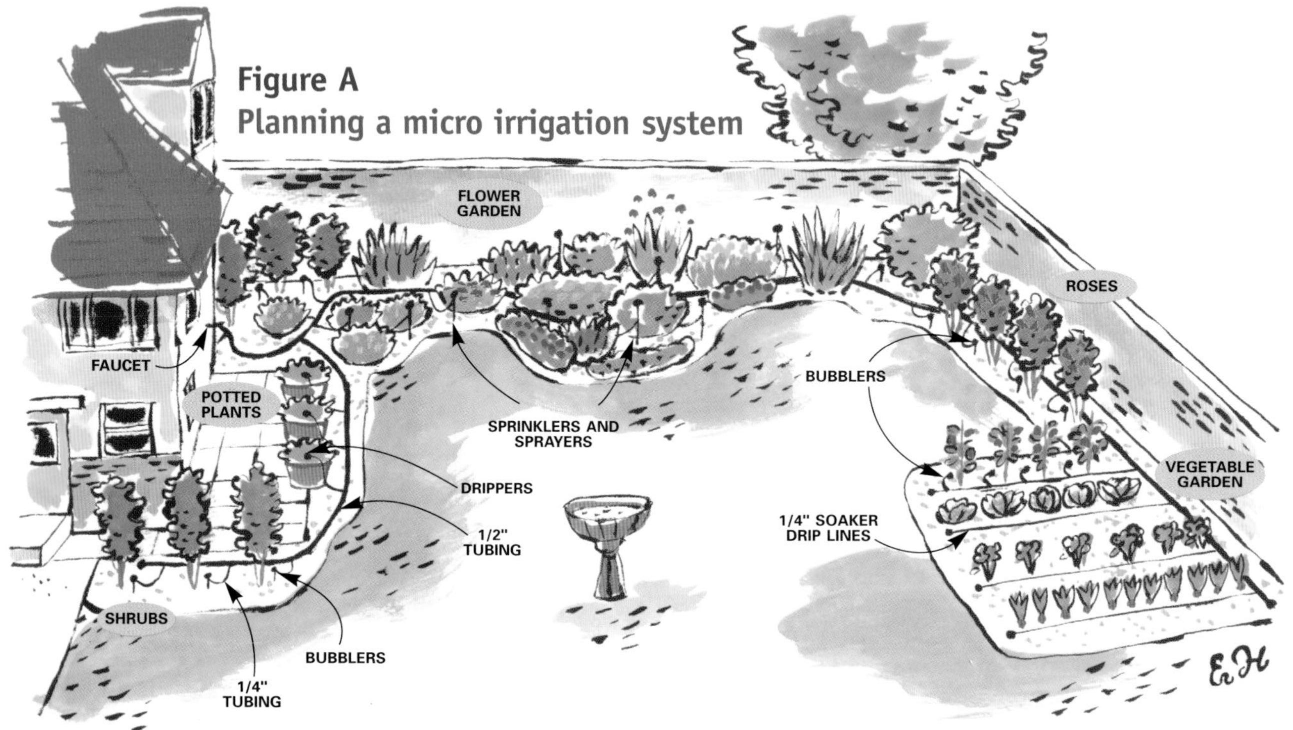

Figure A
Planning a micro irrigation system

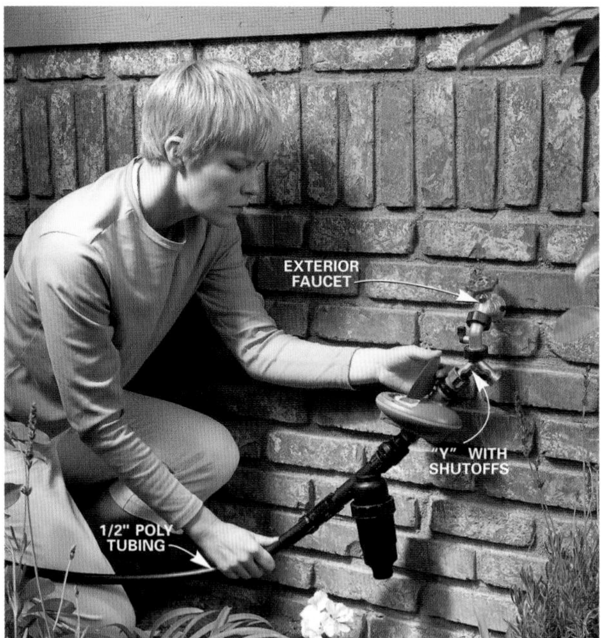

1 MOUNT a "Y" with shutoff valves to your faucet. Then attach the (optional) timer, backflow preventer, filter, pressure regulator and adapter.

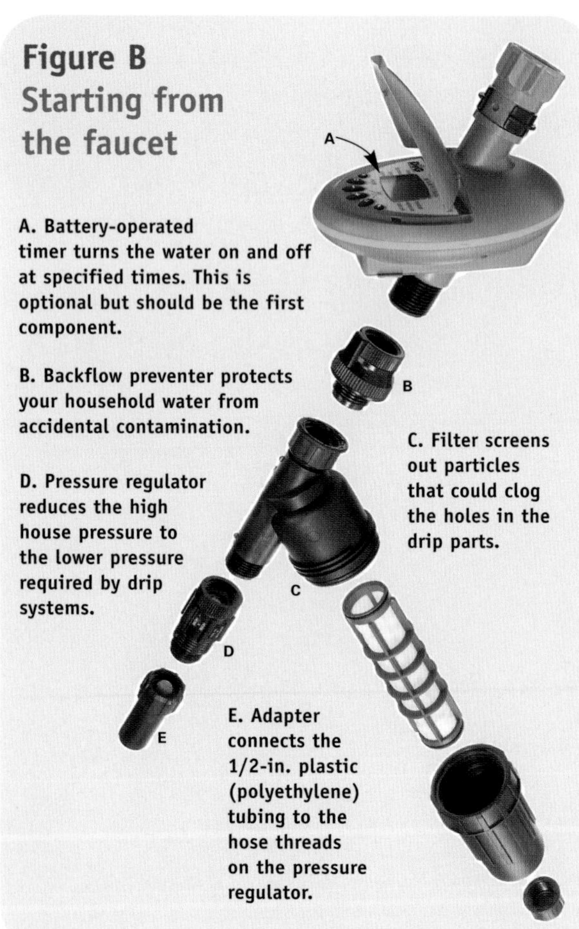

Figure B
Starting from the faucet
A
A. Battery-operated timer turns the water on and off at specified times. This is optional but should be the first component.
B
B. Backflow preventer protects your household water from accidental contamination.
C. Filter screens out particles that could clog the holes in the drip parts.
C
D. Pressure regulator reduces the high house pressure to the lower pressure required by drip systems.
D
E
E. Adapter connects the 1/2-in. plastic (polyethylene) tubing to the hose threads on the pressure regulator.

Make a sketch and plan the system

If this is your first venture into micro irrigation, start small and experiment to get a feel for how the system works. Choose one or two flower beds or a garden and install a simple one-zone system.

The basic planning strategy is to pick the best watering device to serve each type of plant. Then determine a flow rate that supplies adequate water to every plant in the watering zone. Set up the system to run between one and two hours at a time, two or three times a week.

Start by measuring your garden and making a simple sketch. Choose the type and flow rate of the watering devices based on your soil and the plants' water needs. Mark these on the plan and draw in the tubing route to connect them. This will involve a little guesswork. See "Drippers, bubblers, sprinklers and sprayers" on p. 201 for information that will help you choose the right watering device. Try to cover all the root zones of your plants. Don't worry about getting everything perfect at first. Add a few extra of each type of watering device and buy the watering devices, tubing and the basic parts shown in Figure B for the faucet hookup. Once you see how the system works, you'll find it's easy to relocate or add emitters to get a more balanced water flow or better coverage.

Planning rules of thumb:

- Use 1/2 gallons per hour (gph) drippers in clay soil, 1-gph drippers in loam and 2-gph drippers in sandy soil.
- Add the gph rate of all drippers, bubblers, sprayers and sprinklers you plan to use. If you're using 1/2-in. tubing for the main line, limit the total to between 150 and 220 gallons per hour (check with the manufacturer).
- Limit the length of 1/2-in. tubing on one zone to a maximum of about 200 ft.
- Limit the total gph on a length of 1/4-in. tubing to 25 to 30.
- If you're burying lines, call (888) 258-0808 to have your underground utilities marked.

As you add to the system, it's best to divide your yard into groups of plants that have similar watering requirements. With this strategy, you add a separate system (zone), starting at the water source, for each group of plants or area of the yard.

For help with planning a large, more complicated system (and for the best prices), work with a retailer that specializes in micro irrigation (see Buyer's Guide on p. 200).

Begin at the outside faucet

Figure B and Photo 1 show the parts you'll need and the order in which to install them. The Y-splitter with shutoffs allows you to keep the drip system on all the time (and

2 CONNECT the 1/2-in. poly tubing to the faucet end. Then lay the tubing through the garden according to your plan. Stake it down about every 5 or 6 ft.

operated by a controller) and still use your regular garden hose (Photo 1). You don't have to use a controller, but you must use a backflow preventer. Some of these components are available with hose thread or pipe thread, so make sure to match the thread type when you buy parts. Joining hose thread to pipe thread will result in leaks.

Lay the 1/2-in. tubing

Next, run the 1/2-in. tubing to the garden bed (Photo 2) and position it according to your plan. The tubing will be more flexible and easier to work with if you let it sit in the sun for a while to warm up. Remember, you can cover the tubing with decorative mulch later to hide it. Cut the tubing with pruning shears. Use T-fittings to create branches and elbows to make 90-degree bends (Photo 3). Be aware that there are a few different sizes of what's called "1/2-in." tubing, depending on which brand you use. Buy fittings to match the brand of tubing you're using. If you need to join two different brands of tubing or you're not sure which you have, you can buy universal fittings that will work on all diameters of tubing. Use special plastic tubing clamps to nail the tubing to the house or deck.

You can bury 1/2-in. poly tubing in a shallow trench to conceal it as it crosses a path or small section of lawn, but for longer lengths, especially in high-traffic areas, we recommend substituting 1/2-in. PVC pipe instead. Buy adapters to connect the 1/2-in. poly tubing to the ends of the PVC pipe. Check with your local plumbing inspector before burying any pipe to see whether special backflow prevention is required.

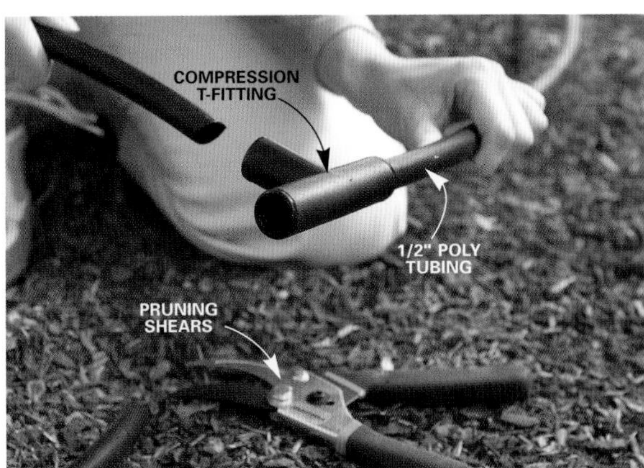

3 CUT the tubing with a pruning shears and install T- and 90-degree fittings where they're needed. Twist and press the tubing firmly into the fitting.

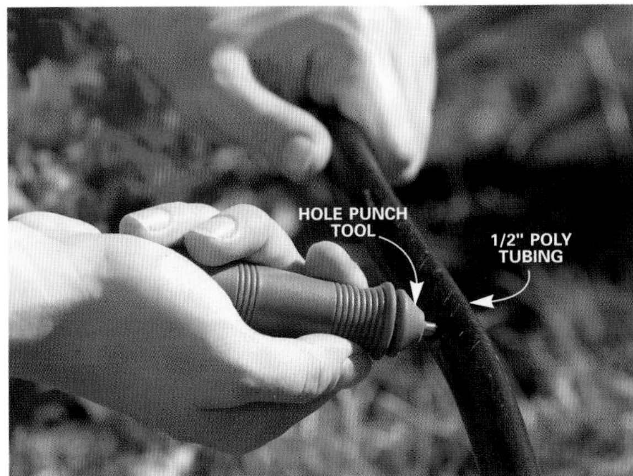

4 PUNCH holes in the tubing wherever you want to install a watering device. Push and twist until the tip of the punch creates a clean hole.

Connect the emitters

Now add the various types of emitters for the particular plants—drippers, sprayers, sprinklers or drip line. The technique is simple. Use a hole punch tool to poke a hole in the tubing wherever you want to add a watering device (Photo 4). You can insert a dripper directly into the hole in the 1/2-in. tubing or use a barbed connector and connect a length of 1/4-in. vinyl tubing. Then connect a watering device to the end of the 1/4-in. tube (Photo 6).

You can buy sprinklers and sprayers as assemblies that include a barbed connector, a short length of 1/4-in. tubing and a plastic stake (Photo 5), or buy the parts separately and assemble them yourself. Remember to buy a selection of 1/4-in. barbed fittings, including T-fittings, elbows, connectors and hole plugs. You can press any of these fittings into a punched hole in the 1/2-in. line and connect 1/4-in. tubes to feed the emitters. T-fittings allow you to run 1/4-in. tubing in opposite directions from the main line or to branch off a 1/4-in. tube. Use connectors to extend a 1/4-in. tube that's too short. If you punch a hole in the wrong spot or want to remove a fitting, push a hole plug into the hole to seal it.

BARBED CONNECTOR

When your installation is complete, run water through the tubing to flush out any dirt. Then cap the ends (Photo 7). Now you're ready to turn on the water and see how your new micro irrigation system works. Let the water run for an hour. Then check around your plants to make sure the root zone has been thoroughly wetted. Fine-tune the system by adjusting the length of time you water or by adding or relocating watering devices.

Maintain your system

- Clean the filter once a month (more often if you have well water with a lot of sediment).
- Inspect the drippers occasionally to make sure they're working.
- In cold climates, prepare for winter by removing the shutoff Y-splitter, backflow preventer, controller, filter and pressure regulator and bringing them inside. Remove end plugs and drain or blow the water out of the system. Replace the caps and plug the faucet end of the tubing as well.

Buyer's Guide

DIG Irrigation Products: (800) 322-9146. www.digcorp.com.

DripWorks: (800) 522-3747. www.dripworks.com.

The Drip Store: (877) 597-1669. www.dripirrigation.com.

Raindrip: (800) FOR-DRIP. www.raindrip.com.

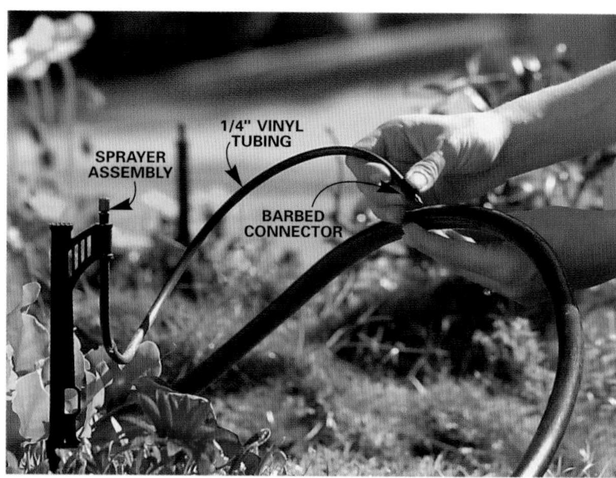

5 **PRESS a barbed connector into the hole in the 1/2-in. tubing. If the 1/4-in. tubing isn't already attached, add a length of 1/4-in. tubing to reach your dripper, sprayer or sprinkler location.**

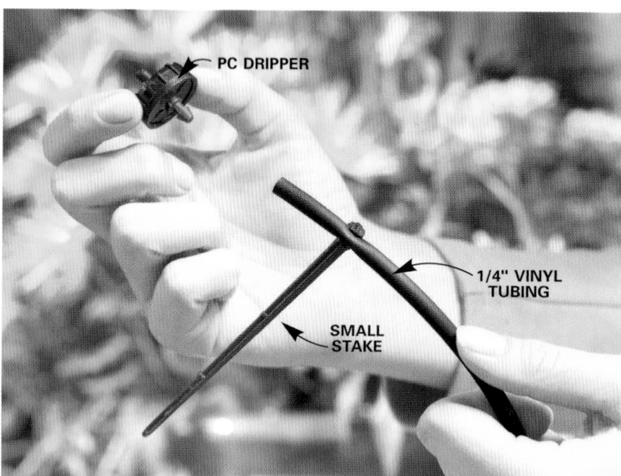

6 **PRESS pressure-compensating (PC) drippers, sprinklers or sprayers onto the end of the 1/4-in. tubing. Use a stake to support the dripper and anchor it in the root zone of the plant.**

7 **FLUSH the system by running water through it. Then use end cap fittings to close the open ends of the 1/2-in. tubing.**

Drippers, bubblers, sprinklers and sprayers

One of the first things you'll notice when you're browsing the brochures or Web sites is a wide variety of watering devices. Here are the basic types and a few things you need to know about each one. While the ones shown here are the most common, there are many other, more specialized emitters. See the micro irrigation catalogs for the other types and their uses.

Drippers (20¢ to 70¢ each)

Use these to water individual plants, or buy "inline" drippers and use them in a series with a 1/4-in. tube. Drippers work great for container plants too. They're color-coded for different flow rates between 1/2 and 4 gph. In general, use lower flow rates for less porous soil, like clay, to allow more time for the water to soak in. Buy pressure-compensating (PC) drippers to maintain a steady flow despite the water pressure.

MIKE KRIVIT

Bubblers (45¢ to 70¢ each)

A cross between drippers and sprayers, many bubblers are adjustable for flows up to 35 gph and diameters to 18 in. Since they put out more water than drippers, they're good for larger plants like roses, tomatoes and shrubs.

Soaker drip line (20¢ to 35¢ per linear foot)

Also called emitter tubing, drip line consists of 1/2-in. or 1/4-in. tubing with built-in drippers. It's available with emitters spaced different distances apart for different flow rates. Drip line is great for vegetable gardens or rows of plants. You can use it to encircle shrubs and large plants, or lay it out in a grid pattern as a substitute for sprinklers in a densely planted flower bed. Use 1/4-in. drip line for maximum flexibility.

Sprinklers (45¢ to $2 each)

These are miniature versions of sprinklers you might use in the yard. Most have flow rates between 14 and 40 gph and cover a radius of 3 to 30 ft. Since most sprinklers have a relatively high flow rate, you can't use more than about 15 or 20 in one zone of 1/2-in. tubing.

Sprayers (45¢ to $1.70 each)

These are like sprinklers without moving parts. You can choose a spray pattern from a quarter circle up to a full circle, or buy sprayers with adjustable spray patterns. They spray from 4 to 34 gph and up to a radius of about 12 ft. Use sprayers to water ground cover or densely planted flower beds.

OLD CARTRIDGE

NEW CARTRIDGE

Repair drippy showers

Constant dripping wastes water and wears on nerves

When your single-handle shower faucet drips and drips, refusing to completely turn off, don't assume you have to replace the whole faucet. Most faucets can be repaired in an hour for less than $50.

Shown here are the fixes for a cartridge-style faucet. Cartridge valves have a single handle and operate when the cartridge slides in and out. Don't confuse them with single-handle ball-style faucets, which have a dome-shaped casing under the handle.

Turn off the water at the fixture shutoff valves or at your home's main valve. Turn on a faucet to make sure the water is off. Remove the handle as shown in Photos 1 and 2. If the handle sticks, try heating it with a hair dryer set on "hot." If you still can't get it off, use a special handle puller ($10 to $20 from a plumbing parts distributor or home center).

Virtually every faucet manufacturer has a different method of securing the cartridge to the faucet body. Look for a clip or spring and remove it (Photo 3). Cartridges are often difficult to pull out. Some manufacturers

Quick tip

THE LOWDOWN ON LOW-FLOW SHOWER-HEADS. A low-flow, water-saving shower-head can easily save up to $10 a year in water and water heating costs.

1 TURN OFF the water supply to the shower. Then pry off the handle cap with a small pocketknife to expose the internal handle screw.

2 **LOOSEN and remove the handle screw. Pull off the handle and set it aside.**

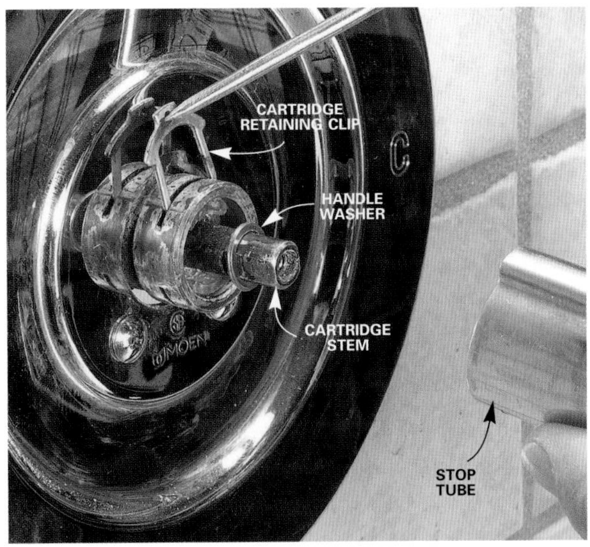

3 **PULL OFF the stop tube. Pry up the cartridge retaining clip with a small screwdriver or awl. Remove the handle washer and then twist the cartridge stem loose and pull it out with pliers.**

include a removal cap with new cartridges. Align the cap with the old cartridge ears and try to twist the cartridge loose. Then pull it out with pliers.

If you can't budge the old cartridge, you'll need a cartridge puller ($20 to $30 from a plumbing parts distributor). Make sure the one you buy works on your brand of faucet. Look on the handle or trim for the faucet brand or manufacturer. A knowledgeable person at a plumbing parts store may be able to identify the brand and model from a photo. Review Photos 4 and 5 for instructions on using a cartridge puller. Make sure you twist the cartridge loose before pulling it out (Photo 4). Take the old cartridge with you to a plumbing parts store or a home center to find an exact replacement ($15 to $25).

Lubricate the cartridge sides, O-rings, retaining clip, cartridge stem and handle screw threads with plumber's grease. Slide the new cartridge into the faucet body. Some cartridges can only be installed one way (to avoid reversing the hot and cold), so follow the enclosed instructions. Reassemble the remaining faucet components.

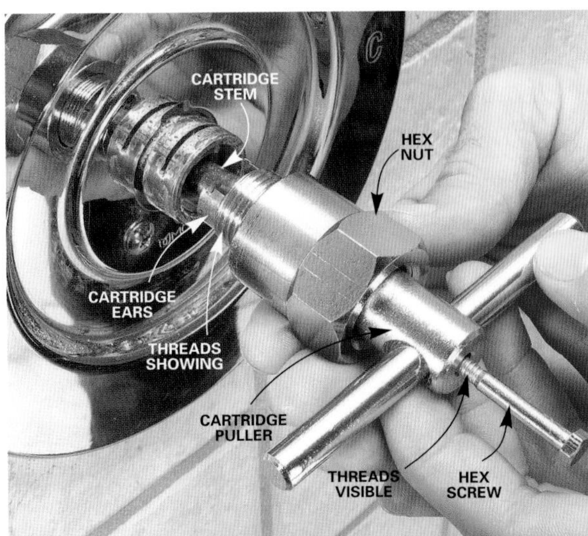

4 **IF IT'S STUCK, use a special cartridge puller. Unscrew the hex screw and hex nut until threads are visible. Slide the puller over the cartridge stem, aligning the tool ears with the cartridge notches, and twist to loosen.**

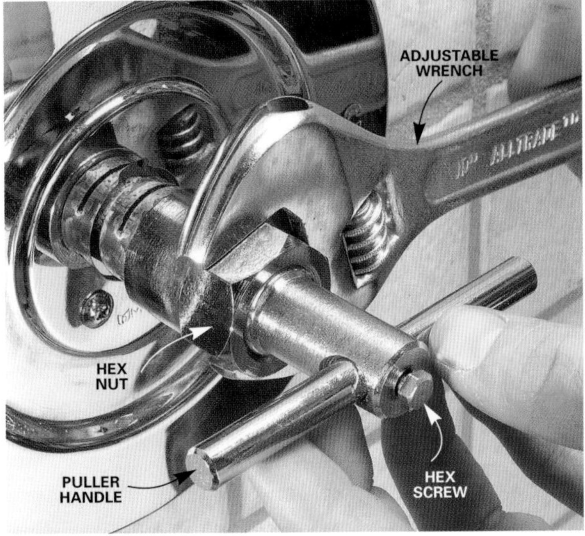

5 **TURN the hex screw by hand until it bottoms out. Snug up the hex nut by hand and tug on the cartridge puller handle. If the cartridge won't pull out, hold the puller handle steady and tighten the hex nut two full turns. Pull the cartridge out of the faucet body. Buy an identical replacement cartridge, align it properly and reassemble the parts.**

Inspect your tires!

And improve your gas mileage

Most drivers don't give their tires a second thought until they make strange noises or, worse yet, go flat and leave them stranded. Here you'll find out how to check your tires' air pressure, when to rotate tires, and the telltale signs of tire wear and what to do about it. You'll drive more safely, improve your gas mileage and extend the life of your tires.

Maintain tire pressure

Check your tire pressure regularly and give your tires a quick inspection every time you fill up with gas (photo above). Pressure is measured in pounds per square inch (psi) with a tire pressure gauge. You can buy one at any auto parts store. The $10-and-up dial and digital gauges perform better in the long run than the less-expensive pencil-style gauges. Tires typically lose pressure slowly (usually about 1 psi per month). If you neglect them, they can get dangerously low, build up excessive heat, wear unevenly and deteriorate faster—all of which spell bad handling and reduced mileage.

To get an accurate reading, check the tire pressure when the tires are "cold." Obviously

DIGITAL GAUGES

DIAL GAUGE

PENCIL GAUGE

Note: For the proper inflation pressure for your vehicle tires, look for an inflation chart on the driver's-side door post or in your manual. Front and rear pressures may differ.

"cold" can mean completely different things in a northern Minnesota winter and an Arizona summer. For tire pressure, however, it simply means the air temperature inside the tires is the same as the air temperature outside the tires. The temperature usually takes about three hours to equalize after your tires are hot from driving. For the proper inflation pressure, look in your owner's manual or look for a sticker on the driver's-side door post. Note: Extremely low temperatures (below 0 degrees F) may cause the inflation valve to stick, and all the air will leak from the tire. So if it's really cold, drive the car a few miles to warm the tires first. The reading may be a bit higher, but at least you won't be stranded.

Rotate regularly

Many auto owners know they should rotate their tires but they still don't do it. When you rotate tires from one wheel to the next, you distribute the wear more evenly over all four tires, giving them a longer life. This service is usually provided free by the tire dealer or you can get it as part of a maintenance contract for just a few dollars. Or take a half hour and do it yourself. Manufacturers differ on the rotation pattern, and the process can differ depending on whether you have a rear-wheel-, front-wheel- or four-wheel-drive auto, so check your owner's manual. Most vehicles should have their tires rotated every 4,000 to 8,000 miles, or about every other oil change.

Watch for uneven wear

Check the condition of your tire treads every month or so and watch for the telltale signs of uneven wear (see Figure B).

Figure A Suggested tire rotation

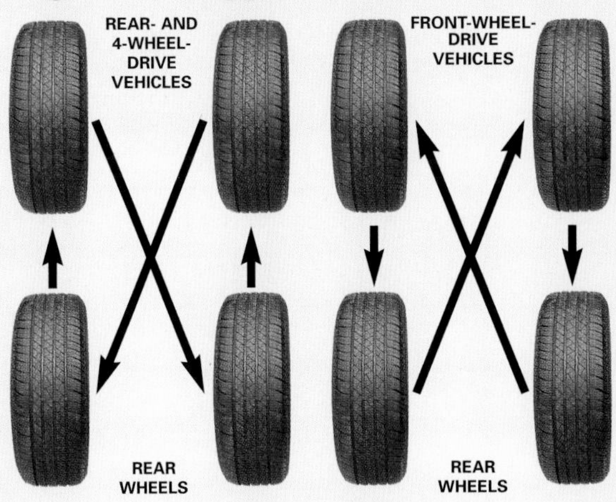

Note: If your vehicle has directional wheels or tires, rotate them front to back on the same side of the vehicle. Check with your dealer or tire manufacturer if you're unsure.

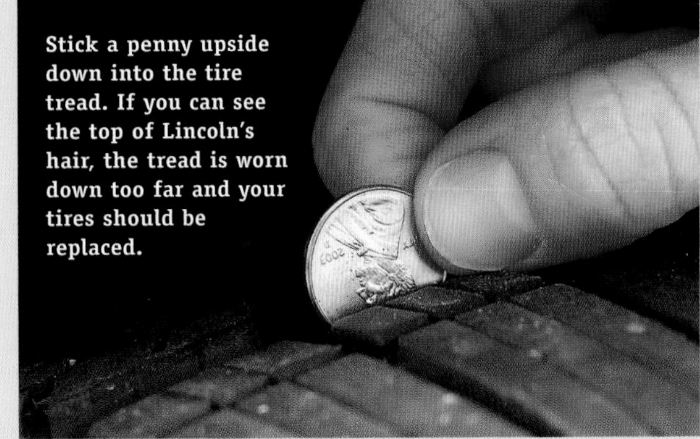

Stick a penny upside down into the tire tread. If you can see the top of Lincoln's hair, the tread is worn down too far and your tires should be replaced.

Figure B Reading tread wear patterns

If your tires show wear on the center of the tread only, you have over-inflated tires. Check the tread depth and replace the tires if necessary or fill them to the proper pressure.

If your tires show wear on the outer edges of the tread, you're probably driving on underinflated tires. Check the tread wear and replace the tires if necessary or fill them to the proper pressure.

If your tires are worn on either the inside or outside of the tread, you'll need to have your vehicle's alignment checked.

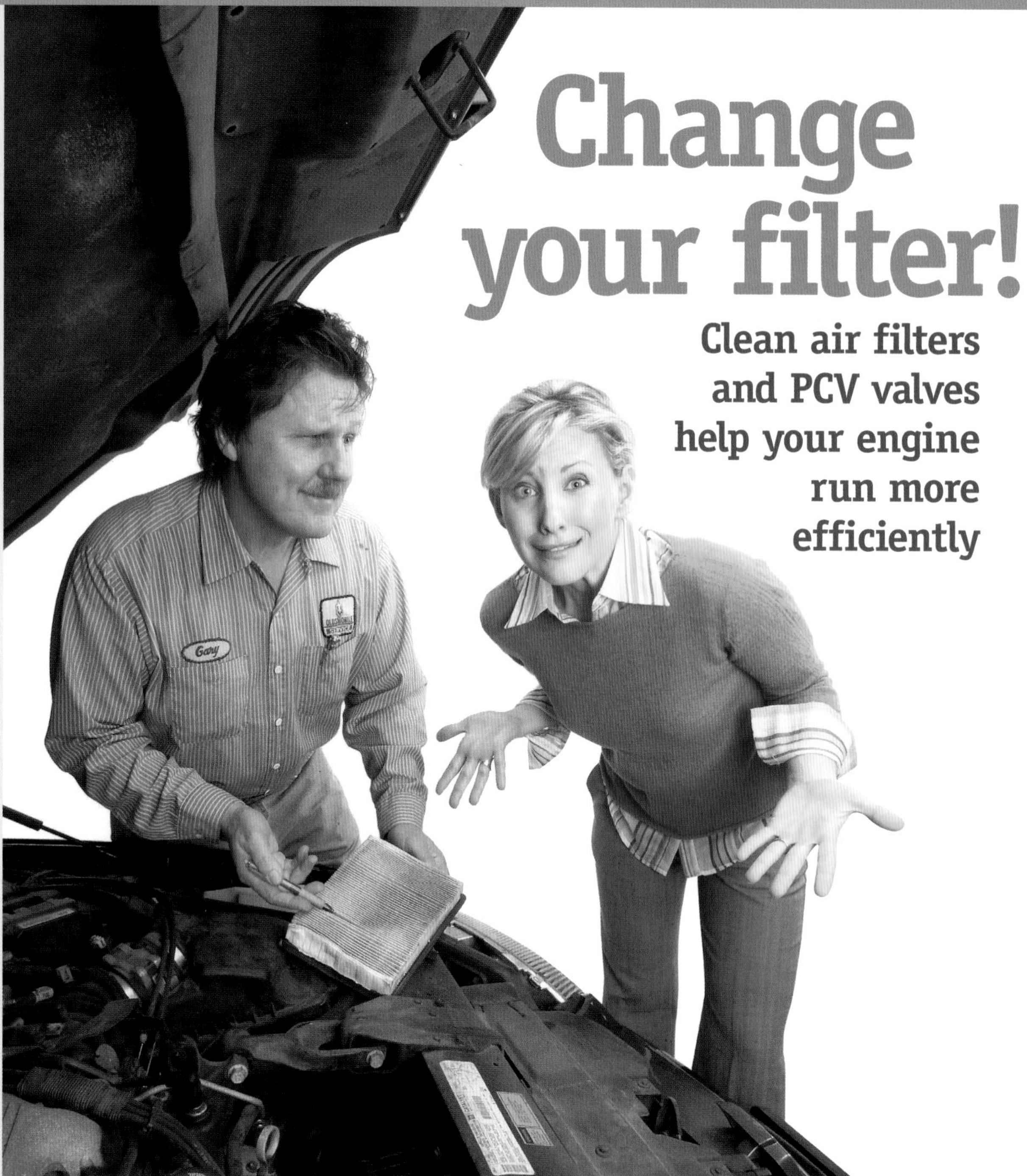

Change your filter!

Clean air filters and PCV valves help your engine run more efficiently

You take your car in for an oil change. The work is almost done when the technician comes out to talk to you. He's holding your air filter and PCV valve and recommending that you replace both because they "look dirty." Without missing a beat, he explains how critical the air filter is to the efficient operation of your car. He tells you that a clogged air filter, or one that's nearly clogged, can easily cost you 10 percent in gas mileage. With gas prices going through the roof, he adds, replacement will probably save you more than the cost of the filter. Plus, a dirty PCV valve, well, that's never a good thing. Then he waits for your decision. It's tough to make up your mind about a $25 air filter and an $11.95 PC-whatchamacallit valve when you don't know what to look for.

It's not difficult to check the air filter and PCV valve yourself. Here's what you need to know:

Air filter check

First, ignore the dirt on the leading edge of the air filter pleats. All air filters accumulate dirt on the leading edge in as little as a few thousand miles. Yet most last for about 12,000 miles. You want to know how much dirt has penetrated deep into the pleats. To test the true condition of your filter, hold a shop light behind it. See how much light passes through the inner pleats and compare yours with the three sample photos (below, right). The filter shown on the left is totally clogged and cost the owner a fortune in wasted gas. The filter in the middle shows a clogged area, but the rest of the filter has decent light transmission. It's borderline, and the owner could probably squeeze 2,000 to 3,000 more miles out of it. It should be replaced at the next oil change interval. The filter on the right shows how much light passes through a new filter.

1 **FOLLOW the black plastic duct to the air filter box. Unscrew or unsnap the latches. Remove the filter. Note that the screen always faces the engine. The pleats face the incoming air.**

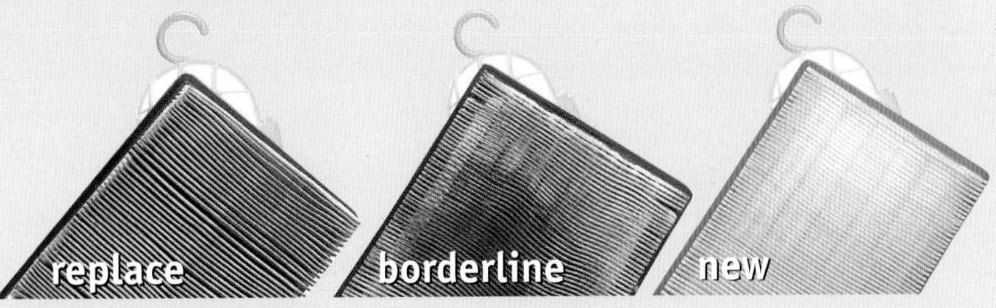

2 **HOLD the filter over a shoplight and compare it with the photos above. Reinstall or replace.**

The PCV story

The PCV (positive crankcase ventilation) valve is a one-way valve that recycles crankcase gases back into the engine to burn. A plugged PCV valve can result in a rough idle and poor mileage. Worse, it can cause costly oil leaks. Always follow your manufacturer's replacement recommendations. And never replace a PCV valve simply because it "looks dirty." All used PCV valves look dirty. Photos 1 and 2 show two ways to check its real condition.

1 **REMOVE the PCV valve from its grommet. With the engine off, shake the valve. If it's good, you'll hear a solid clicking sound.**

2 **OR, CHECK it in place with the engine running. Pull the PCV valve from its housing and place your thumb over the PCV valve opening. You should feel it click. If the click sounds or feels mushy, replace the valve.**

SPARK PLUG BOOT

Worn plug wires and boots can start to leak voltage, resulting in poor combustion and lousy gas mileage.

Replace spark plug wires before they wear out

1 USE your digital camera to record the route of each wire. They have to go back the same way.

Do spark plug wires wear out? You bet. That's because spark plug wires aren't actually made of wire. They're made of delicate carbon fibers. Over time, the carbon breaks down and the fibers separate, causing high electrical resistance. High resistance degrades the spark, resulting in poor combustion, misfires, lousy gas mileage and ultimately a glowing "Check Engine" light. If you let that condition go on too long, the wires can start to leak voltage to nearby engine parts, causing arcing, severe performance problems, and even ignition component failures.

That's why it pays to replace your spark plug wires before they wear out. Change them during spark plug changes (whenever your owner's manual recommends, or between 60,000 and 100,000 miles). Here you'll learn which materials and tools you'll need and all the steps required to do a quality job of your own. You'll save about $80 on shop labor charges and ensure that you won't be

2 **UNCOIL the new spark plug wires and sort them by length.**

3 **USING a wire puller, twist the boot to break the seal from the plug and then pull off the old plug. Match the old wire length to the new wire.**

4 **APPLY dielectric grease to both the plug and the coil/distributor end of each wire. Route the wire and press it onto the plug/coil tower until it clicks.**

Wire Puller

Lisle 51750 Adjustable Spark Plug Wire Puller, $22.95.

Dielectric grease

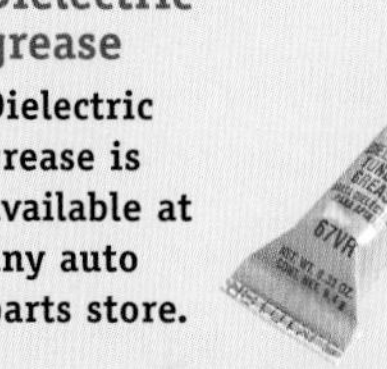

Dielectric grease is available at any auto parts store.

Wire options

The premium replacement exactly matches the factory connectors. The economy wire doesn't.

Economy brand, $22.99

Premium brand, $41.99

Factory

in for the costly diagnostic fees associated with worn spark plug wires. The whole job is pretty easy and will only take about an hour.

Before you start the job, use a digital camera to record how the wires attach to the coil/distributor/coil pack and the path they take to each plug. Notice how each wire wraps around the others and how they are arranged in the plastic retaining clips. They're arranged that way for a reason: to prevent cross-firing and interference with other engine sensors. So be sure to put them back in the same manner.

When you're at the auto parts store, buy a premium set of wires. The economy wire sets don't match the factory connectors, and the individual wires can be either too long or too short for some vehicles. The premium set, shown here, carried a lifetime warranty; the economy set, only two years. Next, invest in a spark plug wire puller tool (Photo 3). A wire puller tool makes removal much easier and saves a lot of busted knuckles. To use it, simply grasp the boot with the rounded jaws, rotate left and right, then pull straight out. This is a tool that's worth the investment.

Some manufacturers precoat the insides of the plug and coil/distributor boots with dielectric silicone grease. The grease prevents the boots from sticking to the plug or coil/distributor. It also provides an additional layer of insulation to prevent voltage from traveling down the inside of the boot. If your set isn't precoated, purchase a small tube of silicone grease and run a bead around the inside of each boot.

Then remove one old wire at a time and match it to a replacement wire of the same length. Route the new wire and push the boot onto the plug or coil/distributor until you feel it click. Repeat the procedure for each wire.

Saving Energy:

Nearly 25 cents of each energy dollar goes to heating the water used in washing machines, dishwashers, showers and sinks. For the most part, water heaters are kept "out of sight and out of mind," hidden away in the basement, garage or far corner of a utility closet. But paying even a little attention to them can yield big energy savings. Lowering the temperature setting to 120 degrees F will both save energy and help prevent scalding accidents. Wrapping your water heater in an insulated jacket can further reduce your water heating costs by up to 10 percent.

Appliances and water heaters that carry the ENERGY STAR label or a higher "energy factor" number may cost more in the short run, but will help conserve energy and money in the long run.

Appliances & Water Heaters

New-generation water heaters

Power-vented units cost more but save big in the long run

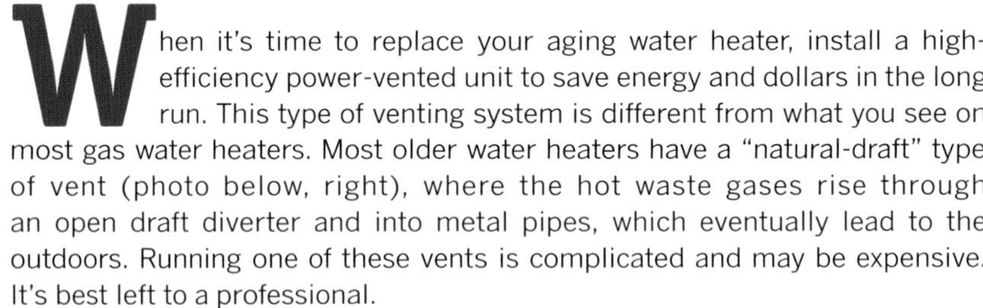

BLOWER

POWER-VENTED WATER HEATER

When it's time to replace your aging water heater, install a high-efficiency power-vented unit to save energy and dollars in the long run. This type of venting system is different from what you see on most gas water heaters. Most older water heaters have a "natural-draft" type of vent (photo below, right), where the hot waste gases rise through an open draft diverter and into metal pipes, which eventually lead to the outdoors. Running one of these vents is complicated and may be expensive. It's best left to a professional.

In contrast, a power-vented type (left) relies on a fan to blow the exhaust gases out. Since this method doesn't rely on the natural buoyancy of hot air, the vent pipes don't have to go upward. They can go out horizontally, which usually makes them much easier to install. Further, the fan dilutes the exhaust with cooler air so you can run the vents with easy-to-assemble PVC pipe. Power venting is an especially good solution for more energy-efficient, tightly built homes, where a good natural draft is difficult to establish.

However, you should be aware of several drawbacks: (1) You may notice the sound of the fan. Ideally the water heater will be in a room away from the main living area so it doesn't become bothersome. (2) You have to provide a standard electrical receptacle near the unit to supply power for the fan. (3) You have to make sure you have adequate "makeup" air to replace the air being blown out. (4) And finally, power-vented water heaters cost at least 50 percent more than a natural-draft water heater. Figure somewhere in the $450 to $650 range, plus installation. You can find power-vented water heaters wherever water heaters are sold; almost every major water heater manufacturer makes them.

If you decide to install one yourself, read the instructions carefully and make sure to follow all venting procedures. And call your local building department and ask if you need a plumbing permit to do the work.

The hot exhaust gases from a natural-draft water heater rise through an open draft diverter and out through a metal duct.

tip Set your water heater's dial to 120 degrees F. If the dial doesn't have numbers, check the water temperature with a cooking thermometer. Higher temperatures increase sediment buildup and the risk of scalding injuries.

A more energy-efficient water heater

Simple maintenance = increased efficiency and life span

Water heaters often work perfectly for a decade or more without any care, so they're easy to neglect. But a few minutes of TLC once a year pays off by extending the tank's life span and maintaining your water heater's efficiency and safety.

First, test the pressure-relief valve located on the top or side of the water heater (Photo 1). This valve opens automatically if the pressure inside the tank gets too high. (Excess pressure can actually cause the tank to explode.) If the valve doesn't release water when you lift the lever, replace the valve ($12 at home centers and hardware stores). Replacement is simple; turn off the water, drain the tank, unscrew the discharge pipe and then unscrew the old valve. Wrap the threads of the new valve with sealant tape and screw it in. If your valve is several years old and has never been tested, it might leak after you test it. In that case, replace the valve.

Next, close the shutoff valve on the cold water supply pipe that feeds the water heater. Then turn on the hot water at any faucet to release the pressure inside the heater's tank. Leave the faucet on until you finish your work. If you have an electric heater, turn off the power at the main panel. With a gas heater, turn the gas control dial to "Off."

Drain the tank to flush out sediments that have settled to the bottom of the tank. Sediment buildup shortens the life of your water heater and adds to your energy bill by reducing its efficiency. Draining 2 or 3 gallons of water is usually enough to flush out sediments, but always let the water flow until you no longer see particles in the bucket. **Caution: The water is scalding hot.**

Don't worry about any gurgling or groaning noises coming from the heater; it's just air entering the system as water drains out. If the drain valve won't close tightly when you're done, drain the tank completely, unscrew the old valve and screw in a new one ($8). To restart the water heater, open the shutoff valve and let the hot water run at any faucet to purge air from the system. Then turn on the power or relight the pilot.

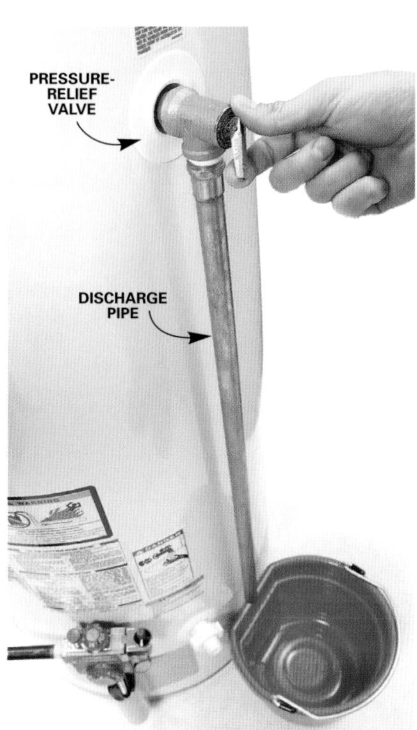

1 PLACE a bucket below the discharge pipe and gently lift the lever on the pressure-relief valve to test it.

2 OPEN the drain valve slowly and let the water run until it's clear and free of sediments. CAUTION: The water is hot!

Electric water heater tune-up

Bad elements and sediment buildup affect efficiency

If you're getting lukewarm water from your electric water heater, most likely one of your water heater's two heating elements—upper or lower—has gone bad. And since the lower element does up to 90 percent of the heating, that one usually wears out first. If you're comfortable with plumbing and electrical tools, you can do the repair yourself, but if you're at all hesitant, call a plumber.

First, shut off the power to the water heater at the fuse or breaker box. In almost every case, you'll remove two fuses or click two breaker handles (they may be pinned together). At the water heater, remove the two access panels and use a voltage meter, neon voltage indicator or voltage-sensing device to make sure there's no voltage running through any of the wires. This is no place to fool around; high-voltage wires, damp floors and water create a dangerous work setting. Make certain there's no power!

Disconnect the two wires attached to the element. Use a water heater continuity tester to test each element (Photo 1). Attach the alligator clip to one screw and touch the probe to the other screw; no light indicates a burned-out element. Perform a second test. Keep the alligator clip in place and touch the probe to the metal plate surrounding the element. If the element is shorted out, the tester bulb will light up.

To replace the element, keep the power off, open the nearest hot water faucet, then drain the unit through a hose connected to the drain valve. Remove the bad element (Photo 2), which may be held in place with four bolts or screwed directly into the tank. It may require a special element wrench for removal. Take the element to a home center or appliance parts store and exactly match the wattage, voltage, length and mounting style of the old element. The one shown cost $8. Install the new element and gasket (Photo 3), reconnect the wires, close the drain valve, refill the tank and check for leaks. If all systems are go, you can turn the power back on.

Unpolished stainless steel elements, specially designed to resist lime buildup and burnout, cost three times as much as the standard element shown, but come with a lifetime warranty. These dark gray, often wavy or U-shaped elements, are a wise investment for homeowners who get their water from a well or other water source high in lime.

There are other, less common causes of lukewarm water. The thermostat controlling each element can go bad, with the upper one being the most likely culprit.

1. Test the element

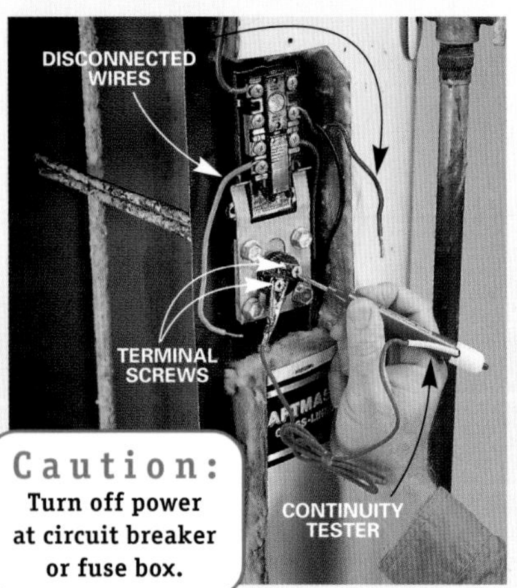

Caution: Turn off power at circuit breaker or fuse box.

2. Remove bad element

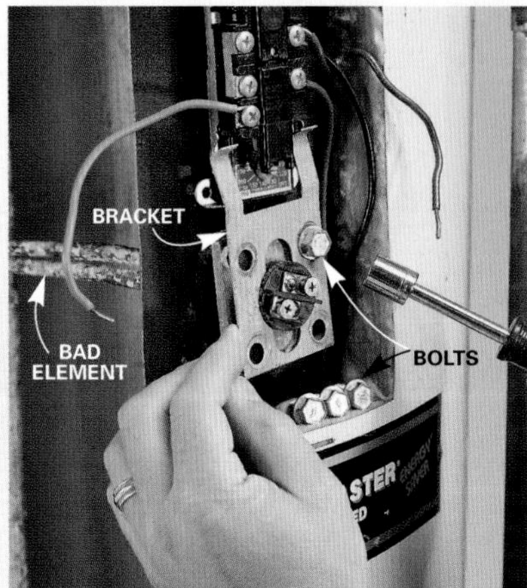

3. Install new element

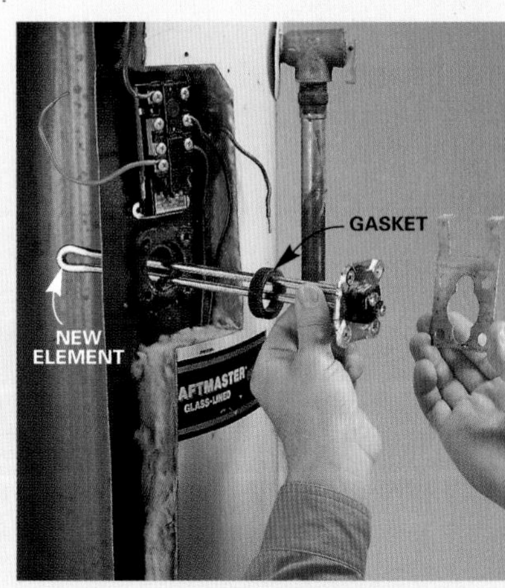

Sediment can lower the efficiency of your water heater. Drain tank and sediment every 6 to 12 months.

SEDIMENT
DRAIN VALVE

Some continuity testers come with instructions on how to conduct a thermostat test. Replacing the thermostat doesn't require draining the tank.

The dip tube can also break off, allowing the cold water to feed into the top of the tank rather than the bottom. This cold water scoots right out the hot water line, rather than starting at the bottom where it gets warmed.

Occasionally, wires leading to the heater get disconnected—but tracking this down is absolutely a pro-only task.

HOT WATER OUTLET PIPE
Distributes hot water throughout house.
COLD WATER INLET PIPE
COLD WATER SHUTOFF VALVE
Shut this off before draining the tank for repairs. Power must be turned off first or elements will burn out.
240-VOLT WIRING
Circuit will be protected by two fuses or circuit breakers.
ELECTRICAL JUNCTION BOX
PRESSURE RELIEF VALVE
Provides safe outlet for overheated or overpressured water to escape.
UPPER THERMOSTAT AND HIGH TEMPERATURE CUTOFF
Thermostat senses water temperature and controls heating element.
OVERFLOW PIPE
Must terminate within 18" of floor for safety.
DIP TUBE
Directs cold water to bottom of tank where it's heated, then rises. In rare cases, tube can break and must be replaced.
LOWER THERMOSTAT
Water temperature (at both thermostats) can be raised or lowered with adjustment screw. The recommended setting is 120 degrees F.
DRAIN VALVE
Remove sediment by attaching hose and draining tank every 6 to 12 months.
Caution: Turn off power first!
ACCESS PANEL
UPPER HEATING ELEMENT
In most units, only one element is on at any given time. Lower element clicks on during non- or low-use periods. Upper element clicks on during heavy use.
FOAM INSULATION
ANODE ROD
Sacrifices itself; it corrodes, rather than the tank. Replacement rod can be installed.
TANK
Most are porcelain or glass-lined steel. If welded seams leak, the entire unit must be replaced.
LOWER HEATING ELEMENT
Does up to 90 percent of all the heating, thus most likely to wear out first.
SEDIMENT AND SCALE
Depending on where your water comes from and how it's treated, your tank may have only a thin layer or several inches of it.

Gas water heater tune-up

Flush the tank, fix broken dip tubes, save energy

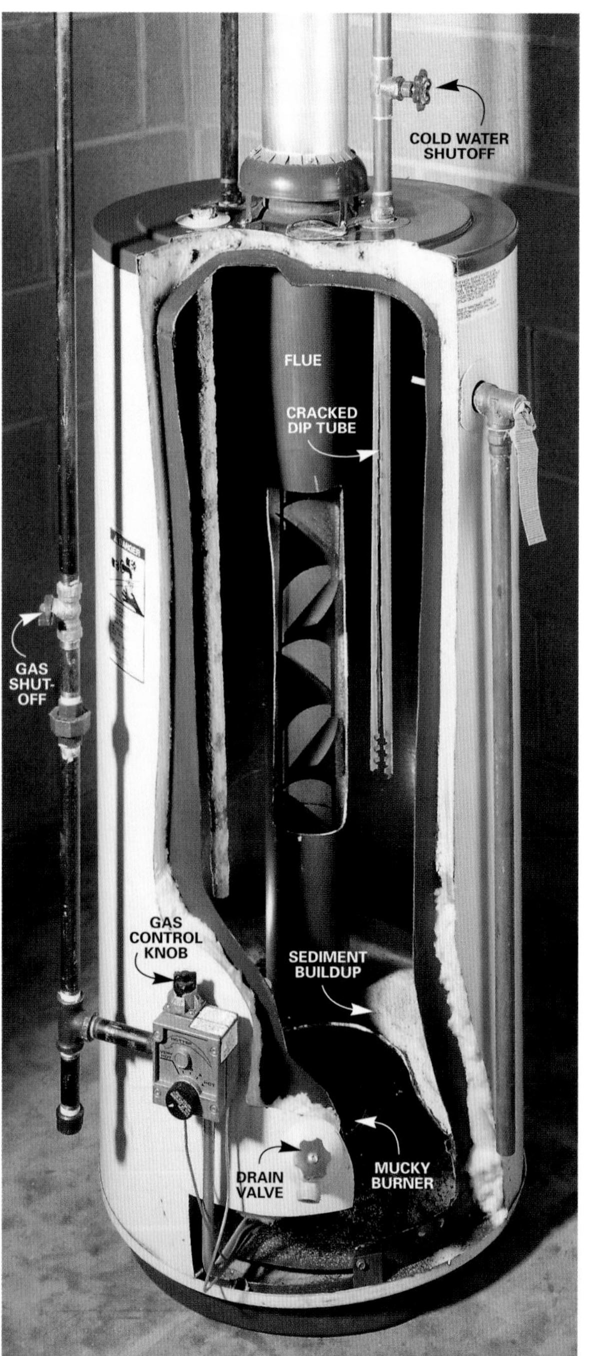

The most likely cause of a sudden hot water shortage from a gas water heater is a broken dip tube. But you should also clean the burner and give the tank a good flushing annually to get the most efficiency and life from your water heater.

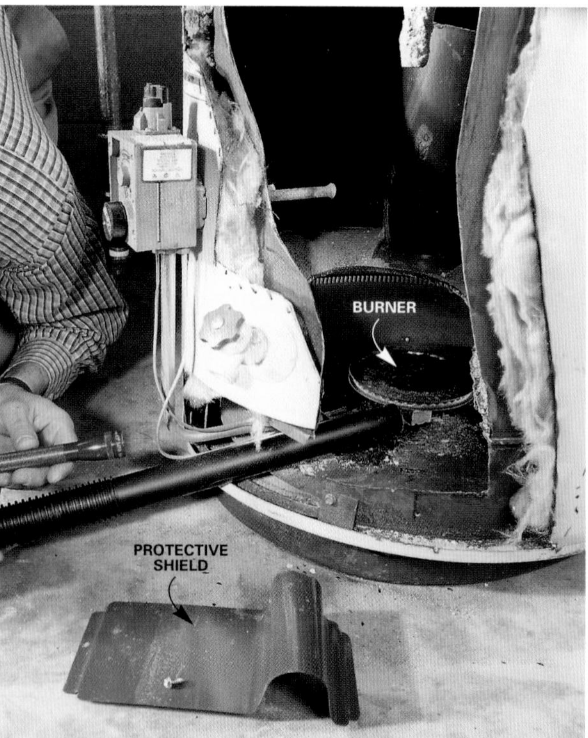

USE a vacuum to clean loose dust, soot and flakes of rust from the burner. These deposits can cause poor combustion, reducing the burner's efficiency.

Quick tip

ELECTRIC VS. GAS WATER HEATERS

In some areas of the country, electric water heaters cost almost three times as much to operate as their natural-gas counterparts. When it's time to replace your electric water heater, consider converting to natural gas or propane.

1

Replace a broken dip tube

The dip tube, which is made of plastic and held in place by a built-in flange, carries the incoming cold water to the bottom of the water heater tank. When the dip tube breaks, cold water enters the tank at the top, mixes with the hot, and makes it seem as though you have very little hot water.

Consider replacing your straight dip tube with one that's curved. It will slow down the buildup of sediment by agitating the particles and keeping them suspended so they are flushed out.

ENERGY STAR WATER HEATERS

Currently there are no ENERGY STAR standards for water heaters. For information on selecting an energy-efficient unit, visit www.eere.energy.gov

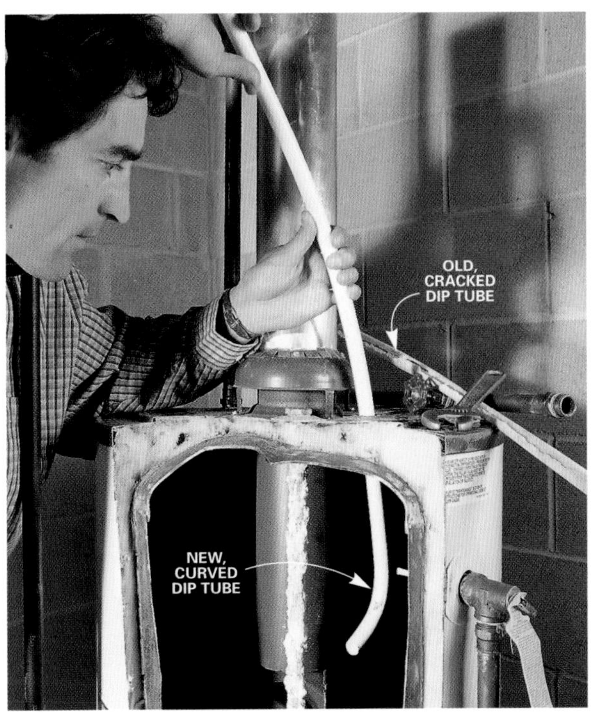

Replace the dip tube by first disconnecting the cold water supply. If you're lucky, there will be a union, which makes disconnecting it easy. You may have to cut the 3/4-in. copper pipe and sweat a joint later. Dig out the old dip tube with your finger. The tube may be cracked like the one in the photo above, or it may be broken or even missing.

2

Flush the tank

Most plumbers will tell you that sediment buildup reduces the capacity of your water heater and lowers its efficiency. Sediment buildup can also contribute to early corrosion and tank failure. That's why it's a good idea to flush the tank annually, especially if your water contains a lot of sediment.

Before you flush your water heater, turn the gas control knob to "Off" and let the water cool. Plan on replacing the drain valve with a 3/4-in. full-port ball valve with water hose adapter and a 3/4-in. x 3-in. galvanized nipple. This setup, coupled with a curved dip tube, will increase the water flow, provide a large opening for debris to escape, and generally help clean the tank better.

Caution: Lever-type ball valves like the one shown can be easily opened by children.

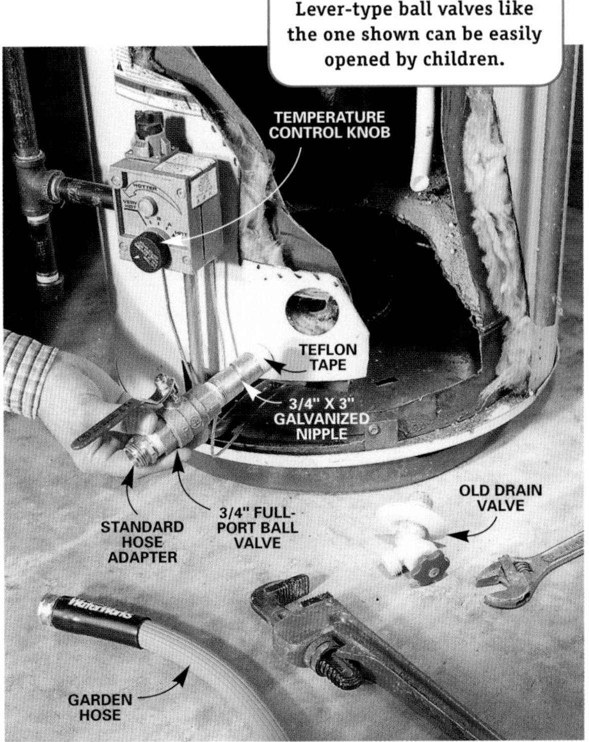

Drain as much water as possible with the factory valve. Then, remove it and install the new valve. Turn the water on and keep the drain valve open. The curved tube will agitate the particles and help with the flushing.

Save energy with a tankless water heater

Tankless water heaters use 30 to 50 percent less energy than units with tanks, saving a typical family about $100 or more per year, depending on water usage. Tankless units (also called "on demand" units) heat water only when you turn on the faucet. They usually operate on natural gas or propane. The main advantage is that they eliminate the extra cost of keeping 40 to 50 gallons of water hot in a storage tank, so you waste less energy. They also offer a continuous supply of hot water, which is ideal for filling a big hot tub or a whirlpool. They're more compact than a standard water heater and mount on a wall.

The primary disadvantage is the upfront cost. The smaller units ($500) that you often see won't produce enough hot water to serve most households. They'll only serve one faucet at a time—a problem if you want to shower while the dishwasher is running. Larger units that can handle the demand of a whole family run $1,000 and up. (Regular tank water heaters cost $300 to $500, and they last 10 to 12 years, compared with 20 years for a tankless unit.)

But because tankless units have high-powered burners, they also have special venting requirements (a dedicated, sealed vent system, which requires professional installation). Natural gas burners often need a larger diameter gas pipe, which could easily add $500 to $1,000 to the initial installation cost.

The bottom line: When you're pricing a unit, be sure to get an estimate or firm bid on installation costs. This is not a do-it-yourself project unless you have pro-level skills. You can find tankless water heaters at many home centers and plumbing specialty stores. Ask if the unit qualifies for a federal tax credit.

Figure A
Tankless water heater details

When a hot-water tap is opened, the heating elements turn on. Water is heated as it flows through the heat exchanger.

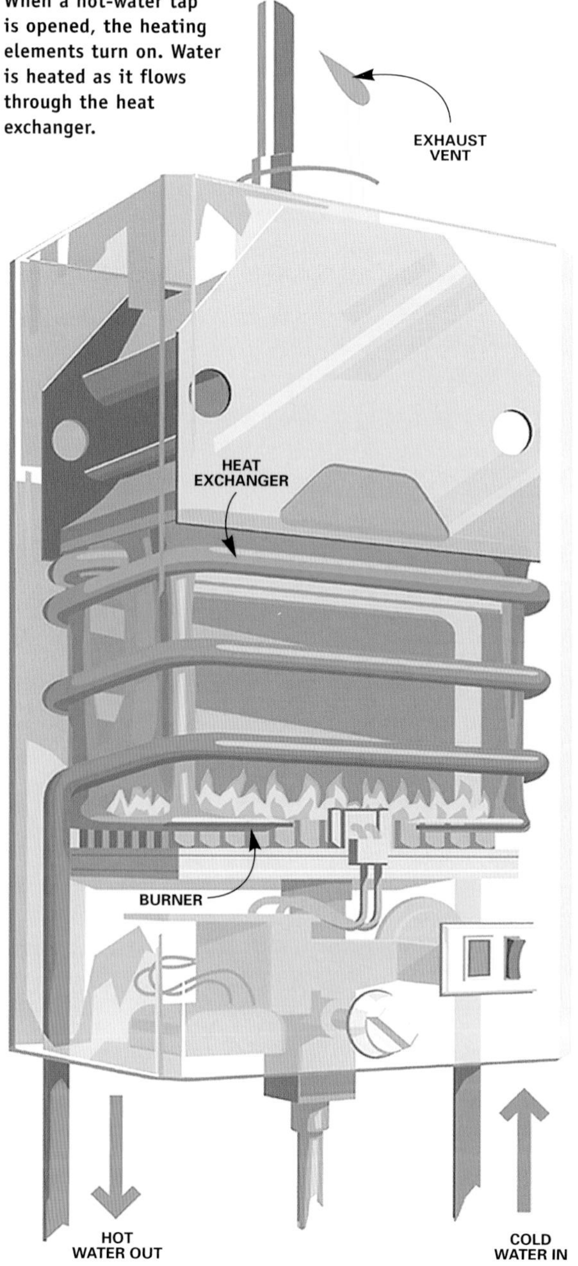

5 minutes to a more efficient refrigerator

You can eliminate more than 70 percent of service calls with this simple cleaning step. Skip this chore and you'll be contributing to your appliance repairman's retirement fund. Not to mention handing over $5 to $10 a month extra to your utility company because the fridge isn't running efficiently. Do it twice a year or more often if you have shedding pets. Their fur clogs up the coils fast.

Condenser coils are located on the back of the fridge or across the bottom. These coils cool and condense the refrigerant. When the coils are clogged with dirt and dust, they can't efficiently release heat. The result is your compressor works harder and longer than it was designed to, using more energy and shortening the life of your fridge. Clean the coils with a coil cleaning brush and vacuum. A coil cleaning brush ($6) does a thorough job and will easily pay for itself (look for one at appliance parts stores). The brush is bendable to fit in tight areas. It can be used for cleaning your dehumidifier and air conditioner coils too.

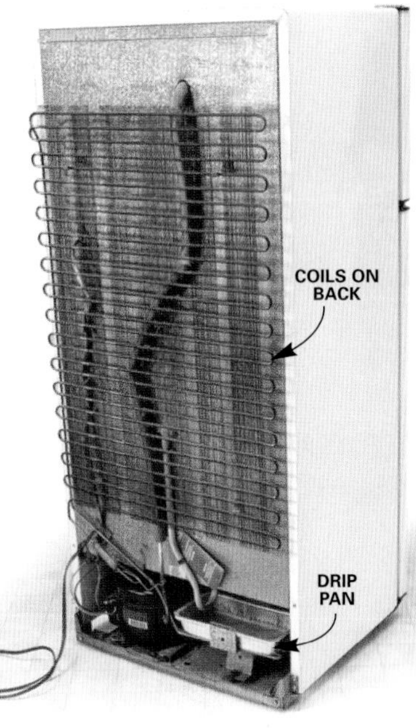

Some refrigerators have the coils on the back of the unit. Brush and vacuum these coils in the same manner as coils found under a refrigerator.

Quick tip

OLD REFRIGERATORS GIVE THE CHILLS

Refrigerators account for more than 15 percent of the electrical usage in most homes. The good news is, today's refrigerators use less than one-half the amount of electricity used by those made 20 years ago.

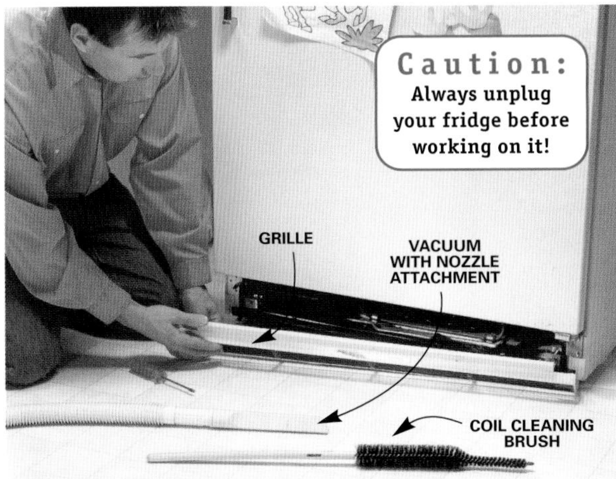

1 UNSNAP the grille at the bottom of the refrigerator to access the coils. If your coils are located on the back, you'll have to roll the fridge out to get at them.

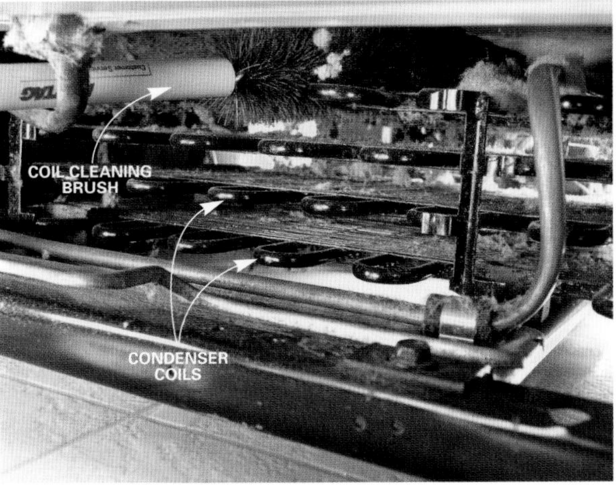

2 CLEAN the coils with a special coil cleaning brush to loosen the dirt and dust. Vacuum the coils as you brush. Be careful not to bend the fan blades. A gentle brushing will do the job.

Maximize your dryer's efficiency

The most likely cause of inefficient clothes drying is a buildup of lint that's constricting the flow of air that carries away moisture, and there are two reasons you should be worried about it. First, a dryer running at 50 percent efficiency means a lot of wasted energy dollars. Second, every year in the United States, 13,000 fires are reported that start at or in the dryer (both gas and electric), and lint buildup is one culprit. To remove that lint and get maximum efficiency from your dryer, first unplug it, then take the following steps.

Minimize obstructions in the duct system by:

1. Replacing any flexible ducting, especially the Slinky-type plastic stuff, with 4-in. rigid metal duct. The smooth sides of rigid metal duct allow the best airflow.
2. Joining the metal duct with metal duct tape instead of sheet metal screws, which can catch lint.
3. Using the fewest 90-degree elbows possible. Every elbow creates as much resistance as 10 ft. of straight duct.
4. Insulating any part of the dryer duct that passes through an unheated area. Otherwise, condensation will form inside the duct, snare the lint and greatly increase lint buildup.
5. Installing a 4 x 4-in. vent hood, instead of one with the standard 2-1/2-in. opening. Installing this larger vent hood is the equivalent of shortening the total duct run by 6 ft.

Clean the dryer's vent system once a year following these three steps:

1. Sweep the inside of the external dryer duct with a 4-in. dryer vent brush (see photo). Get this brush for $15 at an appliance parts store.
2. Vacuum the dryer's lint chute with a homemade attachment made with a piece of 3/4- or 1-in. garden hose fixed through a hole in the plastic cap from a can of spray paint (see photo above, right). In dryers with a top-mounted filter screen, lint tends to collect at the bottom of the lint chute in front of the blower.
3. Scrub the lint screen with a brush and soap and water. Even if you fastidiously remove the lint after each cycle, using fabric softeners in the washer clogs the mesh and restricts airflow.

Vacuum the area under the drum inside the dryer once a year.

This is the real key to avoiding dryer fires and making your motor last. For dryers with a front-mounted lint screen, just remove the kick plate from the bottom front. For dryers with a top-mounted screen (like the one shown), remove the two screws that hold the lint screen chute to the dryer lid. Lift the lid, then remove the two screws at the top of the sides to release the dryer front. Once you have access, use a vacuum with a brush attachment to clean the dryer floor and the motor. If you have a gas dryer, be especially careful. The igniter (glow arm) is extremely fragile. Consult your dryer's instruction manual to locate this delicate piece, then stay away from it.

Note: If the onset of your dryer's inefficiency problem is sudden, check the vent hood outside. Your dryer's vent hood should have a flap that opens only when the dryer is in use. When the flap is missing or stuck open, critters are likely to use this handy shelter to build heated nests.

METAL DUCT TAPE
90° ELBOW
4" X 4" VENT HOOD
RIGID METAL DUCT
HOMEMADE GARDEN HOSE ADAPTER
DRYER LID
LOCATION OF DRYER-FRONT SCREWS
LINT CHUTE
METAL DUCT TAPE
WHERE LINT GATHERS

Quick tip

DRYER VENT LOGIC
If your outside dryer vent doesn't close tightly, replace it. A vent that seals well will keep energy-wasting cold air out in the winter, and unwanted warm air out in the summer.

Energy-Saving Q&A

Better washers and dryers

Q Both my washer and dryer are on their last legs. I'm particularly interested in the pros and cons of a front-load washing machine. What's the story?

A You'll pay more up front for a front-load washing machine, but when it comes to performance and energy savings, they can't be beat. Front-load machines, like the ENERGY STAR-qualified GE model shown below, use less water, so it requires less energy per load to heat the water. It also has a faster spin cycle, which means the clothes come out drier and need to spend less time in the dryer—saving more energy.

Front-load washers offer other bonuses. They're quieter, gentler on clothes (since there's no agitator), handle unbalanced loads better and have a larger capacity.

Quick tip

ATTENTION ALL DRYER SHOPPERS
When shopping for a new dryer, look for one with a moisture sensor that shuts off the machine automatically when your clothes are dry. You'll save energy—and extra wear and tear on your clothes.

Feel cooler this summer with a dehumidifier tune-up

A dehumidifier removes humidity from a home by drawing warm, moist air over cool condenser coils inside the unit. Then, in the same way that humidity collects on a cold glass of lemonade, this humidity drips off the condenser coils into a water collection pan and drains out a hose into a floor drain or fills the pan for emptying. Invest about 30 minutes to improve your dehumidifier's performance and efficiency by conducting a seasonal checkup.

Caution: Begin all appliance maintenance by unplugging the power cord.

1 UNPLUG your appliance Before disassembling the unit, thoroughly read about the maintenance procedures in your owner's manual. Scrub mineral scale out of the water pan and check the drain hose (if used) for kinks.

For this dehumidifier model, pull off the humidistat knob, and then unscrew the hex head screws around the unit to release the front grille and cabinet cover from the chassis. Remove the rear grille and the water pan, then lift off the cabinet cover to gain access to the inner parts (Photo 1).

One reason condenser coils ice up is that accumulated dust "insulates" them and reduces their cooling efficiency, forcing the condenser to work overtime. Prevent this by vacuuming the coils, then any other interior parts (Photo 2). If your unit has a washable filter inside the rear grille or adjacent to the coils, clean it—plus all plastic parts on and inside the unit—with warm water and mild detergent.

tip Avoid another cause of condenser coil icing by running the dehumidifier only in spaces where the temperature is at least 65 degrees F.

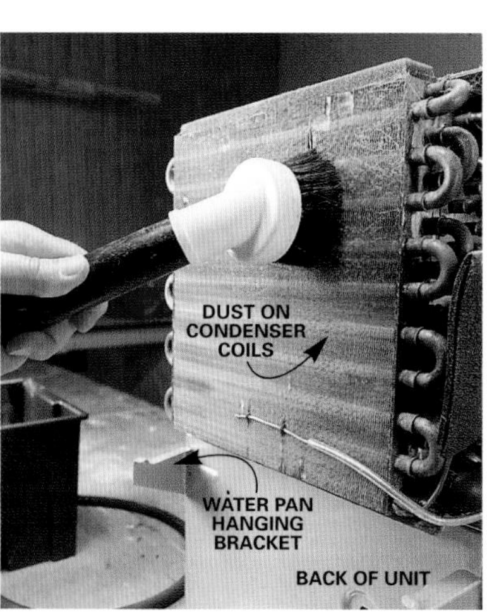

2 VACUUM the condenser coils and other parts inside the dehumidifier. For a better job, wash the coils down with warm water and mild detergent, then thoroughly rinse and dry them.

Dehumidifiers have a pressure-sensitive spring at the back of the cabinet that flattens as the water pan fills up. If the pan is spilling over, change the position of the spring to allow the shutoff switch to activate well before the pan is full (Photo 3).

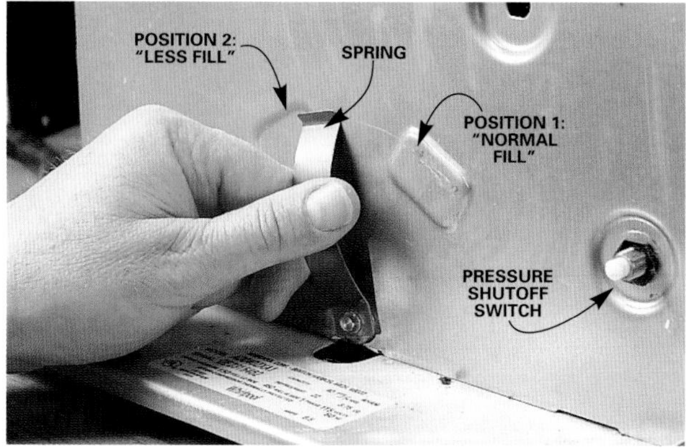

3 CORRECT water pan spillover (on units without drain hoses) by changing the position of the pressure spring to "Position 2." When the pan is full, the spring fully deflects—activating the shutoff switch and killing the power to the unit until the pan is emptied.

Feel warmer this winter with a humidifier tune-up

When heating season approaches, it's time to tune up the portable humidifiers you use to add moisture to the dry air inside your home. Periodically, you need to remove the mineral scale that builds up on the humidifier's electrical heater element and in the water reservoir pan.

The more fouled a heater element becomes with mineral scale, the less efficiently it vaporizes water. Eventually, the element builds up so much scale it stops working. Don't throw it away or buy another humidifier. Invest about 30 minutes of elbow grease and a dollar's worth of white vinegar to get your humidifier up and running. Afterward, clean off accumulated scale once a month to keep it running efficiently.

Most portable humidifiers can be tuned up by following cleaning steps similar to those in Photos 1 – 3. Your humidifier may differ from the one shown, however, so check your owner's manual.

tip Work carefully around the heating element so it doesn't get damaged. Don't chip mineral scale off it with a hammer or screwdriver.

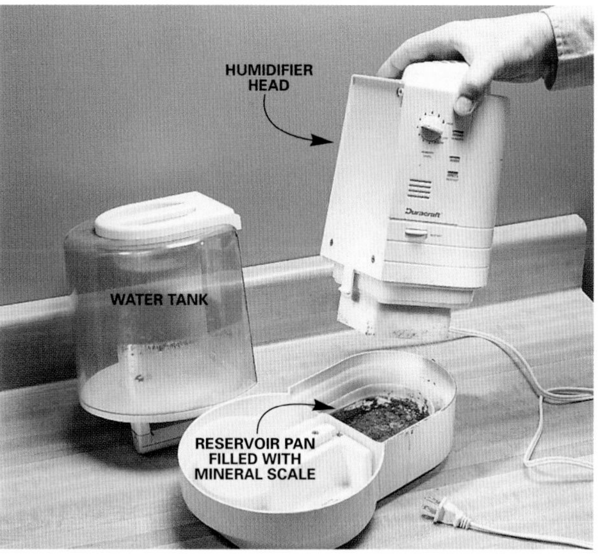

1 UNPLUG the humidifier empty the water tank, and pull off the humidifier head to reveal the reservoir pan. Empty out the water, loose mineral scale and sludge, then give the pan a quick scouring and rinse it well.

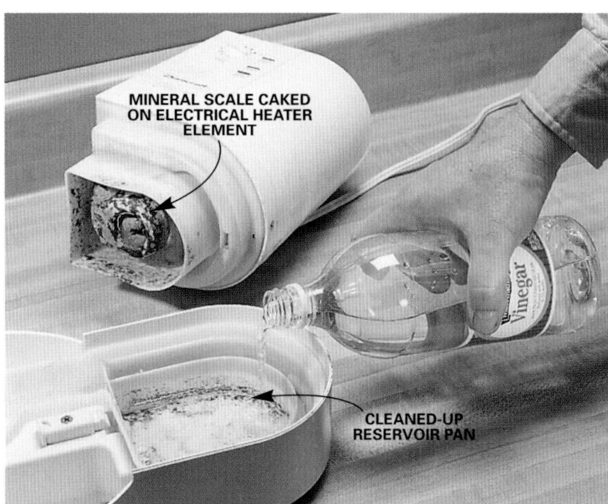

2 FILL the reservoir with white vinegar and reinstall the humidifier head. Leave the humidifier unplugged and soak the heater element in the vinegar overnight to loosen the mineral scale.

3 SCRAPE the mineral scale off the heater element with a utility knife and toothbrush. It's not necessary to scrape down to bare metal everywhere to accomplish your task.

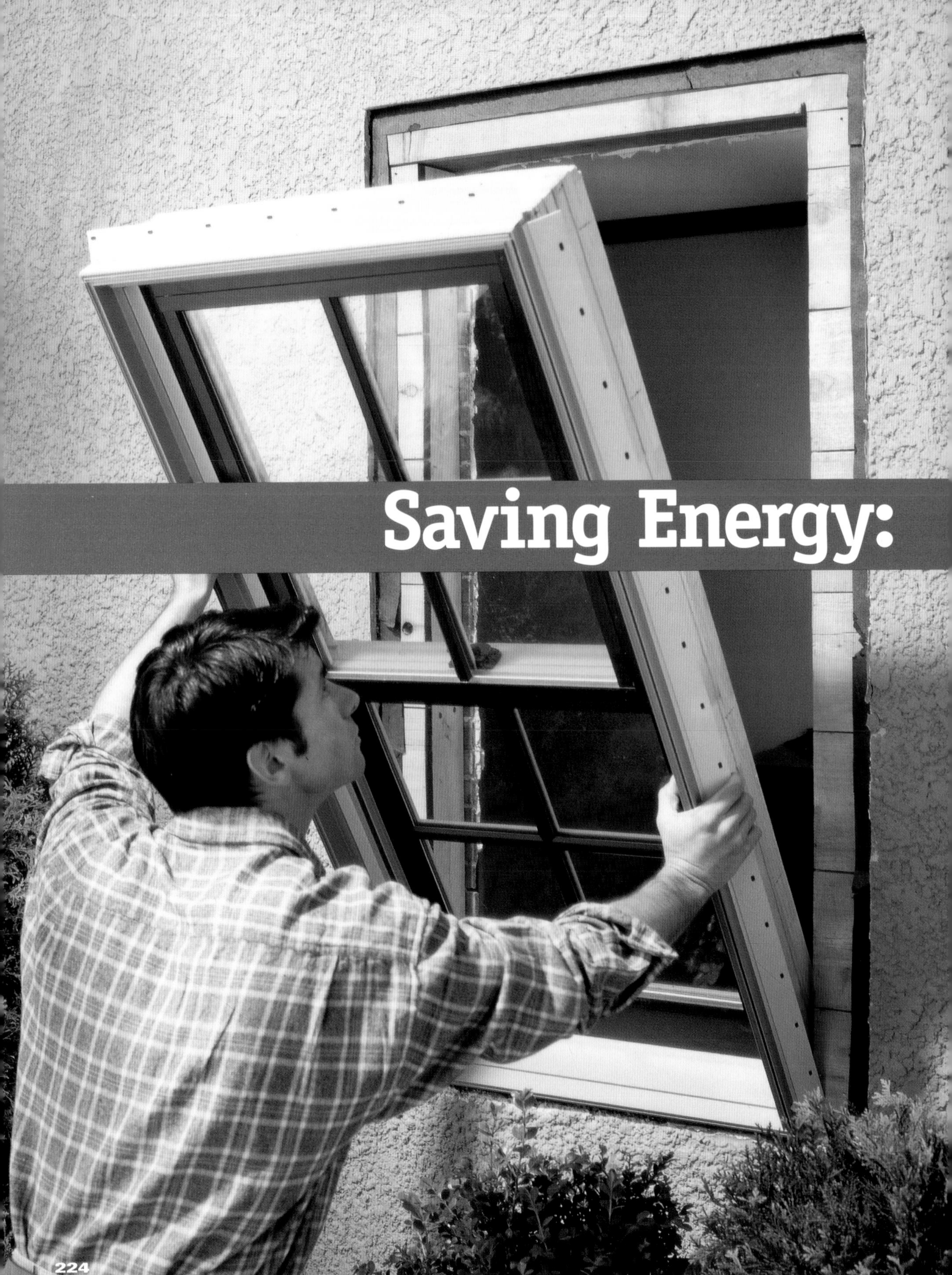

Saving Energy:

There's no better or easier time to integrate energy-efficient building products into your home than when you add on, remodel or build new. The wall and ceiling cavities are readily accessible. And since you'll be buying new windows, doors, appliances and other components anyway, you'll find that energy-efficient models usually cost only a little more and are often no more difficult or expensive to install than non-energy-efficient components.

Of course, if you're starting from scratch, do it right. Using 2x6s instead of 2x4s for your walls will allow you to up the level of insulation. Low-E windows and windows with higher insulating qualities are widely available and are rapidly becoming the norm rather than the exception. New products that help cut down on air infiltration around outlets and switches will make your home less drafty and more energy efficient.

And in the end you'll have a home that's not only more energy efficient but more comfortable as well.

Remodeling

Building and remodeling the "green" home

It's the next big thing. But what is it?

PHOTOS COURTESY OF GE

Above: Solar made simple. GE's Brilliance solar electric power system kit has everything you need to generate your own electricity at home. Learn more at www.gepower.com.

Above, right: Natural, warm, renewable. Cork flooring is do-it-yourself friendly and available in a wide variety of styles. Learn more at www.wicanders.com, www.expanko.com, and www.wecork.com.

Ten years ago, building healthy, energy-efficient homes using environmentally friendly materials was expensive, time consuming and something only a small number of builders, remodelers and consumers were interested in. Things have changed. Today more than half the members of the National Association of Home Builders consider themselves "green builders," and the demand for their homes and remodeling services has grown dramatically.

"Green" is a loose term, which means different things to different people. It can include designing projects to be more energy and water efficient, using sustainable and natural building materials, building smaller, using solar and other alternative forms of energy, or combinations of all of these. Although there are many definitions, the common thread is to build in a way that uses and conserves natural resources wisely in both the short and long term.

Here's a look at the main elements:

PHOTO COURTESY OF ENVIROGLAS PRODUCTS, ALAN KLEHR PHOTOGRAPHER

Left: Terrazzo countertop by EnviroGlas Products, made out of porcelain from old toilets and sinks. www.enviroglasproducts.com

Below: Bamboo—a truly renewable resource. Almost 20 percent of a properly managed bamboo forest can be harvested each year—forever. Materials made from bamboo are super-durable, sustainable, unique and stylish in appearance. The most popular use of bamboo in the U.S. is for tough-as-nails flooring. www.teragren.com

PHOTO COURTESY OF TERAGREN FINE BAMBOO FLOORING, PANELS & VENEER

Use of sustainable, reclaimed and natural building materials

Most green builders keep a close eye not only on which materials they use, but also how much energy is consumed in their manufacture and transporting them to the site.

Those focused on natural building may avoid formaldehyde-based carpets, cabinets and sheathing materials and use more natural and sustainable products like bamboo and cork flooring. Using reclaimed materials such as timbers, doors and trim can be another element of building green. Wood composite decking, trim and other materials made of recycled plastic may also be used.

Generating less waste and scrap, and recycling or repurposing leftover materials is another issue to which green builders give greater consideration.

A more energy-efficient building envelope

Most green homes are built so they require significantly less energy to heat and cool than standard homes. Energy efficiency starts with a properly constructed building envelope or shell, including well-insulated (or super-insulated) walls, high-performance windows and doors, and well-sealed interior vapor barriers and exterior air infiltration barriers, often called "house wraps."

In warm climates, materials like light colored shingles and attic radiant barriers—both help reflect heat—are often included to help lower cooling costs. In cold climates, more attention may be paid to triple pane, or other types of high-efficient windows.

Some energy-efficient building components—like windows—cost more, while others simply require more meticulous care in their installation.

Today more than half the members of the National Association of Home Builders consider themselves "green builders."

Better design and site planning

Many green homes are designed and strategically positioned on the site to increase energy efficiency and decrease impact on the land. Orienting the house to maximize solar gain in the winter, along with designing roof overhangs to provide maximum cooling in the summer are two often-included elements. Positioning operable windows to provide good cross-ventilation can also help lower cooling costs.

Taking advantage of natural light through skylights and windows can help lower lighting costs. Even planting trees strategically to block sun in the summer and block cold winds in the winter can make a home more energy efficient.

Use of alternate sources of energy

In addition to taking advantage of passive solar heating and cooling, many green homes use other forms of alternative energy. Some incorporate roof-mounted photovoltaic cells to generate electricity or solar panels for heating or pre-heating water.

Other alternatives include geothermal heat pumps that extract heat from the earth via a network of pipes buried in the ground, as well as fuel cells and wind power. The combination of building an energy efficient envelope and incorporating alternative forms of energy can make some homes so efficient that heating and cooling costs approach zero.

High-efficiency heating and cooling

Energy-efficient furnaces, boilers and air conditioning equipment are found in most green homes. The best units have efficiency ratings of up to 94 percent, offering substantial energy and dollar savings over furnaces older than 20 years (which may be as little as 50 percent efficient). Since around half of the typical utility bill goes for heating and cooling, the long-range savings are substantial.

High-efficiency appliances and water heaters will also substantially lower energy bills. See "Understanding ENERGY STAR" on p. 26 for more specific details.

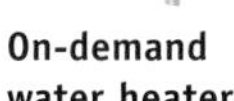

On-demand water heater

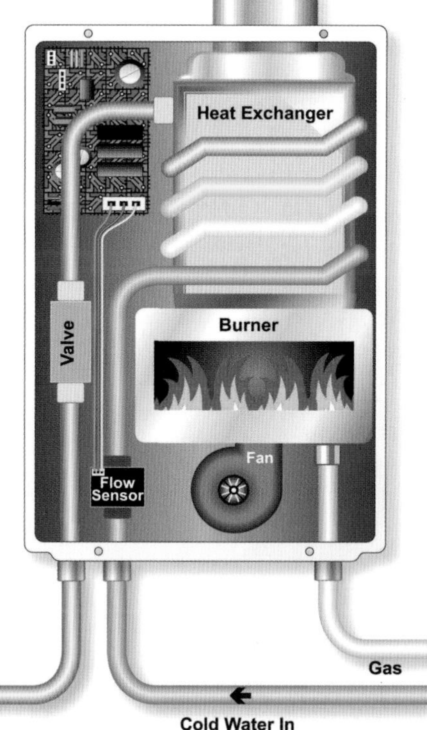

Increased water efficiency

Incorporating water saving faucets, toilets and showerheads is the first step toward water efficiency; purchasing water-efficient washing machines and dishwashers is the second.

Some will go the extra mile and incorporate a smaller lawn or plant drought-resistant plants in order to minimize outdoor watering needs. Gray water recycling, which involves using water from showers, baths, kitchen, laundryroom and other sources for watering lawns is yet another green tactic, but one that should be used following certain precautions. More information can be found at www.graywater.net.

Healthier indoor air quality

A tightly sealed home excels at keeping heated or cooled air inside, but it also excels at keeping mold, moisture, smoke, radon and bacteria in. Some studies show that the level of air pollution inside the home can be two to five times greater than the air outside. Since people spend an average of 90 percent of their time indoors, healthy indoor air is critical.

With a tightly built house, it's important to include some system for exhausting moisture-laden and stale indoor air and bringing in fresh outside air. An air-to-air heat exchanger which uses outgoing warm air to preheat incoming colder air is one product frequently used. These systems require a mini-duct system, so are best installed during new construction or extensive remodeling.

HEPA air filtering devices, that can remove over 99 percent of even the smallest airborne particles, are often included and may be used as freestanding units or integrated into the whole-house heating and cooling system.

Costs and payback

Since building green can be defined in so many ways, pinning exact dollar amounts on the increased initial costs versus the subsequent long-term savings is impossible. Most studies show that costs can range anywhere from 2 to 15 percent more than conventional building, but this varies greatly on degree of homeowner involvement, materials used and design. Federal, state and local governments, along with utility companies, are increasingly offering incentives by way of tax breaks and rebates for those building green.

One should look at building green as an investment: An investment that will pay dividends for as long as you own your home.

Should I buy new windows?

Consider comfort, energy efficiency & the "hassle factor"

Q Many of the windows in my 1964 home are hard to open and don't close tightly. Is it time to chuck them and buy all new windows?

A Tough question. New windows are tempting because they offer so much—smoother operation, lower maintenance, energy savings, fewer drafts and easier cleaning. But they're expensive. Typical residential windows cost $150 to $400 each, depending on their size, materials and features. If you add in the $100 to $300 per window that a pro charges to install them, you're facing a major investment.

Ask yourself the following three questions to evaluate your old windows and weigh the benefits of new ones.

1

Are your old windows a hassle?

Are you sick and tired of nursing your windows along, or are you OK with the minor maintenance jobs that go along with them? Consider:

- **Ease of operation.** Do they lift, swing or slide easily, or do you hesitate to open them when you want fresh air and ventilation?
- **Scraping and painting.** Painted windows require regular maintenance. Otherwise they'll rot and fall apart. New windows with aluminum or vinyl cladding or that are made from vinyl or a composite eliminate this chore.
- **Condensation.** Does condensation regularly collect on the glass, cloud the view and soak the window trim? Higher-efficiency glass in new windows will help reduce this problem.
- **Storm windows.** Do you mind cleaning, maintaining and putting up and taking down storm windows? Do your storms need replacement?
- **Cleaning.** Is this so difficult that you avoid doing it? Many new windows are designed to make cleaning a snap.

2

Are your old windows comfortable?

Single-pane windows often leave rooms feeling chilly and dry in cold weather and overheated in warm, sunny weather. Windows with double-pane glass (p. 233) can greatly improve the comfort of your home. They can block much of the heat of direct sunlight but still allow the light to come through (less need for shades). They'll reduce cold drafts and the chill of cold glass. And they'll reduce condensation, so you can keep the indoor humidity at a higher, more comfortable level in cold weather.

New energy-efficient windows will also save on your fuel bills, but they're expensive. Carefully weigh the pros and cons if your old windows are still in good shape.

New windows offer a host of benefits—smooth operation, low maintenance, fewer drafts, easier cleaning and modest energy savings. But they're expensive, so evaluate the repair and maintenance options for your old windows before taking the plunge.

3

Are your old windows worth repairing?

You can almost always repair and restore old windows if you're willing to set aside the time and can find replacement hardware. But it's not always worth the effort and expense. Major problems include:

- **Rot.** Once rot starts, it's tough to stop unless you commit yourself to replacing rotted wood (a difficult job) and then maintaining it regularly. Consider replacement.
- **Sagging casement (crank-out) windows.** You can usually replace worn-out crank mechanisms, but bent or worn hinges are tougher and replacements don't always solve the problem. Consider new windows.
- **Fogged double-pane glass.** The fogging that occurs between the glass panes can't be fixed. Glass replacement (sometimes the entire sash) is the only solution. This is often difficult and it's expensive if a pro does it. Compare the "fix-it" cost with the cost of a new window.
- **Hard-to-find replacement hardware.** Call the window manufacturer or local window dealer if you can identify the window brand and model number. Many hard-to-find parts are available from Blaine Window Hardware (see Buyer's Guide, p. 233). But often new windows are the only option.

Q What's the best way to replace my windows?

Option 1

A The easiest way to replace windows is to remove the old sashes and slip a window insert into the old frame (photo below). You get the benefits of high-efficiency glass, weathertightness and a maintenance-free exterior with minimal impact on the appearance of your home.

We show two ways to do this in an article on p. 146. You simply measure the frame and order a new wood or vinyl unit to fit it. This always works for double-hung (slide up and down) windows but only sometimes for casements (crank out) and sliding windows. A window dealer will advise you on your options. Or you can opt for sash replacement, which works for double-hungs only.

You can complete the changeout this way in about an hour per window (or much less after learning the ropes on the first one!). But this approach has several drawbacks. The old frame must be rot-free and reasonably square. And you still have to maintain the exterior wood frame and trim.

Option 2

A Completely tear out the old window and frame and put in a new one (photo below). You usually have to go this route with casement and slider windows. This project takes longer and is more difficult because you have to remove the exterior and interior trim, make the new window weathertight and then replace the trim. Plan on spending a whole day per window.

On the plus side, this method allows you to start fresh with a new, weathertight, low-maintenance window. And you have the option of reframing the opening and changing the window size while you're at it.

Keep in mind that complications can arise if your old window doesn't have exterior trim. Sometimes brick, stucco, vinyl siding or other siding materials butt right up against the window frame. In these situations, you may have to remove or cut siding to get the old window out and the new one in, and then patch or restore siding to finish up.

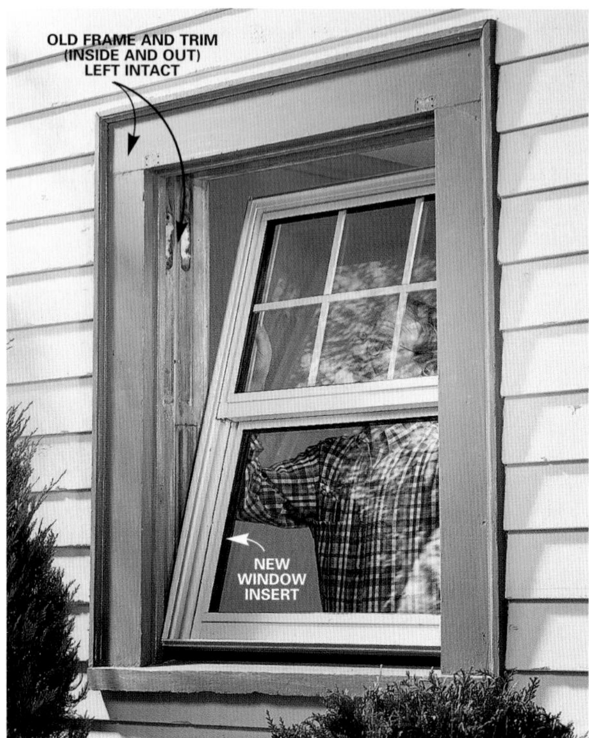

OPTION 1: Wood or vinyl window inserts cost about the same as complete new window units but are easy to install because you leave the old frame and trim intact.

OPTION 2: With new window units, you replace all the old parts with new, ensuring weathertight, long-term performance. But installation is more difficult.

How do I know I'm getting a quality window?

A Quality is a matter of detail. It's best to visit a showroom where you can compare windows of different brands or different models within the same brand. Check these features and answer these questions:

Appearance. Imagine the windows in your home. Does the style of the windows blend well on the interior and exterior? Are the wood or vinyl joints well made? Do the muntins (grids that divide the glass) fit tightly and cleanly? Is the hardware attractive? Unless you're trying to match existing window colors, choose a low-maintenance exterior (such as vinyl or aluminum) so you'll never have to scrape and touch up the paint.

Operation. Try out the display windows. Do they open and close smoothly? Are the cranks, runners and locking devices solid and do they look as though they'll withstand heavy use? Does the window latch firmly without too much effort? Does the weatherstripping fit snugly? Are the screens solidly built and easy to remove?

Cleaning. If cleaning is a priority, can you easily reach both interior and exterior glass? Remove or rotate the sashes to test them.

Service. Are parts available if something should break or wear out? Can you replace the weatherstripping when it wears out? Both these questions favor window companies with long track records because they'll serve their customers well into the future. If the glass breaks or fogs, how difficult and costly is replacement?

Warranties. Compare the warranties for parts and finishes. Probably the most frustrating (and expensive) problem is the failure of the seal between double-pane glass and the resulting fogging. Look for a warranty that covers glass replacement up to 20 years. **Note:** Keep the receipt for your window purchase and the warranty in your records.

Glass selection. Energy-efficient double-pane glass is fairly standard now. But it's almost always worth paying a bit extra for two additional features: a low-E coating and argon gas between the panes. Most manufacturers have two variations of this type of glass, one designed for cold climates and one designed to control sunlight in warmer climates. If you spend more for air conditioning than for heating, choose the warm-climate type, and if you spend more for heating, choose the cold-climate type.

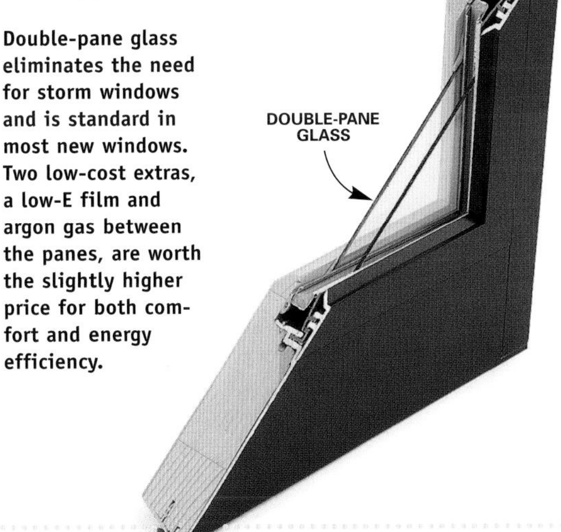

Double-pane glass eliminates the need for storm windows and is standard in most new windows. Two low-cost extras, a low-E film and argon gas between the panes, are worth the slightly higher price for both comfort and energy efficiency.

Should I replace them all at once?

A Balance your home's appearance with your budget. Even if you try for a close match, new windows will probably look a bit different from the old. And even the glass itself (we recommend the low-E) usually looks somewhat different from clear glass. So replacing one or two in a conspicuous area may look bad. One good strategy is to replace all the windows on one side (or level if you have a two-story house) to retain a consistent appearance. Often the windows on one side of a house deteriorate much faster than the others.

Buyer's Guide

REPLACEMENT HARDWARE:
Blaine Window Hardware: (800) 678-1919. www.blainewindow.com

VINYL WINDOWS:
Many sources available for both inserts and complete units; look in your local yellow pages under "Windows, Replacement."

WOOD REPLACEMENT WINDOWS:
Many sources available for complete units. The following manufacturers will custom-size inserts to fit in old frames.

Andersen Corp.: www.andersenwindows.com

Kolbe & Kolbe Millwork: www.kolbe-kolbe.com

Marvin Windows and Doors: www.marvin.com

Pella Corp.: www.pella.com

Weather Shield Mfg.: www.weathershield.com

2x6 vs. 2x4 wall construction

According to an Energy Efficient Building Association study, for an average home with frame construction in a cold climate, 2x6 construction would yield an annual savings of $30 compared with a similarly constructed 2x4 wall. But, in mid-America, where the winters are milder, the savings would be much less. Because a 2x6 frame costs about 20 percent more to build than a 2x4, it would take 75 years to reach the payback point, according to the study. And that's for an entire home; for an addition, the payback would take even longer.

A much better option is to use rigid foam sheathing on a conventional 2x4 wall. A wall built this way costs 10 percent less than a typical 2x6 wall and can be even more energy efficient (see photo at right to compare R-values). The rigid foam sheathing also provides an uninterrupted envelope of insulation to prevent thermal bridging. Thermal bridging occurs when heat is lost by conduction through the studs and nails, lowering the effective R-value of the wall. Another benefit: The rigid foam acts as a wind barrier, stopping cold drafts from sneaking into your walls.

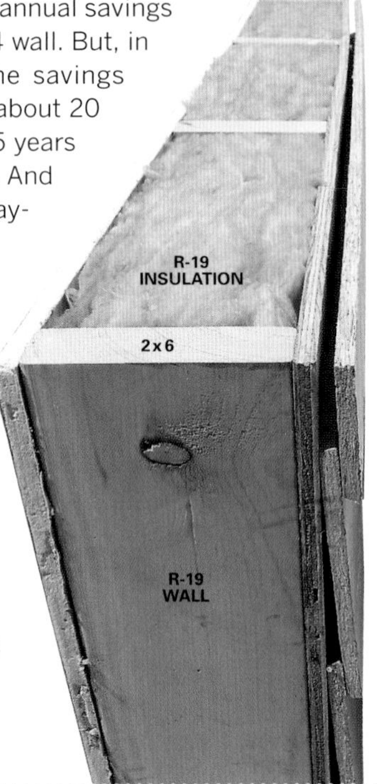

Pay extra for energy-saving features

With energy prices rising, many contractors are offering energy-efficiency upgrades (at an additional price). These might include higher-efficiency windows; guaranteed air sealing; extra-thick insulation; and higher-efficiency heating, cooling or other appliances. If they don't offer this, you can ask what additional measures they (or you) can take to improve your home's energy performance. Then compare the estimated energy savings with the cost of each upgrade. A payback period of seven to 10 years is good. (Simple payback is the time it takes for the savings to equal the original cost.) Keep in mind that upgrades done during the remodeling process always cost less than upgrades added later.

Energy-Saving Q&A

Airtight electrical boxes

Q **Our building inspector told me that I need to use airtight electrical boxes. What are these?**

A Some building codes now require these special boxes to reduce air and moisture movement in exterior walls. Here are three options:

First is a large plastic box (Photo 1) that you nail to the face of a stud, then install a standard electrical box inside it. It's large enough to handle multi-gang electrical boxes. Cut a slit in the side of the box and push the cable through it and wire the box as you normally would. Caulk around the cable where it penetrates the box to seal it. If you're using a plastic vapor barrier, seal it to the box apron with an acoustic (nonhardening) caulk. If you're applying drywall without the vapor barrier behind it, caulk the drywall directly to the box.

Another option is an airtight electrical box (Photo 2) that uses a soft rubber gasket that seals to the drywall. The box also is wrapped in a rubber skin that seals the cables. Make a small slit in the rubber and push the cable through. Install and wire it as you would a standard box.

You can also order these boxes at electrical supply stores.

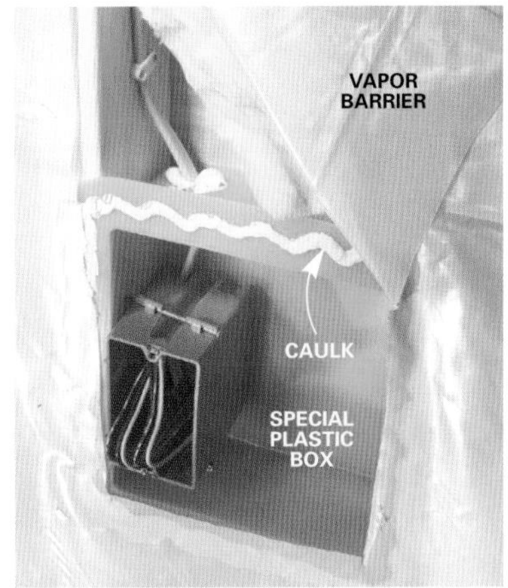

1 **The Lessco Air-Vapor Barrier Box is nailed to the stud and allows use of standard electrical boxes. Slit the top to insert wire, then use caulk to seal as shown. These boxes cost $2.25 to $2.50 each. (Visit www.lessco-airtight.com to find a local dealer.)**

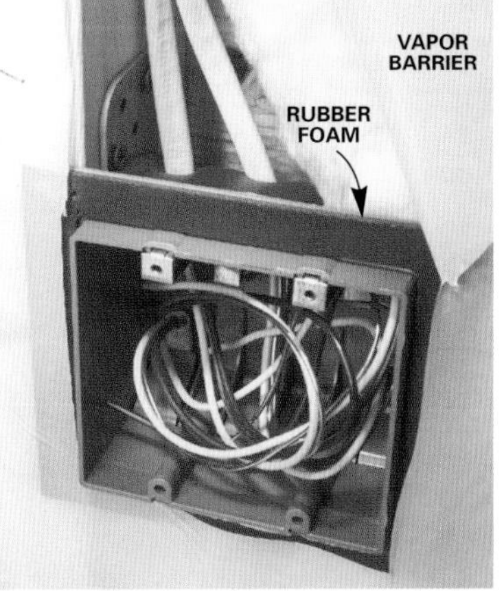

2 **Other airtight electrical boxes use a foam gasket around the drywall flange and where the cable enters to seal out air. These boxes are available at most home centers and well-stocked hardware stores.**

Foam blocks stop air infiltration

Simple foam insulation blocks that fit around electrical boxes (inside the wall cavity) also stop air infiltration.

The blocks save you the time and hassle of buying airtight boxes or caulking regular boxes.

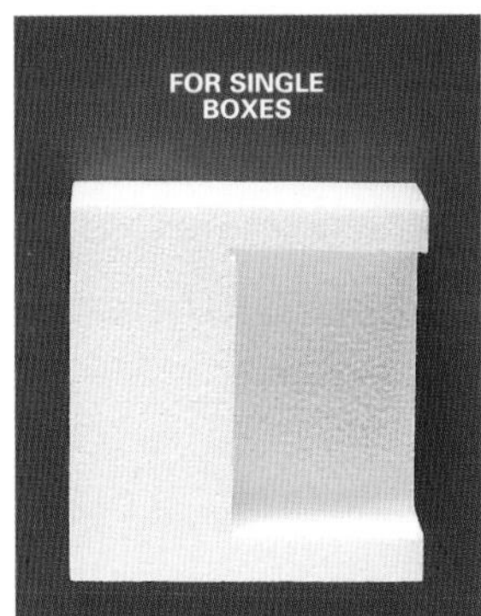

3 **Foam insulation boxes stop air infiltration and install quickly. The units shown cost $2.15 to $3.50 each. (Visit www.energyblock.com for more information.)**

Insulate rim joists and cut heat loss

1 CUT rigid foam insulation into strips with a table saw or a circular saw. Cut the strips to fit between floor joists using a box cutter.

In just a couple of hours, you can seal and insulate your rim joists, which are a major source of heat loss in many homes. Properly insulating and air-sealing rim joists takes patience, so most builders simply stuff in some fiberglass and walk away.

If you have an unfinished basement, you can properly insulate the rim joists in two or three hours. (This will also block tiny passages where spiders and other insects enter your basement!) The materials will cost about $1 per foot of rim joist. Call your local building inspections

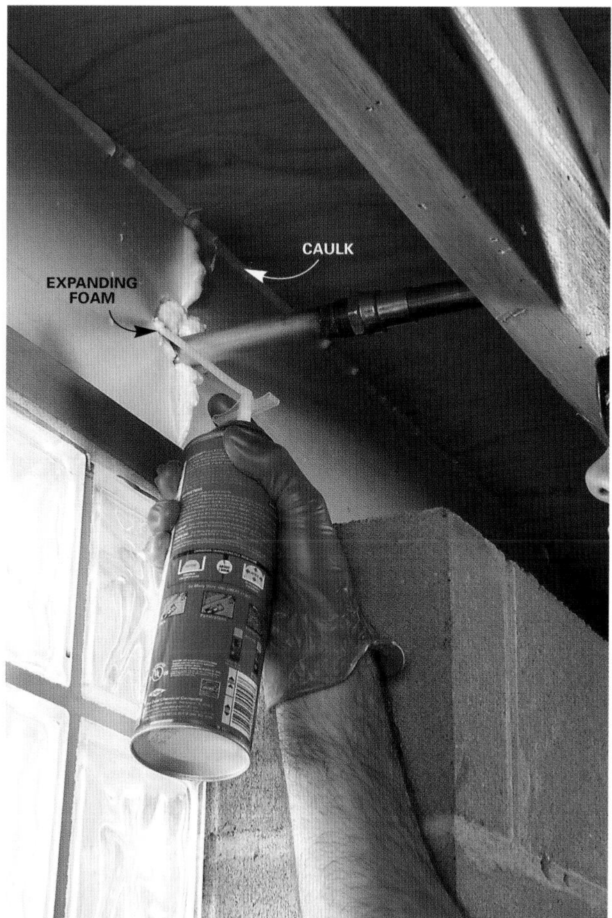

2 **RUN a bead of acrylic caulk around each section of foam to form an airtight barrier. Fill gaps larger than 1/4 in. with expanding foam sealant.**

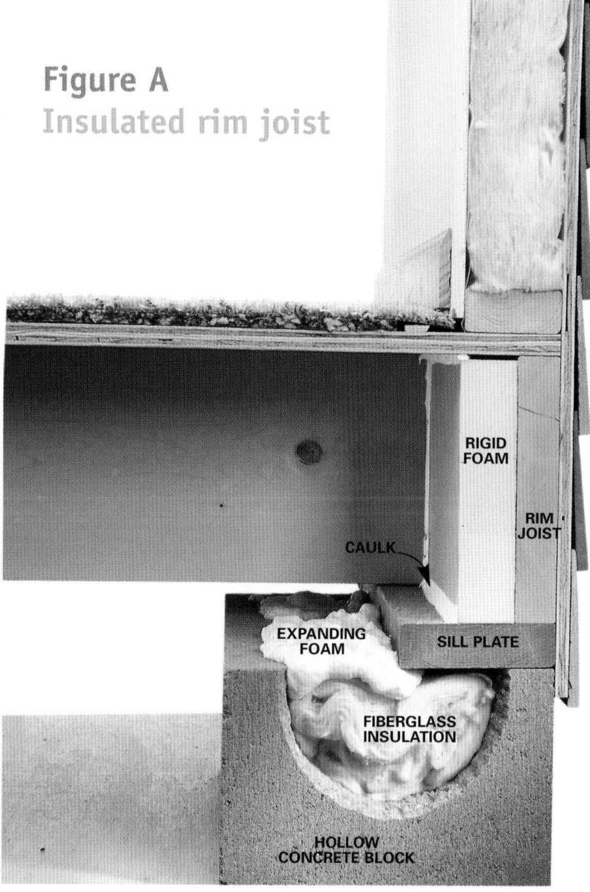

Airtight insulation reduces heat loss through the rim joist. Fiberglass insulation and expanding foam seal the open top of hollow concrete blocks.

department before you begin this project. The inspector may require you to cover the new insulation with drywall (as a fire block) or leave some areas uncovered to allow for termite inspections. You can insulate second-floor rim joists following the same steps shown here if you happen to tear out a ceiling during remodeling.

Rigid foam is the best insulation for rim joists. Shown here is 2-in.-thick (R-10) "extruded polystyrene" ($20 per 4 x 8-ft. sheet). Don't use "expanded polystyrene," which is a less effective air and moisture barrier.

Cut the foam into 8-ft.-long strips 1/8 in. less than the height of the rim joist. A table saw is the fastest way to "rip" these strips, but you can also use a circular saw. Then cut the strips to length to fit between the joists, again cutting them 1/8 in. short (Photo 1). A heavy-duty box cutter ($6) is the best knife for making short cuts and trimming foam; the long blade slices cleanly through the foam (a utility knife blade is too short). Use long sections of foam to cover the rim joists that are parallel to the floor joists (Photo 2). Don't worry about cutting the foam for a tight fit around pipes, cables or other obstructions; you can seal large gaps with expanding foam sealant later.

It's important to create an airtight seal around each section of foam using caulk or expanding foam (Photo 2). Otherwise, moist inside air could condense on the cold rim joist. The resulting dampness can lead to mold and rot. If you have a solid concrete foundation, also run a bead of caulk where the sill plate meets the concrete. If you have a concrete block foundation, also seal the openings on top with expanding foam. Stuff a wad of fiberglass insulation into each opening to support the foam as it hardens (see Figure A).

Replace a bath fan switch with a timer

After a shower, you should run your bath fan for 10 to 30 minutes to clear out moisture, which causes mold, mildew and condensation. Returning later to turn off the fan is a nuisance, but leaving it on is an energy waster. The solution is a timer switch. Old-fashioned rotary timers ($15) produce an annoying buzz and eventually wear out. Silent and reliable electronic timers are a better choice. Models like the one shown here are available at home centers, hardware stores and online at www.rewci.com/timinout.html ($27 plus shipping). Make sure the timer you choose is rated to control electric motors, not just lighting. You'll also need a new cover plate ($3). If you like, you can use this opportunity to upgrade any light switch that shares the same junction box.

Installing a timer isn't difficult, but you should know wiring basics such as how to make connections and detect live wires before you start. Turn off the power to the circuit at the main panel and make sure it's off using a noncontact voltage detector ($8 at home centers and hardware stores). Remove the switch and disconnect the two wires leading to it. Next, you have to determine which of the switch wires is "hot" (supplying power) and which is the "load" leading to the fan. Connect a test light ($4; Photo 1) and turn the power on at the main panel. If the light glows, it's connected to the hot wire. If not, it's connected to the load wire. Turn the power off and mark the hot wire with electrical tape (Photo 2).

To complete the job, connect the timer following the manufacturer's instructions (Photo 2). Don't straighten the hooked ends of the switch wires. Instead, cut them off and strip the insulation to expose fresh wire. You'll have to remove the electrical connectors on the existing neutral (white) and ground wires.

1 With the power off, clip a test light to the ground and to one of the switch wires. Turn on the power. If the light comes on, the wire is hot. If not, the other switch wire is hot.

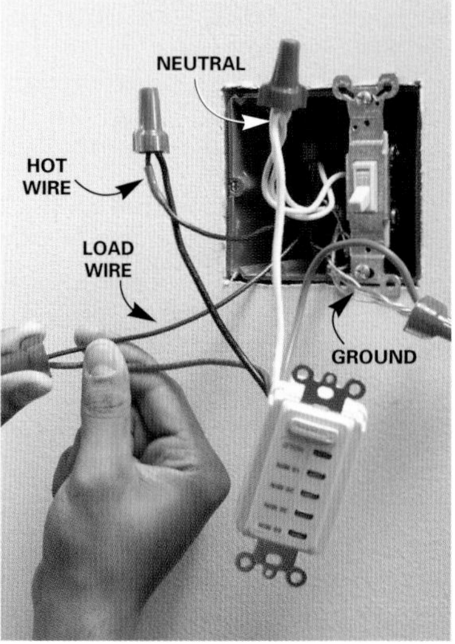

2 Turn off the power again. Connect the timer and tuck the wires neatly into the junction box. Screw on the timer and the cover plate.

Curb heat loss in cathedral ceilings

Light fixtures aren't airtight unless they have an "airtight" rating. But don't plug the holes (see photo). Manufacturers submit fixtures to Underwriter's Laboratories (UL) to receive a safety rating for their designated use. (You'll see a UL rating somewhere on the fixture.) Altering the fixture in any way may compromise its margins for safety.

Recessed lights in cathedral ceilings waste the heat from the lightbulb and the warm air that leaks through the fixture. Also, moist, warm air will flow up against the cold roof sheathing (see photo). Chances are that it'll condense there, wet the wood and eventually cause rot. Unfortunately, there isn't any easy way to know if you have moisture problems and rot until you find water dripping from the ceiling, stains or soft spots in the drywall.

Builders often try to prevent the problem by leaving a 1- to 2-in. airspace for roof ventilation (see photo, right). Roof venting can help dry the wood again in warmer weather, and it'll flush out some of the moisture in cold weather. But it often doesn't work well.

The best solution is to avoid putting any recessed lights in cathedral ceilings. However, if you want them, use type IC "airtight" fixtures (available for $20 at lighting stores and home centers). These fixtures are sealed to stop airflow. In addition, they have gasketed edges to seal them to the drywall.

Replacement can be challenging. If you're lucky, you can pull the old mounting bracket out through the existing hole. Otherwise you have to tear open the ceiling. It's usually best to hire a licensed electrician for this tricky job.

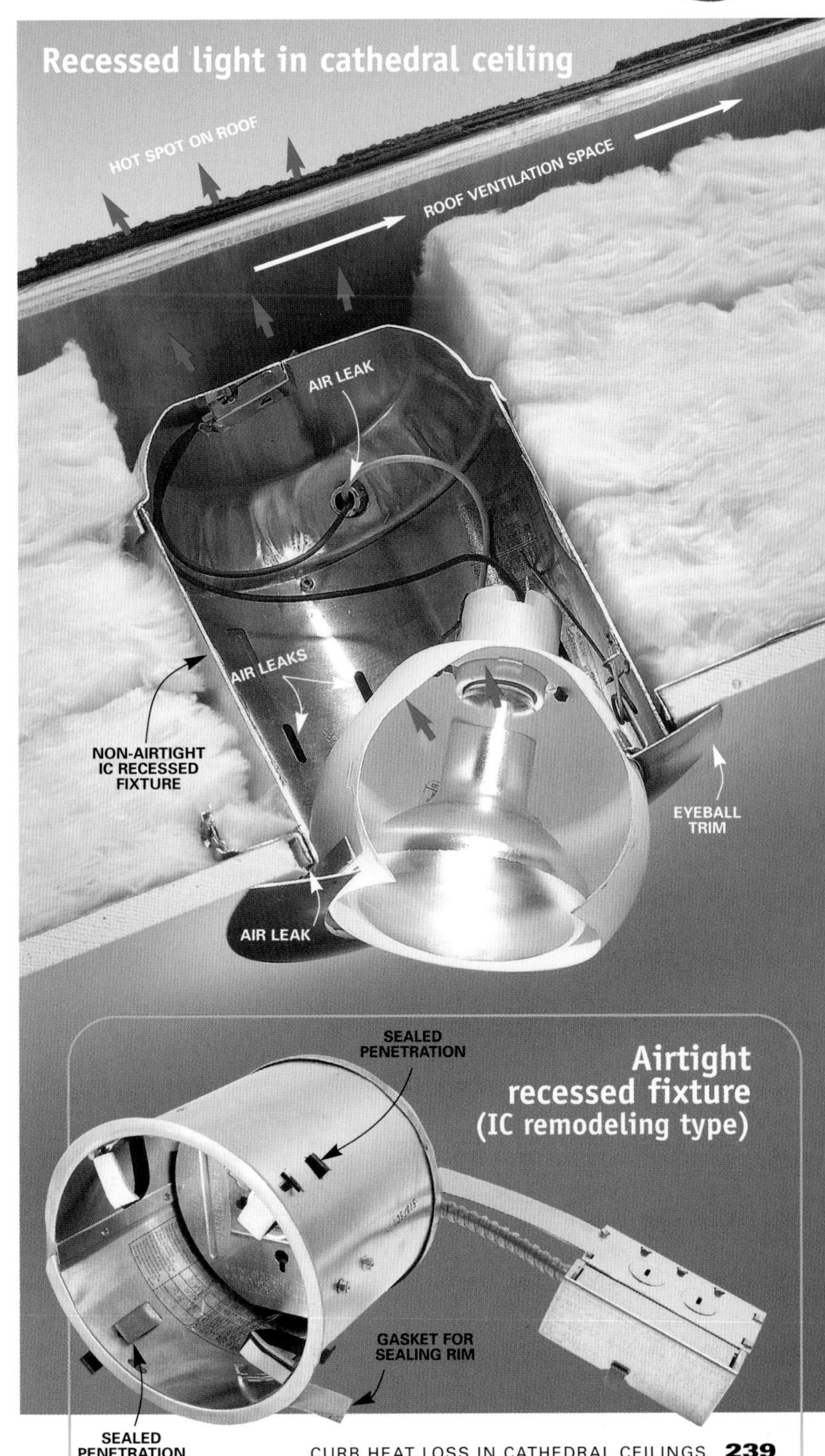

Energy-efficient heat for an

Does your furnace have enough oomph?

If you're looking for an energy-efficient way to heat an addition, weigh your options carefully. If a main rectangular (trunk) line is adjacent, you can tap into the top of it. If it's a round 6-in. branch duct, you should not. However, keep in mind that air distribution within a home is very complex. It's based on how your furnace performs, the local climate, structural features, and the heating and cooling loads of individual rooms.

First, you need to know if your furnace has enough heat output as measured in Btu (British thermal units) and enough blower capacity in cfm (cubic feet per minute) to handle the added square footage.

Next, you must determine the duct size that will deliver the needed cfm and how accessible your basement/crawlspace/attic will be for running new branch ducts from the supply air part of the furnace. Plus, you may need a return air duct to achieve a steady, balanced airflow.

Assuming your head isn't spinning yet, you may need to increase the size of the existing supply trunk line, then step it down to increase the air velocity so properly heated air enters the new room. Then you must decide how many supply lines the room will need, based on variables such as the number of windows and outside walls, the climate, whether your home was built on a slab or basement (heated or not?) and more.

You also have to test the system to avoid a heating system imbalance. The job is even more complex if you have air conditioning in the same ductwork.

Because the job is complex, you're likely to make a mistake and be disappointed by drafts or a

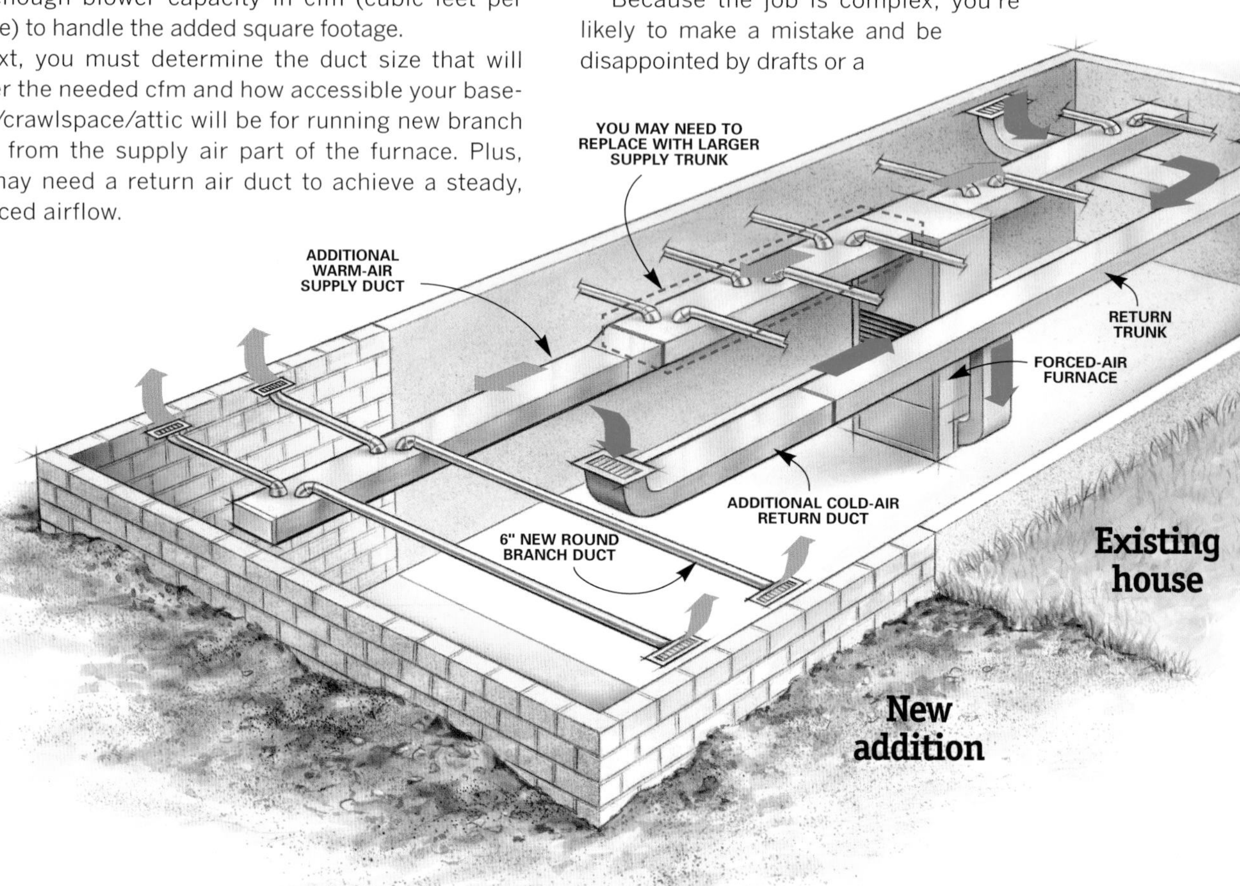

addition

cool room. The two biggest DIYer mistakes are (1) tapping a new duct into a 6-in. round adjacent branch duct and (2) not adding return air ducts.

Best advice? Call in a heating pro. First, pros determine the heat loss/gain for the entire house and for the room addition. That tells them whether the furnace is big enough and how much heat (and cooling) the room needs.

Next, pros size up the existing furnace and duct system, then map and calculate whether a system can handle the added load.

Older furnaces can usually supply the extra heat needed, but the return air ductwork often needs improvement. Newer high-efficiency, forced-air furnaces often don't have spare capacity, so you may have to replace the furnace with a higher capacity one.

If capacity exists, pros size up the new ductwork to make sure heated air reaches the new space at the proper velocity to keep the room at a comfortable temperature and avoid drafts, while maintaining the comfort of other rooms in the house.

Rather than have you replace a furnace that's too small, a pro may recommend other, less expensive options, such as an independent system or electric baseboard heating.

Energy-Saving Products

Energy-wise kitchen appliances

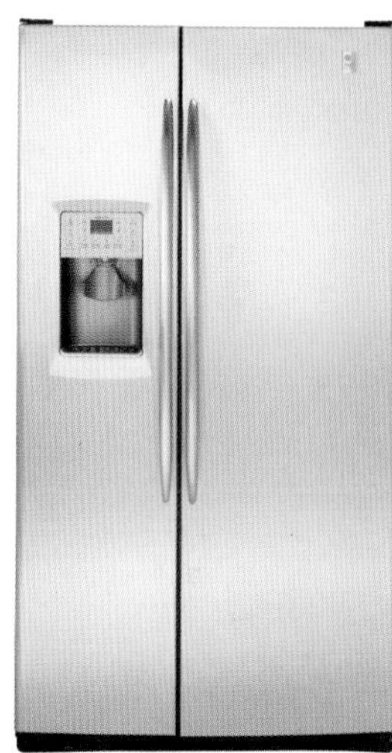

New appliances are usually an integral part of a kitchen-remodeling project, so it's the perfect time to upgrade to more energy-efficient models. For starters, look for the ENERGY STAR label—it's your first indication that the appliance meets strict energy-efficiency standards.

Many new dishwashers save energy in smart new ways. The GE Profile dishwasher, for example, includes a single-rack wash cycle that allows you to wash only the upper rack, using less water. It also has a sensor that automatically adjusts the cycle time and water temperature for each load. All said and done, an energy-efficient dishwasher can save you more than $25 on hot water costs annually.

Since refrigerators can account for up to 15 percent of your annual electric bill, an energy-efficient refrigerator is a wise investment. Door-mounted ice and water dispensers mean less door opening, resulting in less cool air escaping. Some models have condensers that don't require cleaning (which translates into higher energy efficiency) and digital displays that allow you to monitor actual temperatures.

Visit the "Refrigerator Retirement Savings Calculator" at www.energystar.gov to find out the cost of running your old refrigerator versus a new model.

Heating a garage

There are two types of natural-gas heaters that will work to heat a garage: a forced-air garage heater (shown above) that blows warm air like a conventional furnace, and a "low-intensity" infrared tube heater (photo, opposite) that radiates heat. (Avoid "high-intensity" infrared heaters—which visibly glow red—because most aren't approved for residential use.)

Both will burn natural gas (your most economical choice) or LP gas, and both are available in several sizes, so you can choose the one that best heats your space. Both require an electrical hook-up, and both require venting to the outside as well. But the similarities of the two types end there.

Your garage walls and ceiling need to be insulated (minimum of 4 in. thick in the walls, 6 in. thick in the ceiling); otherwise you'll waste energy and money. The basic differences are how the heaters perform and how they feel in terms of comfort.

If you plan to work on woodworking projects in the garage, an infrared heater may work better because it doesn't raise dust or keep dust airborne. A forced-air heater will stir up sawdust, which is a big problem when you're painting or staining.

You won't feel warm as quickly with an infrared heater because it heats objects first, then the air. However, once your concrete floor warms, you'll feel more comfortable because infrared heat is more uniform. But you must keep all objects 3 to 4 ft. away or they'll overheat—and so will you. With forced-air heat, the air is warmer at the ceiling and cooler at your feet. And a forced-air heater will take longer to reheat the space after the garage door has been opened and shut.

Another big difference is the initial cost. Most forced-air units cost half as much as low-intensity infrared tube heaters. The 60,000-Btu Modine Hot Dawg forced-air unit shown cost around $625 (not including the vent kit and thermostat), and the 30,000-Btu Caribe infrared unit shown (including the vent kit) cost around $1,000. However, it's usually less expensive to run the infrared unit, so the cost difference will decrease with frequent use. Check with the manufacturers or a local heating pro for a more exact estimate.

Installation is markedly different too. Infrared heaters must be installed a minimum of 7 ft. above the floor, and must hang down a minimum of 4 in. from the ceiling (check the manufacturer's instructions, as these measurements vary with the size of the heater). It's critical that you make sure objects below are not too close. The 30,000 Btu unit shown requires a minimum 3-ft. distance from heater to objects below. Most infrared heaters are installed at the back of a garage pointed toward the garage door, then aimed downward at a 45-degree angle. They can also be installed between car bays if the garage door opener rail allows and you don't have a tall vehicle.

With a forced-air heater, the installation details aren't as exacting. Most are placed in a corner, near a gas line and an electrical outlet (needed to power the blower). The instructions will indicate the exact spacing required between the unit and the sidewalls or ceiling.

How many Btu you need depends on variables such as the garage size, your climate zone and the temperature you want to work in. A basic rule of thumb for forced-air heaters is 45,000 Btu to heat a two- to 2-1/2-car garage, and 60,000 for a three-car garage. The makers of low-intensity infrared tube heaters say that 30,000 Btu can heat a two- to 2-1/2-car garage, and suggest 50,000 for a three-car garage. Check with a local heating pro or the heater manufacturer for a specific recommendation to fit your needs.

Both heater types need to be vented if powered by natural gas or LP gas. Check the instructions for specific vent pipe sizes and lengths (some models include a vent kit, or you can purchase components separately). Most can be routed either through sidewalls or through the attic and roof.

One other option is an electric infrared heater, if venting or gas-powered heat isn't what you want. Granted, electric heat may cost you more to run, but check with your local electrical utility to see if it offers any type of rebate or off-peak rates that would make this option more cost efficient.

INFRARED TUBE HEATER

Hot Dawg model HD60 from Modine Mfg., (800) 828-4328 (to locate dealer).
Caribe model CGTH-30, Roberts Gordon, (800) 828-7450 (to locate dealer).

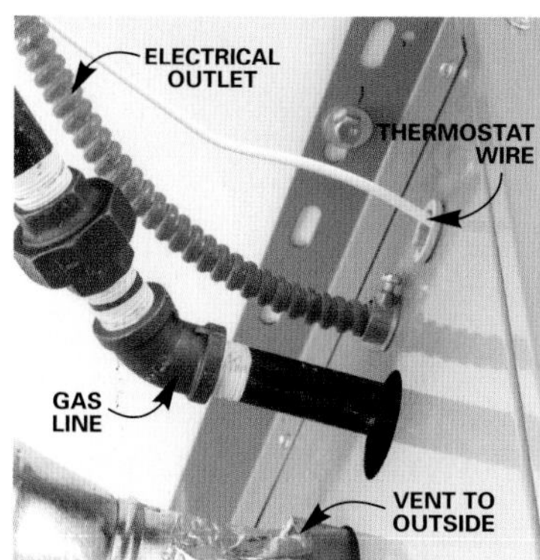

Forced-air heater connections (rear)

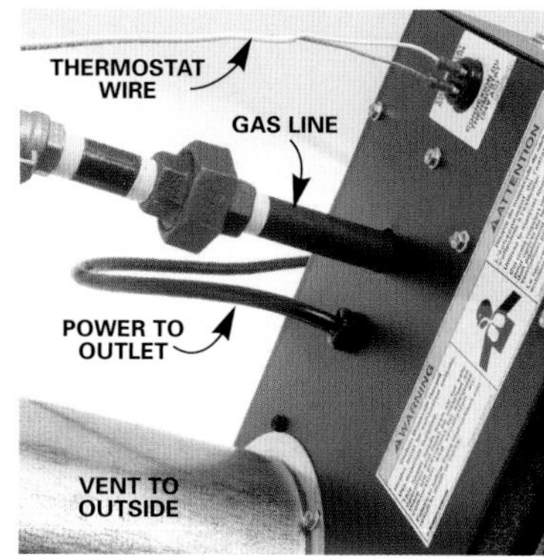

Infrared heater connections (rear)

Forced-air heater:

PROS

- Less expensive initial cost (50 percent less than comparable infrared heater)

CONS

- Noisy
- Loses heat quickly if garage door is opened (longer recovery time)
- Heat rises and stratifies (the air is warmer at ceiling, cooler near floor), but you won't notice it with a 7- or 8-ft. ceiling
- Air movement tends to blow airborne dust around (woodworkers will have to shut down unit before staining and finishing projects)

Low-intensity infrared tube heater:

PROS

- Little noise
- No air movement (dust settles)
- Lower cost to operate
- More uniform heat distribution (no stratification)
- Quicker heat recovery if door is opened/closed (floor and objects retain heat)

CONS

- Higher initial cost (50 percent more than forced-air)
- Correct location of heater is critical (minimum 7 ft. from floor, 3 ft. from objects). Adequate headroom is also critical, because you can overheat if you're working near the unit.

Electric resistance floor heat

A smart do-it-yourself heating alternative for additions & major remodels

Tile floors are popular in bathrooms for their practicality and durability, but even in mild climates, they tend to be too cold for bare feet. Imagine the comfort of stepping out of the shower onto a warm floor, and you'll understand why in-floor electric heating systems have become so popular. For small residential spaces such as bathrooms, simple electric-heating mats borrow the principle of commercial hydronic (water-filled tubing) systems to provide a reliable, affordable heat source.

Embedded in the thin-set mortar used to secure the tile, these mats feature a continuous loop of resistance heating cable amid a thin plastic mesh. There are different systems and types of heating cable available, so shop around. Like other heaters, the system can be controlled by a thermostat, a timer or even an on-off wall switch. Be extra cautious during installation to avoid nicking any wires. Insulate the joist cavity under the floor, if possible.

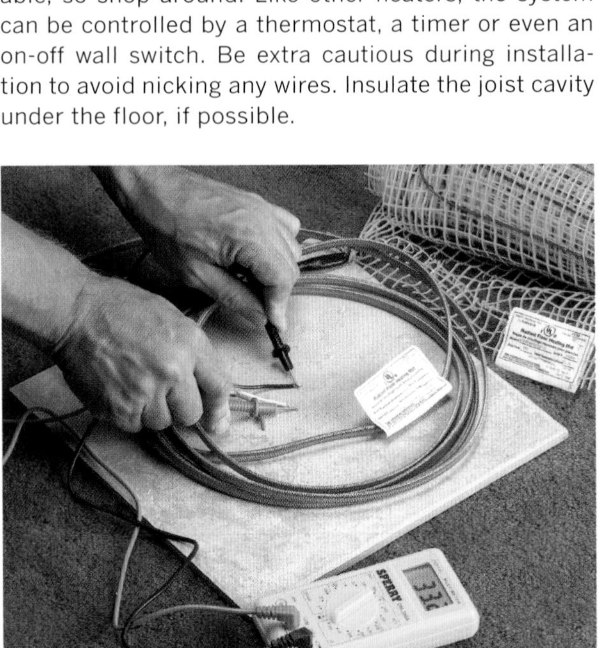

1 TEST the heating cable with a volt-ohm meter to make sure the resistance reading is within 10 percent of the rating on the product label. If it's not, check the manufacturer's instructions before you proceed.

2 AFTER LAYING a cement-board subfloor, test-fit the mat, making sure the heating cable is at least 4 in. away from any walls, fixtures or cabinets. Do not cut the heating cable or allow it to overlap itself.

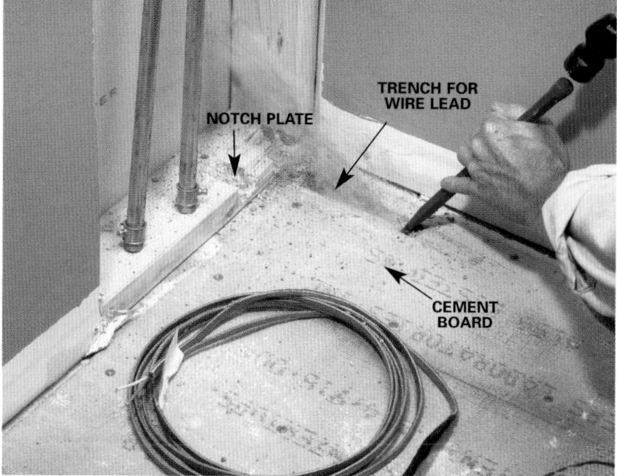

3 CHISEL a shallow trench in the cement board near the wall where the line wiring is, to make room for the mat's thicker wire lead. Also notch the bottom plate for the thermostat cable and power lead.

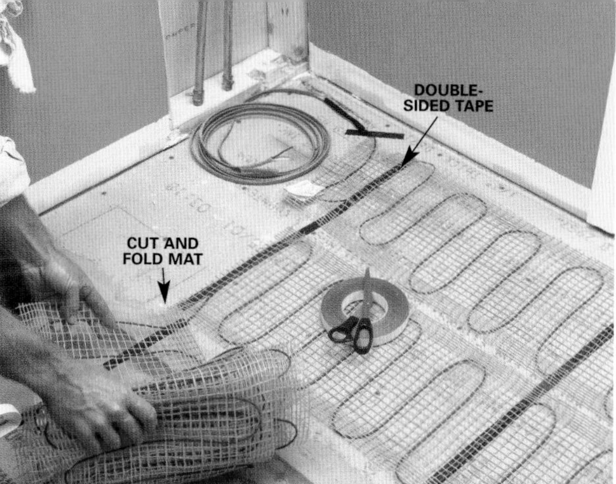

4 SECURE the mat to the cement board subfloor with double-sided tape. At the end of each run, cut the mat, not the heating cable itself, so you can fold it over and reverse direction to start the next course.

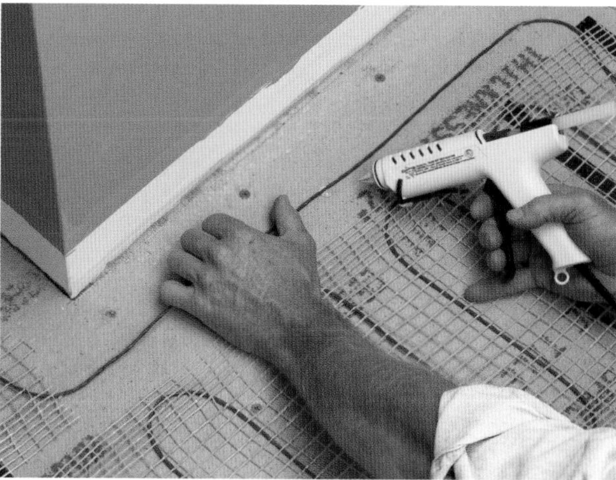

5 FOR SECTIONS where the mat won't fit, such as around a fixture, cut the plastic mesh away and secure the heating cable to the floor with hot-melt glue. Glue down any loose ends or humps in the mat, too.

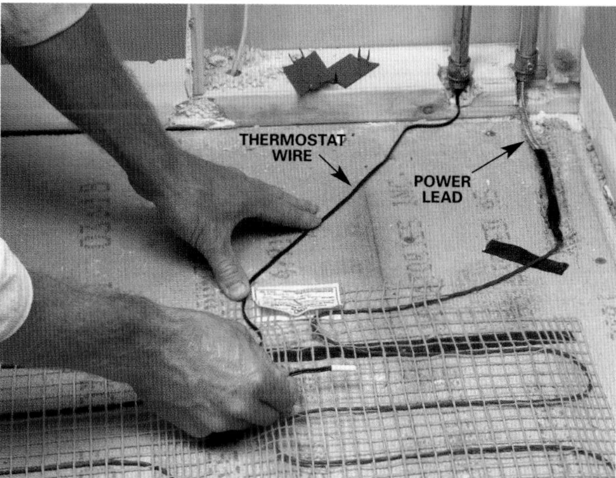

6 FEED the power lead and the thermostat wire through the conduit and to a wall-mounted electrical box. Connect the power lead to the house wiring (it may require a new circuit) and install the thermostat wire and sensor.

7 WITH THE MAT SECURED, use a notched trowel to apply thin-set mortar to cover it and provide a bed for the tile. Take care to avoid nicking or cutting the heating cable with the trowel's sharp edges.

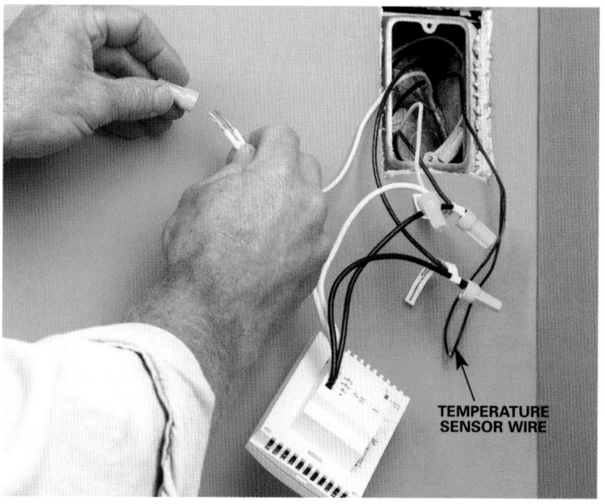

8 AFTER SETTING the tile and doing another continuity-resistance test, wire the wall thermostat. Shut off power to the thermostat while you're working on it. Let mortar cure one week before you turn on the power.

Cozy heat for an addition

Hydronic radiant heating is a good option to consider when adding on to a house with a furnace already working at full capacity. Unlike forced-air heating, which works by blowing warm air through large ducts, hydronic radiant heating circulates hot water through tubes attached to or embedded in a flat surface, usually the floor. The heat then radiates evenly throughout a space, making this arguably the most comfortable way to heat a room.

For truly even heat, choose a system that circulates hot water through code-approved plastic tubing (like PEX) that's embedded in a layer of material and covered by ceramic tile flooring. The material can be lightweight concrete, Gyp-crete or dry-tamped mortar. This cement-like layer, combined with the tile, makes up a great mass that stores the heat for a long time and continues to radiate it even when the water's not circulating. This constant warmth can greatly increase the comfort of a room, especially in a cold climate.

The cost per square foot for a hydronic system will depend on where you live and the size of the job. With a 300-sq.-ft. addition, expect to pay at least $1,500 to have the actual system installed (including water heater, tubing, pump and manifold). Then there's the cost of embedding the tubing. For a fairly small job, the most economical choice is to hire a tile professional to embed the tubing in dry-tamped mortar. That should cost from $3 per sq. ft. on up. Then add the cost of the finished floor. Tile is the best choice.

The cost of a hydronic system for an addition may be about the same as the cost of adding a furnace (vs. replacing). However, operating costs will be lower for the hydronic system, the water heater won't take up as much space as a furnace and ductwork, and you'll probably be more comfortable. To find a hydronics specialist, look in the yellow pages under "Heating Contractors."

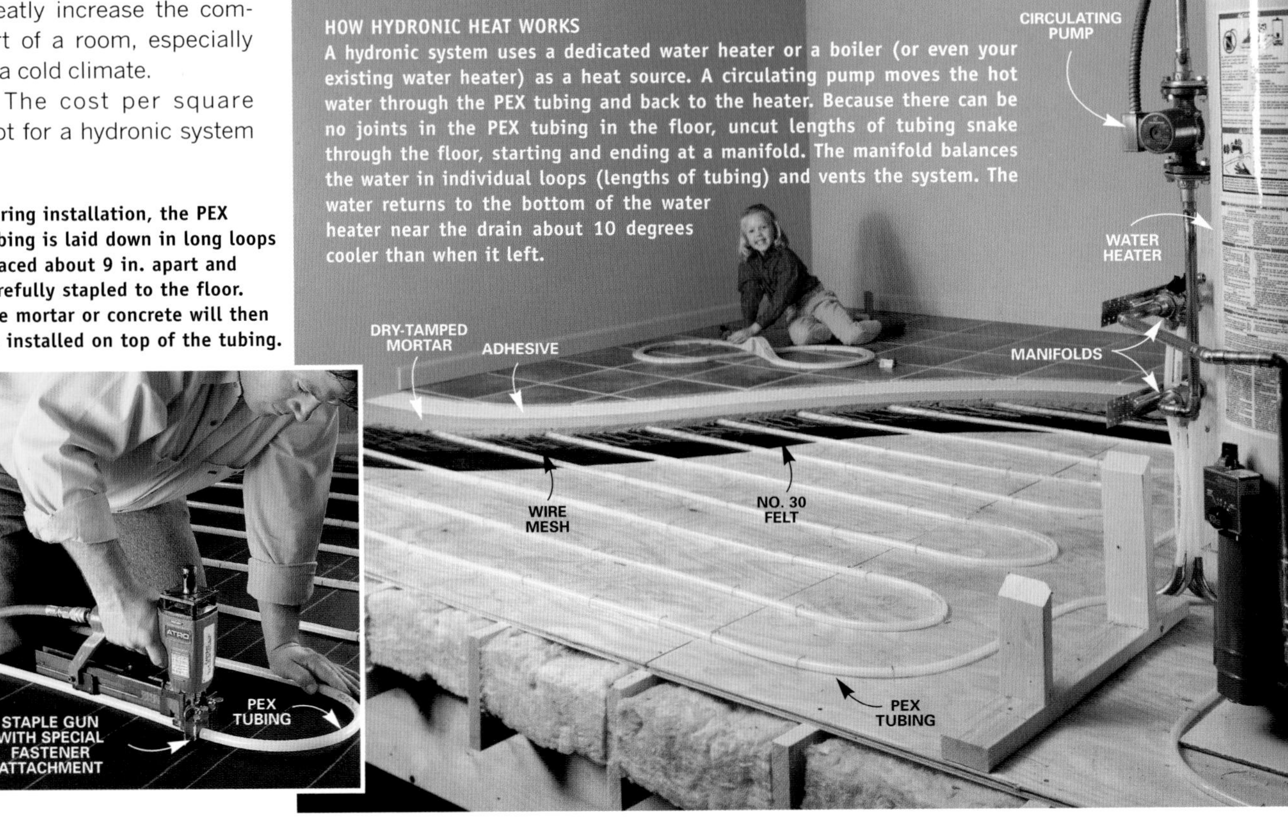

HOW HYDRONIC HEAT WORKS
A hydronic system uses a dedicated water heater or a boiler (or even your existing water heater) as a heat source. A circulating pump moves the hot water through the PEX tubing and back to the heater. Because there can be no joints in the PEX tubing in the floor, uncut lengths of tubing snake through the floor, starting and ending at a manifold. The manifold balances the water in individual loops (lengths of tubing) and vents the system. The water returns to the bottom of the water heater near the drain about 10 degrees cooler than when it left.

During installation, the PEX tubing is laid down in long loops spaced about 9 in. apart and carefully stapled to the floor. The mortar or concrete will then be installed on top of the tubing.

Understanding heat-recovery ventilators

Tightly built energy-efficient homes can experience problems with lingering odors, stale air and high humidity resulting in damaging condensation. Generally, these problems can be solved with ordinary ventilation or by cracking open a window. If you live in a moderately cold climate with high utility rates and conventional methods don't solve your problem, your home may be a candidate for a heat-recovery ventilator (HRV), also called an air-to-air heat exchanger.

Compared with opening a window, an HRV provides continuously controlled ventilation. Heat from stale exhaust air is used to temper the incoming air so fresh air enters your home closer to room temperature; about 70 percent of the heat is transferred. The airstreams don't mingle or contaminate one another, but weave and bypass one another through a series of chambers. Operating costs are about the same as those for a 100-watt incandescent lightbulb.

Most HRVs are designed to ventilate the entire home. Typically, four to eight supply-and-return ducts connect to the HRV. The ideal system exhausts air from moisture-laden rooms, such as the kitchen, bathrooms and laundry room, and dumps the fresh air into a closet, hallway or other space where the cooler air and increased movement won't affect comfort. Adding this kind of whole-house ventilator can be expensive and is normally done by a professional.

It is also possible to install a small plug-in single-room HRV on an exterior wall or in a window. Some models include multiple filters that clean the air as well. For the most effective air mixing, install a wall-mounted unit high on an outside wall, but avoid mounting it up against the ceiling. Keep it away from thermostats and seating areas, in a spot where some fan noise and cool air movement won't be a bother.

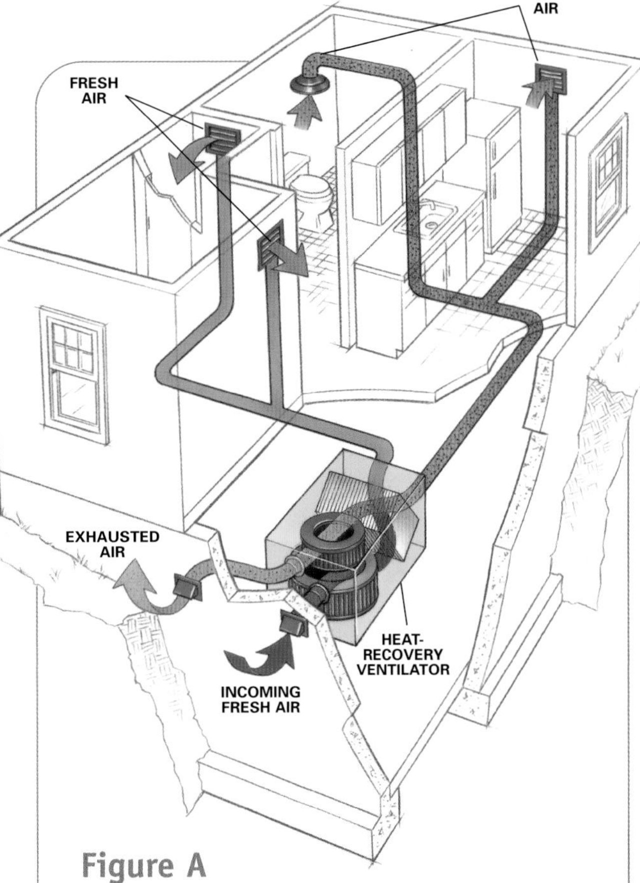

Figure A
How a heat-recovery ventilator works

In an HRV, one fan exhausts stale, moisture-laden indoor air while another draws in fresh outside air. Both air streams pass each other, separately, through a core of many thin metal or plastic surfaces. As it passes through the core, exhaust air from the house transmits its heat through core walls or fins to the cooler outside air coming in. A heater can be added to a supply duct in some systems to further warm the incoming air during severely cold weather. In summer-operating mode, HRVs work in reverse. A drain carries away any condensation.

10 great resources

for learning more about energy efficiency

Lighting

To calculate your savings when replacing standard incandescent bulbs with compact fluorescent bulbs, check out Energy Star's "Light Bulb Calculator" at energystar.gov/ia/partners/promotions/change_light/downloads/bulb.html. Just enter the wattage of your existing bulb and how much you use it each day to determine how much a compact fluorescent bulb will save you.

The Energy Federation is a nonprofit organization that offers energy-efficient lighting and other products to consumers at reasonable prices. You can visit their online catalog at www.energyfederation.org.

Energy-efficient appliances

ENERGY STAR is a joint program run by the U.S. Environmental Protection Agency and the U.S. Department of Energy with the goal of making homes and businesses more energy efficient. One of the ways they do this is to set energy-efficiency guidelines for appliances, heating and cooling equipment, and other products. For more information on specific appliances: Visit their Web site at: www.energystar.gov, call (888) 782-7937, or write U.S. EPA, Energy Star Hotline (6202J), 1200 Pennsylvania Ave NW, Washington, D.C. 20460

Recycling

For information on where and how to recycle batteries from cellular and cordless phones, laptops, camcorders, digital cameras, cordless power tools and other devices, visit the Rechargeable Battery Recycling Corporation Web site at www.rbrc.org. Their Call2Recycle program has established 30,000 collection sites nationwide. Most Lowe's, Sears, Best Buy, Home Depot, Radio Shack, Office Depot, Batteries Plus, Target, Wal-Mart and wireless stores serve as battery drop-off sites.

Refrigerators

To find out how much your refrigerator costs to run per year and how much you can save by replacing it with an energy-efficient model, check out the "Refrigerator Retirement Savings Calculator" at www.energystar.gov./index.cfm?fuseaction=refrig.calculator. Enter the year, size, and configuration of your refrigerator and the program will calculate your savings over one- and five-year periods.

Insulation

To determine how many inches of insulation you need to add to your attic and/or walls to meet U.S. Department of Energy standards, search online for "insulation calculator." You'll find several calculators that determine the thickness you need for various types of insulation. Some also determine how much insulation you'll need to buy.

Energy-efficient and solar products

"Real Goods" carries a wide selection of alternative energy products including solar electric, wind power and transportation. View their online catalog at www.realgoods.com.

Education

The Solar Living Institute offers a wide array of workshops including those on solar and renewable energy, green and natural building and alternative transportation. For more information, check out the "Courses" area at www.solarliving.org or call (707) 472-2450.

Kids can learn more about conserving energy by playing interactive Energy Hog games at www.energyhog.org.

Water

One drippy faucet can waste 20 gallons of water per day; if it's dripping hot water, you'll also be paying to heat all the water that's going down the drain. And a leaky or running toilet can waste 200 gallons per day. For complete information on how to fix or replace a drippy faucet, enter "Repair a Kitchen Faucet" in the search box at www.thefamilyhandyman.com. You'll also find articles on repairing running toilets and dripping showers.

Kids

Your kids can go on a home energy scavenger hunt, become an Energy Hog Buster, and watch superheroes in action at the Alliance to Save Energy's site for kids, www.energyhog.org. The Web site also includes resources for teachers, including an Energy Hog game show, coloring books, and posters.

Fuel Efficiency

Visit www.fueleconomy.gov for information on getting better gas mileage through better driving habits, maintenance, planning and new car purchases. Their Fuel Economy Guide lists mileage estimates for cars built between 1994 and 2014. The site also offers links to Web sites that keep track of the lowest gas prices in your area.

Index

Nails

Nail lengths are identified by numbers from 4 to 60 followed by the letter "d" which stands for "penny." The imperial and metric equivalents are listed here.

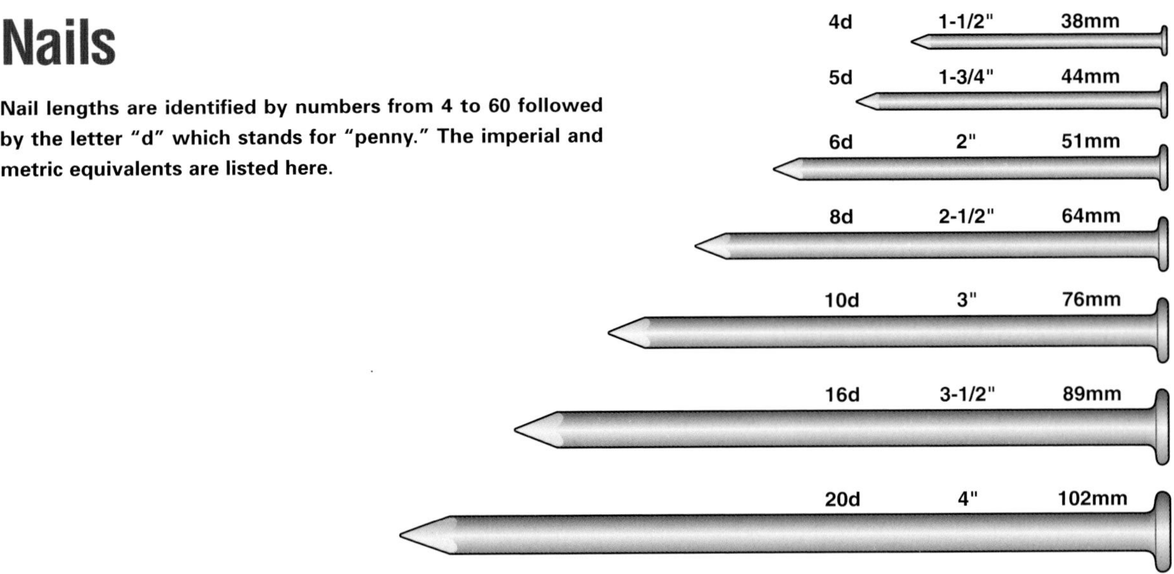

Fractions and metric equivalents

Fractional inches

Inches (in.)	1/64	1/32	1/25	1/16	1/8	1/4	3/8	2/5	1/2	5/8	3/4	7/8
Millimeters (mm)*	0.40	0.79	1.0	1.59	3.18	6.35	9.53	10	12.7	15.9	19.1	22.2
Centimeters (cm)*							0.95	1	1.27	1.59	1.91	2.22

Whole inches (1–12)

Inches (in.)	1	2	3	4	5	6	7	8	9	10	11	12
Feet (ft.)												1
Millimeters (mm)*	25.4	50.8	76.2	101.6	127	152	178	203	229	254	279	305
Centimeters (cm)*	2.54	5.08	7.62	10.16	12.7	15.2	17.8	20.3	22.9	25.4	27.9	30.5
Meters (m)*												.30

Selected large measurements

Inches (in.)	36	39.4
Feet (ft.)	3	3-1/4†
Yards (yd.)	1	1-1/12†
Millimeters (mm)*	914	1,000
Centimeters (cm)*	91.4	100
Meters (m)*	.91	1.00

*Metric values are rounded off. †Approximate fractions.

Metric conversions

Use the tables on these two pages to convert the "English" or "standard" measurements in this book into metric form.

In the "English system to metric system" and "Metric system to English system" charts below, multiply the number in the first column by the number in the third column to arrive at the conversion number in the middle column.

English system to metric system

To change:	Into:	Multiply by:
Inches	Millimeters	25.4
Inches	Centimeters	2.54
Feet	Meters	0.305
Yards	Meters	0.914
Miles	Kilometers	1.609
Square inches	Square centimeters	6.45
Square feet	Square meters	0.093
Square yards	Square meters	0.836
Cubic inches	Cubic centimeters	16.4
Cubic feet	Cubic meters	0.0283
Cubic yards	Cubic meters	0.765
Pints	Liters	0.473
Quarts	Liters	0.946
Gallons	Liters	3.78
Ounces	Grams	28.4
Pounds	Kilograms	0.454
Tons	Metric tons	0.907

Metric system to English system

To change:	Into:	Multiply by:
Millimeters	Inches	0.039
Centimeters	Inches	0.394
Meters	Feet	3.28
Meters	Yards	1.09
Kilometers	Miles	0.621
Square centimeters	Square inches	0.155
Square meters	Square feet	10.8
Square meters	Square yards	1.2
Cubic centimeters	Cubic inches	0.061
Cubic meters	Cubic feet	35.3
Cubic meters	Cubic yards	1.31
Liters	Pints	2.11
Liters	Quarts	1.06
Liters	Gallons	0.264
Grams	Ounces	0.035
Kilograms	Pounds	2.2
Metric tons	Tons	1.1

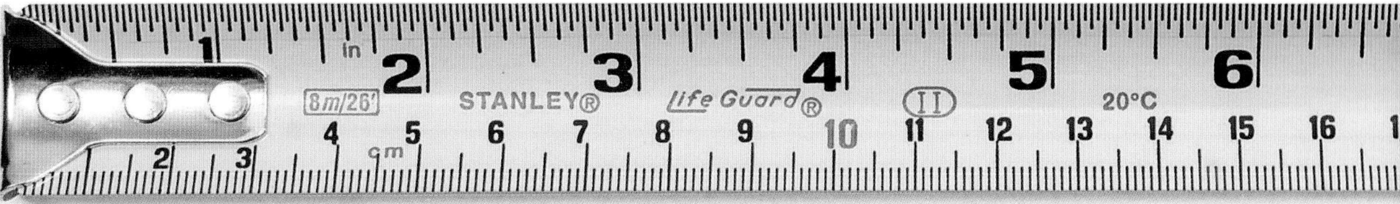

(actual size)